Emergency Planning and Security Measures II

Matthew Pope, CPP

PEARSON
Custom
Publishing

HOMELAND
SECURITY
SERIES

Printed in the United States of America

10 9 8 7 6 5 4 3 2

ISBN 0-536-26132-6

2006340014

SB

Please visit our web site at *www.pearsoncustom.com*

PEARSON CUSTOM PUBLISHING
75 Arlington Street, Suite 300, Boston, MA 02116
A Pearson Education Company

Contents

Introduction: Emergency Planning and Security Measures II

Areal view of Yalova. *Courtesy of AP/Wide World Photos.*

The world that the modern homeland security specialist inherits is one of constant tension between order and destructive chaos. Whether it's the terrorist's bomb or a fire sparked by an exposed wire, the daily mission of the homeland security specialist is to eliminate the possibility of unnecessary chaos.

In Volume I of *Emergency Planning and Security Measures,* we began our study of the challenges, strategies, and methods for protecting commerce and communities from chaos. During this volume you will expand your knowledge base of the immense challenges that the homeland security planning professional must master.

The forces of chaos are arrayed today in a manner unprecedented by history. For almost fifty years, the ultimate chaos of global war was held at bay by the equally matched power of the United States' and the Soviet Union's nuclear arsenal and the paradoxically logical concept of "MAD"—Mutually Assured Destruction.

With the collapse of the Soviet Union in the early 1990s, however, the balance of power shifted dramatically as the United States remained the sole super-power in the world. While this reality considerably lessened tensions around the prospect of an all out global thermonuclear war, the situation, ironically, also gave rise to a host of many new worldwide security risks. The meltdown of the Moscow government and the fracturing of the Soviet Union into fourteen smaller federated states caused a tremendous imbalance in world power relationships. As former Soviet states reverted back into separate nations, new fractious power grabs emerged and reinvigorated old ethnic conflicts in places like Bosnia and Chechnya. With the dissolution of a strong central government, the vast Soviet arsenal of nuclear, biological, and chemical weapons became difficult to account for, and, to this day, a frighteningly large number of these weapons of mass destruction (WMDs) have not been successfully tracked down or recovered.

Add to this the deluge of battlefield weapons that the super-powers poured into the Third World during the Cold War. The inestimable number of hearty Russian Kalishnikov (AK-47) assault rifles floating around the globe has become the mainstay combat weapon of terrorist organizations and guerrillas. As of this writing, one of the greatest threats to American forces in Iraq is Soviet built rocket-propelled grenades in the hands of insurgents. Sophisticated shoulder-fire Stinger surface-to-air missiles built in the United States and given to *mujahadeen* freedom fighters during the Soviet invasion of Afghanistan pose a grave threat today to commercial airlines.

And now terrorists are taking the battle from the physical plane into cyber-space. Every day, computer security experts are learning how to match and repel deliberately manufactured computer viruses and cyber attacks. A surprisingly large number of these attacks are not being launched by bored high school students, but by computer engineers employed by international terrorists and dedicated to determining what chaos they could cause by crashing our electronic infrastructure.

There is the chaos not caused by terrorists at all but by the myriad of opportunities for theft, loss, violence, natural disaster, civil unrest, economic instability, espionage, hazardous materials, and fire. This text will also address the CBRNE Threat. CBRNE is a relatively new comprehensive concept used by security planners. It stands for Chemical, Biological, Radiological, Nuclear, and high Explosive. This, coupled with the threat of cyber-terrorism, is a new type of "super-chaos" representing a challenging new world for the homeland security specialist to function in.

The more sophisticated the world gets and the smaller the global community becomes through telecommunications and rapid transit, the greater the opportunity for spectacular chaos. On the morning of September 11, 2001, nineteen fanatics used a credit card, commercially available chemical mace, and hardware store box cutters to destroy four airliners, seven buildings, and 2,752 lives. They caused the loss of 30 percent of lower Manhattan's office space, 200,000 jobs to be transferred out of New York, and a short-term immediate cost of $27.2 billion in revenue losses.[1] An unbelievably damaging attack carried out through unbelievably low-cost, low-tech means.

This is the world that you inherit as you begin your career as a homeland security specialist. One where the stakes have never been higher and disaster has never been closer. Your education, professionalism, and vigilance may be the only thing that stands between the safety of your community and total chaos.

End Notes

[1] http://www.ccc.nps.navy.mil/si/aug02/homeland.asp

1 Contingency Planning for Information Technology Systems

Overview:

The term "infrastructure" has taken on a new meaning in the last decade or so. With the widespread transfer of data records to electronic media, the mainstreaming of digital processing, and the creation of vast cyber-networks used to transmit, receive and execute instructions to the vital systems that run our national operating systems, a parallel electronic infrastructure has developed as well.

While this new electronic dependency has increased the speed, efficiency, and capacity of our key processes and systems, it has also created some deeply concerning vulnerabilities to our homeland security.

With every new on-ramp added to the information superhighway, there is usually at least one new exposure and vulnerability created as well. New words have entered our lexicon that a little over ten years ago would have sounded like gibberish: "MyDoom," "SoBig," "Blaster."

The "Y2K" bug was one of the first major public issues that brought attention to the possibility of catastrophe caused by massive computer failures worldwide. *Courtesy of PhotoDisc/Getty Images, Inc.*

Even if we don't know exactly what they are, we have a general sense that they are something bad that affects our computers.

This chapter will begin to familiarize you with the major concepts and challenges that pose a threat to our vast electronic infrastructures and jeopardize the ability of our society to function.

Chapter Objectives:

- Explain how electronic infrastructures operate and what vital roles they play in the functioning of nations and communities.
- Describe the malicious and unlawful methods that may be used to weaken, disrupt, and/or damage electronic infrastructures
- Express the contingency planning considerations and computer emergency agencies employed to counter and/or mitigate computer attacks.

Cyber-Security

A leading manufacturer of software systems proudly launches a sophisticated new Internet server program. The program is considered top-of-the-line software and is usually only available to fairly prestigious government and international business clients. In the rush to get the behind-schedule software to market, however, quality assurance testing is dramatically scaled back. As a result, a fatal security flaw in the program's operating code is undetected.

One day, at virtually the exact same moment, hundreds of administrative workers around the globe simultaneously open innocuous looking e-mails from familiar senders. Each e-mail contains the message header "YOUR IMPORTANT FILE TRANSFER FAILED" and a text file attachment. The body of the message text reads, "The message contains Unicode characters and has been sent as a binary attachment." Since it sounds rather official and important, the majority of the recipients click on the text file to try to open it. When they realize there is nothing very important or even intelligible in the text file, most close it and either delete the e-mail or just forget about it and let it sit in their inbox.

What the message recipients don't realize is that a computer program surreptitiously attached to the text file was launched when they clicked on the attachment. What they also don't realize is that the e-mail message was not sent to them by anyone whom they know, or anyone at all. Their IP (Internet Protocol) address was selected at random by the same hidden computer program that has just hidden itself on their own system directory. Even more troubling, the program is now attempting to do the same thing, using their system to pass through to the networks the computer is hooked up to. In every case, the common denominator is that the tainted systems and networks are all running the same new Internet server program, and the malicious program is spreading by exploiting the same security flaw.

After first spreading itself through spoofed, innocuous e-mails, the program then begins exploiting the flawed Internet server program's security hole and generating random IP addresses on multiple networks. Within hours, hundreds of thousands of computers worldwide have been infected, unknown to users and network security professionals. Worse still is that when the program has successfully embedded itself on a computer's system it will read the computer's internal time clock and begin a countdown. At a pre-determined time, every computer with the infected program will automatically launch and cause the computer to log on to the network and simultaneously try to connect to a target IP address, in this case the main Web site of the U.S. Department of Homeland Security. When the attack launches, the Web site, http://www.dhs.gov, will be overwhelmed by traffic and become inaccessible to legitimate traffic that is unable to send or receive information. The site will have to come down for several hours for repairs to be made and possibly even a new IP address to be assigned to the site to deflect any further excessive logon attempts. The U.S. Department of Homeland Security has just been usefully taken out by a Denial of Service (DOS) attack by use of a computer worm. Terrorists have sent a loud message to the American public that even the government agency responsible for homeland security can have its important message denied at will.

Although this scenario is fictitious and grossly oversimplified, it is reminiscent of an actual attempted DOS attack using the "Ida Code Red" worm in July of 2001. The Ida Code Red targeted the White House Web site (www.whitehouse.gov). By good fortune, the U.S. Government learned of the attack just before it was set to launch at midnight Greenwich Mean Time on July 20, 2001 (that would have been 8:00 a.m. in Washington, DC), and the National Infrastructure Protection Center changed the IP address at the last minute to prevent the attack.

To begin our discussion of computer security and contingency planning, let us review some of the most basic computer threats: viruses, Trojans, and worms.

Computer Viruses, Trojans, and Worms

Virus

A virus is a piece of software designed and written to adversely affect your computer by altering the way it works without your knowledge or permission. In more technical terms, a virus is a segment of program code that implants itself to one of your executable files and spreads systematically from one file to another. Computer viruses do not spontaneously generate: They must be written and have a specific purpose. Usually a virus has two distinct functions:

1. Spreads itself from one file to another without your input or knowledge. Technically, this is known as self-replication and propagation.

2. Implements the symptom or damage planned by the perpetrator. This could include erasing a disk, corrupting your programs, or just creating havoc on your computer. Technically, this is known as the virus payload, which can be benign or malignant at the whim of the virus creator.

A benign virus is one that is designed to do no real damage to your computer. For example, a virus that conceals itself until some predetermined date or time and then does nothing more than display some sort of message is considered benign. A malignant virus is one that attempts to inflict malicious damage to your computer, although the damage may not be intentional. There are a significant number of viruses that cause damage due to poor programming and outright bugs in the viral code.

A malicious virus might alter one or more of your programs so that it does not work as it should. The infected program might terminate abnormally, or write incorrect information into your documents. Or the virus might alter the directory information on one of your system areas. This might prevent the partition from mounting; you might not be able to launch one or more programs; or programs might not be able to locate the documents you want to open. Some of the viruses identified are benign; however, a high percentage of them are very malignant. Some of the more malignant viruses will erase your entire hard disk or delete files.

A computer virus is a program designed to replicate and spread on its own, preferably without your knowledge of its existence. Computer viruses spread by attaching themselves to another program (such as your word processing or spreadsheet programs) or to the boot sector of a diskette.

When an infected file is executed, or the computer is started from an infected disk, the virus itself is executed. Often, it lurks in memory, waiting to infect the next program that is run, or the next disk that is accessed. In addition, many viruses also perform a trigger event, such as displaying a message on a certain date, or deleting files after the infected program is run a certain number of times.

While some of these trigger events are benign (such as those that display messages), others can be detrimental. The majority of viruses are harmless, displaying messages or pictures, or doing nothing at all. Other viruses are annoying, slowing down system performance or causing minor changes to the screen display of your computer. Some viruses, however, are truly menacing, causing system crashes, damaged files, and lost data.

The following are the most common types of viruses:

File Infectors

These are viruses that attach themselves to (or replace) .COM and .EXE files, although in some cases they can infect files with extensions .SYS, .DRV, .BIN, .OVL, and .OVY. With this type of virus, uninfected programs usually become infected when they are executed with the virus in memory. In other cases they are infected when they are opened (such as using the DOS DIR command), or the virus simply infects all of the files in the directory it was run from (a direct infector).

Boot Sector Infectors

These are not necessarily fantasies of impending doom. Thus far, computer viruses have hit a variety of systems, including Fortune 500 companies, government agencies, major universities, newspapers, and large networks linking vast numbers of computers and huge volumes of information. Every logical drive, both hard disk and floppy, contains a boot sector. This is true even of disks that are not bootable. This boot sector contains specific information relating to the formatting of the disk and the data stored there. It also contains a small program called the boot program, which loads the DOS system files. The boot program displays the familiar "Non-system Disk or Disk Error" message if the DOS system files are not present. It is also the program that gets infected by viruses. You get a boot sector virus by leaving an infected diskette in a drive and rebooting the machine. When the boot sector program is read and executed, the virus goes into memory and infects your hard drive. Remember, because every disk has a boot sector, it is possible (and most common) to infect a machine from a data disk. NOTE: Both floppy diskettes and hard drives contain boot sectors.

Master Boot Record Infectors

The first physical sector of every hard disk (Side 0, Track 0, Sector 1) contains the disk's Master Boot Record and Partition Table. The Master Boot Record has a small program within it called the Master Boot Program that looks up the values in the partition table for the starting location of the bootable partition, and then tells the system to go there and execute any code it finds. Assuming your disk is set up properly, what it finds in that location (Side 1, Track 0, Sector 1) is a valid boot sector. On floppy disks, these same viruses infect the boot sectors. You get a Master Boot Record virus in exactly the same manner you get a boot sector virus—by leaving an infected diskette in a drive and rebooting the machine. When the boot sector program is read and executed, the virus goes into memory and infects the MBR of your hard drive. Again, because every disk has a boot sector, it is possible (and common) to infect a machine from a data disk.

Multi-Partite Viruses

Multi-partite viruses are a combination of the viruses listed above. They will infect both files and MBRs or both files and boot sectors. These types of viruses are currently rare, but the number of cases is growing steadily.

—Taken from
   http://www.intergov.org/public_information/general_information/view_virus%20types.html

What Is a Computer Virus?

To be defined as a virus, a program must

- replicate itself in order to carry out a mission.
- be dependent on a "host" to carry out the mission.
- create damage to the computer system "infected."

Simple Definition

A virus is a program which reproduces itself, hides in other computer codes without permission, and does undesirable things not intended by its victim.

Virus Effects

- Trivial—simply reproduces or displays messages.
- Minor—alters or deletes infected files.
- Moderate—wipes out entire disk drive.
- Major—slowly corrupts data with pattern, making restoration difficult.
- Severe—slowly corrupts data without pattern, making restoration impossible.
- Unlimited—virus that discovers system administrator's password and mails it to one or more users, tempting them to use it for illegal purposes.

Virus Types

Viruses are classified by the portion of the system they affect. There are five main types:

1. *Boot Viruses*
   - Infect the boot block on a floppy or hard disk.
     Usually replaces the boot block with all or part of a virus program.
   - Most have trigger dates, when booted on that day severe damage will be done.
   - Virus loads into memory and infects other disks.

   Example is "Michelangelo"—on March 6 (Michelangelo's birthday) garbage is written through entire drive.

2. *File Viruses*
   - Infect .EXE or .COM files.
   - Usually append the virus code to the file, new versions hide the virus.
   - Damage is done when program is run and the virus will attach to other files.

   Example is "Friday the 13th"—if the date matches Friday the 13th when the virus is executed, all .EXE files are deleted.

3. *Multi-partite Viruses*
   - Infect both boot blocks and executable files.
   - Combine the capabilities of boot viruses and file viruses.

   Example is "Tequila"—will display graphics and text rather than running programs.

4. *Polymorphic Viruses*
   - Can infect the boot sector, files, or both.
   - Is self-modifying, changes each time it infects a file or disk.
   - Very difficult to detect and remove.

   Example is "Tremor"—triggers three months after infection and displays "-MOMENT-OF-TERROR-IS-THE-BEGINNING-OF-LIFE-" with every warm boot.

5. *Meta Viruses*
   - First viruses to infect data files and to work on multiple platforms.
   - Carried in data files for Microsoft Word documents.

   Example is "Concept"—will infect the global template and all files loaded from then on. Was distributed by Microsoft on a CD-ROM called Microsoft Windows 95 Software Compatibility Test.

Virus Prevention

- Never use a "foreign" disk or CD-ROM without scanning it for viruses.
- Always scan files downloaded from the Internet.
- Never boot your PC from a floppy unless you are certain it is virus free.
- Write-protect your disks to prevent viruses from reproducing onto your disks.

- Use licensed software from a reputable dealer.
- Password protect your PC to prevent copying of files in your absence.
- Make regular backup copies of all your work and system configurations.
- Install and use antivirus software regularly.
- Update your antivirus software regularly so it can detect new viruses.

Computer Trojans

Computer Trojans are malicious computer programs disguised as something useful. The major difference between viruses and Trojans is that viruses reproduce, while a Trojan is just a one-time program that executes its payload as soon as the Trojan is executed. Trojans are the most common way of bringing a virus into a system. A current example of a Trojan is a program called pkz300b.exe that disguises itself as an archiving utility but will delete your entire hard drive when run.

Computer Worms

Computer worms are reproducing programs that run independently and travel across network connections. The main difference between viruses and worms is the method in which they reproduce and spread. A virus is dependant upon a host file or boot sector, and the transfer of files between machines to spread, while a worm can run independently and spread of its own will through network connections. An example of a worm is the famous Internet worm of 1988: Overnight the worm copied itself across the Internet, infecting every Sun-3 and VAX system with so many copies of itself that the systems were unusable. Eventually, several sites disconnected themselves from the Internet to avoid re-infection.

—Taken from *http://ingipsa.usda.gov:8010/itsecurity/computer_viruses.htm*

Computer Emergency Response

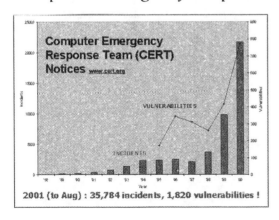

2001 (to Aug) : 35,784 incidents, 1,820 vulnerabilities !

An integral element of security and contingency planning in the electronic infrastructure world is organizational planning for response to computer-based emergencies. Entities from corporations to governments have begun developing polices, procedures, and even teams to identify, respond to, isolate, and neutralize computer attacks and cyber-threats.

The United States Computer Emergency Response Team (US-CERT), which is a hybrid of the Department of Homeland Security and the private industry, is an excellent example of this type of large scale organizational planning. The following is an overview of the mission and objectives of the U.S. CERT:

United States Computer Emergency Readiness Team (US-CERT)
US-CERT is a partnership between the Department of Homeland Security and the public and private sectors. Established to protect the nation's Internet infrastructure, US-CERT coordinates defense against and responses to cyber attacks across the nation.

Frequently Asked Questions about US-CERT
What is US-CERT?
US-CERT was established in September 2003 as a public-private partnership charged with improving computer security preparedness and response to cyber attacks in the United States. As an institution, US-CERT is responsible for:

- Analyzing and reducing cyber threats and vulnerabilities
- Disseminating cyber-threat warning information
- Coordinating incident response activities

US-CERT also provides a way for citizens, businesses, and other institutions to communicate and coordinate directly with the United States government about cyber security.

Why is US-CERT important?
US-CERT is the nation's focal point for preventing, protecting against, and responding to cyber security and vulnerabilities. US-CERT interacts with all federal agencies, private industry, the research community, state and local governments, and others on a 24x7 basis to disseminate reasoned and actionable cyber security information. To provide security information to the public, US-CERT:

- integrates content contributed by numerous organizations from both the public and private sectors
- aggregates and analyzes the various types of data provided by contributing organizations
- serves as the focal point for promoting common and comprehensive analysis of security trends and risks
- maintains quality control standards and works to ensure technical accuracy as well as timeliness

What is US-CERT's relationship to NCSD and DHS?
US-CERT is the operational arm of the National Cyber Security Division (NCSD) at the Department of Homeland Security (DHS). The NCSD was established by DHS to serve as the federal government's cornerstone for cyber security coordination and preparedness, including implementation of the National Strategy to Secure Cyberspace.

What is the relationship between US-CERT and other groups with "CERT" in their name?
Worldwide, there are more than 250 organizations that use the name "CERT" or a similar name and deal with cyber security response. In the United States, the Department of Homeland security created US-CERT to

be the "Computer Emergency Readiness Team" with national responsibility for protecting the nation's information infrastructure by coordinating defense against and response to cyber attacks in the United States. US-CERT and the CERT Coordination Center at Carnegie Mellon University work jointly on these activities. When a cyber security problem warrants it, US-CERT coordinates a response by working with computer security experts. These experts are often part of incident response teams that are from the public and private sector, may include "CERT" or "CIRT" in their names, and originate from within the United States and international locales.

Where is US-CERT located?
US-CERT is located in Washington, DC, and Pittsburgh, PA.

Who runs US-CERT?
US-CERT is the operational arm of the National Cyber Security Division (NCSD) at the Department of Homeland Security. It is a partnership of the NCSD, the CERT/CC, an FFRDC in conjunction with Carnegie Mellon University (BCC), and the public and private sectors. The Department of Homeland Security Cyber Security Chief, Amit Yoran, oversees the operation and administration of US-CERT.

Who are US-CERT's partners?
As it grows, US-CERT will include partnerships with private sector cyber security vendors, academia, federal agencies, Information Sharing and Analysis Centers (ISACs), state and local governments, and domestic and international organizations. Working together, these groups will coordinate national and international efforts to address key cyber security issues.

What is the National Cyber Alert System?
The National Cyber Alert System is America's first cohesive national cyber security system for identifying, analyzing, and prioritizing emerging vulnerabilities and threats. Managed by the US-CERT, the system relays computer security update and warning information to all users. It provides all citizens—from computer security professionals to home computer users with basic skills—with free, timely, actionable information to better secure their computer systems.

How can the National Cyber Alert System help me? How do I subscribe?
The National Cyber Alert System provides valuable cyber security information to all users. You can subscribe to free e-mail lists through the US-CERT Web site. The system sends alerts and other cyber security information that provide guidelines and actions to help you to better secure your portion of cyberspace. You can receive any or all of the following documents through email:

- *Cyber Security Alerts:* Available in two forms—regular for home users and advanced for technical users—Cyber Security Alerts provide timely information about security issues, vulnerabilities, and exploits currently occurring.
  Sign up at www.us-cert.gov/cas.

- *Cyber Security Tips:* Written for non-technical home and corporate computer users, the bi-weekly Cyber Security Tips provide information on computer security best practices.
  Sign up at www.us-cert.gov/cas
- *Cyber Security Bulletins:* Written for technical audiences, Cyber Security Bulletins provide bi-weekly summaries of security issues, new vulnerabilities, potential impact, patches and workarounds, as well as actions recommended to mitigate risk.

How can US-CERT help me?
US-CERT gives you access to valuable educational resources as well as up-to-date computer security information through the National Cyber Alert System and the US-CERT Web site.

What is the Protected Critical Infrastructure Information (PCII) Program? How does the PCII Program protect submitted information?
The PCII Program, established in response to the Critical Infrastructure Information Act of 2002 (CII Act), creates a new framework for protecting certain types of information. The PCII program enables members of the private sector to, for the first time, voluntarily submit confidential information regarding the nation's critical infrastructure to the Department of Homeland Security (DHS) with the assurance that the information will be protected from public disclosure. More details about how information can be protected under the CII Act can be found on the Department of Homeland Security Web site.

—Taken from *http://www.us-cert.gov/capabilities.html*

Computer Contingency Planning

Now that both threats and response mechanisms for computer infrastructure emergencies have been examined, we will want to look at the specific steps and considerations for computer system contingency planning.

The following is the recommended guidance document for information technology contingency planning from the National Institute for Information Technology Systems.

Contingency Planning Guide for Information Technology Systems

Information technology (IT) and automated information systems are vital elements in most business processes. Because these IT resources are so essential to an organization's success, it is critical that the services provided by these systems are able to operate effectively without excessive interruption. Contingency planning supports this requirement by establishing thorough plans, procedures, and technical measures that can enable a system to be recovered quickly and effectively following a service disruption or disaster. Interim measures may include the relocation of IT systems and operations to an alternate site, the recovery of IT functions using alternate equipment, or the performance of IT functions using manual methods.

The National Institute of Standards and Technology's (NIST) Information Technology Laboratory has published a recommended guidance document on contingency planning for federal departments and agencies. (Industry will find the recommendations valuable as well.) NIST Special Publication (SP) 800-34, *Contingency Planning Guide for Information Technology Systems,* by Marianne Swanson, Amy Wohl, Lucinda Pope, Tim Grance, Joan Hash, and Ray Thomas, provides instructions, recommendations, and considerations for government IT contingency planning. NIST SP 800-34 supersedes Federal Information Processing Standard (FIPS) 87, Guidelines for ADP Contingency Planning.

NIST SP 800-34 provides guidance to individuals responsible for preparing and maintaining IT contingency plans. The guide discusses essential contingency plan elements and processes, highlights specific considerations and concerns associated with contingency planning for various types of IT systems, and provides examples to assist readers in developing their own IT contingency plans. This *ITL Bulletin* summarizes the contingency planning guide, which is available at http://csrc.nist.gov/publications/nistpubs/index.html.

Fundamental Contingency Planning Principles

The IT contingency planning guide identifies fundamental planning principles and practices to help personnel develop and maintain effective IT contingency plans. The principles meet most organizational needs; however, each organization may have additional requirements specific to its own processes. The document provides guidance to help personnel evaluate information systems and operations to determine contingency requirements and priorities. The guidance also provides a structured approach to aid planners in developing cost-effective solutions that accurately reflect their IT requirements and integrate contingency planning principles into all aspects of IT operations.

The guidance presented should be considered during every stage of contingency planning, starting with the conceptualization of contingency planning efforts through plan maintenance and disposal of the contingency plan. If used as a planning management tool throughout the contingency planning process, the document and its appendices should provide users with time- and cost-saving practices.

Scope

The guide presents contingency planning principles for the following common IT processing systems:

- Desktop computers and portable systems (laptop and handheld computers)
- Servers
- Web sites
- Local area networks (LANs)
- Wide area networks (WANs)
- Distributed systems
- Mainframe systems

The document discusses common technologies that may be used to support contingency capabilities. Given the broad range of IT designs and configurations, however, as well as the rapid development and obsolescence of products and capabilities, the scope of the discussion is not intended to be comprehensive. Rather, the document describes practices for applying technology to enhance an organization's IT contingency planning capabilities.

The document outlines planning principles that may be applied to a wide variety of incidents that could affect IT system operations. The scope includes minor incidents causing short-term disruptions to disasters that affect normal operations for an extended period. Because IT systems vary in design and application, specific incident types and associated contingency measures are not provided in the document. Instead, the planning guide defines a process that may be followed for any IT system to identify planning requirements and develop an effective contingency plan.

Audience

Managers within federal organizations and those individuals responsible for IT security at system and operational levels can use the principles presented in the document. This description includes the following personnel:

- *Managers* responsible for overseeing IT operations or business processes that rely on IT systems;
- *System administrators* responsible for maintaining daily IT operations;
- *Information System Security Officers (ISSOs)* and other staff responsible for developing, implementing, and maintaining an organization's IT security activities;
- *System engineers and architects* responsible for designing, implementing, or modifying information systems;
- *Users* who employ desktop and portable systems to perform their assigned job functions; and
- *Other personnel* responsible for designing, managing, operating, maintaining, or using information systems.

In addition, emergency management personnel who may need to coordinate facility-level contingency may use this document with IT contingency planning activities. The concepts presented in this document are not specific to government systems and may be used by private and commercial organizations.

Risk Management Process

IT systems are vulnerable to a variety of disruptions, ranging from mild (e.g., short-term power outage, disk drive failure) to severe (e.g., equipment destruction, fire). Many vulnerabilities may be minimized or eliminated through technical, management, or operational solutions as part of the organization's risk management effort; however, it is virtually impossible to completely eliminate all risks. Contingency planning is designed to mitigate the risk of system and service unavailability by focusing effective and efficient recovery solutions.

NIST SP 800-34 discusses the ways in which IT contingency planning fits into an organization's larger risk management, security, and emergency preparedness programs. Other types of emergency-related plans and their relationship to IT contingency planning are described. Finally, the guide explains how integrating contingency planning principles throughout the system development life cycle promotes system compatibility and a cost-effective means to increase an organization's ability to respond quickly and effectively to a disruptive event.

IT Contingency Planning Process
To develop and maintain an effective IT contingency plan, organizations should use the following approach:

1. Develop the contingency planning policy statement.

2. Conduct the business impact analysis (BIA).

3. Identify preventive controls.

4. Develop recovery strategies.

5. Develop an IT contingency plan.

6. Plan testing, training, and exercises.

7. Plan maintenance.

These steps represent key elements in a comprehensive IT contingency planning capability. The responsibility for the planning process generally falls under the auspice of the "contingency planning coordinator" or "contingency planner," who is typically a functional or resource manager within the agency. The coordinator develops the strategy in cooperation with other functional and resource managers associated with the system or the business processes supported by the system. The Contingency Planning Coordinator also typically manages development and execution of the contingency plan. All major applications and general support systems should have a contingency plan.

1. Develop the contingency planning policy statement.
To be effective and to ensure that personnel fully understand the agency's contingency planning requirements, the contingency plan must be based on a clearly defined policy. The contingency planning policy statement should define the agency's overall contingency objectives and establish the organizational framework and responsibilities for IT contingency planning. To be successful, senior management, most likely the chief information officer (CIO), must support a contingency program. These officials should be included in the process to develop the program policy, structure, objectives, and roles and responsibilities. At a minimum, the contingency pol-

icy should comply with federal guidance contained in the documents listed in NIST SP 800-34; agencies should evaluate their respective IT systems, operations, and requirements to determine if additional contingency planning requirements are necessary. Key policy elements are as follows:

- Roles and responsibilities
- Scope as applies to the type(s) of platform(s) and organization functions subject to contingency planning
- Resource requirements
- Training requirements
- Exercise and testing schedules
- Plan maintenance schedule
- Frequency of backups and storage of backup media

2. Conduct the business impact analysis (BIA).
The BIA is a key step in the contingency planning process. The BIA enables the Contingency Planning Coordinator to fully characterize the system requirements, processes, and interdependencies and use this information to determine contingency requirements and priorities. The purpose of the BIA is to correlate specific system components with the critical services that they provide, and based on that information, to characterize the consequences of a disruption to the system components. Key steps are listing critical IT resources, identifying disruption impacts and allowable outage times, and developing recovery priorities.

Results from the BIA should be appropriately incorporated into the analysis and strategy development efforts for the organization's other continuity and recovery plans. NIST SP 800-34 provides a sample BIA process, which helps contingency planning coordinators streamline and focus their contingency plan development activities to achieve a more effective plan.

3. Identify preventive controls.
In some cases, the outage impacts identified in the BIA may be mitigated or eliminated through preventive measures that deter, detect, and/or reduce impacts to the system. Where feasible and cost-effective, preventive methods are preferable to actions that may be necessary to recover the system after a disruption. Preventive controls should be documented in the contingency plan, and personnel associated with the system should be trained on how and when to use the controls. A variety of preventive controls are available, depending on system type and configuration; however, some common measures are listed below:

- Appropriately sized uninterruptible power supplies (UPS) to provide short-term backup power to all system components (including environmental and safety controls)
- Gasoline- or diesel-powered generators to provide long-term backup power
- Air-conditioning systems with adequate excess capacity to permit failure of certain components, such as a compressor

- Fire suppression systems
- Fire and smoke detectors
- Water sensors in the computer room ceiling and floor
- Plastic tarps that may be unrolled over IT equipment to protect it from water damage
- Heat-resistant and waterproof containers for backup media and vital nonelectronic records
- Emergency master system shutdown switch
- Offsite storage of backup media, nonelectronic records, and system documentation
- Technical security controls, such as cryptographic key management and least-privilege access controls
- Frequent, scheduled backups

4. Develop recovery strategies.
Recovery strategies provide a means to restore IT operations quickly and effectively following a service disruption. Strategies should address disruption impacts and allowable outage times identified in the BIA. Several alternatives should be considered when developing the strategy, including cost, allowable outage time, security, and integration with larger, organization-level contingency plans.

The selected recovery strategy should address the potential impacts identified in the BIA and should be integrated into the system architecture during the design and implementation phases of the system life cycle.

The strategy should include a combination of methods that complement one another to provide recovery capability over the full spectrum of incidents. A wide variety of recovery approaches may be considered; the appropriate choice depends on the incident, type of system, and its operational requirements. Specific recovery methods may include commercial contracts with cold, warm, or hot site vendors, mobile sites, mirrored sites, reciprocal agreements with internal or external organizations, and service level agreements (SLAs) with the equipment vendors. In addition, technologies such as Redundant Arrays of Independent Disks (RAID), automatic fail-over, uninterruptible power supply (UPS), and mirrored systems should be considered when developing a system recovery strategy.

5. Develop an IT Contingency Plan.
IT contingency plan development is a critical step in the process of implementing a comprehensive contingency planning program. The plan contains detailed roles, responsibilities, teams, and procedures associated with restoring an IT system following a disruption. The contingency plan should document technical capabilities designed to support contingency operations. The contingency plan should be tailored to the organization and its requirements. Plans need to balance detail with flexibility; usually the more detailed the plan, the less scalable and versatile the approach. The information presented in NIST SP 800-34 is meant to be a guide; however, the

plan format may be modified as needed to better meet the user's specific system, operational, and organization requirements.

In our approach, the contingency plan comprises five main components: *Supporting Information, Notification/Activation, Recovery, Reconstitution, and Plan Appendices.* The first and last components provide essential information to ensure a comprehensive plan. The Notification/Activation, Recovery, and Reconstitution phases address specific actions that the organization should take following a system disruption or emergency.

- The Supporting Information component includes an introduction and concept of operations section that provides essential background or contextual information that makes the contingency plan easier to understand, implement, and maintain. These details aid in understanding the applicability of the guidance, in making decisions on how to use the plan, and in providing information on where associated plans and information outside the scope of the plan may be found.
- The Notification/Activation Phase defines the initial actions taken once a system disruption or emergency has been detected or appears to be imminent. This phase includes activities to notify recovery personnel, assess system damage, and implement the plan. At the completion of the Notification/Activation Phase, recovery staff will be prepared to perform contingency measures to restore system functions on a temporary basis.
- The Recovery Phase begins after the contingency plan has been activated, damage assessment has been completed (if possible), personnel have been notified, and appropriate teams have been mobilized. Recovery phase activities focus on contingency measures to execute temporary IT processing capabilities, repair damage to the original system, and restore operational capabilities at the original or new facility. At the completion of the Recovery Phase, the IT system will be operational and performing the functions designated in the plan. Depending on the recovery strategies defined in the plan, these functions could include temporary manual processing, recovery and operation on an alternate system, or relocation and recovery at an alternate site. Teams with recovery responsibilities should understand and be able to perform these recovery strategies well enough that if the paper plan is unavailable during the initial stages of the event, they can still perform the necessary activities.
- In the Reconstitution Phase, recovery activities are terminated, and normal operations are transferred back to the organization's facility. If the original facility is unrecoverable, the activities in this phase can also be applied to preparing a new facility to support system processing requirements. Once the original or new site is restored to the level that it can support the IT system and its normal processes, the system may be transitioned back to the original or to the new

site. Until the primary system is restored and tested, the contingency system should continue to be operated. The Reconstitution Phase should specify teams responsible for restoring or replacing both the site and the IT system.

- Contingency Plan Appendices provide key details not contained in the main body of the plan. The appendices should reflect the specific technical, operational, and management contingency requirements of the given system. Appendices can include, but are not limited to, contact information for contingency planning team personnel; vendor contact information, including offsite storage and alternate site POCs; standard operating procedures and checklists for system recovery or processes; equipment and system requirements lists of the hardware, software, firmware, and other resources required to support system operations; vendor agreements, reciprocal agreements with other organizations, and other vital records; description of, and directions to, the alternate site; and the BIA.

- Plans should be formatted to provide quick and clear direction in the event those personnel unfamiliar with the plan or the systems are called on to perform recovery operations. Plans should be clear, concise, and easy to implement in an emergency. Where possible, checklists and step-by-step procedures should be used. A concise and well-formatted plan reduces the likelihood of creating an overly complex or confusing plan.

6. Plan Testing, Training, and Exercises.
Plan testing is a critical element of a viable contingency capability. Testing enables plan deficiencies to be identified and addressed. Testing also helps evaluate the ability of the recovery staff to implement the plan quickly and effectively. Each IT contingency plan element should be tested to confirm the accuracy of individual recovery procedures and the overall effectiveness of the plan. The following areas should be addressed in a contingency test:

- System recovery on an alternate platform from backup media
- Coordination among recovery teams
- Internal and external connectivity
- System performance using alternate equipment
- Restoration of normal operations
- Notification procedures

Training for personnel with contingency plan responsibilities should complement testing. Training should be provided at least annually; new hires with plan responsibilities should receive training shortly after they are hired. Ultimately, contingency plan personnel should be trained to the extent that that they are able to execute their respective recovery procedures without aid of the actual document. This is an important goal in the event that paper or electronic versions of the plan are unavailable for the first few hours resulting from the extent of the disaster. Recovery personnel should be trained on the following plan elements:

- Purpose of the plan
- Cross-team coordination and communication
- Reporting procedures
- Security requirements
- Team-specific processes (Notification/Activation, Recovery, and Reconstitution Phases)
- Individual responsibilities (Notification/Activation, Recovery, and Reconstitution Phases)

7. Plan Maintenance.

To be effective, the plan must be maintained in a ready state that accurately reflects system requirements, procedures, organizational structure, and policies. IT systems undergo frequent changes because of shifting business needs, technology upgrades, or new internal or external policies. Therefore, it is essential that the contingency plan be reviewed and updated regularly, as part of the organization's change management process, to ensure new information is documented and contingency measures are revised if required. As a general rule, the plan should be reviewed for accuracy and completeness at least annually or whenever significant changes occur to any element of the plan. Certain elements will require more frequent reviews, such as contact lists. Based on the system type and criticality, it may be reasonable to evaluate plan contents and procedures more frequently.

Following the step-by-step guidance on the contingency planning process, NIST SP 800-34 contains an in-depth discussion of technical contingency planning considerations for specific types of IT systems. Eight appendices complete the document. Appendices give sample formats, address frequently asked questions, discuss human factors, and present a glossary, suggested resources, references, and an index.

NIST SP 800-34, *Contingency Planning Guide for Information Technology Systems,* presents an efficient and cost-effective approach for federal agencies to develop policies and procedures for the timely recovery and restoration of critical IT processes and vital government services to the public.

Disclaimer

Any mention of commercial products or reference to commercial organizations is for information only; it does not imply recommendation or endorsement by NIST nor does it imply that the products mentioned are necessarily the best available for the purpose.

—Taken from: *csrc.nist.gov/publications/nistbul/bulletin06-02.pdf*

Now that we have reviewed the NIST's recommendations for IT contingency planning, we will look at the following report from the United States General Accounting Office. It will provide you with an example of a specific response plan for the Y2K crisis that was anticipated for the millennium change of January 1, 2000.

United States General Accounting Office
Accounting and Information Management Division
Year 2000 Business Continuity and Contingency Planning

Time is running out for solving the Year 2000 problem. Many federal agencies will not be able to renovate and fully test all of their mission critical systems and may face major disruptions in their operations. At the same time, systems that have been renovated and tested may encounter unanticipated Year 2000 problems.

Despite the efforts of each business, state and local government, and federal agency to race against time and to renovate, validate, and implement their mission-critical information systems, every organization remains vulnerable to the disruption of its business processes.

Because most federal organizations are highly dependent on information technology to carry out their business, Year 2000-induced failures of one or more mission critical systems may have a severe impact on their ability to deliver critical services. For example:

- The nation's air transportation may face major delays and disruptions because the airlines may not be able to file flight plans with the Federal Aviation Administration.
- Taxpayers may not receive timely tax refunds because the Internal Revenue Service may be unable to process their tax returns.
- Payments to veterans and retirees may be delayed or disrupted by the failure of mission-critical systems supporting the nation's benefit payment systems.
- College students may not receive student education loans promptly.

The risk of failure is not limited to the organization's internal information systems. Many federal agencies also depend on information and data provided by their business partners—including other federal agencies, hundreds of state and local agencies, international organizations, and private sector entities. Finally, every organization also depends on services provided by the public infrastructure—including power, water, transportation, and voice and data telecommunications.

Because of these risks, agencies must have business continuity and contingency plans to reduce the risk of Year 2000 business failures. Specifically, every federal agency must ensure the continuity of its core business processes by identifying, assessing, managing, and mitigating its Year 2000 risks. This effort should not be limited to the risks posed by the Year 2000-induced failures of internal information systems, but must include the potential Year 2000 failures of others, including business partners and infrastructure service providers. One weak link in the chain of critical dependencies and even the most successful Year 2000 program will fail to protect against major disruption of business operations.

The business continuity planning process focuses on reducing the risk of Year 2000-induced business failures. It safeguards an agency's ability to produce a minimum acceptable level of outputs and services in the event of failures of internal or external mission-critical information systems and services. It also links risk management and mitigation efforts to the agency's Year 2000 program and helps to identify alternate resources and processes needed to operate the agency core business processes. While it does not offer a long-term solution to Year 2000-induced failures, it will help the agency to prepare for a potential crisis and may facilitate the restoration of normal service at the earliest possible time in the most cost-effective manner.

This guide provides a conceptual framework for helping large agencies to manage the risk of potential Year 2000-induced disruptions to their operations. It provides information on the scope and challenge and offers a structured approach for reviewing the adequacy of agency Year 2000 business continuity and contingency planning efforts.

The guide addresses business continuity and contingency planning issues that are common to most large enterprises. Given the many differences among organizations, we are not prescribing a single, rote approach to business continuity planning. Agencies must tailor their Year 2000 business continuity planning efforts in response to their unique needs while ensuring that the guide's concepts and principles are effectively applied in their business environment to achieve necessary results in the most cost-efficient manner.

The guide builds upon our previously issued Year 2000 assessment guide and draws on a variety of other sources, including research and publications of the Gartner Group, the Disaster Recovery Institute of Canada, the Department of Information Resources for the State of Texas, and the Electrical Engineering Institute of England.

The guide addresses four phases supported by program and project management activities:

1. Initiation

2. Business Impact Analysis

3. Contingency Planning

4. Testing

In addition to program and project management, the four phases are united by a common theme of accountability at all levels.

Business Continuity Planning and the Year 2000 Problem
The Year 2000 problem, while technical in nature, is primarily a business problem, with many organizations facing the risk of Year 2000-induced interruptions or failures of their core business processes. Time is running out and many federal organizations may not be able to renovate or replace all of their mission critical systems in time. Organizations must reduce

the risk and potential impact of Year 2000-induced information system failures on their core business processes by implementing rigorous business continuity planning processes.

This guide presents a structured approach to aid federal agencies in business continuity and contingency planning. The guide draws on the work of leading organizations in the information technology industry and incorporates their guidance and practices. Many of the Year 2000-related concepts and practices presented in the guide build upon existing best practices in the contingency and disaster recovery areas.

The guide describes four phases—supported by agency Year 2000 program management—with each phase representing a major Year 2000 business continuity planning project activity or segment.

1.0 Initiation
Executive management needs to be fully aware of the potentially devastating financial, organizational, and political consequences of the failure of one or more mission-critical information systems. Executives responsible for the agency's core business processes must work with the chief information officer, the chief financial officer, and the Year 2000 program manager to reduce the risk of Year 2000-induced business failures. Agency managers must dedicate sufficient resources and staff for the business continuity planning tasks and ensure that senior managers support this effort.

1.1 Establish a business continuity project work group
Establish, within the agency's Year 2000 program office, a business continuity work group. The group should report to executive management and include representatives from the agency's major business units, domain experts in relevant functional areas, business continuity and disaster recovery specialists, operational analysts, and contract specialists. Access to legal advice is also a necessity. This group should work closely with the Year 2000 program manager and staff to ensure access to information on the status of the agency's Year 2000 renovation, validation, and implementation efforts.

1.2 Develop and document a high-level business continuity planning strategy
A high-level business continuity planning strategy provides the agency's executive management with a high-level overview of the Year 2000 business risks and solutions. The strategy should address the project structure, its relationship with the Year 2000 program, metrics and reporting requirements, and the initial cost and schedule estimates.

The risk of business failure is not limited to the organization's internal information systems, but includes risks associated with the potential failure of embedded microprocessors installed in a wide range of building and industrial process control systems. Many federal agencies also depend on information and data provided by their business partners—including other federal agencies, hundreds of state and local agencies, international organizations, and private sector entities. Finally, every organization also depends on services provided by the public infrastructure—including power, water, transportation, and voice and data telecommunications.

1.3 Identify core business processes

Analyze agency business plans and work with business process owners and Year 2000 program staff to identify core business processes and supporting mission-critical systems for each business area. Ensure that all key business dependencies are clearly identified, including infrastructure and external sources of critical supplies and information. Identify executives responsible for the operation and continuity of each core business process. Use ownership of core business processes to promote executive ownership of the planning effort.

1.4 Define roles and assign responsibilities

Define roles and assign responsibilities for leading the planning effort and for performing analyses and designing business alternatives, including contingent operations for sustained and prolonged disruption. Appoint individuals to lead the development of contingency plans for each of the core business processes. Define responsibilities for documenting the business continuity plan and defining the essential operational activities comprising it.

Ensure that individuals responsible for the various business continuity and contingency planning activities are held accountable for the successful completion of individual tasks, and that the core business process owners are responsible and accountable for meeting the milestones for the development and testing of contingency plans for their core business processes.

1.5 Develop a master schedule and milestones

Develop a schedule for the planning effort and the delivery of interim and final products. Link the schedule to critical stages in the Year 2000 program effort. Update as required.

1.6 Implement a risk management process and establish reporting system

Manage the business continuity planning tasks and activities as a subproject within the Year 2000 program office. Assist business units in the development of individual contingency plans. Rank business risks and focus the planning effort on the greatest risk to critical core business processes. Identify project risks and develop metrics.

Establish reporting system, reporting requirements, and formats. Track estimates and after each step is completed update estimates as needed, especially when new information significantly alters the estimates. Estimate and assign risk to each mission-critical system undergoing renovation or replacement. Track and compare actual costs against estimates.

1.7 Assess existing business continuity, contingency, and disaster recovery plans and capabilities

Assess existing business continuity, contingency, and disaster recovery plans for their applicability. Identify weaknesses and strengths of existing plans.

1.8 Implement quality assurance reviews

Task the agency's quality assurance staff to review the business continuity planning processes. For example, use the quality assurance office staff to ensure that the business continuity team reviews existing contingency plans and that the existing contingency and disaster recovery plans are updated and incorporated into the business continuity plan. The quality assurance reviews should examine the worst case scenarios to ensure that a feasible backup strategy—including private sector solutions—can be successfully implemented in a national emergency.

2.0 Business Impact Analysis

The principal objective of the Year 2000 business impact analysis is to determine the effect of mission-critical information system failures on the viability and operations of agency core business processes. During the assessment phase of the Year 2000 program, agencies have assessed the impact of potential Year 2000-induced failures on core business areas and associated processes. The business impact analysis takes this process further and provides greater detail. It examines business process composition and priorities, dependencies, cycles, and service levels, and, most important, the business process dependency on mission-critical information systems.

2.1 Define and document information requirements, methods, and techniques to be used in developing the business continuity plan

Define the information requirements for constructing a business continuity plan. These requirements generally fall into four categories:

1. Business process composition, execution cycles, and support

2. Operational priorities, service levels, dependencies, and relationships,

3. The primary and collateral Year 2000 business risks and the business scope of their impact

4. The costs and benefits of business continuity strategies and alternatives

Each area has detailed information requirements that are essential to providing effective business continuity. For example, the analysis of business process support should provide information on the technical, functional, organizational, and infrastructure support requirements. When collected, analyzed, and synthesized, the information defines a model of critical processes and risks to the business.

2.2 Define and document Year 2000 failure scenarios

Assess business vulnerabilities and their impacts and define the Year 2000 risk scenarios. Assume the loss of all mission-critical information systems due to post-implementation failures or delays in renovation and testing.

Consider the possibility that Year 2000 date problems may be encountered earlier than expected, and address the potential disruption of essential infrastructure services, including electric power, telecommunications, and transportation. Focus agency business continuity and contingency planning efforts on likely failure scenarios.

2.3 Perform risk and impact analyses of each core business process

Monitor the status and progress of the Year 2000 program and review and verify risk metrics and critical milestones for all mission-critical systems undergoing renovation or replacement. Evaluate Year 2000-related risks posed by customers, suppliers, information technology vendors, and business partners.

Determine the impact of internal and external information system failures and infrastructure services on each core business process. Consider acquiring business impact analysis tools. These tools will provide consistent analytical structure and processes and help to standardize the impact analyses throughout the enterprise.

For the core business processes and supporting business areas, analyze both manual and automated functional requirements, manual and automated system support requirements, infrastructure support requirements, suppliers, customers, service levels, processing cycles, and the external and internal business drivers. Identify critical functions, recovery priorities and timing, and dependencies to other systems and processes.

If a core business process receives data from an external organization, contact that organization and obtain the status of its Year 2000 remediation effort. If there are reasons to be concerned, address these concerns in contingency plans.

Estimate the potential cost of service disruptions. In estimating impacts, address the duration of each disruption. Consider using a scorecard to aggregate and track the risk and impact information.

2.4 Assess and document infrastructure risks

Monitor the Year 2000 readiness of the public infrastructure, including power and telecommunications services. Assess the risk of service outages, and the potential impact of outages on the core business processes. Review existing contingency and disaster recovery plans to determine whether emergency services may be available to mitigate outages.

2.5 Define the minimum acceptable level of outputs and services for each core business process

For each core business process, define the minimum acceptable level of output and the recovery time objective.

3.0 Contingency Planning

Contingency planning integrates and acts on the results of business impact analysis. The output of this process is a business continuity plan consisting of a set of contingency plans—with a single plan for each core business process and infrastructure component. Each plan should provide a description of the resources, staff roles, procedures, and timetables needed for its implementation.

3.1 Assess the cost and benefits of identified alternatives and select the best contingency strategy for each core business process

Assess benefits, costs, and risks of alternative contingency strategies. Select a strategy that is practical, cost-effective, and appropriate to the organization. In addition, the alternatives and strategies should provide a high level of confidence in recovery capability.

Three important factors in the selection process are

1. *functionality:* the degree to which the replacement functionality supports the production of a minimum acceptable level of output for a given core business process,

2. *deployment schedule:* the time needed to acquire, test, and implement, and

3. *cost:* life-cycle cost, including acquisition, testing, training, and maintenance.

The goal is to maximize the functionality and speed of business resumption.

3.2 Identify and document contingency plans and implementation modes

Develop a contingency plan including strategies capable of meeting minimum, acceptable output requirements for each core business process. Consider the following strategies:

- quick fix
- partial replacement
- full redundancy or replacement
- outsourcing to the private sector

Consider three basic implementation modes for the quick fix, partial, and full replacement of functionality provided by failed mission-critical systems:

- automated replacement
- semi-automated replacement
- manual replacement

Some core business processes may be fully supported by compliant off-the-shelf application packages that can be purchased and rapidly installed. However, even projects that rely on off-the-shelf replacement packages may fall behind schedule.

A semi-automated alternative can implement "bare bones" functionality, using a combination of compliant off-the-shelf applications, such as accounting software or standard database products. A manual alternative normally requires hiring and training of additional staff. While this is not a desirable solution, in some instances it may be used to replace all or part of a failed automated process. Finally, redundant business services may be provided through outsourcing contracts.

3.3 Define and document triggers for activating contingency plans

Once the business continuity planning team selects the best contingency alternative for each core business process, it must then define triggers that would implement each plan. The information needed to define the implementation triggers for contingency plans is derived from two key sources:

- the deployment schedule for each contingency plan
- the implementation schedule for the renovated or replaced mission-critical systems

The deployment schedule establishes the date at which the contingency plan must be implemented if is to be to be fully tested before December 31, 1999. For example, if the contingency plan calls for an eight-month deployment schedule, the tentative implementation date should be set for April 30, 1999.

3.4 Establish a business resumption team for each core business process

Work with core business process owners to establish business resumption teams and business resumption priorities. These teams would be responsible for managing the implementation of contingency plans and would deal with a wide range of operational problems, including the potential failures of systems thought to be renovated and tested, and the potential failures of external systems and data exchanges.

3.5 Develop and document "zero day" strategy and procedures

Develop a risk-reduction strategy and procedures for the period between Thursday, December 30, 1999, and Monday, January 3. This strategy may include an agency-wide shutdown of all of its information systems on Friday, December 31, 1999, and a phased power-up on Saturday, January 1, 2000. The agency may consider extending the shutdown to infrastructure systems, including local area networks, elevators, and building management systems.

4.0 Testing

The objective of business continuity testing is to evaluate whether individual contingency plans are capable of providing the desired level of support to the agency's core business processes and whether the plans can be implemented within a specified period of time. In instances where a full-scale test may be too costly, the agency may consider end-to-end testing of key contingency plan components. An independent audit of the plan can validate the soundness of the proposed contingency strategy. Similarly, a legal review can provide assurance that the plans comply with government regulations and that liabilities and exposures are being adequately addressed.

4.1 Validate business continuity strategy

Develop and implement a strategy for validating the business continuity plan within the time that remains. A typical strategy defines a minimum number of individual and joint exercises that combine training with testing. There are several common techniques that can be employed, including reviews, rehearsals, and quality assurance audits.

4.2 Develop and document contingency test plans

Define and document the contingency test plans. Review the test plans and make needed changes. Ensure that management approves the plans. Disseminate the documents, provide guidance, and establish a help desk. Test plans should address the following:

- test objectives
- test approach
- required equipment and resources
- necessary personnel
- schedules and locations
- test procedures
- expected results and exit criteria

4.3 Establish test teams and acquire contingency resources

Establish test teams responsible for preparing and executing the contingency plan tests. Test preparation may include hiring and training needed staff.

4.4 Prepare for and execute tests

Assign responsibilities to test team members, including executives, observers, and contractors.

4.5 Validate the capability of contingency plans

Validate the functional capability of each contingency plan. Examine test results for accuracy and consistency and note discrepancies. For each contingency plan, ensure that

- the plan adequately supports a core business function;
- there is adequate capability to manage, record, and track the contingency transactions through the alternative business process;
- the manual activities in particular, and the alternative business process in general, meet an acceptable level of performance;
- an acceptable level of quality control is provided to critical parts of the alternative business process, and an acceptable level of integrity and consistency is provided to alternative databases; and
- an acceptable level of security is provided to the data captured by an alternative data capture mechanism.

4.6 Rehearse business resumption teams

Rehearse business resumption teams to ensure that each team and team member is familiar with business resumption procedures and their roles.

4.7 Update the business continuity plan based upon lessons learned and re-test if necessary

Resolve shortcomings and problems noted during testing and update each continuity plan. When under time constraints, prioritize the problem areas. For example, procedural problems involving internal administrative functions are not as serious as technical problems directly affecting the resumption of operations. Ongoing changes in systems, software, applications, communication, and operations will also require updates to the plan. A retest may be required to ensure that the problems do not recur and that the updated plan does provide the specified capability.

4.8 Update disaster recovery plans and procedures

Update disaster recovery plans. Ensure that all newly developed or acquired contingency applications and other software components are included in the disaster recovery update cycle.

Glossary

The definitions in this glossary were developed by the project staff or were drawn from other sources, including *The Computer Dictionary: The Comprehensive Standard For Business, School, Library, and Home,* Microsoft Press, Washington, DC, 1991; *The Year 2000 Resource Book,* Management Support Technology Corporation, Framingham, MA, 1996; *The Year 2000 and 2-Digit Dates: A Guide for Planning and Implementation,* International Business Machines Corporation, 1997; Denis Howe's "Free Online Dictionary of Computing"; and the Gartner Group's "IT Glossary."

Application
A computer program designed to help people perform a certain type of work. Depending on the work for which it was designed, an application can manipulate text, numbers, graphics, or a combination of these elements.

Architecture
A description of all functional activities to be performed to achieve the desired mission, the system elements needed to perform the functions, and the designation of performance levels of those system elements. An architecture also includes information on the technologies, interfaces, and location of functions and is considered an evolving description of an approach to achieving a desired mission.

Business Area
A grouping of business functions and processes focused on the production of specific outputs.

Business Function
A group of logically related tasks that are performed together to accomplish a mission-oriented objective.

Business Plan
An action plan that the enterprise will follow on a short-term and/or long-term basis. It specifies the strategic and tactical objectives of the enterprise over a period of time. The plan, therefore, will change over time. Although a business plan is usually written in a style unique to a specific enterprise, it should concisely describe "what" is planned, "why" it is planned, "when" it will be implemented, by "whom" it will be implemented, and "how" it will be assessed. The architects of the plan are typically the principals of the enterprise.

Contingency Plan
In the context of the Year 2000 program, a plan for responding to the loss or degradation of essential services due to a Year 2000 problem in an automated system. In general, a contingency plan describes the steps the enterprise would take—including the activation of manual or contract processes—to ensure the continuity of its core business processes in the event of a Year 2000-induced system failure.

Infrastructure
The computer and communication hardware, software, databases, people, facilities, and policies supporting the enterprise's information management functions.

Metrics
Measures by which processes, resources, and products can be assessed.

Mission-Critical System
A system supporting a core business activity or process.

Portfolio
In the context of the Year 2000 program, an inventory—preferably automated—of an agency's information systems and their components grouped by business areas.

Quality Assurance
All the planned and systematic actions necessary to provide adequate confidence that a product or service will satisfy given requirements for quality.

Risk Assessment
An activity performed to identify risks and estimate their probability and the impact of their occurrence; it is used during system development to provide an estimate of damage, loss, or harm that could result from a failure to successfully develop individual system components.

Risk Management
A management approach designed to prevent and reduce risks, including system development risks, and lessen the impact of their occurrence.

Strategic IRM Plan
A long-term, high-level plan that defines how the agency will use information technology to effectively accomplish the agency's missions, goals, and objectives.

Strategic Plan

A long-term, high-level plan that identifies broad business goals and provides a roadmap for their achievement.

Test

The process of exercising a product to identify differences between expected and actual behavior.

Test Facility

An environment that partially represents the production environment but is isolated from it, and is dedicated to the testing and validation of processes, applications, and system components.

Validation

The process of evaluating a system or component during or at the end of the development process to determine whether it satisfies specified requirements.

Year 2000 problem

The potential problems that might be encountered by computer hardware, software, or firmware in processing year-date data for years beyond 2000.

—Taken from: *www.gao.gov/special.pubs/bcpguide.pdf*

Discussion Questions

1) Which of the following is regarded as a threat to computers, networks, and information infrastructures?

   a. Worms

   b. Trojans

   c. Viruses

   d. All of the above

2) In regards to computer security and cyber terrorism, "DOS" stands for

   a. Data Operating System.

   b. Denial of Operating System.

   c. Denial of Service.

   d. Disruption of Operations: Suspected.

3) Which of the following is NOT a type of computer virus?

   a. File Infectors

   b. Serial Port Disruptor

   c. Boot Sector Infector

   d. All of the above

---

4) Computer _____ are simply malicious computer programs disguised as something useful.

5) Computer _____ are reproducing programs that run independently and travel across network connections.

6) The U.S. Computer Emergency Response Team coordinates defense against and responses to _____-_____ across the nation.

7) In information technology contingency planning, BIA is an acronym for _____ _____ _____.

8) A system or function that is regarded as vital to an organization being able to execute its fundamental goals and objectives is known as "mission _____."

9) In regards to contingency plan maintenance, as a general rule, the plan should be reviewed for accuracy and completeness at least _____ or whenever _____ _____ occur.

10) The anticipated potential catastrophic information systems failure that led to a great deal of IT contingency planning in the late 1990s was known as the "_____" bug.

Answers

1) D

2) C

3) B

4) Trojans

5) Worms

6) Cyber attacks

7) Business Impact Analysis

8) Critical

9) Annually, significant changes

10) Y2K

2 The Threat of Terrorism

Overview:

In the previous text, we looked at the events of September 11, 2001, the global terrorist organization known as "Al Qaeda" or "The Base," and the advent of "super-terrorism." In Chapter Two of this text, we will expand the discussion to examine the history, ideology, pathology, and tactics of terrorism.

In terms of controlling and preventing "chaos," terrorism is unique as it seeks to be a form of deliberate chaos. Terrorism could be thought of as "natural disaster meets criminality." While the impact and effect of terrorism tends to have the devastation magnitude of a natural disaster, the conscientious malice of the phenomena is rooted in a criminal pathology. Thus the chaos created by the terrorist is planned and, by their way of thinking, purposeful. Combating terror requires a multi-faceted approach that the professional homeland security specialist must master to achieve effectiveness.

Chapter Objectives:

- *Articulate the history, roots and goals of terrorism*
- *Explain why scholars and officials have such a difficult time coming up with one comprehensive definition of terrorism*
- *Identify the themes and realities that drive terrorism tactics and methodologies*

Defining the Terrorist Threat

One could fill up an entire series of books twice the size of this text and only begin to scratch the surface of what terrorism is. To begin, let us examine some existing attempts to define terrorism.

According to Title 22 of the United States Code, section 2656 f(d), terrorism is defined as

> *Premeditated, politically motivated violence perpetrated against non-combatant targets by subnational groups or clandestine agents, usually intended to influence an audience.*

Whereas *Webster's Dictionary* defines terrorism as

> *The use of force or threats to demoralize, intimidate, and subjugate, especially such use as the political weapon or policy.*

In yet another definition, the Ayatollah Sheikh Muhammad 'Ali Tashkiri of the Organization of the Islamic Conference summed up terrorism this way:

> *Terrorism is an act carried out to achieve an inhuman and corrupt (mufsid) objective, and involving threat to security of any kind, and violation of rights acknowledged by religion and mankind.*

These three definitions pose two very interesting philosophical questions to the homeland security student: "*What is terrorism?*" and "*Who is a terrorist?*"

Notice that according to U.S. federal law's definition, a nation-state cannot carry out terrorism; only "subnational groups" or "clandestine agents" can. The U.S. Government goes so far as to say that nation-states may "sponsor" terrorism (through financing, lending safe haven, sharing intelligence), but the definition seems to stop short of saying that a nation can carry out terrorism, even in cases such as the 1988 bombing of Pan Am Flight 103 over Lockerbie, Scotland, when the bombers were identified as being operatives of the Libyan intelligence services. The difference between being a terrorist and sponsoring terrorism is very nuanced, but it seems legally significant to nations such as the United States.

Whereas the U.S. definition largely addresses legal nuances, and the *Webster's* definition is very general, the Organization of the Islamic Conference's definition of terrorism, on the other hand, seems to deal more with issues of religiosity, morality, and human rights. In stark contrast to Western definitions, the OIC not only identifies "official terrorism" as terror carried out by states and governments, but also identifies it as the more dangerous type.

> *There exists, however, a division based on the type of perpetrators, which must be taken into account. It is the division into official and unofficial terrorism. Official terrorism—which is the more dangerous—consists of all acts that are supported by an internationally recognized quarter or state, whether by the army of that state or individual elements or in the form of an operation for the benefit of the said quarter. Opposing this type of terrorism is unofficial terrorism.*[1]

Some might condemn this definition as irresponsible, as it could be interpreted as justifying "unofficial terrorism" as defense against government repression or "official terrorism," lending a sense of sanction to subnational terrorist groups.

History of Terrorism

Terrorism is not an especially new concept. Use of egregious force, intimidation, and violence designed to coerce through fear dates back for millennia. Zealots, revolutionaries, nationalists, and anarchists have all sought to further their objectives through the manifestation of terrorism.

The following article, from the Center for Defense Information, provides an excellent perspective on historical uses and origins of terrorism.

A Brief History of Terrorism

To begin any history of terrorism (however brief) without first defining what the term means might appear to be putting the cart before the horse. Despite this, no such definition shall be proffered here. Partly, this is for reasons of brevity, but mainly because any effort to first define terrorism would mean restricting any ensuing narrative to this definition. As such, this is not so much a brief history of terrorism as much as a brief history of examples of that which has been (or arguably could be) generally accepted to constitute terrorism. Not everyone will agree that all these examples do so, and there are other instances that could be so construed that are not mentioned at all.

One point is less debatable: terrorism is not new. Indeed, in some respects, that what is today known as terrorism predates by millennia the modern term used to describe it. This is not to say that the act of terrorism has remained static. Rather, as the difficulties involved in defining it reflect, terrorism has evolved considerably over the years, even if retaining some of the same characteristics that have historically typified it.

While it is impossible to definitively ascertain when it was first used, that which we today call terrorism traces its roots back at least some 2,000 years. Moreover, today's terrorism has, in some respects come full circle, with many of its contemporary practitioners motivated by religious convictions—something which drove many of their earliest predecessors. It has also, in the generally accepted usage of the word, often possessed a political dimension. This has colored much of the discourse surrounding terrorism—a phenomenon which is, according to Paul R. Pillar, "a challenge to be managed, not solved."

Religious Roots

Among the earliest such examples were the Sicari and the Zealots, Jewish groups active during the Roman occupation of the first century Middle East. The favored weapon of the Sicari was the sica (the short dagger which gave them their name, which literally means "dagger men"), which they used to murder those (mainly Jews) they deemed apostate and thus selected for execution. The Zealots, who generally targeted Romans and Greeks, give us the modern term Zealot, one translation of which is "a fanatical partisan." Such killings usually took place in daylight and in front of witnesses, with the perpetrators using such acts to send a message to the Roman authorities and those Jews who collaborated with them—a tactic that would also be used by subsequent generations of what would become known as terrorists.

Adherents of other religions also resorted to methods which might today be termed terrorism, such as the Assassins—an eleventh century offshoot of a Shia Muslim sect known as the Ismailis. Like the Zealots-Sicari, the Assassins were also given to stabbing their victims (generally politicians or clerics who refused to adopt the purified version of Islam they were forcibly spreading) in broad daylight. The Assassins—whose name gave us the modern term but literally meant "hashish-eater"—a reference to the ritualistic drug-taking they were (perhaps falsely) rumored to indulge in prior to undertaking missions—also used their actions to send a message. Often, the Assassins' deeds were carried out at religious sites on holy days—a tactic intended to publicize their cause and incite others to it. Like many religiously inspired terrorists today, they also viewed their deaths on such operations as sacrificial and a guarantor that they would enter paradise.

Sacrifice was also a central element of the killings carried out by the Thugees (who bequeathed us the word "thug")—an Indian religious cult who ritually strangled their victims (usually travelers chosen at random) as an offering to the Hindu goddess of terror and destruction, Kali. In this case, the intent was to terrify the victim (a vital consideration in the Thugee ritual) rather than influence any external audience.

Active from the seventh until the mid-nineteenth centuries, the Thugees are reputed to be responsible for as many as one million murders. They were perhaps the last example of religiously-inspired terrorism until the phenomenon reemerged a little over twenty years ago. As David Rapport puts it, "Before the nineteenth century, religion provided the only acceptable justifications for terror." More secularized motivations for such actions did not emerge until the French Revolution, as did the first usage of the term now used to describe them.

Nationalists and Anarchists
The English word "terrorism" comes from the *regime de la terreur* that prevailed in France from 1793–1794. Originally an instrument of the state, the regime was designed to consolidate the power of the newly-installed revolutionary government, protecting it from elements considered "subversive." Always value-laden, terrorism was, initially, a positive term. The French revolutionary leader Maximilien Robespierre viewed it as vital if the new French Republic was to survive its infancy, proclaiming in 1794 that, "Terror is nothing other than justice, prompt, severe, inflexible; it is therefore an emanation of virtue; it is not so much a special principle as

it is a consequence of the general principle of democracy applied to our country's most urgent needs."

Under such justification, some 40,000 people were executed by guillotine—a fate Robespierre and his top lieutenants would themselves suffer later that same year, when his announcement of a new list of subversives led to a counter-inquisition by some in the Revolutionary government who feared their names might be on the latest roll of "traitors." Before long, the Revolution devoured itself in an orgy of paranoiac bloodletting. Meanwhile, terrorism itself began taking on the negative connotations it carries today (terrorists do not generally tend to describe themselves thus), helped initially by the writings of those like the British political philosopher Edmund Burke, who popularized the term "terrorism" in English while demonizing its French revolutionary practitioners.

The newly defined notions of nationalism and citizenship, which both caused and were a result of the French Revolution, also saw the emergence of a new, predominantly secular terrorism. The appearance of political ideologies such as Marxism also created a fertile sense of unrest at the existing order, with terrorism offering a means for change. This led to proposals at the League of Nations for conventions to prevent and punish terrorism as well as the establishment of an international criminal court (neither of which came to aught as they were overshadowed by the events which eventually led to World War II). Despite this, during the interwar years, terrorism increasingly referred to the oppressive measures imposed by various totalitarian regimes, most notably those in Nazi Germany, Fascist Italy, and Stalinist Russia. More recently, other governments, such as those military dictatorships which ruled some South American countries in recent years, or the current regime in Zimbabwe, have also been open to charges of using such methods as a tool of state. Such considerations notwithstanding, some commentators, such as Bruce Hoffman, argue that "such usages are generally termed 'terror' in order to distinguish that phenomenon from 'terrorism,' which is understood to be violence committed by non-state entities." However not everyone agrees that terrorism should be considered a non-governmental undertaking.

For instance, Jessica Stern insists that in deliberately bombarding civilians as a means of attacking enemy morale, states have indeed resorted to terrorism. Per Stern, such instances include not only the allied strategic bombing campaigns of World War II, but the American dropping of atomic bombs on Hiroshima and Nagasaki that ended the Pacific phase of that conflict. This issue remains a contentious one, with individuals such as the World War II British Air Chief "Bomber" Harris alternatively defended and reviled for their belief in the utility and morality of strategic bombing.

Terrorism Since World War II
By contrast, the preponderance of nonstate groups in the terrorism that emerged in the wake of World War II is less debatable. The immediate focus for such activity mainly shifted from Europe itself to that continent's

various colonies. Across the Middle East, Asia, and Africa, nascent nationalist movements resisted European attempts to resume colonial business
as usual after the defeat of the Axis powers. That the colonialists had been
so recently expelled from or subjugated in their overseas empires by the
Japanese provided psychological succor to such indigenous uprisings by
dispelling the myth of European invincibility.

Often, these nationalist and anti-colonial groups conducted guerrilla warfare, which differed from terrorism mainly in that it tended toward larger
bodies of "irregulars" operating along more military lines than their terrorist cousins, and often in the open from a defined geographical area over
which they held sway. Such was the case in China and Indochina, where
such forces conducted insurgencies against the Kuomintang regime and
the French colonial government respectively. Elsewhere, such as with the
fight against French rule in Algeria, these campaigns were fought in both
rural and urban areas and by terrorist and guerrilla means.

Still other such struggles like those in Kenya, Malaysia, Cyprus, and Palestine (all involving the British who, along with the French, bore the brunt
of this new wave of terrorism—a corollary of their large prewar empires)
were fought by groups who can more readily be described as terrorist.
These groups quickly learned to exploit the burgeoning globalization of
the world's media. As Hoffman puts it, "They were the first to recognize
the publicity value inherent in terrorism and to choreograph their violence
for an audience far beyond the immediate geographical loci of their respective struggles." Moreover, in some cases (such as in Algeria, Cyprus, Kenya,
and Israel) terrorism arguably helped such organizations in the successful
realization of their goals. As such, these nationalist and anticolonial groups
are of note in any wider understanding of terrorism.

Through the 1960s and 1970s, the numbers of those groups that might be
described as terrorist swelled to include not only nationalists but those
motivated by ethnic and ideological considerations. The former included
groups such as the Palestinian Liberation Organization (and its many affil-
iates), the Basque ETA, and the Provisional Irish Republican Army, while
the latter comprised organizations such as the Red Army Faction (in what
was then West Germany) and the Italian Red Brigades. As with the emergence of modern terrorism almost a century earlier, the United States was
not immune from this latest wave, although there the identity-crisis-dri-
ven motivations of the white, middle-class Weathermen starkly contrasted
with the ghetto-bred malcontent of the Black Panther movement.

Like their anti-colonialist predecessors of the immediate post-war era, many
of the terrorist groups of this period readily appreciated and adopted methods that would allow them to publicize their goals and accomplishments
internationally. Forerunners in this were the Palestinian groups who pio-
neered the hijacking of a chief symbol and means of the new age of globalization—the jet airliner—as a mode of operation and publicity. One such
group, Black September, staged what was (until the attacks on America of

September 11, 2001) perhaps the greatest terrorist publicity coup then seen, with the seizure and murder of eleven Israeli athletes at the 1972 Olympic Games. Such incidents resulted in the Palestinian groups providing the inspiration (and in some cases mentorship and training) for many of the new generation of terrorists organizations.

Many of these organizations have today declined or ceased to exist altogether, while others, such as the Palestinian, Northern Irish, and Spanish Basque groups, motivated by more enduring causes, remain active today—although some now have made moves toward political rather than terrorist methods. Meanwhile, by the mid-1980s, state-sponsored terrorism re-emerged—the catalyst for the series of attacks against American and other Western targets in the Middle East. Countries such as Iran, Iraq, Libya, and Syria came to the fore as the principle such sponsors of terrorism. Falling into a related category were those countries, such as North Korea, who directly participated in covert acts of what could be described as terrorism.

Such state-sponsored terrorism remains a concern of the international community today (especially its Western constituents), although it has been somewhat overshadowed in recent times by the re-emergence of the religiously inspired terrorist. The latest manifestation of this trend began in 1979, when the revolution that transformed Iran into an Islamic republic led it to use and support terrorism as a means of propagating its ideals beyond its own border. Before long, the trend had spread beyond Iran to places as far away as Japan and the United States, and beyond Islam to every major world religion as well as many minor cults. From the sarin attack on the Tokyo subway by the Aum Shinrikyo in 1995 to the Oklahoma bombing the same year, religion was again added to the complex mix of motivations that led to acts of terrorism. The Al Qaeda attacks of September 11, 2001, brought home to the world, and most particularly the United States, just how dangerous this latest mutation of terrorism is.

Contemporary Terrorism
Today, terrorism influences events on the international stage to a degree hitherto unachieved. Largely, this is due to the attacks of September 2001. Since then, in the United States at least, terrorism has largely been equated to the threat posed by Al Qaeda—a threat inflamed not only by the spectacular and deadly nature of the September 11 attacks themselves, but by the fear that future strikes might be even deadlier and employ weapons of mass destruction.

Whatever global threat may be posed by Al Qaeda and its franchisees, the U.S. view of terrorism nonetheless remains, to a degree, largely egocentric—despite the current administration's rhetoric concerning a so-called "Global War Against Terrorism." This is far from unique. Despite the implications that Al Qaeda actually intends to wage a global insurgency, the citizens of countries such as Colombia or Northern Ireland (to name but two of those long, faced with terrorism) are likely more preoccupied with when and where the next FARC or Real Irish Republican Army attack will occur rather than where the next Al Qaeda strike will fall.

As such considerations indicate, terrorism goes beyond Al Qaeda, which it not only predates but will also outlive. Given this, if terrorism is to be countered most effectively, any understanding of it must go beyond the threat currently posed by that particular organization. Without such a broad-based approach, not only will terrorism be unsolvable (to paraphrase Pillar) but it also risks becoming unmanageable.

—Taken from: *http://www.cdi.org/program/issue/document.cfm*

Pathology of Terrorism

How does a terrorist think? What motivates someone to carry out acts of terrorism? These are among the most challenging questions regarding terrorism. The following thesis prepared for the U.S. Government offers an exhaustive study into the roots and pathologies of individuals who are attracted to the many different international terrorist organizations and will prove to be an excellent resource in your study of terrorism.

The Sociology and Psychology of Terrorism: Who Becomes a Terrorist and Why?

A Report Prepared under an Interagency Agreement
by the Federal Research Division,
Library of Congress
September 1999

Preface
The purpose of this study is to focus attention on the types of individuals and groups that are prone to terrorism (see Glossary) in an effort to help improve U.S. counterterrorist methods and policies.

The emergence of amorphous and largely unknown terrorist individuals and groups operating independently (freelancers) and the new recruitment patterns of some groups, such as recruiting suicide commandos, female and child terrorists, and scientists capable of developing weapons of mass destruction, provide a measure of urgency to increasing our understanding of the psychological and sociological dynamics of terrorist groups and individuals. The approach used in this study is twofold. First, the study examines the relevant literature and assesses the current knowledge of the subject. Second, the study seeks to develop psychological and sociological profiles of foreign terrorist individuals and selected groups to use as case studies in assessing trends, motivations, likely behavior, and actions that might deter such behavior, as well as reveal vulnerabilities that would aid in combating terrorist groups and individuals.

Because this survey is concerned not only with assessing the extensive literature on sociopsychological aspects of terrorism but also providing case studies of about a dozen terrorist groups, it is limited by time constraints and data availability in the amount of attention that it can give to the individual groups, let alone individual leaders or other members. Thus, analysis of the groups and leaders will necessarily be incomplete. A longer study, for example, would allow for the collection and study of the literature produced by each group in the form of autobiographies of former members, group communiqués and manifestos, news media interviews, and other resources. Much information about the terrorist mindset (see Glossary) and decision-making process can be gleaned from such sources. Moreover, there is a language barrier to an examination of the untranslated literature of most of the groups included as case studies herein.

Terrorism databases that profile groups and leaders quickly become outdated, and this report is no exception to that rule. In order to remain current, a terrorism database ideally should be updated periodically. New groups or terrorist leaders may suddenly emerge, and if an established group perpetrates a major terrorist incident, new information on the group is likely to be reported in news media. Even if a group appears to be quiescent, new information may become available about the group from scholarly publications.

There are many variations in the transliteration for both Arabic and Persian. The academic versions tend to be more complex than the popular forms used in the news media and by the Foreign Broadcast Information Service (FBIS). Thus, the latter usages are used in this study. For example, although Ussamah bin Ladin is the proper transliteration, the more commonly used Osama bin Laden is used in this study.

Executive Summary: Mindsets of Mass Destruction

New Types of Post-Cold War Terrorists

In the 1970s and 1980s, it was commonly assumed that terrorist use of weapons of mass destruction (WMD) would be counterproductive because such an act would be widely condemned. "Terrorists want a lot of people watching, not a lot of people dead," Brian Jenkins (1975:15) opined. Jenkins's premise was based on the assumption that terrorist behavior is normative, and that if they exceeded certain constraints and employed WMD they would completely alienate themselves from the public and possibly provoke swift and harsh retaliation. This assumption does seem to apply to certain secular terrorist groups. If a separatist organization such as the Provisional Irish Republic Army (PIRA) or the Basque Fatherland and Liberty (Euzkadi Ta Askatasuna—ETA), for example, were to use WMD, these groups would likely isolate their constituency and undermine sources of funding and political support. When the assumptions about terrorist groups not using WMD were made in the 1970s and 1980s, most of the terrorist groups making headlines were groups with political or nationalist-separatist agenda. Those groups, with some exceptions, such as the Japanese Red Army (JRA—Rengo Sekigun), had reason not to sabotage their ethnic bases of popular support or other domestic or foreign sympathizers of their cause by using WMD.

Trends in terrorism over the past three decades, however, have contradicted the conventional thinking that terrorists are averse to using WMD. It has become increasingly evident that the assumption does not apply to religious terrorist groups or millenarian cults (see Glossary). Indeed, since at least the early 1970s analysts, including (somewhat contradictorily) Jenkins, have predicted that the first groups to employ a weapon of mass destruction would be religious sects with a millenarian, messianic, or apocalyptic mindset.

When the conventional terrorist groups and individuals of the early 1970s are compared with terrorists of the early 1990s, a trend can be seen: the emergence of religious fundamentalist and new religious groups espousing the rhetoric of mass-destruction terrorism. In the 1990s, groups motivated by religious imperatives, such as Aum Shinrikyo, Hizballah, and Al Qaeda, have grown and proliferated. These groups have a different attitude toward violence—one that is extranormative and seeks to maximize violence against the perceived enemy, essentially anyone who is not a fundamentalist Muslim or an Aum Shinrikyo member. Their outlook is one that divides the world simplistically into "them" and "us." With its sarin attack on the Tokyo subway system on March 20, 1995, the doomsday cult Aum Shinrikyo turned the prediction of terrorists using WMD into reality.

Beginning in the early 1990s, Aum Shinrikyo engaged in a systematic program to develop and use WMD. It used chemical or biological WMD in about a dozen largely unreported instances in the first half of the 1990s, although they proved to be no more effective—actually less effective—than conventional weapons because of the terrorists' ineptitude. Nevertheless, it was Aum Shinrikyo's sarin attack on the Tokyo subway on March 20, 1995, that showed the world how dangerous the mindset of a religious terrorist group could be. The attack provided convincing evidence that Aum Shinrikyo probably would not hesitate to use WMD in a U.S. city, if it had an opportunity to do so. These religiously motivated groups would have no reason to take "credit" for such an act of mass destruction, just as Aum Shinrikyo did not take credit for its attack on the Tokyo subway, and just as Osama bin Laden did not take credit for various acts of high-casualty terrorism against U.S. targets in the 1990s. Taking credit means asking for retaliation. Instead, it is enough for these groups to simply take private satisfaction in knowing that they have dealt a harsh blow to what they perceive to be the "Great Satan." Groups unlikely to be deterred by fear of public disapproval, such as Aum Shinrikyo, are the ones who seek chaos as an end in itself.

The contrast between key members of religious extremist groups such as Hizballah, Al Qaeda, and Aum Shinrikyo and conventional terrorists reveals some general trends relating to the personal attributes of terrorists likely to use WMD in coming years. According to psychologist Jerrold M. Post

(1997), the most dangerous terrorist is likely to be the religious terrorist. Post has explained that, unlike the average political or social terrorist, who has a defined mission that is somewhat measurable in terms of media attention or government reaction, the religious terrorist can justify the most heinous acts "in the name of Allah," for example. One could add, "in the name of Aum Shinrikyo's Shoko Asahara."

Psychologist B.J. Berkowitz (1972) describes six psychological types who would be most likely to threaten or try to use WMD: paranoids, paranoid schizophrenics, borderline mental defectives, schizophrenic types, passive-aggressive personality (see Glossary) types, and sociopath (see Glossary) personalities. He considers sociopaths the most likely actually to use WMD. Nuclear terrorism expert Jessica Stern (1999: 77) disagrees. She believes that "schizophrenics and sociopaths, for example, may want to commit acts of mass destruction, but they are less likely than others to succeed." She points out that large-scale dissemination of chemical, biological, or radiological agents requires a group effort, but that "schizophrenics, in particular, often have difficulty functioning in groups. . . ."

Stern's understanding of the WMD terrorist appears to be much more relevant than Berkowitz's earlier stereotype of the insane terrorist. It is clear from the appended case study of Shoko Asahara that he is paranoid. Whether he is schizophrenic or sociopathic is best left to psychologists to determine. The appended case study of Ahmed Ramzi Yousef, mastermind of the World Trade Center (WTC) bombing on February 26, 1993, reported here does not suggest that he is schizophrenic or sociopathic. On the contrary, he appears to be a well-educated, highly intelligent Islamic terrorist. In 1972, Berkowitz could not have been expected to foresee that religiously motivated terrorists would be prone to using WMD as a way of emulating God or for millenarian reasons. This examination of about a dozen groups that have engaged in significant acts of terrorism suggests that the groups most likely to use WMD are indeed religious groups, whether they be wealthy cults like Aum Shinrikyo or well-funded Islamic terrorist groups like Al Qaeda or Hizballah.

The fall of the Berlin Wall in 1989 and the collapse of the Soviet Union in 1991 fundamentally changed the operating structures of European terrorist groups. Whereas groups like the Red Army Faction (Rote Armee Faktion—RAF; see Glossary) were able to use East Germany as a refuge and a source of logistical and financial resources during the Cold War decades, terrorist groups in the post-Cold War period no longer enjoy the support of communist countries. Moreover, state sponsors of international terrorism (see Glossary) toned down their support of terrorist groups. In this new environment where terrorist groups can no longer depend on state support or any significant popular support, they have been restructuring in order to learn how to operate independently.

New breeds of increasingly dangerous religious terrorists emerged in the 1990s. The most dangerous type is the Islamic fundamentalist. A case in point is Ramzi Yousef, who brought together a loosely organized ad hoc group, the so-called Liberation Army, apparently for the sole purpose of carrying out the WTC operation on February 26, 1993. Moreover, by acting independently, the small, self-contained cell led by Yousef prevented authorities from linking it to an established terrorist organization, such as its suspected coordinating group, Osama bin Laden's Al Qaeda, or a possible state sponsor.

The World Trade Center

Aum Shinrikyo is representative of the other type of religious terrorist group, in this case a cult. Shoko Asahara adopted a different approach to terrorism by modeling his organization on the structure of the Japanese government rather than an ad hoc terrorist group. Accordingly, Aum Shinrikyo "ministers" undertook a program to develop WMD by bringing together a core group of bright scientists skilled in the modern technologies of the computer, telecommunications equipment, information databases, and financial networks. They proved themselves capable of developing rudimentary WMD in a relatively short time and demonstrated a willingness to use them in the most lethal ways possible. Aum Shinrikyo's sarin gas attack in the Tokyo subway system in 1995 marked the official debut of terrorism involving WMD. Had a more lethal batch of sarin been used, or had the dissemination procedure been improved slightly, the attack might have killed thousands of people, instead of only a few. Both of these incidents—the WTC bombing and the Tokyo subway sarin attack—had similar casualty totals but could have had massive casualties. Ramzi Yousef's plot to blow up the WTC might have killed an estimated 50,000 people had his team not made a minor error in the placement of the bomb. In any case, these two acts in Manhattan and Tokyo seem an ominous foretaste of the WMD terrorism to come in the first decade of the new millennium.

Statue of Liberty and Twin Towers.
Courtesy of Bettmann/Corbis Images.

Increasingly, terrorist groups are recruiting members with expertise in fields such as communications, computer programming, engineering, finance, and the sciences. Ramzi Yousef graduated from Britain's Swansea University with a degree in engineering. Aum Shinrikyo's Shoko Asahara recruited a scientific team with all the expertise needed to develop WMD. Osama bin Laden also recruits highly skilled professionals in the fields of engineering, medicine, chemistry, physics, computer programming, communications, and so forth. Whereas the skills of the elite terrorist commandos of the 1960s and 1970s were often limited to what they learned in training camp, the terrorists of the 1990s who have carried out major operations have included biologists, chemists, computer specialists, engineers, and physicists.

New Forms of Terrorist-Threat Scenarios

The number of international terrorist incidents has declined in the 1990s, but the potential threat posed by terrorists has increased. The increased threat level, in the form of terrorist actions aimed at achieving a larger scale of destruction than the conventional attacks of the previous three decades, was dramatically demonstrated with the bombing of the WTC. The WTC bombing illustrated how terrorists with technological sophistication are increasingly being recruited to carry out lethal terrorist bombing attacks. The WTC bombing may also have been a harbinger of more destructive attacks of international terrorism in the United States.

Although there are not too many examples, if any, of guerrilla (see Glossary) groups dispatching commandos to carry out a terrorist operation in the United States, the mindsets of four groups discussed herein—two guerrilla/terrorist groups, a terrorist group, and a terrorist cult—are such that these groups pose particularly dangerous actual or potential terrorist threats to U.S. security interests. The two guerrilla/terrorist groups are the Liberation Tigers of Tamil Ealam (LTTE) and Hizballah; the terrorist group is Al Qaeda; and the terrorist cult is Aum Shinrikyo.

The LTTE is not known to have engaged in anti-U.S. terrorism to date, but its suicide commandos have already assassinated a prime minister of India, a president of Sri Lanka, and a former prime minister of Sri Lanka. In August 1999, the LTTE reportedly deployed a ten-member suicide squad in Colombo to assassinate Prime Minister Chandrika Kumaratunga and others. It cannot be safely assumed, however, that the LTTE will restrict its terrorism to the South Asian subcontinent. Prabhakaran has repeatedly warned the Western nations providing military support to Sri Lanka that they are exposing their citizens to possible attacks. The LTTE, which has an extensive international network, should not be underestimated in the terrorist threat that it could potentially pose to the United States, should it perceive this country as actively aiding the Sri Lankan government's counterinsurgency campaign. Prabhakaran is a megalomaniac whose record of ordering the assassinations of heads of state or former presidents, meticulous planning of such actions, compulsion to have the acts photographed and chronicled by LTTE members, and limitless supply of female suicide commandos at his disposal add a dangerous new dimension to potential assassination threats. His highly trained and disciplined Black Tiger commandos are far deadlier than Aum Shinrikyo's inept cultists. There is little protection against the LTTE's trademark weapon: a belt-bomb suicide commando.

Hizballah is likewise quite dangerous. Except for its ongoing terrorist war against Israel, however, it appears to be reactive, often carrying out terrorist attacks for what it perceives to be Western military, cultural, or political threats to the establishment of an Iranian-style Islamic republic in Lebanon.

The threat to U.S. interests posed by Islamic fundamentalist terrorists in particular was underscored by Al Qaeda's bombings of the U.S. embassies in Kenya and Tanzania in August 1998. With those two devastating bombings, Osama bin Laden resurfaced as a potent terrorist threat to U.S. interests worldwide. Bin Laden is the prototype of a new breed of terrorist—the private entrepreneur who puts modern enterprise at the service of a global terrorist network.

With its sarin attack against the Tokyo subway system in March 1995, Aum Shinrikyo has already used WMD and very likely has not abandoned its quest to use such weapons to greater effect. The activities of Aum's large membership in Russia should be of particular concern because Aum Shinrikyo has used its Russian organization to try to obtain WMD, or at least WMD technologies.

The leaders of any of these groups—Prabhakaran, bin Laden, and Asahara—could become paranoid, desperate, or simply vengeful enough to order their suicide devotees to employ the belt-bomb technique against the leader of the Western world. Iranian intelligence leaders could order Hizballah to attack the U.S. leadership in retaliation for some future U.S. or Israeli action, although Iran may now be distancing itself from Hizballah. Whether or not a U.S. president would be a logical target of Asahara, Prabhakaran, or bin Laden is not a particularly useful guideline to assess the probability of such an attack. Indian Prime Minister Rajiv Gandhi was not a logical target for the LTTE, and his assassination had very negative consequences for the LTTE. In Prabhakaran's "psycho-logic," to use Post's term, he may conclude that his cause needs greater international attention, and targeting a country's top leaders is his way of getting attention. Nor does bin Laden need a logical reason, for he believes that he has a mandate from Allah to punish the "Great Satan." Instead of thinking logically, Asahara thinks in terms of a megalomaniac with an apocalyptic outlook. Aum Shinrikyo is a group whose delusional leader is genuinely paranoid about the United States and is known to have plotted to assassinate Japan's emperor. Shoko Asahara's cult is already on record for having made an assassination threat against President Clinton.

If Iran's mullahs or Iraq's Saddam Hussein decide to use terrorists to attack the continental United States, they would likely turn to bin Laden's Al Qaeda. Al Qaeda is among the Islamic groups recruiting increasingly skilled professionals, such as computer and communications technicians, engineers, pharmacists, and physicists, as well as Ukrainian chemists and biologists, Iraqi chemical weapons experts, and others capable of helping to develop WMD. Al Qaeda poses the most serious terrorist threat to U.S. security interests, for Al Qaeda's well-trained terrorists are actively engaged in a terrorist jihad against U.S. interests worldwide.*

These four groups in particular are each capable of perpetrating a horrific act of terrorism in the United States, particularly on the occasion of the new millennium. Aum Shinrikyo has already threatened to use WMD in downtown Manhattan or in Washington, DC, where it could attack the Congress, the Pentagon's Concourse, the White House, or President Clinton. The cult has threatened New York City with WMD, threatened to assassinate President Clinton, unsuccessfully attacked a U.S. naval base in Japan with biological weapons, and plotted in 1994 to attack the White House and the Pentagon with sarin and VX. If the LTTE's serial assassin of heads of state were to become angered by President Clinton, Prabhakaran could react by dispatching a Tamil "belt-bomb girl" to detonate a powerful semtex bomb after approaching the president in a crowd with a garland of flowers or after jumping next to his car.

Al Qaeda's expected retaliation for the U.S. cruise missile attack against Al Qaeda's training facilities in Afghanistan on August 20, 1998, could take several forms of terrorist attack in the nation's capital. Al Qaeda could detonate a Chechen-type building-buster bomb at a federal building. Suicide bomber(s) belonging to Al Qaeda's Martyrdom Battalion could crash-land an aircraft packed with high explosives (C-4 and semtex) into the Pentagon, the headquarters of the Central Intelligence Agency (CIA), or the White House. Ramzi Yousef had planned to do this against the CIA headquarters. In addition, both Al Qaeda and Yousef were linked to a plot to assassinate President Clinton during his visit to the Philippines in early 1995. Following the August 1998 cruise missile attack, at least one Islamic religious leader called for Clinton's assassination, and another stated that "the time is not far off" for when the White House will be destroyed by a nuclear bomb. A horrendous scenario consonant with Al Qaeda's mindset would be its use of a nuclear suitcase bomb against any number of targets in the nation's capital. Bin Laden allegedly has already purchased a number of nuclear suitcase bombs from the Chechen Mafia. Al Qaeda's retaliation, however, is more likely to take the lower-risk form of bombing one or more U.S. airliners with time bombs. Yousef was planning simultaneous bombings of eleven U.S. airliners prior to his capture. Whatever form an attack may take, bin Laden will most likely retaliate in a spectacular way for the cruise missile attack against his Afghan camp in August 1998.

* Author's note: This article was prepared by reseachers in advance of the current world situation. While the overwhelming majority of this article has proven to be extremely well researched and almost prophetic, the author wishes to state that the findings of both objective intelligence sources and the 9/11 Commission have discredited the notion of any operational link between Saddam Hussein's Iraq and the Al Qaeda network regarding the events of September 11th, 2001. The decision to use this article was based on the preponderance of useful historical information and insights into terrorism that it provides, but should not be interpreted as validation of claims of collusion between the former Iraqi government and Al Qaeda.

While nothing is easier than to denounce the evildoer,
nothing is more difficult than to understand him.

—*Fyodor Mikhailovich Dostoevsky*

Introduction

Why do some individuals decide to break with society and embark on a career in terrorism? Do terrorists share common traits or characteristics? Is there a terrorist personality or profile? Can a terrorist profile be developed that could reliably help security personnel to identify potential terrorists, whether they be would-be airplane hijackers, assassins, or suicide bombers? Do some terrorists have a psychotic (see Glossary) personality? Psychological factors relating to terrorism are of particular interest to psychologists, political scientists, and government officials, who would like to be able to predict and prevent the emergence of terrorist groups or to thwart the realization of terrorist actions. This study focuses on individual psychological and sociological characteristics of terrorists of different generations, as well as their groups, in an effort to determine how the terrorist profile may have changed in recent decades, or whether they share any common sociological attributes.

The assumption underlying much of the terrorist profile research in recent decades has been that most terrorists have some common characteristics that can be determined through psychometric analysis of large quantities of biographical data on terrorists. One of the earliest attempts to single out a terrorist personality was done by Charles A. Russell and Bowman H. Miller (1977) (see Attributes of Terrorists).

Ideally, a researcher attempting to profile terrorists in the 1990s would have access to extensive biographical data on several hundred terrorists arrested in various parts of the world and data on terrorists operating in a specific country. If such data were at hand, the researcher could prepare a psychometric study analyzing attributes of the terrorist: educational, occupational, and socioeconomic background; general traits; ideology; marital status; method and place of recruitment; physical appearance; and sex. Researchers have used this approach to study West German and Italian terrorist groups (see Females). Such detailed information would provide more accurate sociological profiles of terrorist groups. Although there appears to be no single terrorist personality, members of a terrorist group(s) may share numerous common sociological traits.

Practically speaking, however, biographical databases on large numbers of terrorists are not readily available. Indeed, such data would be quite difficult to obtain unless one had special access to police files on terrorists around the world. Furthermore, developing an open-source biographical database on enough terrorists to have some scientific validity would require a substantial investment of time. The small number of profiles contained in this study is hardly sufficient to qualify as scientifically representative of terrorists in general, or even of a particular category of terrorists, such as religious fundamentalists or ethnic separatists. Published terrorism databases, such as Edward F. Mickolus's series of chronologies of incidents of international terrorism and the Rand-St. Andrews University Chronology of International Terrorism, are highly informative and contain some useful biographical information on terrorists involved in major incidents, but are largely incident-oriented.

This study is not about terrorism per se. Rather, it is concerned with the perpetrators of terrorism. Prepared from a social sciences perspective, it attempts to synthesize the results of psychological and sociological findings of studies on terrorists published in recent decades and provide a general assessment of what is presently known about the terrorist mind and mindset.

Because of time constraints and a lack of terrorism-related biographical databases, the methodology, but not the scope, of this research has necessarily been modified. In the absence of a database of terrorist biographies, this study is based on the broader database of knowledge contained in academic studies on the psychology and sociology of terrorism published over the past three decades. Using this extensive database of open-source literature available in the Library of Congress and other information drawn from Web sites, such as the Foreign Broadcast Information Service (FBIS), this paper assesses the level of current knowledge of the subject and presents case studies that include sociopsychological profiles of about a dozen selected terrorist groups and more than two dozen terrorist leaders or other individuals implicated in acts of terrorism. Three profiles of noteworthy terrorists of the early 1970s who belonged to other groups are included to provide a better basis of contrast with terrorists of the late 1990s. This paper does not presume to have any scientific validity in terms of general sampling representation of terrorists, but it does provide a preliminary theoretical, analytical, and biographical framework for further research on the general subject or on particular groups or individuals.

By examining the relatively overlooked behaviorist literature on sociopsychological aspects of terrorism, this study attempts to gain psychological and sociological insights into international terrorist groups and individuals. Of particular interest is whether members of at least a dozen terrorist organizations in diverse regions of the world have any psychological or sociological characteristics in common that might be useful in profiling terrorists, if profiling is at all feasible, and in understanding somewhat better the motivations of individuals who become terrorists.

Because this study includes profiles of diverse groups from Western Europe, Asia, the Middle East, and Latin America, care has been taken when making cross-national, cross-cultural, and cross-ideological comparisons. This paper examines such topics as the age, economic and social background, education and occupation, gender, geographical origin, marital status, motivation, recruitment, and religion or ideology of the members of these designated groups as well as others on which relevant data are available.

It is hoped that an examination of the extensive body of behaviorist literature on political and religious terrorism authored by psychologists and sociologists as well as political scientists and other social scientists will provide some answers to questions such as Who are terrorists? How do individuals become terrorists? Do political or religious terrorists have anything in common in their sociopsychological development? How are they recruited? Is there a terrorist mindset, or are terrorist groups too diverse to have a single mindset or common psychological traits? Are there instead different terrorist mindsets?

Terms of Analysis

Defining Terrorism and Terrorists

Unable to achieve their unrealistic goals by conventional means, international terrorists attempt to send an ideological or religious message by terrorizing the general public. Through the choice of their targets, which are often symbolic or representative of the targeted nation, terrorists attempt to create a high-profile impact on the public of their targeted enemy or enemies with their act of violence, despite the limited material resources that are usually at their disposal. In doing so, they hope to demonstrate various points, such as that the targeted government(s) cannot protect its (their) own citizens, or that by assassinating a specific victim they can teach the general public a lesson about espousing viewpoints or policies antithetical to their own. For example, by assassinating Egyptian President Anwar Sadat on October 6, 1981, a year after his historic trip to Jerusalem, the al-Jihad terrorists hoped to convey to the world, and especially to Muslims, the error that he represented.

This tactic is not new. Beginning in AD 48, a Jewish sect called the Zealots carried out terrorist campaigns to force insurrection against the Romans in Judea. These campaigns included the use of assassins (sicari, or daggermen), who would infiltrate Roman-controlled cities and stab Jewish collaborators or Roman legionnaires with a sica (dagger), kidnap members of the Staff of the Temple Guard to hold for ransom, or use poison on a large scale. The Zealots' justification for their killing of other Jews was that these killings demonstrated the consequences of the immorality of collaborating with the Roman invaders, and that the Romans could not protect their Jewish collaborators.

Definitions of terrorism vary widely and are usually inadequate. Even terrorism researchers often neglect to define the term other than by citing the basic U.S. Department of State (1998) definition of terrorism as "premeditated, politically motivated violence perpetrated against noncombatant targets by subnational groups or clandestine agents, usually intended to influence an audience." Although an act of violence that is generally regarded in the United States as an act of terrorism may not be viewed so in another country, the type of violence that distinguishes terrorism from other types of violence, such as ordinary crime or a wartime military action, can still be defined in terms that might qualify as reasonably objective.

This social sciences researcher defines a terrorist action as the calculated use of unexpected, shocking, and unlawful violence against noncombatants (including, in addition to civilians, off-duty military and security personnel in peaceful situations) and other symbolic targets perpetrated by a clandestine member(s) of a subnational group or a clandestine agent(s) for the psychological purpose of publicizing a political or religious cause and/or intimidating or coercing a government(s) or civilian population into accepting demands on behalf of the cause.

In this study, the nouns "terrorist" or "terrorists" do not necessarily refer to everyone within a terrorist organization. Large organizations, such as the Revolutionary Armed Forces of Colombia (FARC), the Irish Republic Army (IRA), or the Kurdistan Workers' Party (PKK), have many members— for example, accountants, cooks, fund-raisers, logistics specialists, medical doctors, or recruiters—who may play only a passive support role. We are not particularly concerned here with the passive support membership of terrorist organizations.

Rather, we are primarily concerned in this study with the leader(s) of terrorist groups and the activists or operators who personally carry out a group's terrorism strategy. The top leaders are of particular interest because there may be significant differences between them and terrorist activists or operatives. In contrast to the top leader(s), the individuals who carry out orders to perpetrate an act of political violence (which they would not necessarily regard as a terrorist act) have generally been recruited into the organization. Thus, their motives for joining may be different. New recruits are often isolated and alienated young people who want to join not only because they identify with the cause and idolize the group's leader, but also because they want to belong to a group for a sense of self-importance and companionship.

The top leaders of several of the groups profiled in this report can be subdivided into contractors or freelancers. The distinction actually highlights an important difference between the old generation of terrorist leaders and the new breed of international terrorists. Contractors are those terrorist leaders whose services are hired by rogue states, or a particular government entity of a rogue regime, such as an intelligence agency. Notable examples of terrorist contractors include Abu Nidal, George Habash of the Popular Front for the Liberation of Palestine (PFLP), and Abu Abbas of the Palestine Liberation Front (PLF). Freelancers are terrorist leaders who are completely independent of a state, but who may collude with a rogue regime on a short-term basis. Prominent examples of freelancers include Sheikh Omar Abdul Rahman, Ahmed Ramzi Yousef, and Osama bin Laden. Contractors like Abu Nidal, George Habash, and Abu Abbas are representative of the old style of high-risk international terrorism. In the 1990s, rogue states, more mindful of the consequences of Western diplomatic, economic, military, and political retaliation were less inclined to risk contracting terrorist organizations. Instead, freelancers operating independently of any state carried out many of the most significant acts of terrorism in the decade.

This study discusses groups that have been officially designated as terrorist groups by the U.S. Department of State. A few of the groups on the official list, however, are guerrilla organizations. These include the FARC, the LTTE, and the PKK. To be sure, the FARC, the LTTE, and the PKK engage in terrorism as well as guerrilla warfare, but categorizing them as terrorist groups and formulating policies to combat them on that basis would be simplistic and a prescription for failure. The FARC, for example, has the official status in Colombia of a political insurgent movement, as a result of a May 1999 accord between the FARC and the Colombian government. To dismiss a guerrilla group, especially one like the FARC which has been fighting for four decades, as only a terrorist group is to misunderstand its political and sociological context.

It is also important to keep in mind that perceptions of what constitutes terrorism will differ from country to country, as well as among various sectors of a country's population. For example, the Nicaraguan elite regarded the Sandinista National Liberation Front (FSLN) as a terrorist group, while much of the rest of the country regarded the FSLN as freedom fighters. A foreign extremist group labeled as terrorist by the Department of State may be regarded in heroic terms by some sectors of the population in another country. Likewise, an action that would be regarded as indisputably terrorist in the United States might not be regarded as a terrorist act in another country's law courts. For example, India's Supreme Court ruled in May 1999 that the assassination of Prime Minister Rajiv Gandhi by a LTTE "belt-bomb girl" was not an act of terrorism because there was no evidence that the four co-conspirators (who received the death penalty) had any desire to strike terror in the country. In addition, the Department of State's labeling of a guerrilla group as a terrorist group may be viewed by the particular group as a hostile act. For example, the LTTE has disputed, unsuccessfully, its designation on October 8, 1997, by the Department of State as a terrorist organization. By labeling the LTTE a terrorist group, the United States compromises its potential role as neutral mediator in Sri Lanka's civil war and waves a red flag at one of the world's deadliest groups, whose leader appears to be a psychopathic (see Glossary) serial killer of heads of state. To be sure, some terrorists are so committed to their cause that they freely acknowledge being terrorists. On hearing that he had been sentenced to 240 years in prison, Ramzi Yousef, mastermind of the WTC bombing, defiantly proclaimed, "I am a terrorist, and I am proud of it."

Terrorist Group Typologies

This study categorizes foreign terrorist groups under one of the following four designated, somewhat arbitrary, typologies: nationalist-separatist, religious fundamentalist, new religious, and social revolutionary. This group classification is based on the assumption that terrorist groups can be categorized by their political background or ideology. The social revolutionary category has also been labeled "idealist." Idealistic terrorists fight for a radical cause, a religious belief, or a political ideology, including anarchism. Although some groups do not fit neatly into any one category, the general typologies are important because all terrorist campaigns are different, and the mindsets of groups within the same general category tend to have more in common than those in different categories. For example, the Irish Republic Army (IRA), Basque Fatherland and Freedom (Euzkadi Ta Askatasuna—ETA), the Palestinian terrorist groups, and the LTTE all have strong nationalistic motivations, whereas the Islamic fundamentalist and the Aum Shinrikyo groups are motivated by religious beliefs. To be at all effective, counterterrorist policies necessarily would vary depending on the typology of the group.

A fifth typology, for right-wing terrorists, is not listed because right-wing terrorists were not specifically designated as being a subject of this study. In any case, there does not appear to be any significant right-wing group on the U.S. Department of State's list of foreign terrorist organizations. Right-wing terrorists are discussed only briefly in this paper (see Attributes of Terrorists). This is not to minimize the threat of right-wing extremists in the United States, who clearly pose a significant terrorist threat to U.S. security, as demonstrated by the Oklahoma City bombing on April 19, 1995.

Approaches to Terrorism Analysis

The Multicausal Approach

Terrorism usually results from multiple causal factors—not only psychological but also economic, political, religious, and sociological factors, among others. There is even an hypothesis that it is caused by physiological factors, as discussed below. Because terrorism is a multicausal phenomenon, it would be simplistic and erroneous to explain an act of terrorism by a single cause, such as the psychological need of the terrorist to perpetrate an act of violence.

For Paul Wilkinson (1977), the causes of revolution and political violence in general are also the causes of terrorism. These include ethnic conflicts, religious and ideological conflicts, poverty, modernization stresses, political inequities, lack of peaceful communications channels, traditions of violence, the existence of a revolutionary group, governmental weakness and ineptness, erosions of confidence in a regime, and deep divisions within governing elites and leadership groups.

The Political Approach

The alternative to the hypothesis that a terrorist is born with certain personality traits that destine him or her to become a terrorist is that the root causes of terrorism can be found in influences emanating from environmental factors. Environments conducive to the rise of terrorism include international and national environments, as well as subnational ones such as universities, where many terrorists first become familiar with Marxist-

Leninist ideology or other revolutionary ideas and get involved with radical groups. Russell and Miller identify universities as the major recruiting ground for terrorists.

Having identified one or more of these or other environments, analysts may distinguish between participants that started the outbreak of violence, on the one hand, and preconditions that allowed the participants to instigate the action, on the other hand. Political scientists Chalmers Johnson (1978) and Martha Crenshaw (1981) have further subdivided preconditions into permissive factors, which engender a terrorist strategy and make it attractive to political dissidents, and direct situational factors, which motivate terrorists. Permissive causes include urbanization, the transportation system (for example, by allowing a terrorist to quickly escape to another country by taking a flight), communications media, weapons availability, and the absence of security measures. An example of a situational factor for Palestinians would be the loss of their homeland of Palestine.

Various examples of international and national or subnational theories of terrorism can be cited. An example of an international environment hypothesis is the view proposed by Brian M. Jenkins (1979) that the failure of rural guerrilla movements in Latin America pushed the rebels into the cities. (This hypothesis, however, overlooks the national causes of Latin American terrorism and fails to explain why rural guerrilla movements continue to thrive in Colombia.) Jenkins also notes that the defeat of Arab armies in the 1967 Six-Day War caused the Palestinians to abandon hope for a conventional military solution to their problem and to turn to terrorist attacks.

The Organizational Approach
Some analysts, such as Crenshaw (1990:250), take an organizational approach to terrorism and see terrorism as a rational strategic course of action decided on by a group. In her view, terrorism is not committed by an individual. Rather, she contends that "acts of terrorism are committed by groups who reach collective decisions based on commonly held beliefs, although the level of individual commitment to the group and its beliefs varies."

Crenshaw has not actually substantiated her contention with case studies that show how decisions are supposedly reached collectively in terrorist groups. That kind of inside information, to be sure, would be quite difficult to obtain without a former decision-maker within a terrorist group providing it in the form of a published autobiography or an interview, or even as a paid police informer. Crenshaw may be partly right, but her organizational approach would seem to be more relevant to guerrilla organizations that are organized along traditional Marxist-Leninist lines, with a general secretariat headed by a secretary general, than to terrorist groups per se. The FARC, for example, is a guerrilla organization, albeit one that is not averse to using terrorism as a tactic. The six members of the FARC's General Secretariat participate in its decision making under the overall leadership of Secretary General Manuel Marulanda Vélez. The hard-line military leaders, however, often exert disproportionate influence over decision making.

Bona fide terrorist groups, like cults, are often totally dominated by a single individual leader, be it Abu Nidal, Ahmed Jibril, Osama bin Laden, or Shoko Asahara. It seems quite improbable that the terrorist groups of such dominating leaders make their decisions collectively. By most accounts, the established terrorist leaders give instructions to their lieutenants to hijack a jetliner, assassinate a particular person, bomb a U.S. Embassy, and so forth, while leaving operational details to their lieutenants to work out. The top leader may listen to his lieutenants' advice, but the top leader makes the final decision and gives the orders.

The Physiological Approach

The physiological approach to terrorism suggests that the role of the media in promoting the spread of terrorism cannot be ignored in any discussion of the causes of terrorism. Thanks to media coverage, the methods, demands, and goals of terrorists are quickly made known to potential terrorists, who may be inspired to imitate them upon becoming stimulated by media accounts of terrorist acts.

The diffusion of terrorism from one place to another received scholarly attention in the early 1980s. David G. Hubbard (1983) takes a physiological approach to analyzing the causes of terrorism. He discusses three substances produced in the body under stress: norepinephrine, a compound produced by the adrenal gland and sympathetic nerve endings and associated with the "fight or flight" (see Glossary) physiological response of individuals in stressful situations; acetylcholine, which is produced by the parasympathetic nerve endings and acts to dampen the accelerated norepinephrine response; and endorphins, which develop in the brain as a response to stress and "narcotize" the brain, being one hundred times more powerful than morphine. Because these substances occur in the terrorist, Hubbard concludes that much terrorist violence is rooted not in the psychology but in the physiology of the terrorist, partly the result of "stereotyped, agitated tissue response" to stress. Hubbard's conclusion suggests a possible explanation for the spread of terrorism, the so-called contagion effect.

Kent Layne Oots and Thomas C. Wiegele (1985) have also proposed a model of terrorist contagion based on physiology. Their model demonstrates that the psychological state of the potential terrorist has important implications for the stability of society. In their analysis, because potential terrorists become aroused in a violence-accepting way by media presentations of terrorism, "terrorists must, by the nature of their actions, have an attitude which allows violence." One of these attitudes, they suspect, may be Machiavellianism because terrorists are disposed to manipulating their victims as well as the press, the public, and the authorities. They note that the potential terrorist "need only see that terrorism has worked for others in order to become aggressively aroused."

According to Oots and Wiegele, an individual moves from being a potential terrorist to being an actual terrorist through a process that is psychological, physiological, and political. "If the neurophysiological model of aggression is realistic," Oots and Wiegele assert, "there is no basis for the argument that terrorism could be eliminated if its sociopolitical causes were eliminated." They characterize the potential terrorist as "a frustrated individual who has become aroused and has repeatedly experienced the fight or flight syndrome. Moreover, after these repeated arousals, the potential terrorist seeks relief through an aggressive act and also seeks, in part, to remove the initial cause of his frustration by achieving the political goal which he has hitherto been denied."

D. Guttman (1979) also sees terrorist actions as being aimed more at the audience than at the immediate victims. It is, after all, the audience that may have to meet the terrorist's demands. Moreover, in Guttman's analysis, the terrorist requires a liberal rather than a right-wing audience for success. Liberals make the terrorist respectable by accepting the ideology that the terrorist alleges informs his or her acts. The terrorist also requires liberal control of the media for the transmission of his or her ideology.

The Psychological Approach
In contrast with political scientists and sociologists, who are interested in the political and social contexts of terrorist groups, the relatively few psychologists who study terrorism are primarily interested in the micro-level of the individual terrorist or terrorist group. The psychological approach is concerned with the study of terrorists per se, their recruitment and induction into terrorist groups, their personalities, beliefs, attitudes, motivations, and careers as terrorists.

General Hypotheses of Terrorism

If one accepts the proposition that political terrorists are made, not born, then the question is what makes a terrorist. Although the scholarly literature on the psychology of terrorism is lacking in full-scale, quantitative studies from which to ascertain trends and develop general theories of terrorism, it does appear to focus on several theories. One, the Olson hypothesis, suggests that participants in revolutionary violence predicate their behavior on a rational cost-benefit calculus and the conclusion that violence is the best available course of action given the social conditions. The notion that a group rationally chooses a terrorism strategy is questionable, however. Indeed, a group's decision to resort to terrorism is often divisive, sometimes resulting in factionalization of the group.

Frustration-Aggression Hypothesis
The frustration-aggression hypothesis (see Glossary) of violence is prominent in the literature. This hypothesis is based mostly on the relative-deprivation hypothesis (see Glossary), as proposed by Ted Robert Gurr (1970), an expert on violent behaviors and movements, and reformulated

by J.C. Davies (1973) to include a gap between rising expectations and need satisfaction. Another proponent of this hypothesis, Joseph Margolin (1977:273–4), argues that "much terrorist behavior is a response to the frustration of various political, economic, and personal needs or objectives." Other scholars, however, have dismissed the frustration-aggression hypothesis as simplistic, based as it is on the erroneous assumption that aggression is always a consequence of frustration.

According to Franco Ferracuti (1982), a University of Rome professor, a better approach than these and other hypotheses, including the Marxist theory, would be a subcultural theory, which takes into account that terrorists live in their own subculture, with their own value systems. Similarly, political scientist Paul Wilkinson (1974:127) faults the frustration-aggression hypothesis for having "very little to say about the social psychology of prejudice and hatred . . ." and fanaticisms that "play a major role in encouraging extreme violence." He believes that "political terrorism cannot be understood outside the context of the development of terroristic, or potentially terroristic, ideologies, beliefs and lifestyles (133)."

Negative Identity Hypothesis
Using Erikson's theory of identity formation, particularly his concept of negative identity, the late political psychologist Jeanne N. Knutson (1981) suggests that the political terrorist consciously assumes a negative identity. One of her examples is a Croatian terrorist who, as a member of an oppressed ethnic minority, was disappointed by the failure of his aspiration to attain a university education and as a result assumed a negative identity by becoming a terrorist. Negative identity involves a vindictive rejection of the role regarded as desirable and proper by an individual's family and community. In Knutson's view, terrorists engage in terrorism as a result of feelings of rage and helplessness over the lack of alternatives. Her political science-oriented viewpoint seems to coincide with the frustration-aggression hypothesis.

Narcissistic Rage Hypothesis
The advocates of the narcissism-aggression hypothesis include psychologists Jerrold M. Post, John W. Crayton, and Richard M. Pearlstein. Taking the terrorists-as-mentally-ill approach, this hypothesis concerns the early development of the terrorist. Basically, if primary narcissism in the form of the "grandiose self" is not neutralized by reality testing, the grandiose self produces individuals who are sociopathic, arrogant, and lacking in regard for others. Similarly, if the psychological form of the "idealized parental ego" is not neutralized by reality testing, it can produce a condition of helpless defeatism, and narcissistic defeat can lead to reactions of rage and a wish to destroy the source of narcissistic injury. "As a specific manifestation of narcissistic rage, terrorism occurs in the context of narcissistic injury," writes Crayton (1983:37–8). For Crayton, terrorism is an attempt to acquire or maintain power or control by intimidation. He suggests that the "meaningful high ideals" of the political terrorist group "protect the group members from experiencing shame."

In Post's view, a particularly striking personality trait of people who are drawn to terrorism "is the reliance placed on the psychological mechanisms of 'externalization' and 'splitting'." These are psychological mechanisms, he explains, that are found in "individuals with narcissistic and borderline personality disturbances." "Splitting," he explains, "is a mechanism characteristic of people whose personality development is shaped by a particular type of psychological damage (narcissistic injury) during childhood." Those individuals with a damaged self-concept have failed to integrate the good and bad parts of the self, which are instead split into the "me" and the "not me." These individuals, who have included Hitler, need an outside enemy to blame for their own inadequacies and weaknesses. The data examined by Post, including a 1982 West German study, indicate that many terrorists have not been successful in their personal, educational, and vocational lives. Thus, they are drawn to terrorist groups, which have an us-versus-them outlook. This hypothesis, however, appears to be contradicted by the increasing number of terrorists who are well-educated professionals, such as chemists, engineers, and physicists.

The psychology of the self is clearly very important in understanding and dealing with terrorist behavior, as in incidents of hostage-barricade terrorism (see Glossary). Crayton points out that humiliating the terrorists in such situations by withholding food, for example, would be counterproductive because "the very basis for their activity stems from their sense of low self-esteem and humiliation."

Using a Freudian analysis of the self and the narcissistic personality, Pearlstein (1991) eruditely applies the psychological concept of narcissism to terrorists. He observes that the political terrorist circumvents the psychopolitical liabilities of accepting himself or herself as a terrorist with a negative identity through a process of rhetorical self-justification that is reinforced by the group's group-think. His hypothesis, however, seems too speculative a construct to be used to analyze terrorist motivation independently of numerous other factors. For example, politically motivated hijackers have rarely acted for self-centered reasons, but rather in the name of the political goals of their groups. It also seems questionable that terrorist suicide-bombers, who deliberately sacrificed themselves in the act, had a narcissistic personality.

The Psychology of the Terrorist

Terrorist Motivation

In addition to drawing on political science and sociology, this study draws on the discipline of psychology, in an attempt to explain terrorist motivation and to answer questions such as who become terrorists and what kind of individuals join terrorist groups and commit public acts of shocking violence. Although there have been numerous attempts to explain terrorism from a psychiatric or psychological perspective, Wilkinson notes that the psychology and beliefs of terrorists have been inadequately explored. Most psychological analyses of terrorists and terrorism, according to psychologist

Maxwell Taylor (1988), have attempted to address what motivates terrorists or to describe personal characteristics of terrorists, on the assumption that terrorists can be identified by these attributes. However, although an understanding of the terrorist mindset would be the key to understanding how and why an individual becomes a terrorist, numerous psychologists have been unable to adequately define it. Indeed, there appears to be a general agreement among psychologists who have studied the subject that there is no one terrorist mindset. This view, however, needs to be clarified.

The topic of the terrorist mindset was discussed at a Rand conference on terrorism coordinated by Brian M. Jenkins in September 1980. The observations made about terrorist mindsets at that conference considered individuals, groups, and individuals as part of a group. The discussion revealed how little was known about the nature of terrorist mindsets, their causes and consequences, and their significance for recruitment, ideology, leader-follower relations, organization, decision making about targets and tactics, escalation of violence, and attempts made by disillusioned terrorists to exit from the terrorist group. Although the current study has examined these aspects of the terrorist mindset, it has done so within the framework of a more general tasking requirement. Additional research and analysis would be needed to focus more closely on the concept of the terrorist mindset and to develop it into a more useful method for profiling terrorist groups and leaders on a more systematic and accurate basis.

Within this field of psychology, the personality dynamics of individual terrorists, including the causes and motivations behind the decision to join a terrorist group and to commit violent acts, have also received attention. Other small-group dynamics that have been of particular interest to researchers include the terrorists' decision-making patterns, problems of leadership and authority, target selection, and group mindset as a pressure tool on the individual.

Attempts to explain terrorism in purely psychological terms ignore the very real economic, political, and social factors that have always motivated radical activists, as well as the possibility that biological or physiological variables may play a role in bringing an individual to the point of perpetrating terrorism. Although this study provides some interdisciplinary context to the study of terrorists and terrorism, it is concerned primarily with the sociopsychological approach. Knutson (1984), executive director of the International Society of Political Psychology until her death in 1982, carried out an extensive international research project on the psychology of political terrorism. The basic premise of terrorists whom she evaluated in depth was "that their violent acts stem from feelings of rage and hopelessness engendered by the belief that society permits no other access to information-dissemination and policy-formation processes."

The social psychology of political terrorism has received extensive analysis in studies of terrorism, but the individual psychology of political and religious terrorism has been largely ignored. Relatively little is known about the terrorist as an individual, and the psychology of terrorists remains poorly understood, despite the fact that there have been a number of individual biographical accounts, as well as sweeping sociopolitical or psychiatric generalizations.

A lack of data and an apparent ambivalence among many academic researchers about the academic value of terrorism research have contributed to the relatively little systematic social and psychological research on terrorism. This is unfortunate because psychology, concerned as it is with behavior and the factors that influence and control behavior, can provide practical, as opposed to conceptual, knowledge of terrorists and terrorism.

A principal reason for the lack of psychometric studies of terrorism is that researchers have little, if any, direct access to terrorists, even imprisoned ones. Occasionally, a researcher has gained special access to a terrorist group, but usually at the cost of compromising the credibility of his/her research. Even if a researcher obtains permission to interview an incarcerated terrorist, such an interview would be of limited value and reliability for the purpose of making generalizations. Most terrorists, including imprisoned ones, would be loath to reveal their group's operational secrets to their interrogators, let alone to journalists or academic researchers, whom the terrorists are likely to view as representatives of the "system" or perhaps even as intelligence agents in disguise. Even if terrorists agree to be interviewed in such circumstances, they may be less than candid in answering questions. For example, most imprisoned Red Army Faction members reportedly declined to be interviewed by West German social scientists. Few researchers or former terrorists write exposés of terrorist groups. Those who do could face retaliation. For example, the LTTE shot to death an anti-LTTE activist, Sabaratnam Sabalingam, in Paris on May 1, 1994, to prevent him from publishing an anti-LTTE book. The LTTE also murdered Dr. Rajani Thiranagama, a Tamil, and one of the four Sri Lankan authors of *The Broken Palmyrah,* which sought to examine the "martyr" cult.

The Process of Joining a Terrorist Group
Individuals who become terrorists often are unemployed, socially alienated individuals who have dropped out of society. Those with little education, such as youths in Algerian ghettos or the Gaza Strip, may try to join a terrorist group out of boredom and a desire to have an action-packed adventure in pursuit of a cause they regard as just. Some individuals may be motivated mainly by a desire to use their special skills, such as bomb-making. The more educated youths may be motivated more by genuine political or religious convictions. The person who becomes a terrorist in Western countries is generally both intellectual and idealistic. Usually, these disenchanted youths, both educated or uneducated, engage in occasional protest and dissidence. Potential terrorist group members often start out as sympathizers of the group. Recruits often come from support organizations, such as prisoner support groups or student activist groups. From sympathizer, one moves to passive supporter. Often, violent encounters

with police or other security forces motivate an already socially alienated individual to join a terrorist group. Although the circumstances vary, the end result of this gradual process is that the individual, often with the help of a family member or friend with terrorist contacts, turns to terrorism. Membership in a terrorist group, however, is highly selective. Over a period as long as a year or more, a recruit generally moves in a slow, gradual fashion toward full membership in a terrorist group.

An individual who drops out of society can just as well become a monk or a hermit instead of a terrorist. For an individual to choose to become a terrorist, he or she would have to be motivated to do so. Having the proper motivation, however, is still not enough. The would-be terrorist would need to have the opportunity to join a terrorist group. And, like most job seekers, he or she would have to be acceptable to the terrorist group, which is a highly exclusive group. Thus, recruits would not only need to have a personality that would allow them to fit into the group, but, ideally, a certain skill needed by the group, such as weapons or communications skills.

The psychology of joining a terrorist group differs depending on the typology of the group. Someone joining an anarchistic or a Marxist-Leninist terrorist group would not likely be able to count on any social support, only social opprobrium, whereas someone joining an ethnic separatist group like ETA or the IRA would enjoy considerable social support and even respect within ethnic enclaves.

Psychologist Eric D. Shaw (1986:365) provides a strong case for what he calls "The Personal Pathway Model," by which terrorists enter their new profession. The components of this pathway include early socialization processes; narcissistic injuries; escalatory events, particularly confrontation with police; and personal connections to terrorist group members, as follows:

The personal pathway model suggests that terrorists came from a selected, at-risk population who have suffered from early damage to their self-esteem. Their subsequent political activities may be consistent with the liberal social philosophies of their families, but go beyond their perception of the contradiction in their family's beliefs and lack of social action. Family political philosophies may also serve to sensitize these persons to the economic and political tensions inherent throughout modern society. As a group, they appear to have been unsuccessful in obtaining a desired traditional place in society, which has contributed to their frustration. The underlying need to belong to a terrorist group is symptomatic of an incomplete or fragmented psychosocial identity. (In Kohut's terms—a defective or fragmented "group self"). Interestingly, the acts of security forces or police are cited as provoking more violent political activity by these individuals and it is often a personal connection to other terrorists that leads to membership in a violent group (shared external targets?).

Increasingly, terrorist organizations in the developing world are recruiting younger members. The only role models for these young people to identify with are often terrorists and guerrillas. Abu Nidal, for example, was able to recruit alienated, poor, and uneducated youths thrilled to be able to identify themselves with a group led by a well-known but mysterious figure.

During the 1980s and early 1990s, thousands of foreign Muslim volunteers (14,000, according to *Jane's Intelligence Review*)—angry, young, and zealous and from many countries, including the United States—flocked to training camps in Afghanistan or the Pakistan-Afghan border region to learn the art of combat. They ranged in age from 17 to 35. Some had university educations, but most were uneducated, unemployed youths without any prospects.

Deborah M. Galvin (1983) notes that a common route of entry into terrorism for female terrorists is through political involvement and belief in a political cause. The Intifada (see Glossary), for example, radicalized many young Palestinians, who later joined terrorist organizations. At least half of the Intifada protesters were young girls. Some women are recruited into terrorist organizations by boyfriends. A significant feature that Galvin feels may characterize the involvement of the female terrorist is the "male or female lover/female accomplice . . . scenario." The lover, a member of the terrorist group, recruits the female into the group. One ETA female member, "Begona," told Eileen MacDonald (1992) that was how she joined at age 25: "I got involved [in ETA] because a man I knew was a member."

A woman who is recruited into a terrorist organization on the basis of her qualifications and motivation is likely to be treated more professionally by her comrades than one who is perceived as lacking in this regard. Two of the PFLP hijackers of Sabena Flight 517 from Brussels to Tel Aviv on May 8, 1972, Therese Halsa, 19, and Rima Tannous, 21, had completely different characters. Therese, the daughter of a middle-class Arab family, was a nursing student when she was recruited into Fatah by a fellow student and was well regarded in the organization. Rima, an orphan of average intelligence, became the mistress of a doctor who introduced her to drugs and recruited her into Fatah. She became totally dependent on some Fatah members, who subjected her to physical and psychological abuse.

Various terrorist groups recruit female and male members from organizations that are lawful. For example, ETA personnel may be members of Egizan ("Act Woman!"), a feminist movement affiliated with ETA's political wing; the Henri Batasuna (Popular Unity) party; or an amnesty group seeking release for ETA members. While working with the amnesty group, a number of women reportedly tended to become frustrated over mistreatment of prisoners and concluded that the only solution was to strike back, which they did by joining the ETA. "Women seemed to become far more emotionally involved than men with the suffering of prisoners," an ETA member, "Txikia," who joined at age 20, told MacDonald, "and when they made the transition from supporter to guerrilla, appeared to carry their deeper sense of commitment with them into battle."

The Terrorist as Mentally Ill

A common stereotype is that someone who commits such abhorrent acts as planting a bomb on an airliner, detonating a vehicle bomb on a city street, or tossing a grenade into a crowded sidewalk café is abnormal. The psychopathological (see Glossary) orientation has dominated the psychological approach to the terrorist's personality. As noted by Taylor, two basic psychological approaches to understanding terrorists have been commonly used: the terrorist is viewed either as mentally ill or as a fanatic. For Walter Laqueur (1977:125), "Terrorists are fanatics and fanaticism frequently makes for cruelty and sadism."

This study is not concerned with the lone terrorist, such as the Unabomber in the United States, who did not belong to any terrorist group. Criminologist Franco Ferracuti has noted that there is "no such thing as an isolated terrorist—that's a mental case." Mentally unbalanced individuals have been especially attracted to airplane hijacking. David G. Hubbard (1971) conducted a psychiatric study of airplane hijackers in 1971 and concluded that skyjacking is used by psychiatrically ill patients as an expression of illness. His study revealed that skyjackers shared several common traits: a violent father, often an alcoholic; a deeply religious mother, often a religious zealot; a sexually shy, timid, and passive personality; younger sisters toward whom the skyjackers acted protectively; and poor achievement, financial failure, and limited earning potential.

Those traits, however, are shared by many people who do not hijack airplanes. Thus, profiles of mentally unstable hijackers would seem to be of little, if any, use in detecting a potential hijacker in advance. A useful profile would probably have to identify physical or behavioral traits that might alert authorities to a potential terrorist before a suspect is allowed to board an aircraft, that is, if hijackers have identifiable personality qualities. In the meantime, weapons detection, passenger identification, and onboard security guards may be the only preventive measures. Even then, an individual wanting to hijack an airplane can often find a way. Japan's Haneda Airport screening procedures failed to detect a large knife that a 28-year-old man carried aboard an All Nippon Airways jumbo jet on July 23, 1999, and used to stab the pilot (who died) and take the plane's controls until overpowered by others. Although police have suggested that the man may have psychiatric problems, the fact that he attempted to divert the plane to the U.S. Yokota Air Base north of Tokyo, at a time when the airbase was a subject of controversy because the newly elected governor of Tokyo had demanded its closure, suggests that he may have had a political or religious motive.

There have been cases of certifiably mentally ill terrorists. Klaus Jünschke, a mental patient, was one of the most ardent members of the Socialist Patients' Collective (SPK), a German terrorist group working with the Baader-

Meinhof Gang (see Glossary). In some instances, political terrorists have clearly exhibited psychopathy (see Glossary). For example, in April 1986 Nezar Hindawi, a freelance Syrian-funded Jordanian terrorist and would-be agent of Syrian intelligence, sent his pregnant Irish girlfriend on an El Al flight to Israel, promising to meet her there to be married. Unknown to her, however, Hindawi had hidden a bomb (provided by the Abu Nidal Organization (ANO)) in a false bottom to her hand luggage. His attempt to bomb the airliner in midair by duping his pregnant girlfriend was thwarted when the bomb was discovered by Heathrow security personnel. Taylor regards Hindawi's behavior in this incident as psychopathic because of Hindawi's willingness to sacrifice his fiancé and unborn child.

Jerrold Post (1990), a leading advocate of the terrorists-as-mentally-ill approach, has his own psychological hypothesis of terrorism. Although he does not take issue with the proposition that terrorists reason logically, Post argues that terrorists' reasoning process is characterized by what he terms "terrorist psycho-logic." In his analysis, terrorists do not willingly resort to terrorism as an intentional choice. Rather, he argues that "political terrorists are driven to commit acts of violence as a consequence of psychological forces, and that their special psycho-logic is constructed to rationalize acts they are psychologically compelled to commit"(1990:25). Post's hypothesis that terrorists are motivated by psychological forces is not convincing and seems to ignore the numerous factors that motivate terrorists, including their ideological convictions.

Post (1997) believes that the most potent form of terrorism stems from those individuals who are bred to hate, from generation to generation, as in Northern Ireland and the Basque country. For these terrorists, in his view, rehabilitation is nearly impossible because ethnic animosity or hatred is "in their blood" and passed from father to son. Post also draws an interesting distinction between "anarchic-ideologues"such as the Italian Red Brigades (Brigate Rosse) and the German RAF (aka the Baader-Meinhof Gang), and the "nationalist-separatist" groups such as the ETA, or the IRA, stating that:

> *There would seem to be a profound difference between terrorists bent on destroying their own society, the "world of their fathers," and those whose terrorist activities carry on the mission of their fathers. To put it in other words, for some, becoming terrorists is an act of retaliation for real and imagined hurts against the society of their parents; for others, it is an act of retaliation against society for the hurt done to their parents. . .This would suggest more conflict, more psychopathology, among those committed to anarchy and destruction of society. . .(1984:243)*

Indeed, author Julian Becker (1984) describes the German terrorists of the Baader-Meinhof Gang as "children without fathers." They were sons and daughters of fathers who had either been killed by Nazis or survived Nazism. Their children despised and rebelled against them because of the shame of Nazism and a defeated Germany. One former RAF female member told MacDonald, "We hated our parents because they were former Nazis, who had never come clean about their past." Similarly, Gunther Wagenlehner (1978:201) concludes that the motives of RAF terrorists were unpolitical and belonged "more to the area of psychopathological disturbances." Wagenlehner found that German terrorists blamed the government for failing to solve their personal problems. Not only was becoming a terrorist "an individual form of liberation" for radical young people with personal problems, but "these students became terrorists because they suffered from acute fear and from aggression and the masochistic desire to be pursued." In short, according to Wagenlehner, the West German anarchists stand out as a major exception to the generally nonpathological characteristics of most terrorists. Psychologist Konrad Kellen (1990:43) arrives at a similar conclusion, noting that most of the West German terrorists "suffer from a deep psychological trauma" that "makes them see the world, including their own actions and the expected effects of those actions, in a grossly unrealistic light" and that motivates them to kill people. Sociologist J. Bowyer Bell (1985) also has noted that European anarchists, unlike other terrorists, belong more to the "province of psychologists than political analysts."

Post's distinction between anarchic-ideologues and ethnic separatists appears to be supported by Rona M. Fields's (1978) psychometric assessment of children in Northern Ireland. Fields found that exposure to terrorism as a child can lead to a proclivity for terrorism as an adult. Thus, a child growing up in violence-plagued West Belfast is more likely to develop into a terrorist as an adult than is a child growing up in peaceful Oslo, Norway, for example. Maxwell Taylor, noting correctly that there are numerous other factors in the development of a terrorist, faults Fields's conclusions for, among other things, a lack of validation with adults. Maxwell Taylor overlooks, however, that Field's study was conducted over an eight-year period. Taylor's point is that Field's conclusions do not take into account that relatively very few children exposed to violence, even in Northern Ireland, grow up to become terrorists.

A number of other psychologists would take issue with another of Post's contentions—that the West German anarchists were more pathological than Irish terrorists. For example, psychiatrist W. Rasch (1979), who interviewed a number of West German terrorists, determined that "no conclusive evidence has been found for the assumption that a significant number of them are disturbed or abnormal." For Rasch the argument that terrorism is pathological behavior only serves to minimize the political or social issues that motivated the terrorists into action. And psychologist Ken Heskin (1984), who has studied the psychology of terrorism in Northern Ireland, notes that, "In fact, there is no psychological evidence that terrorists are diagnosably psychopathic or otherwise clinically disturbed."

Although there may have been instances in which a mentally ill individual led a terrorist group, this has generally not been the case in international terrorism. Some specialists point out, in fact, that there is little reliable evidence to support the notion that terrorists in general are psychologically disturbed individuals. The careful, detailed planning and well-timed execution that have characterized many terrorist operations are hardly typical of mentally disturbed individuals.

There is considerable evidence, on the contrary, that international terrorists are generally quite sane. Crenshaw (1981) has concluded from her studies that "the outstanding common characteristic of terrorists is their normality." This view is shared by a number of psychologists. For example, C.R. McCauley and M.E. Segal (1987) conclude in a review of the social psychology of terrorist groups that "the best-documented generalization is negative; terrorists do not show any striking psychopathology." Heskin (1984) did not find members of the IRA to be emotionally disturbed. It seems clear that terrorists are extremely alienated from society, but alienation does not necessarily mean being mentally ill.

Maxwell Taylor (1984) found that the notion of mental illness has little utility with respect to most terrorist actions. Placing the terrorist within the ranks of the mentally ill, he points out, makes assumptions about terrorist motivations and places terrorist behavior outside the realms of both the normal rules of behavior and the normal process of law. He points out several differences that separate the psychopath from the political terrorist, although the two may not be mutually exclusive, as in the case of Hindawi. One difference is the psychopath's inability to profit from experience. Another important difference is that, in contrast to the terrorist, the purposefulness, if any, of a psychopath's actions is personal. In addition, psychopaths are too unreliable and incapable of being controlled to be of use to terrorist groups. Taylor notes that terrorist groups need discreet activists who do not draw attention to themselves and who can merge back into the crowd after executing an operation. For these reasons, he believes that "it may be inappropriate to think of the terrorist as mentally ill in conventional terms" (1994:92). Taylor and Ethel Quayle (1994:197) conclude that "the active terrorist is not discernibly different in psychological terms from the non-terrorist." In other words, terrorists are recruited from a population that describes most of us. Taylor and Quayle also assert that "in psychological terms, there are no special qualities that characterize the terrorist." Just as there is no necessary reason why people sharing the same career in normal life necessarily have psychological characteristics in common, the fact that terrorists have the same career does not necessarily mean that they have anything in common psychologically.

The selectivity with which terrorist groups recruit new members helps to explain why so few pathologically ill individuals are found within their ranks. Candidates who appear to be potentially dangerous to the terrorist group's survival are screened out. Candidates with unpredictable or uncontrolled behavior lack the personal attributes that the terrorist recruiter is looking for.

Many observers have noted that the personality of the terrorist has a depressive aspect to it, as reflected in the terrorist's death-seeking or death-confronting behavior. The terrorist has often been described by psychologists as incapable of enjoying anything (anhedonic) or forming meaningful interpersonal relationships on a reciprocal level. According to psychologist Risto Fried, the terrorist's interpersonal world is characterized by three categories of people: the terrorist's idealized heroes; the terrorist's enemies; and people one encounters in everyday life, whom the terrorist regards as shadow figures of no consequence. However, Fried (1982:123) notes that some psychologists with extensive experience with some of the most dangerous terrorists "emphasize that the terrorist may be perfectly normal from a clinical point of view, that he may have a psychopathology of a different order, or that his personality may be only a minor factor in his becoming a terrorist if he was recruited into a terrorist group rather than having volunteered for one."

The Terrorist as Suicidal Fanatic

Fanatics

The other of the two approaches that have predominated, the terrorist as fanatic, emphasizes the terrorist's rational qualities and views the terrorist as a cool, logical planning individual whose rewards are ideological and political, rather than financial. This approach takes into account that terrorists are often well-educated and capable of sophisticated, albeit highly biased, rhetoric and political analysis.

Notwithstanding the religious origins of the word, the term "fanaticism" in modern usage has broadened out of the religious context to refer to more generally held extreme beliefs. The terrorist is often labeled as a fanatic, especially in actions that lead to self-destruction. Although fanaticism is not unique to terrorism, it is, like "terrorism," a pejorative term. In psychological terms, the concept of fanaticism carries some implications of mental illness, but as Taylor (1988:97) points out, it "is not a diagnostic category in mental illness." Thus, he believes that "commonly held assumptions about the relationship between fanaticism and mental illness seem to be inappropriate." The fanatic often seems to view the world from a particular perspective lying at the extreme of a continuum.

Two related processes, Taylor points out, are prejudice and authoritarianism, with which fanaticism has a number of cognitive processes in common, such as an unwillingness to compromise, a disdain for other alternative views, the tendency to see things in black-and-white, a rigidity of belief, and a perception of the world that reflects a closed mind. Understanding the nature of fanaticism, he explains, requires recognizing the role of the cultural (religious and social) context. Fanaticism, in Taylor's view, may indeed ". . . be part of the cluster of attributes of the terrorist." However, Taylor emphasizes that the particular cultural context in which the terrorist is operating needs to be taken into account in understanding whether the term might be appropriate.

Suicide Terrorists

Deliberate self-destruction, when the terrorist's death is necessary in order to detonate a bomb or avoid capture, is not a common feature of terrorism in most countries, although it happens occasionally with Islamic fundamentalist terrorists in the Middle East and Tamil terrorists in Sri Lanka and southern India. It is also a feature of North Korean terrorism. The two North Korean agents who blew up Korean Air Flight 858 on November 28, 1987, popped cyanide capsules when confronted by police investigators. Only one of the terrorists succeeded in killing himself, however.

Prior to mid-1985, there were eleven suicide attacks against international targets in the Middle East using vehicle bombs. Three well-known cases were the bombing of the U.S. Embassy in Beirut on April 18, 1983, which killed 63 people; and the separate bombings of the U.S. Marine barracks and the French military headquarters in Lebanon on October 23, 1983, which killed 241 U.S. Marines and 58 French paratroopers, respectively. The first instance, however, was the bombing of Israel's military headquarters in Tyre, in which 141 people were killed. Inspired by these suicide attacks in Lebanon and his closer ties with Iran and Hizballah, Abu Nidal launched "suicide squads" in his attacks against the Rome and Vienna airports in late December 1985, in which an escape route was not planned.

The world leaders in terrorist suicide attacks are not the Islamic fundamentalists, but the Tamils of Sri Lanka. The LTTE's track record for suicide attacks is unrivaled. Its suicide commandos have blown up the prime ministers of two countries (India and Sri Lanka), celebrities, at least one naval battleship, and have regularly used suicide to avoid capture as well as simply a means of protest. LTTE terrorists do not dare not to carry out their irrevocable orders to use their cyanide capsules if captured. No fewer than thirty-five LTTE operatives committed suicide to simply avoid being questioned by investigators in the wake of the Gandhi assassination. Attempting to be circumspect, investigators disguised themselves as doctors in order to question LTTE patients undergoing medical treatment, but, Vijay Karan (1997:46) writes about the LTTE patients, "Their reflexes indoctrinated to react even to the slightest suspicion, all of them instantly popped cyanide capsules." Two were saved only because the investigators forcibly removed the capsules from their mouths, but one investigator suffered a severe bite wound on his hand and had to be hospitalized for some time.

To Western observers, the acts of suicide terrorism by adherents of Islam and Hinduism may be attributable to fanaticism or mental illness or both. From the perspective of the Islamic movement, however, such acts of self-destruction have a cultural and religious context, the historical origins of which can be seen in the behavior of religious sects associated with the Shi'ite movement, notably the Assassins (see Glossary). Similarly, the suicide campaign of the Islamic Resistance Movement (Hamas) in the 1993–94 period involved young Palestinian terrorists, who, acting on individual initiative, attacked Israelis in crowded places, using homemade improvised weapons such as knives and axes. Such attacks were suicidal because escape was not part of the attacker's plan. These attacks were, at least in part, motivated by revenge.

According to scholars of Muslim culture, so-called suicide bombings, however, are seen by Islamists and Tamils alike as instances of martyrdom and should be understood as such. The Arabic term used is *istishad,* a religious term meaning to give one's life in the name of Allah, as opposed to *intihar,* which refers to suicide resulting from personal distress. The latter form of suicide is not condoned in Islamic teachings.

There is a clear correlation between suicide attacks and concurrent events and developments in the Middle East. For example, suicide attacks increased in frequency after the October 1990 clashes between Israeli security forces and Muslim worshippers on Temple Mount, in the Old City of Jerusalem, in which eighteen Muslims were killed. The suicide attacks carried out by Hamas in Afula and Hadera in April 1994 coincided with the talks that preceded the signing by Israel and the PLO of the Cairo agreement. They were also claimed to revenge the massacre of 39 and the wounding of 200 Muslim worshippers in a Hebron mosque by an Israeli settler on February 25, 1994. Attacks perpetrated in Ramat-Gan and in Jerusalem in July and August 1995, respectively, coincided with the discussions concerning the conduct of elections in the Territories, which were concluded in the Oslo II agreement. The primary reason for Hamas's suicide attacks was that they exacted a heavy price in Israeli casualties. Most of the suicide attackers came from the Gaza Strip. Most were bachelors aged 18 to 25, with a high school education, and some with a university education. Hamas or Islamic Jihad operatives sent the attackers on their missions believing they would enter eternal Paradise.

Terrorist Group Dynamics
Unable to study terrorist group dynamics firsthand, social scientists have applied their understanding of small-group behavior to terrorist groups. Some features of terrorist groups, such as pressures toward conformity and consensus, are characteristic of all small groups. For whatever reason individuals assume the role of terrorists, their transformation into terrorists with a political or religious agenda takes place within the structure of the terrorist group. This group provides a sense of belonging, a feeling of self-importance, and a new belief system that defines the terrorist act as morally acceptable and the group's goals as of paramount importance. As Shaw (1988:366) explains:

> *Apparently membership in a terrorist group often provides a solution to the pressing personal needs of which the inability to achieve a desired niche in traditional society is the coup de grace. The terrorist identity offers the individual a role in society, albeit a negative one, which is commensurate with his or her prior expecta-*

> *tions and sufficient to compensate for past losses. Group membership provides a sense of potency, an intense and close interpersonal environment, social status, potential access to wealth and a share in what may be a grandiose but noble social design. The powerful psychological forces of conversion in the group are sufficient to offset traditional social sanctions against violence. To the terrorists their acts may have the moral status of religious warfare or political liberation.*

Terrorist groups are similar to religious sects or cults. They require total commitment by members; they often prohibit relations with outsiders, although this may not be the case with ethnic or separatist terrorist groups whose members are well-integrated into the community; they regulate and sometimes ban sexual relations; they impose conformity; they seek cohesiveness through interdependence and mutual trust; and they attempt to brainwash individual members with their particular ideology. According to Harry C. Holloway, M.D., and Ann E. Norwood, M.D. (1997:417), the joining process for taking on the beliefs, codes, and cult of the terrorist group "involves an interaction between the psychological structure of the terrorist's personality and the ideological factors, group process, structural organization of the terrorist group and cell, and the sociocultural milieu of the group."

Citing Knutson, Ehud Sprinzak (1990:79), an American-educated Israeli political scientist, notes, "It appears that, as radicalization deepens, the collective group identity takes over much of the individual identity of the members; and, at the terrorist stage, the group identity reaches its peak." This group identity becomes of paramount importance. As Post (1990:38) explains: "Terrorists whose only sense of significance comes from being terrorists cannot be forced to give up terrorism, for to do so would be to lose their very reason for being." The terrorist group displays the characteristics of groupthink (see Glossary), as described by I. Janis (1972). Among the characteristics that Janis ascribes to groups demonstrating groupthink are illusions of invulnerability leading to excessive optimism and excessive risk taking, presumptions of the group's morality, one-dimensional perceptions of the enemy as evil, and intolerance of challenges by a group member to shared key beliefs.

Some important principles of group dynamics among legally operating groups can also be usefully applied to the analysis of terrorist group dynamics. One generally accepted principle, as demonstrated by W. Bion (1961), is that individual judgment and behavior are strongly influenced by the powerful forces of group dynamics. Every group, according to Bion, has two opposing forces—a rare tendency to act in a fully cooperative, goal-directed, conflict-free manner to accomplish its stated purposes, and a stronger tendency to sabotage the stated goals. The latter tendency results in a group that defines itself in relation to the outside world and acts as if the only way it can survive is by fighting against or fleeing from the perceived enemy; a group that looks for direction to an omnipotent leader, to whom they subordinate their own independent judgment and act as if they do not have minds of their own; and a group that acts as if the group will bring forth a messiah who will rescue them and create a better world. Post believes that the terrorist group is the apotheosis of the sabotage tendency, regularly exhibiting all three of these symptoms.

Both structure and social origin need to be examined in any assessment of terrorist group dynamics. In Post's (1987) view, structural analysis in particular requires identification of the locus of power. In the autonomous terrorist action cell, the cell leader is within the cell, a situation that tends to promote tension. In contrast, the action cells of a terrorist group with a well-differentiated structure are organized within columns, thereby allowing policy decisions to be developed outside the cells.

Post found that group psychology provides more insights into the ways of terrorists than individual psychology does. After concluding, unconvincingly, that there is no terrorist mindset, he turned his attention to studying the family backgrounds of terrorists. He found that the group dynamics of nationalist-separatist groups and anarchic-ideological groups differ significantly. Members of nationalist-separatist groups are often known in their communities and maintain relationships with friends and family outside the terrorist group, moving in and out of the community with relative ease. In contrast, members of anarchic-ideological groups have irrevocably severed ties with family and community and lack their support. As a result, the terrorist group is the only source of information and security, a situation that produces pressure to conform and to commit acts of terrorism.

Pressures to Conform

Peer pressure, group solidarity, and the psychology of group dynamics help to pressure an individual member to remain in the terrorist group. According to Post (1986), terrorists tend to submerge their own identities into the group, resulting in a kind of "group mind" and group moral code that requires unquestioned obedience to the group. As Crenshaw (1985) has observed, "The group, as selector and interpreter of ideology, is central." Group cohesion increases or decreases depending on the degree of outside danger facing the group.

The need to belong to a group motivates most terrorists who are followers to join a terrorist group. Behavior among terrorists is similar, in Post's analysis, because of this need by alienated individuals to belong. For the new recruit, the terrorist group becomes a substitute family, and the group's leaders become substitute parents. An implied corollary of Post's observation that a key motivation for membership in a terrorist group is the sense of belonging and the fraternity of like-minded individuals is the assumption that there must be considerable apprehension among members that the group could be disbanded. As the group comes under attack from security forces, the tendency would be for the group to become more cohesive.

A member with wavering commitment who attempts to question group decisions or ideology or to quit under outside pressure against the group would likely face very serious sanctions. Terrorist groups are known to retaliate violently against members who seek to drop out. In 1972, when half of the thirty-member Rengo Sekigun (Red Army) terrorist group, which became known as the JRA, objected to the group's strategy, the dissenters, who included a pregnant woman who was thought to be "too bourgeois," were tied to stakes in the northern mountains of Japan, whipped with wires, and left to die of exposure. By most accounts, the decision to join a terrorist group or, for that matter, a terrorist cult like Aum Shinrikyo, is often an irrevocable one.

Pressures to Commit Acts of Violence

Post (1990:35) argues that "individuals become terrorists in order to join terrorist groups and commit acts of terrorism." Joining a terrorist group gives them a sense of "revolutionary heroism" and self-importance that they previously lacked as individuals. Consequently, a leader who is action-oriented is likely to have a stronger position within the group than one who advocates prudence and moderation. Thomas Strentz (1981:89) has pointed out that terrorist groups that operate against democracies often have a field commander whom he calls an "opportunist," that is, an activist, usually a male, whose criminal activity predates his political involvement. Strentz applies the psychological classification of the antisocial personality, also known as a sociopath or psychopath, to the life-style of this type of action-oriented individual. His examples of this personality type include Andreas Baader and Hans Joachim Klein of the Baader-Meinhof Gang and Akira Nihei of the JRA. Although the opportunist is not mentally ill, Strentz explains, he "is oblivious to the needs of others and unencumbered by the capacity to feel guilt or empathy." By most accounts, Baader was unpleasant, constantly abusive toward other members of the group, ill-read, and an action-oriented individual with a criminal past. Often recruited by the group's leader, the opportunist may eventually seek to take over the group, giving rise to increasing tensions between him and the leader. Often the leader will manipulate the opportunist by allowing him the fantasy of leading the group.

On the basis of his observation of underground resistance groups during World War II, J.K. Zawodny (1978) concluded that the primary determinant of underground group decision making is not the external reality but the psychological climate within the group. For action-oriented terrorists, inaction is extremely stressful. For action-oriented members, if the group is not taking action then there is no justification for the group. Action relieves stress by re-affirming to these members that they have a purpose. Thus, in Zawodny's analysis, a terrorist group needs to commit acts of terrorism in order to justify its existence.

Other terrorists may feel that their personal honor depends on the degree of violence that they carry out against the enemy. In 1970, Black September's

Salah Khalef ("Abu Iyad") was captured by the Jordanians and then released after he appealed to his comrades to stop fighting and to lay down their arms. Dobson (1975:52) reports that, according to the Jordanians, Abu Iyad "was subjected to such ridicule by the guerrillas who had fought on that he reacted by turning from moderation to the utmost violence."

Pearlstein points out that other examples of the political terrorist's self-justification of his or her terrorist actions include the terrorist's taking credit for a given terrorist act and forewarning of terrorist acts to come. By taking credit for an act of terrorism, the terrorist or terrorist group not only advertises the group's cause but also communicates a rhetorical self-justification of the terrorist act and the cause for which it was perpetrated. By threatening future terrorism, the terrorist or terrorist group in effect absolves itself of responsibility for any casualties that may result.

Terrorist Rationalization of Violence

Living underground, terrorists gradually become divorced from reality, engaging in what Ferracuti (1982) has described as a "fantasy war." The stresses that accompany their underground, covert lives as terrorists may also have adverse social and psychological consequences for them. Thus, as Taylor (1988:93) points out, although "mental illness may not be a particularly helpful way of conceptualizing terrorism, the acts of terrorism and membership in a terrorist organization may well have implications for the terrorist's mental health."

Albert Bandura (1990) has described four techniques of moral disengagement that a terrorist group can use to insulate itself from the human consequences of its actions. First, by using moral justification terrorists may imagine themselves as the saviors of a constituency threatened by a great evil. For example, Donatella della Porta (1992:286), who interviewed members of left-wing militant groups in Italy and Germany, observed that the militants "began to perceive themselves as members of a heroic community of generous people fighting a war against 'evil.'"

Second, through the technique of displacement of responsibility onto the leader or other members of the group, terrorists portray themselves as functionaries who are merely following their leader's orders. Conversely, the terrorist may blame other members of the group. Groups that are organized into cells and columns may be more capable of carrying out ruthless operations because of the potential for displacement of responsibility. Della Porta's interviews with left-wing militants suggest that the more compartmentalized a group is the more it begins to lose touch with reality, including the actual impact of its own actions. Other manifestations of this displacement technique include accusations made by Asahara, the leader of Aum Shinrikyo, that the Central Intelligence Agency (CIA) used chemical agents against him and the Japanese population.

A third technique is to minimize or ignore the actual suffering of the victims. As Bonnie Cordes (1987) points out, terrorists are able to insulate themselves from moral anxieties provoked by the results of their hit-and-run attacks, such as the use of time bombs, by usually not having to witness first-hand the carnage resulting from them, and by concerning themselves with the reactions of the authorities rather than with civilian casualties. Nevertheless, she notes that "Debates over the justification of violence, the types of targets, and the issue of indiscriminate versus discriminate killing are endemic to a terrorist group." Often, these internal debates result in schisms.

The fourth technique of moral disengagement described by Bandura is to dehumanize victims or, in the case of Islamist groups, to refer to them as "the infidel." Italian and German militants justified violence by depersonalizing their victims as "tools of the system," "pigs," or "watch dogs." Psychologist Frederick Hacker (1996:162) points out that terrorists transform their victims into mere objects, for "terroristic thinking and practices reduce individuals to the status of puppets." Cordes, too, notes the role reversal played by terrorists in characterizing the enemy as the conspirator and oppressor and accusing it of state terrorism, while referring to themselves as "freedom fighters" or "revolutionaries." As Cordes explains, "Renaming themselves, their actions, their victims and their enemies accords the terrorist respectability."

By using semantics to rationalize their terrorist violence, however, terrorists may create their own self-destructive psychological tensions. As David C. Rapoport (1971:42) explains:

> *All terrorists must deny the relevance of guilt and innocence, but in doing so they create an unbearable tension in their own souls, for they are in effect saying that a person is not a person. It is no accident that left-wing terrorists constantly speak of a "pig-society," by convincing themselves that they are confronting animals they hope to stay the remorse which the slaughter of the innocent necessarily generates.*

Expanding on this rationalization of guilt, D. Guttman (1979:525) argues that "the terrorist asserts that he loves only the socially redeeming qualities of his murderous act, not the act itself." By this logic, the conscience of the terrorist is turned against those who oppose his violent ways, not against himself. Thus, in Guttman's analysis, the terrorist has projected his guilt outward. In order to absolve his own guilt, the terrorist must claim that under the circumstances he has no choice but to do what he must do. Although other options actually are open to the terrorist, Guttman believes that the liberal audience legitimizes the terrorist by accepting this rationalization of murder.

Some terrorists, however, have been trained or brainwashed enough not to feel any remorse until confronted with the consequences of their actions. When journalist Eileen MacDonald asked a female ETA commando, "Amaia," how she felt when she heard that her bombs had been successful, she replied, after first denying being responsible for killing anyone: "Satisfaction. The bastards, they deserved it. Yes, I planted bombs that killed people." However, MacDonald felt that Amaia, who had joined the military wing at age 18, had never before questioned the consequences of her actions, and MacDonald's intuition was confirmed as Amaia's mood shifted from bravado to despondency, as she buried her head in her arms, and then groaned, "Oh, God, this is getting hard," and lamented that she had not prepared herself for the interview.

When Kim Hyun Hee (1993:104), the bomber of Korean Air Flight 858, activated the bomb, she had no moral qualms. "At that moment," she writes, "I felt no guilt or remorse at what I was doing; I thought only of completing the mission and not letting my country down." It was not until her 1988 trial, which resulted in a death sentence—she was pardoned a year later because she had been brainwashed—that she felt any remorse. "But being made to confront the victims' grieving families here in this courtroom," she writes, "I finally began to feel, deep down, the sheer horror of the atrocity I'd committed." One related characteristic of Kim, as told by one of her South Korean minders to MacDonald, is that she had not shown any emotion whatsoever to anyone in the two years she (the minder) had known her.

The Terrorist's Ideological or Religious Perception

Terrorists do not perceive the world as members of governments or civil society do. Their belief systems help to determine their strategies and how they react to government policies. As Martha Crenshaw (1988:12) has observed, "The actions of terrorist organizations are based on a subjective interpretation of the world rather than objective reality." The variables from which their belief systems are formed include their political and social environments, cultural traditions, and the internal dynamics of their clandestine groups. Their convictions may seem irrational or delusional to society in general, but the terrorists may nevertheless act rationally in their commitment to acting on their convictions.

According to cognitive theory, an individual's mental activities (perception, memory, and reasoning) are important determinants of behavior. Cognition is an important concept in psychology, for it is the general process by which individuals come to know about and make sense of the world. Terrorists view the world within the narrow lens of their own ideology, whether it be Marxism-Leninism, anarchism, nationalism, Islamic fundamentalism (see Glossary), or some other ideology. Most researchers agree that terrorists generally do not regard themselves as terrorists but rather as soldiers, liberators, martyrs, and legitimate fighters for noble social causes. Those terrorists who recognize that their actions are terroristic are so committed to their cause that they do not really care how they are viewed in the outside world. Others may be just as committed, but loathe to be identified as terrorists as opposed to freedom fighters or national liberators.

Kristen Renwick Monroe and Lina Haddad Kreidie (1997) have found perspective—the idea that we all have a view of the world, a view of ourselves, a view of others, and a view of ourselves in relation to others—to be a very useful tool in understanding fundamentalism, for example. Their underlying hypothesis is that the perspectives of fundamentalists resemble one another and that they differ in significant and consistent ways from the perspectives of nonfundamentalists. Monroe and Kreidie conclude that "fundamentalists see themselves not as individuals but rather as symbols of Islam." They argue that it is a mistake for Western policymakers to treat Islamic fundamentalists as rational actors and dismiss them as irrational when they do not act as predicted by traditional cost/benefit models. "Islamic fundamentalism should not be dealt with simply as another set of political values that can be compromised or negotiated, or even as a system of beliefs or ideology—such as socialism or communism—in which traditional liberal democratic modes of political discourse and interaction are recognized." They point out that "Islamic fundamentalism taps into a quite different political consciousness, one in which religious identity sets and determines the range of options open to the fundamentalist. It extends to all areas of life and respects no separation between the private and the political."

Existing works that attempt to explain religious fundamentalism often rely on modernization theory and point to a crisis of identity, explaining religious fundamentalism as an antidote to the dislocations resulting from rapid change, or modernization. Islamic fundamentalism, in particular, is often explained as a defense against threats posed by modernization to a religious group's traditional identity. Rejecting the idea of fundamentalism as pathology, rational choice theorists point to unequal socioeconomic development as the basic reason for the discontent and alienation these individuals experience. Caught between an Islamic culture that provides moral values and spiritual satisfaction and a modernizing Western culture that provides access to material improvement, many Muslims find an answer to resulting anxiety, alienation, and disorientation through an absolute dedication to an Islamic way of life. Accordingly, the Islamic fundamentalist is commonly depicted as an acutely alienated individual, with dogmatic and rigid beliefs and an inferiority complex, and as idealistic and devoted to an austere lifestyle filled with struggle and sacrifice.

In the 1990s, however, empirical studies of Islamic groups have questioned this view. V. J. Hoffman-Ladd, for example, suggests that fundamentalists are not necessarily ignorant and downtrodden, according to the stereotype, but frequently students and university graduates in the physical sciences, although often students with rural or traditionally religious backgrounds. In his view, fundamentalism is more of a revolt of young people caught between a traditional past and a secular Western education. R. Euben and Bernard Lewis argue separately that there is a cognitive collision between Western and fundamentalist worldviews. Focusing on Sunni fundamentalists, Euben argues that their goals are perceived not as self-interests but rather as moral imperatives, and that their worldviews differ in critical ways from Western worldviews.

By having moral imperatives as their goals, the fundamentalist groups perceive the world through the distorting lens of their religious beliefs. Although the perceptions of the secular Arab terrorist groups are not so clouded by religious beliefs, these groups have their own ideological imperatives that distort their ability to see the world with a reasonable amount of objectivity. As a result, their perception of the world is as distorted as that of the fundamentalists. Consequently, the secular groups are just as likely to misjudge political, economic, and social realities as are the fundamentalist groups. For example, Harold M. Cubert argues that the Popular Front for the Liberation of Palestine (PFLP), guided by Marxist economic ideology, has misjudged the reasons for popular hostility in the Middle East against the West, "for such hostility, where it exists, is generally in response to the threat which Western culture is said to pose to Islamic values in the region rather than the alleged economic exploitation of the region's inhabitants." This trend has made the PFLP's appeals for class warfare irrelevant, whereas calls by Islamist groups for preserving the region's cultural and religious identity have been well-received, at least among the non-secular sectors of the population.

Terrorist Profiling

Hazards of Terrorist Profiling

The isolation of attributes or traits shared by terrorists is a formidable task because there are probably as many variations among terrorists as there may be similarities. Efforts by scholars to create a profile of a "typical" terrorist have had mixed success, if any, and the assumption that there is such a profile has not been proven. Post (1985:103) notes that "behavioral scientists attempting to understand the psychology of individuals drawn to this violent political behavior have not succeeded in identifying a unique 'terrorist mindset.' People who have joined terrorist groups have come from a wide range of cultures, nationalities, and ideological causes, all strata of society, and diverse professions. Their personalities and characteristics are as diverse as those of people in the general population. There seems to be general agreement among psychologists that there is no particular psychological attribute that can be used to describe the terrorist or any "personality" that is distinctive of terrorists.

Some terrorism experts are skeptical about terrorist profiling. For example, Laqueur (1997:129) holds that the search for a "terrorist personality" is a fruitless one. Paul Wilkinson (1997:193) maintains that, "We already know enough about terrorist behavior to discount the crude hypothesis of a 'terrorist personality' or 'phenotype.'"

The U.S. Secret Service once watched for people who fit the popular profile of dangerousness—the lunatic, the loner, the threatener, the hater. That profile, however, was shattered by the assassins themselves. In interviews with assassins in prisons, hospitals, and homes, the Secret Service learned an important lesson—to discard stereotypes. Killers are not necessarily mentally ill, socially isolated, or even male. Now the Secret Service looks for patterns of motive and behavior in potential presidential assassins. The same research methodology applies to potential terrorists. Assassins, like terrorists in general, use common techniques. For example, the terrorist would not necessarily threaten to assassinate a politician in advance, for to do so would make it more difficult to carry out the deed. In its detailed study of eighty-three people who tried to kill a public official or a celebrity in the United States in the past fifty years, the Secret Service found that not one assassin had made a threat. Imprisoned assassins told the Secret Service that a threat would keep them from succeeding, so why would they threaten? This was the second important lesson learned from the study.

The diversity of terrorist groups, each with members of widely divergent national and sociocultural backgrounds, contexts, and goals, underscores the hazards of making generalizations and developing a profile of members of individual groups or of terrorists in general. Post cautions that efforts to provide an overall "terrorist profile" are misleading: "There are nearly as many variants of personality who become involved in terrorist pursuits as there are variants of personality."

Many theories are based on the assumption that the terrorist has an "abnormal" personality with clearly identifiable character traits that can be explained adequately with insights from psychology and psychiatry. Based on his work with various West German terrorists, one German psychologist, L. Sullwold (1981), divided terrorist leaders into two broad classes of personality traits: the extrovert and the hostile neurotic, or one having the syndrome of neurotic hostility. Extroverts are unstable, uninhibited, inconsiderate, self-interested, and unemotional—thrill seekers with little regard for the consequences of their actions. Hostile neurotics share many features of the paranoid personality—they are intolerant of criticism, suspicious, aggressive, and defensive, as well as extremely sensitive to external hostility. Sullwold also distinguishes between leaders and followers, in that leaders are more likely to be people who combine a lack of scruples with extreme self-assurance; they often lead by frightening or pressuring their followers.

Some researchers have created psychological profiles of terrorists by using data provided by former terrorists who became informants, changed their political allegiance, or were captured. Franco Ferracuti conducted one such study of the Red Brigade terrorists in Italy. He analyzed the career and personalities of arrested terrorists by collecting information on demographic variables and by applying psychological tests to construct a typology of terrorists. Like Post, Ferracuti also found, for the most part, the absence of psychopathology (see Glossary), and he observed similar personality characteristics, that is, a basic division between extroverts and hostile neurotics. By reading and studying terrorist literature, such as group communiqués, news media interviews, and memoirs of former members, it would also be possible to ascertain certain vulnerabilities within the group by pinpointing its sensitivities, internal disagreements, and moral weaknesses. This kind of information would assist in developing a psychological profile of the group.

Post points out that the social dynamics of the "anarchic-ideologues," such as the RAF, differ strikingly from the "nationalist-separatists," such as ETA or the Armenian Secret Army for the Liberation of Armenia (ASALA). From studies of terrorists, Post (1990) has observed indications that terrorists, such as those of the ETA, who pursue a conservative goal, such as freedom for the Basque people, have been reared in more traditional, intact, conservative families, whereas anarchistic and left-wing terrorists (such as members of the Meinhof Gang/RAF) come from less conventional, nonintact families. In developing this dichotomy between separatists and anarchists, Post draws on Robert Clark's studies of the social backgrounds of the separatist terrorists of the ETA. Clark also found that ETA terrorists are not alienated and psychologically distressed. Rather, they are psychologically healthy people who are strongly supported by their families and ethnic community.

Post bases his observations of anarchists on a broad-cased investigation of the social background and psychology of 250 terrorists (227 left-wing and 23 right-wing) conducted by a consortium of West German social scientists under the sponsorship of the Ministry of Interior and published in four volumes in 1981–84. According to these West German analyses of RAF and June Second Movement terrorists, some 25 percent of the leftist terrorists had lost one or both parents by the age of fourteen and 79 percent reported severe conflict with other people, especially with parents (33 percent). The German authors conclude in general that the 250 terrorist lives demonstrated a pattern of failure both educationally and vocationally. Post concludes that "nationalist-separatist" terrorists such as the ETA are loyal to parents who are disloyal to their regime, whereas "anarchic-ideologues" are disloyal to their parents' generation, which is identified with the establishment.

Sociological Characteristics of Terrorists in the Cold War Period

A Basic Profile

Profiles of terrorists have included a profile constructed by Charles A. Russell and Bowman H. Miller (1977), which has been widely mentioned in terrorism-related studies, despite its limitations, and another study that involved systematically analyzing biographical and social data on about 250 German terrorists, both left-wing and right-right. Russell and Bowman attempt to draw a sociological portrait or profile of the modern urban terrorist based on a compilation and analysis of more than 350 individual terrorist cadres and leaders from Argentinian, Brazilian, German, Iranian, Irish, Italian, Japanese, Palestinian, Spanish, Turkish, and Uruguayan terrorist groups active during the 1966–76 period, the first decade of the contemporary terrorist era. Russell and Bowman (1977:31) conclude:

> *In summation, one can draw a general composite picture into which fit the great majority of those terrorists from the eighteen urban guerrilla groups examined here. To this point, they have been largely single males aged 22 to 24 . . . who have some university education, if not a college degree. The female terrorists, except for the West German groups and an occasional leading figure in the JRA and PFLP, are preoccupied with support rather than operational roles. . . Whether having turned to terrorism as a university student or only later, most were provided an anarchist or Marxist world view, as well as recruited into terrorist operations while in the university.*

Russell and Miller's profile tends to substantiate some widely reported sociological characteristics of terrorists in the 1970s, such as the youth of most terrorists. Of particular interest is their finding that urban terrorists have largely urban origins and that many terrorist cadres have predominantly middle-class or even upper-class backgrounds and are well-educated, with many having university degrees. However, like most such profiles that are based largely on secondary sources, such as newspaper articles and academic studies, the Russell and Miller profile cannot be regarded as definitive. Furthermore, their methodological approach lacks validity. It is fallacious to assume that one can compare characteristics of members of numerous terrorist groups in various regions of the world and then make generalizations about these traits. For example, the authors' conclusion that terrorists are largely single, young males from urban, middle-class or upper-middle-class backgrounds with some university education would not accurately describe many members of terrorist groups operating in the 1990s. The rank and file of Latin American groups such as the FARC and Shining Path, Middle Eastern groups such as the Armed Islamic Group (Group Islamique Armé—GIA), Hamas, and Hizballah, Asian groups such as the LTTE, and Irish groups such as the IRA are poorly educated. Although the Russell and Miller profile is dated, it can still be used as a basic guide for making some generalizations about typical personal attributes of terrorists, in combination with other information.

Edgar O'Ballance (1979) suggests the following essential characteristics of the "successful" terrorist: dedication, including absolute obedience to the leader of the movement; personal bravery; a lack of feelings of pity or remorse even though victims are likely to include innocent men, women, and children; a fairly high standard of intelligence, for a terrorist must collect and analyze information, devise and implement complex plans, and evade police and security forces; a fairly high degree of sophistication, in order to be able to blend into the first-class section on airliners, stay at first-class hotels, and mix inconspicuously with the international executive set; and have a reasonably good educational background and possession of a fair share of general knowledge (a university degree is almost mandatory), including being able to speak English as well as one other major language.

Increasingly, terrorist groups are recruiting members who possess a high degree of intellectualism and idealism, are highly educated, and are well-trained in a legitimate profession. However, this may not necessarily be the case with the younger, lower ranks of large guerrilla/terrorist organizations in less-developed countries, such as the FARC, the PKK, the LTTE, and Arab groups, as well as with some of the leaders of these groups.

Age

Russell and Miller found that the average age of an active terrorist member (as opposed to a leader) was between 22 and 25, except for Palestinian, German, and Japanese terrorists, who were between 20 and 25 years old. Another source explains that the first generation of RAF terrorists went underground at approximately 22 to 23 years of age, and that the average age shifted to 28 to 30 years for second-generation terrorists (June Second Movement). In summarizing the literature about international terrorists in the 1980s, Taylor (1988) characterizes their demography as being in their early twenties and unmarried, but he notes that there is considerable variability from group to group. Age trends for members of many terrorist groups were dropping in the 1980s, with various groups, such as the LTTE, having many members in the 16- to 17-year-old age level and even members who were preteens. Laqueur notes that Arab and Iranian groups tend to use boys aged 14 to 15 for dangerous missions, in part because they are less likely to question instructions and in part because they are less likely to attract attention.

In many countries wracked by ethnic, political, or religious violence in the developing world, such as Algeria, Colombia, and Sri Lanka, new members of terrorist organizations are recruited at younger and younger ages. Adolescents and preteens in these countries are often receptive to terrorist recruitment because they have witnessed killings first-hand and thus see violence as the only way to deal with grievances and problems.

In general, terrorist leaders tend to be much older. Brazil's Carlos Marighella, considered to be the leading theoretician of urban terrorism, was 58 at the time of his violent death on November 6, 1969. Mario Santucho, leader of Argentina's People's Revolutionary Army (ERP), was 40 at the time of his violent death in July 1976. Raúl Sendic, leader of the Uruguayan Tupamaros, was 42 when his group began operating in the late 1960s. Renato Curcio, leader of the Italian Red Brigades, was 35 at the time of his arrest in early 1976. Leaders of the Baader-Meinhof Gang were in their 30s or 40s. Palestinian terrorist leaders are often in their 40s or 50s.

Educational, Occupational, and Socioeconomic Background

Terrorists in general have more than average education, and very few Western terrorists are uneducated or illiterate. Russell and Miller found that about two-thirds of terrorist group members had some form of university training. The occupations of terrorist recruits have varied widely, and there does not appear to be any occupation in particular that produces terrorists, other than the ranks of the unemployed and students. Between 50 and 70 percent of the younger members of Latin American urban terrorist groups were students. The Free University of Berlin was a particularly fertile recruiting ground for Germany's June Second Movement and Baader-Meinhof Gang.

Highly educated recruits were normally given leadership positions, whether at the cell level or national level. The occupations of terrorist leaders have likewise varied. Older members and leaders frequently were professionals such as doctors, bankers, lawyers, engineers, journalists, university professors, and mid-level government executives. Marighella was a politician and former congressman. The PFLP's George Habash was a medical doctor. The PLO's Yasir Arafat was a graduate engineer. Mario Santucho was an economist. Raúl Sendic and the Baader-Meinhof's Horst Mahler were lawyers. Urika Meinhof was a journalist. The RAF and Red Brigades were composed almost exclusively of disenchanted intellectuals.

It may be somewhat misleading to regard terrorists in general as former professionals. Many terrorists who have been able to remain anonymous probably continue to practice their legitimate professions and moonlight as terrorists only when they receive instructions to carry out a mission. This may be more true about separatist organizations, such as the ETA and IRA, whose members are integrated into their communities, than about members of anarchist groups, such as the former Baader-Meinhof Gang, who are more likely to be on wanted posters, on the run, and too stressed to be able to function in a normal daytime job. In response to police infiltration, the ETA, for example, instituted a system of "sleeping commandos." These passive ETA members, both men and women, lead seemingly normal lives, with regular jobs, but after work they are trained for specific ETA missions. Usually unaware of each others' real identities, they receive coded instructions from an anonymous source. After carrying out their assigned actions, they resume their normal lives. Whereas terrorism for anarchistic groups such as the RAF and Red Brigades was a full-time profession, young ETA members serve an average of only three years before they are rotated back into the mainstream of society.

Russell and Miller found that more than two-thirds of the terrorists surveyed came from middle-class or even upper-class backgrounds. With the main exception of large guerrilla/terrorist organizations such as the FARC, the PKK, the LTTE, and the Palestinian or Islamic fundamentalist terrorist organizations, terrorists come from middle-class families. European and Japanese terrorists are more likely the products of affluence and higher education than of poverty. For example, the RAF and Red Brigades were composed almost exclusively of middle-class dropouts, and most JRA members were from middle-class families and were university dropouts. Well-off young people, particularly in the United States, West Europe, and Japan, have been attracted to political radicalism out of a profound sense of guilt over the plight of the world's largely poor population. The backgrounds of the Baader-Meinhof Gang's members illustrate this in particular: Suzanne Albrecht, daughter of a wealthy maritime lawyer; Baader, the son of an historian; Meinhof, the daughter of an art historian; Horst Mahler, the son of a dentist; Holger Meins, the son of a business executive. According to Russell and Miller, about 80 percent of the Baader-Meinhof Gang had university experience.

Major exceptions to the middle- and upper-class origins of terrorist groups in general include three large organizations examined in this study—the FARC, the LTTE, and the PKK—as well as the paramilitary groups in Northern Ireland. Both the memberships of the Protestant groups, such as the Ulster Volunteer Force, and the Catholic groups, such as the Official IRA, the Provisional IRA, and the Irish National Liberation Army (INLA), are almost all drawn from the working class. These paramilitary groups are also different in that their members normally do not have any university education. Although Latin America has been an exception, terrorists in much of the developing world tend to be drawn from the lower sections of society. The rank and file of Arab terrorist organizations include substantial numbers of poor people, many of them homeless refugees. Arab terrorist leaders are almost all from the middle and upper classes.

General Traits

Terrorists are generally people who feel alienated from society and have a grievance or regard themselves as victims of an injustice. Many are dropouts. They are devoted to their political or religious cause and do not regard their violent actions as criminal. They are loyal to each other but will deal with a disloyal member more harshly than with the enemy. They are people with cunning, skill, and initiative, as well as ruthlessness. To be initiated into the group, the new recruit may be expected to perform an armed robbery or murder. They show no fear, pity, or remorse. The sophistication of the terrorist will vary depending on the significance and context of the terrorist action. The Colombian hostage-takers who infiltrated an embassy party and the Palace of Justice, for example, were far more sophisticated than would be, for example, Punjab terrorists who gun down bus passengers. Terrorists have the ability to use a variety of weapons, vehicles, and communications equipment and are familiar with their physical environment, whether it be a 747 jumbo jet or a national courthouse. A terrorist will rarely operate by himself/herself or in large groups, unless the operation requires taking over a large building, for example.

Members of right-wing terrorist groups in France and Germany, as elsewhere, generally tend to be young, relatively uneducated members of the lower classes (see Table 1, Appendix). Ferracuti and F. Bruno (1981:209) list nine psychological traits common to right-wing terrorists: ambivalence toward authority; poor and defective insight; adherence to conventional behavioral patterns; emotional detachment from the consequences of their actions; disturbances in sexual identity with role uncertainties; superstition, magic, and stereotyped thinking; etero- and auto-destructiveness;

low-level educational reference patterns; and perception of weapons as fetishes and adherence to violent subcultural norms. These traits make up what Ferracuti and Bruno call an "authoritarian-extremist personality." They conclude that right-wing terrorism may be more dangerous than left-wing terrorism because "in right-wing terrorism, the individuals are frequently psychopathological and the ideology is empty: ideology is outside reality, and the terrorists are both more normal and more fanatical."

Marital Status
In the past, most terrorists have been unmarried. Russell and Miller found that, according to arrest statistics, more than 75 to 80 percent of terrorists in the various regions in the late 1970s were single. Encumbering family responsibilities are generally precluded by requirements for mobility, flexibility, initiative, security, and total dedication to a revolutionary cause. Roughly 20 percent of foreign terrorist group memberships apparently consisted of married couples, if Russell and Miller's figure on single terrorists was accurate.

Physical Appearance
Terrorists are healthy and strong but generally undistinguished in appearance and manner. The physical fitness of some may be enhanced by having had extensive commando training. They tend to be of medium height and build to blend easily into crowds. They tend not to have abnormal physiognomy and peculiar features, genetic or acquired, that would facilitate their identification. Their dress and hair styles are inconspicuous. In addition to their normal appearance, they talk and behave like normal people. They may even be well-dressed if, for example, they need to be in the first-class section of an airliner targeted for hijacking. They may resort to disguise or plastic surgery depending on whether they are on police wanted posters.

If a terrorist's face is not known, it is doubtful that a suspected terrorist can be singled out of a crowd only on the basis of physical features. Unlike the *yakuza* (mobsters) in Japan, terrorists generally do not have distinguishing physical features such as colorful tatoos. For example, author Christopher Dobson (1975) describes the Black September's Salah Khalef ("Abu Iyad") as "of medium height and sturdy build, undistinguished in a crowd." When Dobson, hoping for an interview, was introduced to him in Cairo in the early 1970s Abu Iyad made "so little an impression" during the brief encounter that Dobson did not realize until later that he had already met Israel's most-wanted terrorist. Another example is Imad Mughniyah, head of Hizballah's special operations, who is described by Hala Jaber (1997:120) as "someone you would pass in the street without even noticing or giving a second glance."

Origin: Rural or Urban
Guerrilla/terrorist organizations have tended to recruit members from the areas where they are expected to operate because knowing the area of operation is a basic principle of urban terrorism and guerrilla warfare.

According to Russell and Miller, about 90 percent of the Argentine ERP and Montoneros came from the Greater Buenos Aires area. Most of Marighella's followers came from Recife, Rio de Janeiro, Santos, and São Paulo. More than 70 percent of the Tupamaros were natives of Montevideo. Most German and Italian terrorists were from urban areas: the Germans from Hamburg and West Berlin; the Italians from Genoa, Milan, and Rome.

Gender

Males—Most terrorists are male. Well over 80 percent of terrorist operations in the 1966–76 period were directed, led, and executed by males. The number of arrested female terrorists in Latin America suggested that female membership was less than 16 percent. The role of women in Latin American groups such as the Tupamaros was limited to intelligence collection, serving as couriers or nurses, maintaining safehouses, and so forth.

Females—Various terrorism specialists have noted that the number of women involved in terrorism has greatly exceeded the number of women involved in crime. However, no statistics have been offered to substantiate this assertion. Considering that the number of terrorist actions perpetrated worldwide in any given year is probably minuscule in comparison with the common crimes committed in the same period, it is not clear if the assertion is correct. Nevertheless, it indeed seems as if more women are involved in terrorism than actually are, perhaps because they tend to get more attention than women involved in common crime.

Although Russell and Miller's profile is more of a sociological than a psychological profile, some of their conclusions raise psychological issues, such as why women played a more prominent role in left-wing terrorism in the 1966–76 period than in violent crime in general. Russell and Miller's data suggest that the terrorists examined were largely males, but the authors also note the secondary support role played by women in most terrorist organizations, particularly the Uruguayan Tupamaros and several European groups. For example, they point out that women constituted one-third of the personnel of the RAF and June Second Movement, and that nearly 60 percent of the RAF and June Second Movement who were at large in August 1976 were women.

Russell and Miller's contention that "urban terrorism remains a predominantly male phenomenon," with women functioning mainly in a secondary support role, may underestimate the active, operational role played by women in Latin American and West European terrorist organizations in the 1970s and 1980s. Insurgent groups in Latin America in the 1970s and 1980s reportedly included large percentages of female combatants: 30 percent of the Sandinista National Liberation Front (FSLN) combatants in Nicaragua by the late 1970s; one-third of the combined forces of the Farabundo Martí National Liberation Front (FMLN) in El Salvador; and one-half of the Shining Path terrorists in Peru. However, because these percentages may have been inflated by the insurgent groups to impress foreign feminist sympathizers, no firm conclusions can be drawn in the absence of reliable statistical data.

Nevertheless, women have played prominent roles in numerous urban terrorist operations in Latin America. For example, the second in command of the Sandinista takeover of Nicaragua's National Palace in Managua, Nicaragua, in late August 1979, was Dora María Téllez Argüello. Several female terrorists participated in the takeover of the Dominican Embassy in Bogotá, Colombia, by the 19th of April Movement (M-19) in 1980, and one of them played a major role in the hostage negotiations. The late Mélida Anaya Montes ("Ana María") served as second in command of the People's Liberation Forces (Fuerzas Populares de Liberación—FPL) prior to her murder at age 54 by FPL rivals in 1983. Half of the thirty-five M-19 terrorists who raided Colombia's Palace of Justice on November 6, 1985, were women, and they were among the fiercest fighters.

Leftist terrorist groups or operations in general have frequently been led by women. Many women joined German terrorist groups. Germany's Red Zora, a terrorist group active between the late 1970s and 1987, recruited only women and perpetrated many terrorist actions. In 1985 the RAF's twenty-two core activists included thirteen women. In 1991, women formed about 50 percent of the RAF membership and about 80 percent of the group's supporters, according to MacDonald. Of the eight individuals on Germany's "Wanted Terrorists" list in 1991, five were women. Of the twenty-two terrorists being hunted by German police that year, thirteen were women. Infamous German female terrorist leaders have included Susanne Albrecht, Gudrun Ensselin\Esslin, and Ulrike Meinhof of the Baader-Meinhof Gang. There are various theories as to why German women have been so drawn to violent groups. One is that they are more emancipated and liberated than women in other European countries. Another, as suggested to Eileen MacDonald by Astrid Proll, an early member of the Baader-Meinhof Gang, is that the anger of German women is part of a national guilt complex, the feeling that if their mothers had had a voice in Hitler's time many of Hitler's atrocities would not have happened.

Other noted foreign female terrorists have included Fusako Shigenobu of the JRA (Shigenobu, 53, was reported in April 1997 to be with fourteen other JRA members—two other women and twelve men—training FARC guerrillas in terror tactics in the Urabá Region of Colombia); Norma Ester Arostito, who cofounded the Argentine Montoneros and served as its chief ideologist until her violent death in 1976; Margherita Cagol and Susana Ronconi of the Red Brigades; Ellen Mary Margaret McKearney of the IRA; Norma Ester Arostito of the Montoneros; and Geneveve Forest Tarat of the ETA, who played a key role in the spectacular ETA-V bomb assassination of Premier Admiral Carrero Blanco on December 20, 1973, as well as in the bombing of the Café Rolando in Madrid in which eleven people were killed and more than seventy wounded on September 13, 1974. ETA members told journalist Eileen MacDonald that ETA has always had female commandos and operators. Women make up about 10 percent of imprisoned

ETA members, so that may be roughly the percentage of women in ETA ranks.

Infamous female commandos have included Leila Khaled, a beautiful PFLP commando who hijacked a TWA passenger plane on August 29, 1969, and then blew it up after evacuating the passengers, without causing any casualties (see Leila Khaled, Appendix). One of the first female terrorists of modern international terrorism, she probably inspired hundreds of other angry young women around the world who admired the thrilling pictures of her in newspapers and magazines worldwide showing her cradling a weapon, with her head demurely covered. Another PFLP female hijacker, reportedly a Christian Iraqi, was sipping champagne in the cocktail bar of a Japan Air Lines Jumbo jet on July 20, 1973, when the grenade that she was carrying strapped to her waist exploded, killing her.

Women have also played a significant role in Italian terrorist groups. Leonard Weinberg and William Lee Eubank (1987: 248–53) have been able to quantify that role by developing a data file containing information on about 2,512 individuals who were arrested or wanted by police for terrorism from January 1970 through June 1984. Of those people, 451, or 18 percent, were female. Of those females, fewer than 10 percent were affiliated with neofascist groups (see Table 2, Appendix). The rest belonged to leftist terrorist groups, particularly the Red Brigades (Brigate Rosse—BR), which had 215 female members. Weinberg and Eubank found that the Italian women surveyed were represented at all levels of terrorist groups: 33 (7 percent) played leadership roles and 298 (66 percent) were active "regulars" who took part in terrorist actions. (see Table 3, Appendix). Weinberg and Eubank found that before the women became involved in terrorism they tended to move from small and medium-sized communities to big cities (see Table 4, Appendix). The largest group of the women (35 percent) had been students before becoming terrorists, 20 percent had been teachers, and 23 percent had held white-collar jobs as clerks, secretaries, technicians, and nurses (see Table 5, Appendix). Only a few of the women belonged to political parties or trade union organizations, whereas 80 (17 percent) belonged to leftist extraparliamentary movements. Also noteworthy is the fact that 121 (27 percent) were related by family to other terrorists. These researchers concluded that for many women joining a terrorist group resulted from a small-group or family decision.

Characteristics of Female Terrorists

Practicality, Coolness

German intelligence officials told Eileen MacDonald that "absolute practicality . . . was particularly noticeable with women revolutionaries." By this apparently was meant coolness under pressure. However, Germany's female terrorists, such as those in the Baader-Meinhof Gang, have been described by a former member as "all pretty male-dominated; I mean they had male characteristics." These included interests in technical things, such as repairing cars, driving, accounting, and organizing. For example, the RAF's Astrid Proll was a first-rate mechanic, Gudrun Ensslin was in charge of the RAF's finances, and Ulrike Meinhof sought out apartments for the group.

According to Christian Lochte, the Hamburg director of the Office for the Protection of the Constitution, the most important qualities that a female member could bring to terrorist groups, which are fairly unstable, were practicality and pragmatism: "In wartime women are much more capable of keeping things together," Lochte told MacDonald. "This is very important for a group of terrorists, for their dynamics. Especially a group like the RAF, where there are a lot of quarrels about strategy, about daily life. Women come to the forefront in such a group because they are practical."

Galvin points out the tactical value of women in a terrorist group. An attack by a female terrorist is normally less expected than one by a man. "A woman, trading on the impression of being a mother, nonviolent, fragile, even victim like, can more easily pass scrutiny by security forces. . . ." There are numerous examples illustrating the tactical surprise factor that can be achieved by female terrorists. A LTTE female suicide commando was able to get close enough to Indian Prime Minister Rajiv Gandhi on May 21, 1991, to garland him with flowers and then set off her body bomb, killing him, herself, and seventeen others. Nobody suspected the attractive Miss Kim of carrying a bomb aboard a Korean Air Flight 858. And Leila Khaled, dressed in elegant clothes and strapped with grenades, was able to pass through various El Al security checks without arousing suspicion. Female terrorists have also been used to draw male targets into a situation in which they could be kidnapped or assassinated.

Dedication, Inner Strength, Ruthlessness
Lochte also considered female terrorists to be stronger, more dedicated, faster, and more ruthless than male terrorists, as well as more capable of withstanding suffering because "they have better nerves than men, and they can be both passive and active at the same time." The head of the German counterterrorist squad told MacDonald that the difference between the RAF men and women who had been caught after the fall of the Berlin Wall was that the women had been far more reticent about giving information than the men, and when the women did talk it was for reasons of guilt as opposed to getting a reduced prison sentence, as in the case of their male comrades.

According to MacDonald, since the late 1960s, when women began replacing imprisoned or interned male IRA members as active participants, IRA women have played an increasingly important role in "frontline" actions against British troops and Protestant paramilitary units, as well as in terrorist actions against the British public. As a result, in the late 1960s the IRA merged its separate women's sections within the movement into one IRA. MacDonald cites several notorious IRA women terrorists. They include

Marion Price, 19, and her sister (dubbed "the Sisters of Death"), who were part of the IRA's 1973 bombing campaign in London. In the early 1970s, Dr. Rose Dugdale, daughter of a wealthy English family, hijacked a helicopter and used it to try to bomb a police barracks. In 1983, Anna Moore was sentenced to life imprisonment for her role in bombing a Northern Ireland pub in which seventeen were killed. Ella O'Dwyer and Martina Anderson, 23, a former local beauty queen, received life sentences in 1986 for their part in the plot to bomb London and sixteen seaside resorts. Another such terrorist was Mairead Farrell, who was shot dead by the SAS in Gibraltar in 1988. A year before her death, Farrell, who was known for her strong feminist views, said in an interview that she was attracted to the IRA because she was treated the same as "the lads." As of 1992, Evelyn Glenholmes was a fugitive for her role in a series of London bombings.

MacDonald interviewed a few of these and a number of other female IRA terrorists, whom she described as all ordinary, some more friendly than others. Most were unmarried teenagers or in their early twenties when they became involved in IRA terrorism. None had been recruited by a boyfriend. When asked why they joined, all responded with "How could we not?" replies. They all shared a hatred for the British troops (particularly their foul language and manners) and a total conviction that violence was justified. One female IRA volunteer told MacDonald, "Everyone is treated the same. During training, men and women are equally taught the use of explosives and weapons."

Single-Mindedness

Female terrorists can be far more dangerous than male terrorists because of their ability to focus single-mindedly on the cause and the goal. Lochte noted that the case of Susanne Albrecht demonstrated this total dedication to a cause, to the exclusion of all else, even family ties and upbringing. The RAF's Suzanne Albrecht, daughter of a wealthy maritime lawyer, set up a close family friend, Jurgen Ponto, one of West Germany's richest and most powerful men and chairman of the Dresden Bank, for assassination in his home, even though she later admitted to having experienced nothing but kindness and generosity from him. Lochte told MacDonald that if Albrecht had been a man, she would have tried to convince her RAF comrade to pick another target to kidnap. "Her attitude was," Lochte explained, "to achieve the goal, to go straight ahead without any interruptions, any faltering. This attitude is not possible with men." (Albrecht, however, reportedly was submitted to intense pressure by her comrades to exploit her relationship with the banker, and the plan was only to kidnap him rather than kill him.) After many years of observing German terrorists, Lochte concluded, in his comments to MacDonald, that women would not hesitate to shoot at once if they were cornered. "For anyone who loves his life," he told MacDonald, "it is a good idea to shoot the women terrorists first." In his view, woman terrorists feel they need to show that they can be even more ruthless than men.

Germany's neo-Nazi groups also have included female members who have played major roles, according to MacDonald. For example, Sibylle Vorder-brügge, 26, joined a notorious neo-Nazi group in 1980 after becoming infatuated with its leader. She then became a bomb-throwing terrorist expressly to please him. According to MacDonald, she was a good example to Christian Lochte of how women become very dedicated to a cause, even more than men. "One day she had never heard of the neo-Nazis, the next she was a terrorist," Lochte commented. "One day she had no interest in the subject; the next she was 100 percent terrorist; she became a fighter overnight."

Female Motivation for Terrorism

What motivates women to become terrorists? Galvin suggests that women, being more idealistic than men, may be more impelled to perpetrate terrorist activities in response to failure to achieve change or the experience of death or injury to a loved one. Galvin also argues that the female terrorist enters into terrorism with different motivations and expectations than the male terrorist. In contrast to men, who Galvin characterizes as being enticed into terrorism by the promise of "power and glory," females embark on terrorism "attracted by promises of a better life for their children and the desire to meet people's needs that are not being met by an intractable establishment." Considering that females are less likely than males to have early experience with guns, terrorist membership is therefore a more active process for women than for men because women have more to learn. In the view of Susana Ronconi, one of Italy's most notorious and violent terrorists in the 1970s, the ability to commit violence did not have anything to do with gender. Rather, one's personality, background, and experience were far more important.

Companionship is another motivating factor in a woman's joining a terrorist group. MacDonald points out that both Susanna Ronconi and Ulrike Meinhof "craved love, comradeship, and emotional support" from their comrades.

Feminism has also been a motivating ideology for many female terrorists. Many of them have come from societies in which women are repressed, such as Middle Eastern countries and North Korea, or Catholic countries, such as in Latin America, Spain, Ireland, and Italy. Even Germany was repressive for women when the Baader-Meinhof Gang emerged.

Conclusion

Terrorist Profiling

In profiling the terrorist, some generalizations can be made on the basis on this examination of the literature on the psychology and sociology of terrorism published over the past three decades. One finding is that, unfortunately for profiling purposes, there does not appear to be a single terrorist personality. This seems to be the consensus among terrorism psychologists as well as political scientists and sociologists. The personalities of terrorists may be as diverse as the personalities of people in any lawful profession. There do not appear to be any visibly detectable personality traits that would allow authorities to identify a terrorist.

Another finding is that the terrorist is not diagnosably psychopathic or mentally sick. Contrary to the stereotype that the terrorist is a psychopath or otherwise mentally disturbed, the terrorist is actually quite sane, although deluded by an ideological or religious way of viewing the world. The only notable exceptions encountered in this study were the German anarchist terrorists, such as the Baader-Meinhof Gang and their affiliated groups. The German terrorists seem to be a special case, however, because of their inability to come to terms psychologically and emotionally with the shame of having parents who were either passive or active supporters of Hitler.

The highly selective terrorist recruitment process explains why most terrorist groups have only a few pathological members. Candidates who exhibit signs of psychopathy or other mental illness are deselected in the interest of group survival. Terrorist groups need members whose behavior appears to be normal and who would not arouse suspicion. A member who exhibits traits of psychopathy or any noticeable degree of mental illness would only be a liability for the group, whatever his or her skills. That individual could not be depended on to carry out the assigned mission. On the contrary, such an individual would be more likely to sabotage the group by, for example, botching an operation or revealing group secrets if captured. Nor would a psychotic member be likely to enhance group solidarity. A former PKK spokesman has even stated publicly that the PKK's policy was to exclude psychopaths.

This is not to deny, however, that certain psychological types of people may be attracted to terrorism. In his examination of autobiographies, court records, and rare interviews, Jerrold M. Post (1990:27) found that "people with particular personality traits and tendencies are drawn disproportionately to terrorist careers." Authors such as Walter Laqueur, Post notes, "have characterized terrorists as action-oriented, aggressive people who are stimulus-hungry and seek excitement." Even if Post and some other psychologists are correct that individuals with narcissistic personalities and low self-esteem are attracted to terrorism, the early psychological development of individuals in their pre-terrorist lives does not necessarily mean that terrorists are mentally disturbed and can be identified by any particular traits associated with their early psychological backgrounds. Many people in other high-risk professions, including law enforcement, could also be described as "action-oriented, aggressive people who are stimulus-hungry and seek excitement." Post's views notwithstanding, there is actually substantial evidence that terrorists are quite sane.

Although terrorist groups are highly selective in whom they recruit, it is not inconceivable that a psychopathic individual can be a top leader or the top leader of the terrorist group. In fact, the actions and behavior of the ANO's Abu Nidal, the PKK's Abdullah Ocalan, the LTTE's Velupillai Prabhakaran, the FARC's Jorge Briceño Suárez, and Aum Shinrikyo's Shoko Asahara might lead some to believe that they all share psychopathic or sociopathic symptoms. Nevertheless, the question of whether any or all of these guerrilla/terrorist leaders are psychopathic or sociopathic is best left for a qualified psychologist to determine. If the founder of a terrorist group or cult is a psychopath, there is little that the membership could do to remove him, without suffering retaliation. Thus, that leader may never have to be subjected to the group's standards of membership or leadership.

In addition to having normal personalities and not being diagnosably mentally disturbed, a terrorist's other characteristics make him or her practically indistinguishable from normal people, at least in terms of outward appearance. Terrorist groups recruit members who have a normal or average physical appearance. As a result, the terrorist's physical appearance is unlikely to betray his or her identity as a terrorist, except in cases where the terrorist is well known, or security personnel already have a physical description or photo. A terrorist's physical features and dress naturally will vary depending on race, culture, and nationality. Both sexes are involved in a variety of roles, but men predominate in leadership roles. Terrorists tend to be in their twenties and to be healthy and strong; there are relatively few older terrorists, in part because terrorism is a physically demanding occupation. Training alone requires considerable physical fitness. Terrorist leaders are older, ranging from being in their thirties to their sixties.

The younger terrorist who hijacks a jetliner, infiltrates a government building, lobs a grenade into a sidewalk café, attempts to assassinate a head of state, or detonates a body-bomb on a bus will likely be appropriately dressed and acting normal before initiating the attack. The terrorist needs to be inconspicuous in order to approach the target and then to escape after carrying out the attack, if escape is part of the plan. The suicide terrorist also needs to approach a target inconspicuously. This need to appear like a normal citizen would also apply to the FARC, the LTTE, the PKK, and other guerrilla organizations when they use commandos to carry out urban terrorist operations. It should be noted that regular FARC, LTTE, and PKK members wear uniforms and operate in rural areas. These three groups do, however, also engage in occasional acts of urban terrorism, the LTTE more than the FARC and PKK. On those occasions, the LTTE and PKK terrorists wear civilian clothes. FARC guerrillas are more likely to wear uniforms when carrying out their acts of terrorism, such as kidnappings and murders, in small towns.

Terrorist and guerrilla groups do not seem to be identified by any particular social background or educational level. They range from the highly educated and literate intellectuals of the 17 November Revolutionary Organization (17N) to the scientifically savvy "ministers" of the Aum Shinrikyo terrorist cult to the peasant boys and girls forcibly inducted into the FARC, the LTTE, and the PKK guerrilla organizations.

Most terrorist leaders have tended to be well-educated. Examples include Illich Ramírez Sánchez ("The Jackal") and the Shining Path's Abimael Guzmán Reynoso, both of whom are currently in prison. Indeed, terrorists are increasingly well-educated and capable of sophisticated, albeit highly biased, political analysis. In contrast to Abu Nidal, for example, who is a relatively uneducated leader of the old generation and one who appears to be motivated more by vengefulness and greed than any ideology, the new generation of Islamic terrorists, be they key operatives such as the imprisoned Ramzi Yousef, or leaders such as Osama bin Laden, are well-educated and motivated by their religious ideologies. The religiously motivated terrorists are more dangerous than the politically motivated terrorists because they are the ones most likely to develop and use weapons of weapons of mass destruction (WMD) in pursuit of their messianic or apocalyptic visions. The level of intelligence of a terrorist group's leaders may determine the longevity of the group. The fact that the 17 November group has operated successfully for a quarter of a century must be indicative of the intelligence of its leaders.

In short, a terrorist will look, dress, and behave like a normal person, such as a university student, until he or she executes the assigned mission. Therefore, considering that this physical and behavioral description of the terrorist could describe almost any normal young person, terrorist profiling based on personality, physical, or sociological traits would not appear to be particularly useful.

If terrorists cannot be detected by personality or physical traits, are there other early warning indicators that could alert security personnel? The most important indicator would be having intelligence information on the individual, such as a "watch list," a description, and a photo, or at least a threat made by a terrorist group. Even a watch list is not foolproof, however, as demonstrated by the case of Sheikh Omar Abdel Rahman, who, despite having peculiar features and despite being on a terrorist watch list, passed through U.S. Customs unhindered.

Unanticipated stress and nervousness may be a hazard of the profession, and a terrorist's nervousness could alert security personnel in instances where, for example, a hijacker is boarding an aircraft, or hostage-takers posing as visitors are infiltrating a government building. The terrorist undoubtedly has higher levels of stress than most people in lawful professions. However, most terrorists are trained to cope with nervousness. Female terrorists are known to be particularly cool under pressure. Leila Khaled and Kim Hyun Hee mention in their autobiographies how they kept their nervousness under control by reminding themselves of, and being totally convinced of, the importance of their missions.

Indeed, because of their coolness under pressure, their obsessive dedication to the cause of their group, and their need to prove themselves to their male comrades, women make formidable terrorists and have proven to be more dangerous than male terrorists. Hizballah, the LTTE, and PKK are among the groups that have used attractive young women as suicide body-bombers to great effect. Suicide body-bombers are trained to be totally at ease and confident when approaching their target, although not all suicide terrorists are able to act normally in approaching their target.

International terrorists generally appear to be predominately either leftist or Islamic. A profiling system could possibly narrow the statistical probability that an unknown individual boarding an airliner might be a terrorist if it could be accurately determined that most terrorists are of a certain race, culture, religion, or nationality. In the absence of statistical data, however, it cannot be determined here whether members of any particular race, religion, or nationality are responsible for most acts of international terrorism. Until those figures become available, smaller-scale terrorist group profiles might be more useful. For example, a case could be made that U.S. Customs personnel should give extra scrutiny to the passports of young foreigners claiming to be "students" and meeting the following general description: physically fit males in their early twenties of Egyptian, Jordanian, Yemeni, Iraqi, Algerian, Syrian, or Sudanese nationality, or Arabs bearing valid British passports, in that order. These characteristics generally describe the core membership of Osama bin Laden's Arab "Afghans" (see Glossary), also known as the Armed Islamic Movement (AIM), who are being trained to attack the United States with WMD.

Terrorist Group Mindset Profiling

This review of the academic literature on terrorism suggests that the psychological approach by itself is insufficient in understanding what motivates terrorists, and that an interdisciplinary approach is needed to more adequately understand terrorist motivation. Terrorists are motivated not only by psychological factors but also by very real political, social, religious, and economic factors, among others. These factors vary widely. Accordingly, the motivations, goals, and ideologies of ethnic separatist, anarchist, social revolutionary, religious fundamentalist, and new religious terrorist groups differ significantly. Therefore, each terrorist group must be examined within its own cultural, economic, political, and social context to better understand the motivations of its individual members and leaders and their particular ideologies.

Although it may not be possible to isolate a so-called terrorist personality, each terrorist group has its own distinctive mindset. The mindset of a terrorist group reflects the personality and ideology of its top leader and other circumstantial traits, such as typology (religious, social revolutionary, separatist, anarchist, and so forth), a particular ideology or religion, culture, and nationality, as well as group dynamics.

Jerrold Post dismisses the concept of a terrorist mindset on the basis that behavioral scientists have not succeeded in identifying it. Post confuses the issue, however, by treating the term "mindset" as a synonym for personality. The two terms are not synonymous. One's personality is a distinctive pattern of thought, emotion, and behavior that define one's way of interacting with the physical and social environment, whereas a mindset is a fixed mental attitude or a fixed state of mind.

In trying to better define mindset, the term becomes more meaningful when considered within the context of a group. The new terrorist recruit already has a personality when he or she joins the group, but the new member acquires the group's mindset only after being fully indoctrinated and familiarized with its ideology, point of view, leadership attitudes, ways of operating, and so forth. Each group will have its own distinctive mindset, which will be a reflection of the top leader's personality and ideology, as well as group type. For example, the basic mindset of a religious terrorist group, such as Hamas and Hizballah, is Islamic fundamentalism. The basic mindset of an Irish terrorist is anti-British sectarianism and separatism. The basic mindset of an ETA member is anti-Spanish separatism. The basic mindset of a 17 November member is anti-establishment, anti-US, anti-NATO, and anti-German nationalism and Marxism-Leninism. And the basic mindset of an Aum Shinrikyo member is worship of Shoko Asahara, paranoia against the Japanese and U.S. governments, and millenarian, messianic apocalypticism.

Terrorist group mindsets determine how the group and its individual members view the world and how they lash out against it. Knowing the mindset of a group enables a terrorism analyst to better determine the likely targets of the group and its likely behavior under varying circumstances. It is surprising, therefore, that the concept of the terrorist mindset has not received more attention by terrorism specialists. It may not always be possible to profile the individual leaders of a terrorist group, as in the case of the 17 November Revolutionary Organization, but the group's mindset can be profiled if adequate information is available on the group and there is an established record of activities and pronouncements. Even though two groups may both have an Islamic fundamentalist mindset, their individual mindsets will vary because of their different circumstances.

One cannot assume to have a basic understanding of the mindset of a terrorist group without having closely studied the group and its leader(s). Because terrorist groups are clandestine and shadowy, they are more difficult to analyze than guerrilla groups, which operate more openly, like paramilitary organizations. A terrorist group is usually much smaller than a guerrilla organization, but the former may pose a more lethal potential threat to U.S. security interests than the latter by pursuing an active policy of terrorist attacks against U.S. interests. A guerrilla group such as the FARC may kidnap or kill an occasional U.S. citizen or citizens as a result of unauthorized actions by a hardline front commander, but a terrorist group such as the 17 November Revolutionary Organization does so as a matter of policy.

Although Aum Shinrikyo, a dangerous cult, is on U.S. lists of terrorist groups and is widely feared in Japan, it still operates openly and legally, even though a number of its members have been arrested, some have received prison sentences, and others, including Shoko Asahara, have been undergoing trial. It can probably be safely assumed that Aum Shinrikyo will resume its terrorist activities, if not in Japan then elsewhere. Indeed, it appears to be re-organizing, and whatever new form in which this hydra-headed monster emerges is not likely to be any more pleasant than its former incarnation. The question is, What is Aum Shinrikyo planning to help bring about the apocalypse that it has been predicting for the new millennium?

Knowing the mindset of a terrorist group would better enable the terrorism analyst to understand that organization's behavior patterns and the active or potential threat that it poses. Knowing the mindsets, including methods of operation, of terrorist groups would also aid in identifying what group likely perpetrated an unclaimed terrorist action and in predicting the likely actions of a particular group under various circumstances. Indeed, mindset profiling of a terrorist group is an essential mode of analysis for assessing the threat posed by the group. A terrorist group's mindset can be determined to a significant extent through a database analysis of selective features of the group and patterns in its record of terrorist attacks. A computer program could be designed to replicate the mindset of each terrorist group for this purpose.

Promoting Terrorist Group Schisms

All terrorist and guerrillas groups may be susceptible to psychological warfare aimed at dividing their political and military leaders and factions. Guerrilla organizations, however, should not be dealt with like terrorist groups. Although the FARC, the LTTE, and the PKK engage in terrorism, they are primarily guerrilla organizations, and therefore their insurgencies and accompanying terrorism are likely to continue as long as there are no political solutions. In addition to addressing the root causes of a country's terrorist and insurgency problems, effective counterterrorist and counterinsurgency strategies should seek not only to divide a terrorist or guerrilla group's political and military factions but also to reduce the group's rural bases of support through rural development programs and establishment of civil patrols in each village or town.

Another effective counterterrorist strategy would be the identification and capture of a top hardline terrorist or guerrilla leader, especially one who exhibits psychopathic characteristics. Removing the top hard liners of a terrorist group would allow the group to reassess the policies pursued by its captured leader and possibly move in a less violent direction, especially if a more politically astute leader assumes control. This is what appears to be happening in the case of the PKK, which has opted for making peace since the capture of its ruthless, hardline leader, Abdullah Ocalan. A government could simultaneously help members of urban terrorist groups to defect from their groups, for example through an amnesty program, as was done so effectively in Italy. A psychologically sophisticated policy of promoting divisions between political and military leaders as well as defections within guerrilla and terrorist groups is likely to be more effective than a simple military strategy based on the assumption that all members and leaders of the group are hard liners. A military response to terrorism unaccompanied by political countermeasures is likely to promote cohesion within the group. The U.S. Government's focus on bin Laden as the nation's number one terrorist enemy has clearly raised his profile in the Islamic world and swelled the membership ranks of Al Qaeda. Although not yet martyred, bin Laden has become the Ernesto "Che" Guevara of Islamic fundamentalism. As Post (1990:39) has explained:

> *When the autonomous cell comes under external threat, the external danger has the consequence of reducing internal divisiveness and uniting the group against the outside enemy. . . Violent societal counteractions can transform a tiny band of insignificant persons into a major opponent of society, making their "fantasy war," to use Ferracuti's apt term, a "reality."*

How Guerrilla and Terrorist Groups End

A counterterrorist policy should be tailor-made for a particular group, taking into account its historical, cultural, political, and social context, as well as the context of what is known about the psychology of the group or its leaders. The motivations of a terrorist group—both of its members and of its leaders—cannot be adequately understood outside its cultural, economic, political, and social context. Because terrorism is politically or religiously motivated, a counterterrorist policy, to be effective, should be designed to take into account political or religious factors. For example, terrorists were active in Chile during the military regime (1973–90), but counterterrorist operations by democratic governments in the 1990s have reduced them to insignificance. The transition from military rule to democratic government in Chile proved to be the most effective counterterrorist strategy.

In contrast to relatively insignificant political terrorist groups in a number of countries, Islamic terrorist groups, aided by significant worldwide support among Muslim fundamentalists, remain the most serious terrorist threat to U.S. security interests. A U.S. counterterrorist policy, therefore, should avoid making leaders like Osama bin Laden heroes or martyrs for Muslims. To that end, the eye-for-an-eye Israeli policy of striking back for each act of terrorism may be highly counterproductive when applied by the world's only superpower against Islamic terrorism, as in the form of cruise-missile attacks against, or bombings of, suspected terrorist sites. Such actions, although politically popular at home, are seen by millions of Muslims as attacks against the Islamic religion and by people in many countries as superpower bullying and a violation of a country's sovereignty. U.S. counterterrorist military attacks against elusive terrorists may serve only to radicalize large sectors of the Muslim population and damage the U.S. image worldwide.

Rather than retaliate against terrorists with bombs or cruise missiles, legal, political, diplomatic, financial, and psychological warfare measures may be more effective. Applying pressure to state sponsors may be especially effective. Cuba and Libya are two examples of terrorist state sponsors that apparently concluded that sponsoring terrorists was not in their national interests. Iran and Syria may still need to be convinced.

Jeanne Knutson was critical of the reactive and ad hoc nature of U.S. counterterrorism policy, which at that time, in the early 1980s, was considered an entirely police and security task, as opposed to ". . . a *politically* rational, comprehensive strategy to deal with *politically* motivated violence." She found this policy flawed because it dealt with symptoms instead of root causes and instead of eradicating the causes had increased the source of political violence. She charged that this policy routinely radicalized, splintered, and drove underground targeted U.S. groups, thereby only confirming the "we-they" split worldview of these groups. Unfortunately, too many governments still pursue purely military strategies to defeat political and religious extremist groups.

Abroad, Knutson argued, the United States joined military and political alliances to support the eradication of internal dissident groups without any clear political rationale for such a stance. She emphasized that "terrorists are individuals who commit crimes for political reasons," and for this reason "the political system has better means to control and eliminate their activities and even to attack their root causes than do the police and security forces working alone." Thus, she considered it politically and socially unwise to give various national security agencies, including the Federal Bureau of Investigation (FBI), the political role of choosing targets of political violence. She advocated "a necessary stance of neutrality toward national dissident causes—whether the causes involve the territory of historical friend or foe." She cited the neutral U.S. stance toward the Irish Republican Army (IRA) as a case study of how to avoid anti-U.S. terrorism. Her views still seem quite relevant.

Goals of a long-range counterterrorism policy should also include deterring alienated youth from joining a terrorist group in the first place. This may seem an impractical goal, for how does one recognize a potential terrorist, let alone deter him or her from joining a terrorist group? Actually, this is not so impractical in the cases of guerrilla organizations like the FARC, the LTTE, and the PKK, which conscript all the young people in their rural areas of operation who can be rounded up. A counter strategy could be approached within the framework of advertising and civic-action campaigns. A U.S. government-sponsored mass media propaganda campaign undertaken in the Colombian countryside, the Kurdish enclaves, and the

Vanni region of Sri Lanka and tailor-made to fit the local culture and society probably could help to discredit hard liners in the guerrilla/terrorist groups sufficiently to have a serious negative impact on their recruitment efforts. Not only should all young people in the region be educated on the realities of guerrilla life, but a counterterrorist policy should be in place to inhibit them from joining in the first place. If they are inducted, they should be helped or encouraged to leave the group.

The effectiveness of such a campaign would depend in part on how sensitive the campaign is culturally, socially, politically, and economically. It could not succeed, however, without being supplemented by civic-action and rural security programs, especially a program to establish armed self-defense civil patrols among the peasantry. The Peruvian government was able to defeat terrorists operating in the countryside only by creating armed self-defense civil patrols that became its eyes and ears. These patrols not only provided crucial intelligence on the movements of the Shining Path and Tupac Amaru terrorists, but also enabled the rural population to take a stand against them.

There is little evidence that direct government intervention is the major factor in the decline of terrorist groups. Clearly, it was an important factor in certain cases, such as the RAF and with various urban Marxist-Leninist group in Latin America where massive governmental repression was applied (but at unacceptably high cost in human rights abuses). Social and psychological factors may be more important. If, for security reasons, a terrorist group becomes too isolated from the population, as in the case of the RAF and the Uruguayan Tupamaros, the group is prone to losing touch with any base of support that it may have had. Without a measure of popular support, a terrorist group cannot survive. Moreover, if it fails to recruit new members to renew itself by supporting or replacing an aging membership or members who have been killed or captured, it is likely to disintegrate. The terrorist groups that have been active for many years have a significant base of popular support. Taylor and Qualye point out that despite its atrocious terrorist violence, the Provisional IRA in 1994 continued to enjoy the electoral support of between 50,000 and 70,000 people in Northern Ireland. The FARC, the LTTE, and the PKK continue to have strong popular support within their own traditional bases of support.

In the cases of West German and Italian terrorism, counterterrorist operations undoubtedly had a significant impact on terrorist groups. Allowing terrorists an exit can weaken the group. For example, amnesty programs, such as those offered by the Italian government, can help influence terrorists to defect. Reducing support for the group on the local and national levels may also contribute to reducing the group's recruitment pool. Maxwell Taylor and Ethel Quayle have pointed out that penal policies in both countries, such as allowing convicted terrorists reduced sentences and other concessions, even including daytime furloughs from prison to hold a normal job, had a significant impact in affecting the long-term reduction in terrorist violence. Referring to Italy's 1982 Penitence Law, Taylor and Quayle explain that "this law effectively depenalized serious terrorist crime through offering incentives to terrorists to accept their defeat, admit their guilt and inform on others so that the dangers of terrorist violence could be diminished." Similarly, Article 57 of the German Penal Code offers the possibility of reduction of sentence or suspension or deferment of sentence when convicted terrorists renounce terrorism. Former terrorists do not have to renounce their ideological convictions, only their violent methods. To be sure, these legal provisions have not appealed to hard-core terrorists, as evidenced by the apparent re-activation of the Italian Red Brigades in 1999. Nevertheless, for countries with long-running insurgencies, such as Colombia, Sri Lanka, and Turkey, amnesty programs for guerrillas are very important tools for resolving their internal wars.

With regard to guerrilla/terrorist organizations, a major question is how to encourage the political wing to constrain the military wing, or how to discredit or neutralize the military branch. The PKK should serve as an ongoing case study in this regard. Turkey, by its policy of demonizing the PKK and repressing the Kurdish population in its efforts to combat it instead of seeking a political solution, only raised the PKK's status in the eyes of the public and lost the hearts and minds of its Kurdish population. Nevertheless, by capturing Ocalan and by refraining thus far from making him a martyr by hanging him, the Turkish government has inadvertently allowed the PKK to move in a more political direction as advocated by its political leaders, who now have a greater voice in decision making. Thus, the PKK has retreated from Turkey and indicated an interest in pursuing a political as opposed to a military strategy. This is how a guerrilla/terrorist organization should end, by becoming a political party, just as the M-19 did in Colombia and the Armed Forces of National Liberation (FALN) did in El Salvador.

Appendix

Sociopsychological Profiles: Case Studies
Exemplars of International Terrorism in the Early 1970s

Renato Curcio

Significance: Imprisoned leader of the Italian Red Brigades.

Background: The background of Renato Curcio, the imprisoned former main leader of the first-generation Red Brigades (Brigata Rosse), provides some insight into how a university student became Italy's most wanted terrorist. The product of an extramarital affair between Renato Zampa (brother of film director Luigi Zampa) and Yolanda Curcio, Renato Curcio was born near Rome on September 23, 1941. His early years were a difficult time for him and his mother, a housemaid whose itinerant positions with families required long separations. In April 1945, Curcio's beloved uncle, Armando, a Fiat auto worker, was murdered in a Fascist ambush. A poor student, Curcio failed several subjects in his first year of high school and had to repeat the year. He then resumed vocational training classes until moving to Milan to live with his mother. He enrolled in the Ferrini Institute in Albenga, where he became a model student. On completing his degree in 1962, he won a scholarship to study at the new and innovative Institute of Sociology at the University of Trento, where he became absorbed in existential philosophy. During the mid-1960s, he gravitated toward radical politics and Marxism as a byproduct of his interest in existentialism and the self. By the late 1960s, he had become a committed revolutionary and Marxist theoretician. According to Alessandro Silj, three political events transformed him from a radical to an activist and ultimately a political terrorist: two bloody demonstrations at Trento and a massacre by police of farm laborers in 1968. During the 1967–69 period, Curcio was also involved in two Marxist university groups: the Movement for a Negative University and the publication *Lavoro Politico (Political Work)*. Embittered by his expulsion from the radical Red Line faction of Lavoro Politico in August 1969, Curcio decided to drop out of Trento and forego his degree, even though he already had passed his final examinations. Prior to transferring his bases of activities to Milan, Curcio married, in a Catholic ceremony, Margherita (Mara) Cagol, a Trentine sociology major, fellow radical, and daughter of a prosperous Trento merchant. In Milan, Curcio became a full-fledged terrorist. The Red Brigades was formed in the second half of 1970 as a result of the merger of Curcio's Proletarian Left and a radical student and worker group. After getting arrested in February 1971 for occupying a vacant house, the Curcios and the most militant members of the Proletarian Left went completely underground and organized the Red Brigades and spent the next three years, from 1972 to 1975, engaging in a series of bombings and kidnappings of prominent figures. Curcio was captured but freed by Margherita in a raid on the prison five months later. Three weeks after the dramatic prison escape, Margherita was killed in a shootout with the Carabinieri. Curcio was again captured in January 1976, tried, and convicted, and he is still serving a 31-year prison sentence for terrorist activities.

An insight into Curcio's (1973:72) motivation for becoming a terrorist can be found in a letter to his mother written during his initial prison confinement:

> *Yolanda dearest, mother mine, years have passed since the day on which I set out to encounter life and left you alone to deal with life. I have worked, I have studied, I have fought. . .Distant memories stirred. Uncle Armando who carried me astride his shoulders. His limpid and ever smiling eyes that peered far into the distance toward a society of free and equal men. And I loved him like a father. And I picked up the rifle that only death, arriving through the murderous hand of the Nazi-fascists, had wrested from him. . .My enemies are the enemies of humanity and of intelligence, those who have built and build their accursed fortunes on*

the material and intellectual misery of the people. Theirs is the hand that has banged shut the door of my cell. And I cannot be but proud. But I am not merely an "idealist" and it is not enough for me to have, as is said, "a good conscience." For this reason I will continue to fight for communism even from the depths of a prison.

Leila Khaled

Position: First Secretary of the PFLP's Palestinian Popular Women's Committees (PPWC).

Background: Khaled was born on April 13, 1948, in Haifa, Palestine. She left Haifa at age four when her family fled the Israeli occupation and lived in impoverished exile in a United Nations Relief and Works Agency (UNRWA) refugee camp in Sour, Lebanon. By age eight, she had become politically aware of the Palestinian plight. Inspired by a Palestinian revolutionary of the 1930s, Izz Edeen Kassam, she decided to become a revolutionary "in order to liberate my people and myself." The years 1956–59 were her period of political apprenticeship as an activist of the Arab Nationalist Movement (ANM). By the summer of 1962, she was struggling to cope with national, social, class, and sexual oppression but, thanks to her brother's financial support, finally succeeded in attending the American University of Beirut (AUB) in 1962–63, where she scored the second highest average on the AUB entrance exam.

While an AUB student, Khaled received what she refers to as her "real education" in the lecture hall of the Arab Cultural Club (ACC) and in the ranks of the ANM and the General Union of Palestinian Students (GUPS). Her "intellectual companion"at AUB was her American roommate, with whom she would have heated political arguments. In the spring of 1963, Khaled was admitted into the ANM's first paramilitary contingent of university students and was active in ANM underground activities. For lack of funding, she was unable to continue her education after passing her freshman year in the spring of 1963.

In September 1963, Khaled departed for Kuwait, where she obtained a teaching position. After a run-in with the school's principal, who called her to task for her political activities on behalf of the Palestine Liberation Organization (PLO), she returned to Lebanon in late June 1964. She returned to the school in Kuwait that fall but was demoted to elementary teaching. The U.S. invasions of the Dominican Republic and Vietnam in 1965 solidified her hatred of the U.S. Government. The death of Ernesto "Che" Guevara on October 9, 1967, convinced her to join the revolution.

When Fatah renewed its military operations on August 18, 1967, Khaled attempted to work through Fatah's fund-raising activities in Kuwait to liberate Palestine. She pleaded with Yasir Arafat's brother, Fathi Arafat, to be allowed to join Al-Assifah, Fatah's military wing. She found an alternative to Fatah, however, when the Popular Front for the Liberation of Palestine

(PFLP) hijacked an El-Al airplane in July 1968, an action that inspired her to seek contacts with the PFLP in Kuwait. She succeeded when PFLP representative Abu Nidal, whom she described as "a tall, handsome young man" who was "reserved and courteous," met her in a Kuwaiti bookstore. After performing fund-raising for the PFLP, she was allowed to join its Special Operations Squad and underwent intensive training. In her first mission, she hijacked a TWA plane on a flight from Rome to Athens on August 29, 1969, and diverted it to Damascus, where all 113 passengers were released unharmed. Although her identity was revealed to the world by the Syrians, she continued her terrorist career by training to commandeer an El-Al plane. When Jordan's King Hussein launched a military offensive against the Palestinian resistance in Amman in February 1970, Khaled fought in the streets alongside PFLP comrades. That March, in preparation for another hijacking, she left Amman and underwent at least three secret plastic surgery operations over five months by a well-known but very reluctant plastic surgeon in Beirut.

While Khaled was discussing strategy with Dr. Wadi Haddad in his Beirut apartment on July 11, 1970, the apartment was hit by two rockets in the first Israeli attack inside Lebanon, injuring the man's wife and child. On September 6, 1970, Khaled and an accomplice attempted to hijack an El-Al flight from Amsterdam with twelve armed security guards aboard but were overpowered. He was shot to death, but she survived and was detained in London by British police. After twenty-eight days in detention, she was released in a swap for hostages from hijacked planes and escorted on a flight to Cairo and then, on October 12, to Damascus.

Following her release, Khaled went to Beirut and joined a combat unit. In between fighting, she would tour refugee camps and recruit women. She married an Iraqi PFLP member, Bassim, on November 26, 1970, but the marriage was short-lived. She returned to the same Beirut plastic surgeon and had her former face mostly restored. She barely escaped a bed-bomb apparently planted by the Mossad, but her sister was shot dead on Christmas Day 1976. After fading from public view, she surfaced again in 1980, leading a PLO delegation to the United Nations Decade for Women conference in Copenhagen. She attended university in Russia for two years in the early 1980s, but the PFLP ordered her to return to combat in Lebanon before she had completed her studies.

Khaled married a PFLP physician in 1982. She was elected first secretary of the Palestinian Popular Women's Committees (PPWC) in 1986. At the beginning of the 1990s, when she was interviewed by Eileen MacDonald, she was living in the Yarmuk refugee camp in Damascus, still serving as PPWC first secretary and "immediately recognizable as the young Leila."

Since then, Khaled has been living in Amman, Jordan, where she works as a teacher, although still a PFLP member. She was allowed by Israel briefly to enter Palestinian-ruled areas in the West Bank, or at least the Gaza Strip, in February 1996, to vote on amending the Palestinian charter to remove its call for Israel's destruction. She was on a list of 154 members of the Palestine National Council (PNC), an exile-based parliament, who Israel approved for entrance into the Gaza Strip. Khaled said she had renounced terrorism. However, she declined an invitation to attend a meeting in Gaza with President Clinton in December 1998 at which members of the PNC renounced portions of the PLO charter calling for the destruction of Israel. "We are not going to change our identity or our history," she explained to news media.

Kozo Okamoto

Significance: The sole surviving Rengo Sekigun (Japanese Red Army) terrorist of the PFLP's Lod (Tel Aviv) Airport massacre of May 30, 1972, who remains active.

Background: Kozo Okamoto was born in southwestern Japan in 1948. He was the youngest of six children, the son of a retired elementary school principal married to a social worker. The family was reportedly very close when the children were young. His mother died of cancer in 1966, and his father remarried. He is not known to have had a disturbed or unusual childhood. On the contrary, he apparently had a normal and happy childhood. He achieved moderate success at reputable high schools in Kagoshima. However, he failed to qualify for admission at Kyoto University and had to settle for the Faculty of Agriculture at Japan's Kagoshima University, where his grades were mediocre. While a university student, he was not known to be politically active in extremist groups or demonstrations, although he belonged to a student movement and a peace group and became actively concerned with environmental issues. However, Okamoto's older brother, Takeshi, a former student at Kyoto University, introduced him to representatives of the newly formed JRA in Tokyo in early 1970. Soon thereafter, Takeshi participated in the hijacking of a Japan Air Lines jet to Korea. Takeshi's involvement in that action compelled his father to resign his job. Although Kozo had promised his father that he would not follow in his brother's footsteps, Kozo became increasingly involved in carrying out minor tasks for the JRA. Kozo Okamoto was attracted to the JRA more for its action-oriented program than for ideological reasons.

Kozo Okamoto and comrades. *Courtesy of Corbis Images.*

In late February 1972, Okamoto traveled to Beirut, where the JRA said he could meet his brother, and then underwent seven weeks of terrorist training by PFLP personnel in Baalbek. After he and his comrades traveled through Europe posing as tourists, they boarded a flight to Lod Airport on May 30, 1972. Unable to commit suicide as planned following the Lod Airport massacre,

Okamoto was captured and made a full confession only after being promised that he would be allowed to kill himself. During his trial, he freely admitted his act and demonstrated no remorse; he viewed himself as a soldier rather than a terrorist, and to him Lod Airport was a military base in a war zone. Psychiatrists who examined Okamoto certified that he was absolutely sane and rational. To be sure, Okamoto's courtroom speech, including his justification for slaughtering innocent people and his stated hope that he and his two dead comrades would become, in death, "three stars of Orion," was rather bizarre.

By 1975, while in solitary confinement, Okamoto began identifying himself to visitors as a Christian. When his sanity began to deteriorate in 1985, he was moved to a communal cell. That May, he was released as a result of an exchange of Palestinian prisoners for three Israeli soldiers, under a swap conducted by the Popular Front for the Liberation of Palestine-General Command (PFLP-GC) . He arrived to a hero's welcome in Libya on May 20 and was met by JRA leader Fusako Shigenobu. He apparently has continued to operate with the PFLP-GC. On February 15, 1997, he and five JRA comrades were arrested in Lebanon and accused of working with the PFLP-GC and training PFLP-GC cadres in the Bekaa Valley outside Baalbek. According to another report, they were arrested in a Beirut apartment. That August, he and four of his comrades were sentenced to three years in jail (minus time already served and deportation to an undisclosed location) for entering the country with forged passports.

Exemplars of International Terrorism in the Early 1990s

Mahmud Abouhalima

Significance: World Trade Center bomber.

Background: Mahmud Abouhalima was born in a ramshackle industrial suburb fifteen miles south of Alexandria in 1959, the first of four sons of a poor but stern millman, a powerful weight lifter. Mahmud was known as an ordinary, well-rounded, cheerful youth who found comfort in religion. He prayed hard and shunned alcohol. He studied education at Alexandria University and played soccer in his spare time. He developed a deep and growing hatred for Egypt because of his belief that the country offered little hope for his generation's future. As a teenager, he began to hang around with members of an outlawed Islamic Group (Al-Jama Al-Islamiyya), headed by Sheikh Omar Abdel Rahman. In 1981 Abouhalima quit school and left Egypt. He reportedly fought against the Soviets in Afghanistan. In September 1991, now an Afghan veteran, he was granted a tourist visa to visit Germany. In Munich he sought political asylum, claiming that he faced persecution in Egypt because of his membership in the Muslim Brotherhood (Al Ikhwan Al Muslimun). He subsequently made his way to the United States and worked as a taxi driver in Brooklyn, New York. He also allegedly ran a phony coupon-redemption scam. This operation and a similar one run by Zein Isa, a member of the ANO in St. Louis, supposedly funneled about $200 million of the annual $400 million in fraudulent coupon losses allegedly suffered by the industry back to the Middle East to fund terrorist activities, although the figure seems a bit high. On February 26, 1993, the day of the WTC bombing, he was seen by several witnesses with Mohammed A. Salameh at the Jersey City storage facility. Tall and red-haired, Abouhalima ("Mahmud the Red"), 33, was captured in his native Egypt not long after the bombing. He was "hands-on ringleader" and the motorist who drove a getaway car. He is alleged to have planned the WTC bombing and trained his co-conspirators in bomb-testing. He was sentenced to 240 years in federal prison.

Sheikh Omar Abdel Rahman

Significance: World Trade Center bombing co-conspirator.

Background: Omar Abdel Rahman was born in 1938, blinded by diabetes as an infant. He became a religious scholar in Islamic law at Cairo's Al-Azhar University. By the 1960s, he had become increasingly critical of Egypt's government and its institutions, including Al-Azhar University, which he blamed for failing to uphold true Islamic law. One of the defendants accused of assassinating Egyptian President Anwar Sadat on October 6, 1981, Dr. Abdel Rahman was considered an accessory because of his authorization of the assassination through the issuance of a fatwa or Islamic judicial decree, to the assassins. However, he was acquitted because of the ambiguity of his role. In the 1980s, made unwelcome by the Egyptian government, he traveled to Afghanistan, Britain, Pakistan, Saudi Arabia, Sudan, Switzerland, and the United States, exhorting young Muslims to join the mujahideen to fight the Soviets in Afghanistan. Sheikh Abdel Rahman's activities also included leading a puritanical Islamic fundamentalist movement (Al Jamaa al Islamiyya) aimed at overthrowing the regime of President Hosni Mubarak. The movement's methods included terrorist attacks against foreign tourists visiting archaeological sites in Egypt. The sheik has described American and other Western tourists in Egypt as part of a "plague" on his country.

In 1990, after a brief visit back to Egypt, Abdel Rahman fled to Sudan. Later that year, the blind cleric, despite being on the U.S. official list of terrorists, succeeded in entering the United States with a tourist visa obtained at the U.S. Embassy in Sudan. He became the prayer leader of the small El Salem Mosque in Jersey City, New Jersey, where many of the WTC bombing conspirators attended services. He preached violence against the United States and pro-Western governments in the Middle East. Abdel Rahman maintained direct ties with mujahideen fighters and directly aided terrorist groups in Egypt, to whom he would send messages on audiotape. He served as spiritual

Sheikh Omar Abdel Rahman.
Courtesy of Saba/Corbis Images.

mentor of El Sayyid A. Nosair, who assassinated Jewish Defense League founder Rabbi Meir Kahane on November 5, 1990. (Nosair, whose conviction was upheld by a federal appeals court panel on August 16, 1999, knew many members of the WTC bombing group and was visited by some of them in jail.)

Following the WTC bombing on February 26, 1993, Abdel Rahman was implicated in that conspiracy as well as in a plot to bomb other public places in New York, including the Holland and Lincoln tunnels and the United Nations building. He was also implicated in a plot to assassinate U.S. Senator Alfonse d'Amato (R., N.Y.) and United Nations Secretary General Boutros-Ghali. Abdel Rahman and seven others were arrested in connection with this plot in June 1993. In a 1994 retrial of 1981 riot cases in Egypt, Abdel Rahman was convicted in absentia and sentenced to seven years in prison.

On October 1, 1995, Sheikh Abdel Rahman and nine other Islamic fundamentalists were convicted in a federal court in New York of conspiracy to destroy U.S. public buildings and structures. Abdel Rahman was convicted of directing the conspiracy and, under a joint arrangement with Egypt, of attempting to assassinate Mubarak. His conviction and those of his co-conspirators were upheld on August 16, 1999. Despite his imprisonment, at least two Egyptian terrorist groups—Islamic Group (Gamaa Islamiya) and Al-Jihad (see Al-Jihad)—continue to regard him as their spiritual leader. The Gamaa terrorists who massacred fifty-eight tourists near Luxor, Egypt, in November 1997 claimed the attack was a failed hostage takeover intended to force the United States into releasing Abdel Rahman. He is currently serving a life sentence at a federal prison in New York.

Mohammed A. Salameh

Significance: A World Trade Center bomber.

Background: Mohammed A. Salameh was born near Nablus, an Arab town on the West Bank, on September 1, 1967. In his final years in high school, Salameh, according to his brother, "became religious, started to pray and read the Koran with other friends in high school. He stopped most of his past activities and hobbies. . .He was not a fundamentalist. He was interested in Islamic teachings." According to another source, Salameh comes from a long line of guerrilla fighters on his mother's side. His maternal grandfather fought in the 1936 Arab revolt against British rule in Palestine and even as an old man joined the PLO and was jailed by the Israelis. A maternal uncle was arrested in 1968 for "terrorism" and served eighteen years in an Israeli prison before he was released and deported, making his way to Baghdad, where he became number two in the "Western Sector," a PLO terrorist unit under Iraqi influence. Mohammed Salameh earned a degree from the Islamic studies faculty of the University of Jordan. His family went into debt to buy him an airline ticket to the United States, where he wanted to obtain an MBA. Salameh entered the United States on February 17, 1988, on a six-month tourist visa, and apparently lived in Jersey City illegally for the next five years.

He apparently belonged to the Masjid Al-Salam Mosque in Jersey City, whose preachers included fundamentalist Sheikh Omar Abdel Rahman. Slight and bearded, naive, and easy to manipulate, Salameh was arrested in the process of returning to collect the deposit on the van that he had rented to carry the Trade Center bombing materials. On March 4, 1993, Salameh, 26, was charged by the FBI with "aiding and abetting" the WTC bombing on February 26, 1993. He is also believed to be part of the group that stored the explosive material in a Jersey City storage locker.

Ahmed Ramzi Yousef

Significance: Mastermind of the World Trade Center bombing.

Background: Yousef, whose real name is Abd-Al-Basit Balushi, was born either on May 20, 1967, or April 27, 1968, in Kuwait, where he grew up and completed high school. His Pakistani father is believed to have been an engineer with Kuwaiti Airlines for many years. Yousef is Palestinian on his mother's side; his grandmother is Palestinian. He considers himself Palestinian.

In 1989, Yousef graduated from Britain's Swansea University with a degree in engineering. Yousef is believed to have trained and fought in the Afghan War. He and bin Laden reportedly were linked at least as long ago as 1989. In that year, Yousef went to the Philippines and introduced himself as an emissary of Osama bin Laden, sent to support that country's radical Islamic movement, specifically the fundamentalist Abu Sayyaf group. When Iraqi President Saddam Hussein's army invaded Kuwait in August 1990, Yousef was known as a collaborator. After disappearing in Kuwait in 1991, he is next known to have reappeared in the Philippines in December 1991, accompanied by a Libyan missionary named Mohammed Abu Bakr, the leader of the Mullah Forces in Libya. Yousef stayed for three months providing training to Abu Sayyaf guerrillas in the southern Philippines.

Ahmed Ramzi Yousef.
Courtesy of Sygma/Corbis Images.

When he arrived from Pakistan at John F. Kennedy Airport on September 1, 1992, without a visa, Yousef, who was carrying an Iraqi passport, applied for political asylum. Often described as slender, Yousef is six feet tall, weighs 180 pounds, and is considered white, with an olive complexion. He was sometimes clean-shaven, but wears a beard in his FBI wanted poster. Despite his itinerant life as an international terrorist, Yousef is married and has two daughters. A Palestinian friend and fellow terrorist, Ahmad Ajaj, who was traveling with Yousef on September 1, 1992, although apparently at a safe distance, was detained by passport control officers at John F. Kennedy Airport for carrying a false Swedish passport. Ajaj was carrying papers containing formulas for bomb-making material, which prosecutors said were to be used to destroy bridges and tunnels in New York.

Yousef was allowed to stay in the United States while his political asylum case was considered. U.S. immigration officials apparently accepted his false claim that he was a victim of the Gulf War who had been beaten by Iraqi soldiers because the Iraqis suspected that he had worked for Kuwaiti resistance. Yousef moved into an apartment in Jersey City with roommate Mohammad Salameh (q.v.). After participating in the Trade Center bombing on February 26, 1993, Yousef, then 25 or 26 years old, returned to Manila, the Philippines, that same day. In Manila, he plotted "Project Bojinka," a plan to plant bombs aboard U.S. passenger airliners in 1995, using a virtually undetectable bomb that he had created. He was skilled in the art of converting Casio digital watches into timing switches that use light bulb filaments to ignite cotton soaked in nitroglycerine explosive. He carried out a practice run on a Philippine Airlines Flight 434 bound for Tokyo on December 9, 1994. A wearer of contact lenses, Yousef concealed the nitroglycerin compound in a bottle normally used to hold saline solution. His bomb killed a Japanese tourist seated near the explosive, which he left taped under a seat, and wounded 10 others. In March 1993, prosecutors in Manhattan indicted Yousef for his role in the WTC bombing. On January 6, 1995, Manila police raided Yousef's room overlooking Pope John Paul II's motorcade route into the city. Yousef had fled the room after accidentally starting a fire while mixing chemicals. Police found explosives, a map of the Pope's route, clerical robes, and a computer disk describing the plot against the Pope, as well as planned attacks against U.S. airlines. Yousef's fingerprints were on the material, but he had vanished, along with his girlfriend, Carol Santiago. Also found in his room was a letter threatening Filipino interests if a comrade held in custody were not released. It claimed the "ability to make and use chemicals and poisonous gas . . . for use against vital institutions and residential populations and the sources of drinking water." Yousef's foiled plot involved blowing up eleven U.S. commercial aircraft in midair. The bombs were to be made of a stable, liquid form of nitroglycerin designed to pass through airport metal detectors.

For most of the three years before his capture in early 1995, Yousef reportedly resided at the bin Laden-financed Bayt Ashuhada (House of Martyrs) guest house in Peshawar, Pakistan. On February 8, 1995, local authorities arrested Yousef in Islamabad in the Su Casa guest house, also owned by a member of the bin Laden family. Yousef had in his possession the outline of an even greater international terrorist campaign that he was planning, as well as bomb-making products, including two toy cars packed with explosives and flight schedules for United and Delta Airlines. His plans included using a suicide pilot (Said Akhman) to crash a light aircraft filled with powerful explosives into the CIA headquarters in Langley, Virginia, as well as blowing up eleven U.S. airliners simultaneously as they approached U.S. airports. He was then turned over to the FBI and deported to the United

States. On June 21, 1995, Yousef told federal agents that he had planned and executed the WTC bombing.

On September 6, 1996, Yousef was convicted in a New York Federal District Court for trying to bomb U.S. airliners in Asia in 1995. On January 8, 1998, he was sentenced to 240 years in prison. He has remained incarcerated in the new "supermax" prison in Florence, Colorado. His cellmates in adjoining cells in the "Bomber Wing" include Timothy McVeigh, the right-wing terrorist who blew up a federal building in Oklahoma City on April 19, 1995, and Ted Kaczynski, the sociopathic loner known as the Unabomber. The polyglot Yousef has discussed languages with Kaczynski, who speaks Spanish, French, and German, and taught him some Turkish.

Ethnic Separatist Groups

Irish Terrorists

According to a middle-level IRA officer interviewed by Newsweek in 1988, the IRA has plenty of recruits. Each potential enlistee is kept under scrutiny for as long as a year before being allowed to sign up. The Provos are paranoid about informers, so hard drinkers and loudmouths are automatically disqualified from consideration. H.A. Lyons, a Belfast psychiatrist who frequently works with prisoners, told *Newsweek* that the IRA's political murderers are "fairly normal individuals," compared with nonpolitical killers. "They regard themselves as freedom fighters," he said, adding that they feel no remorse for their actions, at least against security forces. As the IRA officer explained to Newsweek:

> *The killing of innocent civilians is a thing that sickens all volunteers, and it must and will stop. But I can live with the killing [of security forces]. There is an occupying army which has taken over our country. I see no difference between the IRA and World War II resistance movements.*

Rona M. Fields noted in 1976 that Belfast "terrorists" are most often adolescent youths from working-class families. By the 1990s, however, that appeared to have changed. According to the profile of Irish terrorists, loyalist and republican, developed by Maxwell Taylor and Ethel Quayle (1994), "The person involved in violent action is likely to be up to 30 years old, or perhaps a little older and usually male." Republican and loyalist leaders tend to be somewhat older. The terrorist is invariably from a working-class background, not because of some Marxist doctrine but because the loyalist and republican areas of Northern Ireland are primarily working class. Quite likely, he is unemployed. "He is either living in the area in which he was born, or has recently left it for operational reasons." His education is probably limited, because he probably left school at age 15 or 16 without formal qualifications. However, according to Taylor and Quayle, recruits in the early 1990s were becoming better educated. Before becoming involved in a violent action, the recruit probably belonged to a junior wing of the group for at least a year. Although not a technically proficient specialist, he is likely to have received weapons or explosives training. The profile notes that the recruits are often well-dressed, or at least appropriately dressed, and easily blend into the community. "Northern Ireland terrorists are frequently articulate and give the impression of being worldly," it states. At the psychological level, Taylor found "a lack of signs of psychopathology, at least in any overt clinical sense" among the members. Irish terrorists can easily justify their violent actions "in terms of their own perception of the world," and do not even object to being called terrorists, although they refer to each other as volunteers or members.

The Provisional Irish Republican Army (PIRA) is generally a homegrown, grassroots organization. In the late 1980s, some members of the PIRA were as young as 12 years of age, but most of those taking part in PIRA operations were in the twenties. Front-line bombers and shooters were younger, better educated, and better trained than the early members were. The PIRA recruits members from the streets.

Kurdistan Workers' Party (PKK) and *Abdullah Ocalan*

Group/Leader Profile
The Kurdistan Workers' Party (Parte Krikaranc Kordesian/Partia Karkaris Kurdistan-PKK) originated in 1972 with a small group of Marxist-oriented university activists in Ankara known as "Apocus." The principal founder of the student-based Apocular group, Abdullah Ocalan ("Apo"—Uncle) was a former student (expelled) in political science at Ankara University, who was prominent in the underground Turkish Communist Party. Ocalan (pronounced Oh-ja-lan or URGE'ah-lohn) was born in 1948 in the village of Omerli in the southeastern Turkish province of Urfa, the son of an impoverished Kurdish farmer and a Turkish mother. In 1974, Apocus formed a university association whose initial focus was on gaining official recognition for Kurdish language and cultural rights. Over the next four years, Ocalan organized the association into the PKK while studying revolutionary theories. In 1978, he formally established the PKK, a clandestine Marxist-Leninist Kurdish political party. During his trial in June 1999, Ocalan blamed harsh Turkish laws for spawning the PKK in 1978, and then for its taking up arms in 1984. "These kinds of laws give birth to rebellion and anarchy," he said. The language ban—now eased—"provokes this revolt."

Several of the founders of the PKK were ethnic Turks. One of the eleven founders of the PKK was Kesire Yildirim, the only female member. She later married Ocalan, but they became estranged when she began questioning his policies and tactics. (She left him in 1988 to join a PKK breakaway faction in Europe.) Unlike other Kurdish groups in the Middle East, the

Abdullah Ocalan. *Courtesy of Corbis Images.*

116

PKK advocated the establishment of a totally independent Kurdish-Marxist republic, Kurdistan, to be located in southeastern Turkey.

In about 1978, influenced by Mao Zedong's revolutionary theory, Ocalan decided to leave the cities and establish the PKK in rural areas. He fled Turkey before the 1980 military coup and lived in exile, mostly in Damascus and in the Lebanese plains under Syrian control, where he set up his PKK headquarters and training camps. In 1983, he recruited and trained at least one hundred field commandos in the Bekaa Valley in Lebanon, where the PKK maintains its Masoum Korkmaz guerrilla training base and headquarters. The PKK's army, the People's Liberation Army of Kurdistan (ARGK), began operating in August 1984. The PKK created the National Liberation Front of Kurdistan (ERNK) in 1985 to bolster its recruitment, intelligence, and propaganda activities.

The PKK's early radical agenda, including its anti-religious rhetoric and violence, alienated the PKK from much of the Kurdish peasantry. Citing various sources, Kurdish specialist Martin van Bruinessen reports that although the PKK had won little popular sympathy by the early 1990s with its brutally violent actions, "It gradually came to enjoy the grudging admiration of many Kurds, both for the prowess and recklessness of its guerrilla fighters and for the courage with which its arrested partisans stood up in court and in prison. . .By the end of 1990, it enjoyed unprecedented popularity in eastern Turkey, although few seemed to actively support it." Ocalan is reportedly regarded by many Kurds as a heroic freedom fighter. However, the "silent majority" of Kurds living in Turkey reportedly oppose the PKK and revile Ocalan.

The charismatic Ocalan was unquestioningly accepted by devoted PKK members, and the PKK reportedly lacked dissenting factions, at least until the early 1990s. The PKK's Leninist structure constrained any internal debate. However, in March 1991 Ocalan admitted at a press conference that he was facing a challenge from a faction within the PKK that wanted him to work for autonomy within Turkey instead of a separate Kurdish state and recognition of the PKK as a political force. When Ocalan, who is said to speak very little Kurdish, agreed to this position and announced a cease-fire in March 1993, the decision was not unanimous, and there was dissension within the PKK leadership over it.

The PKK's recruitment efforts mainly have targeted the poorer classes of peasants and workers, the latter group living in the standard apartment ghettos on the fringes of Turkey's industrial cities. According to a Turkish survey in the southeast cited by Barkey and Fuller, of the 35 percent of those surveyed who responded to a question on how well they knew members of the PKK, 42 percent claimed to have a family member in the PKK. The Turkish government has maintained that the PKK recruits its guerrillas forcibly and then subjects them to "brainwashing" sessions at training camps in Lebanon. According to the official Ankara Journalist Association, "Members of the organization are sent into armed clashes under the influence of drugs. [PKK leaders] keep them under the influence of drugs so as to prevent them from seeing the reality." Scholars also report that the PKK has forced young men to join. In November 1994, the PKK's former American spokesperson, Kani Xulum, told James Ciment that the PKK recruits only those who understand "our strategies and aims" and "we're careful to keep psychopaths" out of the organization. The PKK has laws regarding military conscription. At its 1995 congress, the PKK decided not to recruit youth younger than 16 to fight and to make military service for women voluntary. By the mid-1990s, PKK volunteers increasingly came from emigre families in Germany and the rest of Europe and even Armenia and Australia.

Since it began operating, the PKK's ranks have included a sprinkling of female members. However, according to O'Ballance, "Its claim that they lived and fought equally side by side with their male colleagues can be discounted, although there were some exceptions. Women were employed mainly on propaganda, intelligence, liaison, and educational tasks. The PKK claimed that women accounted for up to 30 percent of its strength." In April 1992, the ARGK claimed that it had a commando force of some 400 armed women guerrillas in the mountains of northern Iraq. James Ciment reported in 1996 that approximately 10 percent of PKK guerrillas are women. Thomas Goltz, a journalist specializing in Turkey, reports that beginning in the mid-1990s, "Many female recruits were specially trained as suicide bombers for use in crowded urban environments like Istanbul's bazaar and even on the beaches favored by European tourists along the Turkish Riviera." For example, a 19-year-old suicide female commando wounded eight policemen in a suicide attack in Istanbul in early July 1999.

The well-funded PKK's recruitment efforts have probably been aided significantly by its mass media outlets, particularly Med-TV, a PKK-dominated Kurdish-language TV station that operates by satellite transmission out of Britain. Ocalan himself often participated, by telephone, in the Med-TV talk shows, using the broadcasts to Turkey and elsewhere to convey messages and make announcements. Med-TV commands a wide viewership among the Kurds in southeast Turkey.

Barkey and Fuller describe the PKK as "primarily a nationalist organization," but one still with ties to the left, although it claimed to have abandoned Marxism-Leninism by the mid-1990s. They report that, according to some Kurdish observers, "Ocalan has begun to show considerably more maturity, realism, and balance since 1993," moving away from ideology toward greater pragmatism. Barley and Graham confirm that the PKK "has been undergoing a significant shift in its political orientation" since the mid-1990s, including moving away from its anti-Islamism and "toward greater reality in its assessment of the current political environment" and the need to reach a political settlement with Turkey.

The PKK leadership's seemingly psychotic vengeful streak became an issue in the assassination of Olaf Palme, the prime minister of Sweden, who was shot and killed while walking in a Stockholm street on February 28, 1986. PKK members immediately became the prime suspects because of the group's extremist reputation. According to John Bulloch and Harvey Morris, "The motive was thought to be no more than a Swedish police determination that the PKK was a terrorist organization, and that as a result a visa had been refused for Ocalan to visit the country, which has a large and growing Kurdish minority." On September 2, 1987, PKK militant Hasan Hayri Guler became the prime suspect. According to *Hurriyet,* a Turkish newspaper, Hasan Hayri Guler reportedly was sent to Stockholm with orders to assassinate Palme in retaliation for the death of a PKK militant in Uppsala, Sweden. (The PKK denied the accusation and hinted that Turkish security forces may have been behind Palme's murder.)

In late 1998, Syria, under intense pressure from Turkey, closed the PKK camps and expelled Ocalan, who began an odyssey through various nations in search of political asylum. In February 1999, he was captured in Kenya and flown to Turkey.

Ocalan had the reputation of being a dogmatic, strict, and hard disciplinarian, even tyrannical. Scholars Henri J. Barkey and Graham E. Fuller, citing a Turkish book, describe him as

> *secretive, withdrawn, suspicious, and lacking in self-confidence. He does not like group discussion; his close associates reportedly seem uncomfortable around him. He does not treat others as equals and he often demeans his subordinates in front of others, demands self-confessions from his lieutenants, and keeps his distance from nearly everyone.*

The ruthlessness with which Kurdish collaborators and PKK defectors were treated by the PKK reflected Ocalan's brutish attitude. Some PKK defectors have also alleged intimidation of guerrillas within PKK camps and units in the field. "If anyone crosses [Ocalan], either with eyes or attitude, he is accused of creating conflict," one defector was quoted by a Danish weekly. "The sinner is then declared a contra-guerrilla, and his punishment is death." According to the *Turkish Daily News,* Ocalan underlined his personal hunger for absolute power at the helm of the PKK in a party publication in 1991 as follows:

> *I establish a thousand relationships every day and destroy a thousand political, organizational, emotional, and ideological relationships. No one is indispensable for me. Especially if there is anyone who eyes the chairmanship of the PKK. I will not hesitate to eradicate them. I will not hesitate in doing away with people.*

Ocalan has also been described as "a smiling, fast-talking and quick-thinking man," but one who "still follows an old Stalinist style of thinking, applying Marxist principles to all problems. . . ." He is reportedly given to exaggeration of his importance and convinced that he and his party alone have the truth. Turkish journalists who have interviewed Ocalan have come away with the impression of a "megalomaniac" and "sick" man who has no respect for or understanding of the "superior values of European civilization." A December 1998 issue of the *Turkish Daily News* quoted Ocalan as saying in one of his many speeches:

> *Everyone should take note of the way I live, what I do, and what I don't do. The way I eat, the way I think, my orders, and even my inactivity should be carefully studied. There will be lessons to be learned from several generations because Apo is a great teacher.*

Ocalan's capture and summary trial initially appeared to have radicalized the PKK. The return of two senior PKK members to the main theater of operations following Ocalan's capture seemed to indicate that a new, more hardline approach was emerging within the PKK leadership. Ali Haidar and Kani Yilmaz, former PKK European representatives, were summoned back to the PKK's main headquarters, now located in the Qandil Mountain Range straddling Iraq and Iran. *Jane's Defence Weekly* reports that their return suggested that the PKK's military wing exercises new authority over the PKK's political or diplomatic representatives, whose approach was seen as failing in the wake of Ocalan's capture. (In addition to Haidar and Yilmaz, the PKK's ruling six-member Presidential Council includes four other senior and long-serving PKK commanders: Cemil Bayik ("Cuma"), Duran Kalkan ("Abbas"), Murat Karayillan ("Cemal"), and Osman Ocalan ("Ferhat")). However, on August 5, 1999, the PKK's Presidential Council declared that the PKK would obey Ocalan's call to abandon its armed struggle and pull out of Turkey. Whether all the PKK groups would do the same or whether the PKK's gesture merely amounted to a tactical retreat remained to be seen. In any case, the rebels began withdrawing from Turkey in late August 1999.

The PKK remains divided between political and military wings. The political wing favors a peaceful political struggle by campaigning for international pressure on Ankara. It is supported by hundreds of thousands of Kurds living in Europe. The military wing consists of about 4,500 guerrillas operating from the mountains of Turkey, northern Iraq, and Iran. It favors continuing the war and stepping up attacks if Ocalan is executed. Karayillan, a leading military hard liner, is reportedly the most powerful member of the Council and slated to take over if Ocalan is executed.

Liberation Tigers of Tamil Eelam (LTTE)

Group Profile

Background

The LTTE is widely regarded as the world's deadliest and fiercest guerrilla/terrorist group and the most ferocious guerrilla organization in South Asia. It is the only terrorist group to have assassinated three heads of government—Indian Prime Minister Rajiv Gandhi in 1991, Sri Lankan President Ranasinghe Premadasa in 1993, and former Prime Minister Dissanayake in 1994. It has also assassinated several prominent political and military figures. The LTTE's ill-conceived Gandhi assassination, however, resulted in the LTTE's loss of a substantial logistical infrastructure, and also the loss of popular support for the LTTE among mainstream Indian Tamils. In 1999, the LTTE made two threats on the life of Sonia Gandhi, who has nevertheless continued to campaign for a seat in parliament.

Also known as the Tamil Tigers, the LTTE is a byproduct of Sri Lanka's ethnic conflict between the majority Sinhalese people and the minority ethnic Tamils, whose percentage of the island's population has been reported with figures ranging from 7 percent to 17 percent. As a result of government actions that violated the rights of the Tamils in Sri Lanka in the 1948–77 period, a large pool of educated and unemployed young people on the island rose up against the government in 1972, under the leadership of the reputed military genius Velupillai Prabhakaran. The Tigers and other Tamil militant groups realized the importance of creating an exclusively Tamil northern province for reasons of security and began their campaign for the independence of Tamil Eelam, in the northern part of the island.

Founders of the military youth movement, Tamil New Tigers, formed the Liberation Tigers of Tamil Eelam on May 5, 1976. In one of its first major terrorist acts, it destroyed an Air Ceylon passenger jet with a time bomb in September 1978. The LTTE is only one of five groups, albeit the supreme one, that have achieved dominance over more than thirty-five Tamil guerrilla groups. Nationalism has remained the driving force behind the Tiger Movement.

Young Tamil Tiger Rebels. *Courtesy of AP/Wide World Photos.*

The Tamil guerrilla movement is mainly composed of groups known as the Tigers, a term applied to the movement's numerous factions. According to Robert C. Oberst:

> *The groups, commonly called "Tigers," are shadowy collections of youths which emerged in the early 1980s as full-fledged politico-military organizations. Prior to that time they were loosely organized, and centered around dominant personalities.*

The bloody ethnic riots of July 1983 polarized the Sinhalese and Tamil communities and became a watershed in the history of Sri Lanka. The riots started by the Sinhalese were a reaction to the death of thirteen soldiers in a Tiger ambush. The end result was that around 500,000 Tamils left for India and the West, seeking asylum. They became the economic backbone of the terrorist campaign, and in the years that followed the Tigers established offices and cells throughout the world, building a network unsurpassed by any other terrorist group. By 1987 the LTTE had emerged as the strongest militant group in Sri Lanka. More than two generations of Tamil youth have now been indoctrinated with separatism.

Membership Profile

The LTTE is an exclusively ethnic organization consisting almost entirely of Tamil Hindu youth. Although a majority of members of the Tamil guerrilla groups are Hindu, a significant number of Tamil Christians reportedly are in the movement. The early supporters of the Tamil independence movement were in their thirties. Since then, the age level has declined sharply. In the 1970s, quotas on university admissions for Tamils prompted younger Tamils to join the insurgency. By 1980 a majority of LTTE combatants were reportedly between 18 and 25 years of age, with only a few in their thirties. In 1990, approximately 75 percent of the second-generation LTTE membership were below 30 years of age, with about 50 percent between the ages of 15 and 21 and about 25 percent between the ages of 25 and 29. Highly motivated and disciplined, most LTTE fighters are subteenagers, according to an Indian authority.

The majority of the rank and file membership belong to the lower middle class. Almost all LTTE cadres have been recruited from the lower-caste strata of Jaffna society. The Tamil Tigers draw their recruits from the Tamils who live in the northern province and some from the eastern province. The cadres drawn from other areas of the northern and eastern provinces are only lower-rung "troops" who do not hold any place of importance or rank. In 1993, the LTTE reportedly had about 10,000 men in its fighting cadres, all Tamils and Hindus.

Deputy Defense Minister General Anuruddha Ratwatte reported in March 1999 that LTTE recruitment had been limited since early 1998 and reduced in strength to a fighting cadre of fewer than 3,000, down from 4,000 to 5,000 members. As a result of its depleted manpower strength, the LTTE has become largely dependent on its Baby Brigade, which is comprised of boys and girls of ages ranging from 10 to 16 years. In May 1999, in an apparently desperate plan to establish a Universal People's Militia, the LTTE began to implement compulsory military training of all people over the age of 15 in areas under LTTE control in the Vanni.

Among the world's child combatants, children feature most prominently in the LTTE, whose fiercest fighting force, the Leopard Brigade (Sirasu puli), is made up of children. In 1983, the LTTE established a training base in the state of Pondicherry in India for recruits under 16, but only one group of children was trained. By early 1984, the nucleus of the LTTE Baby Brigade (Bakuts) was formed. The LTTE trained its first group of women in 1985.

Tamil boy walks past helmet. *Courtesy of Corbis Images.*

In October 1987, the LTTE stepped up its recruitment of women and children and began integrating its child warriors into other units. LTTE leader Prabhakaran reportedly had ordered the mass conscription of children in the remaining areas under LTTE control, especially in the northeastern Mullaittivu District. From late 1995 to mid-1996, the LTTE recruited and trained at least 2,000 Tamils largely drawn from the 600,000 Tamils displaced in the wake of the operations to capture the peninsula. About 1,000 of these were between 12 and 16 years old. In 1998, Sri Lanka's directorate of military intelligence estimated that 60 percent of LTTE fighters were below 18 and that one-third of all LTTE recruits were women. According to an estimate based on LTTE fighters who have been killed in combat, 40 percent of LTTE's force are both males and females between 9 and 18 years of age. Since April 1995, about 60 percent of LTTE personnel killed in combat have been children, mostly girls and boys aged 10 to 16. Children serve everywhere except in leadership positions.

The entire LTTE hardcore and leaders are from Velvettihura or from the "fisher" caste, which has achieved some social standing because of the AK-47s carried by many of its militant members. According to Oberst, many tend to be university-educated, English-speaking professionals with close cultural and personal ties to the West. However, several of the important Tiger groups are led by Tamils who are relatively uneducated and nonprofessional, from a middle-status caste.

LTTE Suicide Commandos
The LTTE has a female military force and uses some females for combat. Indeed, female LTTE terrorists play a key role in the force. An unknown number of LTTE's female commandos are members of the LTTE's elite commando unit known as the Black Tigers. Members of this unit are designated as "suicide commandos" and carry around their necks a glass vial

containing potassium cyanide. Suicide is common in Hindu society, and the Tigers are fanatical Hindus. The cyanide capsule, which LTTE members view as the ultimate symbol of bravery and commitment to a cause, is issued at the final initiation ceremony. An LTTE commando who wears the capsule must use it without fail in the event of an unsuccessful mission, or face some more painful form of death at the hands of the LTTE. One of the first reported instances when LTTE members had to carry out their suicide vow was in October 1987, when the LTTE ordered a group of captured leaders being taken to Colombo to commit suicide.

The Black Tigers include both male and female members. The LTTE "belt-bomb girl" who assassinated Indian Prime Minister Rajiv Gandhi on May 21, 1991, after garlanding him with flowers, was an 18-year-old Sri Lankan Tamil Hindu, who had semtex sachets taped to her body. The blast also killed seventeen others, including an LTTE photographer recording the action. Over the subsequent two months of investigations, as many as twenty-five LTTE members committed suicide to avoid capture.

Although the Gandhi assassination had huge negative repercussions for the LTTE, suicide attacks have remained the LTTE's trademark. On January 31, 1996, an LTTE suicide bomber ran his truck carrying 440 pounds of explosives into the front of the Central Bank of Sri Lanka, killing at least 91 people and wounding 1,400, as well as damaging a dozen office buildings in Sri Lanka's busy financial district. On March 16, 1999, an LTTE "belt-bomb girl" blew herself to bits when she jumped in front of the car of the senior counter-terrorism police officer in an attack just outside Colombo. The car swerved, however, and escaped the full force of the blast. An accomplice of the woman then killed himself by swallowing cyanide. More recently, on July 29, 1999, an LTTE "belt-bomb girl" assassinated Neelan Tiruchelvam, a Harvard-educated, leading Sri Lankan moderate politician and peacemaker, in Colombo by blowing herself or himself up by detonating a body bomb next to the victim's car window.

Leader Profile

Velupillai Prabhakaran
Position: Top leader of the LTTE.

Background: Velupillai Prabhakaran was born on November 27, 1954. He is a native of Velvettihurai, a coastal village near Jaffna, where he hails from the "warrior-fisherman" caste. He is the son of a pious and gentle Hindu government official, an agricultural officer, who was famed for being so incorruptible that he would refuse cups of tea from his subordinates. During his childhood, Prabhakaran spent his days killing birds and squirrels with a slingshot. An average student, he preferred historical novels on the glories of ancient Tamil conquerors to his textbooks. As a youth, he became swept up in the growing militancy in the northern peninsula of Jaffna, which is predominately Tamil. After dropping out of school at age 16, he began to associate with Tamil "activist gangs." On one occasion as a gang member, he participated in a political kidnapping. In 1972 he helped form a

Velupillai Prabhakaran. *Courtesy of Corbis Images.*

militant group called the New Tamil Tigers, becoming its co-leader at 21. He imposed a strict code of conduct over his fifteen gang members: no smoking, no drinking, and no sex. Only through supreme sacrifice, insisted Prabhakaran, could the Tamils achieve their goal of Eelam, or a separate homeland. In his first terrorist action, which earned him nationwide notoriety, Prabhakaran assassinated Jaffna's newly elected mayor, a Tamil politician who was a member of a large Sinhalese political party, on July 27, 1973 (some sources say 1975). Prabhakaran won considerable power and prestige as a result of the deed, which he announced by putting up posters throughout Jaffna to claim responsibility. He became a wanted man and a disgrace to his pacifist father. In the Sri Lankan underworld, in order to lead a gang one must establish a reputation for sudden and decisive violence and have a prior criminal record. Qualifying on both counts, Prabhakaran then was able to consolidate control over his gang, which he renamed Liberation Tigers of Tamil Eelam on May 5, 1976.

In Tamil Nadu, Prabhakaran's exploits in the early 1980s turned him into a folk hero. His fierce eyes glared from calendars. Gradually and ruthlessly, he gained control of the Tamil uprising. Prabhakaran married a fiery beauty named Mathivathani Erambu in 1983. Since then, Tigers have been allowed to wed after five years of combat. Prabhakaran's wife, son, and daughter (a third child may also have been born) are reportedly hiding in Australia.

The LTTE's charismatic "supremo," Prabhakaran has earned a reputation as a military genius. A portly man with a moustache and glittering eyes, he has also been described as "Asia's new Pol Pot," a "ruthless killer," a "megalomaniac," and an "introvert," who is rarely seen in public except before battles or to host farewell banquets for Tigers setting off on suicide missions. He spends time planning murders of civilians, including politicians, and perceived Tamil rivals. Prabhakaran is an enigma even to his most loyal commanders. Asked who his heroes are, Prabhakaran once named actor Clint Eastwood. He has murdered many of his trusted commanders for suspected treason. Nevertheless, he inspires fanatical devotion among his fighters.

Prabhakaran and his chief intelligence officer and military leader, Pottu Amman, are the main LTTE leaders accused in Rajiv Gandhi's assassination. On January 27, 1998, the Colombo High Court issued warrants for the arrest of Prabhakaran, Amman, and eight others accused of killing seventy-eight persons and destroying the Central Bank Building by the bomb explosion in 1996 and perpetrating other criminal acts between July 1, 1995, and January 31, 1996. Prabhakaran has repeatedly warned the Western nations providing military support to Sri Lanka that they are exposing their citizens to possible attacks.

Social Revolutionary Groups

Abu Nidal Organization (ANO)
(aka Fatah—The Revolutionary Council, Black June Organization, Arab Revolutionary Brigades, Revolutionary Organization of Socialist Muslims)

Group Profile
Since 1974 the Abu Nidal Organization (ANO) is said to have killed more than 300 people and wounded more than 650 in 20 countries. In recent years, however, as Abu Nidal has become little more than a symbolic head of the ANO, the ANO appears to have passed into near irrelevance as a terrorist organization.

By mid-1984 the ANO had about 500 members. A highly secretive, mercenary, and vengeful group, ANO has carried out actions under various aliases on several continents on behalf of Middle East intelligence organizations, such as those of Iraq, Syria, Iran, and Libya, as well as other terrorist groups, such as the Shi'ites in southern Lebanon. For many of its attacks, the ANO has used its trademark Polish W.Z.63 submachine gun. Relying primarily on highly motivated young Palestinian students, Abu Nidal has run a highly disciplined and professional organization, but one held together by terror; many members have been accused of treason, deviation, or desertion and eliminated.

For Abu Nidal, the enemy camp comprises everyone who opposes the forceful liberation of Palestine. Together with Zionism and imperialism, a special place in this pantheon is occupied by those in the Arab world supporting the political process, whether Arab regimes or Arafat's PLO. Abu Nidal's Fath (Revolutionary Council) sees itself as the true heir of the authentic Fath, which must be saved from the "founding fathers" (Arafat and his cohorts) who betrayed its heritage. Abu Nidal's Fath represents a model of secular Palestinian fundamentalism, whose sacred goal is the liberation of Palestine.

In 1976–78 Abu Nidal began to establish a corps of dormant agents by forcing young Palestinian students on scholarships in Europe to become his agents. After a short training period in Libya, Iraq, or Syria, they were sent abroad to remain as dormant agents for activation when needed. Despite the ruthlessness of ANO terrorism, ANO members may have a very conservative appearance. Robert Hitchens, a British journalist and reportedly one of the few foreigners to have met Abu Nidal, was highly impressed by the cleanliness of Abu Nidal's headquarters in Baghdad, and by the "immaculate dress of his men," who were "all clean-shaven and properly dressed," as well as very polite.

Recruiting is highly selective. In the early 1980s, members typically came from families or hometowns of earlier members in Lebanon, but by the mid-1980s the ANO began to increase recruitment by drawing from refugee camps. Graduates of the first training program would be driven to southern Lebanon, where they would undergo several weeks of military training. A few weeks later, they would be driven to Damascus airport, issued new code names, and flown to Tripoli, where they would be transferred to ANO training camps.

In the mid-1980s, Abu Nidal continued to recruit from Arab students studying in Europe. Madrid has served as an important source for recruiting these students.

In the 1987–92 period, most of Abu Nidal's trainees at his camp located 170 kilometers south of Tripoli continued to be alienated Palestinian youths recruited from Palestinian refugee camps and towns in Lebanon. They were flown to Libya on Libyan military transports from the Damascus airport in groups of about 100. Abu Nidal's recruitment efforts were directed at very young students whom he would promise to help with education, career prospects, and families. In addition to paying them a good salary, he lauded the students for fulfilling their duty not just to Palestine but to the whole Arab nation by joining his organization, which he claimed was inspired by the noblest Arab virtues.

The selection process became very serious once the new recruits arrived at ANO training camps in Libya. New recruits were made to sign warrants agreeing to be executed if any intelligence connection in their backgrounds were later to be discovered. They were also required to write a highly detailed autobiography for their personal file, to be used for future verification of the information provided. While still on probation, each new recruit would be assigned to a two-man cell with his recruiter and required to stand guard at the Abu Nidal offices, distribute the Abu Nidal magazine, or participate in marches and demonstrations. Some were ordered to do some intelligence tasks, such as surveillance or reporting on neighborhood activities of rival organizations. New recruits were also required to give up alcohol, cigarettes, drugs, and women. They were ordered never to ask the real name of any Abu Nidal member or to reveal their own, and to use only codenames. Throughout their training, recruits were drilled in and lectured on the ANO's ten fundamental principles: commitment, discipline, democratic centralism, obedience to the chain of command, initiative and action, criticism and self-criticism, security and confidentiality, planning and implementation, assessment of experience gained, and thrift. Infractions of the rules brought harsh discipline. Recruits suspected of being infiltrators were tortured and executed.

According to the *Guardian,* by the late 1990s the ANO was no longer considered an active threat, having broken apart in recent years in a series of feuds as Abu Nidal became a recluse in his Libyan haven. According to the *New York Times,* Abu Nidal still had 200 to 300 followers in his organization in 1998, and they have been active in recent years, especially against Arab targets. As of early 1999, however, there were reports that the ANO was being torn apart further by internal feuds, defections, and lack of financing. Half of Abu Nidal's followers in Lebanon and Libya reportedly had defected to Yasser Arafat's Fatah movement and moved to the Gaza Strip.

Leader Profile

Abu Nidal
Position: Leader of the ANO.

Background: Abu Nidal was born Sabri Al-Banna in May 1937 in Jaffa, Palestine, the son of a wealthy orange grower, Khalil Al-Banna, and of his eighth wife. His father was reputed to be one of the wealthiest men in Palestine, primarily from dealing in property. Abu Nidal's family also had homes in Egypt, France, and Turkey. His father died in 1945, when Sabri was attending a French mission school in Jaffa. His more devout older brothers then enrolled him in a private Muslim school in Jerusalem for the next two years, until the once wealthy family was forced into abject poverty. The Israeli government confiscated all of the Al-Banna land in 1948, including more than 6,000 acres of orchards. After living in a refugee camp in Gaza for nine months, the family moved to Nablus on the West Bank, when Sabri Al-Banna was 12 years old. An average student, he graduated from high school in Nablus in 1955.

That year Sabri joined the authoritarian Arab nationalist and violence-prone Ba'ath Party. He also enrolled in the engineering department of Cairo University, but two years later returned to Nablus without having graduated. In 1958, he got a demeaning job as a common laborer with the Arabian-American Oil Company (Aramco) in Saudi Arabia. In 1960, he also set up an electronic contracting shop in Riyadh. His character traits at that time included being an introvert and stubborn. In 1962, while back in Nablus, he married and then returned with his wife to Saudi Arabia. Political discussions with other Palestinian exiles in Saudi Arabia inspired him to become more active in the illegal Ba'ath Party and then to join Fatah. In 1967 he was fired from his Aramco job because of his political activities, imprisoned, and tortured by the Saudis, who then deported him to Nablus. As a result of the Six-Day War and the entrance of Israeli forces into Nablus, he formed his own group called the Palestine Secret Organization, which became more militant in 1968 and began to stir up trouble. He moved his family to Amman, where he joined Fatah, Yasser Arafat's group and the largest of the Palestinian commando organizations.

In 1969, Abu Nidal became the Palestinian Liberation Organization's (PLO) representative in Khartoum, and while there he apparently first came in contact with Iraqi intelligence officers. In August 1970, he moved to Baghdad, where he occupied the same post, and became an agent of the Iraqi intelligence service. After the 1973 Arab-Israeli War, he left Fatah to start his own

Abu Nidal. *Courtesy of Corbis Images.*

organization. With Iraqi weapons, training, and intelligence support, his first major act of terrorism was to seize the Saudi Arabian Embassy in Paris on September 5, 1973. Later, Iraqi officials reportedly admitted that they had commissioned Abu Nidal to carry out the operation.

During 1973–74, the relationship between Abu Nidal and Arafat worsened. Abu Nidal himself has suggested that he left Fatah because of the PLO's willingness to accept a compromised West Bank state instead of the total liberation of Palestine. By mid-1974, Abu Nidal was replaced because of his increasing friendliness with his Iraqi host. In October 1974, Iraq sponsored the Rejection Front. Abu Nidal did not join, however, because of his recent expulsion from the PLO, and he was organizing his own group, the Fatah Revolutionary Council, with the help of the Iraqi leadership. In 1978, Abu Nidal began to retaliate for his ouster from the PLO by assassinating the leading PLO representatives in London, Kuwait, and Paris. He subsequently assassinated the leading PLO representative in Brussels in 1981 and the representatives in Bucharest, Romania, in 1984. Other attempts failed. In 1983, Abu Nidal's hitmen in Lisbon also assassinated one of Arafat's most dovish advisers.

In addition to his terrorist campaign against the PLO, Abu Nidal carried out attacks against Syria. He organized a terrorist group called Black June (named after the month the Syrian troops invaded Lebanon) that bombed Syrian embassies and airline offices in Europe, took hostages at a hotel in Damascus, and attempted to assassinate the Syrian foreign minister. In November 1983, Saddam expelled Abu Nidal from Iraq because of pressure applied by the United States, Jordan, and the United Arab Emirates—all allies of Iraq in the ongoing war against Iran.

Abu Nidal moved his headquarters to Syria. From late 1983 to 1986, Hafiz Al-Assad's government employed ANO to carry out two main objectives: to intimidate Arafat and King Hussein, who were considering taking part in peace plans that excluded Syria, and to attempt to assassinate Jordanian representatives (mainly diplomats). Between 1983 and 1985, the ANO attacked Jordanians in Ankara, Athens, Bucharest, Madrid, New Delhi, and Rome, as well as bombed offices in these capitals. The Gulf states, mainly Saudi Arabia, Kuwait, and the United Arab Emirates were also attacked because they were late in paying him protection money. Other ANO attacks included the machine-gun massacres of El-Al passengers at the Vienna and Rome airports on December 27, 1985.

Abu Nidal's relationship with Syria weakened, however, because Assad treated him as a contract hitman rather than a Palestinian leader and because Britain, the Soviet Union, and the United States applied intense pressures on Assad's regime to end terrorism. After Syrian intelligence caught one of Abu Nidal's lieutenants at the Damascus airport carrying sensitive documents and found weapons that he had stored in Syria without their knowledge, Syria expelled Abu Nidal in 1987. After the expulsion, he moved to Libya.

Abu Nidal appeared to be more secure in Libya. He followed the same pattern that he had established in Iraq and Syria. He organized attacks on the enemies of his friends (Libya's enemies included the United States, Egypt, and the PLO), bombed the U.S. Embassy in Cairo, hijacked planes, and gunned down 21 Jews at an Istanbul synagogue. In Libya, however, internal feuds ripped ANO apart. In 1989-90 hundreds died in battles between Abu Nidal and dissidents supported by the PLO, who sought to take control of his operations in Libya and Lebanon.

A curious feature of Abu Nidal's terrorism is that more than 50 percent of it has been directed against Arab and Palestinian rivals. The ANO's vicious war against the PLO has led to Arab claims that it was secretly manipulated by Israel's Mossad secret service. According to this seemingly far-fetched hypothesis, the Mossad penetrated Abu Nidal's organization and has manipulated Abu Nidal to carry out atrocities that would discredit the Palestinian cause. The hypothesis is based on four main points: Abu Nidal killings have damaged the Palestinian cause to Israel's advantage, the suspicious behavior of some of Abu Nidal's officials, the lack of attacks on Israel, lack of involvement in the Intifada, and Israel's failure to retaliate against Abu Nidal's groups. Another distinctive feature of Abu Nidal's terrorism is that the ANO has generally not concerned itself with captured ANO members, preferring to abandon them to their fate rather than to attempt to bargain for their release. These traits would seem to suggest that the ANO has been more a product of its leader's paranoid psychopathology than his ideology. Abu Nidal's paranoia has also been evident in interviews that he has supposedly given, in which he has indicated his belief that the Vatican was responsible for his fallout with Iraq and is actively hunting down his organization. Wary of being traced or blown up by a remote-controlled device, he allegedly never speaks on a telephone or two-way radio, or drinks anything served to him by others.

In recent years, the aging and ailing Abu Nidal has slipped into relative obscurity. On July 5, 1998, two days after ten ANO members demanded his resignation as ANO chief, the Egyptians arrested Abu Nidal, who was carrying a Tunisian passport under a false name. Egyptian security officers eventually ordered the ten dissident members of his group out of Egypt. Abu Nidal was rumored to be undergoing treatment in the Palestinian Red Crescent Society Hospital in the Cairo suburb of Heliopolis. In mid-December 1998, he went from Egypt to Iraq after fleeing a hospital bed in Cairo, where he had quietly been undergoing treatment for leukemia.

Abu Nidal's physical description seems to vary depending on the source. In 1992 Patrick Seale described Abu Nidal as "a pale-skinned, balding, pot-bellied man, with a long thin nose above a gray mustache." One trainee added that Abu Nidal was not very tall and had blue-green eyes and a plump face.

Popular Front for the Liberation of Palestine-General Command (PFLP-GC)

Group Profile

Ahmad Jibril, a Palestinian who had served as a captain in the Syrian army before joining first the Fatah and later the PFLP, became disillusioned with the PFLP's emphasis on ideology over action and for being too willing to compromise with Israel. Consequently, in August 1968 Jibril formed the PFLP-GC as a breakaway faction of the PFLP. The PFLP-GC is a secular, nationalist organization that seeks to replace Israel with a "secular democratic" state. Like the PFLP, the PFLP-GC has refused to accept Israel's continued existence, but the PFLP-GC has been more strident and uncompromising in its opposition to a negotiated solution to the Palestinian conflict than the PFLP and, unlike the PFLP, has made threats to assassinate Yasir Arafat. Terrorist actions linked to the PFLP-GC have included the hang-glider infiltration of an operative over the Lebanese border in November 1987, the hijacking of four jet airliners on September 6, 1970, and the bombing of a Pan Am Boeing 747 over Lockerbie, Scotland, in 1988, causing 270 deaths. Libyan agents were later charged for the Pan Am bombing, but Jibril and his PFLP-GC have continued to be suspected of some involvement, such as planning the operation and then giving it to the Libyans. In recent years, the PFLP-GC, weakened by reduced support from Syria and Jibril's health problems, has not been associated with any major international terrorist action. Its activities have focused on guerrilla attacks against Israeli forces in southern Lebanon.

In 1991, the PFLP-GC had about 500 members and was attempting to recruit new members. It is known that the PFLP looks for support from the working classes and middle classes, but little has been reported about the PFLP-GC's membership composition. The PFLP-GC's presence in the West Bank and Gaza is negligible, however.

The PFLP has a strict membership process that is the only acceptable form of recruitment. Although it is unclear whether the PFLP-GC uses this or a similar process, the PFLP's recruiting program is nonetheless described here briefly. A PFLP cell, numbering from three to ten members, recruits new members and appoints one member of a comparably sized PFLP circle to guide PFLP trainees through their premembership period. Cells indoctrinate new recruits through the study of PFLP literature and Marxist-Leninist theory. Prior to any training, and during the training period, each recruit is closely monitored and evaluated for personality, ability, and depth of commitment to the Palestinian cause. To qualify for membership, the applicant must be Palestinian or Arab, at least 16 years old, from a "revolutionary class," accept the PFLP's political program and internal rules, already be a participant in one of the PFLP's noncombatant organizations, and be prepared to participate in combat. To reach "trainee" status, the new recruit must submit an application and be recommended by at least two PFLP members, who are held personally responsible for having recommended the candidate. Trainees undergo training for a period of six months to a year. On completing training, the trainee must be formally approved for full membership.

The PFLP-GC political leadership is organized into a General Secretariat, a Political Bureau, and a Central Committee. The PFLP-GC is currently led by its secretary general, Ahmad Jibril. Other top leaders include the assistant secretary general, Talal Naji; and the Political Bureau secretary, Fadl Shururu.

In August 1996, Syrian President Hafiz Al-Asad reportedly asked PFLP-GC chief Ahmad Jibril to leave Syria and go to Iran. However, Jibril apparently was not out of Syria for long. On May 14, 1999, a delegation representing the leadership of the PFLP-GC, led by PFLP-GC Secretary General Ahmad Jibril and comprising PFLP-GC Assistant Secretary General Talal Naji, PFLP-GC Political Bureau Secretary Fadl Shururu, and Central Committee Member Abu Nidal 'Ajjuri, met in Damascus with Iranian President Muhammad Khatami and his delegation, who paid a state visit to the Syrian Arab Republic. Several senior PFLP-GC members quit the group in August 1999 because of Jibril's hard line against peace negotiations.

The PFLP-GC is not known to have been particularly active in recent years, at least in terms of carrying out major acts of terrorism. However, if one of its state sponsors, such as Iran, Libya, and Syria, decides to retaliate against another nation for a perceived offense, the PFLP-GC could be employed for that purpose. The group retains dormant cells in Europe and has close ties to the JRA and Irish terrorists.

Leader Profile

Ahmad Jibril
Position: Secretary General of the PFLP-GC.

Background: Ahmad Jibril was born in the town of Yazur, on land occupied in 1938. Following the Arab-Israeli War in 1948, his family moved to Syria. Late in the second half of the 1950s, he, like other Palestinians, joined the Syrian Army. He attended military college and eventually became

Ahmad Jibril. *Courtesy of Sygma/Corbis Images.*

a demolitions expert and a captain. While remaining an active officer in the Syrian Army, Jibril tried to form his own militant organization, the Palestine Liberation Front (PLF), with a few young Palestinians on the eve of the June 1967 war. Since that time, Jibril has been characterized by two basic constants: not offending or distancing himself from Syria and maintaining a deep-seated hostility toward Fatah and Yasir Arafat. After a brief membership in George Habbash's PFLP, in October 1968 Jibril formed the PFLP-GC, which became known for its military explosives technology.

After a long period of suffering and poverty, Jibril had the good fortune in the mid-1970s of becoming acquainted with Libya's Colonel Muammar Al-Qadhafi in the wake of the downing of a Libyan civilian plane by Israeli fighters over the Sinai. Jibril offered to retaliate, and Qadhafi reportedly gave him millions of dollars to buy gliders and launch kamikaze attacks on an Israeli city. After sending the pilots to certain communist countries for training in suicide missions, Jibril met with Qadhafi and returned the money, saying that twice that amount was needed. Impressed by Jibril's honesty, Qadhafi immediately gave him twice the amount.

Despite his huge quantities of weapons and money, Jibril still suffered from low popularity among Palestinians and a lack of presence in the occupied West Bank and Gaza Strip. Reasons cited for his low popularity included his having grown up in Syrian Army barracks, the nature of his alliance with Syria, and the Fatah movement's isolation of him from the Palestinian scene. Jibril suffered a major setback in 1977, when the PFLP-GC split. In 1982, Jibril fled Beirut in 1982 and began a closer association with Libyan agencies, taking charge of liquidating a large number of Libyan opposition figures and leaders overseas. In early 1983, Jibril suddenly began identifying with Iran, which welcomed him. Eventually, he moved his headquarters and operations center to Tehran. The PFLP-GC began engaging in intelligence operations for Iran among Palestinians in various countries.

Revolutionary Armed Forces of Colombia (FARC)

Group Profile

The membership of the Revolutionary Armed Forces of Colombia (Fuerzas Armadas Revolucionarias de Colombia—FARC) has always come primarily from the countryside. Sociologist James Peter says that 80 percent of the FARC's members are peasants, which explains its vitality and development over time. Most FARC members reportedly are poorly educated, young people from rural areas and who are more attracted to the FARC for its relatively good salary and revolutionary adventurism than for ideology. Many are teenagers, both male and female. Many poor farmers and teenagers join the FARC out of boredom or simply because it pays them about $350 a month, which is $100 more than a Colombian Army conscript. Others may be more idealistic. For example, Ramón, a 17-year-old guerrilla, told a *Washington Post* reporter in February 1999, "I do not know the word 'Marxism,' but I joined the FARC for the cause of the country . . . for the cause of the poor." The FARC has relied on forced conscription in areas where it has had difficulties recruiting or in instances in which landowners are unable to meet FARC demands for "war taxes." In early June 1999, the FARC's Eduardo Devía ("Raul Reyes") pledged to a United Nations representative not to recruit or kidnap more minors.

Although the FARC has traditionally been a primarily peasant-based movement, its membership may have broadened during the 1990s as a result of the steadily expanding area under FARC control. Timothy P. Wickham-Crowley points out that "the most striking single feature of the Colombian guerrilla experience, especially but not only for the FARC, is how thoroughly the entire guerrilla experience has been rooted in local experiences in the countryside." Wickham-Crowley qualifies that traditional characteristic, however, by noting that, according to FARC leader Manuel Marulanda, "There had been an appreciable broadening of the guerrillas' ranks, now including a larger number of urbanites: workers, intellectuals, students, professionals, doctors, lawyers, professors, and priests." If true, this would be surprising considering that the FARC's increasingly terrorist actions, such as mass kidnappings, have had the effect of shifting public opinion in Colombia from apathy toward the isolated rural guerrilla groups to increasing concern and a hardening of attitudes toward the guerrillas.

According to some analysts, the insurgent organization has approximately 20,000 fighters organized in at least 80 fronts throughout the country, which are especially concentrated in specific areas where the FARC has managed to establish a support base within the peasant population. However, that figure is at the higher end of estimates. In 1999, the FARC reportedly had approximately 15,000 heavily armed combatants. The National Army's intelligence directorate puts the figure even lower, saying that the insurgent group has close to 11,000 men—seven blocs that comprise a total of 61 fronts, four columns, and an unknown number of mobile companies.

The FARC was not known to have any women combatants in its ranks in the 1960s, but by the 1980s women were reportedly fighting side by side with FARC men without any special privileges. By 1999 a growing number of FARC troops were women.

In contrast to most other Latin American guerrilla/terrorist groups, FARC leaders generally are poorly educated peasants. The formal education of current FARC leader Manuel Marulanda consists of only four years of grammar school. His predecessor, Jocobo Arenas, had only two years of school. Wickham-Crowley has documented the peasant origins of FARC leaders and the organization in general, both of which were a product of the La Violencia period in 1948, when the government attempted to retake the "independent republics" formed by peasants.

Marulanda's power is limited by the Central General Staff, the FARC's main decision-making body, formed by seven members, including Marulanda. The other six are Jorge Briceño Suárez ("Mono Jojoy"), Guillermo León Saenz Vargas ("Alfonso Cano"), Luis Eduardo Devía ("Raúl Reyes"), Rodrigo Londoño Echeverry ("Timochenko" or "Timoleón"), Luciano Marín Arango ("Iván Márquez"), and Efraín Guzmán Jiménez. Raúl Reyes, Joaquín Gómez and Fabian Ramírez, who have led lengthy military and political careers within the insurgent ranks, have been present during the peace talks with the government in 1999. Raúl Reyes is in charge of finances and international policy; Fabian Ramírez is a commander with the Southern Bloc, one of the organization's largest operations units; and Joaquín Gómez is a member of the Southern Bloc's General Staff.

At the beginning of the 1980s, the FARC leadership decided to send about twenty of its best youth to receive training in the military academies of the now former Soviet Union. The FARC's new second-generation of guerrilla leaders—those young FARC members who completed political-military training abroad and are beginning to assume important military responsibilities—have been educated more for waging war than making peace. Since the mid-1990s, these second-generation FARC military leaders have been gradually assuming greater military responsibilities and taking over from the FARC's first-generation leaders.

The division between so-called moderates and hard liners within the FARC leadership constitutes a significant vulnerability, if it can be exploited. Whereas Marulanda represents the supposedly moderate faction of the FARC and favors a political solution, Jorge Briceño ("Mono Jojoy") represents the FARC hard liners who favor a military solution. Marulanda must know that he will not live long enough to see the FARC take power. Thus, he may prefer to be remembered in history as the FARC leader who made peace possible. However, should Marulanda disappear then Mono Jojoy and his fellow hard liners will likely dominate the FARC. Mono Jojoy, who does not favor the peace process, reportedly has been the primary cause of a rupture between the FARC's political and military branches.

Leader Profiles

Pedro Antonio Marín/Manuel Marulanda Vélez
Position: FARC founder and commander in chief.

Background: Since its inception in May 1966, the FARC has operated under the leadership of Pedro Antonio Marín (aka "Manuel Marulanda Vélez" or "Tirofijo"—Sure Shot). Marín was born into a peasant family in Génova, Quindío Department, a coffee-growing region of west-central Colombia. He says he was born in May 1930, but his father claimed the date was May 12, 1928. He was the oldest of five children, all brothers. His formal education consisted of only four years of elementary school, after which he went to work as a woodcutter, butcher, baker, and candy salesman. His family supported the Liberal Party.

When a civil war erupted in 1948 following the assassination of a Liberal president, Marín and a few cousins took to the mountains. On becoming a guerrilla, Marín adopted the pseudonym of Manuel Marulanda Vélez in tribute to a trade unionist who died while opposing the dispatch of Colombian troops to the Korean War.

A professional survivor, an experienced tactician, and a determined commander, Marulanda Vélez has been officially pronounced dead several times in army communiqués, but he has always reappeared in guerrilla actions. Although only five feet tall, he is a charismatic guerrilla chieftain who has long been personally involved in combat and has inspired unlimited confidence

Manuel Marulanda. *Courtesy of Corbis Images.*

among his followers. He ascended to the top leadership position after the death of Jocobo Arenas from a heart attack in 1990. He is reported to be a member of the Central Committee of the Communist Party of Colombia (Partido Comunista de Colombia—PCC), which has historically been associated with the FARC. According to author Alfredo Rangel Suárez, Marulanda "is not a theoretician by any means, but he is very astute and has a great capacity for command and organization." Rangel Suárez believes that Marulanda is a hardcore Marxist-Leninist. However, Marulanda's peasant origins and his innate sense of military strategy have earned him nationwide recognition as a leader among politicians, leftists, and other guerrilla groups.

Marulanda is not known to have ever married, although he reportedly has numerous children by liaisons with various women. According to journalist María Jimena Duzán, Marulanda lives simply, like a peasant, and without any luxuries, such as cognac. However, he smokes cigarettes.

Jorge Briceño Suárez ("Mono Jojoy")
Position: Second in command of the FARC; commander, Eastern Bloc of the FARC; member, FARC General Secretariat since April 1993.

Background: Jorge Briceño Suárez was born in the Duda region of Colombia, in the jurisdiction of Uribe, Meta Department, in 1949. His father was the legendary guerrilla Juan de la Cruz Varela, and his mother was a peasant woman, Romelia Suárez. He grew up and learned to read and write within the FARC. For years, he was at the side of Manuel Marulanda Vélez ("Tirofijo"—Sure Shot), who is considered his tutor and teacher. Mono Jojoy is a jovial-looking, heavy-set man who wears a handlebar moustache and who normally wears a simple green camouflage uniform and a black beret. He is another of the new second-generation FARC military chiefs who was born in the FARC. Both he and "Eliécer"created the FARC's highly effective school for "special attack tactics," which trains units to strike the enemy without suffering major casualties. Mono Jojoy is credited with introducing the Vietnam War-style specialized commandos that consist of grouping the best men of each front in order to assign them specific high-risk missions. He is one of the most respected guerrilla leaders within FARC ranks. He became second in command when Marulanda succeeded Jocobo Arenas in 1990.

Unlike the other commanders who came to the FARC after university-level studies, Mono Jojoy learned everything about guerrilla warfare in the field. He easily moves among the departments of Boyacá, Cundinamarca, and Meta. He is said to know the Sumapaz region "like the palm of his hand." He is known as a courageous guerrilla, who is obsessed with attacking the Public Force, has little emotion, and is laconic. His great military experience helps to compensate for his low intellectual level. He is said to be unscrupulous and to advocate any form of warfare in pursuit of power, including dialoging with the government as a ruse. Under his command, the Eastern Bloc has earned record amounts of cocaine-trafficking profits. He is opposed to extradition of Colombians, including his brother, Germán Briceño Suárez ("Grannobles"), a FARC hardliner who was charged on July 21, 1999, in the slayings of three U.S. Indian rights activists, who were executed in early 1999. He is contemptuous of the prospect of U.S. military intervention, noting that U.S. soldiers would not last three days in the jungle. However, he would welcome U.S. economic assistance to rural development projects, such as bridge-building.

Germán Briceño Suárez ("Grannobles")
Position: Commander, 10th, 28th, 38th, 45th, and 56th fronts.

Background: Germán Briceño, younger brother of Jorge Briceño Suárez, was born in the Duda region of Colombia, in the jurisdiction of Uribe, Meta Department, in 1953. His father was the legendary guerrilla Juan de la Cruz Varela, and his mother was a peasant woman, Romelia Suárez. At the recommendation of his brother, Germán Briceño became an official member of the FARC in 1980. Even from that early date, Germán Briceño showed himself to be more of a fighter and bolder than his older brother, despite the latter's own reputation for boldness. Germán Briceño was promoted rapidly to commander of the FARC's 30th Front in Cauca Department. After founding a combat training school in that department's Buenos Aires municipality, he began to be known for his meanness. He was reportedly suspended temporarily from the FARC for his excesses against the peasants and his subordinates, but later re-admitted as a commander, thanks to his brother. However, he was transferred to Vichada Department, where he engaged in weapons trafficking and extortion of taxes from coca growers and drug traffickers.

In 1994, after being promoted to his brother's Western Bloc staff, Germán Briceño took over command of the 10th Front, which operates in Arauca Department and along the Venezuelan border. Since then he has also assumed command of the 28th, 38th, 45th, and 56th fronts, operating in the economically and militarily important departments of Arauca, Boyaca, and Casanare. In 1994, he reportedly participated, along with his brother, in the kidnappings and murders of American missionaries Stephen Welsh and Timothy van Dick; the kidnapping of Raymond Rising, an official from the Summer Linguistics Institute; and the kidnappings of industrialist Enrique Mazuera Durán and his son, Mauricio, both of whom have U.S. citizenship. Germán Briceño is also accused of kidnapping British citizen Nigel Breeze, and he is under investigation for the murder of two Colombian Marine Infantry deputy officers and for the kidnappings of Carlos Bastardo, a lieutenant from the Venezuelan navy, as well as about a dozen cattlemen from Venezuela's Apure State. His kidnap victims in Arauca have included the son of Congressman Adalberto Jaimes and Rubén Dario López, owner of the Arauca convention center, along with his wife. He has also ordered the murders of young women who were the girlfriends of police or military officers.

On February 23, 1999, Germán Briceño also kidnapped, without FARC authorization, three U.S. indigenous activists in Arauca and murdered them a week later in Venezuelan territory. The incident resulted in the breaking off of contact between the FARC and the U.S. Department of State. After a so-called FARC internal investigation, he was exonerated, again thanks to his brother, and a guerrilla named Gildardo served as the fall guy. Germán Briceño recovered part of his warrior's reputation by leading an offensive against the army in March and April 1999 that resulted in the deaths of sixty of the army's soldiers. On July 30, 1999, however, Germán Briceño once again carried out an unauthorized action by hijacking a Venezuela Avior commercial flight with eighteen people on board (they were released on August 8).

"Eliécer"
Position: A leading FARC military tactician.

Background: "Eliécer" was born into the FARC in 1957, the son of one of the FARC's founders. He walked though the Colombian jungles at the side of his father. Tall, white, and muscular, he is a member of the so-called second-generation of the FARC. One the FARC's most highly trained guerrillas, he received military training in the Soviet Union. The late FARC ideologist Jocobo Arenas singled out Eliécer for this honor. An outstanding student, Eliécer was awarded various Soviet decorations. He then went to East Germany, where he received not only military training but also learned German and completed various political science courses. Following his stay in East Germany, he received guerrilla combat experience in Central America. Commander "Eliécer" became the FARC's military chief of Antioquia Department at the end of 1995. A modern version of Manuel Marulanda, Eliécer is regarded as cold, calculating, a very good conversationalist, cultured, and intuitive. By 1997 he was regarded as one of the FARC's most important tacticians. He and Mono Jojoy created the FARC's highly effective school for "special attack tactics," which trains units to strike the enemy without suffering major casualties. In Antioquia, Eliécer was assigned to work alongside Efraín Guzmán ("El Cucho"), a member of the FARC Staff and a FARC founder who was 60 years old in 1996.

Revolutionary Organization 17 November (17N)

Group Profile
Since the group's initial appearance with the assassination of U.S. official Richard Welch in an Athens suburb with a Colt .45-caliber magnum automatic pistol on December 23, 1975, no known member of the shadowy Revolutionary Organization 17 November (Epanastatiki Organosi 17 Noemvri—17N) has been apprehended. Thus, the membership and internal dynamics of this small, mysterious, and well-disciplined group remain largely unknown.

It has been claimed in some news media that the identity of no member of 17N is known to Greek, American, or European police and intelligence agencies. However, the group's ability to strike with impunity at its chosen targets for almost a quarter of a century without the apprehension of a single member has reportedly made Western intelligence agencies suspect it of being the instrument of a radicalized Greek intelligence service, the GYP, according to the *Observer* [London]. According to one of the *Observer's* sources, Kurdish bomber Seydo Hazar, 17N leaders work hand-in-glove with elements of the Greek intelligence service. According to the *Observer,* 17N has sheltered the PKK by providing housing and training facilities for its guerrillas. Police were kept away from PKK training camps by 17N leaders who checked the identity of car license plates with Greek officials. Funds were obtained and distributed to the PKK by a retired naval commander who lives on a Greek military base and is a well-known sympathizer of 17N.

What little is known about 17N derives basically from its target selection and its rambling written communiqués that quote Balzac or historical texts, which a member may research in a public library. Named for the 1973 student uprising in Greece protesting the military regime, the group is generally believed to be an ultranationalist, Marxist-Leninist organization that is anti-U.S., anti-Turkey, anti-rich Greeks, anti-German, anti-European Union (EU), and anti-NATO, in that order. It has also been very critical of Greek government policies, such as those regarding Cyprus, relations with Turkey, the presence of U.S. bases in Greece, and Greek membership in NATO and the European Union (EU). In its self-proclaimed role as "vanguard of the working class," 17N has also been critical of Greek government policies regarding a variety of domestic issues. One of the group's goals is to raise the "consciousness of the masses" by focusing on issues of immediate concern to the population. To these ends, the group has alternated its attacks between so-called "watchdogs of the capitalist system" (i.e., U.S. diplomatic and military personnel and "secret services") and "servants of the state" (such as government officials, security forces, or industrialists). It has been responsible for numerous attacks against U.S. interests, including the assassination of four U.S. officials, the wounding of twenty-eight other Americans, and a rocket attack on the U.S. Embassy compound in Athens in February 1996. The group justified its assassination of Welch by blaming the CIA for "contributing to events in Cyprus" and for being "responsible for and supporting the military junta."

Unlike most European Marxist-Leninist terrorist groups that are in their third or fourth generation of membership, the 17N group has been able to retain its original hard-core members. In 1992, according to 17N expert Andrew Corsun, the group's hard-core members were most likely professionals such as lawyers, journalists, and teachers in their late thirties and early forties. If that is the case, most of the group's core membership, which he estimated to be no more than twenty, would today be mostly in their forties. Moreover, the 17N communiques, with a five-pointed star and the name "17N," typically come from the same typewriter that issued the movement's first proclamation in 1975, shortly before Welch's execution. According to the prosecutor who examined the files on 17N accumulated by late Attorney General Dhimitrios Tsevas, the group comprises a small circle of members who are highly educated, have access and informers in the government, and are divided into three echelons: general staff, operators, and auxiliaries. The core members are said to speak in the cultivated Greek of the educated.

There appears to be general agreement among security authorities that the group has between ten and twenty-five members, and that its very small size allows it to maintain its secrecy and security. The origin of the group is still somewhat vague, but it is believed that its founders were part of a resistance group that was formed during the 1967–75 military dictatorship in Greece. It is also believed that Greek Socialist Premier Andreas Papendreou may have played some hand in its beginnings. After democracy returned to Greece in 1975, it is believed that many of the original members went their own way. 17N is considered unique in that it appears not to lead any political movement.

One of the group's operating traits is the fact that more than ten of its attacks in Athens, ranging from its assassination of U.S. Navy Captain George Tsantes on November 15, 1983, to its attack on the German ambassador's residence in early 1999, took place in the so-called Khalandhri Triangle, a triangle comprising apartment blocks under construction in the suburb of Khalandhri and situated between Kifisias, Ethinikis Antistaseos, and Rizariou. The terrorists are believed by authorities to know practically every square foot of this area. Knowing the urban terrain intimately is a basic tenet of urban terrorism, as specified by Carlos Marighella, author of *The Minimanual of the Urban Guerrilla.*

The continuing hard-core membership is suggested by the fact that the group murdered Cosfi Peraticos, scion of a Greek shipping family, in June 1997, with the same Colt .45 that it used to assassinate Richard Welch in 1975. The group has actually used the Colt .45 in more attacks than those in 1975 and 1997 (see Table 6, Appendix). Since the Welch assassination, its signature Colt .45 has been used to kill or wound at least six more of its twenty victims, who include three other American officials and one employee, two Turkish diplomats, and thirteen Greeks. The rest have been killed by another Colt .45, bombs, and anti-tank missiles. The group's repeated use of its Colt .45 and typewriter suggests a trait more typical of a psychopathic serial killer. In the political context of this group, however, it appears to be symbolically important to the group to repeatedly use the same Colt .45 and the same typewriter.

Authorities can tell that the people who make bombs for the 17N organization were apparently trained in the Middle East during the early 1970s. For example, in the bombing of a bank branch in Athens on June 24, 1998, by the May 98 Group, the bomb, comprised of a timing mechanism made with two clocks and a large amount of dynamite, was typical of devices used by 17N, according to senior police officials.

Religious Fundamentalist Groups

Al Qaeda

Group Profile
In February 1998, bin Laden announced the formation of an umbrella organization called the Islamic World Front for the Struggle against the Jews and the Crusaders (Al-Jabhah Al-Islamiyyah Al-'Alamiyyah li-Qital Al-Yahud Wal-Salibiyyin). Among the announced members of this terrorist organization are the Egyptian Al-Jama'a Al-Islamiyyah, the Egyptian Al-Jihad, the Egyptian Armed Group, the Pakistan Scholars Society, the Partisan Movement for Kashmir, the Jihad Movement in Bangladesh, and bin Laden's Afghan military wing of the Advice and Reform Commission (Bodansky: 316). Unlike most terrorist groups, Al Qaeda is more of a home base and financier for a global network of participating Islamic groups.

According to Bodansky (308–9), bin Laden and his close advisers live in a three-chamber cave in eastern Afghanistan, in the mountains near Jalalabad. One room is used as bin Laden's control and communications center and is equipped with a state-of-the-art satellite communications system, which includes, in addition to a satellite telephone, a desktop computer, at least a couple of laptops, and fax machines. Another room is used for storage of weapons such as AK-47s, mortars, and machine guns. A third room houses a large library of Islamic literature and three cots. His immediate staff occupy cave bunkers in nearby mountains.

Bin Laden is ingratiating himself with his hosts, the Taliban, by undertaking a massive reconstruction of Qandahar. In the section reserved for the Taliban elite, bin Laden has built a home of his own, what Bodansky (312) describes as "a massive stone building with a tower surrounded by a tall wall on a side street just across from the Taliban's 'foreign ministry' building." Bin Laden's project includes the construction of defensive military camps around the city. In addition, in the mountains east of Qandahar, bin Laden is building bunkers well concealed and fortified in mountain ravines.

After the U.S. cruise missile attack against his encampment on August 20, 1998, bin Laden began building a new headquarters and communications center in a natural cave system in the Pamir Mountains in Kunduz Province, very close to the border with Tajikistan. According to Bodansky (312–13), the new site will be completed by the first half of 2000.

Bodanksy (326) reports that, since the fall of 1997, bin Laden has been developing chemical weapons at facilities adjacent to the Islamic Center in Soba, one of his farms located southwest of Khartoum, Sudan. Meanwhile, since the summer of 1998, bin Laden has also been preparing terrorist operations using biological, chemical, and possibly radiological weapons at a secret compound near Qandahar.

By 1998 a new generation of mujahideen was being trained at bin Laden's camps in eastern Afghanistan and Pakistan. Bin Laden's Afghan forces consist of more than 10,000 trained fighters, including almost 3,000 Arab Afghans, or Armed Islamic Movement (AIM), which is also known as the International Legion of Islam. According to Bodansky (318–19), Egyptian intelligence reported that these Arab Afghans total 2,830, including 177 Algerians, 594 Egyptians, 410 Jordanians, 53 Moroccans, 32 Palestinians, 162 Syrians, 111 Sudanese, 63 Tunisians, 291 Yemenis, 255 Iraqis, and others from the Gulf states. The remaining 7,000 or so fighters are Bangladeshis, Chechens, Pakistanis, Tajiks, Uzbeks, and other nationalities. Bodansky (318) reports that the 5,000 trainees at one training center in Afghanistan are between 16 and 25 years of age and from all over the world. The Martyrdom Battalions are composed of human bombs being trained to carry out spectacular terrorist operations.

Leader Profiles

Osama bin Laden ("Usama bin Muhammad bin Laden, Shaykh Usama bin Laden, the Prince, the Emir, Abu Abdallah, Mujahid Shaykh, Hajj, the Director")

Position: Head of Al Qaeda.

Background: Usamah bin Mohammad bin Laden, now known in the Western world as Osama bin Laden, was born on July 30, 1957, in Riyadh, Saudi Arabia, the seventeenth son of Mohammad bin Laden. The late Mohammad bin Laden rose from peasant origins in Yemen to become a small-time builder and contractor in Saudi Arabia and eventually the wealthiest construction contractor in Saudi Arabia. He had more than fifty children from several wives. Osama bin Laden's mother was reportedly a Palestinian. Depending on the source of information, she was the least or most favored of his father's ten wives, and Osama was his father's favorite son. He was raised in the Hijaz in western Saudi Arabia, and ultimately Al Medina Al Munawwara. The family patriarch died in the late 1960s, according to one account, but was still active in 1973, according to another account. In any case, he left his sixty-five children a financial empire that today is worth an estimated $10 billion. The Saudi bin Laden Group is now run by Osama's family, which has publicly said it does not condone his violent activities.

After being educated in schools in Jiddah, the main port city on the Red Sea coast, bin Laden studied management and economics in King Abdul Aziz University, also in Jiddah, from 1974 to 1978. As a student, he often went to Beirut to frequent nightclubs, casinos, and bars. However, when his family's construction firm was rebuilding holy mosques in the sacred cities of Mecca and Medina in 1973, bin Laden developed a religious passion for Islam and a strong belief in Islamic law. In the early 1970s, he began to preach the necessity of armed struggle and worldwide monotheism, and he also began to associate with Islamic fundamentalist groups.

Osama bin Laden. *Courtesy of AP/Wide World Photos.*

Bin Laden's religious passion ignited in December 1979, when the Soviet Union invaded Muslim Afghanistan. Bin Laden's worldview of seeing the world in simplistic terms as a struggle between righteous Islam and a doomed West prompted him to join the mujahideen in Pakistan, just a few days after the invasion. In the early 1980s, he returned home to fund, recruit, transport, and train a volunteer force of Arab nationals, called the Islamic Salvation Front (ISF), to fight alongside the existing Afghan mujahideen. He co-founded the Mujahideen Services Bureau (Maktab Al-Khidamar) and transformed it into an international network that recruited Islamic fundamentalists with special knowledge, including engineers, medical doctors, terrorists, and drug smugglers. In addition, bin Laden volunteered the services of the family construction firm to blast new roads through the mountains. As commander of a contingent of Arab troops, he experienced combat against the Soviets first-hand, including the siege of Jalalabad in 1986—one of the fiercest battles of the war, and he earned a reputation as a fearless fighter. Following that battle, bin Laden and other Islamic leaders concluded that they were victims of a U.S. conspiracy to defeat the jihad in Afghanistan and elsewhere.

By the time the Soviet Union had pulled out of Afghanistan in February 1989, bin Laden was leading a fighting force known as "Afghan Arabs," which numbered between 10,000 and 20,000. That year, after the Soviets were forced out of Afghanistan, bin Laden disbanded the ISF and returned to the family construction business in Saudi Arabia. However, now he was a celebrity, whose fiery speeches sold a quarter of a million cassettes. The Saudi government rewarded his hero status with numerous government construction contracts. Following Iraq's invasion of Kuwait on August 2, 1990, bin Laden urged the Saudi government not to compromise its Islamic legitimacy by inviting infidel Americans into Saudi Arabia to defend the country, but he was ignored.

Although bin Laden, unlike most other Islamic leaders, remained loyal to the regime while condemning the U.S. military and economic presence as well as the Iraqi invasion, Saudi officials increasingly began to threaten him to halt his criticism. Consequently, bin Laden and his family and a large band of followers moved to Sudan in 1991. While living modestly in Sudan, bin Laden established a construction company employing many of his former Afghan fighters. In addition to building roads and infrastructure for the Sudanese government, he ran a farm producing sunflower seeds and a tannery exporting goat hides to Italy. Sudan served as a base for his terrorist operations. In 1992, his attention appears to have been directed against Egypt, but he also claimed responsibility that year for attempting to bomb U.S. soldiers in Yemen, and again for attacks in Somalia in 1993. He also financed and help set up at least three terrorist training camps in cooperation with the Sudanese regime, and his construction company worked directly with Sudanese military officials to transport and supply terrorists training in such camps. During the 1992–96 period, he built and equipped twenty-three training camps for mujahideen. While in Sudan, he also established a supposedly detection-proof financial system to support Islamic terrorist activities worldwide.

In the winter of 1993, bin Laden traveled to the Philippines to support the terrorist network that would launch major operations in that country and the United States. In 1993–94, having become convinced that the House of Al-Saud was no longer legitimate, bin Laden began actively supporting Islamic extremists in Saudi Arabia. His calls for insurrection prompted Saudi authorities to revoke his Saudi citizenship on April 7, 1994, for "irresponsible behavior," and he was officially expelled from the country. He subsequently established a new residence and base of operations in the London suburb of Wembley, but was forced to return to Sudan after a few months to avoid being extradited to Saudi Arabia. In early 1995, he began stepping up activities against Egypt and Saudi Arabia.

In mid-May 1996, pressure was applied by the Saudi government on Sudan to exert some form of control over bin Laden. That summer, he uprooted his family again, returning to Afghanistan on board his unmarked, private C-130 military transport plane. Bin Laden established a mountain fortress near the city of Kandahar southwest of Jalalabad, under the protection of the Afghan government. From this location, he continues to fund his training camps and military activities. In particular, bin Laden continues to fund the Kunar camp, which trains terrorists for Al-Jihad and Al-Jama' ah Al-Islamiyyah. After attending a terrorism summit in Khartoum, bin Laden stopped in Tehran in early October 1996 and met with terrorist leaders, including Abu Nidal, to discuss stepping up terrorist activities in the Middle East.

A mysterious figure whose exact involvement with terrorists and terrorist incidents remains elusive, bin Laden has been linked to a number of Islamic extremist groups and individuals with vehement anti-American and anti-Israel ideologies. His name has been connected to many of the world's most deadly terrorist operations, and he is named by the U.S. Department of State as having financial and operational connections with terrorism. Some aspects of bin Laden's known activities have been established during interviews, mainly with Middle Eastern reporters and on three occasions of the release of fatwas (religious rulings) in April 1996, February 1997, and February 1998. Each threatened a jihad against U.S. forces in Saudi Arabia and the Holy Lands, and each called for Muslims to concentrate on "destroying, fighting and killing the enemy."Abdul-Bari Atwan, editor of *Al-Quds Al-Arabi* [London], who interviewed bin Laden at his Afghan headquarters in the Khorassan mountains, reports that:

> *The mujahideen around the man belong to most Arab states, and are of different ages, but most of them are young. They hold high scientific degrees: doctors, engineers, teachers. They left their families and jobs and joined the Afghan Jihad. There is an open front, and there are always volunteers seeking martyrdom. The Arab mujahideen respect their leader, although he does not show any firmness or leading gestures. They all told me that they are ready to die in his defense and that they would take revenge against any quarter that harms him.*

A tall (6′4″ to 6′6″), thin man weighing about 160 pounds and wearing a full beard, bin Laden walks with a cane. He wears long, flowing Arab robes fringed with gold, and wraps his head in a traditional red-and-white checkered headdress. He is said to be soft-spoken, extremely courteous, and even humble. He is described in some sources as ordinary and shy. He speaks only Arabic. Because he has dared to stand up to two superpowers, bin Laden has become an almost mythic figure in the Islamic world. Thanks to the ineffectual U.S. cruise missile attack against his camps in Afghanistan following the bombings in Kenya and Tanzania in August 1998, thousands of Arabs and Muslims, seeing him as a hero under attack by the "Great Satan," have volunteered their service.

In 1998, bin Laden married his oldest daughter to Mullah Muhammad Omar, the Taliban's leader. He himself married a fourth wife, reportedly a young Pushtun related to key Afghan leaders. Thus, Bodansky points out, now that he is related to the Pushtun elite by blood, the ferocious Pushtuns will defend and fight for him and never allow him to be surrendered to outsiders. Bin Laden's son Muhammad, who was born in 1985, rarely leaves his father's side. Muhammad has already received extensive military and terrorist training and carries his own AK-47. He serves as his father's vigilant personal bodyguard.

Ayman al-Zawahiri
Position: Bin Laden's second in command and the undisputed senior military commander.

Background: Al-Zawahiri, who claims to be the supreme leader of the Egyptian Jihad, is responsible for converting bin Laden to Islamic fundamentalism.

Subhi Muhammad Abu-Sunnah ("Abu-Hafs Al-Masri")
Position: Military Commander of Al Qaeda.

Background: A prominent Egyptian fundamentalist leader, he has close ties to bin Laden and has accompanied him on his travels to Arab and foreign countries. He also helped to establish the Al Qaeda organization in Afghanistan in early 1991. He moved his activities with bin Laden to Sudan and then backed to Afghanistan.

Hizballah (Party of God)
Alias: Islamic Jihad

Group Profile

Hizballah, an extremist political-religious movement based in Lebanon, was created and sponsored by a contingent of 2,000 Iranian Revolutionary Guards (IRGs) dispatched to Lebanon by Iran in July 1982, initially as a form of resistance to the Israeli presence in southern Lebanon. Hizballah's followers are Shia Muslims, who are strongly anti-Western and anti-Israeli and totally dedicated to the creation of an Iranian-style Islamic Republic in Lebanon and the removal of non-Islamic influences in the area. Hizballah's following mushroomed in 1982 as both the Iranians and their local allies in Lebanon indoctrinated young and poor Shia peasants and young people in West Beirut's poor Shia suburbs through films, ideological seminars, and radio broadcasts. The Islamic fundamentalist groups in Lebanon have been most successful in recruiting their followers among the slum dwellers of south Beirut. By late 1984, Hizballah is thought to have absorbed all the known major extremist groups in Lebanon.

Hizballah's worldview, published in a 1985 manifesto, states that all Western influence is detrimental to following the true path of Islam. In its eyes, the West, and particularly the United States, is the foremost corrupting influence on the Islamic world today: thus, the United States is known as the "Great Satan." In the same way, the state of Israel is regarded as the product of Western imperialism and Western arrogance. Hizballah believes that the West installed Israel in the region in order to continue dominating it and exploiting its resources. Thus, Israel represents the source of all evil and violence in the region and is seen as an outpost of the United States in the heart of the Islamic Middle East. In Hizballah's eyes, Israel must, therefore, be eradicated.

Hizballah sees itself as the savior of oppressed and dispossessed Muslims. Hizballah's central goals help to explain the nature and scope of its use of terrorism. These include the establishment of an exclusively Shia, Iran-style Islamic state in Lebanon; the complete destruction of the state of Israel and the establishment of Islamic rule over Jerusalem and Palestine; and an implacable opposition to the Middle East peace process, which it has tried to sabotage through terrorism.

The typical Hizballah member in 1990 was a young man in his late teens or early twenties, from a lower middle-class family. In Hizballah's first years, many members were part-time soldiers. By 1990, however, most of the militia and terrorist group members were believed to be full-time "regulars." In the early 1980s, Hizballah used suicide commandos as young as 17, including a beautiful Sunni girl, who killed herself and two Israeli soldiers. In the last decade or so, however, Hizballah has been using only more mature men for special missions and attacks, while continuing to induct youths as young as 17 into its guerrilla ranks. Hizballah's military branch includes not only members recruited from the unemployed, but also doctors, engineers, and other professionals. In 1993, Iranian sources estimated the number of Hizballah's fighters at 5,000 strong, plus 600 citizens from Arab and Islamic countries; the number of the party's political cadres and workers was estimated at 3,000 strong. Within this larger guerrilla organization, Hizballah has small terrorist cells organized on an informal basis. They may consist of the personal following of a particular leader or the relatives of a single extended family.

Hizballah is divided between moderates and radicals. Shaykh Muhammud Husayn Fadlallah, Hizballah's spiritual leader, is considered a moderate leader. The radical camp in 1997 was led by Ibrahim Amin and Hasan Nasrallah. The latter is now Hizballah's secretary general.

Leader Profile

Imad Fayez Mughniyah
Position: Head of Hizballah's Special Operations Command.

Background: Imad Mughniyah was born in about 1961 in southern Lebanon. He has been wanted by the FBI since the mid-1980s. He is a charismatic and extremely violent individual. His physical description, according to Hala Jaber (1997:120), is "short and chubby with a babyish face." Mughniyah served in the PLO's Force 17 as a highly trained security man specializing in explosives. In 1982, after his village in southern Lebanon was occupied by Israeli troops, he and his family took refuge in the southern suburbs of Beirut, where he was soon injured by artillery fire. Disillusioned by the PLO, he joined the IRGs. His first important task apparently was to mastermind the bombing of the Israeli Embassy in Buenos Aires in 1982, in which twenty-two people were killed. On September 2, 1999, Argentina's Supreme Court issued an arrest warrant for Mughniyah for ordering that bombing. His next important tasks, on behalf of Syria and Iran, were the truck bombings that killed 63 people at the U.S. Embassy in Beirut, Lebanon, in April 1983, and another 241 U.S. Marines and sailors at their barracks near Beirut airport the following October; the hijacking of an American airliner in 1985, in which one American was killed; and the 1995 hijacking of TWA flight 847 from Athens to Rome. He also kidnapped most of the Americans who were held hostage in Lebanon, including William Buckley, who was murdered, as well as the British envoy, Terry Waite. In December 1994, his brother was killed by a car bomb placed outside his shop in Beirut.

In mid-February 1997, the pro-Israeli South Lebanese Army radio station reported that Iran's intelligence service dispatched Mughniyah to Lebanon to directly supervise the reorganization of Hizballah's security apparatus concerned with Palestinian affairs in Lebanon and to work as a security liaison between Hizballah and Iranian intelligence. Mughniyah also reportedly controls Hizballah's security apparatus, the Special Operations Command, which handles intelligence and conducts overseas terrorist acts. Operating out of Iran, Lebanon, and Syria, Mughniyah is known to frequently travel on Middle East Airlines (MEA), whose ground crews include

Hizballah members. Although he uses Hizballah as a cover, he reports to the Iranians.

Islamic Resistance Movement (Hamas)

Group Profile

In December 1987, when the Palestinian uprising (Intifada) erupted, Sheikh Ahmed Yassin and other followers of the Muslim Brotherhood Society (Jama'at Al-Ikhwan Al-Muslimin—MB), who had been running welfare, social, and educational services through their mosques, immediately established the Islamic Resistance Movement (Harakat Al Muqawana Al Islamiyyah—Hamas). Hamas's militant wing Al Qassam ('Izz Al-Din Al-Qassam) played a major role in the Intifada. Responsible for attacks on Israeli soldiers, Hamas gained a reputation for ruthlessness and unpredictability.

During the Intifada, two main organizational trends toward decentralization of Hamas developed: Hamas's political leadership moved to the neighboring Arab states, mainly Jordan; and grass-roots leaders, representing young, militant activists, attained increased authority and increased freedom of action within their areas of operation. Hamas's leadership remains divided between those operating inside the Occupied Territories and those operating outside, mainly from Damascus. Mahmoud El-Zahar, Hamas's political leader in Gaza, operated openly until his arrest in early 1996 by Palestinian security forces.

Impatient with the PLO's prolonged efforts to free the Occupied Territories by diplomatic means, Hamas formed an alliance with Iran in November 1992 for support in the continuation of the Intifada. That December, 415 Palestinians suspected of having links with Hamas were expelled from Israel into Lebanon, where they were refused refugee status by Lebanon and neighboring Arab states. They remained for six months in a desert camp until international condemnation of the deportations forced Israel to agree to their return. In September 1993, Hamas opposed the peace accord between Israel and the Palestine Liberation Organization (PLO) and maintained a campaign of violence within Israel aimed at disrupting the Middle East peace process. Its militant wing, Al-Qassam, claimed responsibility for two bomb attacks within Israel in April 1994 and for a further bus bombing in Tel Aviv in October 1994. All were carried out by suicide bombers.

The most persistent image of Hamas in the Western media is that of a terrorist group comprised of suicide bombers in the occupied territories and a radical terrorist faction in Damascus. However, Hamas is also a large socioreligious movement involved in communal work within the Palestinian refugee camps and responsible for many civic-action projects. It runs a whole range of cultural, educational, political, and social activities based on mosques and local community groups. In 1996, most of Hamas's estimated $70 million annual budget was going to support a network of hundreds of mosques, schools, orphanages, clinics, and hospitals in almost every village, town, and refugee camp on the West Bank and Gaza Strip. Consequently, Hamas has massive grass-roots support.

In 1993, Hamas's support reportedly varied from more than 40 percent among the Gaza population as a whole to well over 60 percent in certain Gaza refugee camps, and its support in the West Bank varied from 25 percent to as much as 40 percent. Hamas was reported in early 1996 to enjoy solid support among 15 to 20 percent of the 2 million Palestinians in Gaza and the West Bank. According to Professor Ehud Sprinzak of Hebrew University, Hamas is so popular among 20 to 30 percent of Palestinians not because it has killed and wounded hundreds of Israelis but because it has provided such important community services for the Palestinian population. Moreover, Hamas activists live among the poor and have a reputation for honesty, in contrast with many Palestine Liberation Organization (PLO) activists. Hamas supporters reportedly cross both tribal patterns and family patterns among Palestinians. The same family often has brothers in both the PLO and Hamas.

Hamas's social services also provide both a cover and a recruiting ground for young Hamas terrorists. Hamas members have been recruited from among believers at Hamas-run mosques, which are also used for holding meetings, organizing demonstrations, distributing leaflets, and launching terrorist attacks. Hamas's ability to recruit leading West Bank religious activists into its leadership ranks has broadened its influence.

The Suicide Bombing Strategy

Sprinzak points out that Hamas's opposition to the peace process has never led it to pursue a strategy of suicide bombing. Rather, the group has resorted to this tactic as a way of exacting tactical revenge for humiliating Israeli actions. For example, in a CBS "60 Minutes" interview in 1997, Hassan Salameh, arch terrorist of Hamas, confirmed that the assassination of Yehiya Ayash ("The Engineer") by Israelis had prompted his followers to organize three suicide bombings that stunned Israel in 1996. Salameh thus contradicted what former Labor Party prime minister Shimon Peres and other Israeli leaders had contended, that the bombings resulted from a strategic decision by Hamas to bring down the Israeli government. According to Sprinzak, the wave of Hamas suicide bombings in late 1997, the third in the series, started in response to a series of Israeli insults of Palestinians that have taken place since the beginning of 1997, such as unilateral continuation of settlements. Similarly, Sprinzak notes, Hamas did not initially pursue a policy of bombing city buses. Hamas resorted to this tactic only after February 1994, when Baruch Goldstein, an Israeli physician and army reserve captain, massacred twenty-nine Palestinians praying in a Hebron shrine. The professor's policy prescriptions for reducing Hamas's incentives to commit terrorist atrocities against Israel are to recognize that Hamas is a Palestinian fact of life and to desist from aggressive policies such as unilateral continuation of settlements and assassination of Hamas leaders.

Hamas thrives on the misery and frustration of Palestinians. Its charter, Jerrold Post notes, is pervaded with paranoid rhetoric. The harsh Israeli blockade of Palestinian areas has only strengthened Hamas.

Selection of Suicide Bombers

Hamas's suicide bombers belong to its military wing, Al-Qassam. The Al-Qassam brigades are composed of small, tightly knit cells of fanatics generally in their mid- to late twenties. In Hamas, selection of a suicide bomber begins with members of Hamas's military cells or with members of the Palestinian Islamic Jihad, who circulate among organizations, schools, and mosques of the refugee camps in the West Bank and the Gaza Strip. The recruiter will broach the subject of dying for Allah with a group of students and watch the students' reactions. Students who seem particularly interested in the discussion are immediately singled out for possible "special merit."

In almost every case, these potential bombers—who range in age from 12 to 17 years—have a relative or close friend who was killed, wounded, or jailed during the Israeli occupation. Bombers are also likely to have some longstanding personal frustration, such as the shame they suffered at the hands of friends who chastised them for not throwing stones at the Israeli troops during the Intifada. Theirs is a strong hatred of the enemy that can only be satisfied through a religious act that gives them the courage to take revenge. The suicide bombers are of an age to be regarded by the community as old enough to be responsible for their actions but too young to have wives and children. Hamas claims that its suicide bombers repeatedly volunteer to be allowed to be martyrs. These young persons, conditioned by years of prayer in Hamas mosques, believe that as martyrs they will go to heaven.

These aspiring suicide bombers attend classes in which trained Islamic instructors focus on the verses of the Koran and the Hadith, the sayings of the Prophet that form the basis of Islamic law and that idealize and stress the glory of dying for Allah. Students are promised an afterlife replete with gold palaces, sumptuous feasts, and obliging women. Aside from religion, the indoctrination includes marathon sessions of anti-Israeli propaganda. Students entering the program quickly learn that "the Jews have no right to exist on land that belongs to the Muslims." Students are assigned various tasks to test their commitment. Delivering weapons for use in clandestine activities is a popular way to judge the student's ability to follow orders and keep a secret. Some students are even buried together in mock graves inside a Palestinian cemetery to see if the idea of death spooks them. Students who survive this test are placed in graves by themselves and asked to recite passages from the Koran. It is at this stage that the recruits, organized in small groups of three to five, start resembling members of a cult, mentally isolated from their families and friends.

The support granted by Hamas to the families of suicide bombers and others killed in clashes with Israel are considered vital to Hamas's military operations because they play an important role in recruiting. Graduates of Hamas's suicide schools know that their supreme sacrifice will see their families protected for life. For someone used to a life of poverty, this is a prized reward. Hamas awards monthly stipends in the range of $1,000 to the families of the bombers. Scholarships for siblings and foodstuffs are also made available. Hamas pays for the resettlement of all suicide bomber families who lose their homes as a result of Israeli retribution.

Before embarking on his or her final mission directly from a mosque, the young suicide bomber spends many days chanting the relevant scriptures aloud at the mosque. The mantras inculcate a strong belief in the bomber that Allah and Heaven await. For example, a favorite verse reads: "Think not of those who are slain in Allah's way as dead. No, they live on and find their sustenance in the presence of their Lord." This belief is strong enough to allow the bomber to mingle casually among his intended victims without showing any nervousness.

To ensure the utmost secrecy, a bomber learns how to handle explosives only right before the mission. This practice also minimizes the time in which the bomber could have second thoughts about his martyrdom that could arise from using explosives over time. In the past, it was common for the bomber to leave a written will or make a videotape. This custom is no longer practiced because the General Security Service, the secret service, known by its initials in Hebrew as Shin Bet, has arrested other suicide bombers on the basis of information left on these records. In November 1994, the names of sixty-six Al-Qassam Brigade Martyrs, along with their area of residence, date of martyrdom, and means of martyrdom, were published for the first time. In the late 1990s, the name or the picture of the bomber is sometimes not even released after the suicide attack. Hamas has even stopped publicly celebrating successful suicide attacks. Nevertheless, pictures of past suicide bombers hang on the walls of barber shops inside the refugee camps, and small children collect and trade pictures of suicide bombers. There is even a teenage rock group known as the "Martyrs" that sings the praises of the latest bombers entering heaven.

In late 1997, Iran reportedly escalated its campaign to sabotage the Middle East peace process by training Palestinian suicide bombers. The two suicide bombers who carried out an attack that killed twenty-two Israelis on January 22, 1998, reportedly had recently returned from training in Iran. After their deaths, the Iranian government reportedly made payments to the families of both men. On September 5, 1999, four Hamas terrorists, all Israeli Arabs who had been recruited and trained in the West Bank, attempted to carry out a mission to bomb two Jerusalem-bound buses. However, both bombs apparently had been set to explode much earlier than planned, and both exploded almost simultaneously in the terrorists' cars, one in Tiberias and another in Haifa, as they were en route to their targets.

Leader Profiles

Sheikh Ahmed Yassin
Significance: Hamas founder and spiritual leader.

Background: Ahmed Yassin was born near Ashqe-
lan in the south of Palestine in 1937. After the 1948
Israeli occupation, he lived as a refugee in the Shati
camp in Gaza. He became handicapped and confined to a wheelchair in 1952 as a result of an accident. He is also blind and nearly deaf. He received
a secondary school education in Gaza and worked
as a teacher and preacher there from 1958 until
1978. His association with the Islamic fundamentalist Muslim Brotherhood organization began in the
1950s. He founded the Islamic Center in Gaza in
1973. In 1979, influenced by the 1979 Islamic rev-

Sheik Ahmed Yassin. *Courtesy of Corbis Images.*

olution in Iran, he established Gaza's Islamic Society (Mujamma') and was
its director until 1984. Although he was allowed to use the Israeli media
to criticize Yasir Arafat and the PLO, Yassin was jailed for ten months in
1984 for security reasons. He was a well-respected Muslim Brotherhood
leader in Gaza running welfare and educational services in 1987 when
the Palestinian uprising, Intifada, against Israeli occupation began. He
shortly thereafter formed Hamas. He was arrested in May 1989 and sentenced in Israel to life imprisonment for ordering the killing of Palestinians who had allegedly collaborated with the Israeli Army. He was freed
in early October 1997 in exchange for the release of two Israeli agents
arrested in Jordan after a failed assassination attempt there against a Hamas
leader. Yassin then returned to his home in Gaza. He spent much of the
first half of 1998 on a fund-raising tour of Sudan, Yemen, Saudi Arabia,
Qatar, Kuwait, United Arab Republics, Iran, and Syria, during which he
also received medical treatment in Egypt. Two countries, Saudi Arabia
and Iran, reportedly pledged between $50 million and $300 million for
Hamas's military operations against Israel. After his tour, and in frail health,
Yassin returned to Gaza.

Mohammed Mousa ("Abu Marzook")
Significance: Member, Hamas Political Bureau.

Background: Mohammed Mousa was born in 1951 in Rafah, the Gaza Strip.
He completed his basic education in the Gaza Strip, studied engineering at
Ein Shams University in Cairo, and graduated in 1977. He worked as manager of a factory in the United Arab Emirates (UAE) until 1981. He then
moved to the United States to pursue his doctorate and lived with his family in Falls Church, Virginia, and Brooklyn, New York, for almost fourteen
years prior to his arrest in 1995. In the early 1980s, he became increasingly
involved with militant Muslims in the United States and elsewhere. He co-
founded an umbrella organization called the Islamic Association for Pales-

tine (IAP) and became head of its governing council. The IAP, now head-quartered in Richardson, Texas, established offices in Arizona, California, and Indiana. Beginning in 1987, Mousa allegedly was responsible for launching Hamas terrorist attacks against Israel. In 1989 he became the founding president of the United Association of Studies and Research (UASR), allegedly a covert branch of Hamas responsible for disseminating propaganda and engaging in strategic and political planning, located in Springfield, Virginia. In 1991 he earned a PhD degree in industrial engineering. That year he was elected as chairman of the Hamas Political Bureau, as a result of the arrest of Sheikh Ahmed Yassin in 1989. Known as an ambitious and charismatic figure, Mousa re-organized Hamas by centralizing political, military, and financial control under his leadership and developing foreign funding. Traveling freely between the United States and Europe, Iran, Jordan, Sudan, and Syria, he allegedly helped to establish a large, clandestine financial network as well as death squads that allegedly were responsible for the murder or wounding of many Israelis and suspected Palestinian collaborators. He led the resumption of suicide bombings in protest of the 1993 Oslo accords. In early 1995, under U.S. pressure, Jordanian authorities expelled him from Amman, where he had set up a major Hamas support office. After leaving Amman, he traveled between Damascus and Dubai in the United Arab Emirates, among other places.

On July 28, 1995, Mousa arrived at John F. Kennedy Airport in New York on a flight from London and was detained by Immigration and Naturalization Service (INS) agents for being on a "watch list" of suspected terrorists. Three days later, Israel formally requested Mousa's extradition to face criminal charges of terrorism and conspiracy to commit murder. FBI agents arrested Mousa on August 8, 1995, pending an extradition hearing, and he was jailed at the Federal Metropolitan Correction Center in Manhattan. Mousa dropped his objection to extradition eighteen months later, saying he would rather "suffer martyrdom in Israel than fight extradition through an unjust U.S. court system." Mahmoud Zahar, a top Hamas official in Gaza, then threatened the United States if Mousa were extradited. Wishing to avoid terrorist retaliation, Israel withdrew its extradition request on April 3, 1997. Mousa was thereupon deported to Jordan on May 6, 1997. In August 1999, Jordanian authorities closed the Hamas office in Amman and, on September 22, arrested Mousa and two of his fellow Hamas members. Mousa, who was reportedly holding Yemeni citizenship and both Egyptian and Palestinian travel documents, was again deported.

Emad al-Alami
Significance: A Hamas leader.

Background: Al-Alami was born in the Gaza Strip in 1956. An engineer, he became overall leader of Hamas after the arrest of Mohammed Mousa in 1995. However, in early 1996 he reportedly had less control over all elements of Hamas than Mousa had had. He was based mainly in Damascus, from where he made trips to Teheran.

Mohammed Dief
Position: Al-Qassam leader.

Background: Mohammed Dief is believed to have assumed command of the military brigades of Hamas (Al-Qassam) following the death of Yahya Ayyash ("The Engineer"), who was killed on January 5, 1996. Dief reportedly leads from a small house on the Gaza Strip, although he is known to travel frequently to both Lebanon and Syria. He is currently among the most wanted by Israeli authorities.

Al-Jihad Group
(aka Al-Jihad, Islamic Jihad, New Jihad Group, Vanguards of the Conquest, Tala'i' Al-Fath)

Group Profile
The al-Jihad Organization of Egypt, also known as the Islamic Group, is a militant offshoot of the Muslim Brotherhood movement, an anti-Western Islamic organization that has targeted Egyptian government officials for assassination since its founding in 1928. In 1981, Sheikh 'Umar Abd Al-Rahman (also known as Omar Abdel Rahman), Al-Jihad's blind theologian at the University of Asyut, issued a fatwa, or religious edict, sanctioning the assassination of President Anwar al-Sadat.

In 1981, more than half of Al-Jihad's membership were students or teachers from vocational centers and at least eight universities. However, some of the 302 Al-Jihad members arrested in December 1982 for coup-plotting in the wake of Sadat's assassination included members of the Air Force military intelligence, Army central headquarters, the Central Security Services, and even the Presidential Guard. Others included employees at strategic jobs in broadcasting, the telephone exchange, and municipal services.

Since 1998 there has been a change in the declared policy of the Al-Jihad group. In addition to its bitter ideological conflict with the "heretical" Egyptian government, the organization began calling for attacks against American and Israeli targets. Nassar Asad Al-Tamini of the Islamic Jihad, noting the apparent ease with which biological weapons can be acquired, has suggested using them against Israel. In the eyes of the al-Jihad group, the United States and Israel are the vanguard of a worldwide campaign to destroy Islam and its believers, with the help of the current Egyptian government. This changed attitude was the result of, among other things, the Egyptian Al-Jihad's joining the coalition of Islamic fundamentalist terrorist organizations led by the Afghans. The collaboration between the Egyptian organizations and Al Qaeda played a key role in the formation of Osama bin Laden's "Islamic Front for Jihad against the Jews and the Crusaders." Ayman Al-Zawahiri, Al-Jihad's leader, who was sentenced in absentia to death or to life imprisonment on April 18, 1999, is a close associate of Osama bin Laden and one of the founders of the "Islamic Front for Jihad against the Crusaders and the Jews."

The movement basically seeks to challenge the West on an Islamic basis and establish an Islamic caliphate. However, the goals of the various al-Jihad groups differ in regard to the Palestinian issue. Islamic Jihad wants to liberate Palestine. Others give priority to establishing an Islamic state as a prerequisite for the liberation of Palestine. Islamic Jihad is very hostile toward Arab and Islamic regimes, particularly Jordan, which it considers puppets of the imperialist West. In the spring of 1999, the Islamic Group's leadership and governing council announced that it was giving up armed struggle. Whether that statement was a ruse remains to be seen.

The social background of the al-Jihad remains unclear because the group has never operated fully in public. By the mid-1990s, intellectuals occupied important positions in the leadership of the al-Jihad movements in both Jordan and the Occupied Territories, where it is a powerful force in the unions of engineers, doctors, and students. Their power among workers continues to be weak.

New Religious Groups

Aum Shinrikyo

Group/Leader Profile

The investigation into the sarin gas attack on the Tokyo subway on March 20, 1995, opened a window on Shoko Asahara's cult, Aum Shinrikyo. In 1995, Aum Shinrikyo claimed to have 10,000 supporters in Japan and 30,000 in Russia. Whereas doomsday cults previously had carried out mass suicides, Aum Shinrikyo set itself apart from them by inflicting mass murder on the general public.

What seems most remarkable about this apocalyptic cult is that its leading members include Japan's best and brightest: scientists, computer experts, lawyers, and other highly trained professionals. But according to cult expert Margaret Singer of the University of California at Berkeley, these demographics are not unusual. "Cults actively weed out the stupid and the psychiatric cases and look for people who are lonely, sad, between jobs or jilted," she says. Many observers also suggest that inventive minds turn to Aum Shinrikyo as an extreme reaction against the corporate-centered Japanese society, in which devotion to one's job is valued over individual expression and spiritual growth.

Shoko Asahara. *Courtesy of AP/Wide World Photos.*

Japan's school system of rote memorization, in which individualism and critical thinking and analysis are systematically suppressed, combined with crowded cities and transportation networks, have greatly contributed to the proliferation of cults in Japan, and to the growth of Aum Shinrikyo in particular. Aum Shinrikyo is one of at least 180,000 minor religions active in Japan. There is general agreement that the discipline and competitiveness required of Japan's education system made Aum Shinrikyo seem very attractive to bright university graduates. It provided an alternative lifestyle in which recruits could rebel against their families, friends, and "the system."

Numerous Aum Shinrikyo members were arrested on various charges after the sarin attack on the Tokyo subway system in 1995. According to Manabu Watanabe, none of them claimed innocence; rather, many of them confessed their crimes and showed deep remorse. "These people were proven to be sincere and honest victims of Asahara, the mastermind," Watanabe comments. Aum Shinrikyo became active again in 1997, when the Japanese government decided not to ban it. In 1998, Aum Shinrikyo had about 2,000 members, including 200 of the 380 members who had been arrested.

The story of Aum Shinrikyo is the story of Shoko Asahara, its charismatic and increasingly psychopathic leader. Asahara, whose real name is Chizuo Matsumoto, was born in 1955, the fourth son of a poor weaver of tatami mats, in the small rural village of Yatsushiro on Japan's main southern island of Kyushu. Afflicted with infantile glaucoma, he was blind in one eye and had diminished vision in the other. At age six, he was sent to join his blind older brother at a government-funded boarding school for the blind. Because he had limited vision in one eye, however, he soon developed influence over the blind students, who would pay him for services such as being a guide. Already at that early age, he exhibited a strong tendency to dominate people. His activities as a violence-prone, judo-proficient con artist and avaricious bully had earned him the fear of his classmates, as well as $3,000, by the time he graduated from high school in 1975.

After graduation, Asahara established a lucrative acupuncture clinic in Kumamoto. However, his involvement in a fight in which several people were injured forced him to leave the island for Tokyo in 1977. His stated ambitions at the time included serving as supreme leader of a robot kingdom and even becoming prime minister of Japan. In Tokyo, he again found work as an acupuncturist and also attended a prep school to prepare for the highly competitive Japanese college entrance examinations, which he nevertheless failed. He also began taking an interest in religion, taught himself Chinese, and studied the revolutionary philosophy of Mao Zedong. In the summer of 1977, Asahara met Tomoko Ishii, a young college student; they married in January 1978, and the first of their six children was born in 1979. In 1978, Asahara opened a Chinese herbal medicine and acupuncture clinic southeast of Tokyo and reportedly earned several hundred thousand dollars from the business. In 1981, he joined a new religion called Agon Shu, known for its annual Fire Ceremony and fusing of elements of Early Buddhism, Tantric Buddhism, and Hindu and Taoist yoga. In 1982, he was arrested and convicted for peddling fake Chinese cures, and his business collapsed as a result. Bankrupted, Asahara reportedly earned nearly $200,000 from a hotel scam that year.

In 1984, Asahara quit Agon Shu and, with the help of a few followers who also left Agon Shu, created a yoga training center called Aum, Inc. By the mid-1980s, the center had more than 3,000 followers, and in 1985 Asahara began promoting himself as a holy man. After a spiritual voyage through the Himalayas, he promoted himself as having mystical powers and spiritual bliss.

Beginning in 1986, Aum Shinrikyo began a dual system of membership: ordained and lay. Ordained members had to donate all their belongings, including inheritances, to Aum. Many resisted, and a total of fifty-six ordained members have been reported as missing or dead, including twenty-one who died in the Aum Shinrikyo clinic.

In early 1987, Asahara managed to meet the Dalai Lama. Asahara's megalomania then blossomed. In July 1987, he renamed his yoga schools, which were nonreligious, Aum Supreme Truth (Aum Shinri Kyo) and began developing a personality cult. The next year, Asahara expanded his vision to include the salvation not only of Japan but the world. By the end of 1987, Aum Shinrikyo had 1,500 members concentrated in several of Japan's major cities.

In 1988, Aum Shinrikyo began recruiting new members, assigning only attractive and appealing members as recruiters. It found a fertile recruitment ground in Japan's young, college-educated professionals in their twenties and early thirties from college campuses, dead-end jobs, and fast-track careers. Systematically targeting top universities, Aum Shinrikyo leaders recruited brilliant but alienated young scientists from biology, chemistry, engineering, medical, and physics departments. Many, for example, the computer programmers, were "techno-freaks" who spent much of their time absorbed in comics and their computers. Aum Shinrikyo also enlisted medical doctors to dope patients and perform human experiments. The first young Japanese to be free of financial pressures, the Aum Shinrikyo recruits were wondering if there was more to life than job security and social conformity. However, as Aum Shinrikyo members they had no need to think for themselves. According to David Kaplan and Andrew Marshall, "The high-tech children of postindustrial Japan were fascinated by Aum's dramatic claims to supernatural power, its warnings of an apocalyptic future, its esoteric spiritualism."

Aum's hierarchy had been influenced by Japanese animated movies, cyberpunk fiction and science fiction, virtual reality machines, and computer games. For example, Aum Shinrikyo used Isaac Asimov's classic sci-fi epic in the Foundation Series as a high-tech blueprint for the millennium and beyond. Indeed, Asahara modeled himself on Hari Seldon, the key character in the Foundation Series. The fictional Seldon is a brilliant mathematician who discovers "psychohistory," the science of true prediction, and attempts to save humanity from apocalypse by forming a secret religious society, the Foundation, that can rebuild civilization in a millennium. To do this, Seldon recruits the best minds of his time, and, once a hierarchy of scientist-priests is established, they set about preserving the knowledge of the universe. Like Asimov's scientists in the Foundation Series, Asahara preached that the only way to survive was to create a secret order of beings armed with superior intellect, state-of-the-art technology, and knowledge of the future.

To retain its membership, Aum Shinrikyo used mind-control techniques that are typical of cults worldwide, including brutal forms of physical and psychological punishment for various minor transgressions. New members had to terminate all contacts with the outside world and donate all of their property to Aum. This policy outraged the parents of Aum Shinrikyo members. In addition, in 1989 Aum Shinrikyo began to use murder as a sanction on members wishing to leave the sect.

In July 1989, Aum Shinrikyo became more public when Asahara announced that Aum Shinrikyo would field a slate of twenty-five candidates, including Asahara, in the next election of the lower house of the Japanese parliament. To that end, Aum Shinrikyo formed a political party, Shinrito (Truth Party). All of the Aum Shinrikyo candidates were young professionals between the ages of 25 and 38. In addition, Aum Shinrikyo finally succeeded in getting official recognition as an official religion on August 15, 1989, on a one-year probationary basis.

In the political arena, however, Aum Shinrikyo was a total failure. Its bizarre campaign antics, such as having its followers dance about in front of subway stations wearing huge papier-mâché heads of Asahara, dismayed the public, which gave Aum Shinrikyo a resounding defeat in the 1990 parliamentary elections (a mere 1,783 votes). This humiliation, it is believed, fueled Asahara's paranoia, and he accused the Japanese government of rigging the voting.

Following this public humiliation, Asahara's darker side began to emerge. He began asking his advisers how they might set off vehicle bombs in front of their opponents' offices, and in March 1990, he ordered his chief chemist, Seiichi Endo, to develop a botulin agent.

Beginning that April, when Aum Shinrikyo sent three trucks into the streets of Tokyo to spray poisonous mists, Asahara began to preach a doomsday scenario to his followers and the necessity for Aum Shinrikyo members to militarize and dedicate themselves to protecting Aum Shinrikyo against the coming Armageddon. That April, an Aum Shinrikyo team sprayed botulin poison on the U.S. naval base at Yokosuka outside Tokyo, where the U.S. 7th Fleet docked, but the botulin turned out to be a defective batch.

To prevent its dwindling membership from falling off further, Aum Shinrikyo began to forcefully prevent members from leaving and to recruit abroad. The group's efforts in the United States were not successful; in the early 1990s, Aum Shinrikyo had only a few dozen followers in the New York City area.

By late 1992, Asahara was preaching that Armageddon would occur by the year 2000, and that more than 90 percent of Japan's urban populations would be wiped out by nuclear, biological, and chemical weapons of mass destruction. Apparently, Asahara's plan was to develop the weapons of mass destruction needed for making this Armageddon a reality. In 1992, Aum Shinrikyo began purchasing businesses on a worldwide scale. It set up dummy companies, primarily in Russia and the United States, where its investments served as covers to purchase technology, weapons, and chemicals for its weapons program. During 1992–94, Aum Shinrikyo recruited a number of Russian experts in weapons of mass destruction. Aum's Russian followers included employees in Russia's premier nuclear research facility, the I.V. Kurchatov Institute of Atomic Energy, and the Mendeleyev Chemical Institute. Aum's chemical weapons efforts were more successful than its nuclear efforts. After the Gulf War, Aum's scientists began work on sarin and other related nerve agents.

Aum Shinrikyo found that it could recruit at least one member from almost any Japanese or Russian agency or corporation and turn that recruit into its own agent. For example, in late 1994 Aum Shinrikyo needed access to sensitive military secrets held by the Mitsubishi Heavy Industries (MHI) compound in Hiroshima, so Aum Shinrikyo member Hideo Nakamoto, an MHI senior researcher, obtained MHI uniforms, and Yoshihiro Inoue recruited and converted three paratroopers from the 1st Airborne Brigade, an elite Japanese paratrooper unit. Nakamoto then escorted Inoue and the three paratroopers, wearing MHI uniforms, into the high-security facility, where they downloaded megabytes of restricted files on advanced weapons technology from MHI's mainframe. Other sites raided by the squad included the laser-research lab of NEC, Japan's top computer manufacturer, and the U.S. naval base at Yokosuka. Aum's membership lists included more than twenty serving and former members of the Self-Defense Forces.

Aum's sarin attacks were carried out by highly educated terrorists. Aum's minister of science and technology, Hideo Murai, an astrophysicist, led the cult's first sarin attack in the mountain town Matsumoto on June 27, 1994, by releasing sarin gas near the apartment building in which the judge who had ruled against the cult lived. The attack killed 7 people and poisoned more than 150 others. Robert S. Robbins and Jerrold M. Post note that: "In 1994 Asahara made the delusional claim that U.S. jets were delivering gas attacks on his followers, a projection of his own paranoid psychology. Asahara became increasingly preoccupied not with surviving the coming war but with starting it." That year, Asahara reorganized Aum, using Japan's government as a model.

The five Aum Shinrikyo terrorists who carried out the sarin gas attack on the Tokyo subway on March 20, 1995, included Ikuo Hayashi, 48, head of Aum's Ministry of Healing (aka Medical Treatment Ministry). The other

Table 1. Aum Shinrikyo's Political Leadership, 1995

Leadership Entity	Leader
Founder	Shoko Asahara
Household Agency	Tomomasa Nakagawa
Secretariat	Reika Matsumoto
Ministry of Commerce	Yofune Shirakawa
Ministry of Construction	Kiyohide Hayakawa
Ministry of Defense	Tetsuya Kibe
Ministry of Education	Shigeru Sugiura
Ministry of Finance	Hisako Ishii
Ministry of Foreign Affairs	Fumihiro Joyu
Ministry of Healing	Ikuo Hayashi
Ministry of Health and Welfare	Seiichi Endo
Ministry of Home Affairs	Tomomitsu Niimi
Ministry of Intelligence	Yoshihiro Inoue
Ministry of Justice	Yoshinobu Aoyama
Ministry of Labor	Mayumi Yamamoto
Ministry of Post and Telecommunications	Tomoko Matsumoto
Ministry of Science and Technology	Hideo Murai
Ministry of Vehicles	Naruhito Noda
Eastern Followers Agency	Eriko Iida
New Followers Agency	Sanae Ouchi
Western Followers Agency	Kazuko Miyakozawa

Source: Based on information from D.W. Brackett, *Holy Terror: Armageddon in Tokyo.* New York: Weatherhill, 1996: 104.

four were all vice ministers of Aum's Ministry of Science and Technology and included Masato Yokoyama, 31, an applied-physics graduate; Kenichi Hirose, 30, who graduated at the top of his class in applied physics at the prestigious Waseda University; Yasuo Hayashi, 37, an electronics engineer; and Toru Toyoda, a physicist.

Although no motive has been established for Asahara's alleged role in the nerve gas attacks, some observers suggest that the Tokyo subway attack might have been revenge: all the subway cars struck by the sarin converged at a station beneath a cluster of government offices. Adding credence to this view, Ikuo Hayashi, a doctor who admitted planting gas on one of the Tokyo trains, was quoted in newspapers as saying the goal was to wipe out the Kasumigaseki section of Tokyo, where many government offices are located. "The attack was launched so that the guru's prophecy could come true," Hayashi reportedly told interrogators.

Shoko Egawa, an Aum Shinrikyo critic who has authored at least two books on the cult, observed that Aum Shinrikyo members made no attempt at reviewing the propriety of their own actions during the trial. When their own violations were being questioned, they shifted to generalities and spoke as if they were objective third parties. Their routine tactics, she notes, included shifting stories into religious doctrine and training, making an issue out of a minor error on the part of the other party, evading the main issue, and feigning ignorance when confronted with critical facts.

Authorities arrested a total of 428 Aum Shinrikyo members, and thousands of others quit. The government also stripped Aum Shinrikyo of its tax-exempt status and declared it bankrupt in 1996. Nevertheless, Aum Shinrikyo retained its legal status as a sect and eventually began to regroup. In 1998, its computer equipment front company had sales of $57 million, and its membership had risen to about 2,000. In December 1998, Japan's Public Security Investigation Agency warned in its annual security review that the cult was working to boost its membership and coffers. "Aum is attempting to re-enlist former members and step up recruiting of new members nationwide. It is also initiating advertising campaigns and acquiring necessary capital," the report said.

Key Leader Profiles

Yoshinobu Aoyama
Position: Aum's minister of justice.

Background: Yoshinobu Aoyama was born in 1960. The son of a wealthy Osaka family, he graduated from Kyoto University Law School, where he was the youngest person in his class to pass the national bar exam. He joined Aum Shinrikyo in 1988 and within two years was its chief counsel. He was arrested in 1990 for violation of the National Land Law, and after being released on bail, he involved himself in an effort to prove his innocence. As Aum's attorney, he led a successful defense strategy of expensive countersuits and legal intimidation of Aum Shinrikyo critics. According to Kaplan and Marshall, "He had longish hair, a robotlike delivery, and darting, nervous eyes that made it easy to underestimate him." He was arrested on May 3, 1995.

According to Shoko Egawa, Aoyama's foremost traits during his trial included shifting responsibility and changing the story; speaking emotionally and becoming overly verbose when advocating Aum Shinrikyo positions, but speaking in a completely unemotional voice and making a purely perfunctory apology when addressing a case of obvious violation of the law; engaging in a lengthy dissertation on religious terms; deploying extended empty explanations and religious theory until the listener succumbed to a loss of patience and forgot the main theme of the discussion; deliberately shifting away from the main discussion and responding in a meandering manner to upset the questioner; resorting to counterquestioning and deceiving the other party by refusing to answer and pretending to explain a premise; and showing a complete absence of any remorse for having served the Aum Shinrikyo cult.

Seiichi Endo
Position: Minister of Health and Welfare.

Background: Seiichi Endo, born in 1960, was Aum's health and welfare minister. As a graduate student in biology at Kyoto University, he did experiments in genetic engineering at the medical school's Viral Research Center. Provided with a small but well-equipped biolab from Aum, he conducted research in biological warfare agents, such as botulism and the Ebola virus. In March 1990, three weeks after voters rejected twenty-five Aum Shinrikyo members running for legislative office, Endo and three others went on a trip to collect starter botulinum germs on the northern island of Hokkaido, where Endo had studied as a young man. In late 1993, Asahara also assigned Endo the task of making sarin nerve gas. In a 1994 speech made in Moscow, he discussed the use of Ebola as a potential biological warfare agent. Endo produced the impure sarin that was used for the Tokyo subway attack on March 20, 1995. He was arrested on April 26, 1995, and publicly admitted his role in the sarin attacks in the town of Matsumoto on June 27, 1994, and Tokyo on March 20, 1995.

Kiyohide Hayakawa
Position: Asahara's second in command and minister of construction.

Background: A key senior Aum Shinrikyo member, Kiyohide Hayakawa was born in 1949 in Osaka. He was active in leftist causes in the 1960s and during college. He received a master's degree in environmental planning from Osaka University in 1975. He worked in various architecture firms until 1986, when he joined the Aum's precursor group and soon distinguished himself as director of the Aum's Osaka division. Beginning in 1990, he masterminded Aum's attempt to arm itself and promoted its expansion into Russia. After becoming second in command, he spent a lot of time in Russia developing contacts there for the sect's militarization program. During 1992–95, he visited Russia twenty-one times, spending more than six months there. His visits to Russia became monthly between November 1993 and April 1994. His captured notebooks contain numerous references to nuclear and seismological weapons. Hayakawa participated in the murder of an Aum Shinrikyo member and the family of attorney Tsutsumi Sakamoto, 33, a tenacious Aum Shinrikyo critic, in 1995. He was arrested on April 19, 1995.

Dr. Ikuo Hayashi
Position: Aum's minister of healing.

Background: Ikuo Hayashi, born in 1947, was the son of a Ministry of Health official. He graduated from Keio University's elite medical school, and studied at Mount Sinai Hospital in the United States before joining the Japanese medical system. Handsome and youthful looking, he was a respected doctor and head of cardiopulmonary medicine at a government hospital just outside Tokyo. His behavior changed after an automobile accident in April 1988, when he fell asleep while driving a station wagon and injured a mother and her young daughter. Despondent, he, along with his wife, an anesthesiologist, joined Aum, whereupon he began treating his patients bizarrely, using Aum Shinrikyo techniques. Forced to resign from his hospital position, Dr. Hayashi was put in charge of Aum's new clinic in Tokyo, where patients tended to live only long enough to be brainwashed and to sign over their property to Aum, according to Kaplan and Marshall.

Hayashi was also appointed Aum's minister of healing. Kaplan and Marshall report that "he coldly presided over the wholesale doping, torture, and death of many followers." His activities included using electric shocks to erase memories of 130 suspicious followers. He participated in the sarin attack on the Tokyo subway March 20, 1995.

Arrested on April 8, 1995, Hayashi was sentenced to life in prison on May 26, 1998, for spraying sarin in the Tokyo subway. In trial witness testimony on November 27, 1998, he said that he felt a dilemma over the crimes that he committed because they clashed with his social values, but he used Aum Shinrikyo doctrines to convince himself. Hayashi claimed he followed Asahara's order to commit murders not only out of fear that if he had disobeyed he would have been killed, but also out of a belief that Asahara had some religious power, that he had the God-like ability to see through a person's past, present, and future. Ikuo allegedly abandoned his faith in Asahara.

Yoshihiro Inoue
Position: Aum's minister of intelligence.

Background: Yoshihiro Inoue was born in 1970, the son of a salaried minor official. Kaplan and Marshall describe him as "a quiet boy of middling intelligence who devoured books on Nostradamus and the supernatural." While a high school student in Kyoto, he attended his first Aum Shinrikyo seminar. He became Aum's minister of intelligence and one of its "most ruthless killers," according to Kaplan and Marshall. Unlike other Aum Shinrikyo leaders, Inoue lacked a university degree, having dropped out of college after several months to dedicate his life to Aum, which he had joined as a high school junior. He was so dedicated to Asahara that he declared that he would kill his parents if Asahara ordered it. Inoue was also so articulate, persuasive, and dedicated that, despite his unfriendly face—lifeless black eyes, frowning mouth, and pouting, effeminate lips—he was able to recruit 300 monks and 1,000 new believers, including his own mother and many Tokyo University students. His captured diaries contain his random thoughts and plans concerning future Aum Shinrikyo operations, including a plan to conduct indiscriminate nerve gas attacks in major U.S. cities, including New York City.

In the spring of 1994, Inoue attended a three-day training program run by the former KGB's Alpha Group outside Moscow, where he learned some useful tips on skills such as kidnapping, murder, and so forth. That summer he became Aum's minister of intelligence, a position that he used as a license to abduct runaway followers; kidnap potential cash donors to the cult; torture Aum Shinrikyo members who had violated some regulation; and steal high-technology secrets. That year, Inoue and Tomomitsu Niimi were ordered to plan a sarin and VX gas attack on the White House and the Pentagon. Beginning on December 28, 1994, Inoue led the first of numerous penetrations of the high-security compound of Mitsubishi Heavy Industries (MHI) in Hiroshima to pilfer weapons secrets. He was arrested on May 15, 1995, when police stopped his car at a roadblock outside of Tokyo. During his trial, he allegedly abandoned his faith in Asahara.

Hisako Ishii
Position: Aum's minister of finance.

Background: Hisako Ishii was born in 1960. She joined Aum's yoga classes in 1984, when she was an "office lady" at a major Japanese insurance company. One of Asahara's most devoted disciples, she became Aum's minister of finance and was behind the group's business success. She was also his inseparable mistress, until she gave birth to twins.

At her trial, Ishii spoke of her childhood fear of death, the fact that adults failed to initially reply to her questions concerning death, the fact that she trusted Asahara with pure feelings, and her determination to mature as a person within the Aum Shinrikyo framework. She then proceeded to speak of changes which took place after her arrest:

> *When I experienced a total collapse of the past, more than ten years during which I had matured within the cult as a religious person, I felt I had died. When all that I had believed I had accomplished within myself was destroyed, and I came to the awareness that all was just a fantasy of Asahara imbued in me, that he is not a true religious being, that he is not a guru, and that the Aum Shinrikyo doctrine was wrong, I experienced a form of death separate from the death of a physical being.*

Ishii proceeded to read books banned by the Aum, such as religious books, books on mind-control, and psychology. She testified that as a result she had been resurrected through the process of learning the nature of genuine religion. Despite being impressed by the eloquence of her written statement, Shoko Egawa was dismayed by Ishii's total omission of anything about her feelings for the victims who literally met death as the result of the many crimes committed by the Aum. Although charged with relatively minor offenses, such as concealment of criminals and destruction of evidence, Ishii asserted that she was innocent of each of the charges. She depicted herself merely as an innocent victim taken advantage of by Asahara and stressed her determination to resurrect herself despite all the suffering. She not only refused to testify about her inside knowledge of cult affairs, she cut off any questions of that nature. In May 1998, Ishii announced her resignation from the Aum.

Fumihiro Joyu
Position: Aum's minister of foreign affairs.

Background: Fumihiro Joyu joined Aum Shinrikyo, in 1989, at age 26. He had an advanced degree in telecommunications from Waseda University, where he studied artificial intelligence. He quit his promising new career at Japan's Space Development Agency after only two weeks because it was incompatible with his interests in yoga. He became the sect's spokesman and minister of foreign affairs. As Aum's Moscow chief, Joyu ran the cult's large Moscow center at Alexseyevskaya Square. "Joyu didn't try to hide his contempt for his poor Russian flock," Kaplan and Marshall write. They describe him as "a mini-guru, a cruel and arrogant man who later proved to be Aum's most accomplished liar." They add, "Fluent in English, Joyu was looked upon by most Japanese as a dangerously glib and slippery operator with the ability to lie in two languages." However, with his charismatic, boyish good looks he developed admirers among teenage girls from his appearances on television talk shows. He was arrested on October 7, 1995, on perjury charges. He was scheduled to be released from prison at the end of 1999. He has remained devout to Asahara and was planning to rejoin the Aum Shinrikyo cult.

Takeshi Matsumoto
Position: An Aum Shinrikyo driver.

Background: Born in 1966, Takeshi Matsumoto joined Aum Shinrikyo after telling his parents that he had seen hell. Personable but pathetic, he had dreams of becoming a Grand Prix auto racer. He drove the rental car used to kidnap Kiyoshi Kariya, 68, a notary public whose sister was a runaway Aum Shinrikyo member. Aum Shinrikyo members tortured and murdered Kariya after he refused to reveal his sister's whereabouts. National Police identified Matsumoto from fingerprints on the car rental receipt and put him on their "most wanted" list. His fingerprints were the legal pretext long sought by the National Police to raid Aum Shinrikyo compounds and offices. While on the run, Matsumoto had Dr. Hayashi surgically remove all of his fingerprints and do some abortive facial plastic surgery as well. However, he was arrested in October 1995 and identified by his palm prints. He pleaded guilty to the abduction and confinement of Kariya.

Hideo Murai
Position: Aum's minister of science and technology, minister of distribution supervision, and "engineer of the apocalypse."

Background: Hideo Murai was born in 1954. After graduating from the Physics Department at Osaka University, he entered graduate school, where he studied X-ray emissions of celestial bodies, excelled at computer programming, and earned an advance degree in astrophysics. In 1987, he joined Kobe Steel and worked in research and development. After reading one of Asahara's books, he lost interest in his career. After a trip to Nepal, he quit Kobe Steel in 1989 and, along with his wife, enlisted in a six-month training course at an Aum Shinrikyo commune, where his lifestyle turned ascetic and focused on Asahara's teachings. He quickly rose through the ranks because of his brilliant scientific background, self-confidence, boldness, and devotion to Asahara. He created such devices as the Perfect Salvation Initiation headgear (an electrode-laden shock cap), which netted Aum Shinrikyo about $20 million, and the Astral Teleporter; and he attempted unsuccessfully to develop a botulinus toxin as well as nuclear, laser, and microwave weapons technology. In early 1993, Asahara ordered him to oversee Aum's militarization program. "Widely recognized and feared within Aum, Murai," according to Brackett, "had a reputation as a determined and aggressive leader who liked to stir up trouble for other people." He was directly involved in the murder of the Sakamotos and at least one Aum Shinrikyo member. He led the team that attacked judges' apartments in Matsumoto with sarin gas in June 27, 1994, in which 7 people were killed and 144 injured. Murai also masterminded the sarin attack on the Tokyo subway on March 20, 1995. David Kaplan and Andrew Marshall describe "the cult's deceptively unassuming science chief" as follows: "At first glance, Murai looked more like a provincial schoolteacher than a mad scientist. He had elfin features etched on a perfectly round face, with a fragile build that suggested he could do harm to no one. But a closer look revealed eyes that turned from benign to beady in a blink. His hair was short but disheveled, and he often looked lost in some unreachable thought." Just before he was to be brought in by police for questioning, Murai was stabbed with a butcher's knife by a Korean gangster on April 23, 1995, on prime time TV in front of Aum's Tokyo headquarters, and he died six hours later.

Kiyohide Nakada

Position: vice minister, Ministry of Home Affairs.

Background: Nakada was born in 1948. He is described as having a shiny, shaven head, clipped mustache, and piercing eyes. His distinguishing feature, which is characteristic of a Japanese *yakuza,* or mobster, is a brilliant tattoo stretching from his neck to his calf. For years, he headed a gang affiliated with the Yamaguchi crime syndicate in the city of Nagoya. When he was serving three years in prison on a firearms charge, his wife joined Aum. Although Nakada disapproved of her joining Aum, he himself turned to Aum Shinrikyo when a doctor gave him three months to live because of a failing liver. After a miraculous recovery, he joined Aum, dissolved his gang, and donated his assets to Aum. Nakada became one of Asahara's two former *yakuza* conduits to the underworld. When Aum Shinrikyo began its militarization program in 1994, he became particularly important in obtaining weapons. He eventually became Tomomitsu Niimi's deputy in Aum's Ministry of Home Affairs, charged with enforcing security within the organization. As head of the Action Squad, he was responsible for abducting and killing defecting sect members and opponents of Aum. He was arrested in April 1995.

Tomomasa Nakagawa
Position: head of Aum's Household Agency.

Background: Dr. Tomomasa Nakagawa, 29, an Aum Shinrikyo physician, is alleged to have murdered Satoko Sakamoto, 29, and her infant son with injections of potassium chloride, in 1995. Nakagawa joined Aum Shinrikyo while a medical student at Kyoto Prefectural College of Medicine in February 1988. After passing the national medical exam in April 1988 and practicing medicine for a year, he moved into an Aum Shinrikyo commune in August 1989. As head of the Aum's Household Agency, one of his primary duties was to act as personal doctor to Asahara and his family. He was also actively involved in Aum's sarin production.

Tomomitsu Niimi
Position: Aum's minister of home affairs.

Background: Tomomitsu Niimi was born in 1964. As a university student, he read law, as well as the works of Nostradamus and esoteric Buddhist texts. After graduation, he worked at a food company but quit six months later to join Aum. Kaplan and Marshall describe him as "a slender figure with a long neck, shaven head, and a reptilian smirk that seemed permanently etched upon his face."

As Aum's ferocious minister of home affairs, Niimi presided over Aum's mini-police state. His ten-member hit squad, the New Followers Agency, engaged in spying on, abducting, confining, torturing, and murdering runaway members. He is described by Kaplan and Marshall as Aum's "chief hit man" and a sadistic and ruthless head of security. He allegedly participated in various murders and abductions, including the murder of Shuji Taguchi in 1989, the slaying of the Sakamoto family, and the strangling of a pharmacist in January 1994. In February 1994, he was accidentally exposed to some sarin and lapsed into convulsions, but Dr. Nakagawa was able to save him. In the spring of 1994, he attended a three-day training course conducted by veterans of the former KGB's Alpha Group near Moscow. That year, Niimi and Yoshihiro Inoue were ordered to plan a sarin and VX gas attack on the White House and the Pentagon. On September 20, 1994, Niimi and his hit squad attacked Shoko Egawa, author of two books on Aum, with phosgene gas, but she survived. In January 1995, Niimi sprayed Hiroyuki Nakaoka, head of a cult victims' support group, with VX, but he survived after several weeks in a coma. Niimi also participated in the Tokyo subway attack on March 20, 1995. He was arrested on April 12, 1995. He has remained devout to Asahara.

Toshihiro Ouchi
Position: An Aum Shinrikyo operative.

Background: Ouchi joined the Aum Shinrikyo cult in 1985. Physically large and a long-time Aum Shinrikyo member, Ouchi functioned primarily as a leader of cult followers. Many of the followers and ordained priests of the cult with whom he had been personally associated became involved in crimes, and many remain active cult followers. Ouchi was indicted for involvement in two incidents. One case took place in February 1989 and involved the murder of cult follower Shuji Taguchi, who was making an attempt to leave the cult; the second case involved the destruction of a corpse of a cult follower who had passed away during religious training in June 1993. Ouchi's reluctant behavior gave Asahara doubts about his commitment; hence, he condemned Ouchi as a "cancerous growth on the Aum," assigning him to the Russian chapter in September 1993. Nevertheless, Ouchi continued to serve as an executive cult follower. He recruited new followers in Russia and provided guidance to them. During the investigation of the Sakamoto case that began in March 1995, Ouchi was alarmed when he learned that the Aum Shinrikyo was involved. The knowledge undermined his religious beliefs. He reportedly was shocked when he later received a letter from a former cult follower, who was an intimate friend, that discussed the misguided doctrine of Aum. His faith in Aum Shinrikyo shaken, he gradually began to alter his views about people outside the cult. In early April 1995, Russian police arrested Ouchi, who had been serving as Fumihiro Joyu's deputy in Moscow. Kaplan and Marshall report that Ouchi, "a grinning naïf," was described by one academic as "knowing as much about Russia as the farthest star." During his initial trial in Japan, Ouchi expressed repentance and apologized "as a former official of the Aum."

Masami Tsuchiya
Position: Head of Aum's chemical warfare team.

Background: Masami Tsuchiya was born in 1965. Prior to joining Aum, Tsuchiya was enrolled in a five-year doctoral degree program in organic physics and chemistry at Tsukuba University, one of the top universities in Japan, where his graduate work focused on the application of light to change the structure of molecules. Although described by a professor as "brilliant," Tsuchiya lived in a barren room, was introverted, had no social life, and expressed a desire to become a priest.

Tsuchiya abandoned a career in organic chemistry to join Aum. After suggesting that Aum Shinrikyo produce a Nazi nerve gas called sarin, he was given his own lab (named Satian 7) with one hundred workers and a vast chemical plant to develop chemical weapons. As Aum's chief chemist and head of its chemical warfare team, he played a central role in Aum's manufacture of sarin. Kaplan and Marshall describe Tsuchiya as looking the part of the mad scientist: "His goatee and crew-cut hair framed a broad face with eyebrows that arched high above piercing eyes." Fascinated by

Russia's chemical weapons stockpiles, Tsuchiya spent at least three weeks in Russia in 1993, where he is suspected of meeting with experts in bio-chemical weapons. When he returned to his Mount Fuji lab in the fall of 1993, he began experimenting with sarin, using a Russian formula. He was prepared to build a vast stockpile of nerve agents, such as sarin, blister gas, and others. Although poorly trained workers, leaks of toxic fumes, and repeated setbacks plagued the program, Tsuchiya succeeded in stockpiling 44 pounds of sarin at Satian 7 by mid-June 1994. However, Kaplan and Marshall point out that he was not the only Aum Shinrikyo chemist to make the nerve gas. Tsuchiya also produced other chemical warfare agents such as VX. He had Tomomitsu Niimi, using a VX syringe, test the VX on several unsuspecting individuals. Police arrested Tsuchiya on April 26, 1995. He has remained devout to Asahara.

Table 2. Educational Level and Occupational Background of Right-Wing Terrorists in West Germany, 1980

(In percentages of right-wing terrorists)

Education:	
Volkschule (elementary)	49
Technical	22
Grammar (high school)	17
University	10
Other	2
TOTAL	100
Occupation:	
Self-employed	8
White collar	9
Skilled worker or artisan	41
Unskilled worker	34
Other (unemployed)	8
TOTAL	100

Source: Based on information from Eva Kolinsky, "Terrorism in West Germany." Pages 75–76 in Juliet Lodge, ed., *The Threat of Terrorism*. Boulder, Colorado: Westview Press, 1988.

Table 3. Ideological Profile of Italian Female Terrorists, January 1970–June 1984

Membership in Extraparliamentary Political Organizations Prior to Becoming a Terrorist	Number of Terrorists	Percentage of Total Terrorists
Left	73	91.0
Right	7	9.0
TOTAL	80	100.0
Terrorist Group Affiliation	Number of Terrorists	Percentage of Total Terrorists
Early Left[1]	40	9.0
Early Right[2]	10	2.2
Late Left[3]	366	82.2
Late Right[4]	29	6.5
TOTAL	445	100.0

[1]Partisan Action Groups, Nuclei of Armed Proletarians. Red Brigades, 22 October.
[2]Compass, Mussolini Action Squads, National Front, National Vanguard, New Order, People's Struggle, Revolutionary Action Movement.
[3]Front Line, Red Brigades, Revolutionary Action, Union of Communist Combatants, Worker Autonomy, et alia.
[4]Let Us Build Action, Nuclei of Armed Revolutionaries, Third Position.

Source: Based on information from Leonard Weinberg and William Lee Eubank, "Italian Women Terrorists," *Terrorism: An International Journal,* 9, No. 3, 1987, 250–252.

**Table 4. Prior Occupational Profile of Italian Female Terrorists,
January 1970–June 1984**

Occupation Prior to Becoming a Terrorist	Number of Terrorists	Percentage of Total Terrorists
Clerk, secretary, nurse, technician	57	23.0
Criminal, subproletarian	5	2.0
Free professional (architect, lawyer, physician)	8	3.0
Housewife	11	5.0
Industrialist	5	2.0
Police, military	1	0.0
Small business proprietor, salesperson	3	1.0
Student	86	35.0
Teacher	50	20.0
Worker	18	7.0
TOTAL	244	100.0

Source: Based on information from Leonard Weinberg and William Lee Eubank, "Italian Women Terrorists," *Terrorism: An International Journal,* 9, No. 3, 1987, 250–52.

Table 5. Geographical Profile of Italian Female Terrorists, January 1970–June 1984

Place of Birth (Region)	Number of Terrorists	Percentage of Total Terrorists
North	96	45.0
Center	31	15.0
Rome	30	14.0
South	43	20.0
Foreign-born	12	6.0
TOTAL	212	100.0
Place of Birth (Size of Community)	**Number of Terrorists**	**Percentage of Total Terrorists**
Small community (Less than 100,000)	77	9.0
Medium-sized city (from 100,000 to 1 million)	71	29.0
Big City (more than 1 million)	81	34.0
Foreign-born	12	5.0
TOTAL	241	100.0
Place of Residence (Region)	**Number of Terrorists**	**Percentage of Total Terrorists**
North	246	56.0
Center	54	12.0
Rome	90	21.0
South	49	11.0
TOTAL	241	100.0
Place of Residence (Size of Community)	**Number of Terrorists**	**Percentage of Total Terrorists**
Small community (Less than 100,000)	37	8.0
Medium-sized community (100,000 to 1 million)	106	24.0
Big City (more than 1 million)	297	67.0
TOTAL	440	100.0

Source: Based on information from Leonard Weinberg and William Lee Eubank, "Italian Women Terrorists," *Terrorism: An International Journal*, 9, No. 3, 1987, 250–51.

Table 6. Age and Relationships Profile of Italian Female Terrorists, January 1970–June 1984

Time of Arrest	Number of Terrorists	Percentage of Total Terrorists
Before 1977	46	10.0
After 1977	405	90.0
TOTAL	451	100.0
Age at Time of Arrest	**Number of Terrorists**	**Percentage of Total Terrorists**
15 to 19	28	7.0
20 to 24	170	42.0
25 to 29	106	26.0
30 to 34	63	16.0
35 to 39	21	5.0
40 to 44	9	2.0
45 and over	5	1.0
TOTAL	402	100.0
Role in Organization	**Number of Terrorists**	**Percentage of Total Terrorists**
Supporter	120	27.0
Regular	298	66.0
Leader	33	7.0
TOTAL	451	100.0
Related to Other Terrorists	**Number of Terrorists**	**Percentage of Total Terrorists**
Yes	121	27.0
No	330	73.0
TOTAL	451	100.0
Nature of Relationship to Other Terrorists	**Number of Terrorists**	**Percentage of Total Terrorists**
Marital	81	67.0
Sibling	34	28.0
Parental	1	1.0
Other	5	4.0
TOTAL	121	100.0

Source: Based on information from Leonard Weinberg and William Lee Eubank, "Italian Women Terrorists," *Terrorism: An International Journal,* 9, No. 3, 1987, 250–52.

Table 7. Patterns of Weapons Use by the Revolutionary Organization 17 November, 1975–97

Action	Date	Weapon(s) Used
A masked gunman assassinated U.S. Embassy official Richard Welch in front of his home in an Athens suburb.	December 23, 1975	Colt .45
Gunmen in a passing car shot and fatally wounded Petros Babalis, a former police officer, near his house in central Athens.	January 31, 1979	Colt .45
Gunmen riding on a motorcycle killed Pantalis Petrou, deputy chief of the antiriot police MAT (Units for the Restoration of Order), and seriously wounded his chauffeur in Pangrati, a suburb of Athens.	January 16, 1980	Colt .45
Two men on a motor scooter assassinated U.S. Navy Captain George Tsantes and fatally wounded his driver with the same Colt .45.	November 15, 1983	Colt .45
Two masked gunmen on a motorcycle shot and wounded U.S. Army Master Sgt. Robert Judd, who took evasive action, as he was driving to the Hellenikon base near Athens airport.	April 3, 1984	Colt .45
Two men on a motorcycle shot and wounded U.S. Master Sgt. Richard H. Judd, Jr., as he was driving in Athens.	April 3, 1984	Colt .45
Two men in a car intercepted conservative newspaper publisher Nikos Momferatos's Mercedes and shot him to death and seriously wounded his driver in Kolonaki in the most central part of Athens.	February 21, 1985	Colt .45 and .22-caliber pistol
A gunman riding on the back seat of a motor scooter opened fire on businessman Alexandros Athanasiadis when he stopped for a traffic light on Kifissia Avenue on his way to work, fatally wounding him.	March 1, 1988	Colt .45
Three gunmen ambushed New Democracy (ND) Party deputy Pavlos Bakoyannis, son-in-law of ND Chairman Konstandinos Mitsotakis, as he was waiting for the elevator to his office in Athens. One of the terrorists opened fire on the target from behind, hitting him five times, and then all three casually walked to their getaway car.	September 26, 1989	Colt .45

Three gunmen assassinated the Turkish Deputy Chief of Mission in Athens with seven bullets fired from at least one .45-caliber automatic as he drove to work.	August(?) 1994	Colt .45
Murdered Cosfi Peraticos, scion of a Greek shipping family.	June 1997	Colt .45

Source: Compiled by the author from multiple sources.

Glossary

Afghans—Term applied to veterans of the Afghan War. A number of the would-be mujahideen *(q.v.)*, or Islamic resistance fighters, who flocked to Afghanistan in the 1980s and early 1990s later applied the skills and contacts acquired during the Afghan War and its aftermath to engage in terrorist activities elsewhere. The Afghans also transmitted the knowledge they acquired to a new generation of Muslim militants in countries as different as Algeria, Bosnia-Herzegovina, France, and the Philippines. This new breed of Afghan terrorists, who operate independently of state sponsors, draws on global funding, is savvy about modern weapons and explosives, and is able to take advantage of the most up-to-date means of communication and transportation. Whereas Muslim terrorists were cloistered by nationality prior to the Afghan War, after the war they began working together— Pakistanis, Egyptians, Algerians, and so forth. Al Qaeda's Afghan component is also known as the Armed Islamist Movement (AIM).

Assassins—From the eleventh through the thirteenth century, a sect of Shiite Muslims called the Assassins used assassination as a tool for purifying the Muslim religion. The Assassins' victims, who were generally officials, were killed in public to communicate the error of the targeted official. By carrying out the assassination in public, the Assassin would allow himself to be apprehended and killed in order to demonstrate the purity of his motives and to enter Heaven.

Baader-Meinhof Gang—Journalistic name for the Red Army Faction (Rote Armee Fraktion—RAF) *(q.v.)*. Although the RAF had been reduced to fewer than twenty members by the early 1990s, it may still exist in an inactive status. If so, it would be in at least its second generation of leadership. The group's support network, reportedly involving hundreds of Germans, many of whom are well-educated professionals, helps to account for its possible survival.

fundamentalism—This term is used to refer to people who dedicate their lives to pursuing the fundamentals of their religion.

cult—A journalistic term for an unorthodox system of religious beliefs and rituals that scholars of religion refrain from using.

fight or flight—A theory developed by W.B. Cannon in 1929. When an individual is under stress, the heart rate increases, the lungs operate more efficiently, adrenalin and sugar are released into the bloodstream, and the muscles become infused with blood.

Frustration-Aggression Hypothesis—A hypothesis that every frustration leads to some form of aggression and every aggressive act results from some prior frustration. As defined by Ted Robert Gurr: "The necessary precondition for violent civil conflict is relative deprivation, defined as actors' perception of discrepancy between their value expectations and their environment's apparent value capabilities. This deprivation may be individual or collective."

Groupthink—As originally defined by I.L. Janis, "A mode of thinking that people engage in when the members' strivings for unanimity override the motivation to realistically appraise alternative courses of action."

guerrilla—A revolutionary who engages in insurgency as opposed to terrorism, although guerrillas also use terrorist methods. Usually operating relatively openly in less-developed countries, guerrillas attempt to hold territory and generally attack the state's infrastructure, whereas terrorists usually operate in urban areas and attack more symbolic targets. Guerrillas usually coerce or abduct civilians to join them, whereas terrorists are highly selective in whom they recruit.

international terrorism—Although the Central Intelligence Agency distinguishes between international and transnational terrorism (international being terrorism carried out by individuals or groups controlled by a sovereign state and transnational terrorism being terrorism carried out by autonomous nonstate actors), the distinction is not used in this paper. This is because the distinction is unnecessarily confusing, not self-evident, and lacking in usefulness, whereas the term "state-sponsored terrorism" is self-evident and unambiguous. Moreover, one would have to be extremely well informed to know which terrorist acts are state-sponsored. Thus, the term international terrorism is used here to refer to any act of terrorism affecting the national interests of more than one country. The WTC bombing, for example, was an act of international terrorism because its perpetrators included foreign nationals.

Intifada—The uprising by Palestinians begun in October 1987 against Israeli military occupation of the West Bank and the Gaza Strip. Also the name of the involved Liberation Army of Palestine, a loosely organized group of adult and teenage Palestinians active in 1987–93 in attacks on armed Israeli troops. Their campaign for self-determination included stone-throwing and petrol bombing. Some 1,300 Palestinians and 80 Israelis were killed in the uprising up to the end of 1991.

jihad—An Arabic verbal noun derived from jahada ("to struggle"). Although "holy war" is not a literal translation, it summarizes the essential idea of jihad. In the course of the revival of Islamic fundamentalism *(q.v.)*, the doctrine of jihad has been invoked to justify resistance, including terrorist actions, to combat "un-Islamic" regimes, or perceived external enemies of Islam, such as Israel and the United States.

June Second Movement—An anarchistic leftist group formed in West Berlin in 1971 that sought to resist the liberal democratic establishment in West Berlin through bombings, bank robberies, kidnappings, and murders. The group was named after the anniversary of Benno Ohnejorg's death, who was killed in a demonstration against the visiting Shah of Iran in Berlin on June 2,1967. The group was closely associated with the Red Army Faction *(q.v.)* and after the majority of its members had been arrested by the end of the 1970s, the remainder joined the RAF.

mindset—A noun defined by *American Heritage Dictionary* as: "1. A fixed mental attitude or disposition that predetermines a person's response to and interpretation of situations; 2. an inclination or a habit." *Merriam Webster's Collegiate Dictionary* (10th ed.) defines it as 1. A mental attitude or inclination; 2. a fixed state of mind. The term dates from 1926 but apparently is not included in dictionaries of psychology.

mujahideen—A general designation for Muslim fighters engaged in jihad, as well as the name of various Muslim political and paramilitary groups, such as the Afghan *(q.v.)* Mujahideen.

personality—The distinctive and characteristic patterns of thought, emotion, and behavior that define an individual's personal style of interacting with the physical and social environment.

psychopath—A mentally ill or unstable person, especially one having a psychopathic personality *(q.v.)*, according to *Webster's*.

psychopathy—A mental disorder, especially an extreme mental disorder marked usually by egocentric and antisocial activity, according to *Webster's*.

psychopathology—The study of psychological and behavioral dysfunction occurring in mental disorder or in social disorganization, according to *Webster's*.

psychotic—Of, relating to, or affected with psychosis, which is a fundamental mental derangement (as schizophrenia) characterized by defective or lost contact with reality, according to *Webster's*.

Red Army Faction—The RAF, formerly known as the Baader-Meinhof Gang, was a group of German anarchistic leftist terrorists active from May 11, 1972, to the early 1990s. *(q.v.,* Baader-Meinhof Gang)

sociopath—Basically synonymous with psychopath *(q.v.)*. Sociopathic symptoms in the adult sociopath include an inability to tolerate delay or frustration, a lack of guilt feelings, a relative lack of anxiety, a lack of compassion for others, a hypersensitivity to personal ills, and a lack of responsibility. Many authors prefer the term *sociopath* because this type of person had defective socialization and a deficient childhood.

sociopathic—Of, relating to, or characterized by asocial or antisocial behavior or a psychopathic *(q.v.)* personality, according to *Webster's.*

terrorism—the calculated use of unexpected, shocking, and unlawful violence against noncombatants (including, in addition to civilians, off-duty military and security personnel in peaceful situations) and other symbolic targets perpetrated by a clandestine member(s) of a subnational group or a clandestine agent for the psychological purpose of publicizing a political or religious cause and/or intimidating or coercing a government(s) or civilian population into accepting demands on behalf of the cause.

Bibliography

Alape, Arturo. *Las vidas de Pedro Antonio Marín/Manuel Marulanda Vélez: Tirofijo.* Bogotá: Planeta, 1989.

Alexander, Yonah, and John M. Gleason (eds.) *Behavioral and Quantitative Perspectives on Terrorism.* New York: Pergamon, 1981.

Alexander, Yonah, and Lawrence Zelic Freedman (eds.) *Perspectives on Terrorism.* Wilmington, Delaware: Scholarly Resources, 1983.

Amos II, John W. "Terrorism in the Middle East: The Diffusion of Violence." Pages 149–62 in David Partington (ed.) *Middle East Annual,* 1984. London: G.K. Hall, 1985.

Anonymous. "The Psychology of Terrorism." *Security Digest* 18. Washington: Wilson Center Reports, 1987.

Anonymous. "Terrorism: Psyche or Psychos?" *TVI Journal* 3 (1982):3–11.

Aston, C.C. "Political Hostage—Taking in Western Europe." Pages 57–83 in W. Gutteridge (ed.) *Contemporary Terrorism.* New York: Facts on File, 1986.

Bandura, Albert. "Mechanisms of Moral Disengagement." Pages 161–91 in Walter Reich (ed.) *Origins of Terrorism: Psychologies, Ideologies, Theologies, States of Mind.* Cambridge: Cambridge University Press, 1990.

Barkey, Henri J., and Graham E. Fuller. *Turkey's Kurdish Question.* Carnegie Commission on Preventing Deadly Conflict Series. Lanham, Maryland, and Oxford, England: Rowman and Littlefield, 1998.

Becker, Julian. *Hitler's Children: The Story of the Baader-Meinhof Terrorist Gang.* Philadelphia: J.B. Lippincott, 1977.

Behar, Richard. "The Secret Life of Mahmud the Red," *Time,* October 4, 1993, 55–61.

Bell, J. Bowyer. "Old Trends and Future Realities." *Washington Quarterly,* Spring 1985.

Bell, J. Bowyer. "Psychology of Leaders of Terrorist Groups." *International Journal of Group Tensions* 12 (1982):84–104.

Benedek, E.P. *The Psychiatric Aspects of Terrorism.* Washington: American Psychiatric Association, 1980.

Benson, Mike, Mariah Evans, and Rita Simon. "Women as Political Terrorists." *Research in Law, Deviance, and Social Control* 4 (1982):121–30.

Berkowitz, B.J., et al. *Superviolence: The Threat of Mass Destruction Weapons.* Santa Barbara, California: ADCON Corporation, 1972.

Billig, Otto. "The Lawyer Terrorist and His Comrades," *Political Psychology* 6 (1985) 29-46.

Bodansky, Yossef. *Bin Laden: The Man Who Declared War on America.* Rocklin, Georgia: Prima, 1999.

Bollinger, L. "Terrorist Conduct as a Result of a Psychological Process." In World Congress of Psychiatry, *Psychiatry: The State of the Art* 6. New York: Plenum, 1985.

Brackett, D.W. *Holy Terror: Armageddon in Tokyo.* New York: Weatherhill, 1996.

Bruinessen, Martin van. "Kurdish Society, Ethnicity, Nationalism and Refugee Problems." Pages 33-67 in Philip G. Kreyenbroek and Stefan Sperl (eds.) *The Kurds: A Contemporary Overview.* Routledge/SOAS Politics and Culture in the Middle East Series. London and New York: Routledge, 1992.

Bulloch, John, and Harvey Morris. *No Friends but the Mountains: The Tragic History of the Kurds.* New York and Oxford: Oxford University Press, 1992.

Ciment, James. *The Kurds: State and Minority in Turkey, Iraq and Iran.* Conflict and Crisis in the Post-Cold War World Series. New York: Facts on File, 1996.

Clark, R. "Patterns in the Lives of ETA Members." *Terrorism* 6 No. 3 (1983):423–54.

Cohen, G. *Women of Violence: Memoirs of a Young Terrorist.* Stanford, California: Stanford University Press, 1966.

Combs, Cindy C. *Terrorism in the Twenty-First Century.* Upper Saddle River, New Jersey: Prentice Hall, 1997.

Cooper, H.H.A. "Psychopath as Terrorist." *Legal Medical Quarterly* 2 (1978):253–62.

Cooper, H.H.A. "What Is a Terrorist? A Psychological Perspective." *Legal Medical Quarterly* 1 (1977):16–32.

Corrado, Raymond R. "A Critique of the Mental Disorder Perspective of Political Terrorism," *International Journal of Law and Psychiatry* 4 (1981):293–309.

Cordes, Bonnie. *When Terrorists Do the Talking: Reflections on Terrorist Literature.* Santa Monica, California: Rand, August 1987.

Corsun, Andrew. "Group Profile: The Revolutionary Organization 17 November in Greece (1975–91)." Pages 93–126 in Dennis A. Pluchinsky and Yonah Alexander (eds.) *European Terrorism: Today & Tomorrow.* Washington: Brassey's 1992.

Crayton, John W. "Terrorism and the Psychology of the Self." Pages 33–41 in Lawrence Zelic Freedman and Yonah Alexander (eds.) *Perspectives on Terrorism*. Wilmington, Delaware: Scholarly Resources, 1983.

Crenshaw, Martha. "The Causes of Terrorism." *Comparative Politics* 13 (July 1981):379–99.

Crenshaw, Martha. "Current Research on Terrorism: The Academic Perspective," *Studies in Conflict and Terrorism* 15 (1992):1–11.

Crenshaw, Martha. "An Organization Approach to the Analysis of Political Terrorism." *Orbis* 29 (1985):465–89.

Crenshaw, Martha. "The Psychology of Political Terrorism." Pages 379–413 in Margaret Hermann (ed.) *Handbook of Political Psychology*. San Francisco: Jossey-Bass, 1985.

Crenshaw, Martha. "Questions to Be Answered, Research to Be Done, Knowledge to Be Applied." Pages 247–60 in Walter Reich (ed.) *Origins of Terrorism: Psychologies, Ideologies, Theologies, States of Mind*. Cambridge: Cambridge University Press, 1990.

Crenshaw, Martha. "Theories of Terrorism: Instrumental and Organizational Approaches." Pages 13–31 in David Rapoport (ed.) *Inside Terrorist Organizations*. New York: Columbia University Press, 1988.

Cubert, Harold M. *The PFLP's Changing Role in the Middle East*. London and Portland, Oregon: Frank Cass, 1997.

Daly, L.N. "Terrorism: What Can the Psychiatrist Do?." *Journal of Forensic Sciences* 26 (1981):116–22.

Davies, T.R. "Aggression, Violence, Revolution and War." Pages 234–60 in Jeanne N. Knutson (ed.) *Handbook of Political Psychology*. San Francisco: Jossey-Bass, 1973.

Dedman, Bill. "Secret Service Is Seeking Pattern for School Killers." *New York Times*, June 21, 1999, A10.

Della Porta, Donatella. "Political Socialization in Left-Wing Underground Organizations: Biographies of Italian and German Militants." In Donatella Della Porta (ed.) *Social Movements and Violence: Participation in Underground Organizations*, 4. Greenwich, Connecticut: JAI Press, 1992.

Dobson, Christopher. *Black September: Its Short, Violent History*. London: Robert Hale, 1975.

Dowling, Joseph A. "A Prolegomena to a Psychohistorical Study of Terrorism." In Marius Livingston (ed.) *International Terrorism in the Contemporary World*. Westwood, Connecticut: Greenwood, 1978.

Doyle, Leonard. "The Cold Killers of 17 November Who Always Go Free." *The Observer* [London], September 28, 1997.

Eckstein, Harry. "On the Etiology of Internal Wars." In Ivo K. Feierabend, Rosalind L. Feierabend, and Ted Robert Gurr (eds.) *Anger, Violence and Politics: Theories and Research*. Englewood Cliffs, New Jersey: Prentice-Hall, 1972.

Elliot, John D., and Leslie K. Gibson (eds.) *Contemporary Terrorism: Selected Readings.* Gaithersburg, Maryland: International Association of Chiefs of Police, 1978.

Elliott, Paul. *Brotherhoods of Fear: A History of Violent Organizations.* London: Blandford, 1998.

Entessar, Nader. *Kurdish Ethnonationalism.* Boulder, Colorado: Lynne Rienner, 1992.

Falk, Richard. "The Terrorist Mind-Set: The Moral Universe of Revolutionaries and Functionaries." In Richard Falk (ed.) *Revolutionaries and Functionaries: The Dual Face of Terrorism.* New York: E.P. Dutton, 1988.

Farrell, William R. *Blood and Rage: The Story of the Japanese Red Army.* Lexington, Massachusetts: Lexington Books, 1990.

Ferracuti, Franco. "Ideology and Repentance: Terrorism in Italy." Pages 59–64 in Walter Reich (ed.) *Origins of Terrorism: Psychologies, Ideologies, Theologies, States of Mind.* Cambridge, England: Cambridge University Press, 1990.

Ferracuti, Franco. "Psychiatric Aspects of Terrorism in Italy." In I.L. Barak-Glantz and U.R. Huff (eds.) *The Mad, the Bad, and the Different.* Lexington, Massachusetts: Lexington, 1981.

Ferracuti, Franco. "A Psychiatric Comparative—Analysis of Left and Right Terrorism in Italy." In *World Congress of Psychiatry, Psychiatry: The State of the Art* 6. New York: Plenum, 1985.

Ferracuti, Franco. "A Sociopsychiatric Interpretation of Terrorism." *The Annals of the American Academy of Political and Social Science* 463 (September 1982):129–41.

Ferracuti, Franco, and F. Bruno. "Psychiatric Aspects of Terrorism in Italy." Pages 199–213 in I.L. Barak-Glantz and C.R. Huff (eds.) *The Mad, the Bad and the Different: Essays in Honor of Simon Dinhz.* Lexington, Massachusetts: Lexington Books, 1981.

Fields, Rona M. "Child Terror Victims and Adult Terrorists," *Journal of Psychohistory* 7 No. 1 (Summer 1979):71–76.

Flemming, Peter A., Michael Stohl, and Alex P. Schmid. "The Theoretical Utility of Typologies of Terrorism: Lessons and Opportunities." Pages 153–95 in Michael Stohl (ed.) *The Politics of Terrorism.* Third edition. New York: Marcel Dekker, 1988.

Freedman. Lawrence Zelic. "Terrorism: Problems of the Polistaraxic." Pages 3–18 in Yonah Alexander and L.Z. Freedman (eds.) *Perspectives on Terrorism.* Wilmington, Delaware: Scholarly Resources, 1983.

Freedman, Lawrence Zelic, and Yonah Alexander (eds.) *Perspectives on Terrorism.* Wilmington, Delaware: Scholarly Resources, 1983.

Fried, Risto. "The Psychology of the Terrorist." Pages 119–24 in Brian M. Jenkins (ed.) *Terrorism and Beyond: An International Conference on Terrorism and Low-Level Conflict.* Santa Monica, California: Rand, 1982.

Friedlander, Robert A. "The Psychology of Terrorism: Contemporary Views." In Patrick J. Montana and George S. Roukis (eds.) *Managing Terrorism: Strategies for the Corporate Executive.* Westport, Connecticut: Quorum, 1983.

Foote, Donna. "A Shadow Government: An Insider Describes the Workings of the IRA, Europe's Most Potent Guerrilla Organization," *Newsweek,* September 12, 1988, 37–38.

Galvin, Deborah M. "The Female Terrorist: A Socio-Psychological Perspective." *Behavioral Science and the Law* 1 (1983):19–32.

Georges-Abeyie, Daniel E. "Women as Terrorists." In Lawrence Zelic Freedman and Yonah Alexander (eds.) *Perspectives on Terrorism.* Wilmington, Delaware: Scholarly Resources, 1983.

Goltz, Thomas. "Ankara Dispatch: Just How Authentic Was Abdullah Ocalan's Claim to Represent the Dispossessed of Turkey?" *The New Republic,* March 15, 1999, 14–16.

Greaves, Douglas. "The Definition and Motivation of Terrorism." *Australian Journal of Forensic Science* 13 (1981):160–66.

Gunaratna, Rohan. "LTTE Child Combatants." *Jane's Intelligence Review,* (July 1998)

Gurr, Ted Robert. "Psychological Factors in Civil Violence," *World Politics,* 20 No. 32 (January 1968):245–78.

Gurr, Ted Robert. *Why Men Rebel.* Princeton, New Jersey: Princeton University Press, 1970.

Gutteridge, W (ed.) *Contemporary Terrorism.* New York: Facts on File, 1986.

Guttman, D. "Killers and Consumers: The Terrorist and His Audience," *Social Research* 46 (1979):517–26.

Hacker, Frederick J. *Crusaders, Criminals, Crazies: Terror and Terrorism in Our Time.* New York: W.W. Norton, 1996.

Hacker, Frederick J. "Dialectical Interrelationships of Personal and Political Factors in Terrorism." Pages 19–32 in Lawrence Zelic Freedman and Yonah Alexander (eds.) *Perspectives on Terrorism.* Wilmington, Delaware: Scholarly Resources, 1983.

Hamilton, L.C., and J.D. Hamilton. "Dynamics of Terrorism." *International Studies Quarterly* 27 (1983):39–54;

Harris, Jonathan. "The Mind of the Terrorist." In Jonathan Harris (ed.) *The New Terrorism: Politics of Violence.* New York: Julian Messner, 1983.

Haynal, André, Miklos Molnar, and Gérard de Puymège. *Fanaticism: A Historical and Psychoanalytical Study.* New York: Schocken Books, 1983.

Heskin, Ken. "The Psychology of Terrorism in Ireland." Pages 88–105 in Yonah Alexander and Alan O'Day (eds.) *Terrorism in Ireland.* New York: St. Martin's Press, 1984.

Heyman, E. "The Diffusion of Transnational Terrorism." Pages 190–244 in R. Shultz and S. Sloan (eds.) *Responding to the Terrorist Threat: Security and Crisis Management.* New York: Pergamon, 1980.

Heyman, E., and E. Mickolus. "Imitation by Terrorists: Quantitative Approaches to the Study of Diffusion Patterns in Transnational Terrorism." Pages 175–228 in Yonah Alexander and J.M. Gleason (eds.) *Behavioral and Quantitative Perspectives on Terrorism.* New York: Pergamon, 1980.

Heyman, E., and E. Mickolus. "Observations on Why Violence Spreads." *International Studies Quarterly* 24 (1980):299–305.

Hoffman-Ladd, V.J. "Muslim Fundamentalism: Psychological Profiles." Paper presented at the Fundamentalist Project, M.E. Marty and S.R. Appleby (eds.) 1993.

Holmes, Ronald M., and Stephen T. Holmes. *Profiling Violent Crimes: An Investigative Tool.* Thousand Oaks, California: Sage, 1996.

Holloway, Harry C., and Anne E. Norwood. "Forensic Psychiatric Aspects of Terrorism." Pages 409–451 in R. Gregory Lande, and David T. Armitage (eds.) *Principles and Practice of Military Forensic Psychiatry.* Springfield, Illinois: Charles C. Thomas, 1997.

Hubbard, David G. "The Psychodynamics of Terrorism." Pages 45–53 in Yonah Alexander, T. Adeniran, and R.A. Kilmarx (eds.) *International Violence.* New York: Praeger, 1983.

Hubbard, David G. *The Skyjacker: His Flights of Fantasy.* New York: Macmillan, 1971.

Jaber, Hela. *Hezbollah: Born with a Vengeance.* New York: Columbia University Press, 1977.

Janis, I.L. "Group Identification under Conditions of External Danger." Pages 80–90 in D. Cartwright and A. Zander (eds.) *Group Dynamics.* New York: Free Press, 1968.

Janis, I.L. *Victims of Groupthink.* Boston: Houghton Mifflin, 1972.

Jenkins, Brian M. *High Technology Terrorism and Surrogate Warfare: The Impact of New Technology on Low-Level Violence.* Santa Monica, California: Rand, 1975.

Jenkins, Brian M. "International Terrorism: A New Mode of Conflict." In David Carlton and Carolo Schaerf (eds.) *International Terrorism and World Security.* London: Croom Helm, 1975.

Jenkins, Brian M. "Terrorists at the Threshold." In E. Nobles Lowe and Harry D. Shargel (eds.) *Legal and Other Aspects of Terrorism.* New York: 1979.

Jenkins, Brian M. (ed.) *Terrorism and Beyond: An International Conference on Terrorism and Low-Level Conflict.* Santa Monica, California: Rand, 1982.

Jerome, Richard. "Japan's Mad Messiah: Jailed in Tokyo's Subway Gassing, A Guru is Alone with His Grand Delusions," *People Weekly* 43 No. 23 (June 12, 1995):48.

Johnson, Chalmers. "Perspectives on Terrorism." Reprinted in Walter Laqueur (ed.) *The Terrorism Reader.* New York: New American Library, 1978.

Joshi, Monoj. "On the Razor's Edge: The Liberation Tigers of Tamil Eelam." *Studies in Conflict and Terrorism* 19 No. 1 (1996):19–42.

Juergensmeyer, Mark. *Terror in the Mind of God: The Global Rise of Religious Violence.* Berkeley: University of California Press, 2000.

Kallen, K. *Terrorists—What Are They Like? How Some Terrorists Describe Their World and Actions.* Santa Monica, California: Rand, 1979.

Kaplan, Abraham. "The Psychodynamics of Terrorism." *Terrorism* 1 (1978):237–57.

Kaplan, David, and Andrew Marshall. *The Cult at the End of the World: The Terrifying Story of the Aum Doomsday Cult, from the Subways of Tokyo to the Nuclear Arsenals of Russia.* New York: Crown, 1996.

Karan, Vijay. *War by Stealth: Terrorism in India.* New Delhi: Viking (Penguin Books India), 1997.

Kellen, Konrad. "Ideology and Rebellion: Terrorism in West Germany." Pages 43–58 in Walter Reich (ed.) *Origins of Terrorism: Psychologies, Ideologies, Theologies, States of Mind.* Washington: Woodrow Wilson Center, 1998.

Kellen, Konrad. "Terrorists—What Are They Like? How Some Terrorists Describe Their World and Actions." Pages 125–73 in Brian M. Jenkins (ed.) *Terrorism and Beyond: An International Conference on Terrorism and Low-Level Conflict.* Santa Monica, California: Rand, 1980.

Kent, I., and W. Nicholls. "The Psychodynamics of Terrorism." *Mental Health and Society* 4 (1977):1–8.

Khaled, Leila. *My People Shall Live: The Autobiography of a Revolutionary.* George Hajjar (ed.) London: Hodder and Stoughton, 1973.

Kifner, John. "Alms and Arms: Tactics in a Holy War." *New York Times,* March 15, 1996, A1, A8.

Kim, Hyun Hee. *The Tears of My Soul.* New York: Morrow, 1994.

Knutson, Jeanne N. "Social and Psychodynamic Pressures Toward a Negative Identity." Pages 105–52 in Yonah Alexander and John M. Gleason (eds.) *Behavioral and Quantitative Perspectives on Terrorism.* New York: Pergamon, 1981.

Knutson, Jeanne N. "The Terrorists' Dilemmas: Some Implicit Rules of the Game." *Terrorism* 4 (1980):195-222.

Knutson, Jeanne N. "Toward a United States Policy on Terrorism." *Political Psychology* 5, No. 2 (June 1984):287–94.

Knutson, Jeanne N. (ed.) *Handbook of Political Psychology.* San Francisco: Jossey-Bass, 1973.

Kolinsky, Eva. "Terrorism in West Germany. Pages 75–76 in Juliet Lodge (ed.) *The Threat of Terrorism.* Boulder, Colorado: Westview Press, 1988.

Kovaleski, Serge F. "Rebel Movement on the Rise: Leftist Guerrillas Use Military Force, Not Ideology, to Hold Power." *Washington Post,* February 5, 1999, A27–28.

Kramer, Martin. "The Structure of Shi'ite Terrorism." Pages 43–52 in Anat Kurz (ed.) *Contemporary Trends in World Terrorism.* New York: Praeger, 1987.

Kreyenbroek, Philip G., and Stefan Sperl (eds.) *The Kurds: A Contemporary Overview. Routledge/SOAS Politics and Culture in the Middle East Series.* London and New York: Routledge, 1992.

Kross, Peter. *Spies, Traitors, and Moles: An Espionage and Intelligence Quiz Book.* Lilburn, Georgia: IllumiNet Press, 1998.

Kurz, Anat (ed.) *Contemporary Trends in World Terrorism.* New York: Praeger, 1987.

Kurz, Anat, with Nahman Tal. *Hamas: Radical Islam in a National Struggle.* Tel Aviv: Jaffee Center for Strategic Studies, Tel Aviv University, 1997.

Kushner, Harvey W. "Suicide Bombers: Business as Usual," *Studies in Conflict and Terrorism* 19 No. 4 (1996):329–37.

Kushner, Harvey W. *Terrorism in America: A Structural Approach to Understanding the Terrorist Threat.* Springfield, Illinois: Charles C. Thomas, 1998.

Labeviere, Richard. *Les dollars de la terreur: Les États-Unis et les Islamistes.* Paris: Grasset, 1999.

Laqueur, Walter. *The Age of Terrorism.* Boston: Little, Brown, 1987.

Laqueur, Walter. *Terrorism.* Boston: Little, Brown, 1977.

Lewis, Bernard. "License to Kill: Usama bin Ladin's Declaration of Jihad," *Foreign Affairs* 77 No. 6 (November/December 1998):14–19.

Lodge, Juliet (ed.) *The Threat of Terrorism.* Boulder, Colorado: Westview Press, 1988.

MacDonald, Eileen. *Shoot the Women First.* New York: Random House, 1992.

Margolin, Joseph. "Psychological Perspectives in Terrorism." Pages 273–74 in Yonah Alexander and Seymour Maxwell Finger (eds.) *Terrorism: Interdisciplinary Perspectives.* New York: John Jay, 1977.

Mathiu, Mutuma. "The Kurds Against the World: Why Abdullah Ocalan Is a Hero to Kurds." *World Press Review* 46 No. 5 (May 1999.)

McCauley, C.R., and M.E. Segal. "Social Psychology of Terrorist Groups." In C. Hendrick (ed.) *Group Processes and Intergroup Relations,* Vol. 9 of Annual Review of Social and Personality Psychology. Beverly Hills: Sage, 1987.

McKnight, Gerald. *The Mind of the Terrorist.* London: Michael Joseph, 1974.

Melman, Yossi. *The Master Terrorist: The True Story Behind Abu Nidal.* New York: Adama, 1986.

Merari, Ariel. "Problems Related to the Symptomatic Treatment of Terrorism," *Terrorism* 3 (1980):279–83.

Merari, Ariel, and N. Friedland. "Social Psychological Aspects of Political Terrorism." in S. Oskamp (ed.) *Applied Social Psychology Annual.* Beverly Hills, California: Sage, 1985.

Mickolus, Edward F., with Susan L. Simmons. *Terrorism, 1992–1995: A Chronology of Events and A Selectively Annotated Bibliography.* Westport, Connecticut: Greenwood Press, 1997.

Middendorf, Wolf. "The Personality of the Terrorist." In M. Kravitz (ed.) *International Summaries: A Collection of Selected Translations in Law Enforcement and Criminal Justice* 3. Rockville, Maryland: National Criminal Justice Reference Service, 1979.

Midlarsky, M.I., Martha Crenshaw, and F. Yoshida. "Why Violence Spreads: The Contagion of International Terrorism," *International Studies Quarterly* 24 (1980):262–98.

Milbank, D.L. *International and Transnational Terrorism: Diagnosis and Prognosis.* Washington: Central Intelligence Agency, 1976.

Mishal, Shaul, and Avraham Sela. *Hamas: A Behavioral Profile.* Tel Aviv: The Tami Steinmetz Center for Peace Research, Tel Aviv University, 1997.

Monroe, Kristen Renwick, and Lina Haddad Kreidie. "The Perspective of Islamic Fundamentalists and the Limits of Rational Choice Theory." *Political Psychology* 18 No. 1 (1997):19–43.

Mullen, R.K. "Mass Destruction and Terrorism," *Journal of International Affairs* 32 No. 1 (1978):62–89.

Mylroie, Laurie. "The World Trade Center Bomb: Who Is Ramzi Yousef? And Why It Matters." *U.S. News and World Report,* 118, No. 7, February 20, 1995, 50–54.

Neuburger, Luisella de Cataldo, and Tiziana Valentini. *Women and Terrorism.* New York: St. Martin's Press, 1996.

Neuhauser, P. "The Mind of a German Terrorist: Interview with M.C. Baumann." *Encounter* (September 1978):81–88.

Oberst, Robert C. "Sri Lanka's Tamil Tiger." *Conflict* 8 No. 2/3 (1988): 185–202.

O'Ballance, Edgar. *The Kurdish Struggle, 1920–94.* London: Macmillan Press, 1996.

O'Ballance, Edgar. *The Language of Violence: The Blood Politics of Terrorism.* San Rafael, California: Presidio Press, 1979.

Oots, Kent Layne, and Thomas C. Wiegele. "Terrorist and Victim: Psychiatric and Physiological Approaches from a Social Science Perspective," *Terrorism: An International Journal* 8 No. 1 (1985):1–32.

Paine, L. T*he Terrorists.* London: Robert Hale, 1975.

Pearlstein, Richard M. *The Mind of the Political Terrorist.* Wilmington, Delaware: Scholarly Resources, 1991.

Post, Jerrold. "Current Understanding of Terrorist Motivation and Psychology: Implications for a Differentiated Antiterrorist Policy." *Terrorism* 13 No. 1 (1990):65–71.

Post, Jerrold M. "'Hostilité, Conformité, Fraternité': The Group Dynamics of Terrorist Behavior." *International Journal of Group Psychotherapy* 36 No. 2 (1986):211–24.

Post, Jerrold M. "Individual and Group Dynamics of Terrorist Behavior." In *World Congress of Psychiatry, Psychiatry: The State of the Art* 6. New York: Plenum, 1985.

Post, Jerrold M. "Notes on a Psychodynamic Theory of Terrorist Behavior," *Terrorism: An International Journal* 7 No. 3 (1984):242–56.

Post, Jerrold M. "Rewarding Fire with Fire? Effects of Retaliation on Terrorist Group Dynamics." Pages 103–115 in Anat Kurz (ed.) *Contemporary Trends in World Terrorism.* New York: Praeger, 1987.

Post, Jerrold M. "Terrorist Psycho-Logic: Terrorist Behavior as a Product of Psychological Forces." Pages 25–40 in Walter Reich (ed.) *Origins of Terrorism: Psychologies, Ideologies, Theologies, States of Mind.* Cambridge, England: Cambridge University Press, 1990.

Prunckun, Jr., Henry W. *Shadow of Death: An Analytic Bibliography on Political Violence, Terrorism, and Low-Intensity Conflict.* Lanham, Maryland, and London: Scarecrow Press, 1995.

Rapoport, David C. *Assassination and Terrorism.* Toronto: CBC Merchandising, 1971.

Rapoport, David C. "Fear and Trembling: Terrorism in Three Religious Traditions," *American Political Science Review* 78 No. 3 (1984):655–77.

Rapoport, David C. "Sacred Terror: A Contemporary Example from Islam." Pages 103–30 in Walter Reich (ed.) *Origins of Terrorism: Psychologies, Ideologies, Theologies, States of Mind.* Cambridge, England: Cambridge University Press, 1990.

Rasch, W. "Psychological Dimensions of Political Terrorism in the Federal Republic of Germany," *International Journal of Law and Psychiatry* 2 (1979):79–85.

Reeve, Simon. *The New Jackals: Ramzi Yousef, Osama bin Laden and the Future of Terrorism.* Boston: Simon Reeve/Northeastern University Press, 1999.

Reich, Walter (ed.) *Origins of Terrorism: Psychologies, Ideologies, Theologies, States of Mind.* Cambridge, England: Cambridge University Press, 1990.

Robins, Robert S., and Jerrold M. Post. *Political Paranoia: The Psychopolitics of Hatred.* New Haven, Connecticut: Yale University Press, 1997.

Rogers, John D., Jonathan Spencer, and Jayadeva Uyangoda. "Sri Lanka: Political Violence and Ethnic Conflict," *American Psychologist* 58 No. 7 (July 1998):771–77.

Ronfeldt, David, and William Sater. "The Mindsets of High-Technology Terrorists: Future Implication from an Historical Analog." Pages 15–38 in Yonah Alexander and Charles K. Ebinger (eds.) *Political Terrorism and Energy: The Threat and the Response.* New York: Praeger, 1982.

Rosenberg, Tina. *Children of Cain: Violence and the Violent in Latin America.* New York: Morrow, 1991.

Russell, Charles A., and Bowman H. Miller. "Profile of a Terrorist." Pages 81–95 in John D. Elliott and Leslie K. Gibson (eds.) *Contemporary Terrorism: Selected Readings.* Gaithersburg, Maryland: International Association of Chiefs of Police, 1978.

Russell, Charles A., and Bowman H. Miller. "Profile of a Terrorist." *Terrorism: An International Journal* 1 No. 1 (1977):17–34.

Salewski, Wolfgang D. "The Latest Theory Recognized by Sociological Research in Terrorism and Violence." *Terrorism* 3 (1980):297–301.

Samaranayake, Gamini. "Political Violence in Sri Lanka: A Diagnostic Approach." *Terrorism and Political Violence* 9 No. 2 (Summer 1997):99–119.

Schalk, P. "Resistance and Martyrdom in the Process of State Formation of Tamililam." Pages 61–83 in J. Pettigrew (ed.) *Martyrdom and Political Resistance: Essays From Asia and Europe.* Amsterdam: VU University Press, 1997.

Schalk, P. "Women Fighters of the Liberation Tigers in Tamil Ilam: The Martial Feminism of Atel Palancinkam." *South Asia Research* 14 (1994):163–83.

Schmid, Alex P., and Albert J. Jongman. *Political Terrorism: A New Guide to Actors, Authors, Concepts, Data Bases, Theories, and Literature.* New Brunswick, New Jersey: Transaction Books, 1988.

Schweitzer, Yoram. "Terrorism: A Weapon in the Shi'ite Arsenal." Pages 66–74 in Anat Kurz (ed.) *Contemporary Trends in World Terrorism.* New York: Praeger, 1987.

Shaw, Eric D. "Political Terrorists: Dangers of Diagnosis and an Alternative to the Psychopathology Model." *International Journal of Law and Psychiatry* 8 (1986):359–68.

Shifter, Michael. "Colombia on the Brink: There Goes the Neighborhood," *Foreign Affairs* 78 No. 4 (July/August 1999):14–20.

Silj, Alessandro. *Never Again Without a Rifle: The Origins of Italian Terrorism.* New York: Karz, 1979.

Spaeth, Anthony. "Engineer of Doom: Cult Leader Shoko Asahara Didn't Just Forecast Armageddon, He Planned It (Japan's Aum Shinrikyo Guru Planned to Precipitate World War)." *Time,* 145, No. 24, June 12, 1995, 57.

Sprinzak, Ehud. "The Psychopolitical Formation of Extreme Left Terrorism in a Democracy: The Case of the Weathermen." Pages 65–85 in Walter Reich (ed.) *Origins of Terrorism: Psychologies, Ideologies, Theologies, States of Mind.* Cambridge, England: Cambridge University Press, 1990.

Steinhoff, Patricia G. "Portrait of a Terrorist: An Interview with Kozo Okamoto." *Asian Survey* 16 No. 9 (September 1976):830–45.

Stern, Jessica. *The Ultimate Terrorists.* Cambridge, Massachusetts: Harvard University Press, 1999.

Stohl, Michael (ed.) *The Politics of Terrorism.* Third edition. New York: Marcel Dekker, 1988.

Strentz, Thomas. "The Terrorist Organizational Profile: A Psychological Role Model." Pages 86–104 in Yonah Alexander and John M. Gleason (eds.) *Behavioral and Quantitative Perspectives on Terrorism.* New York: Pergamon, 1981.

Strentz, Thomas. "A Terrorist Psychosocial Profile: Past and Present." *Law Enforcement Bulletin* 57 No. 4 (1988):11–18.

Sullwold, Lilo. "Biographical Features of Terrorists." In *World Congress of Psychiatry, Psychiatry: The State of the Art* 6. New York: Plenum, 1985.

Taheri, Amir. *Holy Terror: Inside the World of Islamic Terrorism.* Bethesda, Maryland: Adler and Adler, 1987.

Tanter, Raymond. *Rogue Regimes: Terrorism and Proliferation.* New York: St. Martin's Griffin, 1999.

Taylor, Maxwell. *The Terrorist.* London: Brassey's, 1988.

Taylor, Maxwell, and Ethel Quayle. *Terrorist Lives.* London and Washington: Brassey's, 1994.

Taylor, Maxwell, and Helen Ryan. "Fanaticism, Political Suicide and Terrorism." *Terrorism* 11 No. 2 (1988):91–111.

Thiranagama, Rajani, Rajan Hoole, Daya Somasundaram, and K. Sritharan. *The Broken Palmyra: The Tamil Crisis in Sri Lanka: An Inside Account.* Claremont, California: Sri Lankan Studies Institute, 1990.

"TVI Profile Report: Fatah Revolutionary Council (FRC)." *TVI Profile* 8 No. 3 (1989):5–8.

"TVI Profile Report: Hizbollah (Party of God)," *TVI Profile* 9 No. 3 (1990):1–6.

"TVI Profile Report: Provisional Irish Republican Army (PIRA)." *TVI Profile* 8 No. 2 (1988):13–15.

United States. Department of State. *Patterns of Global Terrorism, 1998.* Washington, DC: 1999.

Wagenlehner, Gunther. "Motivation for Political Terrorism in West Germany." Pages 195–203 in Marius H. Livingston (ed.) *International Terrorism in the Contemporary World.* Westport, Connecticut: Greenwood Press, 1978.

Warren, Ward W. (ed.) "1996 AFIO Convention on Changing Trends in Terrorism," *Periscope: Newsletter of the Association of Former Intelligence Officers* 22 No. 1 (1997).

Wasmund, Klaus. "The Political Socialization of West German Terrorists." In Peter H. Merkl (ed.) *Political Violence and Terror: Motifs and Motivations.* Berkeley: University of California Press, 1986.

Watanabe, Manabu. "Religion and Violence in Japan Today: A Chronological and Doctrinal Analysis of Aum Shinrikyo." *Terrorism and Political Violence* [London] 10 No. 4 (Winter 1998):80–100.

Wege, Carl Anthony. "The Abu Nidal Organization." *Terrorism* 14 (January–March 1991):59–66.

Weinberg, Leonard, and William Lee Eubank. "Italian Women Terrorists," *Terrorism: An International Journal* 9 No. 3 (1987):241–62.

Wickham-Crowley, Timothy P. *Guerrillas and Revolution in Latin America: A Comparative Study of Insurgents and Regimes since 1956.* Princeton, New Jersey: Princeton University Press, 1992.

Wijesekera, Daya. "The Cult of Suicide and the Liberation Tigers of Tamil Eelam." *Low Intensity Conflict & Law Enforcement* 5 No. 1 (Summer 1996):18–28.

Wijesekera, Daya. "The Liberation Tigers of Tamil Eelam (LTTE): The Asian Mafia." *Low Intensity Conflict & Law Enforcement* 2 No. 2 (Autumn 1993):308–17.

Wilkinson, Paul. "Hamas—An Assessment." *Jane's Intelligence Review* 5 No. 7 (July 1993):31–32.

Wilkinson, Paul. *Political Terrorism.* London: Macmillan, 1974.

Wilkinson, Paul. "Terrorism: International Dimensions." Pages 29–56 in *Contemporary Terrorism.* New York: Facts on File, 1986.

Wolman, Benjamin B. "Psychology of Followers of Terrorist Groups." *International Journal of Group Tensions* 12 (1982):105–21.

Wright, Robin. *Sacred Rage: The Wrath of Militant Islam.* New York: Linden Press/Simon and Schuster, 1985.

Zawodny, J.K. "Internal Organizational Problems and the Sources of Tension of Terrorist Movements as Catalysts of Violence." *Terrorism* 1 No. 3/4 (1978):277–85.

Zisser, Eyal. "Hizballah in Lebanon—At the Crossroads." *Terrorism and Political Violence* 8 No. 2 (Summer 1996):90–110.

Tactics

Whereas, in the past, terror has been employed to suppress citizenry and preserve the authority of the state, in modern times, terrorism, as it is commonly understood in the West, tends to cluster around political objectives of groups seeking change in their daily existence. One of the most caustic flashpoints of this type of struggle is the ongoing conflict between the nation of Israel and the Palestinian people in the Middle East.

Although many attempts have been made to try to draw an equitable resolution to this problem, there have been many frustrations to a lasting peace. Among the barriers to peace is what many consider to be an ongoing campaign of terrorism from the Palestinians. The following excerpt is a catalog of terror events, which some observers regard as preventing peace between Israel and Palestine.

In response to several requests for updates, the RSC continues to compile a partial list of the tactics used in Palestinian terrorism that resulted in the death of innocents. Since Yasser Arafat "renounced" violence in the Oslo Peace Accords on September 13, 1993, at least forty-nine American citizens, including women and children, have been murdered by Palestinian terrorists and at least another eighty-one Americans have been injured by such terrorists. 869 people have been killed by Palestinian terrorism just since September 2000.

- Homicide* bombing on a bus in a bus station: April 13, 1994; February 25, 1996; March 5, 2002; July 17, 2002
- Homicide bombing on a moving bus: October 19, 1994; July 24, 1995; August 21, 1995; March 3, 1996; March 27, 2001; November 29, 2001; December 2, 2001; March 20, 2002; April 10, 2002; June 18, 2002; August 4, 2002; October 10, 2002; November 21, 2002; March 5, 2003; May 18, 2003; June 11, 2003; August 19, 2003
- Homicide bombing at a hitch-hiking post: February 25, 1996; June 19, 2002; September 9, 2003
- Homicide nail-bombing: March 4, 1996; December 5, 2001; March 21, 2002
- Homicide bombing at a café or restaurant: March 21, 1997; December 22, 2000; August 9, 2001; August 12, 2001; January 25, 2002; February 16, 2002; March 9, 2002; March 30, 2002; March 31, 2002; May 27, 2002; June 11, 2002; April 30, 2003; September 9, 2003
- Homicide bombing in a market: July 30, 1997; March 29, 2002; May 19, 2002
- Homicide bombing on a pedestrian/shopping mall: September 4, 1997; May 18, 2001; December 1, 2001; May 22, 2002; November 4, 2002; May 19, 2003
- Homicide bombing on a downtown street: March 4, 2001; April 22, 2001; July 16, 2001; December 9, 2001; January 27, 2002;

March 2, 2002; March 17, 2002; April 12, 2002; September 18, 2002; January 5, 2003; May 17, 2003
- Homicide bombing at a gas station: March 28, 2001; October 27, 2002
- Homicide bombing in a disco: June 1, 2001; May 7, 2002
- Homicide shrapnel-bombing near a hospital: September 4, 2001
- Homicide bombing at a train station: September 9, 2001; April 24, 2003
- Homicide bombing on a kibbutz: October 7, 2001
- Homicide bombing at a border crossing: November 26, 2001
- Homicide bombing at a hotel: March 7, 2002; March 27, 2002
- Homicide bombing in an emergency medical center: March 31, 2002
- Homicide bombing in a grocery store: June 19, 2003; August 12, 2003
- Homicide bombing in a private home: July 7, 2003
- Car-bombing: February 8, 2001; March 27, 2001; May 27, 2001; July 2, 2001; July 9, 2001; August 8, 2001; August 21, 2001; October 1, 2001; December 12, 2001; February 18, 2002; February 27, 2002; April 1, 2002
- Car-bomb attack on a bus: April 6, 1994; April 9, 1995; November 22, 2000; April 29, 2001; June 5, 2002; October 21, 2002
- Car-bomb attack on military vehicle: October 29, 1998
- Car-bomb attack on a market or shopping district: November 2, 2000; January 1, 2001; April 23, 2001; December 1, 2001
- Car-bomb attack on a bus station: May 25, 2001
- Car-bomb attack on a school: May 30, 2001
- Car-bomb attack on a hotel: November 28, 2002
- Remote-detonated bombing: January 22, 1995
- Remote-detonated bombing alongside a bus: November 20, 2000; July 16, 2002
- Remote-detonated bombing on a bus: September 19, 2002
- Remote-detonated bombing in a service taxi: March 1, 2001
- Remote-detonated bombing involving a military vehicle: June 22, 2001; September 5, 2002
- Remote-detonated bombing in a university facility: July 31, 2002
- Bicycle-bombing attack: November 11, 1994
- Driving a bus into a crowd of people: February 14, 2001
- Shooting citizens in their own homes: April 27, 2002; June 8, 2002; June 20, 2002; August 10, 2002; November 10, 2002; January 17, 2003; March 7, 2003
- Shooting students on the playground: May 28, 2002
- Shooting civilian drivers of moving cars: March 19, 2003; May 5, 2003; June 12, 2003; June 17, 2003; June 20, 2003; June 30, 2003; August 29, 2003
- Attack with a mine: November 9, 2002; February 15, 2003
- Attack with grenades: November 15, 2002; November 28, 2002

NOTE: These tactics are in addition to the innumerable instances of gun-fire, kidnapping, stabbing, stoning, and other such acts of Palestinian terrorists.

—Taken from Ministry of Foreign Affairs of the Government of Israel:
http://www.mfa.gov.il/mfa/go.asp?MFAH0i5d0
http://www.mfa.gov.il/mfa/go.asp?MFAH0ia50

Special thanks to Clyde Mark of the Congressional Research Service.

Historical Uses of Terrorism Tactics

At the level of subnational action, the following is a list of tactics, which have been used or attempted in past attacks. This list is for reference only. The good homeland security specialist should always be thinking of new attacks the terrorist may attempt and how to counter them.

- Bombing (suicide, planted, timer-detonated, remote-activated)
- Car/truck bomb
- Military grade explosive (hand grenade, mortar)
- Rocket Propelled Grenade (RPG)
- Missile (shoulder fired, heatseeking)
- Rigging artillery shells
- Hijacking (unlawfully seizing control of a conveyance: airplane, train, bus)
- Hostage taking
- Incendiary device, arson
- Knife attack
- Kidnapping
- Letter bomb
- Mailed hazardous material, chemical, biological (anthrax letters)
- Small arms shooting
- Assasination
- Execution (beheading, stoning, lynching)
- Vandalism
- Bomb threat

Historical Targets of Terrorism

Similarly, the following is a list of common targets of past terror attacks.

- Airport
- Aircraft (civil, cargo, general)
- Banking and financial institutions
- Vacation areas and resorts

Palestinian dressed as a
suicide bomber.
Courtesy of Corbis Images.

Blindfolded American hostages. *Courtesy of
Bettman/Corbis Images.*

Car in flames. *Courtesy of Image Bank/Getty
Images, Inc.*

- Private residences
- Office buildings
- Buses
- Military or cargo convoys
- Commercial ships
- Passenger ships
- Hotels
- Individual business travelers
- Students
- Tourists and tourist destinations
- Executives
- Celebrities
- Diplomats
- Missionaries
- Places of worship
- Embassies
- Government facilities
- Military installations
- Nightclubs
- Casinos
- Fastfood
- Restaurants
- Cafés
- Recreational and entertainment facilities
- Marketplaces
- Pipelines
- Checkpoints/border crossings
- Trains/railways
- Subways
- Taxis

The Concept of Asymmetrical Warfare

"Asymmetry" is a term for an unequal; meaning that two sides of something could not be divided equally or proportionately. Asymmetrical warfare, like terrorism, is another area in which scholars, historians, and officials have had difficulty arriving at one comprehensive definition. Generally speaking, though, asymmetrical warfare is the military term for a conflict in which combatants on both sides are not equally matched in terms of force size, weaponry, technology, funding, and organization.

Chechen fighters in Grozny. *Courtesy of AP/Wide World Photos.*

U.S. Marines in combat gear. *Courtesy of Hulton Archive/Getty Images, Inc.*

Asymmetrical warfare is the "David and Goliath" phenomena, in which one force is larger, better trained, better equipped and better organized than the other. As a result, the smaller and/or less sophisticated force will often resort to different tactics than a conventional military force would. Realizing their inability to withstand a conventional warfighting scenario against a large military power, the smaller force will employ a strategy such as insurgency, attrition, harassment, or terrorism.

Although the term "asymmetrical warfare" was coined only relatively recently, the phenomenon has been around for thousands of years. Here are some examples from history of less sophisticated and smaller forces successfully challenging larger militaries:

- *Teutoberg Forest, 16 AD*—Germanic Tribes ambushed and slaughtered the XVII, XVIII, and XIX Legions of the Roman Army in central Europe. Considered by many historians to be a crucial defeat of Roman military might and the "beginning of the end" for the empire. The Germania Province was at the far northeastern edge of the Roman Empire. When the tribes there did not readily submit to Roman authority, the governor slowly began mounting a large scale military incursion to put down Germanic dissention. A double cross from local leaders who had pledged to aid the Romans, foul weather, hostile terrain, and an overly long convoy line conspired to significantly erode the Roman's fighting readiness. The Germanic tribes employed their advantage of swiftness ironically because they were less heavily armored or well-armed than the

Washington crossing Delaware. *Courtesy of Bettman/ Corbis Images.*

Roman legions. These factors allowed the lightly armed, disorganized tribes to slaughter about 20,000 legionaires and support personnel over a period of three days.

• *The American War for Independence, 1776–1781*—The revolutionary army, navy, and militias of the United States against the combined forces of the then British super-power. General George Washington led the smaller, less well-armed and well-trained Continental Army and Navy, as well as irregular milita forces and mercenaries, in an attrition and harassment campaign against the superior British force. Despite suffering several defeats, enduring great casualties, and a certain degree of ambivalence among Colonists toward the idea of independence, the Americans held out long enough to tie up and exhaust the British, eventually forcing the British army to disengage and give up the American colonies.

• *Dien Bien Phu, 1954*—Following World War II, France attempted to re-exert authority over its colony in Indochina, today known as Vietnam. The Vietnamese were not eager to be subjugated as a colony again and a revolutionary movement known as the "Viet Minh" became the insurgent resistance to the colonial might of the French. Eventually, the insurgency's resilience and the French lack of clear objectives in the conflict began to exhaust the French army and threatened their hold over Indochina. The battle at Dien Bien Phu was an attempt by the French army to drag the Viet Minh insurgency into a conventional battle. The French command hoped that by luring the Viet Minh into a pitched battle they could use their superior military power, artillery, and aerial bombardment to inflict massive casualties on the insurgents. The Viet Minh, however, used their superior knowledge of the land, stealth, and their innovation in logistics transport to surprise the French and lay siege to the fortress at Dien Bien Phu. After two excruciating months, the French, despite their superior military force and funding, had to surrender the fort and, soon after, their colony.

• *Invasion of Afghanistan, 1979–1989*—At the height of the Cold War, the Soviet Union ordered almost 175,000 troops, including armor, artillery, and air power, into Afghanistan to support the unpopular communist government of that nation. Although the Soviets killed upwards of 90,000 Afghanis and injured another 90,000; spent approximately twenty billion equivalent to U.S. dollars; and were armed with a huge array of modern military machinery, they were eventually driven from Afghanistan in defeat due to a passionate, determined, and relentless guerrilla army who was more emotionally committed to defending their homeland than the Soviet army was to invading it.

- *Operation Iraqi Freedom, 2003–*
Operation Iraqi Freedom, currently unfolding as of this writing, is a very relevant and, for many, very emotional study of both symmetrical and asymmetrical modern warfare. The coalition incursion into Iraq began on March 20, 2003. Within about six weeks, on May 1, 2003, major combat operations were declared to be over, although many difficult aspects of the operation lay ahead. By May 1 the "symmetrical" aspect—that is, the conventional warfare between land forces—was con-

Soldier stands guard in Iraq.
Courtesy of AP/Wide World Photos.

cluded. At that time, the Coalition had suffered 139 fatalities. Since then however, over 1,000 more casualties have been incurred through insurgency and terrorism directed against coalition forces.

—Taken from *http://www.cdi.org/press/press_releases/2001/terrorism100501*

The following thesis, from the Center for Defense Information, provides a comprehensive overview of the challenges presented to strategists and military planners regarding asymmetrical warfare.

Reforging the Sword

October 5, 2001

The tragic and shocking attacks of September 11 have raised fundamental questions about the shape and composition of future U.S. forces. An independent defense review published by the Center for Defense Information, and released just before the attacks, provides a roadmap for substantially restructuring the U.S. military to counter new threats in the first quarter of the Twenty-first century.

The review concludes that the U.S. military can, and must, be restructured to successfully undertake fourth-generation warfare against asymmetric threats—the kind of threats posed by terrorist networks. The study places a premium on the need for addressing personnel issues and doctrine, rather than hardware. It argues for boosting the cohesion and initiative-taking of U.S. troops, and asserts that the agility of America's forces should be enhanced by creating lighter, smaller, and more mobile units. In contrast to the recently-issued Quadrennial Defense Review (QDR), the report suggests reductions in legacy forces to free up resources for transformation of other forces and for the other, ever more important, components of national security.

Extracts from the report, *Reforging the Sword: U.S. Forces for a 21st Century Security Strategy,* particularly relevant to asymmetric warfare and counterterrorism are provided below with page references to the full version of the report. Full and condensed versions of the report are available online at www.cdi.org/mrp.

A Different Form of Warfare

At root, the "American way of war" remains focused on a paradigm variously known as attrition, second-generation, or Industrial Age warfare. This style of war-fighting tends to be linear and slow moving, relying on masses of men and material to physically crush (albeit not necessarily through frontal assaults) or threatening to crush an opponent. Industrially, second-generation warfare emulates and relies on mass production techniques to mobilize, train and equip, and deploy military forces. . .

Real third-generation war fighting breaks battlefield linearity by seeking and exploiting a combination of "spaces and timing" vis-a-vis an enemy—that is, creating or at least finding weak points or gaps in enemy thinking and dispositions and taking advantage of these openings before the opponent can rectify them. The objective of this kind of warfare is to collapse the opponent's will to fight early (ideally, even before becoming decisively engaged) by introducing chaos into his intelligence/surveillance-evaluation/command-action/reaction processes. This can be done by anticipating the actions of the opponent and pre-empting his intentions via unexpected thrusts and parries by highly agile, dispersed friendly forces brought together quickly for the mission and just as quickly dispersed when the action is finished. This type of warfare also may free forces from the ponderous support structure characteristic of Industrial Age warfare.

Just as second- and third-generation warfare intermingle, they are both interpenetrated by what some call fourth-generation warfare. This primarily involves land forces (although targets can be naval vessels and air assets)—irregular or guerrilla warfare carried out by groups motivated by ideology, revenge, lust for power, ethnicity, religion, or some other unifying bond. Such irregulars often are associated with, or supported by, regular military forces, but in the late twentieth century this was less often the case. In fact, there are countervailing trends. There are more small groups or very loosely knit organizations which employ terror by threatening to or actually attacking civilian populations and infrastructure—the so-called asymmetric style of warfare. Some receive support, safe harbor, or encouragement from nations while others seem to operate with little support.

Strategies to Win Asymmetric Warfare

"Asymmetric" warfare . . . can be used with telling effect in major theater wars, in smaller-scale contingencies, and in terrorist attacks. . .

Because of U.S. dominance in [second-generation or attrition] warfare, however, opponents instead are likely to fight "asymmetrically"—avoiding U.S. strengths and attacking its vulnerabilities. They are likely to use either third-generation maneuver warfare (with regular armed forces) or, more likely, fourth-generation irregular warfare (with irregular attacks on vulnerable military units, population, infrastructure, culture, and institutions).

Two great military strategists—an ancient one, Sun Tzu, and a twentieth century one, the late John Boyd—explain how to fight and win such warfare. Broadly, these strategists focused on how to win by outmaneuvering an enemy mentally, so as to limit the need for actual combat. Greatly simplified, their ideas suggest that the following are necessary to win asymmetric war:

A New Operational Focus for the Military on Smaller-Scale Contingencies

Smaller-scale contingencies (SSCs) include a variety of military operations of smaller scale and intensity than major theater or regional wars, such as humanitarian, peacekeeping, peace enforcement, noncombatant evacuation operations, and military action to capture a terrorist or deny him shelter. The September 30, 2001, QDR has moved in the direction of giving more prominence to smaller-scale contingencies by eliminating the strategic necessity to be prepared to fight two major regional wars. More, however, must be done to shift resources, doctrine, and training to reflect the increasing demand for such operations.

The large number and variety of [SSCs], however, call for a new focus on these operations as primary missions for the military in their own right, and suggest reshaping a portion of the force away from intense force-on-force combat and toward these more complex expeditionary missions.

Some suggest that these forces should constitute a special constabulary organization structured along military lines. Such units would not have the military's heavy armament but would be more heavily armed than police. (Alternatively, others suggest enlarging regular military police units.)

The experience of units in SSC interventions in Panama, Haiti, Bosnia, Rwanda-Congo, and Kosovo suggests that creating separate quasi-military units may not be the best course. The very unpredictability of SSCs, which can turn from traditional peacekeeping to peace maintenance and even peace enforcement, argue for forces that are trained to operate across most of the spectrum of conflict. The Marine Corps' "three-block war" unit training regimen that includes scenarios for mid-intensity war-fighting, peacekeeping, and humanitarian relief support seems to be appropriate for the majority of situations that U.S. ground forces actually will face in the foreseeable future.

Directions for Transformation of Forces
- Quicken military forces in order to refocus them on smaller-scale contingencies in which they are likely to face asymmetric or fourth-generation warfare. Improve their mobility, agility, flexibility, and strategy and decision-making cycles.
- These changes envision a corresponding change in war-fighting doctrine that moves away from the ponderous and logistics-heavy formations of the twentieth century to a more mobile, agile, responsive

force. Such a force is made possible by incorporating lighter-weight equipment; better command, control, and communications networks; and improved intelligence, surveillance, and reconnaissance—all designed to allow U.S. commanders to get inside an opponent's observation-orientation-decision-action (OODA) cycle.

- Transform some of the active heavy-armored forces into forces more suited to smaller-scale contingencies. Preserve a heavy capability primarily in the reserves.
- Focus transformation and funding on agile forces such as: light- and medium-weight Army, Marine Corps, Special Operations; littoral Navy; lift, close air support, and interdiction Air Force; and defensive nuclear, biological, and chemical forces and equipment.

Help fund the re-orientation with moderate reductions in the forces that are already overwhelmingly dominant in force-on-force combat such as

- open-ocean Navy,
- nuclear and air superiority Air Force,
- heavy active Army, and
- offensive nuclear forces.

Overall Priorities for the Future

- People: fix personnel problems; adequately fund military readiness and "quality of life."
- Doctrine and training: adequately fund training and refine doctrine for third- and fourth-generation warfare and for joint operations with other nations, civilian agencies, international bodies, and nongovernmental organizations.
- Hardware: improve mobility with airlift, sealift, overseas facility infrastructure, and force transformation; develop equipment for interoperability with allies; prioritize development of human intelligence capabilities (and ability to process data into "understanding") over new satellite or other technical data collection and communication systems.
- Other national security tools: adequately fund other components of national security, including the State Department, economic aid programs, and agencies that deal with transnational issues.

Implications for Units and Weapons

The report proposes a strategy of transforming some of the legacy heavy forces into more agile forces for smaller-scale contingencies. That strategy, the reduction in the heavy-armored force-on-force threat, and the potential for greater allied contributions, if realized, could allow a refocusing of resources on transformed forces and a reduction in overall force size.

Pressure to free up funding and resources for transformed forces may be eased for a while, as military budget increases of tens of billions of dollars annually are likely in the wake of September 11. Nevertheless, at some point the extra funding is likely to dry up, and priorities will have to be set more tightly. Recognizing continuing resource constraints, the QDR noted, "the full promise of transformation will be realized as we divest ourselves of legacy forces and they move off the stage and resources move into new concepts, capabilities, and organizations that maximize our war-fighting effectiveness and the combat potential of America's men and women in uniform."

Reductions proposed in *Reforging the Sword* include

- Army divisions,
- three aircraft carrier battle groups, and
- almost four air wings.

The Marine Corps, with its broad mix of ground, air, and sea capabilities, would keep all three active divisions and air wings.

Certain weapons are more suited—and some are less suited—to the proposed strategy. Priorities suggested are as follows:

Continue or accelerate

- light armored vehicle;
- V-22-like transport aircraft;
- aIrlifters;
- communications and other equipment for interoperability with allies;
- littoral-oriented naval vessels; and
- low-density/high-demand aircraft and tankers.

Delay, cancel or cut

- Crusader howitzer;
- Comanche scout/attack helicopter;
- B-2 bomber;
- CVX, DD-21, NSSN;
- F-22; and
- Nuclear weapons.

Special Operations Capabilities

In the unlikely event that it is well-known where and how a weapon of mass destruction (WMD) attack against the United States is being prepared in a foreign country, U.S. forces can of course conduct pre-emptive attacks. U.S. military strategy should ensure that Special Operations and other forces have a capability for long-range raids to attack weapon development, deployment, or launch sites and command structures if necessary to prevent WMD attacks.

Such forces would also be able to conduct operations to capture terrorists.

Intelligence

Boost the human intelligence capabilities that improve knowledge and understanding of foreign cultures and governments.

Apart from taking advantage of external sources of information like NGOs, the Defense Department needs to substantially improve its organic intelligence capabilities and better develop and integrate foreign area knowledge and understanding into deployed units. Intelligence capabilities for SSCs need to focus as much on understanding the society and politics of an area as on targeting hostile weapons.

The United States is already the world leader in collection and communication of raw data and information. The area that needs attention is moving from data to "knowledge" and then to "understanding."

National Missile Defense

As with SSCs, that there will be future terrorism attempts on U.S. soil is agreed by many observers, but when and exactly where are unpredictable. The assumption, endorsed by virtually every recent special commission or blue-ribbon panel, is that within the first quarter of the twenty-first century the American homeland will suffer a significant deliberate attack involving biological, chemical, nuclear, or radiological sources. Such a prediction moves fourth-generation warfare into the first rank of threats and elevates "homeland defense" to a national priority. . .

However likely or unlikely a terrorist attack, it is not clear that the military component of national security is well-equipped to do much about it. National missile defense is the foremost military option, but it has never been satisfactorily explained why an opponent would choose the expensive, technically difficult, and suicidal method of delivering a weapon of mass destruction via missile rather than via truck, boat, or plane. Some scenarios in which it would be useful to have a working missile defense can always be described, but the program becomes a matter of priorities. The strategy proposed here puts other military needs—not least of which is fully funding personnel, training, and spare parts to ensure that today's forces are fully ready—at a higher priority than a missile defense system of high cost, of unknowable reliability in actual use, and that will likely be politically costly in relations with allies and with Russia and China.

Increased and Improved Collaboration and Integration with Allies and Partners

The proposed strategy calls for a major new effort to boost ability and willingness to conduct military operations multinationally. This rests on an assumption that the conditions exist for allies and friends to increase their military capabilities and activities, and that an ambitious initiative to create a new mindset of collaboration could lead to realization of that potential.

A pivotal component of the strategy proposed here is to join more with partners and allies in concerted military, political, and economic action. For this to happen in the military sphere, allies will have to improve their military capabilities and be more politically ready to intervene than they were in the second half of the twentieth century. (And the United States will have to alter its equipment and doctrine to allow for greater interoperability with allies.)

Integrate with allies and partners to collectively engage with areas of conflict, head off conflict if possible, and jointly intervene if not. Work with them to transform their militaries and to improve joint, multinational capabilities.

"Multinational Jointness." In addition to providing improved understanding of foreign-conflict situations, there is substantial untapped potential for improved collaboration with allied or friendly forces in SSC operations. Operating more equally with foreign forces not only can reduce foreign resentment of the United States as a sole global policeman, but also could improve popular support for such operations domestically. The public is likely to look more favorably on operations with other countries where the United States is not bearing almost all of the burden of cost, casualties, and responsibility.

The Defense Department has worked hard to make the services "joint," in terms of common—or at least compatible—communications, headquarters, equipment, and doctrine. A parallel opportunity may exist for integration of allied forces in SSCs along the lines of what the Defense Department has done for the U.S. services—expanding the concept of "jointness" to include foreign military services. If U.S. and a broad range of other nations' forces train units to be integrated into multinational command structures, a force package with a variety of types of units and nationalities could be assembled quickly for specific operations. Clearly, for this to work, much would need to be done in training, doctrine, and equipment to make allied forces more "interoperable" with U.S. forces. Decades of experience in NATO with this issue should provide a solid base to develop improved joint capability in the age of sophisticated electronics.

Improved Collaboration and Integration with NGOs, Other Government Agencies, and International Organizations

"Civilian Jointness." The definition of "joint and combined forces" may also usefully be broadened to include civilian nongovernmental organizations (NGOs), such as relief agencies, and nonmilitary Other Government Agencies (OGAs), including international organizations. These groups often have been operating in an area before intervention forces arrive and can provide essential understanding of the situation and culture where they are located. U.S. forces have cooperated with such organizations during interventions, but these ad hoc efforts could be substantially improved with development and institutionalization of structures and procedures for cooperation and joint tasking beforehand. While experience has shown that personnel in the field will quickly establish informal structures and methods for coordinating and communicating with nonmilitary actors, relying on this combination of luck, personal history, and experience is very risky. Planners should determine definitions of relevant "mission essential tasks," which NGOs/OGAs are best organized to perform them, and how best to allocate them among the nonmilitary actors.

Improved Collaboration and Integration with
Civilian Agencies on Transnational Issues

Transnational problems such as international drug trafficking, illegal migration, crime, environmental conflict or damage, access to water, and health are often tied together in conflict zones. For example, drugs, crime, the environment, and economic issues are deeply intertwined in the conflict in Colombia. If U.S. forces are present in such conflict zones, it is likely they will be exposed to these issues and may have to deal with them. The approach suggested here is that procedures be improved for military units to collaborate more with the civilian agencies that focus on these issues. Current ad hoc arrangements can be made more effective if a high-level effort is undertaken to assess how military, nonmilitary, international (and nongovernment) organizations can best work together to address these complex issues.

Adjusting Forward Deployment and Increasing
Military Engagement and Mobility

Make U.S. forces more "expeditionary." Adust forward deployment by reducing Cold War heavy, permanently-deployed forces and increasing short-term deployments, exercises, training, military-to-military contacts, and engagement with foreign militaries.

This paper takes the view that short-term, rotational deployments, plus increased military-to-military contacts and training, can serve many of the same goals as large permanent forces in an extensive base infrastructure, and that irregular, as opposed to rote, exercises can establish effective military-to-military relationships. It holds that a more flexible and agile form of forward deployment can reduce the political and other costs of the old version.

Precipitous withdrawal is neither called for nor being called for by allies—yet. Any contemplated reductions should be coordinated with allies before actions are initiated, and usually phased withdrawals—unless other demands are made by host nations—should be the rule. Bringing selected forces back to the United States, coupled with regular combined force exercises and aperiodic deployments of military units, will allow the United States to more centrally position forces to respond to emerging contingencies without being seen as isolationist.

—Taken from *http://www.cdi.org/mrp/mrp-press091001.doc*

International Terrorism

2001 Report on Foreign Terrorist Organizations

Released by the Office of the Coordinator for Counterterrorism
October 5, 2001

Background

The Secretary of State designates Foreign Terrorist Organizations (FTOs), in consultation with the Attorney General and the Secretary of the Treasury. These designations are undertaken pursuant to the Immigration and Nationality Act, as amended by the Antiterrorism and Effective Death Penalty Act of 1996. FTO designations are valid for two years, after which they must be redesignated or they automatically expire. Redesignation after two years is a positive act and represents a determination by the Secretary of State that the organization has continued to engage in terrorist activity and still meets the criteria specified in law.

- In October 1997, former Secretary of State Madeleine K. Albright approved the designation of the first thirty groups as Foreign Terrorist Organizations.
- In October 1999, Secretary Albright recertified twenty-seven of these groups' designations but allowed three organizations to drop from the list because their involvement in terrorist activity had ended and they no longer met the criteria for designation.
- Secretary Albright designated one new FTO in 1999 (Al Qaeda) and another in 2000 (Islamic Movement of Uzbekistan).
- Secretary of State Colin L. Powell has designated two new FTOs (Real IRA and AUC) in 2001.
- In October 2001, Secretary Powell recertified the designation of twenty-six of the twenty-eight FTOs whose designation was due to expire, and combined two previously designated groups (Kahane Chai and Kach) into one.

Current List of Designated Foreign Terrorist Organizations (as of October 5, 2001)

1. Abu Nidal Organization (ANO)

2. Abu Sayyaf Group

3. Armed Islamic Group (GIA)

4. Aum Shinrikyo

5. Basque Fatherland and Liberty (ETA)

6. Gama'a Al-Islamiyya (Islamic Group)

7. HAMAS (Islamic Resistance Movement)

8. Harakat ul-Mujahidin (HUM)

9. Hizballah (Party of God)

10. Islamic Movement of Uzbekistan (IMU)

11. Al-Jihad (Egyptian Islamic Jihad)

12. Kahane Chai (Kach)

13. Kurdistan Workers' Party (PKK)

14. Liberation Tigers of Tamil Eelam (LTTE)

15. Mujahedin-e Khalq Organization (MEK)

16. National Liberation Army (ELN)

17. Palestinian Islamic Jihad (PIJ)

18. Palestine Liberation Front (PLF)

19. Popular Front for the Liberation of Palestine (PFLP)

20. PFLP-General Command (PFLP-GC)

21. Al Qaeda

22. Real IRA

23. Revolutionary Armed Forces of Colombia (FARC)

24. Revolutionary Nuclei (formerly ELA)

25. Revolutionary Organization 17 November

26. Revolutionary People's Liberation Army/Front (DHKP/C)

27. Shining Path (Sendero Luminoso, SL)

28. United Self-Defense Forces of Colombia (AUC)

Legal Criteria for Designation

1. The organization must be foreign.

2. The organization must engage in terrorist activity as defined in Section 212 (a)(3)(B) of the Immigration and Nationality Act.*

3. The organization's activities must threaten the security of U.S. nationals or the national security (national defense, foreign relations, or the economic interests) of the United States.

Effects of Designation

Legal

1. It is unlawful for a person in the United States or subject to the jurisdiction of the United States to provide funds or other material support to a designated FTO.

2. Representatives and certain members of a designated FTO, if they are aliens, can be denied visas or excluded from the United States.

3. U.S. financial institutions must block funds of designated FTOs and their agents and report the blockage to the Office of Foreign Assets Control, U.S. Department of the Treasury.

Other Effects

1. Deters donations or contributions to named organizations

2. Heightens public awareness and knowledge of terrorist organizations

3. Signals to other governments our concern about named organizations

4. Stigmatizes and isolates designated terrorist organizations internationally

The Process

The Secretary of State makes decisions concerning the designation and redesignation of FTOs following an exhaustive interagency review process in which all evidence of a group's activity, from both classified and open sources, is scrutinized. The State Department, working closely with the Justice and Treasury Departments and the intelligence community, prepares a detailed "administrative record" which documents the terrorist activity of the designated FTO. Seven days before publishing an FTO designation in the Federal Register, the Department of State provides classified notification to Congress.

Under the statute, designations are subject to judicial review. In the event of a challenge to a group's FTO designation in federal court, the U.S. government relies upon the administrative record to defend the Secretary's decision. These administrative records contain intelligence information and are therefore classified.

FTO designations expire in two years unless renewed. The law allows groups to be added at any time following a decision by the Secretary, in consultation with the Attorney General and the Secretary of the Treasury. The Secretary may also revoke designations after determining that there are grounds for doing so and notifying Congress.

—Taken from *http://www.state.gov/s/ct/rls/rpt/fto*

The Domestic Terrorism Threat

Domestic terrorist groups represent interests that span the full spectrum of political and economic viewpoints, as well as social issues and concerns. It is important to understand, however, that FBI investigations of domestic terrorist groups or individuals are not predicated upon social or political beliefs; rather, FBI investigations are based upon information regarding planned or actual criminal activity. The FBI views domestic terrorism as the unlawful use, or threatened use, of violence by a group or individual that is based and operating entirely within the United States or its territories without foreign direction and which is committed against persons or property with the intent of intimidating or coercing a government or its population in furtherance of political or social objectives. The current domestic terrorist threat primarily comes from right-wing extremist groups, left-wing and Puerto Rican extremist groups, and special interest extremists.

Right-wing extremist groups. Right-wing terrorist groups often adhere to the principles of racial supremacy and embrace anti-government, anti-regulatory beliefs. Generally, extremist right-wing groups engage in activity that is protected by constitutional guarantees of free speech and assembly. Law enforcement becomes involved when the volatile talk of these groups transgresses into unlawful action.

On the national level, formal right-wing hate groups, such as World Church of the Creator (WCOTC) and the Aryan Nations, represent a continuing terrorist threat. Although efforts have been made by some extremist groups to reduce openly racist rhetoric in order to appeal to a broader segment of the population and to focus increased attention on anti-government sentiment, racism-based hatred remains an integral component of these groups, core orientations.

Right-wing extremists continue to represent a serious terrorist threat. Two of the seven planned acts of terrorism prevented in 1999 were potentially large-scale, high-casualty attacks being planned by organized right-wing extremists. In December 1999, individuals associated with an anti-government group and who were planning to attack a large propane storage facility in Elk Grove, California, were arrested by the Sacramento Joint Terrorism Task Force. When arrested, these individuals were in possession of detonation cord, blasting caps, grenade hulls, weapons, and various chemicals, including ammonium nitrate. Also in 1999, the FBI interrupted plans by members of the Southeastern States Alliance—an umbrella organization of militias in Florida, Georgia, South Carolina, Alabama, and other southern states—to steal weapons from national guard armories in Central Florida, attack power lines in several states, and ambush federal law enforcement officers. The goal of this group was to create social and political chaos, thereby forcing the U.S. Government to declare martial law, an act the group believed would lead to a violent overthrow of the government by the American people.

Left-wing and Puerto Rican extremist groups. The second category of domestic terrorists, left-wing groups, generally profess a revolutionary socialist doctrine and view themselves as protectors of the people against the "dehumanizing effects" of capitalism and imperialism. They aim to bring about change in the United States through revolution rather than through the established political process. From the 1960s to the 1980s, leftist-oriented extremist groups posed the most serious domestic terrorist threat to the United States. In the 1980s, however, the fortunes of the leftist movement changed dramatically as law enforcement dismantled the infrastructure of many of these groups and the fall of communism in Eastern Europe deprived the movement of its ideological foundation and patronage.

Terrorist groups seeking to secure full Puerto Rican independence from the United States through violent means represent one of the remaining active vestiges of left-wing terrorism. While these groups believe that bombings alone will not result in change, they view these acts of terrorism as a means by which to draw attention to their desire for independence. During the 1970s and 1980s, numerous leftist groups, including extremist Puerto Rican separatist groups such as the Armed Forces for Puerto Rican National Liberation (FALN—Fuerzas Armadas de Liberacion Nacional Puertorriquena), carried out bombings on the U.S. mainland, primarily in and around New York City. However, just as the leftist threat in general declined dramatically throughout the 1990s, the threat posed by Puerto Rican extremist groups to mainland U.S. communities decreased during the past decade.

Acts of terrorism continue to be perpetrated, however, by violent separatists in Puerto Rico. Three acts of terrorism and one suspected act of terrorism have taken place in various Puerto Rican locales during the past three years. These acts, including the March 1998 bombing of a superaqueduct project in Arecibo, the bombings of bank offices in Rio Piedras and Santa Isabel in June 1998, and the bombing of a highway in Hato Rey, remain under investigation. The extremist Puerto Rican separatist group Los Macheteros is suspected in each of these attacks.

Anarchists and extremist socialist groups—many of which, such as the Workers' World Party, Reclaim the Streets, and Carnival Against Capitalism—have an international presence and, at times, also represent a potential threat in the United States. For example, anarchists, operating individually and in groups, caused much of the damage during the 1999 World Trade Organization ministerial meeting in Seattle.

Special interest extremists. Special interest terrorism differs from traditional right-wing and left-wing terrorism in that extremist special interest groups seek to resolve specific issues, rather than effect more widespread political change. Special interest extremists continue to conduct acts of politically motivated violence to force segments of society, including the general public, to change attitudes about issues considered important to their causes. These groups occupy the extreme fringes of animal rights, pro-life, environmental, anti-nuclear, and other political and social movements. Some special interest extremists—most notably within the animal rights and environmental movements—have turned increasingly toward vandalism and terrorist activity in attempts to further their causes.

In recent years, the Animal Liberation Front (ALF)—an extremist animal rights movement—has become one of the most active extremist elements in the United States. Despite the destructive aspects of ALF's operations, its operational philosophy discourages acts that harm "any animal, human and nonhuman." Animal rights groups in the United States, including ALF, have generally adhered to this mandate. A distinct but related group, the Earth Liberation Front (ELF), claimed responsibility for the arson fires set at a Vail, Colorado, ski resort in October 1998 that destroyed 8 separate structures and caused $12 million in damages. In a communique issued after the fires, ELF claimed that the fires were in retaliation for the resort's planned expansion that would destroy the last remaining habitat in Colorado for the lynx. Eight of the terrorist incidents occurring in the United

States during 1999 have been attributed to either ALF or ELF. Several additional acts committed during 2000 and 2001 are currently being reviewed for possible designation as terrorist incidents.

—Taken from *http://www.fbi.gov/congress/congress01/freeh051001.htm*

U.S. Counterterrorism Policy

The following are the four principles of the official counterterrorism policy of the United States of America:

- Make no concessions to terrorists and strike no deals.
- Bring terrorists to justice for their crimes.
- Isolate and apply pressure on states that sponsor terrorism to force them to change their behavior.
- Bolster the counterterrorism capabilities of those countries that work with the United States and require assistance.

Backgrounder: Terrorism

Emergency Information

Before the September 11, 2001, attacks in New York and the Pentagon, most terrorist incidents in the United States have been bombing attacks, involving detonated and undetonated explosive devices, tear gas, and pipe and fire bombs.

The effects of terrorism can vary significantly from loss of life and injuries to property damage and disruptions in services such as electricity, water supply, public transportation, and communications.

One way governments attempt to reduce our vulnerability to terrorist incidents is by increasing security at airports and other public facilities. The U.S. government also works with other countries to limit the sources of support for terrorism.

What Is Terrorism?

Terrorism is the use of force or violence against persons or property in violation of the criminal laws of the United States for purposes of intimidation, coercion, or ransom. Terrorists often use threats to create fear among the public, to try to convince citizens that their government is powerless to prevent terrorism, and to get immediate publicity for their causes.

The Federal Bureau of Investigation (FBI) categorizes terrorism in the United States as one of two types—domestic terrorism or international terrorism. Domestic terrorism involves groups or individuals whose terrorist activities are directed at elements of our government or population without foreign direction. International terrorism involves groups or individuals whose terrorist activities are foreign-based and/or directed by countries or groups outside the United States or whose activities transcend national boundaries.

Biological and Chemical Weapons

Biological agents are infectious microbes or toxins used to produce illness or death in people, animals, or plants. Biological agents can be dispersed as aerosols or airborne particles. Terrorists may use biological agents to contaminate food or water because they are extremely difficult to detect. Chemical agents kill or incapacitate people, destroy livestock, or ravage crops. Some chemical agents are odorless and tasteless and are difficult to detect. They can have an immediate effect (a few seconds to a few minutes) or a delayed effect (several hours to several days).

Biological and chemical weapons have been used primarily to terrorize an unprotected civilian population and not as a weapon of war. This is because of fear of retaliation and the likelihood that the agent would contaminate the battlefield for a long period of time. The Persian Gulf War in 1991, and other confrontations in the Middle East, were causes for concern in the United States regarding the possibility of chemical or biological warfare. While no incidents occurred, there remains a concern that such weapons could be involved in an accident or be used by terrorists.

Facts About Terrorism (Prior to September 11, 2001)

- On February 29, 1993, a bombing in the parking garage of the World Trade Center in New York City resulted in the deaths of five people and thousands of injuries. The bomb left a crater 200 by 100 feet wide and 5 stories deep. The World Trade Center was the second largest building in the world and houses 100,000 workers and visitors each day.
- The Department of Defense estimates that as many as twenty-six nations may possess chemical agents and/or weapons and an additional twelve may be seeking to develop them.
- The Central Intelligence Agency reports that at least ten countries are believed to possess or be conducting research on biological agents for weaponization.

Terrorism in the United States

- In the United States, most terrorist incidents have involved small extremist groups who use terrorism to achieve a designated objective. Local, state, and federal law enforcement officials monitor suspected terrorist groups and try to prevent or protect against a suspected attack. Additionally, the U.S. Government works with other countries to limit the sources of support for terrorism.
- A terrorist attack can take several forms, depending on the technological means available to the terrorist, the nature of the political issue motivating the attack, and the points of weakness of the terrorist's target. Bombings have been the most frequently used terrorist method in the United States. Other possibilities include an attack at transportation facilities, an attack against utilities or other public services, or an incident involving chemical or biological agents.

211

- Terrorist incidents in this country prior to the September 11, 2001, attack have included bombings of the World Trade Center in New York City, the U.S. Capitol Building in Washington, DC, and Mobil Oil corporate headquarters in New York City.

Fact Sheet: Terrorism

Before
Learn about the nature of terrorism.

- Terrorists look for visible targets where they can avoid detection before or after an attack such as international airports, large cities, major international events, resorts, and high-profile landmarks.
- Learn about the different types of terrorist weapons including explosives, kidnappings, hijackings, arson, and shootings. Prepare to deal with a terrorist incident by adapting many of the same techniques used to prepare for other crises.
- Be alert and aware of the surrounding area. The very nature of terrorism suggests that there may be little or no warning.
- Take precautions when traveling. Be aware of conspicuous or unusual behavior. Do not accept packages from strangers. Do not leave luggage unattended.
- Learn where emergency exits are located. Think ahead about how to evacuate a building, subway, or congested public area in a hurry. Learn where staircases are located.
- Notice your immediate surroundings. Be aware of heavy or breakable objects that could move, fall, or break in an explosion.

Preparing for a Building Explosion
The use of explosives by terrorists can result in collapsed buildings and fires. People who live or work in a multi-level building can do the following:

- Review emergency evacuation procedures. Know where fire exits are located.
- Keep fire extinguishers in working order. Know where they are located and how to use them. Learn first aid. Contact the local chapter of the American Red Cross for additional information.
- Keep the following items in a designated place on each floor of the building:
  Portable, battery-operated radio and extra batteries
  Several flashlights and extra batteries
  First aid kit and manual
  Several hard hats
  Fluorescent tape to rope off dangerous areas

Bomb Threats
If you receive a bomb threat, get as much information from the caller as possible. Keep the caller on the line and record everything that is said. Notify the police and the building management.

After you've been notified of a bomb threat, do not touch any suspicious packages. Clear the area around the suspicious package and notify the police immediately. In evacuating a building, avoid standing in front of windows or other potentially hazardous areas. Do not restrict sidewalks or streets to be used by emergency officials.

During

In a building explosion, get out of the building as quickly and calmly as possible. If items are falling off of bookshelves or from the ceiling, get under a sturdy table or desk. Tips if there is a fire are as follows:

- Stay low to the floor and exit the building as quickly as possible.
- Cover nose and mouth with a wet cloth.
- When approaching a closed door, use the palm of your hand and forearm to feel the lower, middle, and upper parts of the door. If it is not hot, brace yourself against the door and open it slowly. If it is hot to the touch, do not open the door—seek an alternate escape route.
- Heavy smoke and poisonous gases collect first along the ceiling. Stay below the smoke at all times.

After

If you are trapped in debris, do as follows:

- Use a flashlight.
- Stay in your area so that you don't kick up dust. Cover your mouth with a handkerchief or clothing.
- Tap on a pipe or wall so that rescuers can hear where you are. Use a whistle if one is available. Shout only as a last resort—shouting can cause a person to inhale dangerous amounts of dust.

Assisting Victims

- Untrained persons should not attempt to rescue people who are inside a collapsed building. Wait for emergency personnel to arrive.

Chemical Agents

Chemical agents are poisonous gases, liquids, or solids that have toxic effects on people, animals, or plants. Most chemical agents cause serious injuries or death. Severity of injuries depends on the type and amount of the chemical agent used and the duration of exposure.

Were a chemical agent attack to occur, authorities would instruct citizens to either seek shelter where they are and seal the premises or evacuate immediately. Exposure to chemical agents can be fatal. Leaving the shelter to rescue or assist victims can be a deadly decision. There is no assistance that the untrained can offer that would likely be of any value to the victims of chemical agents.

Biological Agents

Biological agents are organisms or toxins that have illness-producing effects on people, livestock, and crops.

Because biological agents cannot necessarily be detected and may take time to grow and cause a disease, it is almost impossible to know that a biological attack has occurred. If government officials become aware of a biological attack through an informant or warning by terrorists, they would most likely instruct citizens to either seek shelter where they are and seal the premises or evacuate immediately.

A person affected by a biological agent requires the immediate attention of professional medical personnel. Some agents are contagious, and victims may need to be quarantined. Also, some medical facilities may not receive victims for fear of contaminating the hospital population.

—Taken from *http://www.fema.gov/hazards/terrorism/terrorf.shtm*

Endnotes

[1] Ayatollah Sheikh Muhammad 'Ali Taskhiri, Vol V No. , Towards a Definition of Terrorism, June 22–26, 1987, http://www.al-islam.org/al-tawhid/definition-terrorism.htm

[2] http://www.cdi.org/program/issue/document.cfm

* "Homicide bombing" is a political variant of the traditional term "suicide bombing." The variant is designed to draw attention more to the aggressive nature of suicide bombing and its victimization of others beyond just the bomber.

*INADMISSIBLE ALIENS—Section 212(a)(3)(B) of the Immigration and Nationality Act (8 U.S.C. 1182(a)(3)(B)) is amended—
(1) in clause (i), by amending subclauses (IV) and (V) to read as follows:
"(IV) is a representative (as defined in clause (iv)) of a terrorist organization, including an organization designated as a foreign terrorist organization by the Secretary under section 219," or
"(V) is a member of a terrorist organization, including an organization designated as a foreign terrorist organization by the Secretary under section 219,"; and
(2) in clause (iii)—
(A) in subclause (IV), by striking "organization" and inserting "organization, including an organization designated as a foreign terrorist organization by the Secretary under section 219,";
(B) in subclause (V), by striking "organization," and inserting "organization (including an organization designated as a foreign terrorist organization by the Secretary under section 219),"; and
(C) by adding at the end the following:
"(VI)(aa) Any other act committed by an alien that constitutes aiding or abetting another individual who has conducted, is conducting, or is planning to conduct a terrorist activity, or aiding or abetting a terrorist organization, including an organization designated as a foreign terrorist organization by the Secretary under section 219."

Discussion Questions

1) According to the U.S. government's official definition, terrorism is only conducted by subnational and clandestine agents.

        True   False

2) According to the Islamic Conference, "unofficial" terrorism is the response to "official" terrorism.

        True   False

3) Prior to September 11, 2001, terrorism wasn't generally a concern for most people in the world.

        True   False

4) A successful terrorist attack may serve to inspire others to join or form terrorists organizations.

        True   False

5) To date, no terrorist organization has yet used a weapon of mass destruction (WMD) successfully in an attack.

        True   False

6) Asymmetrical warfare refers to combat situations where both forces are equally matched in terms of numbers and technology, and conventional tactics are employed.

        True   False

7) In some instances, terrorists can become so dedicated to their ideological cause, they are willing to fasten an explosive device to themselves in a suicide attack.

        True   False

8) Terrorism is an overseas concern for the United States and shouldn't be regarded as a domestic problem.

        True   False

9) The Central Intelligence Agency reports that at least ten countries are believed to possess or be conducting research on biological agents for weaponization.

        True   False

10) The official counterterrorism policy of the United States permits negotiations and deals to be struck with terrorists in emergency circumstances.

        True   False

Answers
1) True
2) True
3) False
4) True
5) False
6) False
7) True
8) False
9) True
10) False

3 Chemical and Biological Warfare

Inspector examining nuclear weapon. *Courtesy of Bettmann/ Corbis Images.*

Overview:

"Weapons of Mass Destruction" (WMD) has become a familiar, if not always understood, term in our modern lexicon. Specifically, the term refers to a weapon system, contained within itself, that is capable of producing the same type of devastation that a whole military force, or a series of weapons used simultaneously, might cause. Their portability, rapid deployment, ability to be secreted, and widespread global proliferation makes these weapons concerning enough, but what is exceptionally disturbing for homeland security planners is the horrific nature of these weapons. A compact weapon, capable of inflicting terrible damage, both physically and psychologically, that could be acquired by the highest bidder and transported covertly into a target society is a nightmare scenario for security specialists.

In this chapter we will begin discussing the theory and principles of chemical and biological weapons as WMD. Nuclear and radiological weapons will be discussed in the following chapter.

Chapter Objectives:

- *Explain what the characteristics are that qualify certain weapons as "chemical" and "biological."*
- *Explain how battlefield chemical and biological weapons have become a concern for terrorism.*
- *Describe how chemical and biological weapons may be created by rogue states and terrorist organizations.*
- *Identify historical incidents in which chemical and biological weapons have been used.*

219

Chemical and Biological Warfare Defined

Chemical Warfare (CW)

All aspects of military operations involving the deployment of lethal and incapacitating munitions/agents and the warning and protective measures associated with offensive operations. Since riot control agents and herbicides are not considered chemical warfare agents, those two items will be referred to separately or under the broader term "chemical," which is generally used to include all types of chemical munitions/agents collectively. The term "chemical warfare weapons" may be used when it is desired to reflect both lethal and incapacitating munitions/agents of either chemical or biological origin.

Biological Warfare

The use of biological agents (bacteria, viruses, fungi, and biologically derived toxins) directed at a military force in an effort to cause mass casualties and death.

—Taken from *http://www.vdh.state.vt.us/common/define.htm*

War, it has been said, is the extension of policy by other means. War should be the last resort, the use of force in critical situations for which no peaceful resolution can reasonably be found. To that end, warfare is a desperate science, one in which the goal is to completely decimate and destroy the enemy's ability to resist and counter strike.

Thus, in the history of warfare all options are usually considered viable. War is not an elegant affair; horror and brutality have often been employed and done so indiscriminately. Occasionally, however, certain acts and events have been considered so morally repugnant and outrageous that their use is seen as something to avoid, even under the worst circumstances.

When World War I ended in 1918, the global community was staggered by the horrific loss of life and overall destruction. As the first truly mechanized war in the new industrial world, the resultant level of devastation was something not previously seen before. Many thought that World War I was to be the "war to end all wars." The League of Nations was formed afterward as the first attempt at an international body to try to resolve conflicts peacefully without war. Another convention to come out of WWI was the banning of certain types of weapons designed to sicken and poison combatants. This was the first international attempt to prohibit the use of chemical and biological weapons in warfare. The horrors of mustard gas, a chemical blistering agent, on battlefield troops so disturbed the world consciousness that future conventions on the rules of warfare prohibited the use of such weaponry in the future.

To this day, the Geneva Protocol (February 28, 1928), the most commonly regarded document proscribing the rules of war in international law, prohibits the use of "asphyxiating, poisonous or other gases, and of all analogous liquids,

Three soldiers falling from gas attack. *Courtesy of Hulton Archive/Getty Images, Inc.*

materials or devices, as well as the use of bacteriological methods of warfare." This, of course, has not completely stopped the production and experimentation with such weaponry. A number of nations, including the United States and Soviet Union, continued through the Cold War to develop stockpiles of chemical and biological weapons as a method of ensuring national security by not letting the one develop a weapons technology with which the other could not compete. As of the late 1990s, the United States reported having approximately 30,000 tons of chemical weapons stockpiled, although the American government has begun destroying them in the interest of global security.

Chemical and biological weapons are designed to use a single shell, warhead, or some other dispersal method to release a toxin that will maim, poison, cripple, and/or kill an enemy. Whereas, in conventional warfare, combatants are injured by high-velocity projectiles such as bullets and shrapnel, chemical and biological warfare relies on deliberately released clouds, sprays, mists, powders, and/or vapors to introduce a toxin to the bodies of multiple enemy personnel simultaneously. The efficacy of chemical and biological warfare (CW/BW) is threefold:

1) On a practical level, it has the potential to disable and destroy larger numbers of enemy combatants more efficiently than traditional warfighting methods.

2) On a strategic level, CW/BW can serve as a "force multiplier" increasing the destructive capability of a relatively small combatant force against an opponent.

3) On a psychological level, the particularly gruesome nature of the injuries and fatalities caused by CW/BW makes it a powerful deterring and demoralizing force to one's enemies.

In modern times, chemical and biological weapons have been effectively used in both combat and terrorism scenarios.

- Between 1967 and 1971, the United States used aircraft to spray approximately nineteen million gallons of a powerful defoliant known as Agent Orange during the Vietnam War. The herbicide was employed as an effort to destroy the dense jungle foliage that provided the Viet Cong with cover and concealment. Agent Orange became notorious for its toxic side effects on Vietnamese soldiers and citizens, as well as American military personnel, who were exposed to the chemical.

- During the bloody war between Iraq and Iran, from 1980 to 1988, it is estimated that approximately 100,000 Iranian soldiers and civilians may have been exposed to deadly chemical agents such as sarin and soman (blister agents similar to mustard gas).

- The Iraqi government also used lethal nerve gas against the Kurdish village of Halabja in the northern part of Iraq on March 16, 1988; approximately 5,000 Kurdish villagers were killed in that attack.

History of Chemical Warfare

The following is a brief history of chemical warfare. As you will see, chemical warfare, like terrorism, is not a new concept at all.

- **429 BC**—Spartans ignite pitch and sulphur to create toxic fumes in the Peloponnesian War.
- **424 BC**—Toxic fumes used in siege of Delium during the Peloponnesian War.
- **1456**—City of Belgrade defeats invading Turks by igniting rags dipped in poison to create a toxic cloud.
- **April 24, 1863**—The U.S. War Department issues General Order 100, proclaiming "the use of poison in any manner, be it to poison wells, or foods, or arms, is wholly excluded from modern warfare."
- **World War I**—The use of chemical agents in WWI caused an estimated 1,300,000 casualties, including 90,000 deaths.
- **1914**—French begin using tear gas in grenades, and Germans retaliate with tear gas in artillery shells. This was the first significant use of chemical warfare in WWI.
- **April 22, 1915**—Germans attack the French with chlorine gas at Ypres, France.
- **September 25, 1915**—First British chemical weapons attack; chlorine gas is used against Germans at the Battle of Loos.
- **February 26, 1918**—Germans launch the first projectile attack against U.S. troops with phosgene and chloropicrin shells. The first major use of gas against American forces.
- **June 1918**—First U.S. use of gas in warfare.
- **June 28, 1918**—The United States begins its formal chemical weapons program with the establishment of the Chemical Warfare Service.
- **1919**—British use Adamsite against the Bolsheviks during the Russian Civil War.
- **1922, 1927**—The Spanish use chemical weapons against the Rif rebels in Spanish Morocco.
- **1936**—Italy uses mustard gas against Ethiopians during its invasion of Abyssinia.
- **1942**—Nazis begin using Zyklon B (hydrocyanic acid) in gas chambers for the mass murder of concentration camp prisoners.
- **December 1943**—A U.S. ship loaded with mustard bombs is attacked by Germans in the port of Bari, Italy; eighty-three U.S. troops die in poisoned waters.

- **April 1945**—Germans manufacture and stockpile large amounts of tabun and sarin nerve gases but do not use them.
- **1962–1970**—United States uses treat gas and four types of defoliant, including Agent Orange, in Vietnam.
- **1963, 1967**—Egypt uses chemical weapons (phosgene, mustard) against Yemen.
- **1975, 1983**—Alleged use of Yellow Rain (trichothecene mycotoxins) by Soviet-backed forces in Laos and Kampuchea. There is evidence to suggest use of T-2 toxin, but an alternative hypothesis suggests that the yellow spots labelled Yellow Rain were caused by swarms of defecating bees.
- **1979**—The U.S. Government alleges Soviets use of chemical weapons in Afghanistan, including "yellow rain."
- **August 1983**—Iraq begins using chemical weapons (mustard gas), Iran-Iraq War.
- **1984**—First ever use of nerve agent tabun on the battlefield, by Iraq during Iran-Iraq War.
- **1987, 1988**—Iraq uses chemical weapons (hydrogen cyanide, mustard gas) in its Anfal Campaign against the Kurds, most notably in the Halabja Massacre of 1988.
- **March 20, 1995**—The Tokyo Subway sarin gas attack killed nearly a dozen people and incapacitated or injured approximately 5,000 others. Thousands did not die from the Tokyo attack due to impurity of the agent. A tiny drop of sarin, which was originally developed in Germany in the 1930s, can kill within minutes after skin contact or inhalation of its vapor. Like all other nerve agents, sarin blocks the action of acetylcholinesterase, an enzyme necessary for the transmission of nerve impulses.

—Taken from *http://www.wilpf.int.ch/disarmament/chemicalweapons.htm,* by permission of the Women's International League for Peace and Freedom

A Chemical Weapons Atlas

Few states admit that they possess chemical weapons. In recent years, only the United States, Russia, Iraq, and now India, have done so. The United States, which has started to destroy its chemical weapons, has a stockpile of about 30,000 tons. Russia has declared 40,000 tons. Iraq, which acknowledged after the Gulf War that it had such weapons, claims that its chemical agents and munitions were destroyed during and after the war. India recently admitted to having chemical weapons, but only for "defensive" purposes.

In any event, four nations make a short list indeed. And now that the Chemical Weapons Convention has entered into force, many people believe that the struggle to banish lethal chemical munitions has been won. But it is too early to celebrate.

Developing and dealing in chemical weapons has always been a back-alley business that nations have mainly conducted in secret. And it could continue in much the same way, unless members of the international community are willing to speak up in public about chemical-weapons activities.

Yet states largely refuse to do so. Even the new Organization for the Prohibition of Chemical Weapons (which is implementing the Chemical Weapons Convention) keeps the mandatory declarations of past and present chemical-weapons activities confidential.

Such secrecy, however, is misguided, because it keeps the public ignorant of the true extent of the proliferation problem and allows states that have or are developing chemical weapons to continue to manufacture and stockpile them.

In the United States, the discussion of the proliferation of chemical weapons is highly politicized. Typically, U.S. officials will only point their fingers at the current list of "rogue nations." For instance, in testimony before the Senate Select Committee on Intelligence last February, CIA Director George Tenet said that some twenty countries, among them Iran, Iraq, and Syria, have or are actively developing chemical and biological weapons. By identifying only three states by name, Tenet chose, or was directed, to name one less state than his predecessor John Deutch had named the year before. He omitted North Korea. This omission is particularly troubling in light of the testimony—at the same Senate hearing—by the director of the Defense Intelligence Agency (DIA), Lt. Gen. Patrick Hughes, that "a Korean war scenario remains our primary near-term military concern."

The public deserves to be fully informed about the proliferation of chemical weapons and should have the same on-the-record information U.S. policy makers use. Chemical weapons threaten not only soldiers, who may have protective gear, but also civilians.

Consider what happened when the United States failed to respond to Iraq's use of chemical weapons in the early 1980s. Recently declassified intelligence reports indicate that the United States knew by 1983 that Iraq had—and had used—lethal agents. It also knew that, with the help of foreign firms, Iraq was building a major new chemical weapons facility. Yet the United States and its allies continued to support Iraq with loans and other forms of assistance. Unrestrained, Iraq used chemical weapons repeatedly during the Iraq-Iran War. Later, it attacked Kurdish villagers in northern Iraq with mustard and nerve gas.

The failure of the international community to condemn Iraq for using chemical weapons and the failure to control the trade in chemicals had other unforeseen consequences. As a Defense Department report indicates, Iran initiated a chemical warfare program "in response to Iraq's use of mustard gas against Iranian troops." And, partially as a result of the U.S. Government's earlier silence, American troops faced the prospect of Iraq's chemical and biological arsenal in the Gulf War.

This also encouraged other governments to believe they would not be censured if they initiated chemical weapons programs. As a 1992 DIA report concludes, Third World countries believed they were free to stockpile chemical weapons "without the fear of repercussions from the international community."

Perhaps this attitude will change as the Organization for the Prohibition of Chemical Weapons does its work, but the process might be speeded up if the U.S. Government disclosed what it knows about chemical weapons activities throughout the world.

Meanwhile, how much can be known without more government disclosure? Through official documents released under the Freedom of Information Act and press reports citing U.S. government officials, it is possible to identify most of the states suspected of trading in or manufacturing chemical weapons.

There are two caveats about using these sources: Intelligence reports often characterize a state as having a "chemical warfare capability" without indicating whether that state is developing weapons or already has a stockpile of chemical munitions. Then, too, it is difficult or impossible to verify U.S. intelligence reports independently. Nonetheless, they are on-the-record assessments that U.S. policy makers use and often share with NATO partners and other allies.

The Middle East

The Middle East and North Africa are enmeshed in a destabilizing arms race. Here the belief that one state possessed weapons of mass destruction prompted another to establish its own program, which led to another state acquiring chemical weapons, that led another state, and so on.

The race has gone on in earnest since the 1960s, and currently more than half of the states in the region have, or are suspected of having, offensive chemical weapons.

- **Egypt.** According to a Special National Intelligence Estimate, "Implications on Soviet Use of Chemical and Toxin Weapons for U.S. Security Interests," a 1983 report representing the judgment of the CIA, the DIA, the National Security Agency, and the intelligence arms of the State and Treasury Departments, Egypt was "the first country in the Middle East to obtain chemical weapons training, indoctrination, and materiel." (Egypt may or may not have been motivated by Israel's construction of the Dimona nuclear reactor in 1958.)

  Egypt was also the first Middle Eastern country to use chemical weapons. It employed phosgene and mustard agent against Yemeni Royalist forces in the mid-1960s, and some reports claim that it also used an organophosphate nerve agent.

  A 1990 DIA study, "Offensive Chemical Warfare Programs in the Middle East," concluded that Egypt was continuing to conduct research related to chemical agents. The report identified a production facility, but details were deleted.

- **Israel.** According to the same DIA study, Israel developed its own offensive chemical weapons program in response to a perceived Arab chemical-weapon threat. In 1974, Lt. Gen. E. H. Almquist told a Senate Armed Forces Committee that the Israeli program was operational. The 1990 DIA study reports that Israel maintains a chemical warfare testing facility. Newspaper reports suggest the facility is in the Negev desert.

- **Syria.** Syria began developing chemical weapons in the 1970s, in response to the Israeli threat, according to a 1993 DIA report, "Chemical Warfare Assessments Syria." The 1990 DIA survey reports that Syria received chemical weapons from Egypt in the 1970s, and indigenous production began in the 1980s.

  Today, Syria is believed to have a large stockpile of chemical munitions. It allegedly has two means of delivery: a 500-kilogram aerial bomb, and chemical warheads for Scud-B missiles. The 1990 DIA report named two chemical munitions storage depots, at Khan Abu Shamat and Furqlus, and indicated that the Centre D'Etude et Recherche Scientifique, near Damascus, was the primary research facility. Recent newspaper articles, citing U.S. reconnaissance, report that Syria is building a new chemical-weapons factory near the city of Aleppo.

- **Iran.** According to the 1990 DIA report, Iran's program was developed in response to the Iraqi use of chemical weapons during the Iran-Iraq War. The DIA concluded that by the end of the war. the Iranian military had been able to field mustard and phosgene, although it reportedly used them in limited quantities only.

  The same report stated that Iran had artillery shells and bombs filled with chemical agents. A 1992 DIA report, "Weapons Acquisition Strategy Iran," added that Iran was developing ballistic missiles with the assistance of China and North Korea, both of which are reported to have chemical-agent warheads for their surface-to-surface missiles.

- **Iraq.** Since the end of the Gulf War, U.N. specialists have destroyed more than 480,000 liters of Iraq's chemical agents and 1.8 million liters of precursor chemicals. But this may not be the full extent of that country's large and sophisticated chemical weapons program. Iraq is believed to have a number of secret depots where agents or precursors are stored.

  Rolf Ekeus, the former head of the U.N. Special Commission charged with eliminating Iraq's weapons of mass destruction, said in a June 24 interview with the *New York Times* that he doubts the entire stockpile has been found. Iraq has made repeated attempts to import proscribed equipment and attempted to hide chemicals, munitions, and equipment from U.N. inspectors. "We have documentary evidence about orders from the leadership to preserve a strategic capability," Ekeus said. He believes that Iraq wants "to keep the production equipment ready to produce at any given moment." A 1995 DIA assessment concluded that Iraq was still conducting research and development.

- **Libya.** According to a publicly released Defense Department survey, "Proliferation: Threat and Response," Libya obtained its first chemical agents from Iran, using them against Chad in 1987.

  Libya opened its own production facility in Rabta in 1988. The report concludes that the Rabta facility may have produced as much as one hundred tons of blister and nerve agent before a suspicious fire closed it down in 1990. Many newspaper reports, citing U.S. intelligence sources, indicate that Libya is building a second facility in an underground location at Tarhunah.

- **Saudi Arabia.** U.S. analysts suspect that Saudi Arabia has a limited chemical warfare capability in part because it acquired fifty CSS-2 ballistic missiles from China. These highly inaccurate missiles are thought to be suitable only for delivering chemical agents.

  The sections on Saudi Arabia in the declassified portions of the 1992 and 1993 editions of the DIA's annual assessment of weapons of mass destruction (prepared for the Senate Select Committee on Intelligence) are heavily deleted. In addition, Gulf War-related documents recently released by the Defense Department indicate that the United States suspected at that time that Saudi Arabia had chemical agents.

Asia

There are many chemical-weapon suspects in Asia. China, India, Pakistan, North Korea, and Taiwan appear to have developed chemical weapons in response to regional tensions. Burma, on the other hand, apparently wanted chemical weapons for domestic use.

- **North Korea.** North Korea's chemical weapons stockpile is probably the largest in the region. According to a 1995 DIA assessment, "Worldwide Chemical Warfare Threat Current and Projected," North Korea has had a chemical weapons program since the 1960s. The 1996 Defense Department survey concludes that North Korea can produce "large quantities" of blister, blood, and nerve agents.

  North Korea could deliver these agents by artillery, rocket launcher, mortar, and spray tank. The Defense Department notes that the North Korean military has been trained to operate in a chemical environment and North Korean civilians have been trained in chemical defense.

- **South Korea.** South Korea is also suspected by U.S. intelligence of having chemical weapons. South Korea has the chemical infrastructure and technical capability to produce chemical agents, and newspaper reports from the late 1980s cite U.S. government sources claiming that South Korea had a chemical weapons program. A 1986 U.S. Army Scientific and Technical Intelligence Bulletin, "Expanding Chemical Warfare Capability: A Cause for Concern," included a heavily edited section on South Korea. South Korea is regularly included in the annual DIA assessments of the proliferation of weapons of mass destruction, but details are deleted. (U.S. chemical munitions may also be stockpiled in South Korea.)

- **India.** According to a 1991 DIA assessment, India has the technical capability and industrial base needed to produce precursors and chemical agents, and it is expected to acquire chemical weapons over the next two decades. Development is expected to be "paced by the parallel Pakistani program." As required of a party to the chemical weapons treaty, India admitted this year that it had produced and stockpiled chemical munitions for "defensive purposes."

  Several Indian companies have been implicated in highly suspicious chemicals shipments and are involved in the construction of chemical plants in states that are developing chemical weapons. The United States has sanctioned some Indian companies for these activities.

- **Pakistan.** The 1996 Defense Department report indicates that Pakistan can produce chemical agents and munitions with dual-use chemical precursors procured from foreign sources. Its goal now is to achieve self-sufficiency in producing precursors. According to a 1993 DIA report, "Weapons Acquisition Strategy Pakistan," Pakistan has artillery projectiles and rockets that can be made chemical-capable.

- **China.** China has a mature chemical warfare capability, according to the 1996 Defense Department report on proliferation. Given China's advanced technical know-how, it must also be assumed that China can field its chemical agents in a wide variety of munitions, including ballistic missiles. China is also a serious proliferation concern, and a number of Chinese companies and individuals have been sanctioned by the U.S. Government for their proliferation activities.

- **Taiwan.** The 1983 Special National Intelligence Estimate, cited in the Defense & Foreign Affairs Handbook, reported that Taiwan had "an aggressive high-priority program to develop both offensive and defensive capabilities"—but that information was deleted from the declassified version. In 1988, the director of naval intelligence told a congressional committee that Taiwan was developing a chemical weapons capability, and, in 1989, he reported that it may be operational.

- **Burma.** Another Asian state thought to produce chemical weapons is Burma (Myanmar). Its program, under development in 1983, may or may not be active today. U.S. officials told Congress in 1988 and 1991 that Burma was developing or had developed chemical weapons. According to the 1992 DIA survey produced for the Senate Select Committee on Intelligence, Burma has "chemical weapons and artillery for delivering chemical agents." On the other hand, the 1993 edition of the DIA report indicates that Burma is no longer developing chemical weapons. There have been many reports that Burma used chemical agents against insurgents.

- **Vietnam.** In congressional testimony in 1988, the director of naval intelligence indicated that Vietnam was in the process of developing, or already had, chemical weapons. Newspaper reports suggest that Vietnam may have obtained chemical weapons from the former Soviet Union.

  Vietnam also captured large stocks of U.S. riot-control agents during and at the end of the Vietnam War. No public references have been made recently to an indigenous production capacity.

Europe

During the Cold War it was generally assumed that all the NATO and Warsaw Pact states had access to the superpowers' chemical weapons, and it was an accepted idea that chemical warfare would be likely in the event of a war between the two alliances. Since the dissolution of the Soviet Union and the Warsaw Pact, and the withdrawal of U.S. chemical munitions, it is unclear which European states may still have access to chemical weapons.

According to U.S. intelligence, the only European states that developed indigenous production capabilities were Yugoslavia, Romania, the former Czechoslovakia, and France. (Britain produced large quantities of chemical weapons in the World War II-era, but it disposed of them in the 1950s, dumping some in the sea and incinerating the rest.) Some other states, including Bulgaria, may still retain munitions left behind by Russian forces.

- **The former Yugoslavia.** The former Yugoslavia has a "CW production capability" according to the Defense Department's Bosnia Country Handbook, issued in 1995. After a year-long research project, Human Rights Watch concluded that before the breakup of Yugoslavia, the Yugoslav National Army produced and weaponized sarin, sulfur mustard, BZ (a psychochemical incapacitant), and irritants CS and CN. The army apparently had also developed and/or produced bombs, artillery shells, and rockets to deliver these munitions, some of which it produced in quantity.

  When Yugoslavia broke apart, much of the program was inherited by the army of the Federal Republic of Yugoslavia (Serbia). The program apparently remains active. Bosnian officers interviewed by

Human Rights Watch reported that the Bosnian government also produced crude chemical weapons during the 1992–95 war.

- **Romania.** The declassified version of the DIA's 1995 "Chemical Warfare Assessment Romania" is heavily edited, but the U.S. National Ground Intelligence Agency did identify research and production facilities and chemical-weapons stockpiles and storage facilities in Romania. A 1982 classified report, the Army-commissioned "Warsaw Pact Scientific Resources of Chemical/Biological Defense," indicated that Romania had a large chemical-warfare program, adding that it had developed a cheaper method for synthesizing sarin.

- **The former Czechoslovakia.** According to the 1992 and 1993 DIA assessments, the Czech Republic and Slovakia had confirmed pilot-plant chemical capabilities that probably included sarin, soman, and possibly VX, but the study concluded that they did not appear to be producing chemical agents at the time.

- **France.** France probably does not have an active program, but it presumably has a stockpile of chemical weapons. In a heavily censored 1978 report, "Chemical and Biological Capabilities NATO Countries (France, Italy & West Germany)," U.S. intelligence concluded that France had produced and stockpiled a number of chemical agents and munitions, including aerosol bombs. During the 1980s, France was identified as having chemical weapons in surveys published by the *New York Times,* the *Christian Science Monitor,* and the *Wall Street Journal,* all citing U.S. intelligence sources.

  In 1987, Foreign Minister Jean-Bernard Raimond announced that France had decided to acquire new chemical weapons, but it is not known how far this program had advanced before the Chemical Weapons Convention was signed in Paris in 1993.

- **Bulgaria.** According to the declassified version of a 1995 DIA report, "Chemical Agent Threat Current and Projected," Bulgaria has a stockpile of chemical munitions of Soviet origin, but no indigenous production capability. Details of the stockpile were deleted.

Sub-Saharan Africa

South Africa is the only state in southern Africa with a possible chemical weapons program. The 1992 and 1993 DIA reports mentioned South Africa, but details were deleted. Public evidence suggests that at one point South Africa had an active program. Justice Minister Dullah Omar told a June 10, 1996, press conference that South Africa had initiated a well-funded chemical program in 1980, with procurement of equipment and materials handled through a sophisticated network of front companies.

Lt. Gen. Niel Knobel, the surgeon general of the South African Defense Force, claims that "all lethal, incapacitating, and irritating chemical and biological agents" were destroyed in 1990, but this claim has not been verified. Newspaper reports citing U.S. intelligence sources suggest that former employees of South Africa's chemical weapons program may have helped Libya and other states develop chemical weapons.

Looking to the Future

Many of the countries described in this survey have signed and/or ratified the Chemical Weapons Convention. Now that it is in force, the treaty, and its implementing body, the Organization for the Prohibition of Chemical Weapons, should do much to counter current proliferation tendencies, and it should reduce the number of states with chemical warfare capabilities. All parties to the convention are required to declare past and present chemical weapons research, development, production, and stockpiling, although their declarations will remain confidential unless the states independently publicize their declarations. (Britain released much of its declaration and India has recently admitted to having a program.)

The policy of confidentiality is unfortunate, because it is openness that will stop the proliferation of chemical weapons. Much of the success of the Chemical Weapons Convention will rest on states' willingness to cooperate and freely exchange information about current and past shipments of the precursors and equipment that are used to produce military agents and munitions.

Acknowledging the spread of weapons and information on suspected chemical weapons programs will make it much more difficult to conceal illegal programs or to maintain stockpiles. Public investigation of neighbors' allegations will also reduce the incentive for countries neighboring suspected chemical weapons-capable states to develop chemical weapons.

Under the provisions of the Chemical Weapons Convention, an accused state must allow a thorough investigation. If it denies inspectors access, it will face both sanctions and the stigma that comes with being identified as a potential possessor of chemical weapons. Under the treaty, neighboring states can also request international assistance to protect their populations, eliminating the need to develop their own weapons as deterrents.

Any attempt to control the proliferation of chemical weapons, however, must be linked to an objective assessment of their spread. The United States should establish a firm policy that no state—no matter how close an ally—should be allowed to maintain a secret capability to produce and use chemical munitions. It should therefore reveal the identities of all states it believes have chemical weapons programs.

Are sea-dumped chemical munitions ticking time bombs, as some say? Or do they constitute a classic nonproblem that can be reasonably ignored?

The first intensive dumping efforts came immediately after World War II. In 1945, for instance, soon after the Allies had destroyed the German war machine, British sailors loaded twenty old, deteriorating merchant vessels with captured German nerve gas shells and headed to the Baltic. When they reached the coast of Norway, the sailors put on gas masks, placed explosives aboard the ships, and waited. One by one, the ships blew up, taking thousands of tons of poison gas to the sea bottom.

Two decades later, in June 1967, the U.S. military loaded the S.S. Corporal Eric Gibson with nerve gas rockets containing VX and sarin at Colt's Neck Naval Pier in Monmouth County, New Jersey. The navy towed the vessel to a spot 200 miles east of Atlantic City, where it was scuttled in 7,200 feet (2,194 meters) of water.

These are just two of the more than one hundred sea dumpings of chemical weapons that took place from 1945 to 1970 in every ocean except the Arctic. Many scientists, environmentalists, and defense experts consider these scattered sites to be a potentially deadly legacy of the three major twentieth century wars—World War I, World War II, and the Cold War.

"There are many questions that need answers," said Kyle B. Olson, a senior member of the Arms Control and Proliferation Center of TASC, an Arlington, Virginia, defense consulting firm specializing in a number of arms control and security-related issues. "The rate of the deterioration of the munitions is unclear, and not all the sea-dumpings sites are known."

Don't Ask, Don't Tell

The Chemical Weapons Convention, which was concluded in 1992 after more than a decade of negotiations, has been hailed as a major milestone in the history of arms control and disarmament. As the first treaty to eliminate a class of weapons, the convention has some of the most stringent verification measures ever included in an arms-control agreement.

The CWC, however, does not cover sea-dumped chemical weapons; in fact, it makes a clear exception for them. "The CWC does not provide the legal basis to cover chemical weapons that were dumped before 1985," Thomas Stock of the Stockholm International Peace Research Institute (SIPRI) wrote in the recently published anthology of essays *Sea-Dumped Chemical Weapons: Aspects, Problems, and Solutions.* "Any declaration by a treaty party is voluntary. As long as those chemical weapons remain sea-dumped, there is no obligation to destroy them."

But given the volume, the lack of oversight, and years of indifference, many experts worry that sea-dumped chemical weapons are a time bomb bound to explode at some point. "The commitment of the chemical weapons signatories to destroy all chemical weapons stockpiles should be extended, under a collateral agreement, to include those dumped on the seabed, where the state of the ammunition can hardly be expected to be less hazardous than above ground," says Brigitte Sauerwein, a Geneva-based security consultant and co-author of *European Security in the 1990s: Challenges and Perspectives.*

Such dangerous weapons, of course, could not be openly dumped at sea today, but the decision to do so in the era between the end of World War II and the dawning of the age of environmental consciousness is understandable, given the times. "From the 1940s to the 1960s, the level of security and openness about the environment was less than it is now," said Greg Williams, national spokesperson for the Kentucky Environmental Coalition, an organization that works for the safe disposal of chemical weapons. "It's still a struggle, but back then nobody batted an eye about the environment."

Dumping Nazi Stockpiles

After the defeat of Germany, the Allies found Nazi arsenals containing mines, grenades, aerial bombs, and artillery shells filled with yperite and its derivatives, chlorine-containing substances (phosgene), arsenic-containing compounds (levisite), and organophosphorous compounds (tabun). The Allies felt they had to act quickly, because the stockpiles could kill millions and there were concerns that German soldiers were still hiding out and might want to get the weapons. The United States, France, Britain, and Russia held hurried discussions and established a special group, the Continental Committee on Dumping, which would coordinate disposal.

The group also decided that the occupying powers in each zone could destroy the chemical weapons on their territory in a manner that was most convenient to them. The captured German chemical weapons totaled 296,103 tons. The American zone had 93,995 tons; the British 122,508; the Russian 70,500; and the French 9,250.

The United States transferred all of its captured chemical weapons to five German munitions depots for decontamination, detonation, and incineration. Those munitions that were to be scuttled at sea—the majority of the Nazi weapons cache—were packed by German workers in wicker baskets, the thinking being that the wicker would absorb the liquid mustard if it leaked out of the bomb shells.

The United States subsequently launched Operation Davey Jones Locker, and from June 1946 to August 1948, the country conducted 5 dumpings of chemical weapons in the Scandinavian region, totaling between 30,000 and 40,000 tons. Nine ships were scuttled in the Skagerrak Strait and 2 more in the North Sea at depths of 2,130 to 3,870 feet (650 to 1,180 meters). The last U.S. dumpings of captured German chemical weapons are believed to have taken place in 1958.

"Sea dumping was thought to be the quickest and best way to do disposal because the materials would be dissipated at sea," Olson explained. "So they loaded up barges and captured German ships and submarines with the stuff, took them out to sea, and dumped them."

Alexander Kaffka, a researcher at the Russian Academy of Sciences, chairman of the Conversation for Environment International Foundation (CFE), and editor of *Sea Dumped Chemical Weapons,* added, "There were some important safety rules envisaged at the time; for instance, to dump only in deep waters and far from the shores. But the rules were often broken, which led to the most dangerous kind of dumping—at shallow depths, in straits, and in areas of active fishing."

The Baltic Sea, one of the major dump sites used by the United States, Russia, and Britain, has a mean depth of only 170 feet (51 meters). As soon as World War II ended, 46,000 tons of chemical weapons were dumped in the Baltic areas known as the Gotland Deep, Bornholm Deep, and the Little Belt, according to information submitted to the 1994 Helsinki Commission. The Russians alone are reported to have dumped 30,000 tons in an area 2,000 square kilometers in size near the Gotland and Bornholm Islands.

According to Eugeniusz Andrulewicz of the Institute of Meteorology and Water Management at Gdynia, Poland, "There are indications that during transport to the dumping area east of Bornholm and southeast of Gotland, the munitions were partially overthrown from ships en route. Some munitions were dumped in wooden cases, which remained floating for some time and might have drifted outside the intended dumping area."

Between 1945 and 1949, the British dumped 34 shiploads carrying 127,000 tons of chemical and conventional weapons in the Norwegian Trench, much of it 25 miles east of the town of Arendal in a 2,300-foot (700 meters) deep site. The British also dumped more chemical weapons at a site 20 miles west of the Irish coast.

In the 1950s and 1960s, the Allies continued dumping chemical weapons at sea. Recently declassified British government records reveal that in 1955 and 1956 the British conducted Operation Sandcastle in which weapons containing cyanide, drums of sarin and tabun nerve gas, the agent phosgene, and large quantities of mustard gas were loaded in containers on three old merchant ships and scuttled in deep water in the Atlantic Ocean, west of the Outer Hebrides and eighty miles northeast of the coast of Northern Ireland. In a letter sent in February 1995 to the Celtic League, an Irish environmental group, the British Ministry of Defense admitted that two cases containing chemical agents leaked during the operation, although no one was harmed.

During the 1950s, the United States conducted an ambitious nerve gas program, manufacturing what would eventually total 400,000 M-55 rockets, each of which was capable of delivering a 10.8-pound payload of sarin. When the U.S. Army discovered in 1966 that some of the rockets were leaking, it launched Operation Chase ("Cut Holes and Sink 'Em"). In two scuttlings undertaken in 1967 and 1968, 51,180 nerve gas rockets were dropped 150 miles off the coast of New York in depths measuring from 6,390 to 7,200 feet (1,950 to 2,190 meters). The last chase operation took place in 1970 off the coast of Florida and involved dumping solid concrete vaults of gb-filled M-55 rockets, an amount equal to 39 filled railroad boxcars.

In all, the United States is responsible for 60 sea dumpings totaling about 100,000 tons of chemical weapons filled with toxic materials, according to a 1993 study by the U.S. Arms Control and Disarmament Agency (ACDA). The U.S. sites are located in the Gulf of Mexico, off the coast of New Jersey, California, Florida, and South Carolina, and near India, Italy, Norway, Denmark, Japan, and Australia.

Official information bearing upon sea dumpings—especially those in the late 1940s—is far from comprehensive. The ACDA report "Special Study on the Sea Disposal of Chemical Munitions" revealed that 40,000 cubic feet of government military records at the National Records Center in Washington, DC, were destroyed in the early 1950s because of a lack of storage facilities.

The report also revealed that "records from various posts and camps where chemical weapons were stored or used were supposed to have been shipped to the Washington National Records Center, but the military archivist [at the center] cautioned that many were never forwarded. This suggests that some bases or installations may possess meaningful chemical weapons records."

Dumping Stops, But Questions Linger
The United States stopped sea dumping in 1970 after public opposition arose to an army plan to dump 27,000 tons of chemicals and munitions; at the same time, a study released by the National Academy of Sciences recommended that the army avoid sea dumping. Two years later, Congress passed the Marine Protection Research and Sanctuaries Act of 1972, which prohibited further ocean dumping of chemical weapons. Since then, the U.S. Army has accumulated nearly 400,000 chemical weapons at 8 sites across the country and has spent much time and money developing plans to dispose of them; yet there has been little official concern about chemical weapons previously dumped at sea. The United States made its last probe in 1974, examining the condition of 12,508 nerve gas rockets unloaded off the coast of Florida and found no sign of leakage. According to a report of the probe prepared by the U.S. Naval Research Laboratory, "There is life . . . even on the sunken ship." The army says that it has no plans to do any more probes. "There would be a tremendous cost associated with any additional probes," said U.S. Army spokesperson Maj. Gary Milner. "Besides, results of the probes conducted in the 1970s indicated that there is no need for continuing monitoring."

The ACDA study puts the cost of the current U.S. disposal program at between $8.5 and $9.5 billion and warned that "the costs associated with recovering sea-dumped CW materiel would tax an already burdened system trying to dispose of just the present CW stock."

Let Sleeping Dogs Lie?
A number of scientists and some respected international organizations believe it is best to leave the underwater sites alone, especially if they are in deep water. In 1994, for example, the Helsinki Commission (officially known as the Baltic Marine Environment Protection Commission) recommended that chemical weapons dumped in the Baltic Sea be left undis-

turbed and concluded that they pose no immediate danger to the marine environment.

Many experts disagree with that conclusion. They point out that during the past four decades there have been several incidents involving sea-dumped chemical weapons in the Baltic. For example, mustard bombs have been recovered on German and Polish beaches, and fishing nets have been contaminated.

Moreover, there are too many uncertainties about the chemical weapons at the bottom of the Baltic to draw any firm conclusions. For instance, the rate of deterioration of the munitions is unclear, not all of the dump sites are known, and the behavior of the leaking chemical weapons in the Baltic is not understood. "There is no question incidents have occurred and the environment has been affected," Olson said. "So the truth is nobody knows for certain what is happening at the bottom of the Baltic."

Although no probes have been conducted in more than two decades, the U.S. Government has looked, however lightly, at the environmental implications of the issue. As part of the 1993 study, ACDA conducted a literature search to "identify possible chemical reactions of sea water with containers, of sea water with munitions fills [agents or their decomposition products], and of fills with containers in sea water at the ambient ocean temperatures and turbidity."

Specific temperature and turbidity profiles could not be obtained, but ACDA's report cited a Norwegian Defense Research Establishment (NDRE) study that investigated whether ships scuttled in the Skagerrak posed any environmental hazard. The NDRE study concluded that "no effect on sea life is to be expected if any of the chemical agents leak out." The ACDA report, however, also revealed that a Danish study cited over 150 cases where Danish fisherman hauled in some type of chemical agent, mostly mustard. These findings led ACDA to conclude that "what this suggests is that additional research may be needed to ascertain the answers to a number of questions."

Critics of the U.S. Government's approach to the issue agree that more research should be done, but they insist the dump sites must also be monitored in the meantime. Their worst-case scenario goes something like this: No effort is made to monitor the sites, and one day—without warning—many of the sea-dumped weapons begin to leak. Toxic agents then enter the food chain, pollute the water, deplete the world's endangered fish stocks, cause serious environmental damage, and create toxic effects with possible genetic consequences. "It's only a matter of time before we have a serious accident," warns Greg Williams of the Kentucky Environmental Coalition.

Wayne Landis, an expert in environmental toxicology and a professor at Western Washington University in Bellingham, has been one of the most vocal critics of the U.S. Government's refusal to conduct probes. In testimony before the U.S. District Court of the District of Hawaii in 1990, Landis said that not enough is known about nerve gas agents like VX and GB to accurately evaluate the environmental impact of an accidental release into the aquatic environment. He warned that an accident involving nerve agents would have "devastating toxicological consequences."

Many other scientists share Landis's belief that nobody really knows what is happening at the bottom of the sea. In his essay in *Sea-Dumped Chemical Weapons,* SIPRI's Thomas Stock noted, "The available information on the poisoning of the marine environment and fish by released chemical warfare agents is very limited and mostly related to laboratory investigations.

"The complex ecosystem of the Baltic Sea has been studied at length," Stock wrote. "However, most investigations have been performed regarding normal environmental contaminants. There is no real expertise available on the bioaccumulation of such agents in marine organisms. Assessing the potential threat to marine environments after the massive release of chemical warfare agents from dumped chemical weapons requires more detailed scientific investigations."

Not My Problem
Although many questions need to be answered, the issue has had a low priority among states and international organizations. A number of reasons help explain the indifference. For one thing, the issue is politically sensitive because it raises the question of accountability. Many dumping operations were conducted secretly without notifying neighboring states. "Not only the countries that undertook the dumping operations, but also those that were informed but allowed dumping in proximity to their shores, without making it public, have been reluctant to discuss the problem," Kaffka said. "That's why so many governments keep insisting the situation is safe."

Paul Rusman, a scientist at Groningen University in the Netherlands, said, "Without adding to conspiracy theories, governments may reasonably fear the consequences of more detailed knowledge of this issue more than the possible political and financial risks involved in leaving the problem at rest, since, for any government that does not have to cope with special interests such as fishermen, this must look like a no-win situation."

Another factor is the complexity of the issue and the huge commitment of money and resources it would demand. Serious work would require highly qualified specialists in various fields; expensive expeditions, underwater exploration and monitoring equipment; complicated and extensive laboratory and archival research; and intergovernmental support and collaboration over a long period of time. The work would also be dangerous, with the potential for high-profile accidents with serious, widespread consequences.

If monitoring reveals a significant problem, is it a problem that can be easily addressed, or might remediation make things worse? "The problem of remediation probably cannot be easily addressed in any circumstance,"

Rusman said. "Remediation will not make things worse, but demoting shells is always a risky business, especially when the shells are leaking."

Despite the complexity of the issue, a few organizations have responded to the challenge and are now working to find solutions. The Helsinki Commission has put the issue on its agenda, and in January 1995, the Rockefeller Foundation funded, and the Conversation for Environment International Foundation organized, a conference titled "The Advanced Workshops on Sea Dumped Chemical Weapons" at Kaliningrad, Russia, the first attempt to address the issue on a comprehensive basis.

The CFE organized a second conference on sea-dumped chemical munitions, funded by NATO's Scientific and Environmental Division, at Bellagio, Italy in April 1996. Attendees—including academics, environmentalists, military specialists, and journalists—drafted an action plan to "overcome the inertia and reluctance of governments and international organizations to tackle the problem of sea-dumped chemical weapons which is a potential time bomb."

"Some of the evidence I saw at the conference gives sufficient cause for concern," Rusman said. "The fact is we still simply know too little about the present condition of the dumped chemicals present worldwide to enable us to lean back in relaxation."

Among its recommendations, the conference called for a risk assessment to be carried out in collaboration with international bodies and institutions and urged that those dump sites identified as being most at risk be constantly monitored. Funds for the risk assessment would come from the governments of the countries concerned, private donors, and other international organizations.

Conference participants concluded that know-how and personnel from the world's defense industries could be used to deal with the problem: Given post-Cold War cuts in defense spending, the clean-up effort could prove to be a lucrative avenue for companies looking for profitable defense conversion opportunities. The U.S. Government's own reports reveal that while costs would be high, the technological problems could be overcome.

"This ecological problem has direct relevance to the military industry," Kaffka explained. "Almost all of the resources that are needed can be obtained from the defense industries of the countries involved. It represents an excellent opportunity for fruitful cooperation between the defense conversion sector and the environmental community."

E. J. Hogendoorn is a researcher at Human Rights Watch in Washington, DC, under whose auspices this research was conducted.

—Taken from *http://www.bullatomsci.org/issues/1997/so97/so97hogendoom.htm*

History of Biological Warfare and the Current Threat

The universal symbol for "Bio-Hazard."

USAMRIID's Medical Management of Biological Casualties Handbook

Fourth Edition, February 2001

The use of biological weapons in warfare has been recorded throughout history. Two of the earliest reported uses occurred in the sixth century BC, with the Assyrians poisoning enemy wells with rye ergot, and Solon's use of the purgative herb hellebore during the siege of Krissa. In 1346, plague broke out in the Tartar army during its siege of Kaffa (at present day Feodosia in Crimea). The attackers hurled the corpses of plague victims over the city walls; the plague epidemic that followed forced the defenders to surrender, and some infected people who left Kaffa may have started the Black Death pandemic that spread throughout Europe. Russian troops may have used the same tactic against Sweden in 1710.

On several occasions, smallpox was used as a biological weapon. Pizarro is said to have presented South American natives with variola-contaminated clothing in the fifteenth century, and the English did the same when Sir Jeffery Amherst provided Indians loyal to the French with smallpox-laden blankets during the French and Indian War of 1754–1767. Native Americans defending Fort Carillon sustained epidemic casualties which directly contributed to the loss of the fort to the English.

In this century, there is evidence that during World War I, German agents inoculated horses and cattle with glanders in the United States before the animals were shipped to France. In 1937, Japan started an ambitious biological warfare program, located fourty miles south of Harbin, Manchuria, in a laboratory complex code-named "Unit 731." Studies directed by Japanese General Ishii continued there until 1945, when the complex was burned. A post-World War II investigation revealed that the Japanese researched numerous organisms and used prisoners of war as research subjects. Slightly less than 1,000 human autopsies apparently were carried out at "Unit 731," mostly on victims exposed to aerosolized anthrax. Many more prisoners and Chinese nationals may have died in this facility—some have estimated up to 3,000 human deaths. After reports of Japanese planes dropping plague-infected fleas, a plague epidemic ensued in China and Manchuria. By 1945, the Japanese program had stockpiled 400 kilograms of anthrax to be used in a specially designed fragmentation bomb.

In 1943, the United States began research into the use of biological agents for offensive purposes. This work was started, interestingly enough, in response to a perceived German biological warfare (BW) threat as opposed to a Japanese one. The United States conducted this research at Camp Detrick (now

Fort Detrick), which was a small National Guard airfield prior to that time, and produced agents at other sites until 1969, when President Nixon stopped all offensive biological and toxin weapon research and production by executive order. Between May 1971 and May 1972, all stockpiles of biological agents and munitions from the now defunct U.S. program were destroyed in the presence of monitors representing the United States Department of Agriculture, the Department of Health, Education, and Welfare, and the states of Arkansas, Colorado, and Maryland. Included among the destroyed agents were *Bacillus anthracis,* botulinum toxin, *Francisella tularensis, Coxiella burnetii,* Venezuelan equine encephalitis virus, *Brucella suis,* and Staphylococcal enterotoxin B. The United States began a medical defensive program in 1953 that continues today at USAMRIID.

In 1972, the United States, United Kingdom, and Soviet Union signed the Convention on the Prohibition of the Development, Production and Stockpiling of Bacteriological (Biological) and Toxin Weapons and on Their Destruction, commonly called the Biological Weapons Convention. Over 140 countries have since added their ratification. This treaty prohibits the stockpiling of biological agents for offensive military purposes and also forbids research into such offensive employment of biological agents. However, despite this historic agreement among nations, biological warfare research continued to flourish in many countries hostile to the United States. Moreover, there have been several cases of suspected or actual use of biological weapons. Among the most notorious of these were the "yellow rain" incidents in Southeast Asia, the use of ricin as an assassination weapon in London in 1978, and the accidental release of anthrax spores at Sverdlovsk in 1979.

Testimony from the late 1970s indicated that Laos and Kampuchea were attacked by planes and helicopters delivering aerosols of several colors. After being exposed, people and animals became disoriented and ill, and a small percentage of those stricken died. Some of these clouds were thought to be comprised of trichothecene toxins (in particular, T2 mycotoxin). These attacks are grouped under the label "yellow rain." There has been a great deal of controversy about whether these clouds were truly biological warfare agents. Some have argued that the clouds were nothing more than feces produced by swarms of bees.

In 1978, a Bulgarian exile named Georgi Markov was attacked in London with a device disguised as an umbrella. The device injected a tiny pellet filled with ricin toxin into the subcutaneous tissue of his leg while he was waiting for a bus. He died several days later. On autopsy, the tiny pellet was found and determined to contain the toxin. It was later revealed that the Bulgarian secret service carried out the assassination, and the technology to commit the crime was supplied by the former Soviet Union.

In April 1979, an incident occurred in Sverdlovsk (now Yekaterinburg) in the former Soviet Union which appeared to be an accidental aerosol release of *Bacillus anthracis* spores from a Soviet military microbiology facility,

Compound 19. Residents living downwind from this compound developed high fever and difficulty breathing, and a large number died. The Soviet Ministry of Health blamed the deaths on the consumption of contaminated meat, and for years controversy raged in the press over the actual cause of the outbreak. All evidence available to the United States government indicated a massive release of *aerosolized B. anthracis* spores. In the summer of 1992, U.S. intelligence officials were proven correct when the new Russian President, Boris Yeltsin, acknowledged that the Sverdlovsk incident was in fact related to military developments at the microbiology facility. In 1994, Meselson and colleagues published an in-depth analysis of the Sverdlovsk incident (*Science* 266:1202–1208). They documented that all of the cases from 1979 occurred within a narrow zone extending four kilometers downwind in a southerly direction from Compound 19. There were sixty-six fatalities of the seventy-seven patients identified.

In August 1991, the United Nations carried out its first inspection of Iraq's biological warfare capabilities in the aftermath of the Gulf War. On August 2, 1991, representatives of the Iraqi government announced to leaders of United Nations Special Commission Team 7 that they had conducted research into the offensive use of *Bacillus anthracis,* botulinum toxins, and *Clostridium perfringens* (presumably one of its toxins). This open admission of biological weapons research verified many of the concerns of the U.S. intelligence community. Iraq had extensive and redundant research facilities at Salman Pak and other sites, many of which were destroyed during the war.

In 1995, further information on Iraq's offensive program was made available to United Nations inspectors. Iraq conducted research and development work on anthrax, botulinum toxins, *Clostridium perfringens,* aflatoxins, wheat cover smut, and ricin. Field trials were conducted with *Bacillus subtilis* (a simulant for anthrax), botulinum toxin, and aflatoxin. Biological agents were tested in various delivery systems, including rockets, aerial bombs, and spray tanks. In December 1990, the Iraqis filled one hundred R400 bombs with botulinum toxin, fifty with anthrax, and sixteen with aflatoxin. In addition, thirteen Al Hussein (SCUD) warheads were filled with botulinum toxin, ten with anthrax, and two with aflatoxin. These weapons were deployed in January 1991 to four locations. In all, Iraq produced 19,000 liters of concentrated botulinum toxin (nearly 10,000 liters filled into munitions); 8,500 liters of concentrated anthrax (6,500 liters filled into munitions); and 2,200 liters of aflatoxin (1,580 liters filled into munitions).

The threat of biological warfare has increased in the last two decades, with a number of countries working on the offensive use of these agents. The extensive program of the former Soviet Union is now primarily under the control of Russia. Former Russian president Boris Yeltsin stated that he would put an end to further offensive biological research; however, the degree to which the program was scaled back is not known. Recent revelations from a senior BW program manager who defected from Russia in 1992 outlined a remarkably robust biological warfare program, which included active research into genetic engineering, binary biologicals and chimeras, and industrial capacity to produce agents. There is also growing concern that the smallpox virus, now stored in only two laboratories at the CDC in Atlanta and the Institute for Viral Precautions in Moscow, may be in other countries around the globe.

There is intense concern in the West about the possibility of proliferation or enhancement of offensive programs in countries hostile to the western democracies, due to the potential hiring of expatriate Russian scientists. It was reported in January 1998 that Iraq had sent about a dozen scientists involved in BW research to Libya to help that country develop a biological warfare complex disguised as a medical facility in the Tripoli area. In a report issued in November 1997, Secretary of Defense William Cohen singled out Libya, Iraq, Iran, and Syria as countries "aggressively seeking" nuclear, biological, and chemical weapons.

Finally, there is an increasing amount of concern over the possibility of the terrorist use of biological agents to threaten either military or civilian populations. There have been cases of extremist groups trying to obtain microorganisms that could be used as biological weapons. The 1995 sarin nerve agent attack in the Tokyo subway system raised awareness that terrorist organizations could potentially acquire or develop WMD for use against civilian populations. Subsequent investigations revealed the organization had attempted to release botulinum toxins and anthrax on several occasions. The Department of Defense has been leading a federal effort to train the first responders in 120 American cities to be prepared to act in case of a domestic terrorist incident involving WMD. The program will be handed over to the Department of Justice on October 1, 2000. In the past two years, first responders, public health and medical personnel, and law enforcement agencies have dealt with the exponential increase in biological weapons hoaxes around the country.

Certainly the threat of biological weapons being used against U.S. military forces and civilians is broader and more likely in various geographic scenarios than at any point in our history. Therefore, awareness of this potential threat and education of our leaders, medical care providers, and public health agencies on how to combat it is crucial.

—Taken from *http://www.health.state.ri.us/environment/biot/history.htm*

Has Any American City Ever Faced Biological Warfare?

by George Beres

Threats of terrorism have taken many forms in recent weeks. But none more pervasive than the biological. First, crop-duster planes were grounded nationally. Then cases of anthrax disease were reported in Florida. Suddenly the nation awoke to prospects of germ warfare as one of the terrible realities of international terrorism.

But the frightening prospects, while new to the rest of the nation, were an old story in Oregon—a 17-year-old story that involved a conspiracy to cause sickness in one Oregon community by spreading cultivated germs at public food counters.

In the wake of the September 11, 2001, airliner attacks on New York City and Washington, DC, the federal government began exploring possibilities for biological follow-up attacks. That revived memories of the poisoning of residents of The Dalles in north central Oregon by members of the Rajneeshees cult in 1984. Now departed, the controversial religious commune in the early 1980s had bought and settled on a 64,000-acre plot of land in Wasco County, a few miles from The Dalles.

I was reminded of the Rajneeshees while reading a new Simon & Schuster book, *Germs,* by *New York Times* reporter Judith Miller. In an accident of good timing, it appeared in bookstores for the first time on September 11. Its opening chapter describes the sickness conspiracy that in 1984 hit The Dalles, a town of some 20,000 on Interstate 84, near the edge of the Columbia River. The Oregon poisoning incident got greater national exposure when mentioned by a guest authority on biological warfare during the "Lehrer NewsHour" of Public Television, October 1. More attention came in the October 3 edition of *Time Magazine,* which mentioned it as "America's First Bioterrorism Attack."

For all the attention it now gets, early investigation of The Dalles trauma was a comedy of errors in the judgment of Jim Weaver, then an Oregon congressman in Washington.

Weaver told me: "I'd gotten familiar with the 'bug' of choice in The Dalles, salmonella, during my college days studying biology. I knew the area because I chaired the Congressional committee that approved Bureau of Land Management transfers, such as that sought by the Rajneeshees." Weaver was impatient with preliminary investigations of the state that suggested food handlers had carelessly infected salad bar food. "I said that was ridiculous," recalled Weaver. "Data from a study done by the Center for Disease Control clearly showed it was poisoning from the outside. State health authorities simply did not want to face the truth. They were scared of causing panic."

The reason for the poison plot was simple politics. The Dalles had a big proportion of Wasco County's voters. Conspirators among the 4,000 new residents of the cult-compound figured their bloc of votes could swing the election their way and give them control of the county, if many voters in The Dalles were too sick to go to the polls. The Rajneeshees had a surprisingly sophisticated medical lab. There they developed the germ culture for salmonellosis, which they then began to spread in salad bars of the town's restaurants. For its size, The Dalles had a high proportion of restaurants—thirty-five—because of the heavy traffic of Interstate 84.

"Big Mom" of the cult, Ma Anand Sheela, was personal secretary to the Bhagwan leader of the commune. She was accused of masterminding the poison plot, and soon had a public identity outside the commune exceeding that of the Bhagwan. Her co-conspirator, Ma Anand Puja, was accused of developing the germ cultures in the lab. Her scientific aberrations earned her a nickname with Nazi German connotations: "Nurse Mengele."

The commune was well-funded and tightly controlled. It had several jet planes and a helicopter, and a sixty-man police force. Rep. Weaver got on the case after a visit from legendary Oregon Olympics track coach Bill Bowerman, whose family had property in Wasco County. He was concerned about what he considered disruptions by the Rajneeshees and worried about the unexplainable incidence of illness. His son, Tom, a Eugene businessman, said he thought at first that germs allegedly cultivated by the cult "were more obnoxious than lethal."

Former Oregon Supreme Court justice Ed Fadeley, then president of the Oregon Senate, took the issue more seriously: "I felt the Wasco County situation might have grave health implications, and that the germs had the potential for killing people." Weaver sought the expertise of the leading authority on salmonella at the University of Washington. The scientist told him: "You must have a madman loose down there." But he added to Weaver's frustration by refusing to make the statement publicly.

Dave Frohnmayer, University of Oregon's president, was the Oregon attorney general who investigated the growing list of complaints directed at the Rajneeshees. He led a task force that discovered glass vials of bacterial disease in the cult lab. Some evidence suggested a separate plot to kill eleven people, including an *Oregonian* reporter.

At that point, the Bagwhan, leaving behind his fleet of Rolls-Royces, fled in one of his jets. He was caught at a North Carolina refueling point. He paid a fine of $400,000. When Frohnmayer could not get the U.S. Government interested, the guru—who had turned on the two "Mas" and accused them of trying to create a fascist community—was allowed to leave the country. Both "Mas," Sheela and Puja, were extradited from their West Germany sanctuary, and sentenced to twenty-four-year prison terms. They served four years in a California prison before being paroled and fleeing the country.

The conspiracy went public in a big way when Rep. Weaver made a speech on the subject in Congress on February 28, 1985, earning it a place in the public record through publication in the "Congressional Record." But it did him no good among doubting constituents. "This came at the height of concern with political correctness," said Weaver. "Some people criticized me for what they called bigotry against a religious minority. Students spat on me when I visited the University of Oregon. The Oregon press villified me when I kept pushing the investigation."

What bothered the Congressman most was what he calls self-censorship by the media. When the Congressional Research Service did a study of what appeared in the national press, it found the only published reference to the poisoning controversy made outside Oregon was one sentence in the *New York Times*. Weaver believes many public officials were afraid of creating a panic by making public the investigation. He feels Secretary of State Norma Paulus took the issue seriously, as did Frohnmayer, "although he was not forceful enough in pursuing the case."

In April 1985, Weaver got a letter on stationery of the Rajneeshees Medical Association. It sought from him an apology for "choosing to hide behind legislative immunity" while criticizing members of the commune in the Congress.

"They, and we, are lucky they left Oregon," said Weaver. "Only now do we recognize how easy it is to get pathogens from a germ bank if you have the identity of a medical corporation. As we face new threats since September 11, we're learning how vital it is for our intelligence operatives to get information from informers."

Long retired from the Congress, Weaver has discarded some records from his term of office, but has kept four boxes of documented data from the Rajneeshees case.

"It is frightening when one considers how bad it might have become," he says. "When the FBI eventually investigated the cult's medical lab, it found experimental cultures of the AIDS virus."

Today, almost two decades after the "germ attack" in Oregon, I share with many uncertainty over what to expect next in a world of conflict that has vastly changed. If this new battleground threatens to explode in our midst, the lessons of The Dalles in Oregon could guide U.S. security agencies now facing a new kind of alert.

—Taken from *http://www.hnn.us/articles/355.html*

Biological and Chemical Terrorism: Strategic Plan for Preparedness and Response

Recommendations of the CDC Strategic Planning Workgroup

". . . And he that will not apply new remedies must expect new evils; for time is the greatest innovator. . . ."

—*The Essays by Sir Francis Bacon, 1601*

Summary
The U.S. national civilian vulnerability to the deliberate use of biological and chemical agents has been highlighted by recognition of substantial biological weapons development programs and arsenals in foreign countries, attempts to acquire or possess biological agents by militants, and

high-profile terrorist attacks. Evaluation of this vulnerability has focused on the role public health will have detecting and managing the probable covert biological terrorist incident with the realization that the U.S. local, state, and federal infrastructure is already strained as a result of other important public health problems. In partnership with representatives for local and state health departments, other federal agencies, and medical and public health professional associations, CDC has developed a strategic plan to address the deliberate dissemination of biological or chemical agents. The plan contains recommendations to reduce United States vulnerability to biological and chemical terrorism—preparedness planning, detection and surveillance, laboratory analysis, emergency response, and communication systems. Training and research are integral components for achieving these recommendations. Success of the plan hinges on strengthening the relationships between medical and public health professionals and on building new partnerships with emergency management, the military, and law enforcement professionals.

Introduction

An act of biological or chemical terrorism might range from dissemination of aerosolized anthrax spores to food product contamination, and predicting when and how such an attack might occur is not possible. However, the possibility of biological or chemical terrorism should not be ignored, especially in light of events during the past ten years (e.g., the sarin gas attack in the Tokyo subway, and the discovery of military bioweapons programs in Iraq and the former Soviet Union). Preparing the nation to address this threat is a formidable challenge, but the consequences of being unprepared could be devastating.

The public health infrastructure must be prepared to prevent illness and injury that would result from biological and chemical terrorism, especially a covert terrorist attack. As with emerging infectious diseases, early detection and control of biological or chemical attacks depends on a strong and flexible public health system at the local, state, and federal levels. In addition, primary healthcare providers throughout the United States must be vigilant because they will probably be the first to observe and report unusual illnesses or injuries.

This report is a summary of the recommendations made by CDC's Strategic Planning Workgroup in "Preparedness and Response to Biological and Chemical Terrorism: A Strategic Plan" (CDC, unpublished report, 2000), which outlines steps for strengthening public health and healthcare capacity to protect the United States against these dangers. This strategic plan marks the first time that CDC has joined with law enforcement, intelligence, and defense agencies in addition to traditional CDC partners to address a national security threat. As a reflection of the need for broad-based public health involvement in terrorism preparedness and planning, staff from CDC's centers, institute, and offices participated in developing the strategic plan, including the

- National Center for Infectious Diseases,
- National Center for Environmental Health,
- Public Health Practice Program Office,
- Epidemiology Program Office,
- National Institute for Occupational Safety and Health,
- Office of Health and Safety,
- National Immunization Program, and
- National Center for Injury Prevention and Control.

The Agency for Toxic Substances and Disease Registry (ATSDR) is also participating with CDC in this effort and will provide expertise in the area of industrial chemical terrorism. In this report, the term CDC includes ATSDR when activities related to chemical terrorism are discussed. In addition, colleagues from local, state, and federal agencies; emergency medical services (EMS); professional societies; universities and medical centers; and private industry provided suggestions and constructive criticism.

Combating biological and chemical terrorism will require capitalizing on advances in technology, information systems, and medical sciences. Preparedness will also require a re-examination of core public health activities (e.g., disease surveillance) in light of these advances. Preparedness efforts by public health agencies and primary healthcare providers to detect and respond to biological and chemical terrorism will have the added benefit of strengthening the U.S. capacity for identifying and controlling injuries and emerging infectious diseases.

U.S. Vulnerability to Biological and Chemical Terrorism
Terrorist incidents in the United States and elsewhere involving bacterial pathogens, nerve gas, and a lethal plant toxin (i.e., ricin), have demonstrated that the United States is vulnerable to biological and chemical threats as well as explosives. Recipes for preparing "homemade" agents are readily available, and reports of arsenals of military bioweapons raise the possibility that terrorists might have access to highly dangerous agents, which have been engineered for mass dissemination as small-particle aerosols. Such agents as the variola virus, the causative agent of smallpox, are highly contagious and often fatal. Responding to large-scale outbreaks caused by these agents will require the rapid mobilization of public health workers, emergency responders, and private healthcare providers. Large-scale outbreaks will also require rapid procurement and distribution of large quantities of drugs and vaccines, which must be available quickly.

Overt Versus Covert Terrorist Attacks
In the past, most planning for emergency response to terrorism has been concerned with overt attacks (e.g., bombings). Chemical terrorism acts are likely to be overt because the effects of chemical agents absorbed through inhalation or by absorption through the skin or mucous membranes are usually immediate and obvious. Such attacks elicit immediate response from police, fire, and EMS personnel.

In contrast, attacks with biological agents are more likely to be covert. They present different challenges and require an additional dimension of emergency planning that involves the public health infrastructure (Box 1). Covert dissemination of a biological agent in a public place will not have an immediate impact because of the delay between exposure and onset of illness (i.e., the incubation period). Consequently, the first casualties of a covert attack probably will be identified by physicians or other primary health-care providers. For example, in the event of a covert release of the contagious variola virus, patients will appear in doctors' offices, clinics, and emergency rooms during the first or second week, complaining of fever, back pain, headache, nausea, and other symptoms of what initially might appear to be an ordinary viral infection. As the disease progresses, these persons will develop the papular rash characteristic of early-stage smallpox, a rash that physicians might not recognize immediately. By the time the rash becomes pustular and patients begin to die, the terrorists would be far away and the disease disseminated through the population by person-to-person contact. Only a short window of opportunity will exist between the time the first cases are identified and a second wave of the population becomes ill. During that brief period, public health officials will need to determine that an attack has occurred, identify the organism, and prevent more casualties through prevention strategies (e.g., mass vaccination or prophylactic treatment). As person-to-person contact continues, successive waves of transmission could carry infection to other worldwide localities. These issues might also be relevant for other person-to-person transmissible etiologic agents (e.g., plague or certain viral hemorrhagic fevers).

Certain chemical agents can also be delivered covertly through contaminated food or water. In 1999, the vulnerability of the food supply was illustrated in Belgium, when chickens were unintentionally exposed to dioxin-contaminated fat used to make animal feed. Because the contamination was not discovered for months, the dioxin, a cancer-causing chemical that does not cause immediate symptoms in humans, was probably present in chicken meat and eggs sold in Europe during early 1999. This

---

BOX 1. Local Public Health Agency Preparedness

- Because the initial detection of a covert biological or chemical attack will probably occur at the local level, disease surveillance systems at state and local health agencies must be capable of detecting unusual patterns of disease or injury, including those caused by unusual or unknown threat agents.
- Because the initial response to a covert biological or chemical attack will probably be made at the local level, epidemiologists at state and local health agencies must have expertise and resources for responding to reports of clusters of rare, unusual, or unexplained illnesses.

incident underscores the need for prompt diagnoses of unusual or suspicious health problems in animals as well as humans, a lesson that was also demonstrated by the recent outbreak of mosquito-borne West Nile virus in birds and humans in New York City in 1999. The dioxin episode also demonstrates how a covert act of foodborne biological or chemical terrorism could affect commerce and human or animal health.

Focusing Preparedness Activities

Early detection of and response to biological or chemical terrorism are crucial. Without special preparation at the local and state levels, a large-scale attack with variola virus, aerosolized anthrax spores, a nerve gas, or a foodborne biological or chemical agent could overwhelm the local and perhaps national public health infrastructure. Large numbers of patients, including both infected persons and the "worried well," would seek medical attention, with a corresponding need for medical supplies, diagnostic tests, and hospital beds. Emergency responders, healthcare workers, and public health officials could be at special risk, and everyday life would be disrupted as a result of widespread fear of contagion.

Preparedness for terrorist-caused outbreaks and injuries is an essential component of the U.S. public health surveillance and response system, which is designed to protect the population against any unusual public health event (e.g., influenza pandemics, contaminated municipal water supplies, or intentional dissemination of *Yersinia pestis,* the causative agent of plague). The epidemiologic skills, surveillance methods, diagnostic techniques, and physical resources required to detect and investigate unusual or unknown diseases, as well as syndromes or injuries caused by chemical accidents, are similar to those needed to identify and respond to an attack with a biological or chemical agent. However, public health agencies must prepare also for the special features a terrorist attack probably would have (e.g., mass casualties or the use of rare agents) (Boxes 2–5). Terrorists might use combinations of these agents, attack in more than one location simultaneously, use new agents, or use organisms that are not on the critical list (e.g., common, drug-resistant, or genetically engineered pathogens). Lists of critical biological and chemical agents will need to be modified as new information becomes available. In addition, each state and locality will need to adapt the lists to local conditions and preparedness needs by using the criteria provided in CDC's strategic plan.

Potential biological and chemical agents are numerous, and the public health infrastructure must be equipped to quickly resolve crises that would arise from a biological or chemical attack. However, to best protect the public, the preparedness efforts must be focused on agents that might have the greatest impact on U.S. health and security, especially agents that are highly contagious or that can be engineered for widespread dissemination via small-particle aerosols. Preparing the nation to address these dangers is a major challenge to U.S. public health systems and healthcare providers. Early detection requires increased biological and chemical terrorism awareness among front-line healthcare providers because

BOX 2. Preparing Public Health agencies for Biological Attacks

Steps in Preparing for Biological Attacks

- Enhance epidemiologic capacity to detect and respond to biological attacks.
- Supply diagnostic re-agents to state and local public health agencies.
- Establish communication programs to ensure delivery of accurate information.
- Enhance bioterrorism-related education and training for healthcare professionals.
- Prepare educational materials that will inform and re-assure the public during and after a biological attack.
- Stockpile appropriate vaccines and drugs.
- Establish molecular surveillance for microbial strains, including unusual or drug-resistant strains.
- Support the development of diagnostic tests.
- Encourage research on antiviral drugs and vaccines.

BOX 3. Critical Biological Agents

Category A

The U.S. public health system and primary healthcare providers must be prepared to address varied biological agents, including pathogens that are rarely seen in the United States. High-priority agents include organisms that pose a risk to national security because they

- can be easily disseminated or transmitted person-to-person;
- cause high mortality, with potential for major public health impact;
- might cause public panic and social disruption; and
- require special action for public health preparedness (Box 2).

Category A agents include

- variola major (smallpox);
- *Bacillus anthracis* (anthrax);
- *Yersinia pestis* (plague);
- *Clostridium botulinum toxin* (botulism);
- *Francisella tularensis* (tularaemia);
- filoviruses,
  - Ebola hemorrhagic fever,
  - Marburg hemorrhagic fever; and
- arenaviruses,
  - Lassa (Lassa fever),
  - Junin (Argentine hemorrhagic fever) and related viruses.

Category B

Second highest priority agents include those that

- are moderately easy to disseminate;
- cause moderate morbidity and low mortality; and
- require specific enhancements of CDC's diagnostic capacity and enhanced disease surveillance.

Category B agents include

- *Coxiella burnetti* (Q fever);
- *Brucella species* (brucellosis);
- *Burkholderia mallei* (glanders);
- alphaviruses,
    - ○ Venezuelan encephalomyelitis,
    - ○ eastern and western equine encephalomyelitis;
- ricin toxin from *Ricinus communis* (castor beans);
- epsilon toxin of *Clostridium perfringens;* and
- *Staphylococcus* enterotoxin B.

A subset of List B agents includes pathogens that are food- or waterborne.

These pathogens include but are not limited to

- *Salmonella* species,
- *Shigella dysenteriae,*
- *Escherichia coli* O157:H7,
- *Vibrio cholerae,* and
- *Cryptosporidium parvum.*

Category C

Third highest priority agents include emerging pathogens that could be engineered for mass dissemination in the future because of

- availability;
- ease of production and dissemination; and
- potential for high morbidity and mortality and major health impact.

Category C agents include

- Nipah virus,
- hantaviruses,
- tickborne hemorrhagic fever viruses,
- tickborne encephalitis viruses,
- yellow fever, and
- multidrug-resistant tuberculosis.

Preparedness for List C agents requires ongoing research to improve disease detection, diagnosis, treatment, and prevention. Knowing in advance which newly emergent pathogens might be employed by terrorists is not possible; therefore, linking bioterrorism preparedness efforts with ongoing disease surveillance and outbreak response activities as defined in CDC's emerging infectious disease strategy is imperative.*

*CDC. "Preventing emerging infectious diseases: a strategy for the 21st century." Atlanta, Georgia: U.S. Department of Health and Human Services, 1998.

BOX 4. Preparing Public Health Agencies for Chemical Attacks

Steps in Preparing for Chemical Attacks

- Enhance epidemiologic capacity for detecting and responding to chemical attacks.
- Enhance awareness of chemical terrorism among emergency medical service personnel, police officers, firefighters, physicians, and nurses.
- Stockpile chemical antidotes.
- Develop and provide bioassays for detection and diagnosis of chemical injuries.
- Prepare educational materials to inform the public during and after a chemical attack

---

BOX 5. Chemical Agents

Chemical agents that might be used by terrorists range from warfare agents to toxic chemicals commonly used in industry. Criteria for determining priority chemical agents include

- chemical agents already known to be used as weaponry;
- availability of chemical agents to potential terrorists;
- chemical agents likely to cause major morbidity or mortality;
- potential of agents for causing public panic and social disruption; and
- agents that require special action for public health preparedness (Box 4).

Categories of chemical agents include

- nerve agents,
  - tabun (ethyl N,N-dimethylphosphoramidocyanidate),
  - sarin (isopropyl methylphosphanofluoridate),
  - soman (pinacolyl methyl phosphonofluoridate),
  - GF (cyclohexylmethylphosphonofluoridate),
  - VX (o-ethyl-[S]-[2-diisopropylaminoethyl]-methylphosphonothiolate);
- blood agents,
  - hydrogen cyanide,
  - cyanogen chloride;
- blister agents,
  - lewisite (an aliphatic arsenic compound, 2-chlorovinyldichloroarsine),
  - nitrogen and sulfur mustards,
  - phosgene oxime;
- heavy metals,
  - arsenic,
  - lead,
  - mercury;

- Volatile toxins,
  - benzene,
  - chloroform,
  - trihalomethanes;
- pulmonary agents,
  - phosgene,
  - chlorine,
  - vinyl chloride;
- incapacitating agents,
  - BZ (3-quinuclidinyl benzilate);
- pesticides, persistent and nonpersistent;
- dioxins, furans, and polychlorinated biphenyls (PCBs);
- explosive nitro compounds and oxidizers,
  - ammonium nitrate combined with fuel oil;
- flammable industrial gases and liquids,
  - gasoline,
  - propane;
- poison industrial gases, liquids, and solids,
  - cyanides,
  - nitriles; and
- corrosive industrial acids and bases,
  - nitric acid,
  - sulfuric acid.

Because of the hundreds of new chemicals introduced internationally each month, treating exposed persons by clinical syndrome rather than by specific agent is more useful for public health planning and emergency medical response purposes. Public health agencies and first responders might render the most aggressive, timely, and clinically relevant treatment possible by using treatment modalities based on syndromic categories (e.g., burns and trauma, cardiorespiratory failure, neurologic damage, and shock). These activities must be linked with authorities responsible for environmental sampling and decontamination.

they are in the best position to report suspicious illnesses and injuries. Also, early detection will require improved communication systems between those providers and public health officials. In addition, state and local healthcare agencies must have enhanced capacity to investigate unusual events and unexplained illnesses, and diagnostic laboratories must be equipped to identify biological and chemical agents that rarely are seen in the United States. Fundamental to these efforts is comprehensive, integrated training designed to ensure core competency in public health preparedness and the highest levels of scientific expertise among local, state, and federal partners.

Key Focus Areas
CDC's strategic plan is based on the following five focus areas, with each area integrating training and research:

- preparedness and prevention;
- detection and surveillance;
- diagnosis and characterization of biological and chemical agents;
- response; and
- communication.

Preparedness and Prevention
Detection, diagnosis, and mitigation of illness and injury caused by biological and chemical terrorism is a complex process that involves numerous partners and activities. Meeting this challenge will require special emergency preparedness in all cities and states. CDC will provide public health guidelines, support, and technical assistance to local and state public health agencies as they develop coordinated preparedness plans and response protocols. CDC also will provide self-assessment tools for terrorism preparedness, including performance standards, attack simulations, and other exercises. In addition, CDC will encourage and support applied research to develop innovative tools and strategies to prevent or mitigate illness and injury caused by biological and chemical terrorism.

Detection and Surveillance
Early detection is essential for ensuring a prompt response to a biological or chemical attack, including the provision of prophylactic medicines, chemical antidotes, or vaccines. CDC will integrate surveillance for illness and injury resulting from biological and chemical terrorism into the U.S. disease surveillance systems, while developing new mechanisms for detecting, evaluating, and reporting suspicious events that might represent covert terrorist acts. As part of this effort, CDC and state and local health agencies will form partnerships with front-line medical personnel in hospital emergency departments, hospital care facilities, poison control centers, and other offices to enhance detection and reporting of unexplained injuries and illnesses as part of routine surveillance mechanisms for biological and chemical terrorism.

Diagnosis and Characterization of Biological and Chemical Agents
CDC and its partners will create a multilevel laboratory response network for bioterrorism (LRNB). That network will link clinical labs to public health agencies in all states, districts, territories, and selected cities and counties and to state-of-the-art facilities that can analyze biological agents (Figure 1). As part of this effort, CDC will transfer diagnostic technology to state health laboratories and others who will perform initial testing. CDC will also create an in-house rapid-response and advanced technology (RRAT) laboratory. This laboratory will provide around-the-clock diagnostic confirmatory and reference support for terrorism response teams. This network will include the regional chemical laboratories for diagnosing human exposure to chemical agents and provide links with other departments (e.g., the

Figure 1. Multilevel Laboratory Response Network for Bioterrorism That Will Link Clinical Labs to Public Health Agencies

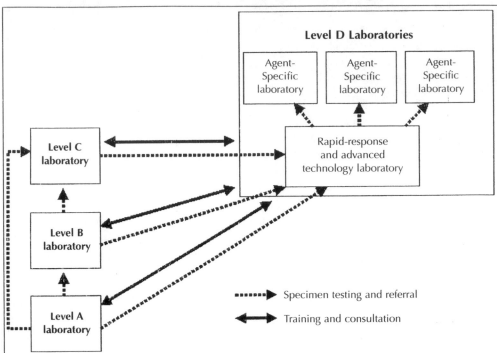

Functional Levels of the Laboratory Response Network for Bioterrorism

Level A: Early detection of intentional dissemination of biological agents—Level A laboratories will be public health and hospital laboratories with low-level biosafety facilities. Level A laboratories will use clinical data and standard microbiological tests to decide which specimens and isolates should be forwarded to higher level biocontainment laboratories. Level A laboratory staff will be trained in the safe collection, packaging, labeling, and shipping of samples that might contain dangerous pathogens.

Level B: Core capacity for agent isolation and presumptive-level testing of suspect specimens—Level B laboratories will be state and local public health agency laboratories that can test for specific agents and forward organisms or specimens to higher level biocontainment laboratories. Level B laboratories will minimize false positives and protect Level C laboratories from overload. Ultimately, Level B laboratories will maintain capacity to perform confirmatory testing and characterize drug susceptibility.

Level C: Advanced capacity for rapid identification—Level C laboratories, which could be located at state health agencies, academic research centers, or federal facilities, will perform advanced and specialized testing. Ultimately, Level C laboratories will have the capacity to perform toxicity testing and employ advanced diagnostic technologies (e.g., nucleic acid amplification and molecular fingerprinting). Level C laboratories will participate in the evaluation of new tests and reagents and determine which assays could be transferred to Level B laboratories.

Level D: Highest level containment and expertise in the diagnosis of rare and dangerous biological agents—Level D laboratories will be specialized federal laboratories with unique experience in diagnosis of rare diseases (e.g., smallpox and Ebola). Level D laboratories also will develop or evaluate new tests and methods and have the resources to maintain a strain bank of biological agents. Level D laboratories will maintain the highest biocontainment facilities and will be able to conduct all tests performed in Level A, B, and C laboratories, as well as additional confirmatory testing and characterization, as needed. They will also have the capacity to detect genetically engineered agents.

U.S. Environmental Protection Agency, which is responsible for environmental sampling).

Response
A comprehensive public health response to a biological or chemical terrorist event involves epidemiologic investigation, medical treatment and prophylaxis for affected persons, and the initiation of disease prevention or environmental decontamination measures. CDC will assist state and local health agencies in developing resources and expertise for investigating unusual events and unexplained illnesses. In the event of a confirmed terrorist attack, CDC will coordinate with other federal agencies in accord with Presidential Decision Directive (PDD) 39. PDD 39 designates the Federal Bureau of Investigation as the lead agency for the crisis plan and charges the Federal Emergency Management Agency with ensuring that the federal response management is adequate to respond to the consequences of terrorism. If requested by a state health agency, CDC will deploy response teams to investigate unexplained or suspicious illnesses or unusual etiologic agents and provide on-site consultation regarding medical management and disease control. To ensure the availability, procurement, and delivery of medical supplies, devices, and equipment that might be needed to respond to terrorist-caused illness or injury, CDC will maintain a national pharmaceutical stockpile.

Communication Systems
U.S. preparedness to mitigate the public health consequences of biological and chemical terrorism depends on the coordinated activities of well-trained healthcare and public health personnel throughout the United States who have access to up-to-the-minute emergency information. Effective communication with the public through the news media will also be essential to limit terrorists' ability to induce public panic and disrupt daily life. During the next five years, CDC will work with state and local health agencies to develop a) a state-of-the-art communication system that will support disease surveillance; b) rapid notification and information exchange regarding disease outbreaks that are possibly related to bioterrorism; c) dissemination of diagnostic results and emergency health information; and d) coordination of emergency response activities. Through this network and similar mechanisms, CDC will provide terrorism-related training to epidemiologists and laboratorians, emergency responders, emergency department personnel and other front-line healthcare providers, and health and safety personnel.

Partnerships and Implementation
Implementation of the objectives outlined in CDC's strategic plan will be coordinated through CDC's Bioterrorism Preparedness and Response Program. Program personnel are charged with a) helping build local and state preparedness, b) developing U.S. expertise regarding potential threat agents, and c) coordinating response activities during actual bioterrorist events. Program staff have established priorities for 2000–2002 regarding the focus areas (Box 6). Implementation will require collaboration with

BOX 6. Implementation Priorities Regarding Focus Areas for 2000–2002

Preparedness and Prevention

- Maintain a public health preparedness and response cooperative agreement that provides support to state health agencies who are working with local agencies in developing coordinated bioterrorism plans and protocols.
- Establish a national public health distance-learning system that provides biological and chemical terrorism preparedness training to healthcare workers and to state and local public health workers.
- Disseminate public health guidelines and performance standards on biological and chemical terrorism preparedness planning for use by state and local health agencies.

Detection and Surveillance

- Strengthen state and local surveillance systems for illness and injury resulting from pathogens and chemical substances that are on CDC's critical agents list.
- Develop new algorithms and statistical methods for searching medical databases on a real-time basis for evidence of suspicious events.
- Establish criteria for investigating and evaluating suspicious clusters of human or animal disease or injury and triggers for notifying law enforcement of suspected acts of biological or chemical terrorism.

Diagnosis and Characterization of Biological and Chemical Agents

- Establish a multilevel laboratory response network for bioterrorism that links public health agencies to advanced capacity facilities for the identification and reporting of critical biological agents.
- Establish regional chemical terrorism laboratories that will provide diagnostic capacity during terrorist attacks involving chemical agents.
- Establish a rapid-response and advanced technology laboratory within CDC to provide around-the-clock diagnostic support to bioterrorism response teams and expedite molecular characterization of critical biological agents.

Response

- Assist state and local health agencies in organizing response capacities to rapidly deploy in the event of an overt attack or a suspicious outbreak that might be the result of a covert attack.
- Ensure that procedures are in place for rapid mobilization of CDC terrorism response teams that will provide on-site assistance to local health workers, security agents, and law enforcement officers.
- Establish a national pharmaceutical stockpile to provide medical supplies in the event of a terrorist attack that involves biological or chemical agents.

- Establish a national electronic infrastructure to improve exchange of emergency health information among local, state, and federal health agencies.
- Implement an emergency communication plan that ensures rapid dissemination of health information to the public during actual, threatened, or suspected acts of biological or chemical terrorism.
- Create a Web site that disseminates bioterrorism preparedness and training information, as well as other bioterrorism-related emergency information, to public health and healthcare workers and the public.

state and local public health agencies, as well as with other persons and groups, including

- public health organizations,
- medical research centers,
- healthcare providers and their networks,
- professional societies,
- medical examiners,
- emergency response units and responder organizations,
- safety and medical equipment manufacturers,
- the U.S. Office of Emergency Preparedness and other Department of Health and Human Services agencies,
- other federal agencies, and
- international organizations.

Recommendations
Implementing CDC's strategic preparedness and response plan by 2004 will ensure the following outcomes:

- U.S. public health agencies and healthcare providers will be prepared to mitigate illness and injuries that result from acts of biological and chemical terrorism.
- Public health surveillance for infectious diseases and injuries—including events that might indicate terrorist activity—will be timely and complete, and reporting of suspected terrorist events will be integrated with the evolving, comprehensive networks of the national public health surveillance system.
- The national laboratory response network for bioterrorism will be extended to include facilities in all fifty states. The network will include CDC's environmental health laboratory for chemical terrorism and four regional facilities.
- State and federal public health departments will be equipped with state-of-the-art tools for rapid epidemiological investigation and control of suspected or confirmed acts of biological or chemical terrorism, and a designated stock of terrorism-related medical supplies will be available through a national pharmaceutical stockpile.

- A cadre of well-trained healthcare and public health workers will be available in every state. Their terrorism-related activities will be coordinated through a rapid and efficient communication system that links U.S. public health agencies and their partners.

Conclusion

Recent threats and use of biological and chemical agents against civilians have exposed U.S. vulnerability and highlighted the need to enhance our capacity to detect and control terrorist acts. The United States must be protected from an extensive range of critical biological and chemical agents, including some that have been developed and stockpiled for military use. Even without threat of war, investment in national defense ensures preparedness and acts as a deterrent against hostile acts. Similarly, investment in the public health system provides the best civil defense against bioterrorism. Tools developed in response to terrorist threats serve a dual purpose. They help detect rare or unusual disease outbreaks and respond to health emergencies, including naturally occurring outbreaks or industrial injuries that might resemble terrorist events in their unpredictability and ability to cause mass casualties (e.g., a pandemic influenza outbreak or a large-scale chemical spill). Terrorism-preparedness activities described in CDC's plan, including the development of a public health communication infrastructure, a multilevel network of diagnostic laboratories, and an integrated disease surveillance system, will improve our ability to investigate rapidly and control public health threats that emerge in the twenty-first century.

References

1. Okumura T., Suzuki K., Fukuda A., et al. "Tokyo subway sarin attack; disaster management, Part 1: Community emergency response." *Acad Emerg Med* 5 (1998):613–7.

2. Davis, C. J. "Nuclear blindness: an overview of the biological weapons programs of the former Soviet Union and Iraq." *Emerg Infect Dis* 5 (1999):509–12.

3. Török T. J., Tauxe R. V., Wise R. P., et al. "Large community outbreak of Salmonellosis caused by intentional contamination of restaurant salad bars." *JAMA* 278 (1997):389–95.

4. Tucker J. B. "Chemical/biological terrorism: coping with a new threat." *Politics and the Life Sciences* 15 (1996):167–184.

5. *Uncle Fester. Silent death.* 2nd ed. Port Townsend, WA: Loompanics Unlimited, 1997.

6. Ashraf H. European dioxin-contaminated food crisis grows and grows [news]. *Lancet* 353 (1999):2049.

7. Janofsky M. Looking for motives in plague case. *New York Times.* May 28, 1995: A18.

8. Federal Emergency Management Agency. Federal response plan. Washington, DC: Government Printing Office, 1999. Available at <http://www.fema.gov/r-n-r/frp>. Accessed February 3, 2000.

—Taken from *http://www.cdc.gov/mmwrhtml/rr4904a1.htm*

Chemical and Biological Agents

Individual Chemical Agents

Nerve Agents

Health Effects:
- Physostigmine cholinesterase inhibitors (reversible)
- Organophosphorus cholinesterase inhibitors (irreversible)
- Disable enzymes responsible for transmitting nerve impulses.
- Initial effects of organophosphorus agents occur within 1–10 minutes of exposure
- Death
  - Within 15 minutes for tabun, sarin, and soman
  - From 4–42 hours for VX.

Agents include:
- tabun (NATO military designation, GA);
- sarin (NATO military designation, GB);
- soman (NATO military designation, GD);
- GF (Cyclohexyl methylphosphonofluoridate);
- VX (Methylphosphonothioic acid S-(2-(bis(1-methylethyl)amino) ethyl) O-ethyl ester);
- GE (Phosphonofluoridic acid, ethyl-, isopropyl ester);
- VE (Phosphonothioic acid, ethyl-, S-(2-(diethylamino)ethyl) O-ethyl ester);
- VG (Amiton); and
- VM (Phosphonothioic acid, methyl-, S-(2-(diethylamino)ethyl) O-ethyl ester).

Blister/Vesicant Agents

Health Effects:
- Vesicants
  - Skin blisters
  - Damage eyes, mucous membranes, respiratory tract, and internal organs
  - Initial effects rapid
- Mustard agents
  - Destroy different substances within cells of living tissue
  - Initial effects occur 12 to 24 hours after exposure
- Symptoms variable
- Acute mortality low
- Death can occur from complications after lung injury

Agents include
- lewisite (L);
- mustard-Lewisite (HL);
- nitrogen mustards (HN-1, HN-2, HN-3);
- phosgene oxime (CX); and
- sulfur mustards (H, HD, HT).

Blood Agents

Health Effects:
- Highly volatile
- Rapidly acting
- seizures
- respiratory failure
- cardiac arrest

Agents include
- cyanogen chloride (CK), and
- hydrogen cyanide (AC).

Pulmonary Agents

Health Effects:
- Liquids dispersed in gas form
- Damage the respiratory tract and cause severe pulmonary edema in about four hours, leading to eventual death. Effects are variable
- Rapid or delayed depending on the specific agent.

Agents include
- chlorine,
- chloropicrin (PS),
- diphosgene (DP), and
- phosgene (CG).

—Taken from *http://sis.nlm.nih.gov/Tox/ChemWar.html*

Chemical and Biological Agents Used in Attacks

Mustard Gas—WWI (1914–1918)

What Sulfur Mustard Is
- Sulfur mustard is a type of chemical warfare agent. These kinds of agents are called vesicants or blistering agents because they cause blistering of the skin and mucous membranes on contact.
- Sulfur mustard is also known as "mustard gas or mustard agent," or by the military designations H, HD, and HT.
- Sulfur mustard sometimes smells like garlic, onions, or mustard and sometimes has no odor. It can be a vapor (the gaseous form of a liquid), an oily-textured liquid, or a solid.

- Sulfur mustard can be clear to yellow or brown when it is in liquid or solid form.

Where Sulfur Mustard Is Found and How It Is Used
- Sulfur mustard is not found naturally in the environment.
- Sulfur mustard was introduced in World War I as a chemical warfare agent. Until recently, it was available for use in the treatment of a skin condition called psoriasis. Currently, it has no medical use.

How People Can Be Exposed to Sulfur Mustard
- If sulfur mustard is released into the air as a vapor, people can be exposed through skin contact, eye contact, or breathing. Sulfur mustard vapor can be carried long distances by wind.
- If sulfur mustard is released into water, people can be exposed by drinking the contaminated water or getting it on their skin.
- People can be exposed by coming in contact with liquid sulfur mustard.
- Sulfur mustard can last from 1 to 2 days in the environment under average weather conditions and from weeks to months under very cold conditions.
- Sulfur mustard breaks down slowly in the body, so repeated exposure may have a cumulative effect (that is, it can build up in the body).

How Sulfur Mustard Works
- Adverse health effects caused by sulfur mustard depend on the amount people are exposed to, the route of exposure, and the length of time that people are exposed.
- Sulfur mustard is a powerful irritant and blistering agent that damages the skin, eyes, and respiratory (breathing) tract.
- It damages DNA, a vital component of cells in the body.
- Sulfur mustard vapor is heavier than air, so it will settle in low-lying areas.

Immediate Signs and Symptoms of Sulfur Mustard Exposure
- Exposure to sulfur mustard is usually not fatal. When sulfur mustard was used during World War I, it killed fewer than 5 percent of the people who were exposed and got medical care.
- People may not know right away that they have been exposed, because sulfur mustard often has no smell or has a smell that might not cause alarm.
- Typically, signs and symptoms do not occur immediately. Depending on the severity of the exposure, symptoms may not occur for 2 to 24 hours. Some people are more sensitive to sulfur mustard than are other people, and may have symptoms sooner.
- Sulfur mustard can have the following effects on specific parts of the body:

- *Skin:* redness and itching of the skin may occur 2 to 48 hours after exposure and change eventually to yellow blistering of the skin.
- *Eyes:* irritation, pain, swelling, and tearing may occur within 3 to12 hours of a mild to moderate exposure. A severe exposure may cause symptoms within 1 to 2 hours and may include the symptoms of a mild or moderate exposure plus light sensitivity, severe pain, or blindness (lasting up to 10 days).
- *Respiratory tract:* runny nose, sneezing, hoarseness, bloody nose, sinus pain, shortness of breath, and cough within 12 to 24 hours of a mild exposure and within 2 to 4 hours of a severe exposure.
- *Digestive tract:* abdominal pain, diarrhea, fever, nausea, and vomiting.
- Showing these signs and symptoms does not necessarily mean that a person has been exposed to sulfur mustard.

What the Long-term Health Effects May Be

- Exposure to sulfur mustard liquid is more likely to produce second- and third-degree burns and later scarring than is exposure to sulfur mustard vapor. Extensive skin burning can be fatal.
- Extensive breathing in of the vapors can cause chronic respiratory disease, repeated respiratory infections, or death.
- Extensive eye exposure can cause permanent blindness.
- Exposure to sulfur mustard may increase a person's risk for lung and respiratory cancer.

How People Can Protect Themselves and What They Should Do If They Are Exposed to Sulfur Mustard

- Because no antidote exists for sulfur mustard exposure, the best thing to do is avoid it. Immediately leave the area where the sulfur mustard was released. Try to find higher ground, because sulfur mustard is heavier than air and will settle in low-lying areas.
- If avoiding sulfur mustard exposure is not possible, rapidly remove the sulfur mustard from the body. Getting the sulfur mustard off as soon as possible after exposure is the only effective way to prevent or decrease tissue damage to the body.
- Quickly remove any clothing that has liquid sulfur mustard on it. If possible, seal the clothing in a plastic bag, and then seal that bag inside a second plastic bag.
- Immediately wash any exposed part of the body (eyes, skin, etc.) thoroughly with plain, clean water. Eyes need to be flushed with water for 5 to 10 minutes. Do NOT cover eyes with bandages, but do protect them with dark glasses or goggles.
- If someone has ingested sulfur mustard, do NOT induce vomiting. Give the person milk to drink.
- Seek medical attention right away. Dial 911 and explain what has happened.

How Sulfur Mustard Exposure Is Treated

The most important factor is removing sulfur mustard from the body. Exposure to sulfur mustard is treated by giving the victim supportive medical care to minimize the effects of the exposure. Though no antidote exists for sulfur mustard, exposure is usually not fatal.

—Taken from *http://www.bt.cdc.gov/agent/sulfurmustard/basics/facts.asp*

Salmonella—The Dalles, Oregon (1984)

What Is Salmonellosis?

Salmonellosis is an infection with a bacteria called salmonella. Most persons infected with salmonella develop diarrhea, fever, and abdominal cramps twelve to seventy-two hours after infection. The illness usually lasts four to seven days, and most persons recover without treatment. However, in some persons the diarrhea may be so severe that the patient needs to be hospitalized. In these patients, the salmonella infection may spread from the intestines to the blood stream, and then to other body sites and can cause death unless the person is treated promptly with antibiotics. The elderly, infants, and those with impaired immune systems are more likely to have a severe illness.

What Sort of Germ Is Salmonella?

The salmonella germ is actually a group of bacteria that can cause diarrheal illness in humans. They are microscopic living creatures that pass from the feces of people or animals to other people or other animals. There are many different kinds of salmonella bacteria. Salmonella serotype Typhimurium and salmonella serotype Enteritidis are the most common in the United States. Salmonella has been known to cause illness for over 100 years. They were discovered by a American scientist named Salmon, for whom they are named.

How Can Salmonella Infections Be Diagnosed?

Many different kinds of illnesses can cause diarrhea, fever, or abdominal cramps. Determining that salmonella is the cause of the illness depends on laboratory tests that identify salmonella in the stools of an infected person. These tests are sometimes not performed unless the laboratory is instructed specifically to look for the organism. Once salmonella has been identified, further testing can determine its specific type, and which antibiotics could be used to treat it.

How Can Salmonella Infections Be Treated?

Salmonella infections usually resolve in 5–7 days and often do not require treatment unless the patient becomes severely dehydrated or the infection spreads from the intestines. Persons with severe diarrhea may require rehydration, often with intravenous fluids. Antibiotics are not usually necessary unless the infection spreads from the intestines, then it can be treated with ampicillin, gentamicin, trimethoprim/sulfamethoxazole, or ciprofloxacin. Unfortunately, some salmonella bacteria have become resistant to antibiotics, largely as a result of the use of antibiotics to promote the growth of feed animals.

Are There Long Term Consequences to a Salmonella Infection?
Persons with diarrhea usually recover completely, although it may be several months before their bowel habits are entirely normal. A small number of persons who are infected with salmonella will go on to develop pains in their joints, irritation of the eyes, and painful urination. This is called Reiter's syndrome. It can last for months or years and can lead to chronic arthritis which is difficult to treat. Antibiotic treatment does not make a difference in whether or not the person later develops arthritis.

How Do People Catch Salmonella?
Salmonella live in the intestinal tracts of humans and other animals, including birds. Salmonella are usually transmitted to humans by eating foods contaminated with animal feces. Contaminated foods usually look and smell normal. Contaminated foods are often of animal origin, such as beef, poultry, milk, or eggs, but all foods, including vegetables, may become contaminated. Many raw foods of animal origin are frequently contaminated, but fortunately, thorough cooking kills salmonella. Food may also become contaminated by the unwashed hands of an infected food handler, who forgot to wash his or her hands with soap after using the bathroom.

Salmonella may also be found in the feces of some pets, especially those with diarrhea, and people can become infected if they do not wash their hands after contact with these feces. Reptiles are particularly likely to harbor salmonella and people should always wash their hands immediately after handling a reptile, even if the reptile is healthy. Adults should also be careful that children wash their hands after handling a reptile.

What Can a Person Do to Prevent This Illness?
There is no vaccine to prevent salmonellosis. Since foods of animal origin may be contaminated with salmonella, people should not eat raw or undercooked eggs, poultry, or meat. Raw eggs may be unrecognized in some foods such as homemade hollandaise sauce, caesar and other salad dressings, tiramisu, homemade ice cream, homemade mayonnaise, cookie dough, and frostings. Poultry and meat, including hamburgers, should be well-cooked, not pink in the middle. Persons also should not consume raw or unpasteurized milk or other dairy products. Produce should be thoroughly washed before consuming.

Cross-contamination of foods should be avoided. Uncooked meats should be keep separate from produce, cooked foods, and ready-to-eat foods. Hands, cutting boards, counters, knives, and other utensils should be washed thoroughly after handling uncooked foods. Hands should be washed before handling any food, and between handling different food items.

People who have salmonellosis should not prepare food or pour water for others until they have been shown to no longer be carrying the salmonella bacterium. People should wash their hands after contact with animal feces. Since reptiles are particularly likely to have salmonella, everyone should immediately wash their hands after handling reptiles. Reptiles (including turtles) are not appropriate pets for small children and should not be in the same house as an infant.

How Common Is Salmonellosis?

Every year, approximately 40,000 cases of salmonellosis are reported in the United States. Because many milder cases are not diagnosed or reported, the actual number of infections may be thirty or more times greater. Salmonellosis is more common in the summer than winter.

Children are the most likely to get salmonellosis. Young children, the elderly, and the immunocompromised are the most likely to have severe infections. It is estimated that approximately 600 persons die each year with acute salmonellosis.

What Else Can Be Done to Prevent Salmonellosis?

It is important for the public health department to know about cases of salmonellosis. It is important for clinical laboratories to send isolates of salmonella to the city, county, or state public health laboratories so the specific type can be determined and compared with other salmonella in the community. If many cases occur at the same time, it may mean that a restaurant, food, or water supply has a problem which needs correction by the public health department.

Some prevention steps occur everyday without you thinking about it. Pasteurization of milk and treating municipal water supplies are highly effective prevention measures that have been in place for many years. In the 1970s, small pet turtles were a common source of salmonellosis in the United States, and in 1975, the sale of small turtles was halted in this country. Improvements in farm animal hygiene, in slaughter plant practices, and in vegetable and fruit harvesting and packing operations may help prevent salmonellosis caused by contaminated foods. Better education of food industry workers in basic food safety and restaurant inspection procedures may prevent cross-contamination and other food handling errors that can lead to outbreaks. Wider use of pasteurized egg in restaurants, hospitals, and nursing homes is an important prevention measure. In the future, irradiation or other treatments may greatly reduce contamination of raw meat.

—Taken from *http://www.cdc.gov/ncidod/dbmd/diseaseinfo/salmonellosis_t.htm*

Sarin Gas Attack—Tokyo, 12 Dead, 6,000 Sickened (1995)

What Sarin Is

- Sarin is a human-made chemical warfare agent classified as a nerve agent. Nerve agents are the most toxic and rapidly acting of the known chemical warfare agents. They are similar to certain kinds of pesticides (insect killers) called organophosphates in terms of how they work and what kind of harmful effects they cause. However, nerve agents are much more potent than organophosphate pesticides.

- Sarin originally was developed in 1938 in Germany as a pesticide.
- Sarin is a clear, colorless, and tasteless liquid that has no odor in its pure form. However, sarin can evaporate into a vapor (gas) and spread into the environment.
- Sarin is also known as GB.

Where Sarin Is Found and How It Is Used

- Sarin and other nerve agents may have been used in chemical warfare during the Iran-Iraq War in the 1980s.
- Sarin was used in two terrorist attacks in Japan in 1994 and 1995.
- Sarin is not found naturally in the environment.

How People Can Be Exposed to Sarin

- Following release of sarin into the air, people can be exposed through skin contact or eye contact. They can also be exposed by breathing air that contains sarin.
- Sarin mixes easily with water, so it could be used to poison water. Following release of sarin into water, people can be exposed by touching or drinking water that contains sarin.
- Following contamination of food with sarin, people can be exposed by eating the contaminated food.
- A person's clothing can release sarin for about thirty minutes after it has come in contact with sarin vapor, which can lead to exposure of other people.
- Because sarin breaks down slowly in the body, people who are repeatedly exposed to sarin may suffer more harmful health effects.
- Because sarin vapor is heavier than air, it will sink to low-lying areas and create a greater exposure hazard there.

How Sarin Works

- The extent of poisoning caused by sarin depends on the amount of sarin to which a person was exposed, how the person was exposed, and the length of time of the exposure.
- Symptoms will appear within a few seconds after exposure to the vapor form of sarin and within a few minutes up to eighteen hours after exposure to the liquid form.
- All the nerve agents cause their toxic effects by preventing the proper operation of the chemical that acts as the body's "off switch" for glands and muscles. Without an "off switch," the glands and muscles are constantly being stimulated. They may tire and no longer be able to sustain breathing function.
- Sarin is the most volatile of the nerve agents, which means that it can easily and quickly evaporate from a liquid into a vapor and spread into the environment. People can be exposed to the vapor even if they do not come in contact with the liquid form of sarin.

- Because it evaporates so quickly, sarin presents an immediate but short-lived threat.

Immediate Signs and Symptoms of Sarin Exposure
People may not know that they were exposed because sarin has no odor.

People exposed to a low or moderate dose of sarin by breathing contaminated air, eating contaminated food, drinking contaminated water, or touching contaminated surfaces may experience some or all of the following symptoms within seconds to hours of exposure:

- Runny nose
- Watery eyes
- Small, pinpoint pupils
- Eye pain
- Blurred vision
- Drooling and excessive sweating
- Cough
- Chest tightness
- Rapid breathing
- Diarrhea
- Increased urination
- Confusion
- Drowsiness
- Weakness
- Headache
- Nausea, vomiting, and/or abdominal pain
- Slow or fast heart rate
- Low or high blood pressure

Even a small drop of sarin on the skin can cause sweating and muscle twitching where sarin touched the skin.

Exposure to large doses of sarin by any route may result in the following harmful health effects:

- Loss of consciousness
- Convulsions
- Paralysis
- Respiratory failure possibly leading to death

Showing these signs and symptoms does not necessarily mean that a person has been exposed to sarin.

What the Long-term Health Effects Are
Mild or moderately exposed people usually recover completely. Severely exposed people are not likely to survive. Unlike some organophosphate pesticides, nerve agents have not been associated with neurological problems lasting more than one to two weeks after the exposure.

How people can protect themselves, and what they should do if they are exposed to sarin.

Recovery from sarin exposure is possible with treatment, but the antidotes available must be used quickly to be effective. Therefore, the best thing to do is avoid exposure:

- Leave the area where the sarin was released and get to fresh air. Quickly moving to an area where fresh air is available is highly effective in reducing the possibility of death from exposure to sarin vapor.
- If the sarin release was outdoors, move away from the area where the sarin was released. Go to the highest ground possible, because sarin is heavier than air and will sink to low-lying areas.
- If the sarin release was indoors, get out of the building.
- If people think they may have been exposed, they should remove their clothing, rapidly wash their entire body with soap and water, and get medical care as quickly as possible.

Removing and Disposing of Clothing

- Quickly take off clothing that has liquid sarin on it. Any clothing that has to be pulled over the head should be cut off the body instead of pulled over the head. If possible, seal the clothing in a plastic bag. Then seal the first plastic bag in a second plastic bag. Removing and sealing the clothing in this way will help protect people from any chemicals that might be on their clothes.
- If clothes were placed in plastic bags, inform either the local or state health department or emergency personnel upon their arrival. Do not handle the plastic bags.
- If helping other people remove their clothing, try to avoid touching any contaminated areas, and remove the clothing as quickly as possible.

Washing the Body

- As quickly as possible, wash any liquid sarin from the skin with large amounts of soap and water. Washing with soap and water will help protect people from any chemicals on their bodies.
- Rinse the eyes with plain water for ten to fifteen minutes if they are burning or if vision is blurred.
- If sarin has been swallowed, do not induce vomiting or give fluids to drink.
- Seek medical attention immediately. Dial 911 and explain what has happened.

How Sarin Exposure Is Treated

Treatment consists of removing sarin from the body as soon as possible and providing supportive medical care in a hospital setting. Antidotes are available for sarin. They are most useful if given as soon as possible after exposure.

—Taken from *http://www.bt.cdc.gov/agent/ricin/erc9009-86-3.asp*

Anthrax—USA—Five Fatalities (2001)

What Is Anthrax?

Anthrax is a serious disease caused by *Bacillus anthracis,* a bacterium that forms spores. A bacterium is a very small organism made up of one cell. Many bacteria can cause disease. A spore is a cell that is dormant (asleep) but may come to life with the right conditions.

There are three types of anthrax:

- skin (cutaneous)
- lungs (inhalation)
- digestive (gastrointestinal)

How Do You Get It?

Anthrax is not known to spread from one person to another.

- Anthrax from animals. Humans can become infected with anthrax by handling products from infected animals or by breathing in anthrax spores from infected animal products (like wool, for example). People also can become infected with gastrointestinal anthrax by eating undercooked meat from infected animals.
- Anthrax as a weapon. Anthrax also can be used as a weapon. This happened in the United States in 2001. Anthrax was deliberately spread through the postal system by sending letters with powder containing anthrax. This caused twenty-two cases of anthrax infection.

How Dangerous Is Anthrax?

The Centers for Disease Control and Prevention classifies agents with recognized bioterrorism potential into three priority areas (A, B and C). Anthrax is classified as a Category A agent. Category A agents are those that

- pose the greatest possible threat for a bad effect on public health;
- may spread across a large area or need public awareness; and
- need a great deal of planning to protect the public's health.

In most cases, early treatment with antibiotics can cure cutaneous anthrax. Even if untreated, 80 percent of people who become infected with cutaneous anthrax do not die. Gastrointestinal anthrax is more serious because between one-fourth and more than half of cases lead to death. Inhalation anthrax is much more severe. In 2001, about half of the cases of inhalation anthrax ended in death.

What Are the Symptoms?

The symptoms (warning signs) of anthrax are different depending on the type of the disease:

- Cutaneous: The first symptom is a small sore that develops into a blister. The blister then develops into a skin ulcer with a black area in the center. The sore, blister, and ulcer do not hurt.
- Gastrointestinal: The first symptoms are nausea, loss of appetite, bloody diarrhea, and fever, followed by bad stomach pain.

- Inhalation: The first symptoms of inhalation anthrax are like cold or flu symptoms and can include a sore throat, mild fever and muscle aches. Later symptoms include cough, chest discomfort, shortness of breath, tiredness, and muscle aches. (Caution: Do not assume that just because a person has cold or flu symptoms that they have inhalation anthrax.)

How Soon Do Infected People Get Sick?
Symptoms can appear within seven days of coming in contact with the bacterium for all three types of anthrax. For inhalation anthrax, symptoms can appear within a week or can take up to forty-two days to appear.

How Is Anthrax Treated?
Antibiotics are used to treat all three types of anthrax. Early identification and treatment are important.

- Prevention after exposure. Treatment is different for a person who is exposed to anthrax, but is not yet sick. Healthcare providers will use antibiotics (such as ciprofloxacin, doxycycline, or penicillin) combined with the anthrax vaccine to prevent anthrax infection.
- Treatment after infection. Treatment is usually a sixty-day course of antibiotics. Success depends on the type of anthrax and how soon treatment begins.

Can Anthrax Be Prevented?
Vaccination. There is a vaccine to prevent anthrax, but it is not yet available for the general public. Anyone who may be exposed to anthrax, including certain members of the U.S. armed forces, laboratory workers, and workers who may enter or re-enter contaminated areas, may get the vaccine. Also, in the event of an attack using anthrax as a weapon, people exposed would get the vaccine.

What Should I Do if I Think I Have Anthrax?
If you are showing symptoms of anthrax infection, call your healthcare provider right away.

What Should I Do if I Think I Have Been Exposed to Anthrax?
Contact local law enforcement immediately if you think that you may have been exposed to anthrax. This includes being exposed to a suspicious package or envelope that contains powder.

What Is CDC Doing to Prepare for a Possible Anthrax Attack?
CDC is working with state and local health authorities to prepare for an anthrax attack. Activities include

- developing plans and procedures to respond to an attack using anthrax;
- training and equipping emergency response teams to help state and local governments control infection, gather samples, and perform tests; educating healthcare providers, media, and the general public about what to do in the event of an attack;

- working closely with health departments, veterinarians, and laboratories to watch for suspected cases of anthrax; developing a national electronic database to track potential cases of anthrax;
- ensuring that there are enough safe laboratories for quickly testing of suspected anthrax cases; and
- working with hospitals, laboratories, emergency response teams, and healthcare providers to make sure they have the supplies they need in case of an attack.

—Taken from *http://www.bt.cdc.gov/agent/anthrax/needtoknow.asp*

Ricin—USA—No Fatalities (2004)

What Ricin Is
- Ricin is a poison that can be made from the waste left over from processing castor beans.
- It can be in the form of a powder, a mist, or a pellet, or it can be dissolved in water or weak acid.
- It is a stable substance. For example, it is not affected much by extreme conditions such as very hot or very cold temperatures.

Where Ricin Is Found and How It Is Used
- Castor beans are processed throughout the world to make castor oil. Ricin is part of the waste "mash" produced when castor oil is made.
- Ricin has some potential medical uses, such as bone marrow transplants and cancer treatment (to kill cancer cells).

How You Could Be Exposed to Ricin
- It would take a deliberate act to make ricin and use it to poison people. Accidental exposure to ricin is highly unlikely.
- People can breathe in ricin mist or powder and be poisoned.
- Ricin can also get into water or food and then be swallowed.
- Pellets of ricin, or ricin dissolved in a liquid, can be injected into people's bodies.
- Depending on the route of exposure (such as injection or inhalation), as little as 500 micrograms of ricin could be enough to kill an adult. A 500-microgram dose of ricin would be about the size of the head of a pin. A greater amount would likely be needed to kill people if the ricin were swallowed.
- In 1978, Georgi Markov, a Bulgarian writer and journalist who was living in London, died after he was attacked by a man with an umbrella. The umbrella had been rigged to inject a poison ricin pellet under Markov's skin.
- Some reports have indicated that ricin may have been used in the Iran-Iraq war during the 1980s and that quantities of ricin were found in Al Qaeda caves in Afghanistan.
- Ricin poisoning is not contagious. It cannot be spread from person to person through casual contact.

How Ricin Works
- Ricin works by getting inside the cells of a person's body and pre-venting the cells from making the proteins they need. Without the proteins, cells die. Eventually this is harmful to the whole body, and death may occur.
- Effects of ricin poisoning depend on whether ricin was inhaled, ingested, or injected.

Signs and Symptoms of Ricin Exposure
- The major symptoms of ricin poisoning depend on the route of exposure and the dose received, though many organs may be affected in severe cases.
- Initial symptoms of ricin poisoning by inhalation may occur within eight hours of exposure. Following ingestion of ricin, initial symp-toms typically occur in less than six hours.

Inhalation: Within a few hours of inhaling significant amounts of ricin, the likely symptoms would be respiratory distress (difficulty breathing), fever, cough, nausea, and tightness in the chest. Heavy sweating may follow as well as fluid building up in the lungs (pulmonary edema). This would make breathing even more difficult, and the skin might turn blue. Excess fluid in the lungs would be diagnosed by x-ray or by listening to the chest with a stethoscope. Finally, low blood pressure and respiratory failure may occur, leading to death. In cases of known exposure to ricin, people having res-piratory symptoms that started within twelve hours of inhaling ricin should seek medical care.

Ingestion: If someone swallows a significant amount of ricin, he or she would develop vomiting and diarrhea that may become bloody. Severe dehydration may be the result, followed by low blood pressure. Other signs or symptoms may include hallucinations, seizures, and blood in the urine. Within several days, the person's liver, spleen, and kidneys might stop work-ing, and the person could die.

Skin and eye exposure: Ricin in the powder or mist form can cause red-ness and pain of the skin and the eyes.

Death from ricin poisoning could take place within thirty-six to seventy-two hours of exposure, depending on the route of exposure (inhalation, ingestion, or injection) and the dose received. If death has not occurred in three to five days, the victim usually recovers.

Showing these signs and symptoms does not necessarily mean that a per-son has been exposed to ricin.

How Ricin Poisoning Is Treated
Because no antidote exists for ricin, the most important factor is avoiding ricin exposure in the first place. If exposure cannot be avoided, the most important factor is then getting the ricin off or out of the body as quickly as possible. Ricin poisoning is treated by giving victims supportive med-

ical care to minimize the effects of the poisoning. The types of supportive medical care would depend on several factors, such as the route by which victims were poisoned (that is, whether poisoning was by inhalation, ingestion, or skin or eye exposure). Care could include such measures as helping victims breathe, giving them intravenous fluids (fluids given through a needle inserted into a vein), giving them medications to treat conditions such as seizure and low blood pressure, flushing their stomachs with activated charcoal (if the ricin has been very recently ingested), or washing out their eyes with water if their eyes are irritated.

How You Can Know Whether You Have Been Exposed to Ricin
- If we suspect that people have inhaled ricin, a potential clue would be that a large number of people who had been close to each other suddenly developed fever, cough, and excess fluid in their lungs. These symptoms could be followed by severe breathing problems and possibly death.
- No widely available, reliable test exists to confirm that a person has been exposed to ricin.

How You Can Protect Yourself, and What to Do If You Are Exposed to Ricin
- First, get fresh air by leaving the area where the ricin was released. Moving to an area with fresh air is a good way to reduce the possibility of death from exposure to ricin.
- If the ricin release was outside, move away from the area where the ricin was released.
- If the ricin release was indoors, get out of the building.
- If you are near a release of ricin, emergency coordinators may tell you to either evacuate the area or to "shelter in place" inside a building to avoid being exposed to the chemical.
- If you think you may have been exposed to ricin, you should remove your clothing, rapidly wash your entire body with soap and water, and get medical care as quickly as possible.

Removing Your Clothing
- Quickly take off clothing that may have ricin on it. Any clothing that has to be pulled over the head should be cut off the body instead of pulled over the head.
- If you are helping other people remove their clothing, try to avoid touching any contaminated areas, and remove the clothing as quickly as possible.

Washing Yourself
- As quickly as possible, wash any ricin from your skin with large amounts of soap and water. Washing with soap and water will help protect people from any chemicals on their bodies.
- If your eyes are burning or your vision is blurred, rinse your eyes with plain water for ten to fifteen minutes. If you wear contacts, remove them and put them with the contaminated clothing. Do not

put the contacts back in your eyes (even if they are not disposable contacts). If you wear eyeglasses, wash them with soap and water. You can put your eyeglasses back on after you wash them.

Disposing of Your Clothes

- After you have washed yourself, place your clothing inside a plastic bag. Avoid touching contaminated areas of the clothing. If you can't avoid touching contaminated areas, or you aren't sure where the contaminated areas are, wear rubber gloves, turn the bag inside out and use it to pick up the clothing, or put the clothing in the bag using tongs, tool handles, sticks, or similar objects. Anything that touches the contaminated clothing should also be placed in the bag. If you wear contacts, put them in the plastic bag, too.
- Seal the bag, and then seal that bag inside another plastic bag. Disposing of your clothing in this way will help protect you and other people from any chemicals that might be on your clothes.
- When the local or state health department or emergency personnel arrive, tell them what you did with your clothes. The health department or emergency personnel will arrange for further disposal. Do not handle the plastic bags yourself.
- If someone has ingested ricin, do not induce vomiting or give fluids to drink.
- Seek medical attention right away. Dial 911 and explain what has happened.

Other Biological Threats

What is Tularemia?

Tularemia is a potentially serious illness that occurs naturally in the United States. It is caused by the bacterium *Francisella tularensis* found in animals (especially rodents, rabbits, and hares).

What Are the Symptoms of Tularemia?

Symptoms of tularemia could include

- sudden fever;
- chills;
- headaches;
- diarrhea;
- muscle aches;
- joint pain;
- dry cough; and
- progressive weakness.

People can also catch pneumonia and develop chest pain, bloody sputum and can have trouble breathing and even sometimes stop breathing.

Other symptoms of tularemia depend on how a person was exposed to the tularemia bacteria. These symptoms can include ulcers on the skin or mouth, swollen and painful lymph glands, swollen and painful eyes, and a sore throat.

How Does Tularemia Spread?
People can get tularemia many different ways:

- being bitten by an infected tick, deerfly or other insect
- handling infected animal carcasses
- eating or drinking contaminated food or water
- breathing in the bacteria *F. tularensis*

Tularemia is not known to be spread from person to person. People who have tularemia do not need to be isolated. People who have been exposed to the tularemia bacteria should be treated as soon as possible. The disease can be fatal if it is not treated with the right antibiotics.

How Soon Do Infected People Get Sick?
Symptoms usually appear three to five days after exposure to the bacteria, but can take as long as fourteen days.

What Should I Do If I Think I Have Tularemia?
Consult your doctor at the first sign of illness. Be sure to let the doctor know if you are pregnant or have a weakened immune system.

How Is Tularemia Treated?
Your doctor will most likely prescribe antibiotics, which must be taken according to the directions supplied with your prescription to ensure the best possible result. Let your doctor know if you have any allergy to antibiotics.

A vaccine for tularemia is under review by the Food and Drug Administration and is not currently available in the United States.

What Can I Do to Prevent Becoming Infected with Tularemia?
Tularemia occurs naturally in many parts of the United States. Use insect repellent containing DEET on your skin, or treat clothing with repellent containing permethrin, to prevent insect bites. Wash your hands often, using soap and warm water, especially after handling animal carcasses. Be sure to cook your food thoroughly and that your water is from a safe source.

Note any change in the behavior of your pets (especially rodents, rabbits, and hares) or livestock, and consult a veterinarian if they develop unusual symptoms.

Can Tularemia Be Used As a Weapon?
Francisella tularensis is very infectious. A small number (10–50 or so organisms) can cause disease. If F. tularensis were used as a weapon, the bacteria would likely be made airborne for exposure by inhalation. People who inhale an infectious aerosol would generally experience severe respiratory illness, including life-threatening pneumonia and systemic infection, if they are not treated. The bacteria that cause tularemia occur widely in nature and could be isolated and grown in quantity in a laboratory,

although manufacturing an effective aerosol weapn would require considerable sophistication.

What Is CDC Doing About Tularemia?

The CDC operates a national program for bioterrorism preparedness and response that incorporates a broad range of public health partnerships. Other things CDC is doing include

- stockpiling antibiotics to treat infected people;
- coordinating a nation-wide program where states share information about tularemia; and
- creating new education tools and programs for health professionals, the public, and the media.

—Taken from *http://www.bt.cdc.gov/agent/tularemia*

Smallpox

The Disease

Smallpox is a serious, contagious, and sometimes fatal infectious disease. There is no specific treatment for smallpox disease, and the only prevention is vaccination. The name smallpox is derived from the Latin word for "spotted" and refers to the raised bumps that appear on the face and body of an infected person.

There are two clinical forms of smallpox. Variola major is the severe and most common form of smallpox, with a more extensive rash and higher fever. There are four types of variola major smallpox: ordinary (the most frequent type, accounting for 90 percent or more of cases); modified (mild and occurring in previously vaccinated persons); flat; and hemorrhagic (both rare and very severe). Historically, variola major has an overall fatality rate of about 30 percent; however, flat and hemorrhagic smallpox usually are fatal. Variola minor is a less common presentation of smallpox, and a much less severe disease, with death rates historically of 1 percent or less.

Smallpox outbreaks have occurred from time to time for thousands of years, but the disease is now eradicated after a successful worldwide vaccination program. The last case of smallpox in the United States was in 1949. The last naturally occurring case in the world was in Somalia in 1977. After the disease was eliminated from the world, routine vaccination against smallpox among the general public was stopped because it was no longer necessary for prevention.

Where Smallpox Comes From

Smallpox is caused by the variola virus that emerged in human populations thousands of years ago. Except for laboratory stockpiles, the variola virus has been eliminated. However, in the aftermath of the events of September and October 2001, there is heightened concern that the variola virus might be used as an agent of bioterrorism. For this reason, the U.S. Government is taking precautions for dealing with a smallpox outbreak.

Transmission

Generally, direct and fairly prolonged face-to-face contact is required to spread smallpox from one person to another. Smallpox also can be spread through direct contact with infected bodily fluids or contaminated objects such as bedding or clothing. Rarely, smallpox has been spread by virus carried in the air in enclosed settings such as buildings, buses, and trains. Humans are the only natural hosts of variola. Smallpox is not known to be transmitted by insects or animals.

A person with smallpox is sometimes contagious with onset of fever (prodrome phase), but the person becomes most contagious with the onset of rash. At this stage the infected person is usually very sick and not able to move around in the community. The infected person is contagious until the last smallpox scab falls off.

Smallpox Disease

- Incubation Period
  (Duration: seven to seventeen days)
  Not contagious
  Exposure to the virus is followed by an incubation period during which people do not have any symptoms and may feel fine. This incubation period averages about twelve to fourteen days but can range from seven to seventeen days. During this time, people are not contagious.

- Initial Symptoms (Prodrome)
  (Duration: two to four days)
  Sometimes contagious[1]
  The first symptoms of smallpox include fever, malaise, head and body aches, and sometimes vomiting. The fever is usually high, in the range of 101 to 104 degrees Fahrenheit. At this time, people are usually too sick to carry on their normal activities. This is called the prodrome phase and may last for two to four days.

- Early Rash
  (Duration: about four days)
  Most contagious
  A rash emerges first as small red spots on the tongue and in the mouth. These spots develop into sores that break open and spread large amounts of the virus into the mouth and throat. At this time, the person becomes most contagious.
  Around the time the sores in the mouth break down, a rash appears on the skin, starting on the face and spreading to the arms and legs and then to the hands and feet. Usually the rash spreads to all parts of the body within twenty-four hours. As the rash appears, the fever usually falls and the person may start to feel better. By the third day of the rash, the rash becomes raised bumps.
  By the fourth day, the bumps fill with a thick, opaque fluid and often have a depression in the center that looks like a bellybutton. (This

is a major distinguishing characteristic of smallpox.) Fever often will rise again at this time and remain high until scabs form over the bumps.

- Pustular Rash
  (Duration: about five days)
  Contagious
  The bumps become pustules—sharply raised, usually round and firm to the touch as if there's a small round object under the skin. People often say the bumps feel like BB pellets embedded in the skin.

- Pustules and Scabs
  (Duration: about five days)
  Contagious
  The pustules begin to form a crust and then scab.
  By the end of the second week after the rash appears, most of the sores have scabbed over.

- Resolving Scabs
  (Duration: about six days)
  Contagious
  The scabs begin to fall off, leaving marks on the skin that eventually become pitted scars. Most scabs will have fallen off three weeks after the rash appears. The person is contagious to others until all of the scabs have fallen off.

- Scabs resolved
  Not contagious
  Scabs have fallen off. Person is no longer contagious.

UNSCOM—International Weapons Inspectors

Three members of toxic waste management team. *Courtesy of PhotoEdit.*

With the end of the Cold War, the proliferation of weapons—particularly chemical, biological, and radiological—became an acute global security concern. While the threat of all-out nuclear war may have seemed to recede, the post-Cold War power vacuum, the disintegration of the Soviet central government, and the widespread distribution of sophisticated military hardware on "low-intensity" battlefields across the Third World created a disturbing reality in which such some of the most lethal weaponry available was now unaccounted for.

A number of multinational efforts have begun over the past decade and a half in order to locate, identify, and ideally disarm Cold War-era weaponry that had been distributed throughout the globe. Some of these weapons were left over from conflicts, while others were the remnants of weapons development programs in nations such as Iraq. The United Nations Special Commission (UNSCOM) is an exceptional example of one of these efforts. From 1991 through 1998, UNSCOM teams of weapons experts scoured the post-Gulf War Iraq in order to account for chemical, biological and nuclear weapons developed by Saddam Hussein's Ba'ath regime during the previous two decades.

The following overview of UNSCOM's mission is provided as a means of helping you understand the challenges and tactics of weapons containment efforts.

Establishment

By its resolution 687 of April 3, 1991, the Security Council established the terms and conditions for a formal cease-fire between Iraq and the coalition of Member States cooperating with Kuwait. Section C of this resolution deals with the elimination, under international supervision, of Iraq's weapons of mass destruction and ballistic missiles with a range greater than 150 kilometres (km), together with related items and production facilities. It also calls for measures to ensure that the acquisition and production of prohibited items are not resumed. The Special Commission was set up to implement the non-nuclear provisions of the resolution and to assist the International Atomic Energy Agency (IAEA) in the nuclear areas. The precise terms are laid out in paragraphs seven to thirteen of the resolution.

Composition

On April 18, 1991, after Iraq had formally accepted the provisions of resolution 687, the secretary-general submitted to the Security Council his report regarding the establishment of the United Nations Special Commission (UNSCOM). Following acceptance by the Security Council of the report on April 19 the secretary-general appointed Ambassador Rolf Ekéus (Sweden) as the executive chairman of the Special Commission. On May 1, 1991, the Secretary-General appointed twenty other members of the Commission, from

Australia, Austria, Belgium, Canada, China, the Czech Republic, Finland, France, Germany, Indonesia, Italy, Japan, the Netherlands, Nigeria, Norway, Poland, the Russian Federation, the United Kingdom, the United States, and Venezuela. Mr. Richard Butler (Australia) replaced Ambassador Rolf Ekéus as the executive chairman on July 1, 1997. The current deputy executive chairman is Mr. Charles Duelfer (United States).

Mandate

The Commission's mandate is the following: to carry out immediate on-site inspections of Iraq's biological, chemical, and missile capabilities; to take possession for destruction, removal, or rendering harmless of all chemical and biological weapons and all stocks of agents and all related subsystems and components and all research, development, support, and manufacturing facilities; to supervise the destruction by Iraq of all its ballistic missiles with a range greater than 150 km and related major parts, and repair and production facilities; and to monitor and verify Iraq's compliance with its undertaking not to use, develop, construct, or acquire any of the items specified above. The Commission is also requested to assist the director general of IAEA, which, under resolution 687, has been requested to undertake activities similar to those of the Commission but specifically in the nuclear field. Further, the Commission is entrusted to designate for inspection any additional site necessary for ensuring the fulfillment of the mandates given to the Commission and IAEA.

UNSCOM/IAEA Rights, Privileges and Immunities

While Security Council resolution 687 mandated UNSCOM and the IAEA to conduct inspections in Iraq, it was necessary to establish the detailed modalities and legal basis on which such inspections would be conducted. This was achieved through an exchange of letters in May 1991 involving the secretary-general of the United Nations, the executive chairman of UNSCOM and the minister for Foreign Affairs of Iraq. The letters constituted an agreement between the United Nations and Iraq under which Iraq was to accord to members of UNSCOM, to officials of the United Nations, the IAEA and specialized agencies of the United Nations system, and to technical experts and specialists in Iraq for the purposes of fulfilling the mandate all rights contained in the relevant provisions of the Convention on the Privileges and Immunities of the United Nations of 1946, and the Convention on the Privileges and Immunities of the UN Specialized Agencies of 1947. As agreed in the exchange of letters, Iraq was also to accord to UNSCOM:

- "Unrestricted freedom of entry and exit without delay or hindrance of personnel, property, supplies, equipment, spare parts and other items as well as means of transport, including expeditious issuance of entry and exit visas";
- "Unrestricted freedom of movement without advance notice within Iraq of the personnel of the Special Commission and its equipment and means of transport";

- "The right to unimpeded access to any site or facility for the purpose of the on-site inspection [pursuant to the mandate] whether such a site be above or below ground. . . Any number of sites, facilities or locations may be subject to inspection simultaneously";
- "The right to request, receive, examine and copy any record, data or information or examine, retain, move or photograph, including videotape, any item relevant to the Special Commission's activities and to conduct interviews";
- "The right to designate any site whatsoever for observation, inspection or other monitoring activity and for storage, destruction or rendering harmless" of the items described in operative paragraphs 8, 9 and 12 of resolution 687;
- "The right to install equipment or construct facilities for observation, inspection, testing or other monitoring activity and for storage, destruction or rendering harmless" of those items;
- "The right to take photographs, whether from the ground or from the air, relevant to the Special Commission's activities";
- "The right to take and analyse samples of any kind as well as to remove and export samples for off-site analysis"; and
- "The right to unrestricted communication by radio, satellite or other forms of communication."

Iraq was also to:

- "Provide at no cost to the United Nations . . . all such premises as may be necessary for the accommodation and fulfillment of the functions of the Special Commission," to be under the exclusive control of the Executive Chairman of the Special Commission; and
- "Without prejudice to the use by the Special Commission of its own security, . . . ensure the security and safety of the Special Commission and its personnel."

These rights, privileges and immunities have proved to be essential to the effective fulfillment of the Commission's and IAEA's mandate. They remain in force and have since been clarified and supplemented by specific provisions of Security Council resolution 707 (1991) and of UNSCOM's and the IAEA's plans for ongoing monitoring and verification.

Members of inspection teams from UNSCOM and the IAEA, and personnel assigned to serve at the BMVC, except for regular U.N. Secretariat or IAEA support staff, enjoy the privileges and immunities which are accorded to experts on mission under the various multilateral treaties governing the privileges and immunities of the U.N. and the IAEA.

Organization, Structure and Functioning of the Commission
Full sessions of the members of the Commission are held approximately twice yearly in New York to discuss policy issues and to assess the results of operations to date.

Following the establishment of the Commission as a subsidiary organ of the Security Council, the Office of the Executive Chairman of the Special Commission—a full-time office to assist the Chairman in the exercise of his functions—was set up at United Nations Headquarters in New York, with offices in Bahrain and Baghdad.

Reporting Requirements

The executive chairman reports to the U.N. Security Council on the activities of the commission on a formal basis through the secretary-general twice a year. These written reports to the Council are submitted in April and November and cover the activities and issues of the previous six months. In addition, the executive chairman briefs the Council orally and through the submission of written reports several times a year, as and when necessary.

Offices

The Special Commission's operations are planned and managed under the direction of the executive chairman from New York. The staff there includes technical experts, analysts, data processors, logistics personnel as well as political/diplomatic and administrative support staff. The Bahrain office serves as the assembly and training point for inspection teams as well as a logistics and supply point, while the Baghdad office provides the required communications and logistical support in the field. The Baghdad office now includes the Monitoring and Verification Center, which is responsible for the maintenance and operation of the monitoring system and also houses Baghdad based inspection teams. The total staff compliment (excluding the aircrews that provide transport to and within Iraq, some forty-five persons) is approximately 120.

Finance

The Special Commission is not financed from assessed contributions to the United Nations. The costs of its operations are to be borne by the government of Iraq. However, this will not happen until the embargo on the sale of oil from Iraq is lifted. In the meantime, in the main, the cash requirements of the commission have been met through funds released from the escrow account established under resolution 778 for the receipt of Iraqi frozen assets. In addition, the commission has received some voluntary contributions from a number of States. As of the end of 1996, the commission had spent close to $120 million from these two main sources since its beginnings in 1991. Security Council resolution 986 of 1995, which authorizes the sale of limited amounts of Iraqi oil to pay for the import of humanitarian supplies (mainly food and medicine), allows for some of the funds realized from the sale of oil to be used to meet the current operating costs of the commission. The provisions of the resolution were accepted by Iraq in November 1996. Iraq began to export limited quantities of oil in December 1996 and funds have been available to the commission since that time. The commission's cash requirements are approximately $15 million per six months. The provisions of resolution

986 are renewable every six months provided the Security Council and Iraq agree.

Support

The commission's cash requirements come in addition to the generous assistance provided by governments through the provision of aircraft, facilities, equipment, materials and expert personnel. If given a monetary value, this "in-kind" assistance would amount to approximately twice that of the commission's cash expenditures.

Member States and the United Nations Secretariat have provided the commission staff. Inspection teams have consisted of personnel made available by governments, members of the commission, the United Nations Secretariat, and, in the nuclear field, inspectors and staff of the IAEA. The nuclear teams are organized by the IAEA, with the assistance and cooperation of the Special Commission. The inspectors are selected on the basis of their technical qualifications and expertise, with due regard to drawing them from as many member states as possible within the range of available capabilities and experience. By the end of April 1997, more than 1,000 individuals from over 40 countries had served on inspection teams.

Operational Activities

The implementation of section C of resolution 687 (1991) entails a three-stage process. These stages are not mutually exclusive. Indeed, there is much overlap:

(a) An inspection and survey phase to gather the information necessary to make an informed assessment of Iraq's capabilities and facilities in the nuclear, chemical, biological and ballistic missile fields.

(b) The disposal of weapons of mass destruction, facilities and other related items through destruction, removal or rendering harmless and the destruction of ballistic missiles with a range greater than 150 km, including launchers, other items and repair and production facilities.

(c) Long-term monitoring to ensure ongoing verification of Iraq's compliance with its obligations under paragraph 10 of resolution 687 —principally not to reacquire banned capabilities—in accordance with the plans prepared by the Special Commission and IAEA and approved by the Security Council in its resolution 715 of 1991.

In the pursuit of the first two tasks, by the end of April 1997, 188 inspection missions had been fielded by the commission and IAEA. Of these missions, 158 were related to non-nuclear matters; 43 chemical (including three destruction visits), 49 biological, 3 joint chemical and biological (one of which was conducted in conjunction with a nuclear inspection), and 53 ballistic missile. Thirty nuclear inspections have been undertaken by the IAEA with the assistance and cooperation of the Special Commission. In addition, there has been an inspection of a computer centre in connection with computers suspected to have been used for prohibited activities. An export/import mission was also conducted in 1995 in connection with the plans for the export/import monitoring mechanism called for in paragraph seven of Security Council resolution 715 (1991).

The inspections undertaken have had to be energetic, rigorous and intrusive because of the failure of Iraq to adopt the candid and open approach to the full, final and complete disclosure of all aspects of its weapons programmes called for in Security Council resolutions 687 and 707. Despite the obstacles placed in the way by Iraq, the commission has been able to compile much information about Iraq's capabilities and facilities of concern to it.

Compliance Monitoring
The third stage of the commission's mandate represents its long-term operation. Its main purpose is to monitor and verify Iraq's compliance with its unconditional obligation not to use, retain possess, develop, construct, or otherwise acquire any weapons or related items prohibited under section C of resolution 687 (1991). As requested in that resolution, the secretary-general and the IAEA director general prepared and submitted to the Security Council two separate but closely coordinated plans for compliance monitoring. By approving these plans, under its resolution 715 (1991) of October 11, 1991, the council mandated the Special Commission to implement the plan for ongoing monitoring and verification of permitted chemical, biological and ballistic missile activities. The council also requested the commission to assist and cooperate with IAEA in the implementation of the plan for ongoing monitoring and verification in the nuclear field.

Under the plans, Iraq is obliged to provide, on a regular basis, full, complete, correct and timely information on activities, sites, facilities, material or other items, both military and civilian, that might be used for purposes prohibited under resolutions 687 (1991) and 707 (1991). Furthermore, the Special Commission and IAEA have the right to carry out inspections, at any time and without hindrance, of any site, facility, activity, material or other items in Iraq. They may conduct unannounced inspections and inspections at short notice. They may inspect on the ground or by aerial surveillance any number of declared or designated sites or facilities.

Both plans entered into force immediately upon their approval by the Security Council on October 11, 1991. Despite the mandatory nature of the resolution adopting the plans, Iraq initially failed to state its recognition of or act upon its obligations under resolution 715 (1991) or the plans. At its meeting on March 11–12, 1992, the Security Council demanded that Iraq meet all its obligations, including those arising from council resolution 715 (1991) and the plans for ongoing monitoring and verification approved by the council. On June 27, 1992, seven months after the Council resolution was adopted, Iraq gave the commission initial declarations concerning non-nuclear activities which need to be monitored. Iraq finally accepted the terms of resolution 715 in late 1993. As a result the commission was able to establish its monitoring activities carried out from its Baghdad Monitoring and Verification Center (BMVC).

Export and Import Control Mechanism
Paragraph seven of Security Council Resolution 715 requested the Sanctions Committee established under Resolution 661, the Special Commission and the director general of the IAEA to develop a mechanism for monitoring any future sales or supplies by other countries to Iraq of dual use items that might have applications in WMD programmes. This was seen as being an essential element of the commission's overall efforts to monitor Iraq's compliance with its obligations not to reacquire banned weapon capabilities. If monitoring and verification represent the internal element of that effort, the export/import mechanism represents the external element.

The commission and the IAEA presented a draft concept paper to the Sanctions Committee in May 1994 containing a proposal for a system of notification by both Iraq and the exporting country of dual-purpose items to be exported to Iraq. The mechanism was not to require licensing by the commission. Rather, Iraq would inform a joint unit, to be set up by the commission and the IAEA of its intention to import dual-purpose items as defined in the annexes to the commission and IAEA plans for monitoring and verification. The unit, which staff from both the commission and IAEA, will maintain offices in New York and Baghdad. The exporting country would be obliged inter alia to report on contracts to export such items and, once the details were known, on the contract number, the date of shipment, the point of entry into Iraq and the end user in Iraq. Upon arrival of the goods in Iraq, Iraq would notify the joint unit of receipt. Monitoring groups would then inspect the items at the site of end use to assess their purpose, to tag and inventory them as necessary, and to incorporate the items into the monitoring plan for that site. Any country which became aware of attempts by Iraq to acquire proscribed items would also be required to report such attempts. The process would be underpinned by ongoing monitoring and verification activities, the rights of the commission and the IAEA of no-notice inspection anywhere in Iraq, aerial surveillance activities and information received from other sources. Proscribed items or dual-purpose items imported for proscribed activities would be subject to destruction under the terms of Resolution 687. The assumption would be that imports of dual-purpose items not declared by Iraq were for proscribed purposes.

This paper was discussed by the committee informally. Revisions to the annexes were presented to the Security Council in March 1995. Although there has been no change in the status of the sanctions regime imposed on Iraq under resolution 661, it had been clear for some time that items relevant to the mandate established by the council were being imported into the country or were destined for Iraq. Thus there was an immediate requirement to put the export/import mechanism in place, in order to ensure the comprehensiveness of the commission's and the IAEA's overall monitoring system in Iraq.

The mechanism was put forward to the Council in a letter dated December 7, 1995, from the chairman of the Sanctions Committee. A Security Council resolution, 1051, (with the council acting under Chapter VII of the United Nations Charter, thereby making the requirement to notify such exports an obligation on all states) was adopted unanimously on March 27, 1996.

Under the export/import mechanism, the import of items relevant to the commission's and the IAEA's mandate is notified by both the government of Iraq and the government of the supplier. Resolution 1051 of March 1997 called upon Iraq to implement the system within sixty days of the passage of the resolution, namely May 26, 1996. In advance of that date, the government of Iraq was provided with the necessary documentation to implement the notification system and a mission composed of experts from the commission and the IAEA was dispatched to Baghdad to explain the requirements of the system. Concurrently, the first Export/Import Monitoring Group was established at the BMVC to receive Iraq's notification forms and to take action, as required.

Since the inception of the system, the government of Iraq has made a number of notifications concerning imports, principally of notifiable chemical and biological related materials. In order to receive and to process notifications of the export to Iraq of notifiable items, the commission and the IAEA have established a joint unit at the United Nations Headquarters in New York.

Resolution 1051 required notifications by governments of suppliers of notifiable goods to be provided as from "the date the secretary-general and the director general of the IAEA, after their consultations with the members of the council and other interested states, report to the council indicating that they are satisfied with the preparedness of states for the effective implementation of the mechanism." The chairman of the commission wrote to the members of the council and former major suppliers to Iraq noting that informal contacts with a number of states appeared to indicate that they were, or would shortly be, in a position to provide the necessary notifications. As a consequence of various consultations a recommendation was made to the secretary-general and the director general of the IAEA that they report to the council that notifications should be provided commencing on October 1, 1996. Such a decision was made and was transmitted to all States on September 30, 1996. This important element of the commission's and the IAEA's ongoing monitoring and verification system is now in place and notifications have started to arrive at the joint unit.

—Taken from *http://www.un.org/Depts/unscom/unscom.htm*

Endnote

[1]Smallpox may be contagious during the *prodrome* phase, but is most infectious during the first seven to ten days following rash onset.

Discussion Questions

1) "Weapons of mass destruction" are a special class of armaments which only include chemical and biological weapons.

       True   False

2) Biological warfare is described as "the use of biological agents (bacteria, viruses, fungi, and biologically derived toxins) directed at a military force in an effort to cause mass casualties and death."

       True   False

3) Chemical and biological warfare may be tactically effective because it serves as a "force multiplier."

       True   False

4) The Geneva Protocol of 1928 theoretically prohibited the use of chemical weapons, although some nations continued to develop them.

       True   False

5) To date, chemical and biological weapons have only been used in declared war situations and never against civilian populations.

       True   False

6) Currently, the United States is exceptionally well-prepared to prevent chemical and biological terrorism and very few improvements will be needed to really protect the general population.

       True   False

7) Which of the following is a health effect caused by a blood agent?
   a) Seizures
   b) Respiratory failure
   c) Cardiac arrest
   d) All of the above

8) Which of the following is NOT a nerve agent?
   a) Tabun
   b) Sarin
   c) Lewisite
   d) All of the Above

9) Which of the following is a means by which anthrax may enter the body?
   a) Inhalation (lungs)
   b) Cutaneous (skin)
   c) Ingestion (mouth)
   d) All of the above

10) When disposing of clothing which may have been exposed to ricin, and after washing any affected areas on your body, you should place your clothing inside a plastic bag and avoid touching contaminated areas of the clothing.

         True   False

Answers

1) False

2) True

3) True

4) True

5) False

6) False

7) D

8) C

9) D

10) True

4

Emergency Response to Chemical/ Biological Attacks

Two men in protective gear carrying hazardous material.
Courtesy of Hulton Archive/Getty Images, Inc.

Overview:

What happens if a chemical or biological weapon that disappeared off the traditional battlefield resurfaces on mainstreet, or the football stadium, or the local mall? What if a well-funded terrorist organization such as Al-Qaeda locates the right former Cold War weapons scientist with the knowledge and possibly even some of the material required to make even a low-yield WMD? How will the general public react to a terrorist's bomb that goes off in a crowded venue if there is even the suspicion that the device was laced with a contaminant?

These questions, and many others, are the kinds that must be pondered by the homeland security specialist. Part of your career will be to prepare mentally, physically, and emotionally to prevent and respond to an attack of this magnitude.

Chapter Objectives:

- *State the major principles of emergency response for a chemical/ biological attack*
- *State the benefits of conducting "mass casualty exercises"*
- *Identify the types and uses of chemical protective clothing*
- *Describe the standards for the transportation of hazardous materials*

Definition: Mass Casualty/Mass Fatality

Many people confuse the term "mass casualty" with "mass fatality." Mass casualty refers to an event in which responders must triage, treat, and care for multiple injured victims. Mass fatality, as the name implies, means first responders are dealing with a situation in which there are multiple deaths. On September 11, 2001, at the World Trade Center site, for example, emergency medical personnel and local hospitals set up multiple triage centers to begin dealing with what they thought were going to an influx of casualties. Sadly, many of these doctors reported a lack of casualties in need of treatment. The collapse and utter destruction of the twin towers produced more of a mass fatality situation than a mass casualty.

Chemical Weapons Improved Response Program (CW IRP)

The Chemical Weapons Improved Response Program (CW IRP) is part of the Domestic Preparedness program, enacted under the Nunn-Lugar-Domenici legislation to prepare the United States for possible acts of domestic terrorism. The CW IRP is designed to increase our country's readiness posture by enhancing the capability of civilian emergency responders to safely and effectively respond to a potential terrorist incident that involves the use of chemical warfare agents.

The CW IRP is a long-term think tank approach that focuses on high priority responder needs when responding to the scene of CW terrorism. The program is seeking to develop both technical and operational solutions that are applicable to both rural and metropolitan communities.

The program's approach is to conduct parallel operational and scientific research that consist of a series of workshops, scientific investigations, and functional exercises that systematically develops, tests, and validates chemical weapons incident response procedures. Participants in this program include local, state and federal government agencies; law enforcement; firefighters; emergency medical services technicians; hazardous materials technicians; emergency management professionals; Military Reserves; and the National Guard.

The chemical warfare expertise of the U.S. Army Soldier and Biological Chemical Command of the Aberdeen Proving Ground, Maryland, is joined with fire service, law enforcement, public health, and emergency management professionals. The primary focus is the Baltimore Metropolitan region with active participation from Philadelphia, New York, Los Angeles and Washington, DC, that provides a national perspective. The team is uniquely qualified to address the tough problems facing the nation's emergency responders in dealing with chemical terrorism.

BALTEX Exercises

The Baltimore exercises, referred to as BALTEX, are a series of facilitated and specialized functional tabletop and functional exercises that bring together emergency responders and emergency management personnel from all levels of government to thoroughly examine the issues associated with the response to a wide variety of chemical terrorist event scenarios.

Each BALTEX exercise is intended to increase in complexity and focus on different aspects of the "total response" while always building on lessons learned from previous exercises. Through this process, participants identify deficiencies in knowledge, equipment, and procedures that inhibit safe and efficient response. Notional procedural concepts and equipment requirements are also identified which often require detailed scientific investigation. These concepts and requirements are refined, tested, and finally are operationally validated in a BALTEX functional exercise.

Typical areas of emphasis in a BALTEX exercise include

- emergency responder protection
- emergency responder detection capabilities and methods of enhancement;
- mass casualty decontamination techniques;
- crime scene preservation and law enforcement personnel protection; and
- command and control of response assets.

Technical Initiatives

- **Mass Casualty Decontamination**—The focus of emergency responder partners is to evaluate technologies and methodologies that permit rapid decontamination of large numbers of casualties. In addition, partners will also research all known documentation pertaining to decontamination of chemical warfare agents from the skin.
- **Chemical Detector Assessment**—The objective is to determine the ability of available chemical weapons detectors to meet the needs of the first responder community and provide guidelines for the use and purchase of such items. The approach involves conducting detector market surveys of military and commercial detectors, testing for agent sensitivity and false alarms, as well as the assessment of the detector role across the range of first responder needs.
- **Firefighter Protective Clothing Assessment**—Evaluation of the degree of protection against chemical agents afforded by standard firefighter turn-out gear during quick rescue operations. The approach has involved conducting man-in-simulant testing to measure protection factors of structural turn-out gear. The studies also include evaluation of field expedient methods of increasing protection of the ensemble, and the use of data to develop guidelines that can be used by incident commanders to make risk based decisions.
- **Positive Pressure Ventilation Testing**—The use of Positive Pressure Ventilation is being evaluated as a mitigation tool to quickly reduce the levels of contamination in a structure, thus making the environment less hazardous for emergency responders. These types of

systems are commonly used by firefighters to vent smoke out of burning buildings.

- **Personal Protective Equipment for Law Enforcement and Emergency Medical Personnel**—Law enforcement officers have volunteered for man-in-simulant studies. Such studies evaluate a range of low cost PPE options for personnel operating on the perimeter (cold zone only) of an incident, where low levels of contamination are expected to be present.

- **Medical Health Response to Chemical Terrorism**—The development of a generic medical response template to handle the catastrophic number of casualties that could be generated from a chemical terrorism incident. This plan will address issues that hospitals and health care providers would face in a chemical WMD incident and explore methodologies of handling victims during such an incident.

—Taken from *http://www2.sbccom.army.mil/hld/cwirp/index.htm*

U.S. Department of Labor: Occupational Safety & Health Administration Technical Manual

Introduction

The purpose of chemical protective clothing and equipment is to shield or isolate individuals from the chemical, physical, and biological hazards that may be encountered during hazardous materials operations. During chemical operations, it is not always apparent when exposure occurs. Many chemicals pose invisible hazards and offer no warning properties.

These guidelines describe the various types of clothing that are appropriate for use in various chemical operations and provides recommendations in their selection and use. The final paragraph discusses heat stress and other key physiological factors that must be considered in connection with protective clothing use.

It is important that protective clothing users realize that no single combination of protective equipment and clothing is capable of protecting you against all hazards. Thus protective clothing should be used in conjunction with other protective methods. For example, engineering or administrative controls to limit chemical contact with personnel should always be considered as an alternative measure for preventing chemical exposure. The use of protective clothing can itself create significant wearer hazards, such as heat stress, physical and psychological stress, in addition to impaired vision, mobility, and communication. In general, the greater the level of chemical protective clothing, the greater the associated risks. For any given situation, equipment and clothing should be selected that provide an adequate level of protection. Overprotection as well as underprotection can be hazardous and should be avoided.

Descriptions
Protective Clothing Applications

Protective clothing must be worn whenever the wearer faces potential hazards arising from chemical exposure. Some examples include

- emergency response;
- chemical manufacturing and process industries;
- hazardous waste site cleanup and disposal;
- asbestos removal and other particulate operations; and
- agricultural application of pesticides.

Within each application, there are several operations which require chemical protective clothing. For example, in emergency response, the following activities dictate chemical protective clothing use:

- **Site Survey:** The initial investigation of a hazardous materials incident; these situations are usually characterized by a large degree of uncertainty and mandate the highest levels of protection.
- **Rescue:** Entering a hazardous materials area for the purpose of removing an exposure victim; special considerations must be given to how

the selected protective clothing may affect the ability of the wearer to carry out rescue and to the contamination of the victim.

- **Spill Mitigation:** Entering a hazardous materials area to prevent a potential spill or to reduce the hazards from an existing spill (i.e., applying a chlorine kit on railroad tank car). Protective clothing must accommodate the required tasks without sacrificing adequate protection.

- **Emergency Monitoring:** Outfitting personnel in protective clothing for the primary purpose of observing a hazardous materials incident without entry into the spill site. This may be applied to monitoring contract activity for spill cleanup.

- **Decontamination:** Applying decontamination procedures to personnel or equipment leaving the site; in general a lower level of protective clothing is used by personnel involved in decontamination.

The Clothing Ensemble

The approach in selecting personal protective clothing must encompass an "ensemble" of clothing and equipment items which are easily integrated to provide both an appropriate level of protection and still allow one to carry out activities involving chemicals. In many cases, simple protective clothing by itself may be sufficient to prevent chemical exposure, such as wearing gloves in combination with a splash apron and faceshield (or safety goggles).

The following is a checklist of components that may form the chemical protective ensemble:

- Protective clothing (suit, coveralls, hoods, gloves, boots)
- Respiratory equipment (SCBA, combination SCBA/SAR, air purifying respirators)
- Cooling system (ice vest, air circulation, water circulation);
- Communications device
- Head protection
- Eye protection
- Ear protection
- Inner garment
- Outer protection (overgloves, overboots, flashcover)

Factors that affect the selection of ensemble components include the following:

- How each item accommodates the integration of other ensemble components. Some ensemble components may be incompatible due to how they are worn (e.g., some SCBAs may not fit within a particular chemical protective suit or allow acceptable mobility when worn).
- The ease of interfacing ensemble components without sacrificing required performance (e.g., a poorly fitting overglove that greatly reduces wearer dexterity).

- Limiting the number of equipment items to reduce donning time and complexity (e.g., some communications devices are built into SCBA's which as a unit are NIOSH certified).

Level of Protection

Table VIII:1-1 lists ensemble components based on the widely used EPA Levels of Protection: Levels A, B, C, and D. These lists can be used as the starting point for ensemble creation; however, each ensemble must be tailored to the specific situation in order to provide the most appropriate level of protection. For example, if an emergency response activity involves a highly contaminated area or if the potential of contamination is high, it may be advisable to wear a disposable covering such as Tyvek coveralls or PVC splash suits over the protective ensemble.

Table VIII:1-1. EPA Levels of Protection

LEVEL A:

Vapor protective suit (meets NFPA 1991)
Pressure-demand, full-face SCBA
Inner chemical-resistant gloves, chemical-resistant safety boots, two-way radio communication

OPTIONAL: Cooling system, outer gloves, hard hat

Protection Provided: Highest available level of respiratory, skin, and eye protection from solid, liquid, and gaseous chemicals.

Used When: The chemical(s) have been identified and have high level of hazards to respiratory system, skin, and eyes. Substances are present with known or suspected skin toxicity or carcinogenity. Operations must be conducted in confined or poorly ventilated areas.

Limitations: Protective clothing must resist permeation by the chemical or mixtures present. Ensemble items must allow integration without loss of performance.

LEVEL B:

Liquid splash-protective suit (meets NFPA 1992)
Pressure-demand, full-facepiece SCBA
Inner chemical-resistant gloves, chemical-resistant safety boots, two-way radio communications
Hard hat.

OPTIONAL: Cooling system, outer gloves

Protection Provided: Provides same level of respiratory protection as Level A, but less skin protection. Liquid splash protection, but no protection against chemical vapors or gases.

Used When: The chemical(s) have been identified but do not require a high level of skin protection. Initial site surveys are required until higher levels of hazards are identified. The primary hazards associated with site entry are from liquid and not vapor contact.

Limitations: Protective clothing items must resist penetration by the chemicals or mixtures present. Ensemble items must allow integration without loss of performance.

LEVEL C:

Support Function Protective Garment (meets NFPA 1993)
Full-facepiece, air-purifying, canister-equipped respirator
Chemical resistant gloves and safety boots
Two-way communications system, hard hat

OPTIONAL: Faceshield, escape SCBA

Protection Provided: The same level of skin protection as Level B, but a lower level of respiratory protection. Liquid splash protection but no protection to chemical vapors or gases.

Used When: Contact with site chemical(s) will not affect the skin. Air contaminants have been identified and concentrations measured. A canister is available which can remove the contaminant. The site and its hazards have been completely characterized.

Limitations: Protective clothing items must resist penetration by the chemical or mixtures present. Chemical airborne concentration must be less than IDLH levels. The atmosphere must contain at least 19.5 percent oxygen.

Not Acceptable for Chemical Emergency Response

LEVEL D:

Coveralls, safety boots/shoes, safety glasses or chemical splash goggles

OPTIONAL: Gloves, escape SCBA, face-shield

Protection Provided: No respiratory protection, minimal skin protection.

Used When: The atmosphere contains no known hazard. Work functions preclude splashes, immersion, potential for inhalation, or direct contact with hazard chemicals.

Limitations: This level should not be worn in the Hot Zone. The atmosphere must contain at least 19.5 percent oxygen.

Not Acceptable for Chemical Emergency Response

The type of equipment used and the overall level of protection should be reevaluated periodically as the amount of information about the chemical situation or process increases, and when workers are required to perform different tasks. Personnel should upgrade or downgrade their level of protection only with concurrence with the site supervisor, safety officer, or plant industrial hygienist.

The recommendations in Table VIII:1-1 serve only as guidelines. It is important for you to realize that selecting items by how they are designed or configured alone is not sufficient to ensure adequate protection. In other words, just having the right components to form an ensemble is not enough. The EPA levels of protection do not define what performance the selected clothing or equipment must offer. Many of these considerations are described in the "limiting criteria" column of Table VIII:1-1. Additional factors relevant to the various clothing and equipment items are described in subsequent paragraphs.

Ensemble Selection Factors

- **Chemical Hazards.** Chemicals present a variety of hazards such as toxicity, corrosiveness, flammability, reactivity, and oxygen deficiency. Depending on the chemicals present, any combination of hazards may exist.
- **Physical Environment.** Chemical exposure can happen anywhere: in industrial settings, on the highways, or in residential areas. It may occur either indoors or outdoors; the environment may be extremely hot, cold, or moderate; the exposure site may be relatively uncluttered or rugged, presenting a number of physical hazards; chemical handling activities may involve entering confined spaces, heavy lifting, climbing a ladder, or crawling on the ground. The choice of ensemble components must account for these conditions.
- **Duration of Exposure.** The protective qualities of ensemble components may be limited to certain exposure levels (e.g., material chemical resistance, air supply). The decision for ensemble use time must be made assuming the worst case exposure so that safety margins can be applied to increase the protection available to the worker.
- **Protective Clothing or Equipment Available.** Hopefully, an array of different clothing or equipment is available to workers to meet all intended applications. Reliance on one particular clothing or equipment item may severely limit a facility's ability to handle a broad range of chemical exposures. In its acquisition of equipment and clothing, the safety department or other responsible authority should attempt to provide a high degree of flexibility while choosing protective clothing and equipment that is easily integrated and provides protection against each conceivable hazard.

Classification of Protective Clothing

Personal protective clothing includes the following:

- Fully encapsulating suits
- Nonencapsulating suits
- Gloves, boots, and hoods
- Firefighter's protective clothing
- Proximity, or approach clothing
- Blast or fragmentation suits; and
- Radiation-protective suits

Firefighter turnout clothing, proximity gear, blast suits, and radiation suits by themselves are not acceptable for providing adequate protection from hazardous chemicals.

Table VIII:1-2 describes various types of protection clothing available, details the type of protection they offer, and lists factors to consider in their selection and use.

Table VIII:1-2. Types of Protective Clothing for Full Body Protection

Description	Type of Protection	Use Considerations
Fully encapsulating suit One-piece garment. Boots and gloves may be integral, attached and replaceable, or separate.	Protects against splashes, dust gases, and vapors.	Does not allow body heat to escape. May contribute to heat stress in wearer, particularly if worn in conjunction with a closed-circuit SCBA; a cooling garment may be needed. Impairs worker mobility, vision, and communication.
Nonencapsulating suit jacket, hood, pants or bib overalls, and one-piece coveralls.	Protects against splashes, dust, and other materials but not against gases and vapors. Does not protect parts of head or neck.	Do not use where gas-tight or pervasive splashing protection is required. May contribute to heat stress in wearer. Tape-seal connections between pant cuffs and boots and between gloves and sleeves.
Aprons, leggings, and sleeve protectors. Fully sleeved and gloved apron. Separate coverings for arms and legs. Commonly worn over non-encapsulating suit.	Provides additional splash protection of chest, forearms, and legs.	Whenever possible, should be used over a nonencapsulating suit to minimize potential heat stress. Useful for sampling, labeling, and analysis operations. Should be used only when there is a low probability of total body contact with contaminants.
Firefighters' protective clothing. Gloves, helmet, running or bunker coat, running or bunker pants (NFPA No. 1971, 1972, 1973, and boots (1974).	Protects against heat, hot water, and some particles. Does not protect against gases and vapors, or chemical permeation or degradation. NFPA Standard No. 1971 specifies that a garment consists of an outer shell, an inner liner and a vapor barrier with a minimum water penetration of 25 lb/in^2 (1.8 kg/cm^2) to prevent passage of hot water.	Decontamination is difficult. Should not be worn in areas where protection against gases, vapors, chemical splashes or permeation is required.

Proximity garment (approach suit). One- or two-piece overgarment with boot covers, gloves, and hood of aluminized nylon or cotton fabric. Normally worn over other protective clothing, fire-fighters' bunker gear, or flame-retardant coveralls.	Protects against splashes, dust, gases, and vapors.	Does not allow body heat to escape. May contribute to heat stress in wearer, particularly if worn in conjunction with a closed-circuit SCBA; a cooling garment may be needed. Impairs worker mobility, vision, and communication.
Blast and fragmentation suit. Blast and fragmenta-tion vests and clothing, bomb blankets, and bomb carriers.	Provides some protection against very small detona-tions. Bomb blankets and baskets can help redirect a blast.	Does not provide for hearing protection.
Radiation-contamination protective suit. Various types of protective clothing designed to prevent contamination of the body by radioactive particles.	Protects against alpha and beta particles. Does not protect against gamma radiation.	Designed to prevent skin contamination. If radiation is detected on site, consult an experienced radiation expert and evacuate personnel until the radiation hazard has been evaluated.
Flame/fire retardant coveralls. Normally worn as an undergarment.	Provides protection from flash fires.	Adds bulk and may exacerbate heat stress problems and impair mobility.

Classification of Chemical Protective Clothing. Table VIII:1-3 provides a listing of clothing classifications. Clothing can be classified by design, performance, and service life.

Table VIII:1-3. Classification of Chemical Protective Clothing

By Design	By Performance	By Service Life
gloves boots aprons, jackets, coveralls, full body suits	particulate protection liquid-splash protection vapor protection	single use limited use reusable

Design. Categorizing clothing by design is mainly a means for describing what areas of the body the clothing item is intended to protect.

In emergency response, hazardous waste site cleanup, and dangerous chemical operations, the only acceptable types of protective clothing include fully or totally encapsulating suits and nonencapsulating or "splash" suits plus accessory clothing items such as chemically resistant gloves or boots. These descriptions apply to how the clothing is designed and not to its performance.

Performance. The National Fire Protection Association (NFPA) has classified suits by their performance as follows:

Vapor-protective suits (NFPA Standard 1991) provide "gas-tight" integrity and are intended for response situations where no chemical contact is permissible. This type of suit would be equivalent to the clothing required in EPA's Level A.

Liquid splash-protective suits (NFPA Standard 1992) offer protection against liquid chemicals in the form of splashes, but not against continuous liquid contact or chemical vapors or gases. Essentially, the type of clothing would meet the EPA Level B needs. It is important to note, however, that by wearing liquid splash-protective clothing, the wearer accepts exposure to chemical vapors or gases because this clothing does not offer gas-tight performance. The use of duct tape to seal clothing interfaces does not provide the type of wearer encapsulation necessary for protection against vapors or gases.

Support function protective garments (NFPA Standard 1993) must also provide liquid splash protection but offer limited physical protection. These garments may comprise several separate protective clothing components (i.e., coveralls, hoods, gloves, and boots). They are intended for use in non-emergency, nonflammable situations where the chemical hazards have been completely characterized. Examples of support functions include proximity to chemical processes, decontamination, hazardous waste cleanup, and training. Support function protective garments should not be used in chemical emergency response or in situations where chemical hazards remain uncharacterized.

These NFPA standards define minimum performance requirements for the manufacture of chemical protective suits. Each standard requires rigorous testing of the suit and the materials that comprise the suit in terms of overall protection, chemical resistance, and physical properties. Suits that are found compliant by an independent certification and testing organization may be labeled by the manufacturer as meeting the requirements of the respective NFPA standard. Manufacturers also have to supply documentation showing all test results and characteristics of their protective suits.

Protective clothing should completely cover both the wearer and his or her breathing apparatus. In general, respiratory protective equipment is not designed to resist chemical contamination. Level A protection (vapor-protective suits) require this configuration. Level B ensembles may be configured either with the SCBA on the outside or inside. However, it is strongly recommended that the wearer's respiratory equipment be worn inside the ensemble to prevent its failure and to reduce decontamination problems. Level C ensembles use cartridge or canister type respirators which are generally worn outside the clothing.

Service Life

Clothing item service life is an end user decision depending on the costs and risks associated with clothing decontamination and reuse. For example, a Saranex/Tyvek garment may be designed to be a coverall (covering the wearer's torso, arms, and legs) intended for liquid splash protection, which is disposable after a single use.

Protective clothing may be labeled as

- reusable, for multiple wearings; or
- disposable, for one-time use.

The distinctions between these types of clothing are both vague and complicated. Disposable clothing is generally lightweight and inexpensive. Reusable clothing is often more rugged and costly. Nevertheless, extensive contamination of any garment may render it disposable. The basis of this classification really depends on the costs involved in purchasing, maintaining, and re-using protective clothing versus the alternative of disposal following exposure. If an end user can anticipate obtaining several uses out of a garment while still maintaining adequate protection from that garment at lower cost than its disposal, the suit becomes re-usable. Yet, the key assumption in this determination is the viability of the garment following exposure. This issue is further discussed in the paragraph on decontamination.

Protective Clothing Selection Factors

Clothing Design. Manufacturers sell clothing in a variety of styles and configurations.

Design Considerations

- Clothing configuration
- Components and options
- Sizes
- Ease of donning and doffing
- Clothing construction
- Accommodation of other selected ensemble equipment
- Comfort
- Restriction of mobility

Material Chemical Resistance. Ideally, the chosen material(s) must resist permeation, degradation, and penetration by the respective chemicals.

Permeation is the process by which a chemical dissolves in or moves through a material on a molecular basis. In most cases, there will be no visible evidence of chemicals permeating a material.

Permeation breakthrough time is the most common result used to assess material chemical compatibility. The rate of permeation is a function of several factors such as chemical concentration, material thickness, humidity, temperature, and pressure. Most material testing is done with 100 percent chemical over an extended exposure period. The time it takes chemical to permeate through the material is the breakthrough time. An acceptable material is one where the breakthrough time exceeds the expected period of garment use. However, temperature and pressure effects may enhance permeation and reduce the magnitude of this safety factor. For example, small increases in ambient temperature can significantly reduce breakthrough time and the protective barrier properties of a protective clothing material.

Degradation involves physical changes in a material as the result of a chemical exposure, use, or ambient conditions (e.g., sunlight). The most common observations of material degradation are discoloration, swelling, loss of physical strength, or deterioration.

Penetration is the movement of chemicals through zippers, seams, or imperfections in a protective clothing material.

It is important to note that no material protects against all chemicals and combinations of chemicals, and that no currently available material is an effective barrier to any prolonged chemical exposure.

Sources of information include:

- *Guidelines for the Selection of Chemical Protective Clothing,* Third Edition. This reference provides a matrix of clothing material recommendations for approximately 500 chemicals based on an evaluation of chemical resistance test data, vendor literature, and raw material suppliers. The major limitation for these guidelines are their presentation of recommendations by generic material class. Numerous test results have shown that similar materials from different manufacturers may give widely different performance. That is to say manufacturer A's butyl rubber glove may protect against chemical X, but a butyl glove made by manufacturer B may not.
- *Quick Selection Guide to Chemical Protective Clothing.* Pocket size guide that provides chemical resistance data and recommendations for 11 generic materials against over 400 chemicals. The guide is color-coded by material-chemical recommendation. As with the *Guidelines* . . . above, the major limitation of this reference is its dependence on generic data.
- Vendor data or recommendations. The best source of current information on material compatibility should be available from the manufacturer of the selected clothing. Many vendors supply charts which show actual test data or their own recommendations for specific chemicals. However, *unless vendor data or the recommendations are well-documented, end users must approach this information with caution.* Material recommendations must be based on data obtained from tests performed to standard ASTM methods. Simple ratings of "poor," "good," or "excellent" give no indication of how the material may perform against various chemicals.

Mixtures of chemicals can be significantly more aggressive towards protective clothing materials than any single chemical alone. One permeating chemical may pull another with it through the material. Very little data is available for chemical mixtures. Other situations may involve unidentified substances. In both the case of mixtures and unknowns, serious consideration must be given to deciding which protective clothing is selected. If clothing must be used without test data, garments with materials having the broadest chemical resistance should be worn, i.e. materials which demonstrate the best chemical resistance against the widest range of chemicals.

Physical Properties

As with chemical resistance, manufacturer materials offer wide ranges of physical qualities in terms of strength, resistance to physical hazards, and operation in extreme environmental conditions. Comprehensive manufacturing standards such as the NFPA Standards set specific limits on these material properties, but only for limited applications, (i.e., emergency response.)

End users in other applications may assess material physical properties by posing the following questions:

- Does the material have sufficient strength to withstand the physical strength of the tasks at hand?
- Will the material resist tears, punctures, cuts, and abrasions?
- Will the material withstand repeated use after contamination and decontamination?
- Is the material flexible or pliable enough to allow end users to perform needed tasks?
- Will the material maintain its protective integrity and flexibility under hot and cold extremes?
- Is the material flame-resistant or self-extinguishing (if these hazards are present)?
- Are garment seams in the clothing constructed so they provide the same physical integrity as the garment material?

Ease of Decontamination. The degree of difficulty in decontaminating protective clothing may dictate whether disposable or re-usable clothing is used, or a combination of both.

Cost. Protective clothing end users must endeavor to obtain the broadest protective equipment they can buy with available resources to meet their specific application.

Chemical Protective Clothing Standards. Protective clothing buyers may wish to specify clothing that meets specific standards, such as 1910.120 or the NFPA standards (see paragraph on classification by performance). The NFPA standards do not apply to all forms of protective clothing and applications.

General Guidelines

Decide if the clothing item is intended to provide vapor, liquid-splash, or particulate protection.

Vapor protective suits also provide liquid-splash and particulate protection. Liquid-splash protective garments also provide particulate protection. Many garments may be labeled as totally encapsulating but do not provide gas-tight integrity due to inadequate seams or closures. Gas-tight integrity can only be determined by performing a pressure or inflation test and a leak detection test of the respective protective suit. This test involves

- closing off suit exhalation valves;
- inflating the suit to a prespecified pressure; and
- observing whether the suit holds the above pressure for a designated period.
  ASTM Standard Practice F1052 (1987 Edition) offers a procedure for conducting this test.

Splash suits must still cover the entire body when combined with the respirator, gloves, and boots. Applying duct tape to a splash suit does not make it protect against vapors. Particulate protective suits may not need to cover the entire body, depending on the hazards posed by the particulate. In general, gloves, boots, and some form of face protection are required. Clothing items may only be needed to cover a limited area of the body such as gloves on hands. The nature of the hazards and the expected exposure will determine if clothing should provide partial or full body protection.

Determine if the clothing item provides full body protection

- Vapor-protective or totally encapsulating suit will meet this requirement by passing gas-tight integrity tests.
- Liquid splash-protective suits are generally sold incomplete (i.e., fewer gloves and boots).
- Missing clothing items must be obtained separately and match or exceed the performance of the garment.
- Buying a PVC glove for a PVC splash suit does not mean that you obtain the same level of protection. This determination must be made by comparing chemical resistance data.

Evaluate manufacturing chemical resistance data provided with the clothing

Manufacturers of vapor-protective suits should provide permeation resistance data for their products, while liquid and particulate penetration resistance data should accompany liquid splash and particulate protective garments respectively. Ideally, data should be provided for every primary material in the suit or clothing item. For suits, this includes the garment, visor, gloves, boots, and seams.

Closing off suit exhalation valves

Permeation data should include the following:

- Chemical name
- Breakthrough time (shows how soon the chemical permeates)
- Permeation rate (shows the rate that the chemical comes through)
- System sensitivity (allows comparison of test results from different laboratories)
- A citation that the data was obtained in accordance with ASTM Standard Test Method F739-85

If no data are provided or if the data lack any one of the above items, the manufacturer should be asked to supply the missing data. Manufacturers that provide only numerical or qualitative ratings must support their recommendations with complete test data.

Liquid penetration data should include a pass or fail determination for each chemical listed, and a citation that testing was conducted in accordance with ASTM Standard Test Method F903-86. Protective suits which are certified to NFPA 1991 or NFPA 1992 will meet all of the above requirements.

Particulate penetration data should show some measure of material efficiency in preventing particulate penetration in terms of particulate type or size and percentage held out. Unfortunately, no standard tests are available in this area and end users may have little basis for company products.

Suit materials which show no breakthrough or no penetration to a large number of chemicals are likely to have a broad range of chemical resistance. (Breakthrough times greater than one hour are usually considered to be an indication of acceptable performance.) Manufacturers should provide data on the ASTM Standard Guide F1001-86 chemicals. These fifteen liquid and six gaseous chemicals listed in Table VIII:1-4 below represent a cross-section of different chemical classes and challenges for protective clothing materials. Manufacturers should also provide test data on other chemicals as well. If there are specific chemicals within your operating area that have not been tested, ask the manufacturer for test data on these chemicals.

Obtain and examine the manufacturer's instruction or technical manual

This manual should document all the features of the clothing, particularly suits, and describe what material(s) are used in its construction. It should cite specific limitations for the clothing and what restrictions apply to its use. Procedures and recommendations should be supplied for at least the following:

- Donning and doffing
- Inspection, maintenance, and storage
- Decontamination
- Use

The manufacturer's instructions should be thorough enough to allow the end users to wear and use the clothing without a large number of questions.

Table VIII:1-4. Recommended Chemicals to Evaluate the Performance of Protective Clothing Materials

Chemical	Class
Acetone	Ketone
Acetonitrile	Nitrile
Ammonia	Strong base (gas)
1,3-Butadiene	Olefin (gas)
Carbpm Dosi;fode	Sulfur-containing organic
Chlorine	Inorganic gas
Dichloromethane	Chlorinated hydrocarbon
Diethylamine	Amine
Dimethyl formamide	Amide
Ethyl Acetate	Ester
Ethyl Oxide	Oxygen heterocyclic gas
Hexane	Aliphatic hydrocarbon
Hydrogen Chloride	Acid gas
Methanol	Alcohol
Methyl Chloride	Chlorinated hydrocarbon (gas)
Nitrobenzene	Nitrogen-containing organic
Sodium Hydroxide	Inorganic base
Sulfuric Acid	Inorganic acid
Tetrachloroethylene	Chlorinated hydrocarbon
Tetrahydrofuran	Oxygen heterocyclic
Toluene	Aromatic hydrocarbon

Obtain and inspect sample clothing item garments

Examine the quality of clothing construction and other features that will impact its wearing. The questions listed under "Protective Clothing Selection Factors, Clothing Design" should be considered. If possible, representative clothing items should be obtained in advance and inspected prior to purchase, and discussed with someone who has experience in their use. It is also helpful to try out representative garments prior to purchase by suiting personnel in the garment and having them run through exercises to simulate expected activities.

Field selection of chemical protective clothing

Even when end users have gone through a very careful selection process, a number of situations will arise when no information is available to judge whether their protective clothing will provide adequate protection. These situations include

- chemicals that have not been tested with the garment materials;
- mixtures of two or more different chemicals;
- chemicals that cannot be readily identified;
- extreme environmental conditions (hot temperatures); and
- lack of data in all clothing components (e.g., seams, visors).

Testing material specimens using newly developed field test kits may offer one means for making an on-site clothing selection. A portable test kit has been developed by the EPA using a simple weight-loss method that allows field qualification of protective clothing materials within one hour.

Use of this kit may overcome the absence of data and provide additional criteria for clothing selection.

Selection of chemical protective clothing is a complex task and should be performed by personnel with both extensive training and experience.

Under all conditions, clothing should be selected by evaluating its performance characteristics against the requirements and limitations imposed by the application.

Management Program
Written Management Program
A written Chemical Protective Clothing Management Program should be established by all end users who routinely select and use protective clothing. Reference should be made to 1910.120 for those covered.

The written management program should include policy statements, procedures, and guidelines. Copies should be made available to all personnel who may use protective clothing in the course of their duties or job. Technical data on clothing, maintenance manuals, relevant regulations, and other essential information should also be made available.

The two basic objectives of any management program should be to protect the wearer from safety and health hazards, and to prevent injury to the wearer from incorrect use and/or malfunction of the chemical protective clothing. To accomplish these goals, a comprehensive management program should include hazard identification; medical monitoring; environmental surveillance; selection, use, maintenance, and decontamination of chemical protective clothing; and training.

Program Review and Evaluation. The management program should be reviewed at least annually. Elements which should be considered in the review include

- the number of person-hours that personnel wear various forms of chemical protective clothing and other equipment;
- accident and illness experience;
- levels of exposure;
- adequacy of equipment selection;
- adequacy of the operational guidelines;
- adequacy of decontamination, cleaning, inspection, maintenance, and storage programs;
- adequacy and effectiveness of training and fitting programs;
- coordination with overall safety and health program;
- the degree of fulfillment of program objectives;
- the adequacy of program records;
- recommendations for program improvement and modification; and
- program costs.

The results of the program evaluation should be made available to all end users and presented to top management so that program changes may be implemented.

Types of Standard Operating Procedures. Personal protective clothing and equipment can offer a high degree of protection only if it is used properly. Standard Operating Procedures (SOP's) should be established for all workers involved in handling hazardous chemicals. Areas that should be addressed include

- selection of protective ensemble components;
- protective clothing and equipment donning, doffing, and use;
- decontamination procedures;
- inspection, storage, and maintenance of protective clothing/equipment; and
- training.

Selection of Protective Clothing Components

Protective clothing and equipment SOPs must take into consideration the factors presented in the Clothing Ensemble and Protective Clothing Applications sections of this chapter. All clothing and equipment selections should provide a decision tree that relates chemical hazards and information to levels of protection and performance needed.

Responsibility in selecting appropriate protective clothing should be vested in a specific individual who is trained in both chemical hazards and protective clothing use such as a safety officer or industrial hygienist. Only chemical protective suits labeled as compliant with the appropriate performance requirements should be used. In cases where the chemical hazards are known in advance or encountered routinely, clothing selection should be predetermined. That is, specific clothing items should be identified in specific chemical operations without the opportunity for individual selection of other clothing items.

Clothing Donning, Doffing, and Use

The procedures below are given for vapor protective or liquid-splash protective suit ensembles and should be included in the training program.

Donning the Ensemble

A routine should be established and practiced periodically for donning the various ensemble configurations that a facility or team may use. Assistance should be provided for donning and doffing since these operations are difficult to perform alone, and solo efforts may increase the possibility of ensemble damage.

Table VIII:1-5, on the following page, lists sample procedures for donning a totally encapsulating suit/SCBA ensemble. These procedures should be modified depending on the suit and accessory equipment used. The procedures assume the wearer has previous training in respirator use and decontamination procedures.

Once the equipment has been donned, its fit should be evaluated. If the clothing is too small, it will restrict movement, increase the likelihood of tearing the suit material, and accelerate wearer fatigue. If the clothing is too large, the possibility of snagging the material is increased, and the

Table VIII:1-5. Sample Donning Procedures

Inspect clothing and respiratory equipment before donning (see paragraph on Inspection).

Adjust hard hat or headpiece if worn, to fit user's head.

Open back closure used to change air tank (if suit has one) before donning suit.

Standing or sitting, step into the legs of the suit; ensure proper placement of the feet within the suit; then gather the suit around the waist.

Put on chemical-resistant safety boots over the feet of the suit. Tape the leg cuff over the tops of the boots.

If additional chemical-resistant safety boots are required, put these on now.

Some one-piece suits have heavy-soled protective feet. With these suits, wear short, chemical-resistant safety boots inside the suit.

Put on air tank and harness assembly of the SCBA. Don the facepiece and adjust it to be secure, but comfortable. Do not connect the breathing hose. Open valve on air tank.

Perform negative and positive respirator facepiece seal test procedures.

To conduct a negative-pressure test, close the inlet part with the palm of the hand or squeeze the breathing tube so it does not pass air, and gently inhale for about ten seconds. Any inward rushing of air indicates a poor fit. Note that a leaking facepiece may be drawn tightly to the face to form a good seal, giving a false indication of adequate fit.

To conduct a positive-pressure test, gently exhale while covering the exhalation valve to ensure that a positive pressure can be built up. Failure to build a positive pressure indicates a poor fit.

Depending on type of suit:

Put on long-sleeved inner gloves (similar to surgical gloves). Secure gloves to sleeves, for suits with detachable gloves (if not done prior to entering the suit).

Additional overgloves, worn over attached suit gloves, may be donned later.

Put sleeves of suit over arms as assistant pulls suit up and over the SCBA. Have assistant adjust suit around SCBA and shoulders to ensure unrestricted motion.

Put on hard hat, if needed.

Raise hood over head carefully so as not to disrupt face seal of SCBA mask. Adjust hood to give satisfactory comfort.

Begin to secure the suit by closing all fasteners on opening until there is only adequate room to connect the breathing hose. Secure all belts and/or adjustable leg, head, and waistbands.

Connect the breathing hose while opening the main valve.

Have assistant first ensure that wearer is breathing properly and then make final closure of the suit.

Have assistant check all closures.

Have assistant observe the wearer for a period of time to ensure that the wearer is comfortable, psychologically stable, and that the equipment is functioning properly.

dexterity and coordination of the wearer may be compromised. In either case, the wearer should be recalled and better-fitting clothing provided.

Doffing an Ensemble
Exact procedures for removing a totally encapsulating suit/SCBA ensemble must be established and followed in order to prevent contaminant

migration from the response scene and transfer of contaminants to the wearer's body, the doffing assistant, and others.

Sample doffing procedures are provided in Table VIII:1-6 below. These procedures should be performed only after decontamination of the suited end user. They require a suitably attired assistance. Throughout the procedures, both wearer and assistant should avoid any direct contact with the outside surface of the suit.

Table VIII:1-6. Sample Doffing Procedures

If sufficient air supply is available to allow appropriate decontamination before removal:

1. Remove any extraneous or disposable clothing, boot covers, outer gloves, and tape.
2. Have assistant loosen and remove the wearer's safety shoes or boots.
3. Have assistant open the suit completely and lift the hood over the head of the wearer and rest it on top of the SCBA tank.
4. Remove arms, one at a time, from suit. Once arms are free, have assistant lift the suit up and away from the SCBA backpack—avoiding any contact between the outside surface of the suit and the wearer's body—and lay the suit out flat behind the wearer. Leave internal gloves on, if any.
5. Sitting, if possible, remove both legs from the suit.
6. Follow procedure for doffing SCBA.
7. After suit is removed, remove internal gloves by rolling them off the hand, inside out.
8. Remove internal clothing and thoroughly cleanse the body.

If the low-pressure warning alarm has sounded, signifying that approximately five minutes of air remain:

9. Remove disposable clothing.
10. Quickly scrub and hose off, especially around the entrance/exit zipper.
11. Open the zipper enough to allow access to the regulator and breathing hose.
12. Immediately attach an appropriate canister to the breathing hose (the type and fittings should be predetermined). Although this provides some protection against any contamination still present, it voids the certification of the unit.

Follow Steps 1 through 8 of the regular doffing procedure above. Take extra care to avoid contaminating the assistant and the wearer.

User Monitoring and Training

The wearer must understand all aspects of clothing/equipment operation and their limitations; this is especially important for fully encapsulating ensembles where misuse could potentially result in suffocation. During protective clothing use, end users should be encouraged to report any perceived problems or difficulties to their supervisor. These malfunctions include, but are not limited to

- degradation of the protection ensemble;
- perception of odors;
- skin irritation;
- unusual residues on clothing material;

- discomfort;
- resistance to breathing;
- fatigue due to respirator use;
- interference with vision or communication;
- restriction of movement; and
- physiological responses such as rapid pulse, nausea, or chest pain.

Before end users undertake any activity in their chemical protective ensembles, the anticipated duration of use should be established. Several factors limit the length of a mission, including

- air supply consumption as affected by wearer work rate, fitness, body size, and breathing patterns;
- suit ensemble permeation, degradation, and penetration by chemical contaminants, including expected leakage through suit or respirator exhaust valves (ensemble protection factor);
- ambient temperature as it influences material chemical resistance and flexibility, suit and respirator exhaust valve performance, and wearer heat stress; and
- coolant supply (if necessary).

Decontamination Procedures
Definition and Types
Decontamination is the process of removing or neutralizing contaminants that have accumulated on personnel and equipment. This process is critical to health and safety at hazardous material response sites. Decontamination protects end users from hazardous substances that may contaminate and eventually permeate the protective clothing, respiratory equipment, tools, vehicles, and other equipment used in the vicinity of the chemical hazard; it protects all plant or site personnel by minimizing the transfer of harmful materials into clean areas; it helps prevent mixing of incompatible chemicals; and it protects the community by preventing uncontrolled transportation of contaminants from the site.

There are two types of decontamination:

- **Gross decontamination:** To allow end user to safely exit or doff the chemical protective clothing.
- **Decontamination:** For reuse of chemical protective clothing.

Prevention of Contamination. The first step in decontamination is to establish standard operating procedures that minimize contact with chemicals and thus the potential for contamination. For example:

- Stress work practices that minimize contact with hazardous substances (e.g., do not walk through areas of obvious contamination, do not directly touch potentially hazardous substances).
- Use remote sampling, handling, and container-opening techniques (e.g., drum grapples, pneumatic impact wrenches).

- Protect monitoring and sampling instruments by bagging. Make openings in the bags for sample ports and sensors that must contact site materials.
- Wear disposable outer garments and use disposable equipment where appropriate.
- Cover equipment and tools with a strippable coating that can be removed during decontamination.
- Encase the source of contaminants, (e.g., with plastic sheeting or overpacks).
- Ensure all closures and ensemble component interfaces are completely secured and that no open pockets that could serve to collect contaminant are present.

Types of Contamination
- **Surface Contaminants.** Surface contaminants may be easy to detect and remove.
- **Permeated Contaminants.** Contaminants that have permeated a material are difficult or impossible to detect and remove. If contaminants that have permeated a material are not removed by decontamination, they may continue to permeate the material where they can cause an unexpected exposure.

Four major factors affect the extent of permeation:

- **Contact time.** The longer a contaminant is in contact with an object, the greater the probability and extent of permeation. For this reason, minimizing contact time is one of the most important objectives of a decontamination program.
- **Concentration.** Molecules flow from areas of high concentration to areas of low concentration. As concentrations of chemicals increase, the potential for permeation of personal protective clothing increases.
- **Temperature.** An increase in temperature generally increases the permeation rate of contaminants.
- **Physical state of chemicals.** As a rule, gases, vapors, and low-viscosity liquids tend to permeate more readily than high-viscosity liquids or solids.

Decontamination Methods
Decontamination methods either (1) physically remove contaminants; (2) inactivate contaminants by chemical detoxification or disinfection/sterilization; or (3) remove contaminants by a combination of both physical and chemical means.

In general, gross decontamination is accomplished using detergents (surfactants) in water combined with a physical scrubbing action. This process will remove most forms of surface contamination including dusts, many inorganic chemicals, and some organic chemicals. Soapy water scrubbing of protective suits may not be effective in removing oily or tacky organic substances (e.g., PCBs in transformer oil). Furthermore, this form of decontamination is unlikely to remove any contamination that has permeated or penetrated the suit materials. Using organic solvents such as petroleum distillates may allow easier removal of heavy organic contamination but may result in other problems, including

- permeation into clothing components, pulling the contaminant with it;
- spreading localized contaminant into other areas of the clothing; and
- generating large volumes of contaminated solvents that require disposal.

One promising method for removing internal or matrix contamination is the forced circulation of heated air over clothing items for extended periods of time. This allows many organic chemicals to migrate out of the materials and evaporate into the heated air. The process does require, however, that the contaminating chemicals be volatile. Additionally, low-level heat may accelerate the removal of plasticizer from garment materials and affect the adhesives involved in garment seams.

Unfortunately, both manufacturers and protective clothing authorities provide few specific recommendations for decontamination. There is no definitive list with specific methods recommended for specific chemicals and materials. Much depends on the individual chemical-material combination involved.

Testing the Effectiveness of Decontamination
Protective clothing or equipment reuse depends on demonstrating that adequate decontamination has taken place. Decontamination methods vary in their effectiveness and unfortunately there are no completely accurate methods for nondestructively evaluating clothing or equipment contamination levels.

Methods which may assist in a determination include the following:

- Visual examination of protective clothing for signs of discoloration, corrosive effects, or any degradation of external materials. However, many contaminants do not leave any visible evidence.
- Wipe sampling of external surfaces for subsequent analysis; this may or may not be effective for determining levels of surface contamination and depends heavily on the material-chemical combination. These methods will not detect permeated contamination.
- Evaluation of the cleaning solution. This method cannot quantify clean method effectiveness since the original contamination levels are unknown. The method can only show if the chemical has been removed by the cleaning solution. If a number of garments have been contaminated, it may be advisable to sacrifice one garment for destructive testing by a qualified laboratory with analysis of contamination levels on and inside the garment.

Decontamination Plan

A decontamination plan should be developed and set up before any personnel or equipment are allowed to enter areas where the potential for exposure to hazardous substances exists. The decontamination plan should

- determine the number and layout of decontamination stations;
- determine the decontamination equipment needed;
- determine appropriate decontamination methods;
- establish procedures to prevent contamination of clean areas;
- establish methods and procedures to minimize wearer contact with contaminants during removal of personal protective clothing; and
- establish methods for disposing of clothing and equipment that are not completely decontaminated.

The plan should be revised whenever the type of personal protective clothing or equipment changes, the use conditions change, or the chemical hazards are reassessed based on new information.

The decontamination process should consist of a series of procedures performed in a specific sequence. For chemical protective ensembles, outer, more heavily contaminated items (e.g., outer boots and gloves) should be decontaminated and removed first, followed by decontamination and removal of inner, less contaminated items (e.g., jackets and pants). Each procedure should be performed at a separate station in order to prevent cross contamination. The sequence of stations is called the decontamination line.

Stations should be separated physically to prevent cross contamination and should be arranged in order of decreasing contamination, preferably in a straight line. Separate flow patterns and stations should be provided to isolate workers from different contamination zones containing incompatible wastes. Entry and exit points to exposed areas should be conspicuously marked. Dressing stations for entry to the decontamination area should be separate from redressing areas for exit from the decontamination area. Personnel who wish to enter clean areas of the decontamination facility, such as locker rooms, should be completely decontaminated.

All equipment used for decontamination must be decontaminated and/or disposed of properly. Buckets, brushes, clothing, tools, and other contaminated equipment should be collected, placed in containers, and labeled. Also, all spent solutions and wash water should be collected and disposed of properly. Clothing that is not completely decontaminated should be placed in plastic bags, pending further decontamination and/or disposal.

Decontamination of workers who initially come in contact with personnel and equipment leaving exposure or contamination areas will require more protection from contaminants than decontamination workers who are assigned to the last station in the decontamination line. In some cases, decontamination personnel should wear the same levels of protective clothing as workers in the exposure or contaminated areas. In other cases, decontamination personnel may be sufficiently protected by wearing one level lower protection (e.g., wearing Level B protection while decontaminating workers who are wearing Level A).

Decontamination for Protective Clothing Reuse. Due to the difficulty in assessing contamination levels in chemical protective clothing before and after exposure, the responsible supervisor or safety professional must determine if the respective clothing can be reused. This decision involves considerable risk in determining clothing to be contaminant-free. Reuse can be considered if, in the estimate of the supervisor,

- no "significant" exposures have occurred;
- decontamination methods have been successful in reducing contamination levels to safe or acceptable concentrations;
- contamination by known or suspected carcinogens should warrant automatic disposal. Use of disposable suits is highly recommended when extensive contamination is expected.

Emergency Decontamination

In addition to routine decontamination procedures, emergency decontamination procedures must be established. In an emergency, the primary concern is to prevent the loss of life or severe injury to personnel. If immediate medical treatment is required to save a life, decontamination should be delayed until the victim is stabilized. If decontamination can be performed without interfering with essential life-saving techniques or first aid, or if a worker has been contaminated with an extremely toxic or corrosive material that could cause severe injury or loss of life, decontamination should be continued.

If an emergency due to a heat-related illness develops, protective clothing should be removed from the victim as soon as possible to reduce the heat stress. During an emergency, provisions must also be made for protecting medical personnel and disposing of contaminated clothing and equipment.

Inspection, Storage, and Maintenance

The end user in donning protective clothing and equipment must take all necessary steps to ensure that the protective ensemble will perform as expected. During emergencies is not the right time to discover discrepancies in the protective clothing. Teach end user care for his clothing and other protective equipment in the same manner as parachutists care for parachutes. Following a standard program for inspection, proper storage, and maintenance along with realizing protective clothing/equipment limitations is the best way to avoid chemical exposure during emergency response.

Inspection

An effective chemical protective clothing inspection program should feature five different inspections:

- Inspection and operational testing of equipment received as new from the factory or distributor.
- Inspection of equipment as it is selected for a particular chemical operation.
- Inspection of equipment after use or training and prior to maintenance.
- Periodic inspection of stored equipment.
- Periodic inspection when a question arises concerning the appropriateness of selected equipment, or when problems with similar equipment are discovered.

Each inspection will cover different areas with varying degrees of depth. Those personnel responsible for clothing inspection should follow manufacturer directions; many vendors provide detailed inspection procedures. The generic inspection checklist provided in Table VIII:1-7 may serve as an initial guide for developing more extensive procedures.

Records must be kept of all inspection procedures. Individual identification numbers should be assigned to all reusable pieces of equipment (many clothing and equipment items may already have serial numbers), and records should be maintained by that number. At a minimum, each inspection should record

- clothing/equipment item ID number;
- date of the inspection;
- person making the inspection;
- results of the inspection; and
- any unusual conditions noted.
- periodic review of these records can provide an indication of protective clothing which requires excessive maintenance and can also serve to identify clothing that is susceptible to failure.

Table VIII:1-7. Sample PPE Inspection Checklists

Clothing	
Before use:	Determine that the clothing material is correct for the specified task at hand.
Visually inspect for:	Imperfect seams; Nonuniform coatings; Tears; and Malfunctioning closures.
Hold up to light and check for pinholes	
Flex product:	Observe for cracks. Observe for other signs or shelf deterioration.
If the product has been used previously, inspect inside and out for signs of chemical attack:	Discoloration Swelling Stiffness

Table VIII:1-7. Continued

During the work task, periodically inspect for:	Evidence of chemical attack such as discoloration, swelling, stiffening and softening. Keep in mind, however, that chemical permeation can occur without any visible effects. Closure failure Tears Punctures Seam discontinuities
Gloves	
Before use:	Pressurize glove to check for pinholes. Either blow into glove, then roll gauntlet towards fingers or inflate glove and hold under water. In either case, no air should escape.
Fully Encapsulating Suits	
Before use:	Check the operation of pressure relief valves Inspect the fitting of wrists, ankles, and neck Check faceshield, if so equipped, for cracks crazing fogginess

Storage

Clothing must be stored properly to prevent damage or malfunction from exposure to dust, moisture, sunlight, damaging chemicals, extreme temperatures, and impact. Procedures are needed for both initial receipt of equipment and after use or exposure of that equipment. Many manufacturers specify recommended procedures for storing their products. These should be followed to avoid equipment failure resulting from improper storage.

Some guidelines for general storage of chemical protective clothing include the following:

- Potentially contaminated clothing should be stored in an area separate from street clothing or unused protective clothing.
- Potentially contaminated clothing should be stored in a well-ventilated area, with good air flow around each item, if possible.
- Different types and materials of clothing and gloves should be stored separately to prevent issuing the wrong material by mistake (e.g., many glove materials are black and cannot be identified by appearance alone).
- Protective clothing should be folded or hung in accordance with manufacturer instructions.

Maintenance

Manufacturers frequently restrict the sale of certain protective suit parts to individuals or groups who are specially trained, equipped, or authorized by the manufacturer to purchase them. Explicit procedures should be adopted to ensure that the appropriate level of maintenance is performed only by those individuals who have this specialized training and equipment. In no case should you attempt to repair equipment without checking with the person in your facility who is responsible for chemical protective clothing maintenance.

The following classification scheme is recommended to divide the types of permissible or nonpermissible repairs:

- **Level 1:** User or wearer maintenance, requiring a few common tools or no tools at all.
- **Level 2:** Maintenance that can be performed by the response team's maintenance shop, if adequately equipped and trained.
- **Level 3:** Specialized maintenance that can be performed only by the factory or an authorized repair person.

Each facility should adopt the above scheme and list which repairs fall into each category for each type of protective clothing and equipment. Many manufacturers will also indicate which repairs, if performed in the field, void the warranty of their products. All repairs made must be recorded on the records for the specific clothing along with appropriate inspection results.

Training

Benefits. Training in the use of protective clothing
- allows the user to become familiar with the equipment in a non-hazardous, nonemergency condition;
- instills confidence of the user in his/her equipment; and
- makes the user aware of the limitations and capabilities of the equipment;
- increases worker efficiency in performing various tasks; and
- reduces the likelihood of accidents during chemical operations.

Content. Training should be completed prior to actual clothing use in a nonhazardous environment and should be repeated at the frequency required by OSHA SARA III legislation. As a minimum the training should point out the user's responsibilities and explain the following, using both classroom and field training when necessary:

- The proper use and maintenance of selected protective clothing, including capabilities and limitations.
- The nature of the hazards and the consequences of not using the protective clothing.
- The human factors influencing protective clothing performance.
- Instructions in inspecting, donning, checking, fitting, and using protective clothing.
- Use of protective clothing in normal air for a long familiarity period.
- The user's responsibility (if any) for decontamination, cleaning, maintenance, and repair of protective clothing.

- Emergency procedures and self-rescue in the event of protective clothing/ equipment failure.
- The buddy system.

The discomfort and inconvenience of wearing chemical protective clothing and equipment can create a resistance to its conscientious use. One essential aspect of training is to make the user aware of the need for protective clothing and to instill motivation for the proper use and maintenance of that protective clothing.

Risks

Heat Stress. Wearing full body chemical protective clothing puts the wearer at considerable risk of developing heat stress. This can result in health effects ranging from transient heat fatigue to serious illness or death. Heat stress is caused by a number of interacting factors, including

- environmental conditions;
- type of protective ensemble worn;
- the work activity required; and
- the individual characteristics of the responder.

When selecting chemical protective clothing and equipment, each item's benefit should be carefully evaluated for its potential for increasing the risk of heat stress. For example, if a lighter, less insulating suit can be worn without a sacrifice in protection, then it should be. Because the incidence of heat stress depends on a variety of factors, all workers wearing full body chemical protective ensembles should be monitored.

The following physiological factors should be monitored.

Heart Rate. Count the radial pulse during a thirty-second period as early as possible in any rest period. If the heart rate exceeds 110 beats per minute at the beginning of the rest period, the next work cycle should be shortened by one-third.

Oral Temperature
Do not permit an end user to wear protective clothing and engage in work when his or her oral temperature exceeds 100.6°F (38.1°C).

Use a clinical thermometer (three minutes under the tongue) or similar device to measure oral temperature at the end of the work period (before drinking), as follows:

- If the oral temperature exceeds 99.6°F (37.6°C), shorten the next work period by at least one-third.
- If the oral temperature exceeds 99.6°F (37.6°C) at the beginning of a response period, shorten the mission time by one-third.

Body Water Loss. Measure the end user's weight on a scale accurate to plus or minus 0.25 pounds prior to any response activity. Compare this weight with his or her normal body weight to determine if enough fluids have been consumed to prevent dehydration. Weights should be taken while the end user wears similar clothing, or ideally, in the nude. The body water loss should not exceed 1.5 percent of the total body weight loss from a response.

Bibliography

Barker, R.L. and Coletta, G.C. *Performance of Protective Clothing.* American Society for Testing Materials: Philadelphia, 1986.

Forsberg, K. and Keith, L.H. *Chemical Protective Clothing Performance Index Book.* John Wiley & Sons: New York, 1989.

Forsberg, K. and Mansdorf, S.Z. *Quick Selection Guide to Chemical Protective Clothing.* Van Nostrand-Reinhold: New York, 1989.

Perkins, J.L. and Stull, J.O., ed. *Chemical Protective Clothing Performance in Chemical Emergency Response.* American Society for Testing Materials: Philadelphia, 1989.

Schwope, A.D., et al. *Guidelines for the Selection of Chemical Protective Clothing.* Third Ed. ACGIH: Cincinnati, 1987.

Managing Hazardous Materials

The homeland security specialist must be aware that not every potential biological or chemical terrorist attack could be the introduction of a hazardous weapon into a target environment. Another very viable and, in many ways, simpler means of initiating a hazardous materials attack would be to sabotage or damage an industrial or government facility that uses toxic materials as a part of its daily operations. These could include laboratories, powerplants, petrochemical sites, nuclear reactors, waste treatment centers, hazardous materials storage and disposal facilities, and manufacturing plants.

A conventional explosive device placed near a hazardous material container, deliberate sabotage of a transfer pipes carrying toxins, or the deliberate venting of harmful gases into the environment are all methods by which a terrorist, turn civil grade hazardous materials into weapons.

The first line of defense against this type of attack is sound facility life safety and security planning and hazardous materials management. As a security specialist, you may be called upon to monitor and even manage a life safety monitoring system designed to prevent an authorized release of hazardous materials.

Process Plant Security Programs for Managing Risks from Deliberate Releases and Diversions of Hazardous Materials[*]
by Paul Raybutt

Process plants may be subject to terrorist and criminal acts that can result in the deliberate catastrophic release or diversion of hazardous materials. Presently, many plants may not be prepared to handle such threats, although various measures are available to manage these risks. They include traditional physical security measures that must be applied to protect assets

[*] Taken from *Security Management* magazine, November 2002, by permission of ASIS International. © 2002 ASIS International, 1625 Prince Street, Alexandria, VA 22314.

which are hazardous materials. Such measures help protect plants against penetration by adversaries trying to reach the hazardous materials. Additionally, safeguards must be employed to help protect against releases in the event the security measures do not prevent adversaries from reaching the hazardous materials.

Certain combinations of security measures and safeguards should be considered by all process plants as part of a basic security program. As the risk increases, more and stronger measures should be taken. Since many plants have not considered these issues previously, it is useful to provide examples of security programs that can be implemented to manage various risk levels. In this paper, a classification scheme is described for security measures and safeguards to protect against deliberate acts, and security programs are described for four levels of increasing security. These programs provide a starting point for implementing a security program according to the particular circumstances faced by a facility. Existing safeguards that protect against accidental releases may also protect against deliberate releases and diversions, but it is unlikely they will be sufficient. They may need to be strengthened, and additional safeguards and security measures may be required.

Introduction

Many process plants contain hazardous materials that, if released, can adversely impact the health and safety of workers and the public, and damage the environment.

These include chemical plants, oil refineries, and companies that handle hazardous chemicals such as ammonia and chlorine in large quantities. Hazardous material releases can result from extraordinary events such as accidents, natural events, or deliberate acts. Accidents occur when people make errors or mistakes, or equipment fails. Natural events are phenomena such as lightning strikes and flooding, sometimes called external events. Deliberate acts are performed with the intention of causing harm and include terrorism, sabotage, vandalism, and theft. Various threat scenarios are possible and the risk from them must be managed with a process security program.

Accidental and natural events are addressed by Process Safety Management and Risk Management Programs which are required by government regulation. OSHA's Process Safety Management (PSM) standard, 29 CFR 1910.119 was promulgated in 1992 and EPA's Risk Management (RM) Program rule, 40 CFR Part 68, became effective in 1999. Over the past few years, concern has developed about the risk from deliberate acts. Public debate began when EPA considered placing off-site consequence analyses from RM Plans on the Internet and concern was expressed that the information could be used by terrorists to plan attacks against plants. This concern has been underlined by the events of September 11, 2001. The risk of terrorism and criminal acts against process plants is clearly real. Appropriate security measures and safeguards must be employed. Unfortunately, it is believed that security at some chemical plants may be very poor. Therefore, immediate action may be needed.

Chemical plants must ensure they are appropriately secure from attack by adversaries.

United States legislators and industry have recognized this need. The Chemical Security Act of 2001 (S. 1602) was introduced by Senators Corzine (D-NJ), Jeffords (D-VT), Boxer (D-CA), and Clinton (D-NY) on October 31, 2001, and referred to the Committee on Environment and Public Works. The American Chemistry Council (ACC) published "Site Security Guidelines for the US Chemical Industry" in October 2001, in cooperation with the Society of Organic Chemical Manufacturers and the Chlorine Institute. ACC mandated enhanced security for its members on January 29, 2002, and promised a new Security Code by June 2002 under Responsible Care.

Presently, there are no standards for companies to use in implementing a process security program. The ACC guidelines provide suggestions on measures to consider but they do not provide specifications for programs. Some standards are under development. For example, the National Fire Protection Association has proposed two standards for an overall security program to protect premises, people, property, and information specific to a particular occupancy. These are NFPA 730, Premises Security Code, and NFPA 731, Installation of Premises Security Equipment. However, process security covers a range of issues and it will be challenging to develop standards that address them all. For example, physical security, computer and information security, and protection against releases must all be addressed. This goes beyond normal considerations either for protecting valuable assets or for preventing accidental releases of hazardous materials.

Security Measures and Safeguards

Both security and safety programs typically use defense in depth to protect against threats and accidents. This is called rings of protection in security and layers of protection in safety. Generally, security protection tries to prevent access to hazardous materials while safety protection tries to prevent their release. In process safety, the term safeguards is usually intended to convey measures to protect against accidents. In process security, various security measures that do not necessarily assist in protecting against accidents are needed to protect against threats. These can be called secureguards. Some safeguards may act as secureguards and vice versa. In process security management, safeguards and secureguards must be combined into a program to provide overall protection.

In process security, protection rings/layers can be classified as follows:

- Prevention
- Detection
- Control
- Mitigation

- Prevention secureguards can be divided into perimeter and interior secureguards.
- Perimeter prevention secureguards include the following:
  Buffer zones, setbacks and clear zones
  Physical barriers to personnel entry (e.g., fencing, locks)
  Physical barriers to vehicle entry
  Facility access controls (e.g., identification, personnel and vehicle logs, gates, turnstiles, escorts, searches, bag/parcel inspection)
  Shipment security (e.g., screening deliveries for bombs, checking incoming vehicles for intruders and outgoing vehicles for diverted materials)
  Guards and guard dogs
- Interior prevention secureguards include the following:
  Personnel security (e.g., screening, ID badges, labor relations, actions on termination)
  Information security (e.g. controlled use of radios and telephones, document control, internet and intranet restrictions)
  Cyber security (e.g., firewall; encryption; passwords; virus, worm and trojan horse protection; separation of functions)
  Security awareness program for employees and contractors
  Access control to sensitive areas (e.g., control rooms, utilities)
  Access control to hazardous materials areas
  Area lighting
  Hardening of control rooms, utilities and other critical support systems
  Vehicle controls
  Vehicle barriers for sensitive and hazardous materials areas
  Locking manual valves
  Projectile shields
  Process design including inherent security
  Detection secureguards include:
  Surveillance system
  Intrusion detection and alarms
  Cyber intrusion detection
  Site inspections by guards on rounds
- Control secureguards include the following:
  Layout (e.g., location of hazardous materials and critical support systems)
  Good housekeeping practices (e.g., keeping sight lines free of obstruction in hazardous materials areas, frequent emptying of trash containers)
- Mitigation secureguards include the following:
  Law enforcement response
  Safeguards can be classified similarly.
- Prevention safeguards include the following:
  Process design, including inherent safety

> Inventory control, minimize amounts present and monitor for diversion

- Detection safeguards include:
  Release detection
  Monitoring process parameters
- Control safeguards include the following:
  Excess flow check valves
  Automatic shutoff valves
  Extraordinary event emergency shutdown procedures
- Mitigation safeguards include the following::
  Buffer zones
  Secondary containment (e.g., double-walled vessels)
  Release containment (e.g., dikes)
  Vapor cloud suppression (e.g., deluge systems)
  Emergency response
  Evacuation plans
  Chemical antidotes stockpiled

The defense-in-depth concept is based on the premise that multiple layers or rings of protection ensure some level of protection in the event that one or more layers or rings fails. A second concept important for process security is the use of both high-profile and low-profile systems. High-profile systems are intended to be noticed by and discourage adversaries while low-profile systems provide protection against determined adversaries who are not discouraged by the high-profile systems but may not readily detect the low-profile systems. A third concept for process security is to ensure there is an appropriate balance between secureguards and safeguards. Usually, plants should not favor protecting against either penetration or releases but rather utilize measures that provide a balance between the two types of protection. This diversity provides more reliable security and safety.

Examples of Security Programs
Four programs are described of increasing sophistication.

Level 1 Program
This program provides a combination of secureguards and safeguards that should be considered by all facilities handling hazardous materials. Consider implementing these measures:

- Coordination with law enforcement
- Screening of employees and contractors
- Fencing around the entire facility with top guard
- Gates with locks
- Key and lock management program
- Secure points of intrusion
- Personnel identification on entry
- ID badges
- Visitor escorts
- Guards at gates

- Visual inspection of bags/parcels
- Appropriate employee/contractor termination procedures
- Security awareness program
- Document control for sensitive information
- Restrictions on in-plant signs
- Restrictions on electronic dissemination of information (e.g., intranet and internet)
- Cyber security
- Secure communications to law enforcement
- Good housekeeping practices
- Inventory control
- Monitoring process parameters
- Extraordinary event emergency shutdown procedures
- Release detection
- Release containment
- Vapor cloud suppression
- Emergency response
- Evacuation plans

Most plants should implement these measures or their equivalent.

Typically, justification should be provided to exclude any of them from a basic security program.

Level 2 Program
This program can be used to protect facilities containing more hazardous materials or larger quantities, or for which the threat level is higher, or when a company wants to take a more conservative risk management approach. Consider implementing Program 1 measures plus the following:

- Retractable vehicle booms at gates
- Prohibition of entrance to facility by anyone other than employees or contractors
- Guard patrols within facility
- Random checks of incoming and outgoing vehicles
- Area lighting
- Restrictions on vehicle access
- Locking manual valves

Level 3 Program
This program provides measures for increased security that may be appropriate when large populations are at risk, for example, close to major metropolitan areas. Consider implementing measures from the previous programs plus the following:

- Vehicle blocking system at entries (e.g., retractable bollards)
- Double exterior fence with tanglefoot
- Guards stationed at key interior locations
- Checks of all incoming and outgoing vehicles

- Use of smart keys
- Prohibition of radio conversations about sensitive topics
- Access control to sensitive areas, (e.g., control rooms, utilities)
- Access control to hazardous materials areas
- Analyze transaction histories for critical computer systems
- Cyber intrusion detection
- Surveillance system
- Perimeter intrusion detection and alarms
- Panic alarms
- Additional excess flow check valves
- Additional automatic shutoff valves
- Secondary containment

Level 4 Program

This program offers all reasonable available measures short of creating an armed encampment. In addition to the measures described for the previous programs, consider the following:

- Vehicle barriers around perimeter (e.g., trenches)
- Secondary fences around hazardous materials areas and sensitive areas
- Armed guards
- Guard dogs
- x-ray screening of bags/parcels/packages
- Radio voice encryption
- Perform counter-surveillance to detect information gathering
- Hardening of control rooms, utilities and other critical support systems
- Backup computer and critical support systems
- Vehicle barriers for sensitive and hazardous materials areas
- Projectile shields
- Interior area intrusion detection and alarms
- Chemical antidotes stockpiled

Considerations for New Facilities

New plants provide opportunities for managing security and safety that may not be available for existing plants. For example, buffer zones are used to provide space between a facility and its neighbors. Existing facilities may not have this option due to the proximity of other buildings or the unavailability of land for purchase, but it is an important consideration for a new facility, both for security and safety reasons. Buffer zones act both as a preventive secureguard and a mitigation safeguard. They may deter adversaries by decreasing the visibility of the facility and providing for easier observation of approaching assailants. They also increase the distance from public receptors and thus decrease the risk of exposure.

New facilities also offer the opportunity to use inherent safety and security concepts.

The goal is to produce a facility that is "benign by design" by eliminating or reducing features that make the process attractive to criminals or terrorists. Although this is best considered during design, it is also possible to retrofit some features for existing facilities.

Process design also offers the opportunity to consider equipment that is appropriately resistant to attack, for example, increased wall thicknesses, double-walled construction, mounding, and underground installation. Where possible, weak points such as sight glasses and flex hoses should be avoided. Protection for critical support systems such as computers, utilities, and communications should also be addressed during design, for example, placing wiring in rigid conduit.

Layout of equipment and buildings is part of the design process for a new facility.

Generally, hazardous materials and sensitive areas should be located away from the facility perimeter for improved security. The most vulnerable locations should be the hardest for adversaries to reach. Sensitive areas include control rooms, computer rooms, motor control centers, rack rooms, server rooms, telecommunication rooms, and utilities.

Measures for security and safety may sometimes be in opposition. For example, in the past few years, a number of companies have relocated control rooms away from process areas to improve process safety as part of facility siting studies. In some cases these relocations may have resulted in a less secure facility. However, if companies are aware of the need to manage both process security and process safety, reasonable compromises are usually possible. Another example of such a conflict is the placement of hazardous materials storage areas within buildings to restrict access for security purposes. This may increase the risk of exposure to personnel from accidental releases unless special precautions are taken.

Conclusions

Four programs have been described using combinations of secureguards and safeguards to protect against deliberate releases or diversions of hazardous materials.

They provide increasing levels of protection. No one program will be right for every facility since each facility is unique. These programs do not necessarily provide all the measures that should be provided for a facility. However, they do provide reference points for facilities who wish to improve their current process security programs.

References

1. *Final Rule on Process Safety Management of Highly Hazardous Chemicals; Explosives and Blasting Agents,* 29 CFR 1910.119, Occupational Safety and Health Administration, published 2/24/1992 and effective 5/26/92.

2. *Accidental Release Prevention Requirements: Risk Management Programs Under Clean Air Act Section 112(r)(7)—Final Rule (the Risk Management Program or RMP Rule),* 40 CFR Part 68, Environmental Protection Agency, signed May 24, 1996, published and effective June 20, 1996.

3. "Chemical Accident Prevention: Site Security," EPA Alert, EPA-K-550-F00-002, Office of Solid Waste and Emergency Response, February, 2000.

4. R. M. Burnham, "Potential Effects of Electronic Dissemination of Chemical 'Worst-Case Scenarios' Data" Statement before the US Senate Subcommittee on Clean Air, Wetlands, Private Property and Nuclear Safety, March 16, 1999.

5. *Industrial Chemicals and Terrorism: Human Health Threat Analysis, Mitigation and Prevention,* Agency for Toxic Substances and Disease Registry (ATSDR) Report, 1999.

6. *Site Security Guidelines for the US Chemical Industry,* American Chemistry Council, October, 2001.

7. American Chemistry Council Press Release, January 29, 2002.

8. P. Baybutt, *Process Security Management Systems: Protecting Plants Against Threats, submitted for publication, 2002.*

9. P. Baybutt, *Inherent Security, Protecting Process Plants Against Threats,* submitted for publication, 2002.

Sample Hazardous Material Containment Policy

The following is a working hazardous material containment policy currently in use with a major research facility. This document should provide an in-depth examination of what considerations are required by security and safety planners when faced with the challenge of proper handling and safe storage.

Secondary Containment of Hazardous Material and Waste

1. Overview

Secondary containment is a means of surrounding one or more primary storage containers or equipment containing hazardous material or waste so that spills and leaks are automatically contained in the event of primary container or equipment failure. This chapter provides guidance on the application of secondary containment for hazardous material, hazardous waste, and some nonhazardous waste in equipment or containers. Secondary containment provides the following benefits:

- Reduces the health, safety, or environmental risk posed by stored hazardous material and waste
- Prevents releases and costly cleanups of hazardous material and waste to the soil, surface water, and ground water

- Reduces the urgency of responding to and reporting spills to regulatory agencies

2. Policy

Secondary containment must be provided for hazardous material and waste at SLAC in compliance with all applicable

- regulations:
  Federal
  State
  Local;
- DOE orders;
- Storm Water Pollution Prevention Program (SWPPP); and
- Best Management Practices (BMPs).

At the discretion of the responsible department and ES&H, secondary containment may also be provided in cases where it is not specifically called for by regulations, but will reduce health, safety, and environmental risks. Factors that may affect the decision include the following:

- Location and proximity to site boundary or sensitive environmental areas.
- Special personnel or safety concerns.
- History of leaks.
- Equipment or article age.
- Future uses.
- Volume and type of hazardous material present.

S&H and the responsible department may also, after a thorough evaluation of circumstances, factors, and liabilities, make exceptions or reduce the stringency of secondary containment policy requirements where conditions warrant it. When secondary containment is not practical, a documented engineering or risk-based assessment is required. Part of the risk-based assessment may include the use of alternatives to secondary containment such as drip pans, frequent inspections, or leak detection equipment. The assessment will be performed and documented by Environmental Protection and Restoration (EPR).

3. Scope

This document provides guidance on the use of secondary containment for

- oil-filled equipment;
- hazardous material (including substances and chemicals); and
- hazardous and Toxic Substance Control Act (TSCA) waste.

Note:

Oil-filled equipment may contain Polychlorinated Biphenyls (PCBs). This equipment may require more stringent secondary containment requirements, particularly for PCB waste storage.

3.1 Compressed Gases

The scope of this document does not include secondary containment for compressed gases. Regulations do not currently require spill control, drainage, and containment for the storage of highly toxic or toxic compressed gases. Secondary containment or diversionary structures may be required, however, for specific applications as determined by the Safety Overview Committee.

Note:

For technical and regulatory guidance, refer to the Toxic Gas Model Ordinance. Copies are available from EPR.

3.2 Combustible and Flammable Liquids

Secondary containment designed to accommodate fire suppression or extinguishing volumes for combustible and flammable liquids will not be addressed in this document. Additional requirements to provide sufficient secondary containment capacity based on sprinkler volumes will be evaluated by the Safety, Health, and Assurance (SHA) Department and the department responsible for the secondary containment.

Note:

Considerations of secondary containment limitations are subordinate to the task of safely controlling and extinguishing a fire.

4. Responsibilities

4.1 Environmental Protection and Restoration

The Environmental Protection and Restoration Department in the ES&H Division

- provides information and guidance about requirements for secondary containment for hazardous and non-hazardous liquids; and
- reviews applicable regulations and provides guidance on secondary containment for hazardous materials and hazardous waste storage.

4.2 Safety, Health, and Assurance Department

The SHA Department in the ES&H Division

- inspects secondary containments for compliance with SLAC policy; and
- Provides guidance on fire-suppression systems for secondary containment associated with flammable and combustible liquids; and other worker safety and Industrial Hygiene (IH) issues.

4.3 Plant Engineering Department

The Plant Engineering Department (PED) shall do as follows:

- Restrict access to secondary containment for electrical equipment under their control when safety warrants it.
- Maintain, clean, and drain secondary containment under their control.

Note:
PED will design and construct custom-made secondary containment, upon request. They will also verify that custom-made secondary containment meets construction specifications, upon request.

4.4 Building or Area Managers
Building or area managers who are responsible for secondary containers in their area shall do as follows:

- Maintain, clean, and drain secondary containment under their control.
- Review the floor drain systems to ensure that secondary containment is properly located.
- Ensure that appropriate containment measures are taken to preclude uncontrolled discharge either into the sewer or storm drain system.
- Restrict access to secondary containment for electrical equipment under their control when safety warrants it.

4.5 Facilities Department
The Facilities Department (FAC) shall do as follows:

- Restrict access to secondary containment for electrical equipment under their control when safety warrants it.
- Maintain, clean, and drain secondary containment under FAC control.
- Review the floor drain systems to ensure that secondary containment is properly located to protect storm drain and sanitary sewer systems.

4.6 Hazardous Waste Material Coordinators
Hazardous Waste Material Coordinators (HWMCs) shall ensure that hazardous material and waste in Waste Accumulation Areas (WAAs) are stored and managed properly within secondary containment.

4.7 Managers and Supervisors
Managers and supervisors responsible for areas that contain hazardous material or waste shall do as follows:

- Ensure that secondary containment is provided where required.
- Ensure that secondary containment is located properly.
- Assign personnel to inspect secondary containment.
- Take corrective actions in response to deficiencies in secondary containment.
- Contact the EPR Department for guidance on regulations and selection of secondary containment when necessary.
- Contact PED if a custom-made secondary containment is needed.
- Ensure that prefabricated secondary containment meets specifications.

- Ensure that secondary containment for equipment containing polychlorinated biphenyls (PCBs) and for tank trucks meets specifications.
- Restrict access to secondary containment under their control when safety warrants it.
- Designate an individual to inspect secondary containment.
- Ensure that hazardous material and waste are stored properly within secondary containment.
- Ensure that secondary containment is kept clean and free of rain-water and debris.
- Ensure that leaks and spills discovered in secondary containment are corrected immediately or as soon as feasible.
- Ensure that secondary containment under their control is maintained, cleaned, and drained as needed.

4.8 All Others

All other persons on the SLAC premises, including subcontractors, users, and visitors who are working at SLAC must do as follows:

- Obtain the safety and environmental protection training appropriate for their work assignments.
- Inform themselves of the physical and chemical hazards in their work area(s), and the potential environmental implications of their work processes.
- Wear PPE and monitoring devices that are appropriate for their work assignments.
- Perform their work functions in a safe and environmentally responsible manner and within the constraints set by the WS Set.
- Contact security to stop any activity that presents an immediate safety hazard or threat to the environment, or is in violation of any safety or environmental standard contained in the WSSet.
- Report, to their supervisors or to Security, any activities that present an immediate safety hazard or threat to the environment, or are in violation of any safety or environmental standards contained in the WS Set.
- Prepare for emergencies by knowing how to summon assistance.

Note:

No one may discharge any water from secondary containments unless following approved ES&H procedures.

5. Requirements

Secondary containment must be provided for hazardous material and waste at SLAC in compliance with all applicable federal, state, and local regulations, and DOE orders. Managers and supervisors are responsible for ensuring that secondary containment is provided where required.

Note:

In some cases, existing secondary containment must be retrofitted to comply with requirements.

Secondary containment is required for the following:

- Total volumes of liquid hazardous material and waste greater than 55 gallons.
- Any volume of hazardous waste or any volume of extremely hazardous material.
- Overhead lines and pipes that carry hazardous material or waste when feasible. (In this case, secondary containment is provided by using double-walled lines or pipes.)
- All storage facilities containing hazardous material, hazardous waste, or oil-filled equipment.
- In situations where it is not specifically called for by regulations, but will substantially reduce health, safety, and environmental risks. Such situations will be reviewed on a case-by-case basis between the responsible manager or department and EPR.
- Non-hazardous liquids (such as low-conductivity water), when their release could violate environmental permits and result in illegal discharges to the sanitary sewer or storm drain.

Note:
Contact EPR for more information about secondary containment for non-hazardous liquids.

In cases where secondary containment is required but is not feasible, the responsible department must perform and document an engineering evaluation or a risk-based assessment to determine:

- Potential environment-, safety-, and health-related risks.
- Alternatives to secondary containment.

Note:
Contact EPR for assistance and review in risk evaluation.

Secondary containment is not required for the following:

- Equipment that has been completely drained of hazardous material.
- Hazardous material that is solid under normal conditions or the conditions that are likely to occur.

6. Types of Secondary Containment
Secondary containment measures may consist of one or more of the following:

- Dikes, berms, or retaining walls
- Curbing
- Drainage systems
- Spill-diversion ponds
- Retention ponds
- Sorbent material
- Sumps

There are two main types of secondary containment:

- Prefabricated
- Custom-made

6.1 Prefabricated

Prefabricated secondary containments are usually the most cost-effective type. Prefabricated secondary containments come in a wide range of sizes. They are typically made of:

- Stainless steel and epoxy-coated steel.
- Polyethylene plastic.

Note:

Prefabricated buildings are also available. See Section 6.1.3, "Prefabricated Buildings for Hazardous Material Storage."

6.1.1 Stainless Steel and Epoxy-coated Steel

Secondary containments made of stainless or epoxy-coated steel are

- durable;
- capable of withstanding significant loads;
- heavy;
- incompatible with some chemicals. For more information, consult the manufacturer; and
- more expensive than secondary containments made of polyethylene plastic.

6.1.2 Polyethylene Plastic

Secondary containments made of polyethylene plastic are as follows:

- Lightweight
- Compatible with most chemicals
- Inexpensive
- Subject to gradual degradation when exposed to ultraviolet rays or warm temperatures

6.1.3 Prefabricated Buildings for Hazardous Material Storage

Some departments at SLAC have successfully used prefabricated hazardous-material storage buildings to store large volumes of hazardous material. Using prefabricated hazardous-material storage buildings as secondary containment has several advantages.

Prefabricated hazardous-material storage buildings

- have built-in secondary containment;
- can be purchased with multiple "rooms" that can be used for segregating incompatible material;
- can be equipped with fire-suppression systems if they are used to store flammable or combustible liquids;
- can be locked to restrict access;

- are semi-mobile and can be relocated if storage requirements change; and
- are durable.

6.2 Custom-made

Custom-made secondary containments are usually made of epoxy- or elastomeric-coated reinforced concrete.

If you need a custom-made secondary containment, contact PED, who will, upon request, design and construct custom-made secondary containment for SLAC, in compliance with applicable regulations and appropriate design specifications.

If subcontractors are used to design and construct a custom-made secondary containment, PED will evaluate, upon request, the design and construction of the secondary containment for compliance with design specifications. EPR will evaluate secondary containment for compliance with applicable regulations.

Note:
Custom-made secondary containments must be assessed for seismic safety.

7. Selecting Secondary Containment

If unsure about the type of secondary containment to use, consult the Secondary Containment Technical Basis Document (SC-TBD)1, or contact PED and EPR.

The SC-TBD may be accessed in the ES&H Document room or on the Web at http://www.slac.stanford.edu/esh/techbas/.

8. Secondary Containment Locations

Secondary containments shall be located such that they

- do not pose a potential threat to the environment;
- are not located near or immediately upstream of a sewer or storm drain, as a release of hazardous material or waste to these drains can damage the environment;
- are not located near high-traffic areas such as roads and paths; and
- can be easily accessible in an emergency.

9. Secondary Containment Specifications

Secondary containments must meet the applicable specifications as described in the

SC-TBD. Secondary containment specifications include the following:

- Capacity
- Roofing
- Fire-suppression systems
- Ventilation
- Leak detection systems
- Curbing

- Sumps
- Lockable drain valves

10. Special Requirements

There are three types of items that require secondary containment with special specifications: hazardous waste storage tanks, PCB-containing equipment, and tank trucks used for storage of hazardous material. For specific information, refer to the SC-TBD.

11. Labeling and Marking

For all other secondary containments, the identifier may be the primary container(s).

WAAs are to be uniquely identified. A number will be assigned by the manager of the secondary containment and/or oil-filled equipment database. Association of a secondary containment with the article inside will enable better management to ensure that capacity requirements, compatibility, and inspections are met. In areas such as WAAs or the Centralized Waste Management Area (CWMA), where the inventory of containers for liquid hazardous material or waste may change frequently, it is recommended that HWMCs (or the responsible manager or supervisor) determine and post the maximum volume of a single container and the maximum total volume that may be stored in the secondary containment.

12. Restricting Access

Managers and supervisors must restrict access to secondary containment in their areas when safety warrants it. PED, FAC, HWMCs, or responsible managers or supervisors are responsible for restricting access to secondary containment for electrical equipment when safety warrants it. Access may be restricted with locks, barriers, or other means. Examples of secondary containment whose access must be restricted for safety reasons include the following:

- CWMAs and some of the WAAs
- Secondary containment for high-voltage electrical equipment
- Secondary containment for PCB-containing equipment that are located at SLAC outside of the controlled area fence

If you are unsure whether access should be restricted to a secondary containment or are unsure about the best method for restricting access, contact

- SHA for secondary containments that may be associated with confined spaces;
- HWMCs for WAAs;
- PED or responsible department for high-voltage electrical equipment and PCB-containing equipment.

341

13. Inspections

Managers and supervisors responsible for areas that contain hazardous material or waste must designate an individual to inspect secondary containments. Secondary containments must be inspected, at a minimum, according to the schedule in Table 21-1.

Table 21-1. Secondary Containment Inspection Schedule

Daily—Leaking equipment containing PCBs at a concentration greater than 500 ppm
Weekly—Tanks containing hazardous waste
Weekly—Secondary containments storing PCB waste
Monthly—Equipment and tanks containing hazardous material
Monthly—Secondary containment other than tanks containing hazardous waste
Quarterly—Equipment containing PCBs at a concentration greater than 500 ppm

Note:
Immediately report any spills, leaks, accumulation of rainwater in, or deterioration of secondary containment to the HWMC, responsible department, or the building manager for that area.

13.1 Responsibility for Inspections
The department that manages the equipment stored within the secondary containment is responsible for all inspections. If spillage is found, the spill should be reported immediately to the HWMC, supervisor, or building manager for the area.

Note:
All deficiencies of secondary containment must be corrected under the authority of the building or area manager responsible for that secondary containment

13.2 Frequency of Inspections
The frequency of inspection of secondary containments to be performed will be governed by the most restrictive requirements, if various categories of equipment or containers are contained within. Specifically, those secondary containments that contain oil-filled equipment will be inspected in conjunction with the requirements set forth in the Oil-filled Equipment Management Program. Those containing PCBs will generally be more frequent than those that do not.

Those secondary containments that contain hazardous materials will be treated the same as those that contain hazardous wastes, since there is a potential that hazardous materials may become hazardous wastes if mishandled or spilled. Inspections of secondary containments for hazardous materials are to be performed monthly. Inspections of hazardous waste-containment areas, WAAs, and hazardous waste-tank systems will be performed weekly.

The inspector should look for accumulation from spills, leaks, or precipitation, and for deterioration of containers and/or the containment system caused by corrosion or other factors. Inspections will be documented and made available for review.

The responsible department shall periodically inspect areas used for containment storage or transfer. The inspector should look for accumulation from spills, leaks, or precipitation and for deterioration of containers and/or the containment system caused by corrosion or other factors. In the case of absorbent materials and drip pans, the inspector should be attentive to saturation and freeboard levels such that the container capacity is not exceeded.

14. Compatibility of Stored Materials
Areas that contain hazardous material or waste must be stored properly within secondary containment. A chart on material compatibility is available from SLAC Stores.

HWMCs must ensure that hazardous material and waste in WAAs are stored properly within secondary containment by

- storing only compatible materials within a secondary containment; and
- using separate secondary containment for incompatible materials.

Note:
Do not store outdoors or near water sources any liquid hazardous material or waste that reacts with water.

15. Maintenance
Secondary containment surfaces must be maintained in good condition and be kept free of cracks or gaps. The surface coating must be maintained so that it is impervious to the material being contained.

16. General Housekeeping
Water and debris within secondary containments may be contaminated. For this reason, secondary containments should be kept dry, clean, and free of debris. The department responsible for the containment should inspect the containment for potential sources of contamination.

Rainwater must be removed from secondary containments in a timely manner so that overflow is prevented. Water or debris that is collected in the secondary containments should be removed so that it does not become hazardous waste.

Note:
A secondary containment should be thoroughly cleaned after it has been contaminated with any hazardous material or waste to prevent rainwater from becoming contaminated if it enters into the secondary containment.

Accumulations of noncombustible and combustible debris should be removed as soon as practicable. Combustible materials, including brooms and boards, must never be stored within secondary containments containing electrical equipment or PCBs and should be removed at least five (5) meters away from the equipment. Leaking valves should have absorbent pads placed below them or plastic bags secured around them to prevent contamination of the secondary containment area.

17. Leaks and Spills

Report any leaks and spills in secondary containments to the responsible manager or supervisor. Managers and supervisors must ensure that leaks and spills discovered in secondary containments are corrected immediately or as soon as feasible. Leaks and spills from PCB-containing equipment must be immediately cleaned up and disposed of as PCB-contaminated waste.

Note:
Spills must be evaluated and responded to as described in the "Spills" chapter of this manual.

18. Alternatives to Secondary Containment

In some applications, drip pans may serve as a suitable alternative spill-prevention measure. These would cover absorbents (such as pads or kitty litter), and other spill containment devices that are neither designed nor intended to contain at least the entire volume of fluid of the equipment or container. Drip pans or buckets are sometimes employed as a means of containing and managing a minor leak of equipment that is located within some type of secondary containment. In some cases, secondary containments are not feasible, such as underneath klystrons. Drip pans may be used under these conditions.

Drip pans that are utilized to contain minor leaks from equipment or containers do not need to conform to the requirements for secondary containments. However, if a leak of regulated material is involved, it must be managed in accordance with SLAC's hazardous waste policy.

SLAC generators are not allowed to store hazardous waste for more than forty-five days. This will ensure that WM can dispose of the waste within the legally required ninety-day limit. Consult with WM to arrange for disposal.

Other alternatives to secondary containment may include frequent inspections or leak detection systems. Consult with EPR for further information.

19. Moving Secondary Containment

Before moving a secondary containment to a new location, notify the following:

- Building manager for the building or area from which the secondary containment will be removed.
- Building manager for the building or area to which the secondary will be moved.
- PED to update the oil-filled equipment inventory database.
- EPR Department.

20. Closure or Transfers

A secondary containment may outlive the useful service life of the equipment or container stored within. The responsible department is charged with the maintenance of the equipment or container to ensure the proper handling of the secondary containment. When the equipment or container is removed, a decision has to be made whether to transfer ownership and responsibility to another group or decommission the secondary containment.

If ownership is to be transferred to another group or department who has use for the secondary containment, it must first be cleaned and decontaminated by the transferring group. Sampling and analysis may be required to verify the level of cleanliness. The secondary containment must then be officially transferred, via a memo, giving jurisdiction to the new owner. A copy of the memo associating the new owner with the secondary containment will be provided by the old owner.

The new owner will now assume responsibility for the subsequent maintenance, upgrades, and cleaning of this secondary containment.

Note:
It is the responsibility of the new owner to ensure that any equipment or container stored within is compatible with the secondary containment requirements.

If no new owner for the secondary containment can be found, no jurisdictional transfer occurs and the secondary containment remains the responsibility of the owner. It must continue to be maintained, cleaned, and drained of any accumulated rainwater according to proper procedure unless the secondary containment will no longer be used. Speculative use of the secondary containment is not encouraged.

If the secondary containment is to be decommissioned, the containment may be breached so that any water accumulation is self-draining. If the secondary containment is to be decommissioned and dismantled, the dismantling will include any associated costs incurred for disposal. Site remediation may be involved and must be coordinated with the appropriate EPR personnel.

—Taken from *www.slac.stanford.edu/esh/eshmanual/ESHch21.pdf*

The following document from the U.S. Department of Human Services, Public Health Service, will provide you with an excellent insight into the considerations for planning and managing public health crises involving hazardous materials.

Managing Hazardous Materials Incidents Volume I, Emergency Medical Services

U.S. Department of Human Services, Public Health Service, Agency for Toxic Substance and Disease Registry

Introduction
The presence of hazardous materials or toxic chemicals at an incident location or other emergency situation adds a new dimension of risk to those handling and treating casualties. The fundamental difference between a hazardous materials incident and other emergencies is the potential

for acute risk from contamination to both patient and responder. In some cases, traditional practices must be altered to avoid compounding a critical situation.

Emergency medical services (EMS) must protect their personnel on-site and en route to the hospital, and other people within the hospital, while providing the best care for the chemically contaminated patient. This guide is intended to help emergency medical services plan for incidents that involve hazardous materials and improve their ability to respond to these incidents appropriately.

To ensure appropriate and timely patient care, as well as optimal worker protection, emergency personnel must have an understanding of decontamination procedures and personal protective equipment that they do not generally receive in the course of their routine professional training. They should also be aware of community resources that could be called upon to assist in emergency response.

Current training curricula for emergency physicians, nurses, and emergency medical technicians (EMTs) often do not adequately prepare these professionals to either manage the contaminated individual or decontaminate patients exposed to toxic substances. High-quality, specific, and concise guidance is needed to describe appropriate procedures to be followed by emergency medical personnel to safely care for a patient, as well as to protect responders, equipment, hospital personnel, and others from risk of exposure. In response to this need, the Agency for Toxic Substances and Disease Registry (ATSDR) has contracted for the production of two documents: (I) *Emergency Medical Services: A Planning Guide for the Management of Contaminated Patients* and (II) *Hospital Emergency Departments: A Planning Guide for the Management of Contaminated Patients.* The second document is designed for use by emergency department personnel to minimize their risks of exposure within the emergency department and to provide for the safe and effective treatment of chemically contaminated patients.

This guide for emergency response personnel is designed to familiarize readers with the concepts, terminology, and key considerations that affect the management of incidents of chemical contamination. It has been developed not only to present uniform guidance for emergency care of chemically contaminated patients, but also to provide basic information critical to advance planning and implementation of emergency medical services strategies. It is intended to illustrate the characteristics of hazardous materials incidents that mandate modifications to traditional emergency response, and the preparatory actions that should be taken to respond effectively to hazardous materials incidents.

All community emergency response systems and hospitals may not be prepared to respond to a hazardous chemical incident to the same degree. This document may be used to assess capabilities with respect to potential community hazards, and to develop response plans using national and community specific resources. Worker safety and training are also key factors in effective management of medical emergencies, and this document is also intended to provide source material for developing local training and safety protocols.

Emergency Medical Services Response to Hazardous Materials Incidents outlines general principles for hazard recognition, chemical exposure, and personal protective equipment. In addition, the hazard recognition section presents generalized guidance for determining whether a given situation constitutes a hazardous materials incident and details various hazardous materials classification systems. Basic toxicological and chemical terminology that emergency personnel need to effectively conduct patient assessments is presented, as well as an outline of personal protective equipment such as respiratory devices and protective clothing.

Response and Patient Management includes guidelines for preparation and response to a potential hazardous materials incident. In addition, this chapter discusses patient assessment and decontamination guidelines.

Lastly, Systems Approach to Planning details the Joint Commission on Accreditation of Healthcare Organizations (JCAHO) guidelines for emergency preparedness and hazardous materials and waste programs. Government and private planning activities are also outlined, such as those established under the Superfund Amendments and Reauthorization Act (SARA) Title III, the National Response Team, the Community Awareness Emergency Response (CAER) program, and the Chemical Emergency Preparedness Program (CEPP). This chapter discusses the need for hazard identification and risk analysis pertaining to hazardous materials located in the community or that could be a threat to the community given existing transportation routes.

Although this guidance document has been developed to provide for the safety of responders, as well as the needs of patients, it is not all-encompassing. Supplemental material that is vital to successful response to hazardous materials contamination is cited within the document. These supplementary materials should be reviewed before preparing any strategic plans or before conducting training exercises on this topic. This document cannot be regarded as a substitute for comprehensive instruction and training for hazardous materials incidents.

Emergency Medical Services Response to Hazardous Materials Incident Hazard Recognition
When dispatched to the scene of an incident, emergency response personnel may not be aware that the incident involves hazardous materials. As a result, emergency medical services personnel should always be alert to the possibility that they may be dealing with a chemically contaminated individual, and should ask the victims and dispatch personnel about the nature of the incident. Although an injury at a hazardous material incident

need not invariably involve a chemical exposure (it could have resulted from a purely physical occurrence, such as slipping off a ladder), as a routine precaution, the involvement of hazardous materials should be considered a possibility in such situations. As outlined in the National Fire Academy/National Emergency Training Center manual, *Recognizing and Identifying Hazardous Materials,* there are six clues that may confirm the presence of hazardous materials. These clues are included in this guidance document to facilitate and expedite prompt identification of any hazardous materials at the scene of the incident. Dispatch personnel familiar with these clues will subsequently find the communication with field personnel enhanced. For example, patient symptoms reported from the field—such as nausea, dizziness, burning eyes, or cyanosis—could suggest to the dispatch staff the presence of hazardous materials. Knowledgeable dispatch staff could then request field personnel to examine the site for these six clues:

- **Occupancy and Location.** Community preplanning should identify the specific sites that contain hazardous materials. In addition, emergency personnel should be alert to the obvious locations in their communities that use hazardous materials—for example, laboratories, factories, farm and paint supply outlets, and construction sites.
- **Container Shape.** Department of Transportation (DOT) regulations dictate certain shapes for transport of hazardous materials. There are three categories of packaging: stationary bulk storage containers at fixed facilities that come in a variety of sizes and shapes; bulk transport vehicles such as rail and truck tank cars that can vary in shape depending upon the cargo; and smaller hazardous materials that may be packaged in fiberboard boxes, drums, or cylinders with labeling.

- **Markings/Colors.** Transportation vehicles must use DOT markings, including identification (ID) numbers. Identification numbers, located on both ends and both sides, are required on all cargo tanks, portable tanks, rail tank cars, and other small packages that carry hazardous materials. A marking system designed by the National Fire Protection Association (NFPA) identifies hazardous materials at terminals and industrial sites but does not provide product specific information. This system uses a diamond divided into four quadrants. Each quadrant represents a different consideration: the left blue section refers to health; the top red quarter pertains to flammability; the right yellow area is for reactivity; and the bottom white quadrant highlights special information. In addition, a number from zero through four indicates the relative risk of the hazard, with zero being the minimum risk.

- **Placards/Labels.** These convey information by use of colors, symbols, Hazard Communication Standard, American National Standard Institute (ANSI) Standards for Precautionary Labeling of

Hazardous Industrial Chemicals, United Nations Hazard class numbers, and either hazard class wording or four-digit identification numbers. Placards are used when hazardous materials are in bulk such as in cargo tanks; labels designate hazardous materials on small packages.

- **Shipping Papers.** These can clarify what is labeled "dangerous" on placards. They should provide the shipping-name, hazard class, ED number, and quantity, and may indicate "waste" or "poison." (Shipping papers must accompany all hazardous material shipments.)

- **Senses.** Odor, vapor clouds, dead animals or dead fish, fire, and irritation to skin or eyes can signal the presence of hazardous materials. Generally, if one detects the odor of hazardous materials, one should assume that exposure has occurred. Some chemicals, however, can impair an individual's sense of smell (i.e., hydrogen sulfide), and others have no odor at all (i.e., carbon monoxide).

Appendix A provides illustrations and greater detail on the National Fire Protection Association 704M system, the Department of Transportation hazardous materials marking, labeling, and placarding guide, and the Department of Labor Material Safety Data Sheet (MSDS). It is important that any and all available clues are used in the process of substance identification, especially the most obvious, such as the information provided on a label or in shipping papers (shipping papers should remain at the incident scene for use by other response personnel). The aim of the health provider should be to make a product-specific identification. Every effort should be taken to prevent exposure to chemicals. Identifying the hazardous material and obtaining information on its physical characteristics and toxicity are steps that are vital to the effective management of the hazardous materials incident. Since each compound has its own unique set of physical and toxicological properties, early and accurate identification of the hazardous material involved in the incident allows the emergency responders and emergency department staff to initiate appropriate scene management steps.

Many printed resources are available to provide information concerning response and planning for hazardous materials incidents. A selected bibliography is included at the end of each section; however, this is not a complete list of the materials available. Printed reference materials provide several advantages: they are readily available, can be transported in the response vehicle, are not dependent on a power source or subject to malfunction, and are relatively inexpensive. Disadvantages include the difficulty in determining a correct identity for an unknown chemical, materials are often out of date and cannot be easily updated, and no single volume is capable of providing all the information that may be needed.

There is also a vast array of telephone and computer-based information sources concerning hazardous materials. They can help you by describing the toxic effects of the chemical, its relative potency, and the potential for secondary contamination and by recommending decontamination procedures.

They may also provide advice on the adequacy of specific types of protective gear. Table 1 is a partial listing of the many information resources available by telephone. Table 2 is a list of suggested telephone numbers that should be filled in for your community. Planning is an essential part of every response, and these resources will also provide guidance that can be used in forming an effective response plan. Table 3 provides a partial listing of the available computerized and on-line information sources. It should be noted that not all online databases are peer reviewed. Therefore, some medical management information may be based only on DOT or MSDS data. Care and planning should be used when selecting information sources.

Computerized information sources are basically two types: (a) call-up systems that are addressed via telephone lines and (b) database systems that are housed on a local computer disc. Each system contains large amounts of information on many hazardous materials and can be searched to help identify the material involved. They are updated frequently at no extra cost to the subscriber and are extremely portable with today's computer systems. Computer databases can be expensive, as can the initial cost of the equipment. Most systems will require the operator to have some knowledge of computer terms and search protocols. Also, mechanical equipment may fail and should not be counted on as a sole source of information.

Principles of Toxicology for Emergency Department Personnel

Exposure to hazardous chemicals may produce a wide range of adverse health effects. The likelihood of an adverse health effect occurring, and the severity of the effect, are dependent on the toxicity of the chemical, route of exposure, and the nature and extent of exposure to that substance. In order to better understand potential health effects, emergency department personnel should have an understanding of the basic principles and terminology of toxicology.

Toxicology is the study of the nature, effects, and detection of poisons in living organisms. Some examples of these adverse effects, sometimes called toxic end points, include carcinogenicity (development of cancer), hepatotoxicity (liver damage), neurotoxicity (nervous system damage), and nephrotoxicity (kidney damage). This is by no means a complete list of toxic end points, but rather a selection of effects that might be encountered (Table 4).

Toxic chemicals often produce injuries at the site at which they come into contact with the body. A chemical injury at the site of contact with the body, typically the skin and the mucous membranes of the eyes, nose, mouth, or respiratory tract, is termed a local toxic effect. For example, irritant gases, such as chlorine and ammonia, can produce a localized toxic

Table 1. Telephone Information and Technical Support References

Resource	Contact	Services Provided
CHEMTRAC	1-800-424-9300	24-hour emergency number. Connection with manufacturers and/or shippers who will provide (Chemical Transportation Emergency advice on handling rescue gear needed, decontamination considerations, etc. Also provides Center access to Chlorine Emergency Response Plan (CHLOREP).
ATSDR	1-404-639-0615	24-hour emergency number for health-related support in hazard materials emergencies, (Agency for Toxic Substances including on-site assistance, if necessary, and Disease Registry).
Bureau of Explosives	1-202-639-2222	24-hour emergency number for hazardous materials incidents involving railroads.
Emergency Planning and Community Right-To-Know Information Hotline	1-800-535-0202	8:30 am–7:30 pm (EST) Provides information on SARA Title III. Provides list of extremely hazardous substances and planning guidelines.
EPA (Environmental Protection Agency)		Environmental response team available.
Regional Offices		
Region I	(617) 565-3698	CT, ME, MA, NH, RI, VT
Region II	(212) 264-0504	NJ, NY, PR, VI
Region III	(215) 597-0980	DE, DC,MD, PA, VA, WV
Region IV	(404) 347-3454	AL, FL, GA, KY, MS, NC, SC, TN
Region V	(312) 886-7579	IL, IN, MI, MN, OH, WI
Region VI	(214) 655-6760	AR, LA, NM, OK, TX
Region VII	(913) 236-2850	IA, KS, MO, NE
Region VIII	(303) 293-1720	CO, MT, ND, SD, UT, WY
Region IX	(415) 974-7460	AM, SAMOA, AZ, CA, GU, HI, NV, Trust Territory of the Pacific Isl., Marshall Isl., Palau, Ponape
Region X	(206) 442-2782	AK, ID, OR, WA
National Animal Poison Control Center	1-217-333-3611	24-hour consultation concerning animal poisonings or chemical contamination. Provides an emergency response team to investigate incidents and perform laboratory analysis.
National Response Center	1-800-424-8802	For reporting transportation incidents where hazardous materials are responsible for death, serious injury, property damage in excess of $50,000, or continuing danger to life and property.

Table 2. Local Telephone Information and Technical Support Resource Worksheet

Resource (fill in future reference)	Contact	Services Provided (fill in for future reference)
EPA Regional Office		
Regional Poison Control Center		
State Emergency Response Commission		
State Health Department		
Community Fire Department		
Community Police Department		
Local Emergency Planning Committee		
Local Health Department		
State Department of Natural Resources		

Table 3. Computerized Data Sources of Information and Technical Support

Data Systems	Contact	Description
ANSWER	ANSWER Specialized Information Svcs. National Library of Medicine Building 38A 8600 Rockville Pike Bethesda, Maryland 20894 (301) 496-6531	National Library of Medicine's Workstation of Emergency Response (ANSWER)—to advise emergency response health professionals on potential hazardous chemical emergencies.
CAMEO	CAMEO Database Manager National Oceanic and Atmospheric Administration (NOAA) Hazardous Materials Response Branch, N/OMA-34 7600 Sand Point Way, NE Seattle, Washington 98115 (206) 526-6317	Computer-Aided Management of Emergency Operations available to on-scene responder. Chemical identification database assists in: identifying substance involved, predicting downwind concentrations, providing response recommenations, and identifying potential hazards.
CHRIS	CIS, Inc. Fein Management Associates 7215 York Road Baltimore, Maryland 21212 (800) 247-8737	Chemical Hazard Response Information System, developed by the Coast Guard and comprised reviews on fire hazards, fire fighting recommendations, reactivities,

		physicochemical properties, health hazards, use of protective clothing, and shipping information for over chemicals.
HAZARDTEXT	Micromedex, Inc. 660 Bannock Street Denver, Colorado 80203-3527 (800) 525-9083	Assists responders dealing with incidents involving hazardous materials such as spills, leaks, and fires. Emergency medical treatment and recommendations for initial hazardous response are presented.
HMIS	David W. Donaldson Information Sys. Specialist Dept. of Trans/RSPA/OHMT 400 7th Street, S.W. Washington, DC 20590 (202) 366-5869	Hazardous Material Information Systems provides name and emergency phone number of manufacturer, chemical formula, NIOSH number, firefighting, spill, and leak procedures.
HSDB	Toxicology Data Network (TOXNET) National Library of Medicine Toxicology Information Program 8600 Rockville Pike Bethesda, Maryland 20894 (301) 496-6531	Hazardous Substances Data Bank, compiled by the National Library of Medicine, provides reviews on the toxicity, hazards, and regulatory status of over 4,000 frequently used chemicals.
1st MEDICAL RESPONSE PROTOCOLS	Micromedex, Inc. 660 Bannock Street Denver, Colorado 80203-3527 (800) 525-9083	For use in developing training programs and establishing protocls for first aid or initial workplace response to a medical emergency.
MEDITEXT	Micromedex, Inc. 660 Bannock Street Denver, Colorado 80203-3527 (800) 525-9083	Provides recommendations regarding the evaluation and treatment of exposure to industrial chemicals.
OHMTADS	CIS, Inc. Fein Management Associates 7215 York Road Baltimore, Maryland 80203-3527 (800) 247-8737	Oil and Hazardous Materials Technical Assistance Data Systems provides effects of spilled chemical compounds and their hazardous characteristics and properties, assists in identifying unknown substances, and recommends procedures for handling and cleanup.
TOMES	Micromedex, Inc. 660 Bannock Street Denver, Colorado 80203-3527 (800) 525-9083	The Tomes Plus Information Systems is a series of comprehensive data bases on a single CD-ROM disc. It provides information regarding hazardous properties of chemicals and medical effects from exposure. The Tomes Plus database contains Meditext, Hazardtext, HSDB CHRIS, OHMTADS, and 1st Medical Response Protocols.

Table 3. Continued

Data Systems	Contact	Description
TOXNET	Toxicology Data Network (TOXNET) National Library of Medicine Toxicology Information Prog. (301) 496-6531	Computerized system of three toxicologically oriented data banks operated by the National Library of Medicine—the Hazardous Substances Data Bank, the Registry of Toxic Effects of Chemical Substances, and the Chemical Carcinogenesis Research Information System. TOXNET provides information on the health effects of exposure to industrial and environmental substances.

Table 4. Examples of Adverse Health Effects from Exposure to Toxic Chemicals

Toxic End Point	Target Organ Systems	Example of Causative	Health Effect	
			Acute	Chronic
Carcinogenicity	Multiple Sites	Benzene	Dermatitis Tightness in Chest	Aleukemia Myeloblastic leukemia
Hepatotoxicity	Liver	Carbon Tetrachloride	Vomiting Vesication Dizziness	Liver Necrosis Fatty Liver
Neurotoxicity	Nervous System	Lead	Nausea Vomiting Abdominal Pain	Wrist Drop IQ Deficits Encephalopathy
Nephrotoxicity	Kidney	Cadmium	Vomiting Diarrhea Chest Pain	Kidney Damage Anemia

effect in the respiratory tract; corrosive acids and bases can produce a local damage to the skin. In addition, a toxic chemical may be absorbed into the bloodstream and distributed to other parts of the body. These compounds may then produce systemic effects. For example, many pesticides are absorbed by the skin, distributed to other sites in the body, and produce adverse effects such as seizures or other neurological problems. It is important for medical providers to recognize that exposure to chemical compounds can result not only in the development of a single systemic effect but also in the development of multiple systemic effects or a combination of systemic and local effects.

Routes and Extent of Exposure

There are three main routes of chemical exposure: inhalation, skin contact, and ingestion. Inhalation results in the introduction of toxic compounds into the respiratory system. Most of the compounds that are commonly inhaled are gases or vapors of volatile liquids; however, solids and liquids can be inhaled as dusts or aerosols. Inhalation of toxic agents generally results in a rapid and effective absorption of the compound into the bloodstream because of the large surface area of the lung tissue and number of blood vessels in the lungs. Skin contact exposure does not typically result in as rapid systemic dosage as inhalation, although some chemicals are readily absorbed through the skin. Many organic compounds are lipid (fat) soluble and can therefore be rapidly absorbed through the skin. Some materials that come in contact with the eyes can also be absorbed. Ingestion is a less common route of exposure for emergency response personnel at hazardous materials incidents. However, incidental hand-to-mouth contact, smoking, and swallowing of saliva and mucus containing trapped airborne contaminants can cause exposure by this route. In addition, emergency medical personnel in both hospital or prehospital settings will see chemical exposures in patients who have ingested toxic substances as a result of accidental poisonings or suicide attempts.

Compounds can also be introduced into the body by injection; however, injection exposure is an unlikely scenario involving spills or discharges of hazardous materials.

The route by which personnel are exposed to a compound plays a role in determining the total amount of the compound taken up by the body because a compound may be absorbed following exposure by one route more readily than by another. In addition to the route of exposure, the amount of the compound absorbed by the body depends on the duration of exposure to the compound and the concentration of the compound to which one is exposed. Therefore, a complex relationship exists between the total amount of the compound absorbed by the body (dose) and the concentration of that compound in the environment. This relationship is important for emergency response personnel to understand because the adverse effects produced by a toxic compound are often related to the dose of that compound received by a patient. However, because we usually monitor only the concentration of the toxic substance in the environment (e.g., parts per million (ppm) of a compound in air), the actual dose of the compound received by the patient is seldom known. Factors specific to the exposed patient, such as size of the skin surface area exposed, presence of open wounds or breaks in the skin, and rate and depth of respiration, are important in estimating the dose of the compound received by the patient.

Dose-Response Relationship

As mentioned above, the effect produced by a toxic compound is a function of the dose of the compound received by the organism. This principle, termed the dose-response relationship, is a key concept in toxicology.

Many factors affect the normal dose-response relationship and should be considered when attempting to extrapolate toxicity data to a specific situation (Table 5).

Typically, as the dose increases, the severity of the toxic response increases. For example, humans exposed to 100 ppm of tetrachloroethylene, a solvent that is commonly used for dry-cleaning fabrics, may experience relatively mild symptoms, such as headache and drowsiness. However, exposure to 200 ppm tetrachloroethylene can result in a loss of motor coordination in some individuals. Exposure to 1,500 ppm tetrachloroethylene for 30 minutes may result in a loss of consciousness (Table 6). As shown in Table 6, the severity of the toxic effect is also dependent on the duration of exposure, a factor that influences the dose of the compound in the body.

Toxicity information is often expressed as the dose of the compound that causes an effect in a percentage of the exposed subjects, which are mostly experimental animals. These dose-response terms are often found in Material Safety Data Sheets (MSDS) and other sources of health information.

Table 5. Classification of Factors Influencing Toxicity

Type	Examples
1. Factors related to the chemical.	Composition (salt, freebase, etc.); physical characteristics (size, liquid, solid, etc.); physical properties (volatility, solubility, etc.); presence of impurities; breakdown products; carriers
2. Factors related to exposure.	Dose; concentration; route of exposure (inhalation, ingestion, etc.) duration
3. Factors related to person exposed.	Heredity; immunology; nutrition; hormones; age; sex; health status; preceding diseases
4. Factors related to environment.	Media (air, water, soil, etc.) additional chemicals present; temperature; air pressure

Table 6. Dose-Response Relationship for Humans Inhaling Tetrachloroethylene Vapors

Levels in Air	Duration of Exposure	Effect on Nervous System
50 ppm	Odor threshold	
100 ppm	7 hours	Headache, drowsiness
200 ppm	2 hours	Dizziness, uncoordination
600 ppm	10 minutes	Dizziness, loss of inhibitions
1000 ppm	1–2 minutes	Marked dizziness, intolerable eye and respiratory tract irritation
1500 ppm	30 minutes	Coma

One dose-response term that is commonly used is the lethal dose 50 (LD50), the dose which is lethal to 50 percent of an animal population from exposure by any route other than inhalation when given all in one dose. Another similar term is the lethal concentration 50 (LC50), which is the concentration of a material in air that on the basis of respiratory exposure in laboratory tests is expected to kill 50 percent of a group of test animals when administered as a single exposure (usually 1 hour). Table 7 lists a number of chemicals that may be encountered in dealing with hazardous materials incidents, and the reported acute LD50 of these compounds when they are administered orally to rats.

From Table 7, it can be seen that a dose of 3,000–3,800 mg/kg tetrachloroethylene is lethal to 50 percent of rats that received the compound orally; however, only 6.4 to 10 mg/kg of sodium cyanide is required to produce the same effect. Therefore, compounds with low LD50 values are more acutely toxic than substances with larger LD50 values.

The LD50 values that appear in an MSDS or in the literature must be used with caution by emergency medical personnel. These values are an index of only one type of response and give no indication of the ability of the compound to cause nonlethal, adverse, or chronic effects. Furthermore, LD50 values typically come from experimental animal studies. Because of the anatomical and physiological differences between animals and humans, it is difficult to compare the effects seen in experimental animal studies to the effects expected in humans exposed to hazardous materials in the field. Therefore, emergency medical personnel should remember that the LD50 and LC50 values are only useful for comparing the relative toxicity of compounds and should only be used to determine if one chemical is more toxic than another.

Responses to toxic chemicals may differ among individuals because of the physiological variability that is present in the human population. For example, an individual may be more likely to experience an adverse health effect after exposure to a toxic chemical because of a reduced ability to metabolize that compound. The presence of pre-existing medical conditions can also increase one's susceptibility to toxic chemicals. Respiratory

Table 7. Acute LD50 Values for Representative Chemicals When Administered Orally to Rats

Chemical	Acute Oral LD50 (mg/kg)*
Sodium cyanide	6.4–10
Pentachlorophenol	50–230
Chloride	83–560
Lindane	88–91
Toluene	2,600–7,000
Tetrachloroethylene	3,000–3,800

*Milligrams of the compound administered per kilogram body weight of the experimental animal.

distress in patients or workers with asthma may be triggered by exposure to toxic chemicals at lower levels than might be expected to produce the same effect in individuals without respiratory disease. Factors such as age, personal habits (smoking, diet), previous exposure to toxic chemicals, and medications may also increase one's sensitivity to toxic chemicals. Therefore, exposure to concentrations of toxic compounds that would not be expected to result in the development of a toxic response in most individuals may cause an effect in susceptible individuals. Not all chemicals, however, have a threshold level. Some chemicals that produce cancer (carcinogens) may produce a response (tumors) at any dose level. Any exposure to these compounds may be associated with some risk of developing cancer. Thus, literature values for levels which are not likely to produce an effect do not guarantee that an effect will not occur.

Exposure Limits

The various occupational exposure limits found in the literature or in an MSDS are based primarily on time-weighted average limits, ceiling values, or ceiling concentration limits to which the worker can be exposed to without adverse effects. Examples of these are listed in Table 8. The values listed in Table 8 were established to provide worker protection in occupational settings. Because the settings in which these values are appropriate are quite different than an uncontrolled spill site, it is difficult to interpret how these values should be used by emergency medical personnel dealing with a hazardous materials incident. At best, TLV, PEL, IDLH, and REL values can be used as a benchmark for determining relative toxicity, and perhaps assist in selecting appropriate levels of Personal Protective Equipment (PPE). Furthermore, these occupational exposure limits are only useful if the appropriate instrumentation is available for measuring the levels of toxic chemicals in the air at the chemical spill site. Of the above occupational exposure limit values, only the OSHA values are regulatory limits. The ACGIH values are for guidance only and are not regulatory limits. In addition, the ACGIH limits have certain caveats that may or may not affect the usefulness of the values. Some of these conditions are individual susceptibility or aggravation of a pre-existing condition. Nevertheless, all emergency medical personnel responsible for the management of chemically contaminated patients should be familiar with these exposure limits because they will be encountered in various documents dealing with patient care or the selection of PPE.

This brief discussion highlights some fundamental concepts of toxicology. Emergency medical personnel responsible for managing chemically contaminated patients are encouraged to obtain further training in recognizing and treating health effects related to chemical exposure. Also, a list of general references in toxicology is provided at the end of this section that will allow emergency medical personnel to undertake a more in-depth examination of the principles of toxicology.

Table 8. Occupational Exposure Limits

Value	Abbreviation	Definition
Threshold Limit Value (3 Types) (ACGIH)	TLV	Refers to airborne concentrations of substances and represents conditions under which it is believed that nearly all workers may be repeatedly exposed day after day without adverse effect.
1) Threshold Limit Value-Time-Weighted Average (ACGIH)	TLV-TWA	The time-weighted average concentration for a normal eight-hour workday and a forty-hour workweek, to which nearly all workers may be repeatedly exposed, day after day, without adverse effect.
2) Threshold Limit Value Short-Term Exposure Limit	TLV-STEL	The concentration to which workers can be exposed continuously for a short period of time without suffering from 1) irritation, 2) chronic or irreversible tissue damage, or 3) narcosis of sufficient degree to increase the likelihood of accidental injury, impair self-rescue or materially reduce work efficiency, and provided that the daily TLV-TWA is not exceeded.
3) Threshold Limit Value-Ceiling (ACGIH)	TLV-C	The concentration that should not be exceeded during any part of the working exposure.
Permissible Exposure Limit (OSHA)**	PEL	Same as TLV-TWA.
Immediately Dangerous to Life and Health (OSHA)**	IDLH	A maximum concentration (in air) from which one could to escape within thirty minutes without any escape-impairing symptoms or any irreversible health effects.
Recommended Exposure Limit (NIOSH)***	REL	Highest allowable airborne concentration that is not expected to injure a worker, expressed as a ceiling limit or time-weighted average for an eight- or ten-hour work day.

* American Conference of Governmental Industrial Hygienists.

** Occupational Safety and Health Administration.

*** National Institute for Occupational Safety and Health.

Personnel Protection and Safety Principles

This section is designed to provide those emergency medical personnel who receive a relatively large number of contaminated victims, because of their proximity to a chemical industrial area or transport corridor, with information on protective equipment and safety principles. However, in the vast majority of cases, EMS staff will not experience a large enough number of cases to keep them optimally trained or their equipment properly maintained. For example, respirators and their cartridges must be properly fitted, tested, and stored. Staff must be initially trained in the proficient use of PPE, specifically respiratory equipment, and must maintain that proficiency. Equipment must be maintained according to OSHA standards. Many EMS, given their workload mix, may not be able to expend the funds and time necessary to accomplish this task. In these cases, the EMS should make arrangements with the local fire department or hazardous materials (hazmat) team to be ready, if the situation warrants, to decontaminate patients, including those who are transported to a hospital before they are decontaminated. Considerations in determining what an EMS's capabilities should be include the number of incidents occurring locally (several per week versus only a few per year) and proximity to industries or transportation routes that have a potential for a hazardous materials incident (see SARA Title III).

Federal Regulations Pertaining to Use of Personal Protective Equipment (PPE)

The term Personal Protective Equipment (PPE) is used in this document to refer to both personal protective clothing and equipment. The purpose of PPE is to shield or isolate individuals from the chemical, physical, and biological hazards that may be encountered at a hazardous materials incident.

Recent new OSHA standards mandate specific training requirements (eight hours of initial training or sufficient experience to demonstrate competency) for employees engaged in emergency response to hazardous substances incidents at the first responders operations level. Additionally, each employer must develop a safety and health program and provide for emergency response. These standards also are intended to provide additional protection for those who respond to hazardous materials incidents, such as firefighters, police officers, and EMS personnel. OSHA's March 6,1989, 29 CFR 1910.120 final rule as it applies to emergency medical personnel states that: "Training shall be based on the duties and functions to be performed by each responder of an emergency response organization" (p. 9329).

Training Is Essential Before Any Individual Attempts to Use PPE

No single combination of protective equipment and clothing is capable of protecting against all hazards. Thus, PPE should be used in conjunction with other protective methods. The use of PPE can itself create significant worker hazards, such as heat stress, physical and psychological stress, and impaired vision, mobility, and communication. In general, the greater the level of PPE protection, the greater are the associated risks. For any given situation, equipment and clothing should be selected that provide an adequate level of protection. Overprotection can be as hazardous as underprotection and should be avoided. Personnel should not be expected to use PPE without adequate training. The two basic objectives of any PPE program should be to protect the wearer from safety and health hazard and to prevent injury to the wearer from incorrect use and/or malfunction of the PPE. To accomplish these goals, a comprehensive PPE program should include hazard identification; medical monitoring; environmental surveillance; selection, use, maintenance, and decontamination of PPE; and training.

Levels of Protection

The Environmental Protection Agency (EPA) has assigned four levels of protection to assist in determining which combinations of respiratory protection and protective clothing should be employed:

- Level A protection should be worn when the highest level of respiratory, skin, eye, and mucous membrane protection is needed. It consists of a fully-encapsulating chemical-resistant suit and self-contained breathing apparatus (SCBA).
- Level B protection should be selected when the highest level of respiratory protection is needed but a lesser level of skin and eye protection is sufficient. It differs from Level A only in that it provides splash protection by use of chemical-resistant clothing (overalls, long sleeves, jacket, and SCBA).
- Level C protection should be selected when the type of airborne substances is known, concentration is measured, criteria for using air-purifying respirators are met, and skin and eye exposures are unlikely. This involves a full-facepiece, air-purifying, canister-equipped respirator and chemical-resistant clothing. It provides the same level of skin protection as Level B, but a lower level of respiratory protection.
- Level D is primarily a work uniform. It should not be worn on any site where respiratory or skin hazards exist. It provides no respiratory protection and minimal skin protection.

Figure 1 and Figure 2 illustrates these four levels of protection. For more information on this area, Appendix C outlines the protective equipment recommended for each level of protection.

Factors to be considered in selecting the proper level of protection include the routes of entry for the chemical, degree of contact, and the specific task assigned to the user. Activities can also be used to determine which level of protection should be chosen. EPA and NIOSH recommend that initial entry into unknown environments, unknown container sampling, and entry into a confined space that has not been chemically characterized warrants at least "Level B" protection.

Routes of Entry

PPE is designed to provide emergency medical personnel with protection from hazardous materials that can affect the body by one of three primary routes of entry: inhalation, ingestion, and direct contact. Inhalation occurs when emergency personnel breathe in chemical fumes or vapors. Respirators are designed to protect the wearer from contamination by inhalation and must be fitted properly and tested frequently to ensure continued protection. Ingestion usually is the result of a health care provider

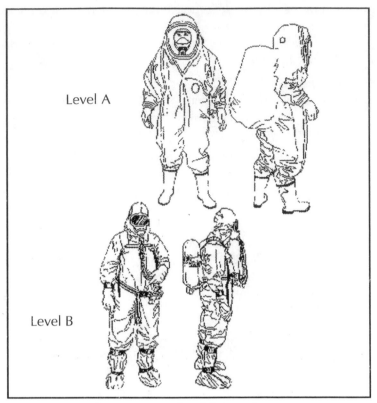

Level A

Level B

Figure 1. Levels of Protection

transferring hazardous materials from his hand or clothing to his mouth. This can occur unwittingly when an individual wipes his mouth with his hand or sleeve. Direct contact refers to chemical contact with the skin or eye. Skin is protected by garments, and full-face respirators protect against ingestion and direct contact. Mucous membranes in the mouth, nose, throat, inner ear, and respiratory system are affected by one or more of the three primary routes of entry. Many hazardous materials adhere to and assimilate with the moist environment provided by these membranes, become trapped or lodged in the mucus, and, subsequently, absorbed or ingested.

Chemical Protective Clothing (CPC)
Protective clothing is designed to prevent direct contact of a chemical contaminant with the skin or body of the user. However, there is not one single material that will afford protection against all substances. Thus, multilayered garments are often employed, which may reduce dexterity and agility. CPC is designed to afford the wearer a known degree of protection from a known type, a known concentration, and a known length of exposure to a hazardous material, but only if it is properly fitted and worn correctly. Improperly worn equipment can expose and endanger the wearer. One factor to keep in mind during the selection process is that most protective clothing is designed to be impermeable to moisture,

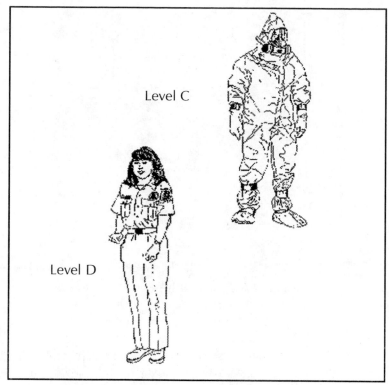

Level C

Level D

Figure 2. Levels of Protection (continued)

thus limiting the transfer of heat from the body through natural evaporation. This is a particularly important factor in hot environments or for strenuous tasks since such garments can increase the likelihood of heat injury.

The effectiveness of protective clothing can be reduced by three actions: degradation, permeation, and penetration. Chemical degradation occurs when the characteristics of the material in use are altered through contact with chemical substances. Examples of degradation include cracking and brittleness and other changes in the structural characteristics of the garment. Degradation can also result in an increased permeation rate through the garment, that is, the molecular absorption by or passage through the protective material of a chemical substance.

Permeation is the process in which chemical compounds cross the protective barrier of CPC because of passive diffusion. The rate at which a compound permeates CPC is dependent on factors such as the chemical properties of the compound, the nature of the protective barrier in the CPC, and the concentration of the chemical on the surface of the CPC. Most manufacturers of CPC provide charts on the breakthrough time, or the time it takes for the chemical to permeate the material of a protective suit, for a wide range of chemical compounds.

Penetration occurs when there is an opening or a puncture in the protective material. These openings can include unsealed seams, button holes,

Hazmat team in full protective gear.

and zippers. Often such openings are the result of faulty manufacture or problems with the inherent design of the suit. Protective clothing is available in a wide assortment of forms, ranging from fully-encapsulating body suits to gloves, hard hats, earplugs, and boot covers. CPC comes in a variety of materials, offering a range of protection against a number of chemicals. Emergency medical personnel must evaluate the properties of the chemical versus the properties of the material. Selection of which kinds of CPC to use will depend on the specific chemical and on the specific tasks to be performed.

Respiratory Protection

Substantial information is available for the correct selection, training, and use of respirators. The correct respirator must be selected for the specific hazard in question. Material safety data sheets (if available) often specify the type of respirator that will protect users from risks. The manufacturers suggest the types of hazards their respirators are capable of protecting against. There are two basic types of respirators: atmosphere-supplying and air-purifying. Atmosphere-supplying respirators include self-contained breathing apparatus (SCBA) and supplied-air respirators (SAR). OSHA has requirements under 29 CFR 1910.134 which specify certain aspects of a respiratory protection standard, and these are mandatory legal minimums for a program to be operated. In addition, NIOSH has established comprehensive requirements for the certification of respiratory protection equipment.

Air-Purifying Respirators (APRS)

An air-purifying respirator depends on ambient air purified through a filtering element before inhalation. Three basic types of APRs are used by emergency personnel: chemical cartridges or canisters, disposables, and powered air. The major advantage of the APR system is the increased mobility it affords the wearer. However, the respirator can only be used where there is sufficient oxygen (19.5 percent) since it depends on ambient air to function. In addition, the APR should not be used when substances with poor warning properties are known to be involved.

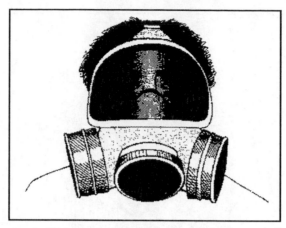

Figure 3. A Chemical Cartridge Air-Purifying Respirator

The most commonly used APR depends on cartridges (Figure 3) or canisters to purify the air by chemical reaction, filtration, adsorption, or absorption. Cartridges and canisters are designed for specific materials at specific concentrations. To aid the user, manufacturers have color-coded the cartridges/canisters to indicate the chemical or class of chemicals the device is effective against. NIOSH recommends that use of a cartridge not exceed one work shift. However, if "breakthrough" of the contaminant occurs first, then the cartridge or canister must be immediately replaced. After use, cartridges and canisters should be considered contaminated and disposed of accordingly.

Disposable APRs are usually designed for use with particulates, such as asbestos. However, some are approved for use with other contaminants. These respirators are customarily half-masks that cover the face from nose to chin, but do not provide eye protection. Once used, the entire respirator is usually discarded. This type of APR depends on a filter to trap particulates. Filters may also be used in combination with cartridges and canisters to provide an individual with increased protection from particulates. The use of half-mask APRs is not generally recommended by most emergency response organizations.

Atmosphere-Supplying Respirators

Atmosphere-supplying respirators consist of two basic types: the self-contained breathing apparatus (SCBA), which contains its own air supply, and the supplied-air respirator (SAR), which depends on an air supply provided through a line linked to a distant ambient air source. Figure 4 illustrates an example of each.

Self-Contained Breathing Apparatus (SCBA)

A self-contained breathing apparatus respirator is composed of a facepiece connected by a hose to a compressed air source. There are three varieties of SCBAs: closed-circuit, open-circuit, and escape. Open-circuit SCBAs, most often used in emergency response, provide clean air from a cylinder

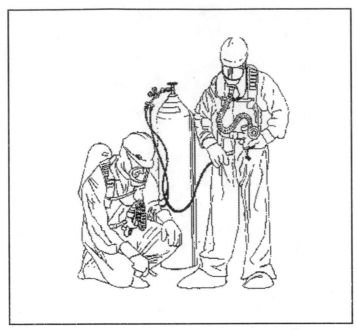

**Figure 4. A Self-Contained Breathing Apparatus/
Supplied-Air Respirator**

to the wearer, who exhales into the atmosphere. Closed-circuit SCBAs, also known as "rebreathers," recycle exhaled gases and contain a small cylinder of oxygen to supplement the exhaled air of the wearer. Escape SCBAs provide air for a limited amount of time and should only be used for emergency escapes from a dangerous situation.

The most common SCBA is the open-circuit, positive-pressure type. In this type, air is supplied to the wearer from a cylinder and supplied to the facepiece under positive pressure. In contrast to the negative-pressure units, a higher air pressure is maintained inside the facepiece than outside. This affords the SCBA wearer the highest level of protection against airborne contaminants since any leakage may force the contaminant out. There is a potential danger when wearing a negative-pressure type apparatus that contaminant may enter the face mask if it is not properly sealed. The use of a negative-pressure SCBA is prohibited by OSHA under 29 CFR 1910.120(q)(iv) in incidents where personnel are exposed to hazardous materials. However, one disadvantage of SCBAs is that they are bulky and heavy, and can be used for only the period of time allowed by air in the tank.

Personnel Must Be Fit-Tested for Use of All Respirators
A tiny space between the respirator and you could permit exposure to a hazard by allowing contaminated air in. Anyone attempting to wear any type of respirator should be trained and drilled in its proper use.

Furthermore, equipment must be inspected and checked for serviceability on a routine basis.

Supplied-Air Respirators (SARS)

Supplied-air respirators differ from SCBAs in that the air is supplied through a line that is connected to a source away from the contaminated area. SARs are available in both positive- and negative-pressure models. However, only positive- and negative- pressure models. However only positive-pressure SARs are recommended for use at hazardous materials incidents. One major advantage the SAR has over the SCBA device is that the SAR allows an individual to work for a longer period. In addition, the SAR is less bulky than the SCBA. However, by necessity, a worker must retrace his steps to stay connected to the SAR, and therefore cannot leave the contaminated work area by a different exit.

Site Control

Hazardous materials incidents can and often do attract large numbers of people and equipment, complicating the imposition of adequate controls to minimize risks of human injury or death, property damage, and environmental degradation.

An Incident Command System (ICS) allows for the coordination and management of facilities, equipment, personnel, and communications during a hazardous materials incident. In order to keep the contaminants onsite, an Incident Commander (IC) is responsible for the control of the scene, which includes delineating work zones, establishing levels of protection, and implementing decontamination activities.

Rules to keep in mind to enhance control at the site of a chemical incident include the following: inactive individuals and equipment should be kept at a safe distance from the area of possible contamination; public access from all directions must be restricted as soon as possible; media access should be limited to the staging area, and any closer approach should involve escort by a designated public Information Officer.

Work Zones

NIOSH/OSHA/USCG/EPA recommend dividing the incident into three zones, establishing access control points, and delineating a contamination reduction corridor. Figure 5 presents a diagram of the recommended zones. The Exclusion Zone (hot zone) should encompass all known or suspected hazardous material contamination. The respective radius of the Contamination Reduction Zone (warm zone) is determined by the length of the decontamination corridor, containing all of the needed "decon" stations. The Support Zone (cold zone) should be "clean"—free of hazardous material contamination of all kinds, including discarded protective clothing and respiratory equipment. The command post and staging areas for necessary support equipment should be located upwind and uphill of the Exclusion Zone in the support area. Equipment that may eventually be needed should be kept in staging areas beyond the crowd-control line. Access to

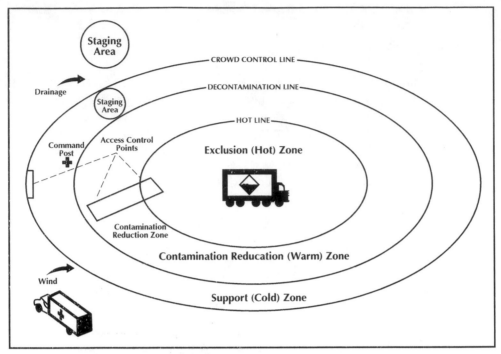

Figure 5. NIOSH/OSHA/USCG/EPA/Recommended Zones

the different zones should be tightly controlled and limited to as few locations as possible.

Decontamination of Emergency Medical Service Personnel

Decontamination is the process of removing or neutralizing harmful materials that have gathered on personnel and/or equipment during the response to a chemical incident. Many stories are told of seemingly successful rescue, transport, and treatment of chemically contaminated individuals by unsuspecting emergency personnel who in the process contaminate themselves, the equipment, and the facilities they encounter along the way. Decontamination is of the utmost importance because it

- protects all incident personnel by sharply limiting the transfer of hazardous materials from the contaminated area into clean zones;
- protects the community by preventing transportation of hazardous materials from the incident to other sites in the community by secondary contamination; and
- protects workers by reducing the contamination and resultant permeation of or degradation to their protective clothing and equipment.

This section will only address the steps necessary for dealing with worker decontamination. Patient decontamination will be addressed in Section 11. It should be stressed that in order to carry out proper decontamination, personnel must have received at least the same degree of training as required for workers who respond to hazardous materials incidents. It should be noted that the design of the decontamination process should take into account the degree of hazard and should be appropriate for the situation. For example, a nine-station decontamination process, as presented in (Figure 6), need not be set up if only a boot-wash station would suffice.

Avoiding contact is the easiest method of decontamination—that is, not to get the material on the worker or his protective equipment in the first place. However, if contamination is unavoidable, then proper decontamination or disposal of the worker's outer gear is recommended. Segregation and proper disposal of the outer gear in a polyethylene bag or steel drum is recommended. With extremely hazardous materials, it may be necessary to dispose of equipment as well.

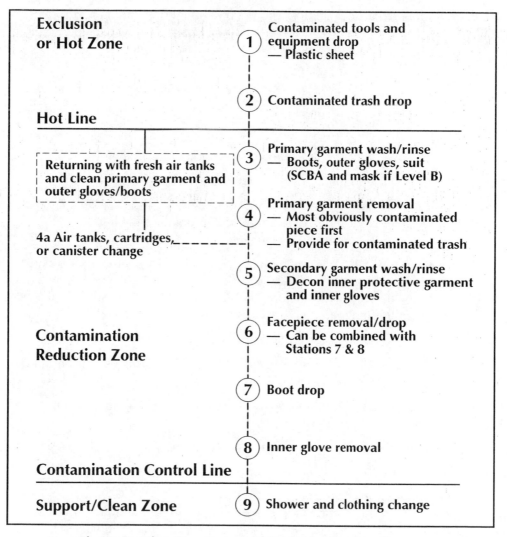

Figure 6. Nine-Step Personnel Decontamination Plan.

Physical decontamination of protective clothing and equipment can be achieved in some cases by several different means. These all include the systematic removal of contaminants by washing, usually with soap and water, and then rinsing. In rare cases, the use of solvents may be necessary. There is a trend toward dry decontamination, which involves using disposable clothing (e.g., suits, boots, and gloves) and systematically removing these garments in a manner that precludes contact with the contaminant. The appropriate procedure will depend on the contaminant and its physical properties. A thorough work-up of the chemical involved and its properties or expert consultation is necessary to make these kinds of decisions.

Care must be taken to ensure that decontamination methods, because of their physical properties, do not introduce fresh hazards into the situation. Additionally, the residues of the decontamination process must be treated as hazardous wastes. The decontamination stations and process should be confined to the Contamination Reduction Zone. Steps for dry decontamination (not using water) are outlined in Figure 7.

Decontamination of EMS Personnel
EMS personnel should remove protective clothing in the following sequence.

1. Remove tape securing gloves to suit.

2. Remove outer gloves turning them inside out as they are removed.

3. Remove suit turning it inside out and avoid shaking.

4. Remove plastic shoe cover from one foot and step over "clean line." Remove other shoe cover and put that foot over the line.

5. Remove mask. The last staff member removing his/her mask may want to wash all masks with soapy water before removing suit and gloves. Place masks in plastic bag and hand over the clean line, and place in second bag held by another member of the staff. Send for decontamination.

6. Remove inner gloves and discard in drum inside dirty area.

7. Close off dirty area until level of contamination is established and the area improperly cleaned.

8. Personnel should then move to a shower area, remove scrub suit, and place it in a plastic bag.

9. Shower and redress in normal working attire.

Note: Double-bag clothing and label appropriately.

Communications
Effective communications are essential to maintaining incident control. These include a dedicated radio frequency and a sufficient number of radios for distribution to all participating agencies. Another network links the

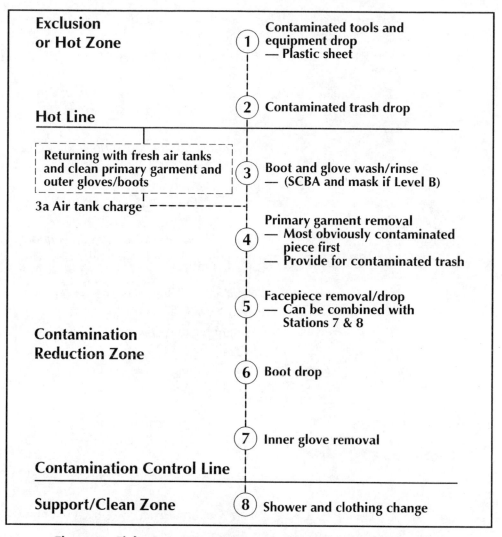

Figure 7. Eight-Step Dry Decontamination Plan for Personnel

on-scene command post to support groups. Other networks that may have to be activated include one linking EMTs to the hospital emergency room and one dedicated for use by the teams in the Exclusion Zone. If a sufficient number of radios are not available for use in the Exclusion Zone, then line of sight must be maintained at all times for those personnel in the zone. Often when an Incident Command System is activated, one person is assigned to manage communications.

Selected Bibliography

American Conference of Governmental Industrial Hygienists. Guidelines for the Selection of Chemical Protective Clothing. Cincinnati, Ohio, 1983.

Arena, J. M. *Poisoning: Toxicology, Symptoms, Treatments.* Fifth Edition. Charles C. Thomas, Springfield, Illinois, 1986.

Browning, E. *Toxicity and Metabolism of Industrial Solvents.* Elsevier, Amsterdam, 1965.

Klaassen, C. D., Amdur, M. O., Doull, J., eds. *Casarett and Doull's Toxicology: The Basic Science of Poisons.* Third Edition. Macmillan Publishing Company, New York, 1986.

Clayton, G. D., Clayton, F .E. *Patty's Industrial Hygiene and Toxicology.* Revised Edition. John Wiley and Sons, New York, 1985.

Chemical Manufacturers Association (CMA), and the Association of American Railroads. Terms for Personal Protective Equipment. CMA, Washington, DC, October 1987.

Dreisbach, R. H., Robertson, W. O. *Handbook of Poisoning: Prevention, Diagnosis, and Treatment.* Twelfth Edition. Lange Medical, Los Altos, California, 1986.

Ellenhorn, M. J., Barceloux, D. G. *Medical Toxicology: Diagnosis and Treatment of Human Poisoning.* Elsevier, New York, 1988.

EPA Region VII. Chemical Response Planning and Operations. EPA Region VII, EPA, Washington, DC, January 1989.

Goldfrank, L. R. *Goldfrank's Toxicological Emergencies, A Comprehensive Handbook in Problem Solving.* Third Edition. Appleton Century Crofts, New York, 1986.

Gosselin, R. E., Smith, R. P., Hodge, H. C. *Clinical Toxicology of Commercial Products.* Fifth Edition. Williams and Wilkins Publishers, Baltimore, Maryland, 1984.

Hayes, A. W., ed. *Principles and Methods of Toxicology.* Raven, New York, 1989.

Hodgson, E., Levi, P.E. *A Textbook of Modern Toxicology.* Elsevier, New York, 1987.

Levine, S. P., Martin, W. F. *Protecting Personnel at Hazardous Waste Sites.* Butterworth Publishers, Boston, Massachusetts, 1985.

Lu, F. C. *Basic Toxicology: Fundamentals, Target Organs, and Risk Assessment.* Hemisphere, Washington, DC, 1985.

National Fire Academy/National Emergency Training Center, *Recognizing and Identifying Hazardous Materials.* National Audio-Visual Center, Capitol Heights, Maryland, 1985.

Sax, N. I. *Dangerous Properties of Industrial Materials.* Seventh Edition. Van Nostrand Reinhold Publishing Corp., New York, New York, 1988.

Schwope, A. D., Costas, P. P., Jackson, J. 0., Weitzman, D. J. *Guidelines for the Selection of Chemical Protective Clothing.* Third Edition. American Conference of Governmental Industrial Hygienists, Cincinnati, Ohio, 1987.

Windholz, M., eds. *The Merck Index.* Tenth Edition. Merck and Co., Rahway, New Jersey, 1983.

Response and Patient Management

In the protocol for responding to potential hazardous materials incidents, the following primary considerations should be included: activities to undertake en route to the scene and upon arrival at the scene; guidelines for assessment, decontamination, and treatment of victims; and patient transport to the hospital.

En Route to a Hazardous Materials Scene

First responders need to be alert for hazardous materials when responding to every call. Hazardous materials can be obvious (i.e., noxious fumes, gasoline, or corrosive liquid spills) or they can be unnoticeable (odorless, but poisonous and/or flammable vapors and liquids, or radioactive). If a vehicle has a diamond-shaped placard or an orange-numbered panel on the side or rear, the cargo should be assumed to be hazardous. Unfortunately, not all hazardous materials carriers will be clearly marked. For example, delivery trucks regularly carry hazardous materials that can be released in a collision, yet rarely are marked. Therefore, first responders should use caution when attempting rescue at any incident scene. The hazard, or lack thereof, must be determined immediately—before first responders enter a chemically contaminated area.

The responder should pay attention to certain clues en route to an incident scene that could tip off the possibility of hazardous material involvement. Billowing smoke or clouds of vapor could give advanced warning that a dangerous substance may be involved. Senses are one of the best ways to detect chemicals, particularly the sense of smell. However, if you smell something you are too close and should remove yourself to a safe distance until you know more about the source of the odor. Failure to do so could cause injury. The nature of an incident should also be a key to identifying the possibility of a hazardous materials involvement. Tank trucks, train wrecks, and incidents at fixed facilities where chemicals are used could indicate hazardous materials involvement. The dispatcher may have clues that could indicate hazardous materials precautions are necessary. These could include the nature of an incident (e.g., leaking tank) and the nature of injuries (e.g., twenty workers with shortness of breath).

It is important that emergency responders pay attention to factors such as wind direction and topography when approaching a suspected hazardous materials incident. Responders should always approach upwind and upgrade from an incident, taking note that low-lying areas such as stream beds and gulleys, or in urban areas, places such as courtyards or tall buildings, may contain vapor clouds that prevent dispersal by the wind.

Responders should also attempt to gather as much information as possible while en route to an incident. Using resources outlined under Hazard Recognition, they can relay this information to a predesignated information center (e.g., regional poison control center, ATSDR) to obtain information about definitive care procedures including

- possible health effects;
- PPE required;
- treatment/antidote therapy; and
- decontamination procedures.

Information that will be needed to determine appropriate care will include the following:

- Knowledge of whether a chemical may be involved
- Chemical name of substance involved
- State of material (solid, liquid, gas)
- Quantities involved
- Number of victims
- Signs or symptoms
- Nature of exposure (inhalation, dermal, etc.)
- Length of exposure.

If a hazardous substance is involved and has been identified, responders should locate information concerning that substance using appropriate references, such as Material Safety Data Sheets (MSDS), the Department of Transportation (DOT) Emergency Response Guidebook, and CHEMTREC, as outlined under Hazard Recognition. This information can also help responders identify possible health hazards, including the nature of possible injuries; routes of exposure; proper level of PPE required; and the appropriate safe distance from the hazard to protect EMS personnel, the public, and property from exposure or other dangers, such as explosion or fire. This information may be available from a command post if one has been established. Emergency Medical Services Response to Hazardous Materials Incidents outlines these procedures for PPE, and Systems Approach To Planning describes guidelines for planning.

Communications with other agencies or services involved should also begin en route to an incident. If an Incident Command System (ICS) is implemented, interactions with an incident commander will identify the best route of approach, the possible dangers involved, and the estimated number of injuries. Communications between on-site response personnel and receiving facilities should be kept open to relay as much advance information as possible. Communications with other services should include the fire department, police, and hazardous materials response team (if one exists).

Arrival at the Scene
Many first responders (police, fire-rescue, and EMS personnel, including physicians and nurses) are accustomed to immediately attending an injured victim; often they disregard the possibility of danger to themselves. Consequently, a rescuer entering a contaminated area also risks exposure and the potential for becoming a victim. Even though rescue of any injured patient is important, it should only be attempted after it is certain that the

responders themselves will not become injured. Responders must use judgement when assessing the dangers involved in a possible hazardous materials incident. Patient care should not be delayed unnecessarily when only minimal risk is involved, but many factors must be considered in determining the level of danger. Training and experience are essential for decision making and those decisions, at best, are often a judgement call. As a rule, however, rescue should not be attempted by individuals who are not properly trained and equipped with appropriate PPE. Rescue should only be attempted by trained and equipped emergency personnel, fire department, or hazardous materials response team personnel. Figure 8 represents a typical decision tree that may be used in making decisions about risk and response.

Upon arrival at a scene, an initial assessment of the situation and the size of the incident should be conducted. Additional support should be requested, if necessary. Sources of on-scene assistance may include the following:

- Fire Departments
- Police Departments
- Health Departments
- Hazardous Materials Response Teams
- Local Industry Response Teams

Unless otherwise directed, responders should park upwind, upgrade, pointing away from, and a safe distance from any incident where hazardous materials are suspected. Safe distances for specific chemicals may be determined using the DOT Emergency Response Guidebook, by consulting CHEMTREC, or by using other response references. Responders should not drive or walk through any spilled or released materials (i.e., smoke and vapors as well as puddles). Also, a first-in responder should confirm that local authorities have been notified and are aware that hazardous materials might be involved.

Don't:

- Drive or walk through any spilled materials.
- Allow unnecessary contamination of equipment.
- Attempt to recover shipping papers or manifests unless adequately protected.
- Become exposed while approaching a scene.
- Approach anyone coming from contaminated areas.
- Attempt rescue unless trained and equipped with appropriate PPE for the situation.

For first-in responders, the first priority is scene isolation. KEEP OTHERS AWAY! KEEP UNNECESSARY EQUIPMENT FROM BECOMING CONTAMINATED.

Immediately establish an Exclusion (Hot) Zone, but do not become exposed in doing so (see Figure 5). The Exclusion Zone should encompass all contaminated areas, and no one should be allowed to cross into that zone.

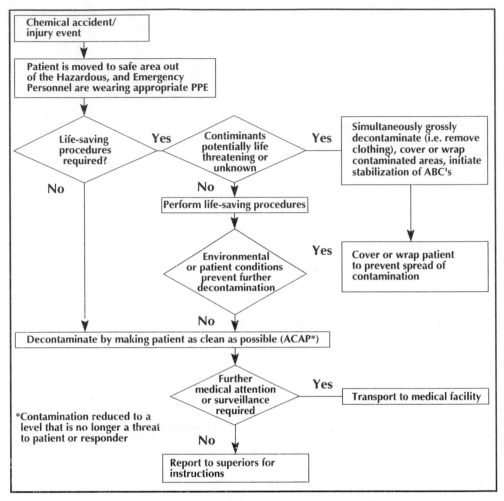

Figure 8. Sample EMS Decision Tree for Chemical Incidents

Assume that anyone leaving the Exclusion Zone is contaminated and should be assessed and decontaminated if necessary. Additional zones, such as Contamination Reduction (Warm), Support/Clean (Cold), and Crowd Control, should be determined as soon as the opportunity becomes available. Do not remove nonambulatory patients from the Exclusion Zone unless properly trained personnel with the appropriate PPE are available and decontamination has been accomplished.

Not all hazardous substances have color or odor. Therefore, a responder with appropriate PPE may be required for rescue. If an incident commander has been identified, report to him or her and coordinate patient access and emergency care activities. Unless appropriately trained and protected, responders must not attempt entry into the Exclusion Zone to rescue patients or to recover shipping papers or manifests.

Do not approach any victims without first consulting with the incident commander. No rescue should be attempted unless the responder is trained and equipped with appropriate PPE for the situation. Likewise, response personnel should not approach anyone coming from contaminated areas (particularly those potentially contaminated) until given permission by the incident commander.

It must be emphasized that EMS responders who have not been trained should stay out of the hot zone and decontamination area. Sophisticated protective gear should only be used by those with proper knowledge and experience. If decontamination is carried out before the patient is transported to the EMS personnel at the perimeter, then no special gear may be needed.

Assessment, Decontamination, and Initial Treatment of Patients
Primary goals for emergency personnel in a hazardous materials incident include termination of exposure to the patient, removal of the patient from danger, and patient treatment—while not jeopardizing the safety of rescue personnel. Termination of exposure can best be accomplished by removing the patient from the exposure area and removing contaminants from the patient. If the patient is removed from the possibility of additional exposure or other dangers and the patient is no longer contaminated, the level of protection for personnel can be downgraded to a level that will better facilitate the provision of patient care. The potential for additional or increased danger to patient and responder prohibits any treatment inside the Exclusion Zone other than basic life support. The probability of contact with hazardous substances either by subsequent release of materials still in the area, along with the dangers of fire or explosion, and the restriction of movement by necessary PPE outweighs the time saved by attempting patient care in a dangerous area. Gross management of Airway, Breathing, and Circulation (ABC) is all that should be undertaken while there is potential for further injury to patient or response personnel.

One of the most important steps in scene hazard assessment should be obtaining immediate assistance from a regional poison control center. The poison center can help determine the risk for secondary contamination, the need for special protective gear and decontamination procedures, and the toxic effects of the chemical.

Primary assessment can be undertaken while simultaneously performing decontamination in the Contamination Reduction Zone. Priority should be given to the ABC: Airway, Breathing, and Circulation. Once life-threatening matters have been addressed, rescue personnel can then direct attention to secondary patient assessment. It is important to remember that appropriate personal protective equipment and clothing must be worn until the threat of secondary exposure is no longer a danger. Therefore, the sooner the patient becomes decontaminated the sooner response personnel may reduce protective measures or downgrade the level of protection.

During initial patient stabilization, a gross decontamination should simultaneously be performed. This consists of cutting away or otherwise removing all suspected contaminated clothing, including jewelry and watches, and brushing or wiping off any obvious contamination. Care should be taken to protect any open wounds from contamination. Every effort should be made by personnel to avoid contact with any potentially hazardous substance.

Effective decontamination consists of making the patient As Clean As Possible (ACAP). This means that the contamination has been reduced to a level that is no longer a threat to the patient or the responder.

Decontamination

Directives for decontamination include the reduction of external contamination, containment of the contamination present, and prevention of the further spread of potentially dangerous substances. In other words, remove what you can and contain what you can't. With a few exceptions, intact skin is less absorptive than injured flesh, mucous membranes, or eyes. Therefore, decontamination should begin at the head of the patient and proceed downward with initial attention to contaminated eyes and open wounds. Once wounds have been cleaned, care should be exercised so as not to recontaminate them. This can be aided by covering the wounds with a waterproof dressing. For some chemicals, such as strong alkali, it may be necessary to flush exposed eyes with water or normal saline for several hours. Table 9 outlines the minimum equipment that is required for decontamination of patients by emergency response personnel. These lists are not detailed; they are only provided to guide departments in developing their own equipment lists based on their community needs and requirements. Many chemical substances, even though highly toxic, carry no intrinsic risk for contamination to others. Most toxic gases, such as

Table 9. Suggested Decontamination Equipment

At a minimum, the protective equipment listed is necessary to participate in decontamination procedures. Protective equipment used for decontamination should be no less than one level below that used for entry into the hazardous environment. Positive-pressure, self-contained breathing apparatus (SCBA) and fully encapsulated suits may be necessary in extreme cases.

Containment equipment	Sponges and soft brushes
Pool or tank	Large plastic bags for contaminated clothing
Tarps	Small plastic bags for patients' valuables
six-mil construction plastic	Tags and waterproof pens to mark bags
Saw horses to support backboards	Disposable clothes and shoes for
Fiberglass backboards	ambulatory patients
Supports for ambulatory patients	Towels and blankets
Water supply	Clear, zip-front bags to minimize
Scissors for clothing removal	contamination to transport personnel
Mild detergent (dishwashing liquid)	and ambulances
Five-gallon buckets	Tape (duct, four-inch)

carbon monoxide or arsine, are highly poisonous, but once the victim has been brought out of the exposure area and into the fresh air, the amount of leftover gas in and around the patient simply cannot poison others. Even many chemicals that have the potential for spreading contamination can be made less hazardous by simply diluting them with copious amounts of water.

External decontamination should be performed using the least aggressive methods. Limit mechanical or chemical irritation to the skin to prevent increased permeability. Wash contaminated areas gently under a gentle spray of water, and wash with a soft sponge using a mild soap such as dish-washing liquid. Use warm, never hot, water. The degree of decontamination should be completed based on the nature of the contaminant, the form of contaminant, the patient's condition, environmental conditions, and resources available. Care should be taken so that contaminants are not introduced into open wounds. Responders should try to contain all runoff from decontamination procedures for proper disposal. The patient should be isolated from the environment to prevent the spread of any remaining contaminants.

Ensure that all potentially contaminated patient clothing and belongings have been removed. Properly label bags that contain clothing or other potentially contaminated articles. Contaminated clothing and belongings should not be transported with the patient in the ambulance unless the incident commander approves, and the clothing and belongings have been adequately bagged.

Decontamination
- Decontaminate from the head down.
  - Take care not to introduce contaminants into open wounds.
  - Decontaminate exposed wounds and eyes before intact skin areas.
  - Cover wounds with a water-proof dressing after decontamination.
- For external contamination, begin with the least aggressive methods
  - Limit mechanical or chemical irritation of the skin.
  - Wash contaminated area gently under a stream of water, and scrub with a soft brush or surgical sponge.
  - Use warm, never hot, water.
- Remove contaminants to the level that they are no longer a threat to patient or response personnel.
- Isolate the patient from the environment to prevent the spread of any remaining contaminants.
- If possible, contain all runoff from decontamination procedures for proper disposal.
- Ensure that all potentially contaminated patient clothing and belongings have been removed.
  - Properly label bags that contain clothing or other potentially contaminated articles.

Considerations for Patient Treatment

Basically, a contaminated patient is like any other patient and may be treated as such except that responders must protect themselves and others from dangers due to contamination. Response personnel must first address life-threatening issues and then decontamination and supportive measures. Primary surveys will be accomplished simultaneously with decontamination; and secondary surveys should be completed as conditions allow. The chemical-specific information received from the hazardous materials response resources should be incorporated into the proper patient treatment procedures. In multiple patient situations, proper triage procedures should be implemented using local community emergency response plans (see, SARA Title III). Treat presenting signs and symptoms as appropriate and when conditions allow. The sooner a patient has been decontaminated the sooner he or she can be treated like a "normal" patient. Administer orders of the designated poison control center when conditions allow. Unless required by life-threatening conditions prophylactic invasive procedures, such as intravenous injections (IVs) or intubation, should be performed only in fully decontaminated areas where conditions permit. These procedures may create a direct route for introducing the hazardous material into the patient. Oxygen should be given using a bag valve mask with reservoir device (rebreather) or manually triggered oxygen-powered breathing device. The contaminated atmosphere should not mix with the oxygen if possible. Reassess the patient frequently because many hazardous materials have latent physiological effects. While some cases may require treatment with antidotes, most cases will be handled with symptomatic care.

Patient Treatment

- Assign highest priorities to ABC and decontamination.
- Complete primary and secondary surveys as conditions allow. Bear in mind the chemical specific information received from the designated poison control or information center.
- In multiple patient situations, begin proper triage procedures.
- Treat presenting signs and symptoms as appropriate and when conditions allow.
- Administer orders of the designated poison control center when conditions allow.
- Perform invasive procedures only in uncontaminated areas.
- Reassess the patient frequently because many chemicals have latent physiological effects.
- Delay prophylactic measures until the patient is decontaminated.

Patient Transport to Hospital

When transporting a contaminated patient by ambulance, special care should be exercised in preventing contamination of the ambulance and subsequent patients. Exposed surfaces that the contaminated patient is likely to come into contact with should be covered with plastic sheeting.

Fiberglass backboards and disposable sheeting are recommended. If a wood backboard is used, it should be covered with disposable sheeting or it may have to be discarded afterwards. Equipment that comes in contact with the patient should be segregated for disposal or decontamination. EMS personnel should wear protective clothing appropriate for conditions (e.g., surgical gloves, CPC, etc.), and respirators, if indicated (see Section I, PPE). Table 10 outlines suggested equipment required for care and transport of contaminated patients. Like other listings provided, it is only for guidance, and items may be added or deleted with experience.

The patient should be as clean as reasonably possible before transport, and further contact with contaminants should be avoided. Protective clothing should be worn by response personnel as appropriate. If decontamination cannot be performed adequately, responders should make every attempt to prevent the spread of contamination and at the very least remove patient clothing, wrap the patient in blankets, followed by body bags or plastic or rubber sheets to lessen the likelihood of contamination to equipment and others. Considerations should be made for chemicals that pre-

Table 10. Supplies Needed to Prepare the Ambulance for Care of a Patient Contaminated with Hazardous Materials

Enough 6-mil construction plastic* cut to size to:
   —Cover floor of ambulance
   —Cover squad seat
   —Cover litter
Disposable sheets
One box of plastic trash bags to contain contaminated medical supply waste, gloves and the victim's clothes, and the like
Personal protection:
   —CVC disposable suits with built-in hoods and booty/boot covers
   —Positive-pressure SCBA
   —Full-face mask respirator with an orange- and purple-type cartridge (acid gas, organic vapor, highly toxic dust, mist and fumes, and radionuclides-rated cartridge)
   —Poly Vinyl Chloride (PVC) or duct tape for taping closures
   —Two-piece rainwear
   —Rubber boots with steel toes
   —Nitrite gloves with 14-inch cuffs
   —Duct tape to seal suit seams if necessary

If the fire department's protective clothing is used, rainwear should be worn as an overgarment. Hydrocarbons and other chemicals may permeate the "bunker clothes."

NOTE: The protective equipment listed is to be used for patent care situations after initial decontamination. It is meant to be used when complete decontamination of the patients cannot be guaranteed or when assisting with decontamination procedures (in extreme cases positive-pressure SCBA and encapsulated suits may be required for decontamination procedures). It is not meant to be used in rescue operations of victims found in a hazardous area. Under no circumstances should this equipment be relied upon for entry into hazardous environments. Protective equipment for entry must be appropriate to and compatible with the products involved.This may include positive-pressure SCBA and fully encapsulated suits. Many factors must be taken into consideration when determining the appropriate level of protection. Consequently, selection of protccdve equipment must be done by a qualified individual.

*Wet plastic is slippery; stability is important.

sent the added danger of accelerated skin absorption due to heat. In these cases body bags and plastic or rubber sheets should not be used. Minimize contamination from shoes. The name of the involved chemicals, if identified, and any other data available, should be recorded before leaving the scene. Oxygen should be administered by rebreather mask for any victim with respiratory problems unless contraindicated (e.g., paraquat). Eyes that have been exposed should be irrigated with available saline or water, and such irrigation should be continued en route to the hospital. Personnel also should be alert for any respiratory distress.

In an ambulance during transport, personnel should use appropriate respiratory protection. Provide the maximum fresh air ventilation (e.g., open windows) that weather conditions permit to the patient and driver's compartment regardless of the presence or absence of odors.

Recontact the receiving hospital and provide an update on treatment provided or required and any other information received from the designated poison control center. Instructions for the procedure to enter the hospital with a contaminated patient should also be requested. Facilities receiving a potential hazardous material patient will need as much information as possible.

A checklist should be developed and made available for all vehicles and telephone or radio communication centers. Information that will aid in initiating appropriate actions includes the following:

- Type and nature of incident
- Number of patients
- Signs/symptoms being experienced by the patients
- Nature of injuries
- Name of chemical(s) involved
- Information available at the site concerning the chemical(s)
- Extent of patient decontamination in the field
- Estimated time of arrival

The ambulance should park in an area away from the emergency room or go directly to a predesignated decontamination center or area, thereby limiting exposure to hospital facilities. In order to protect staff and other patients, the patient should not be brought into the emergency department before ambulance personnel receive permission from the hospital staff.

Upon the release of the patient to the hospital, any equipment that is believed to have become contaminated should be double-bagged. The use of disposable equipment is recommended whenever possible. Contaminated articles should be kept sealed until the Incident Commander or his designee gives further instructions. If possible, send any material safety data sheets concerning the involved hazardous materials with the patient.

The ambulance should not go back into service unless the vehicle is clean. This again emphasizes the importance of thorough patient decontamination; if the patient is clean, then the vehicle (interior) is clean. After the patient is unloaded from the ambulance, a check should be made with the hospital to determine where the ambulance can be safely decontaminated, and whether equipment is available for this purpose. When decontamination is required, the most appropriate method should be identified using information resources. In most cases soap and water are adequate for decontaminating of the vehicle.

Transport to Hospital
- Recontact the receiving hospital.
- Update the hospital on treatment provided and any other information received from the designated poison control center.
- Obtain instructions on approaching and entering the hospital.
- Avoid contact with contaminants; provide protection to the vehicle; wear protective clothing as appropriate.
- Get patient as clean as possible prior to transport.
- Administer oxygen by mask for any patient with respiratory problems (except as contraindicated).
- Before leaving the scene, write down the name of the involved chemicals, if identified, and any other data available.
- Provide fresh air ventilation to patient and driver's compartment.
- Continue to irrigate eyes that have been exposed with normal saline or water en route to the hospital and be alert for any respiratory distress.
- Park the ambulance in an area away from the emergency department, or go directly to a predesignated decontamination area.
- Do not bring patients into the emergency department before ambulance personnel receive permission from the hospital staff.
- After unloading the patient, check with the hospital to determine where the ambulance can be safely decontaminated and the availability of equipment for this purpose.
- Decontaminate exposed personnel.

Air Transportation of Chemically Exposed Patients
There is a potential danger in transporting patients in a helicopter from a hazardous materials incident. Often decontamination is not complete, and the flight crew could experience difficulty breathing or seeing. Also the area of the incident needs to be clearly communicated with the flight crew to avoid traveling through an unsafe area. Furthermore, the downdraft from the helicopter could affect vapors or fumes on the scene. Considerations should be made for each specific incident and chemical.

Critique
As soon as possible after each incident, all participating units should send personnel involved to review the measures that were taken by each unit or agency. The purpose of this review is to examine which activities succeeded and which did not, and to evaluate the overall coordination effort.

Patient Management Under Mass Casualty Conditions
Involving Hazardous Chemicals

Basic medical procedures in a large-scale hazardous materials incident are not substantially different from life-saving measures in other mass casualty disasters. Primary attention to the ABC (Airway, Breathing, and Circulation) continues to have first priority.

There are, however, several important differences in disasters involving hazardous materials. A chemical mass casualty incident may also require setting up mass screening and decontamination centers. It may also be necessary to establish casualty collection points to provide stabilizing care in the field prior to transport. A major chemical disaster may accompany other disasters such as an earthquake. Such an event would drastically increase the number of casualties and the complexity of the medical care that must be provided (crushing and broken bones vs. gas inhalation, for example). This would require increased numbers of personnel, perhaps more sophisticated medical equipment, and a better transport system for taking stabilized victims out of the area. Training in the appropriate procedures to be followed is essential for potential responders to a hazardous materials incident involving mass casualties. Triage may be complicated for chemical exposure by delayed onset of signs and symptoms. The patient, injured or not, must be decontaminated before being transported to the emergency department to protect EMS and emergency department staff.

Selected Bibliography

Cashman, J. R. *Hazardous Materials Emergencies, Response and Control.* Revised, second edition. Lancaster, PA: Technomic Publishing Co., 1988.

Currance, P. L., Bronstein, A. C. *Emergency Care for Hazardous Materials Exposure.* St. Louis, MI: C.V. Mosby, 1988.

Department of Transportation (DOT). *Emergency Response Guidebook.* Washington, DC, 1987; DOTP-5800.5

Federal Emergency Management Agency (FEMA). *Disaster Planning Guidelines for Fire Chiefs.* Prepared by International Association of Fire Chiefs, Inc: February 1981. Washington, DC: FEMA.

Federal Emergency Management Agency (FEMA). *Guidance for Developing State and Local Radiological Emergency Response Plans and Preparedness for Transportation-Accidents.* Washington, DC: FEMA, 1985.

Federal Emergency Management Agency (FEMA). *Hazardous Materials Management System: A Guide for Local Emergency Managers.* Prepared by the Multnomah County Office of Emergency Management: July 198 1. Washington, DC: FEMA.

Federal Emergency Management Agency (FEMA). *Hospital Emergency Department Management of Radiation Accidents.* Washington, DC: FEMA, 1984.

Goldfrank, L. R. Goldfrank's Toxicological Emergencies, A Comprehensive Handbook in Problem Solving. New York: Appleton Century Crofts, 1986.

Haddad, L. M., Winchester, J. F. *Clinical Management of poisoning and Overdose.* Philadelphia: WB Saunders Co., 1983.

Leonard, R. B., Ricks, R. *Emergency Department Radiation Accident Protocol, Annals of Emergency Medicine,* September, 1980.

Noji, E. K., Kelen, G. D. *Manual of Toxicologic Emergencies.* Chicago: Year Book Medical Publishers, 1989.

Noll, G., Hildebrand, M. S., Yvorra, J. G. *Hazardous Materials, Managing the Incident.* Fire Protection Publications, Stillwater, OK: Oklahoma State University, 1988.

Ricks, R. C. *Hospital Emergency Department Management of Radiation Accidents.* Oak Ridge, TN: Oak Ridge Associated Universities, 1984.

Stutz, D. R., Ricks, R., Olsen, M. *Hazardous Materials Injuries, a Handbook of Prehospital Care.* Greenbelt, MD: Bradford Communications Corporation,1982.

Systems Approach to Planning
The Role of the EMS in a Systems Approach to Planning

The potential for hazardous materials incidents exists almost everywhere. While occurring infrequently, chemical incidents are capable of endangering the health of specific individuals and the emergency personnel directed to assist them. People who have been seriously injured by a hazardous material have a greater chance of recovery without complications when appropriate emergency treatment is provided by trained prehospital EMS personnel at the scene, and the patient is transported to a facility having the most appropriate personnel and technical resources to manage his or her care. This requires an integrated emergency medical response. However, many local governments, private businesses, and hospitals do not have a tested integrated hazardous materials response plan in place that involves all of the responders. This has resulted in several problems, including the following:

- On-site incidents have been poorly managed by first responders.
- Communication channels between the private sector and the public sector or among public responders have not been clearly identified and formalized.
- The medical community has not been firmly integrated into many response systems and may not be prepared to treat multiple casualties resulting from a serious hazardous materials incident.

EMS are a crucial link in the community response system for emergency preparedness planning. Not only are hospitals asked to treat patients who have been chemically contaminated at remote sites, but as repositories of hazardous materials themselves, are potential sites of hazardous materials incidents. Coordination and communication between hospitals and other elements of an Emergency Medical Services plan can best be achieved by hospital staff and physicians fully participating at local meetings for hazmat planning and protocol review.

EMS must acknowledge their role as a component of the community-wide emergency response system. Administrators must familiarize themselves with the contingency planning of other components, such as fire, police, and health departments, and understand what services are expected from hospitals. Optimally, EMS staff should be represented on planning committees that develop and periodically review these contingency plans.

A common characteristic of the successful management of chemical incidents is adequate contingency planning. Planning requires the involvement of an array of community institutions—fire and police departments and community hospitals. Not every hospital or EMS in an area needs to have an emergency department capable of handling hazardous materials patients. In fact many communities have centralized such services into one major area hospital or shock trauma center.

However, all hospitals should be capable of performing decontamination and basic care since some patients may come in on their own—not through the Emergency Medical Services (EMS) Systems. In addition, emergency department personnel must be knowledgeable about where to send patients for further specialized care.

The Spectrum of Hazardous Materials Incidents

Local and state EMS agencies should be able to participate in the response to a range of hazmat incidents from the individual level to the multi-casualty to the disaster level. The hospital and emergency medical responders are key components of the local response system. Planning should integrate hospital and EMS personnel, equipment, and supply needs into the state and local hazmat plans. In turn, the hospital must be familiar with these plans and know how to use them if it is involved in a incident that overwhelms its capabilities.

- Individual patient—a single individual is contaminated and must be transported to an emergency department:
  - Can be an occupational or accidental exposure.
  - May pose a problem in rural areas with small hospitals, or where there are low levels of hazmat skills and experience for EMTs.
- Multi-casualty—this situation is usually limited to a single location:
  - Involves normal systems of transportation.
  - Patients are usually treated at the same level facility as a single emergency response, but the demand on all systems is much greater.
- Disaster—disrupts a large segment of the community:
  - May involve several locations.

- ○ May involve additional units to the normal responders; such units are not part of the local EMS system, and these units may not know how it works.
- • May involve long-range mutual aid; normal systems of transportation (ambulances) are inadequate or disrupted.
- • Patients may be treated locally at different facilities providing various levels of care, or even outside of the area altogether.

While transportation incidents attract larger media attention, statistics show that almost 75 percent of all acute hazardous materials events, excluding fuel spills, occur in the fixed locations where they are used or stored. In addition, events resulting in death and injury occur almost 1.5 times as often in plants as in transit.

Hazardous material incidents range from small releases at a factory site to rapidly expanding events that endanger a community. Regardless of its size, an incident's successful management depends on preplanning. This preplanning often requires coordination between local, state, and federal agencies, and industries, as well as those in the community who use and maintain stocks of potentially hazardous materials. Contributions to hazardous materials planning come from a variety of sources: regulations from the Joint Commission on Accreditation of Healthcare Organizations, state and local planning committees established by SARA Title III, state EMS agencies, and federal agencies.

Joint Commission on Accreditation of Healthcare Organizations (JCAHO)

In drawing up contingency plans, administrators of hospitals have significant guidance available from the Joint Commission on Accreditation of Healthcare Organizations (JCAHO). The JCAHO establishes standards that must be met before a hospital can receive accreditation. A comprehensive accreditation survey occurs once every three years, with intermittent evaluation if a specific area of weakness is identified at the time of full review.

The Key Indicator Probe (KIP) system in the Plant Technology and Safety Management Standards is a valuable addition to the accreditation process. Before the JCAHO survey is conducted, KIPs define what the accreditation survey expects a hospital to have completed in order to comply with a specific standard. For example, JCAHO standard PL.1.11.1 describes the hospital's role in community-wide emergency preparedness plans. The description of the hospital's role in community-wide emergency preparedness plans is the key indicator. The probe for this key indicator presents the question: Is the role of this facility and other health care organizations and community civil services addressed in the program?

Additionally, JCAHO standard PL.1.11.2 discusses procedures in response to environmental or man-made events. For the key indicator item "information about how the hospital plans to implement specific procedures in response to environmental or man-made events," there are five probes.

These include: 1) Has the organization identified alternate sources of essential utilities? 2) Is there an emergency communication system? 3) Is there a procedure for identifying an alternate care site? 4) Are facilities available for radioactive or chemical isolation and decontamination? and 5) Is there a workable plan for total facility evacuation? JCAHO Accreditation Standards for Hospitals 1989 outlines the JCAHO standards and indicator probes that are relevant for treating chemically contaminated patients.

The emergency department standards include: 1) current toxicologic reference materials and antidote information (ER.5.2), 2) a list of referral and consultation services (ER.5.3), and 3) equipment for chemical incidents (ER.6.8.3). In addition, JCAHO standards and key indicator probes for a hazardous materials and wastes program (PL.1.10) and an emergency preparedness program (PL.1.11) are provided. A hospital can more readily comply with some JCAHO standards by using community response and public information systems mandated by SARA Title III.

JCAHO Accreditation Standards for Hospitals, 1989

ER.5.2 Current toxicologic reference materials and antidote information are readily available in the emergency department/service, along with the telephone number of the regional poison control information center.

ER.5.3 A list of referral and consultation services is prominently displayed and includes, as appropriate, the regional coordinating office for radiologic emergency assistance, antivenin service, county coroner or medical examiner, police department, state and local health departments, ambulance transport and rescue services, tissue donation centers, and special care services not provided by the hospital.

ER.6.8.3 Standard drugs, antivenin (in geographic areas as indicated), common poison antidotes, syringes and needles, parenteral fluids and infusion sets, plasma substitutes and blood administration sets, and surgical supplies are available for immediate use.

PL.I.10 There is a hazardous materials and wastes program, designed and operated in accordance with applicable law and regulation, to identify and control hazardous materials and wastes; the program includes:

PL.1.10.1 policies and procedures for identifying, handling, storing, using, and disposing of hazardous materials from receipt through use and hazardous wastes from generation to final disposal;

PL.1.10.2 training for and, as appropriate, monitoring of personnel who manage and/or regularly come into contact with hazardous materials and/or wastes;

PL.1.10.3 monitoring of compliance with the program's requirements; and

PL.1.10.4 evaluation of the effectiveness of the program, with reports to the safety committee and to those responsible for other appropriate monitoring activities.

PL.1.11 There is an emergency preparedness program designed to manage the consequences of natural disasters or other emergencies that disrupt the hospital's ability to provide care and treatment; the program includes:

PL.1.11.1 a description of the hospital's role in community wide emergency preparedness plans;

PL.1.11.2 information about how the hospital plans to implement specific procedures in response to environmental or man-made events;

PL.1.11.3 provisions for the management of space, supplies, communications, and security;

PL.1.11.4 provisions for the management of staff, including distribution and assignment of responsibilities and functions;

PL.1.11.5 provisions for the management of patients, including scheduling of services, control of patient information, and admission, transfer, and discharge;

PL.1.11.6 staff training in their roles during emergencies; and

PL.1.11.7 semi-annual implementations of the plan, either in response to an emergency or in a planned drill.

PL.I.11.7.1 The hospital's performance during implementation of the plan is evaluated, documented, and reported to the safety committee through the hospital-wide information collection and evaluation system.

Key Items
PL.1.10.3 Monitoring of compliance with the program's requirements and probes.

   a. Are reports of hazardous materials and waste-monitoring programs presented to the safety committee?
   b. Are all hazardous materials and waste incident reports reviewed by the safety committee?

PL.1.10.4 Evaluation of the effectiveness of the program, with reports to the safety committee and to those responsible for other appropriate monitoring activities.

   a. Does the safety officer or other responsible individual(s) compare the results of the program with standards established by law, regulation, or the organization to evaluate the effectiveness of the program?
   b. Is the analysis reported to the safety committee and others as appropriate?

PL.1.11 There is an emergency preparedness program designed to manage the consequences of natural disasters or other emergency situations that disrupt the hospital's ability to provide care and treatment; the program includes the following:

Is there a current written program at the facility that addresses the responsibilities of the medical staff, the nursing staff, and support services during a variety of applicable emergencies, both within the organization and in the surrounding community?

PL.1.11.1 a description of the hospital's role in community-wide emergency preparedness plans;

Is the role of this facility and other health care organizations and community civil services addressed in the program?

PL.1.11.2 information about how the hospital plans to implement specific procedures in response to environmental or man-made events;

    a. Has the organization identified alternate sources of essential utilities?
    b. Is there an emergency communication system?
    c. Is there a procedure for identifying an alternate care site?
    d. Are facilities available for radioactive or chemical isolation and decontamination?
    e. Is there a workable plan for total facility evacuation?

PL.1.11.3 provisions for the management of space, supplies, communications, and security; Does the facility's plan address the use of space, replenishment of supplies, and the loss of communication, security, and utilities?

PL.1.11.4 provisions for the management of staff, including distribution and assignment of responsibilities and functions;

    a. Does the program list staff roles and responsibilities during emergencies?
    b. Is there a reliable method for notifying staff of an emergency?
    c. Is there a procedure for assigning available staff that reflects staffing changes on various shifts and days?
    d. Was the plan tested during drills or actual implementation?
    e. Are staff lists current?

PL.1.11.5 provisions for the management of patients, including scheduling of services, control of patient information, and admission, transfer, and discharge;

Does the plan include procedures for

    a. modification or discontinuation of less than essential services?
    b. moving of patients within the facility?
    c. relocating patients outside the facility in the event of an emergency?
    d. provision of appropriate medical staff services and physical facilities to implement the plan?

PL.1.11.6 staff training in their roles during emergencies; and

    a. Is there documentation of the training and education of all personnel who have an assigned role in the emergency preparedness program?

b. Can a random sample of staff adequately describe training they have received in the emergency preparedness program and in the fire plan?

PL.I.11.7 semiannual implementation of the plan, either in response to an actual emergency or in a planned drill.

Is there evidence of semiannual implementation, either in response to an emergency, or in a planned drill?

NOTE: Drills separated by at least four months are acceptable.

NOTE: Organizations that offer emergency services and/or are designated as disaster receiving stations must have at least one implementation per year that includes an influx of patients.

PL.1.11.7.1 The hospital's performance during implementation of the plan is evaluated, documented, and reported to the safety committee through the hospital-wide information collection and evaluation system.

Is there evidence

a. of evaluation of the emergency preparedness plan gathered from previous drills, changes in the mission or capability of hospitals, and changes in the community?
b. in the community of a review of the effectiveness of the program, and changes made where appropriate?
c. of critiques of each implementation addressing elements of hospital preparedness, staff preparedness, and patient management?
d. for each critique, evidence of identification of problems, corrective actions taken, and recommendations for modification of the program?
e. of a random sample of staff being asked about the drill?

NOTE: Some organizations may not participate in a community-wide emergency plan. In these cases, item (b) is not applicable, and compliance with PL.1.11.7.1 will be scored:

1. a,c,d,e

2. 3 of 4

3. 2 of 4

4. 1 of 4

5. none in place

SARA Title III

Title III of the Superfund Amendments and Reauthorization Act (SARA), passed by Congress in 1986, provides for an infrastructure in states and local communities to plan for effective response to hazardous material emergencies. In addition, the legislation also provides for public access to information on the presence and releases of specified hazardous chemicals in communities.

Title III, "The Emergency Planning and Community Right-to-Know Act of 1986," required that each state establish a State Emergency Response Commission (SERC), which consists of members with technical expertise in emergency response, environmental and natural resources, public health, occupational safety, media, and transportation. The SERC is responsible for establishing local emergency planning districts (usually on a county level), appointing and overseeing local emergency planning committees (LEPC), establishing procedures for handling public requests for information, and reviewing LEPC emergency plans.

SARA Title III requires that the local committees must include, at a minimum, representatives from the following groups: state and local officials, law enforcement, civil defense, firefighting, environmental, hospital, media, first aid, health, transportation, and facility owners or operators subject to the emergency planning requirements. The LEPC was primarily responsible for preparing a comprehensive emergency response plan for its district by October 1988, and for making information on hazardous chemicals, which is submitted under Title III, available to the public. Using information about the presence of potentially hazardous chemicals reported by businesses and other facilities under Title III, the LEPC was to have developed its plan.

As part of the planning process, the LEPC must evaluate available resources for developing, implementing, and exercising the plan. The plan must include the following:

- identification of facilities subject to planning provisions under Title III
- identification of transportation routes for extremely hazardous substances
- identification of risk-related facilities
- methods and procedures for response
- designated community and facility coordinators
- procedures for public notification
- methods for determining release occurrence and area affected
- description of emergency equipment and facilities and those responsible
- evacuation plans and training programs

Under Title III's planning provisions, EPA was mandated by Congress to establish a list of chemicals to help focus local emergency planning activities. In April 1987, EPA listed 406 Extremely Hazardous Substances (EHS) and established a Threshold Planning Quantity (TPQ) for each. If any business or facility contains one of these EHS, in an amount equal to or greater than its respective TPQ, the facility owner or operator is required to notify the SERC and LEPC. These facilities must name a facility coordinator to work with the LEPC for specific inclusion of that facility in the local plan.

Representative facilities covered under the planning provisions include not only major chemical manufacturing facilities, but also a wide variety of chemical users, such as farmers, dry cleaners, and other service-related businesses. Exemptions under this provision apply only to vessels (ship/boat), federal facilities, and transportation. Storage incidental to transportation is exempt provided that the EHS are still moving under active shipping papers and have not reached the final consignee.

Accidental releases of EHS and other hazardous substances identified in the Comprehensive Environmental Response, Compensation, and Liability Act of 1980 (CERCLA) must be reported to the LEPC and SERC. This requirement ensures immediate notification to local response personnel. Other provisions of Title HI provide further information on the presence, storage, and emissions of hazardous and toxic chemicals. These data further assist the LEPC in obtaining a fuller picture of chemical risk in the local district.

Emergency medical personnel can be better prepared for response to incidents that involve contaminated victims by actively participating in the LEPC planning process. Title III provides for the submission of information on hazardous and toxic chemicals as presented above. In addition, Title III contains a specific provision for the disclosure of chemical identity by facility owners or operators on chemicals for which facilities have made trade secret claims. Access to chemical identity assists health professionals, physicians, and nurses in obtaining further information for diagnostic purposes during emergencies and for prevention and treatment measures during nonemergencies.

The State Emergency Medical Services (EMS) Agency

Planning for hazardous materials incidents should include the appropriate linkage to the state EMS agency. The state agencies are responsible for overseeing a network of local EMS units, and thus are an essential part of the planning process. Often this body is part of the SERC.

Duties of the agencies vary from state to state. However, EMS agencies usually are responsible for medical management and medical control of first responders. EMS agencies develop medical mutual aid agreements between counties, and establish procedures for distribution of casualties between hospitals. In addition, these agencies maintain an inventory of disaster medical supplies. Further, EMS agencies develop and maintain communications protocols for on-site activities: between receiving hospitals and the base hospital, between base hospitals and ambulances, and between all hospitals and the Regional Poison Control Center. EMS agencies also work with counties in designating field casualty decontamination and collection points for a major disaster.

Suggested planning activities may include:

- **Medical Direction**—The local EMS agency should be contacted for information on how medical control is provided for the EMS system.

- **Patient Destination**—Hospital emergency departments are able to provide supportive care. However, in some cases it may be more appropriate to take the victim to a hospital that has expertise in handling certain kinds of poison exposures. The plan should include directions for obtaining this information. One option is to go through the Regional Poison Control Center via the base hospital. The poison center will often know which hospitals are best prepared for which substances.
- **Decontamination and Medical Management Protocols**—The literature on the clinical management of hazardous materials exposures is sometimes inconsistent in its recommendations. Provision should be made in the plan for obtaining field and hospital medical management information from experienced physicians. For example, the Regional Poison Control Center can provide decontamination and medical management protocols via facsimile transmission or telephone to all receiving hospitals, and through the base hospital or via cellular telephone to EMTs in the field. They also have rapid access to experts.
- **Coordination with Burn Centers, Hyperbaric Chamber Facilities, and Other Specialty Centers** provision should be made to alert and coordinate patient destination with various specialty care centers.

Federal Emergency Response Activities

Contingency planning is essential to the successful implementation of any system designed to manage chemically contaminated patients and to promptly contain the hazard itself. Contingency plans require a coordinated community response that may also involve state and federal agencies. Preplanning and coordination of services are equally critical at the national level. A National Contingency Plan (NCP) has been established by the federal government to promote coordination of resources and services of federal and state response systems. To oversee this plan, a National Response Team (NRT) and National Response Center, a network of Regional Response Teams (RRTs), and a group of On-Scene Coordinators (OSCs) have been established.

The Hazardous Materials Emergency Planning Guide, referred to as NRT-1, provides guidance to help local communities prepare for potential hazardous materials incidents. The NRT-1 can be used by local communities developing their own plan, as well as by LEPCs formed in accordance with the "Emergency Planning and Community Right-to-Know Act" (SARA Title III) of 1986.

The objectives of the Hazardous Materials Emergency Planning Guide are to

- focus communities on emergency preparedness and response;
- provide communities with information that can be used to organize the emergency planning task;

- furnish criteria for risk and hazard assessments and assist communities in determining whether a hazardous materials incidents plan is needed, in addition to the district-wide plan developed by the LEPC;
- help LEPCs and individual communities prepare a plan that is appropriate for their needs and consistent with their capabilities; and
- provide a method for revising, testing, and maintaining community emergency plans.

The NRT-1 is published by the National Response Team, and was developed cooperatively by its fourteen federal member agencies: the Department of Defense, Department of the Interior, Department of Transportation (Research and Special Programs Administration and U.S. Coast Guard), Environmental Protection Agency (EPA), Department of Commerce (National Oceanic and Atmospheric Administration (NOAA), Federal Emergency, Management Agency (FEMA), Department of State, Department of Agriculture, Department of Health and Human Services (Agency for Toxic Substances and Disease Registry), Department of Justice, Department of Labor (Occupational Safety and Health Administration), Nuclear Regulatory Commission, and the Department of Energy. The NRT-1 represents a concerted effort by federal agencies to consolidate their general hazardous material planning guidance into an integrated federal document.

NRT-1 states that an emergency plan must include response procedures of facilities and local emergency and medical personnel, as well as a description of emergency equipment and facilities in the community. It also recommends that hospital, emergency medical service, and health department personnel be included as members of an emergency planning team. As previously mentioned, SARA Title III requires medical, hospital, and first aid personnel to be members of the local emergency planning committee. The NRT-I describes relevant publications that provide specific operational guidance to emergency responders, such as the DOT's Emergency Response Guidebook for first responders, which provides guidance for firefighters, police, and other emergency services personnel to help them protect themselves and the public during the initial minutes immediately following a hazardous materials incident.

In addition, the document provides information on the Chemical Manufacturers Association's (CMA) Community Awareness Emergency Response (CAER) and the Chemical Transportation Emergency Center (CHEMTREC) programs. The CAER program encourages local facilities to inform local residents, public officials, and emergency response organizations about industry operations and to integrate their on-site emergency response plans with the planning efforts of the local community. In some areas of the country, the chemical industry has established physician networks. The purpose of the networks is to develop a better dialogue between company physicians and local health authorities. CAER has outlined that the following specific steps be taken: review the plant emergency plan, improve employee awareness and training, prepare a community relations plan, inventory the status of local emergency planning, develop a briefing paper, prepare a list of initial contacts, meet with initial contacts and identify key officials, establish a coordinating group, and begin implementation steps. On the federal level, EPA and FEMA provide technical assistance and guidance to local and state planners through the SARA Title III program.

The NRT-1 document also recommends that contingency plans include standard operating procedures for entering and leaving sites; accountability for personnel entering and leaving sites; decontamination procedures; recommended safety and health equipment; and personal safety precautions. The document suggests that emergency plans include a list of emergency response equipment appropriate to various degrees of hazard using the EPA levels of protection (A, B, C, and D). Further, it recommends that the list include the type of respirator (e.g., self-contained breathing apparatus, supplied-air respirator, or air-purifying respirator), the type of clothing that must be worn, and the equipment needed to protect the head, eyes, face, ears, hands, arms, and feet.

In addition, the NRT-I recommends that medical personnel be made aware of significant chemical hazards in the community to train properly and prepare for possible hazardous materials incidents. It also states that emergency medical teams and hospital personnel must be trained in the proper methods for decontaminating and treating persons exposed to hazardous chemicals.

Hazard Analysis

Hazard analysis is a necessary step in comprehensive emergency planning for a community. It is a three-step decision-making process comprised of hazard identification, vulnerability analysis, and risk analysis. The first task in conducting analysis is to complete an inventory of the hazardous materials present in the community and describe the nature of the hazard. This is a key step because it permits planners to describe and evaluate risks and to allocate resources accordingly. However, the task of analyzing all relevant hazards may not prove cost-effective to many communities. The planning committee therefore should assign priorities to the hazards found in its community and establish affordable limits for analysis. It should be noted that several federal agencies (e.g., DOT, FEMA, and EPA) report that frequently encountered substances often pose the most prevalent dangers. These materials include fuels and chemicals, such as chlorine, ammonia, and hydrochloric and sulfuric acids. Such materials should be given special attention by the LEPC in the planning process.

In this context, a hazard is any situation that is capable of causing injury or impairing an individual's health. During the process of identifying hazards, facilities or transportation routes will be pinpointed that contain materials that are potentially dangerous to humans. The identification of hazards also should provide the following information:

- The types, quantities, and location of hazardous materials in the community, or transported through a community
- The nature of the hazard that would accompany incidents, such as explosions, spills, fires, and venting to the atmosphere

Hazards should be identified at as many facilities in the community as possible. These include the obvious ones such as chemical plants, refineries, petroleum plants, and storage facilities and warehouses. In requesting information directly from facilities, remember that SARA Title III planning provisions require certain facilities to provide the LEPC with any information on the facility that the committee needs to develop and implement its plan. Local emergency planning committees may provide assistance here, particularly if the LEPC has industry representatives on it. It is essential that these industries or businesses understand the role these data play in ensuring a sound emergency response plan. As previously stated, placing business or industrial representatives on the community-wide planning committee as required under SARA Title III may assist in gaining their cooperation. The cooperation and assistance of a facility that regularly deals with hazardous materials presents the local planning unit with a wide array of services. For example, such a facility can provide technical experts, spill prevention control and countermeasure (SPCC) plans, training and safe handling instructions, and cleanup capabilities.

In addition, hospitals and educational and governmental facilities should not be overlooked since they all contain a variety of chemicals. Major transportation routes and transfer points, such as airports, vessels in port, railroad yards, and trucking terminals, should be included in the overall hazards identification plan. SARA Title III planning provisions, for example, address many of these potential risk areas by requiring the following: facility cooperation in plan preparation, a wide range of chemical handlers (manufacturers to service-related businesses), and specific risk areas to be addressed in the plan (i.e., transportation).

Risk analysis includes the probable damage that may occur if a chemical incident occurs. Information that is necessary for a risk analysis includes

- the type of risk to humans, such as an acute, chronic, or delayed reaction;
- the groups that are at highest risk; and
- the type of risk to the environment, such as permanent damage or recoverable condition.

Many documents can be of assistance in conducting a risk analysis. Risk analysis in transportation settings has been outlined in the DOT's "Community Teamwork: Working Together To Promote Hazardous Materials Safety, A Guide for Local Officials." In conjunction with FEMA and DOT, EPA published a supplement to NRT-1 in December 1987. This document, entitled Technical Guidance for Hazards Analysis and often referred to as the "Green Book," provides technical assistance to LEPCs in assessing the lethal hazards associated with potential airborne releases of extremely hazardous substances.

Selected Bibliography

Department of Transportation. *Community Teamwork: Working Together to Promote Hazardous Materials Safety, A Guide for Local Officials.* Washington, DC: May 1983.

Environmental Protection Agency and Federal Emergency Management Agency. *Technical Guidance for Hazardous Analysis: Emergency Planning for Extremely Hazardous Substances.* Washington, DC: Environmental Protection Agency, December 1987.

Federal Emergency Management Agency. *Guide for Development of State and Local Emergency Operations Plan.* Washington, DC, October 1985; CPG 1-8.

Federal Emergency Management Agency. *Planning Guide and Check list for Hazardous Materials.* U.S. Government Printing Office, Washington, DC, July 1981; FEMA-10.

National Institute for Occupational Safety and Health/Occupational Safety and Health Administration. *Pocket Guide to Chemical Hazards.* Washington, DC: U.S. Government Printing Office, 1985.

National Response Team. Hazardous Materials Emergency Planning Guide. Washington, DC: U.S. Government Printing Office, 1987; NRT 2100.

SARA Title III Compliance Guidebook, Government Institutes, Inc., 1988; ISBN: 0-86587-749-1.

Appendix A: Hazardous Materials Classification Systems

- National Fire Protection Association, 704M System
  - Department of Transportation DOT Chart 9
  - Example of Department of Labor Material Safety Data Sheet NFPA 704M

System Notes: Health (BLUE)
In general, health hazard in firefighting is that of a single exposure which may vary from a few seconds up to an hour. The physical exertion demanded in firefighting or other emergency conditions may be expected to intensify the effects of any exposure. Only hazards arising out of an inherent property of the material are considered. The following explanation is based upon protective equipment normally used by firefighters.

4. Hazard D Levels should be used when materials are too dangerous to expose firefighters to. A few whiffs of the vapor could cause death or the vapor or liquid could be fatal on penetrating the firefighter's normal full protective clothing. The normal full protective clothing and breathing apparatus available to the average fire department will not provide adequate protection against inhalation or skin contact with these materials.

3 Materials extremely hazardous to health but areas may be entered with extreme care. Full protective clothing—including self-contained breathing apparatus, coat, pants, gloves, boots, and bands around legs, arms, and waist—should be provided. No skin surface should be exposed.

2 Material hazardous to health, but areas may be entered freely with full-faced mask self-contained breathing apparatus which provides eye protection.

1 Materials only slightly hazardous to health. It may be desirable to wear self-contained breathing apparatus.

0 Materials which on exposure under fire conditions would offer no hazard—beyond that of ordinary combustible material.

Flammability (RED)
Susceptibility to burning is the basis for assigning degrees within this category. The method of attacking the fire is influenced by this susceptibility factor.

4 Very flammable gases or very volatile flammable liquids. Shut off flow and keep cooling water streams on exposed tanks or containers.

3 Materials which can be ignited under almost all normal temperature conditions. Water may be ineffective because of the low flash point.

2 Materials which must be moderately heated before ignition will occur. Water spray may be used to extinguish the fire because the material can be cooled below its flash point.

1 Material that must be preheated before ignition will occur. Water may cause frothing if it gets below the surface of the liquid and turns to steam. However, water fog gently applied to the surface will cause a frothing which will extinguish the fire.

0 Materials that will not burn.

Reactivity (STABILITY) (YELLOW)
The assignment of degrees in the reactivity category is based upon the susceptibility of materials to release energy either by themselves or in combination with water. Fire exposure was one of the factors considered along with conditions of shock and pressure.

4 Materials which (in themselves) are readily capable of detonation or of explosive decomposition or explosive reaction at normal temperatures and pressures. Includes materials which are sensitive to mechanical or localized thermal shock. If a chemical with this hazard rating is in an advanced or massive fire, the area should be evacuated.

3 Materials which (in themselves) are capable of detonation or of explosive decomposition or of explosive reaction which require a strong initiating source which must be heated under confinement before initiation. Includes materials which are sensitive to thermal or mechanical shock at

elevated temperatures and pressures or which react explosively with water without requiting heat or confinement. Fire fighting should be done from an explosive-resistant location.

2 Materials which (in themselves) are normally unstable and readily undergo violent chemical change but do not detonate. Includes materials which can undergo chemical change with rapid release of energy at normal temperatures and pressures or which can unrgo violent chemical change at elevated temperatures and pressures. Also includes those materials which may react violently with water or which may form potentially explosive mixtures with water. In advanced or massive fires, firefighting should be done from a safe distance or from a protected location.

1 Materials which (in themselves) are normally stable but which may become unstable at elevated temperatures and pressures or which may react with water with some release of energy but not violently. Caution must be used in approaching the fire and applying water.

0 Materials which (in themselves) are normally stable even under fire exposure conditions and which are not reactive with water. Normal firefighting procedures may be used.

U.S. Department of Transportation Research and Special Programs Administration Hazardous Materials Marking, Labeling & Placarding
June 15, 1993 Guide

This Marking, Labeling and Placarding Guide will assist shippers, carriers, fire departments, police, emergency response personnel, and others in complying with, and enforcing the regulations governing the safe transport of hazardous materials by highway, rail, water and air.

The information and illustrations presented in this guide are intended to serve as an introduction to regulations governing hazardous materials transportation. The guide should be read in conjunction with the Hazardous Materials Regulations (HMR; 49 CFR 100-199). Published annually, and amended periodically, the HMR are the key to compliance and contain the information needed to comply with the requirements for the safe transport of hazardous materials.

** The DOT Chart 9 and the guidelines for Hazardous Materials Warning Labels can be ordered from the Publication Warehouse (404) 639-6360.

Material Safety Data Sheets
The Material Safety Data Sheet (MSDS) has become a major source of chemical information. It is the key document used to provide hazard information to employees and can become an invaluable tool for emergency personnel when used in a chemical emergency.

Occupational Safety and Health (OSHA) Hazard Communication Standard (29 CFR 1910.1200) requires all manufacturers of pure chemicals and/or mixtures to evaluate their products and relate, via MSDS, any hazards that may be encountered while handling these materials. This standard is intended for all workplaces, manufacturing and non-manufacturing alike. The Environmental Protection Agency's (EPA) Emergency Response and Community Right-to-Know Act of 1986 ensures the availability of MSDS to emergency response personnel such as fire departments, first aid crews, and hospital emergency room staff.

MSDS contain a wealth of information which may be understood with a minimum of training. It is the purpose of this document to briefly explain the format and information found in properly prepared MSDS.

SECTION 1—Figure 9
This section identifies the material by product or trade name and chemical name. It is the product or trade name that is usually found on the container labels although the chemical name is also required by some states. Section I will also contain the manufacturer's name, address, and telephone number.

SECTION 2—Figure 9
This section lists the chemical ingredients of the material if they are known or suspected to be hazardous. Hazardous materials which are not carcinogens must be reported if they represent 1 percent or more of the product. Carcinogens must be reported and identified as such if their levels are O.1 percent or higher. Also included in this section are Threshold Limit Values (TLV) and OSHA Permissible Exposure Limit (PEL).

SECTION 3—Figure 9
Section 3 provides physical data about the product that can be utilized for proper identification. Included are specifics such as color, odor, specific gravity (weight), vapor pressure, and boiling point.

SECTION 4—Figure 9
Section 4 includes fire and explosion hazard data. This information is especially useful when devising both in-house and community contingency plans. Plant first responders, local fire departments, and HAZMAT teams need unlimited access to this information.

SECTION 5—Figure 9
This section contains information on the reactivity of the product. It will list other chemicals which, when mixed with the product, will result in a chemical reaction. If a product is water reactive it will be noted in this section.

Also, hazardous decomposition products such as carbon monoxide and other hazardous gases formed and emitted during chemical reactions or during fires are listed. It is imperative that this section be carefully noted by firefighters, both in-house and local.

SECTION 6—Figure 9

Section 6 contains health hazard data. It will describe any acute (short-term exposure) and/or chronic (long-term exposure) effects on the body. These will include routes (inhalation, skin, ingestion) of overexposure and the bodily organs affected as well as the signs and symptoms of overexposure. First aid procedures will also be found in this section.

SECTION 7—Figure 9

Section 7 lists the procedures that should be used if the product spills or leaks, including waste disposal methods.

SECTION 8—Figure 9

Section 8 contains information regarding the proper personal protective equipment (PPE) necessary to handle the product in a manner which will minimize exposure. Ventilation practices are also listed in this section.

Summary

A Material Safety Data Sheet can aid in making the right decisions on health and safety issues in a plant or in a community. Yet, it must be noted that it is but one of many references that should be used to make final determinations. MSDS are offered by manufacturers for identification and verification and are not the last word on safety and health practices.

1. Material Safety Data Sheet

Product name	CAS #
Chemical nature	
% Activity	

2. Physical Data

Boiling point, 760 mm HG		Freeze point	
Specific gravity		Vapor Pressure at 20°C	
Vapor Density		Solubility in H_2O	
Percent volatiles by weight		Ionic Nature	

Appearance and Odor

3. Chemical Ingredients

Material	%	TLV (Units)

4. Fire and Explosion Hazard Data

Flash point (test methods)		Auto-ignition temperature		
Flammable limits in air, % by volume		Lower		Upper
Extinguishing media				
Special fire fighting procedures				
Unusual fire and explosion hazards				

Figure 9. Sample Material Safety Data Sheet

5. Health Hazard Data

Threshold limit value

Effects of exposure

Emergency and First Aid procedures

6. Reactive Data

Stability		Conditions to avoid	
Unstable	Stable		
Compatibility			
Hazardous recomposition products			
Hazardous polymerization		Conditions to avoid	

7. Spill or Leak Procedures

Steps to be taken or material
is released or spilled

Waste disposal method

8. Special Protection Information

Respiratory protection

Ventilation	Local exhaust		Special	
	Mechanical		Other	
Protective gloves			Eye protection	
Other protective equipment				

9. Special Precautions

Precautionary labeling	
Other handling and storage conditions	

Figure 9. Sample Material Safety Data Sheet (continued)

Table 11. Appendix B Types of Respiratory Protection

Type of Respirator	Advantages	Disadvantages
Air Purifying Air-Purifying Respirator (Including powered air-purifying respirators [PAPRs])	Enhanced mobility. Lighter in weight than an SCBA. Generally weighs two pounds (one kg) or less (except for PAPRS).	Cannot be used in IDLH or oxygen-deficient atmospheres (less than 19.5 percent oxygen at sea level). Limited duration of protection. May be hard to gauge safe operating time in field conditions. Only protects against specific chemicals, and up to specific concentrations. Use requires monitoring of contaminant and oxygen levels. Can only be used: (1) against gas and vapor contaminants with adequate warning properties or (2) for specific gases or vapors provided that the service is known and a safety factor is applied, or if the unit has an ESLI (end-of-service-life-indicator).
Atmosphere-Supplying Self-Contained Breathing Apparatus (SCBA)	Provides the highest available level of protection against airborne contaminants and oxygen deficiency. Provides the highest available level of protection under strenuous work conditions.	Bulky, heavy (up to 35 pounds). Finite air supply limits work duration. May impair movement in confined spaces.
Positive-Pressure Supplied-Air Respirator (SAR) (also called air line respirator)	Enables longer work periods than an SCBA. Less bulky and heavy than an SCBA. SAR equipment weighs less than five pounds (or around fifteen pounds, if escape SCBA protection isincluded). Protects against most airborne contaminants	Not approved for use in atmospheres immediately dangerous to life or health (IDLH) or in oxygen-deficient atmospheres unless equipped with an emergency egress unit, such as an escape-only SCBA that can provide immediate emergency respiratory protection in case of air line failure. Impairs mobility. Mine Safety and Health Administration/NIOSH certification limits hose length to 300 feet (90 meters). As the length of the hose is increased, the minimum approved airflow may not be delivered at the faceplate.

Table 11. Continued

Type of Respirator	Advantages	Disadvantages
		Air line is vulnerable to damage, chemical contamination, and degradation. Decontamination of hoses may be difficult. Worker must retrace steps to leave work area. Requires supervision/monitoring of the air supply line.

Table 12. Appendix C Levels of Protection*

Level of Protection	Equipment	Protection Provided	Should Be Used When:	Limiting Criteria
A	Recommended: Pressure-demand, fully incapsulating, chemical-resistant suit. Inner chemical-resistant safety boots/shoes. Two-way radio communication. OPTIONAL: Cooling unit. Coveralls. Long cotton underwear. Hard hat. Disposable gloves and boot covers.	The highest available level of respiratory, skin, and eye protection.	The chemical substance has been identified and requires the highest level of protection for skin, eyes, and the respiratory system based on either: –Measured (or potential for) high concentration of atmospheric vapors, gases, or particulates or –Site operations and work functions involving a high potential for splash, immersion, or exposure to unexpected vapors, gases or particulates of materials that are harmful to skin or capable of being absorbed through the contact skin. Substances with a high degree of hazard to the skin are known or suspected to be present, and skin contact is possible. Operations must be conducted in confined, poorly ventilated areas until the absence of conditions.	Fully-encapsulated suit material must be compatible with the substance involved.

* Reprinted from NIOSH/OSHA/USCG/EPA1

Occupational Safety and Health Guidance Manual for Hazardous Waste Site Activities, Department of Health and Human Services, October 1985.

Transportation of Hazardous Materials

Finally, this chapter will examine the requirements for the transportation of hazardous materials. A constant threat for all security planners is transportation; materials and goods in transit are often at their most vulnerable. Attacking an enemy's supply convoy is a popular tactic in warfare. Armored car companies generate millions in revenue every year offering their services to securely transport cash and valuables. Theives cost manufacturers billions through the jacking of goods in shipment. Similarly, hazardous materials must likewise be transported in accordance to very specific requirements. The deliberate derailment of a train carrying chlorine; the hijacking of a truck transporting radioactive waste; the piercing of the hull of a ship loaded with diesel fuel: these are but some of the methods a terrorist might use to conceivably turn a hazardous material conveyance into a WMD.

The following is an overview of the U.S. Government's laws and requirements for the transportation of hazardous materials.

U.S. Department of Transportation
Introduction—Hazardous Materials Transportation Act

Purpose and Organization

The Hazardous Materials Transportation Act of 1975 (HMTA), is the major transportation-related statute affecting transportation of hazardous cargoes. The objective of the HMTA according to the policy stated by Congress is ". . . To improve the regulatory and enforcement authority of the Secretary of Transportation to protect the Nation adequately against risks to life and property which are inherent in the transportation of hazardous materials in commerce."

Regulations apply to ". . . any person who transports, or causes to be transported or shipped, a hazardous material; or who manufactures, fabricates, marks, maintains, reconditions, repairs, or tests a package or container which is represented, marked, certified, or sold by such person for use in the transportation in commerce of certain hazardous materials."

Enforcement of the HMTA is shared by each of the following administrations under delegations from the Secretary of the Department of Transportation (DOT):

- Research and Special Programs Administration (RSPA)—Responsible for container manufacturers, reconditioners, and retesters and shares authority over shippers of hazardous materials.
- Federal Highway Administration (FHA)—Enforces all regulations pertaining to motor carriers.
- Federal Railroad Administration (FRA)—Enforces all regulations pertaining to rail carriers.
- Federal Aviation Administration (FAA)—Enforces all regulations pertaining to air carriers.

- Coast Guard—Enforces all regulations pertaining to shipments by water.

Material Designation and Hazard Communication

The Hazardous Materials Table (49 CFR Part 172.101) designates specific materials as hazardous for the purpose of transportation. It also classifies each material and specifies requirements pertaining to its packaging, labeling, and transportation. Hazard communication consists of documentation and identification of packaging and vehicles. This information is communicated in the following formats:

- Shipping papers
- Package marking
- Package labeling
- Vehicle placarding

Upon determining the proper shipping name (i.e., the name of the hazardous material shown in Hazardous Materials Table), the Hazardous Materials Table will specify the correct packaging. Packaging authorized for the transportation of hazardous materials is either manufactured to DOT standards or does not meet DOT standards, but is approved for shipments of less hazardous materials and limited quantities. The shipper is responsible for determining the shipping name. The shipper must also ascertain the hazard class, United Nations Identification number (if required), labels, packaging requirements, and quantity limitations.

The Hazardous Materials Transportation Act (HMTA) pre-empts state and local governmental requirements, unless that requirement affords an equal or greater level of protection to the public than the HMTA requirement.

New Hazardous Materials Transportation Regulations

DOT, motivated by a need for international harmony in hazardous materials transportation rules, has promulgated new rules, published on December 21, 1990, which comprehensively revised the Hazardous Materials Regulations (HMR), with respect to hazard communication, classification, and packaging requirements, based on United Nations recommendations. One intended effect of the rule was to facilitate the international transportation of hazardous materials by ensuring a basic consistency between the Hazardous Materials Regulation and international regulations.

Classification of Hazardous Materials

The DOT has broad authority to regulate hazardous materials that are in transport, including the discretion to determine which materials shall be classified as "hazardous." These materials are placed in one of nine categories, based on their chemical and physical properties. Based on the classification of the material, the DOT is also responsible for determining the appropriate packaging materials for shipping or transport. Finally, also based on the material classification, strict guidelines are furnished for proper labeling/marking of packages of hazardous materials offered for transport, and for placarding of transport vehicles.

- Class 1: Explosives
  - Division 1.1 Explosives with a mass explosion hazard
  - Division 1.2 Explosives with a projection hazard
  - Division 1.3 Explosives with predominantly a fire hazard
  - Division 1.4 Explosives with no significant blast hazard
  - Division 1.5 Very insensitive explosives
  - Division 1.6 Extremely insensitive explosive articles
- Class 2: Gases
  - Division 2.1 Flammable gases
  - Division 2.2 Nonflammable gases
  - Division 2.3 Poison gas
  - Division 2.4 Corrosive gases
- Class 3: Flammable liquids.
  - Division 3.1 Flashpoint below −18°C (0°F)
  - Division 3.2 Flashpoint −18°C and above, but less than 23°C (73°F)
  - Division 3.3 Flashpoint 23°C and up to 61°C (141°F)
- Class 4: Flammable solids; spontaneously combustible materials; and materials that are dangerous when wet
  - Division 4.1 Flammable solids
  - Division 4.2 Spontaneously combustible materials
  - Division 4.3 Materials that are dangerous when wet
- Class 5: Oxidizers and organic peroxides
  - Division 5.1 Oxidizers
  - Division 5.2 Organic peroxides
- Class 6: Poisons and etiologic materials
  - Division 6.1 Poisonous materials
  - Division 6.2 Etiologic (infectious) materials
- Class 7: Radioactive materials
  - Any material, or combination of materials, that spontaneously gives off ionizing radiation. It has a specific activity greater than 0.002 microcuries per gram.
- Class 8: Corrosives
  - A material, liquid or solid, that causes visible destruction or irreversible alteration to human skin or a liquid that has a severe corrosion rate on steel or aluminum.
- Class 9: Miscellaneous
  - A material which presents a hazard during transport, but which is not included in any other hazard class (such as a hazardous substance or a hazardous waste).
- ORM-D: Other regulated material
  - A material which, although otherwise subjected to regulations, presents a limited hazard during transportation due to its form, quantity, and packaging.

Hazard Identification: Labeling and Placarding, Marking and Shipping Papers

Hazard communication forms the backbone of emergency response, and response begins with identification. The primary mission of DOT hazard communication is to alert the public and transportation workers of the presence of hazardous materials, and to insure that incompatible materials are segregated when placed in the same transport vehicle, storage area (or lab!). The distinctive DOT system of labeling and placarding provides another visual clue for responders to a hazardous material incident.

Hazard markings, labels and placards are a common approach to warning the public of hazards that may be encountered. The DOT uses labels, defined as 4" x 4" colored diamond with warning words and graphics, affixed to the outside of the shipping container or box. Labels are required on the outside of the package regardless of the quantity shipped. The DOT requires placards, a much larger version of the labels, to be displayed on tank cars, cargo tanks, portable tanks and bulk packaging. Requirements for placarding are dependent upon the identity and quantity shipped. "Markings" are required to convey specific information about the enclosed hazard and the person responsible.

Placards and Labels

Placards are used to represent the hazard classes of materials contained within freight containers, motor vehicles or train car. Labels communicate the same hazards for smaller containers and packages offered for transport. Examples of the placards and labels used for the various hazard classes follow.

1) This placard or label is used to designate explosive materials, specifically Class 1.1, 1.2, and 1.3 explosives. Explosives that belong to classes 1.4, 1.5, and 1.6 will have that specified, with the class designation replacing the exploding ball. This placard is required when transporting ANY quantity of a Class 1.1, 1.2, or 1.3 explosive, or over 1001 lbs of a Class 1.4 or 1.5, explosive.

2) These placards and labels are used to designate compressed gases. Given the diverse chemical properties of compressed gases, this class is subdivided into flammable gases (Class 2.1), nonflammable gases or oxygen, (Class 2.2) and poisonous gases (Class 2.3).

This placard is required when transporting over 1001 lbs of Class 2.1 or 2.2, or when transporting ANY quantity of poisonous (Class 2.3) gas.

3) This is the label or placard used to designate flammable liquids. Certain common flammable liquids have their own placards, where the name of the material (such as gasoline and fuel oil) replaces the word "FLAMMABLE." Also, materials that fit the definition of a combustible material have the word "COMBUSTIBLE" replacing the word "FLAMMABLE."

This placard is required when transporting over 1001 lbs of flammable materials.

4) The below placards and labels are used to indicate the cargo contains flammable solids (Class 4.1), materials that are pyrophoric (i.e., ignite in the presence of oxygen) (Class 4.2), and those that react adversely when exposed to water (or humidity!) (Class 4.3). These placards are required when transporting over 1001 lbs of Class 4.1 or 4.2 materials, or when transporting ANY quantity of a water reactive material (Class 4.3).

5) This placard or label is used to designate a cargo that contains oxidizing materials (Class 5.1). In addition, this class contains materials that are classified as organic peroxides (Class 5.2), and in that case the label would read "ORGANIC PEROXIDES" rather than "OXIDIZER."

Placards are required when transporting over 1001 lbs of oxidizers or organic peroxides.

6) This class contains poisonous liquids that are designated as inhalation hazards. If the material is toxic but not an inhalation hazard it is placed in Class 6.1. Materials in these classes may NOT be transported in the same cargo as foodstuffs, feed, or any other edible substances intended for humans or animals.

In addition to the POISON label, packages of 110 gallon capacity or less, and that are recognized as "inhalation hazards," must also be marked "INHALATION HAZARD."

Placarding is required when transporting ANY quantity of Class 6 material, and when transporting over 1001 lbs of a Class 6.1 material.

7) This label is required on all radioactive materials and equipment. Packages containing radioactive species must be clearly labeled with 2 labels on opposite sides of the package. This class is divided into 3 divisions—I, II and III.

Placarding is required on ANY quantity of radioactive material rated as III; it is not required on materials rated as I or II.

8) This placard/label is used to designate any corrosive liquid. Placarding is required whenever the quantity exceeds 1001 lbs of a corrosive liquid.

9) Class 9 materials are those that have not been placed in a hazard class, but may still pose some degree of danger in transport. Placarding is not required for materials that are not classified. However, you may placard a material that presents a hazard during transport and weighs more than 1001 lbs.

This applies to placarding only and is required when 1001 lbs or more of material is transported and it is composed of 2 or more hazard categories. It will replace the specific placards for the individual classes. An exception is when one single class in a multiple class transport exceeds 5000 lbs, in which case the placard for the large load class must be displayed.

Markings

Each person offering for transport a hazardous material must ensure the package, container or vehicle carries the markings appropriate for the corresponding hazard. Specific rules and requirements are outlined in CFR 49 172.300. The following requirements are generally true, though exceptions are the rule!

- The proper shipping name and the proper identification number (preceded by UN or NA as appropriate).
- The identification number, when required, may be displayed separately from the warning placard. If so it must consist of black writing on an orange background. If the identification number is displayed on the warning placard itself, it shall be black writing on a white background and will replace the warning wording on the placard, but not the graphic. The iden-

tification number must be affixed to each side and each end if the packaging has a capacity of 1,000 gallons or more. It must be affixed on opposite ends if the packaging capacity is less than 1,000 gallons.
- The markings must be durable, in English, and printed legibly.
- They must be displayed on a background of sharply contrasting color.
- They must be unobscured by labels or attachments.
- The markings must be placed sufficiently far from other markings, such as advertising, so as not to detract from them or less their effectiveness.

In addition to the above general requirements, some materials require that specific markings be displayed on packages and on vehicles when offered for transport. The guidelines for these materials are as follows:

- For radioactive materials, each package must have its weight clearly marked on the outside of the package. The packaging type (TYPE A or TYPE B) must be clearly marked on the outside of the package.
- Liquid hazardous materials in non-bulk packaging must be packaged with the closures upward and be legibly marked with package orientation markings pointing in the correct upright direction. Markings that depict arrows for purposes other than to indicate the upward position may not be used on hazardous liquid materials. This requirement does not apply to packaging where the interior package is a metal cylinder.
- Bulk packages which contain materials that are poisonous if inhaled must be marked with the warning "INHALATION HAZARD" on two opposing sides. Nonbulk packages must be marked with the word "POISON" within 6 inches of the closure.
- Nonbulk packages of materials classified as ORM-D must be marked on at least one side or end with the ORM-D designation directly below the proper shipping name of the material. This marking is certification by the person offering the material for transport that the description, classification, packaging, marking, and labeling are all correct and appropriate for the material.

Shipping Papers
Whenever a hazardous material is offered for transport, it must be accompanied by proper shipping papers, which fully identify the hazards involved.

The description must fulfill the following requirements:

1. If a hazardous material and a nonhazardous material are described on the same shipping papers, the hazardous material must be
   o named first;

     o shown in contrasting (highlighted) color on all copies of the form;

     o identified with an "X" in the column marked "HM."

2. The shipping description must furnish

     o proper shipping name;

     o hazard class or division (this from column 3 of the Hazardous Materials Table);

     o identification number (this from column 4 of the Hazardous Materials Table);

     o packing group (this from column 5 of the Hazardous Materials Table); and

     o except for empty packages, the total quantity, including unit for measurement, of the hazardous material.

3. Entry must be legible and in English.

4. Unless specifically authorized or required, the description may not contain codes or abbreviations.

5. Additional information must follow the basic description.

6. Must contain the name of the shipper when transported by water.

7. If more than one page is required, the first page must indicate multiple pages, i.e., "page 1 of 3."

8. Shipping paper must show an emergency response telephone number.

9. Shipping paper must contain shipper's certification. An example of the shipping paper entry is as follows:

Hazardous Material Shipping Papers

TO:

Consignee

Street

Destination Zip

FROM:

Shipper

Street

Origin Zip

Route:

Vehicle Number

US DOT Hazmat Reg. No.

No. Shipping Units HM

Kind of Packages, Description of Articles

(IF HAZARDOUS MATERIALS—PROPER SHIPPING NAME)

Hazard

Class

I.D.

Number

Packing

Group

WEIGHT (subject to correction)

Rate

LABELS REQUIRED (or exemption)

—Taken from *http://safety.science.tamu.edu/dot.html*

Endnote

[1]www.primatech.com/info/paper_process_plant_security_programs_for_
managing_risks_from_deliberate_rele a-180k

Discussion Questions

1) A Mass _____ Incident is one in which a first responder must address multiple fatal injuries.

2) _____ _____ _____ is the focus of emergency responder partners to evaluate technologies and methodologies that permit rapid decontamination of large numbers of casualties.

3) The purpose of chemical protective clothing and equipment is to _____ or _____ individuals from the chemical, physical, and biological hazards that may be encountered during hazardous materials operations.

4) Level ___ protective equipment offers the highest available level of respiratory, skin, and eye protection from solid, liquid, and gaseous chemicals.

5) A _____ _____ is the initial investigation of a hazardous materials incident; these situations are usually characterized by a large degree of uncertainty and mandate the highest levels of protection.

6) The first task in conducting a community hazard analysis is to complete a(n) _____ of the hazardous materials present in the community and describe the nature of the hazard.

7) During decontamination operations, the exclusionary zone is also known as the _____ zone.

8) The most common SCBA is the open-circuit, _____-_____ type.

9) The _____ _____ _____ _____ has become a major source of chemical information. It is the key document used to provide hazard information to employees and can become an invaluable tool for emergency personnel when used in a chemical emergency.

10) Wearing full-body chemical protective clothing puts the wearer at considerable risk of developing _____ _____. This can result in health effects ranging from transient heat fatigue to serious illness or death.

Answers

1) Fatality

2) Mass Casualty Decontamination

3) Shield, isolate

4) A

5) Site survey

6) Inventory

7) Hot

8) Pressure positive

9) Material Data Safety Sheet

10) Heat stress

5 Improvised Explosive Devices (IEDs)

Overview:

Although considerable concern and discussion have rightly been generated in recent years regarding the awesome threat from chemical and biological weapons, conventional explosives still remain a far more present and widely experienced hazard.

Throughout Chapter Five, we will examine the threats, modalities, and methods of constructing Improvised Explosive Devices (IEDs). As the name implies, an IED is an often crude, but effective, explosive weapon fashioned from widely available or salvaged materials. Sometimes the devices are conspicuously hazardous looking, and other times they are innocuous or not readily apparent as a weapon. The homeland security specialist must be familiar with the reality of IEDs, and how to mitigate the threat they represent.

Chapter Objectives:

- *Define "Improvised Explosive Device."*
- *Identify common means and methods for constructing an IED.*
- *Explain how terrorists and insurgents use IEDs against both combatants and noncombatants.*

Humvee on fire. *Courtesy of Corbis Images.*

The means, materials, and instructions for manufacturing explosive devices are frighteningly available. When Timothy McVeigh murdered 168 people with a massive truck bomb at the Murrah Federal Building in Oklahoma City, the explosive device he had created consisted of almost two tons of ammonium nitrate, a chemical found in common fertilizer. In the fall of 1994, a McVeigh co-conspirator allegedly purchased, in cash, eighty 50-pound bags of fertilizer from a farming cooperative in Kansas. Although the purchase was unusually large, and in cash, there was no law against purchasing massive quantities of fertilizer.

In the summer of 1997, eco-terrorists destroyed a $1.3 million slaughterhouse to protest animal cruelty. The weapon used was a homemade incendiary device converting everyday fuel additives to a form of napalm. In combat situations all around the globe, crude improvised bombs are being used to attack and harass conventional forces.

The word "improvise" generally means to either do something impromptu, or to create something out of necessity from whatever materials happen to be available. The IED is in many ways an ideal terrorist weapon because the materials used are often widely available, inexpensive, and difficult to trace. Similarly IEDs can also be easily transported, difficult to immediately recognize, and their lethality may be enhanced by using everyday items such as nails, ball bearings, or scrap metal. In other cases, simply placing an IED in a metal trashcan or mailbox may dramatically increase the ability of the device to maim and kill, turning the container into a source of shrapnel.

One of the most frightening things about IEDs is how easy it can be in some situations to overlook them, or not immediately recognize them as a bomb device. In many respects, one of the best strategies for dealing with an IED threat is always adhering to the simple security specialist principle: JDLR—Just Doesn't Look Right. Always be looking for that thing that seems out of place, unexplained, suspect, or just gives you that "gut feeling." The following will give you some information on common IEDs and safety rules.

Improvised Explosive Devices

Safety Rules

- Primary rule: If a suspected device is encountered, it should not be handled, and the area should be secured.
- Secondary rule: Always assume that there is more than one device present, whether it is a bombing, a threat, or a device that has been located.
- Never pick up or disassemble a pipe bomb or any other IED, even if someone else has.
- The powder in the threads can set it off, or it may have a timer and/or movement switch.

Common Improvised Devices

Pipe bombs are the most common and readily assembled device. Once ignited, the confined filler material produces heat and gas, and the nearly instantaneous build-up of pressure results in the pipe bomb's explosion. If the pipe bomb is filled with high explosives, then it is basically a hand grenade, and the pipe is ripped into many small, very high-velocity fragments at the time of detonation.

Time bombs are designed to give the bomber time to get away from the scene before the bomb detonates.

Molotov cocktails are incendiary destructive devices.

Booby-trapped bombs are devices fired by an unsuspecting person who disturbs an apparently harmless object or performs a presumably safe act.

Having the components of an explosive device in your possession without a certificate of possession for the explosives will constitute the crime of possession of a destructive device.

Just Because It Isn't Real Doesn't Mean It's Not a Crime!

ORS 166.385 Possession of hoax destructive device. (1) A person commits the crime of Possession of a Hoax Destructive Device if the person knowingly places another person in fear of serious physical injury by

a. possessing, manufacturing, selling, delivering, placing or causing to be placed a hoax destructive device; or
b. sending a hoax destructive device to another person

—Taken from *http://www.osp.state.or.us/html/improvised_explosives.html*

IEDs New Reality of Iraq Duty

Marine Corps Base Camp Pendleton, Calif. (Dec 19, 2003)—They look innocent enough. A soda can lying on the side of a road. Maybe a lump of overturned dirt or even a war trophy to show off after a deployment. Problem is they're turning out to be one of the deadliest weapons Coalition forces face in Iraq.

Building on fire. *Courtesy of AP/Wide World Photos.*

They're called improvised explosive devices, and they're largely to blame for many of the casualties inflicted on U.S. and allied troops on duty in Iraq. With Marines soon returning to the region, they too will have to face this often deceptive and sometimes undetectable tool of war.

"Improvised explosive devices are made on hand of readily available materials," said Master Gunnery Sgt. Samuel A. Larter, staff noncommissioned officer in-charge for 1st Explosive Ordnance Platoon with 1st Force Serce Support Group. "It is not a manufactured device like military munitions. They can be as simple or as complex as the builder decides."

FBI Lends a Hand

It's gotten so much attention, in fact, that the Federal Bureau of Investigation held a weeklong course at Marine Corps Air Station Yuma, Arizona, to show Marines the devastating effects of IEDs. Similar training was conducted here at Camp Pendleton and Marine Corps Air Station Miramar.

Special Agent Kevin G. Miles, a bomb technician with the FBI, has been training Marines in the explosive ordnance disposal field and in force protection billets alongside law enforcement officials.

According to Miles, the training teaches students to look for information that could lead to who made the bomb, what explosives were used, and just what advanced technologies were used in the weapon.

"The students learn how to identify what kind of material was used in making a bomb, so they know what resources are available to the terrorists," Miles said.

As the weeklong course progressed, students received instruction on how to identify explosives, telltale signs they leave behind, and the power they pack.

Seized guns and explosives in front of film on bin Laden. *Courtesy of Corbis Images.*

During the Yuma exercise, explosives ranging from dynamite to a home-made bomb were used to destroy a fuel tanker. The explosion caused collateral damage to one car parked to the side and to one parked in front of the large truck. Another explosion in the trunk of a car reduced it to a smoldering heap.

After examining evidence gathered from the burned debris, students pieced together what type of materials were used, how much was used—and, most importantly, who did it.

"With this type of attack, students see that the first explosion is designed to lure Marines, law enforcement, or paramedics to the scene," Miles said. "A short time later the second bomb in the car, which is not parked far away, is detonated, causing even more injuries."

Examples of IEDs
The truck bombing of the Marine barracks on Oct. 23, 1983, in Beirut, Lebanon, and the events of September 11, 2001, are examples of IED attacks, Larter said.

"They run the spectrum from the most simple—being basically a piece of pipe filled with a rapidly burning or explosive material and a piece of fuse stuck into it—to the far end that would be an improvised nuclear device, a full-fledged thermonuclear bomb home-built," Larter said. "The problem we run into in Iraq now is that everyone has free access to explosives and military ordnance because of all the caches and ammunition supply points that were abandoned during the war."

It's not just bomb-laden trucks, though.

Larter described some of the different IEDs that have been used in Iraq; not surprisingly, suicide vests were among the varied types.

Special Agent Scott Thorilin, a bomb technician with the Federal Bureau of Investigation, describes what materials are used to make explosives during a class on improvised explosive devices at Marine Corps Air Station Yuma, Ariz. Dec. 10, 2003. The detonation was part of a class given to Marines to help them guard against improvised explosive devices.
Photo by Sgt. Enrique S. Diaz.

"One of our teams recovered 280 of them [suicide vests] from a facility where they were making them in Iraq," Larter said.

Designed with twenty pounds of plastic explosive and lined with steel ball bearings, the leather vests "would have been devastating had they gotten out and been used," Larter said.

"The sheer amount of explosives and the way they packed the ball bearings, they had a giant, improvised claymore," he said.

Guarding Against IEDs

Master Sgt. Michael R. Button, an EOD team leader with 1st FSSG, said many of the casualties occurred because forces in Iraq are letting down their guard.

"They have become predictable," Button said. "Their movements are all on major main supply routes and they are using the same ones over, and over and over."

"They are used to the point where these people are setting these things up, they are taking the time to bring in a broke-down vehicle to block a lane to channel them into a kill zone and these are all observed sites where they have somebody sitting a couple hundred yards away and when they see the military convoy coming along, they fire it (IED)," said Button.

"Any place in the world where they are using IEDs or vehicle IEDs is because whoever the target is has become predictable," he added.

It's common sense and attention to the surrounding area that Marines should rely upon to guard against IEDs, Button said.

"The big thing that most Marines are pretty good about because units are always briefing them is if it is not something you were issued, don't pick it up," Button said. "They know the Marines will want to take military hardware. Anything they think a guy is going to bend over and pick up and want to take with them, they run the risk of booby trap."

Gut Instinct

"Trust your instinct. If you're in a situation where it doesn't feel right, it probably isn't," Miles added.

Unfortunately, children could be a sign of enemy presence.

"Americans don't look at children as part of the problem," said Gunnery Sgt. Rik L. Rarick, assistant operations and training chief for Marine Corps

Base. "Like a drug dealer in New York, he is not going to go out and sell the drugs himself. He is going to use the kids, so even if they get caught, they cannot be prosecuted."

Most well-known to Marines, though, is the danger of redundancy and routine, which leads to predictability.

"If you develop a schedule, someone is going to pick up on it," Button stated. "As soon as you develop a pattern, you make yourself vulnerable."

Federal Bureau of Investigation agents destroy a vehicle to simulate a terrorist attack at Marine Corps Air Station Yuma, Ariz. Dec. 10, 2003. Although the bomb was located in the trunk, only a charred frame shows it was ever a car. *Photo by Sgt. Enrique S. Diaz.*

It's a matter of keeping a sharp eye and a keen sense of awareness to guard against IEDs.

One of the most important resources Marines can use to stay alive is each other, Miles said.

"I was in Al Kut, my second night there . . . my teammate and I were called out for a Russian hand grenade in a can filled full with gasoline," explained Gunnery Sgt. William W. Moore, an EOD team leader 1st Force Service Support Group, of the earlier stages of the war. "They had pulled the pin and the spoon was resting against the side of the can. The way they had put it there, it actually defeated itself."

With the spoon caught on the side of the can, "it didn't allow the striker to go home and set off the explosive train," Moore said. "It was a huge threat then, and it has become more of a threat now. Iraq is an extremely dangerous place."

Identification and Addressing an IED Situation

The U.S. State Department's Office of Diplomatic Security has issued the following document regarding identfication and addressing an IED. Although no document or set of instructions regarding explosive devices could address every possible scenario or situation, the following should provide you with a good, working example of an IED recogniton and response procedure.

Department of State Publication 10428 Bureau of Diplomatic Security Bomb Threat Awareness

Introduction
This pamphlet is intended to provide an overview of improvised explosive devices (IEDs). IED is a term for an explosive device that is constructed

in an improvised manner designed to kill, maim, or destroy property. These devices are categorized by their container (i.e., vehicle bombs) and by the way they are initiated. IEDs are homemade and usually constructed for a specific target.

This pamphlet will provide you with basic information and should not be used in dealing with or dismantling an IED. Explosive ordnance disposal (EOD) technicians and local bomb squads are trained to accomplish this mission.

Descriptions
The design and placement of an IED is up to the imagination of the bomber. First and foremost it is an object, regardless of its disguise, that is not supposed to be there. The best and most effective defense is to be aware of your surroundings. Based on your threat, if you think it does not belong in your area, consider it suspicious.

External Appearances of an IED
IEDs can be contained in almost anything. The item must be carried or driven to where it will placed, so concealment or masking of the device will be necessary. The outer container can be, but not limited to the following:

> **Pipe Bombs**—steel or PCV pipe section with end caps in nearly any configuration are the most prevalent type of containers.
> **Briefcase/Box/Back-pack**—any style, color, or size; even as small as a cigarette pack.

WARNING! If an object is considered suspicious, **do not touch it or move it. Evacuate the area and notify authorities.** Any movement, however slight, may cause it to function.

Sampling of Possible Pipe Bomb Configurations
Internally Fused Pipe Bomb
Cigarette Pack Bomb (Small But Deadly)

Postal Service Mail—Because mail screening procedures implemented worldwide have proven successful, terrorists are looking for other ways to deliver devices. There is a long list of possible indicators; these are some of the most common:

- The package or letter has no postage, noncancelled postage, excessive postage, has been hand-delivered, or dropped off by a friend
- Sender is unknown or no return address available
- Addressee does not normally receive mail at that address
- Common words are misspelled
- Package emits a peculiar or suspicious odor
- Letter or package seems heavy or bulky for its size
- Package makes a ticking, buzzing, or whirring noise
- An unidentified person calls to ask if the letter or package was received

If the letter or parcel exhibits some of the indicators above, it could be considered suspect and the proper authorities should be notified. Never accept unexpected packages at your home, and make sure family members and clerical staff refuse unexpected mail.

Vehicle Bombs—By far the most devastating (may contain thousands of pounds of explosives), vehicle bombs can be the easiest to conceal. Indicators may include inappropriate decals or an unfamiliar vehicle parked in your area. The device can be placed anywhere in the vehicle.

A vehicle bomb is intended to create mass casualties or cause extensive property damage.

Existing Objects—Items that seem to have a purpose can be substituted or used as the bomb container. Some examples are fire extinguishers, propane bottles, trashcans, gasoline cans, or books.

Internal Components
All devices require a firing train that consists of a fusing system, detonator, and main charge (explosive or incendiary). Any switch that can turn something on or off can be used to activate a device. Fusing systems can be categorized into the following:

> **Time**—preset to detonate or arm the device at an unknown interval of time. The timer may be mechanical such as a kitchen timer, wind-up wristwatch, pocket watch, or electronic, i.e., digital wristwatches, integrated circuit chips, or solid-state timers.
> **Victim activated**—may be designed to function by pressure, pull, movement, vibration, tension release, or tilting the item. Booby-trapped is the best way to describe it.
> **Command**—sending a signal via radio frequency or through a hidden wire from a remote location.
> **Environmental**—designed to function when there is a change in temperature, pressure, light, sound, or magnetic field.
> **Cap Detonator or Blasting cap**—The detonator is a small explosive component, widely available from military and commercial sources, which can be initiated by a variety of mechanical and electrical devices. With the increased availability of blasting caps, fabrication and use of improvised detonators are on the decline. However, the possibility of encountering one cannot be excluded.

> Main charges can be used to burn, detonate, or both, depending on the bombers desired effect. Explosives fall into three general categories.

> **Commercial Explosives**—used for property demolition, mining and blasting operations. Commercial explosives come in assorted shapes and consistencies including binary (two-part), slurries, gels, and standard dynamites.
> **Military Explosives**—differ from commercial explosives in several respects. Military explosives must have high rates of detonation,

be relatively insensitive, and be usable underwater. TNT, C_4 plastic explosives, and military dynamite are some of the more common explosives associated with the military.

Improvised Explosives—when manufactured explosives are not available, it is relatively easy to obtain all of the ingredients necessary to make improvised explosives, such as ammonium nitrate (fertilizer), and potassium/sodium chlorate.

Incendiary—improvised devices may be designed to burn. Included are some common materials used in incendiary devices: gasoline, iodine crystals, magnesium, glycerin, and aluminum powder.

Unknown—Because of the vast variety of explosives and incendiary materials, any unknown solid, powder, crystal, or liquid should be treated with respect and not handled.

Where IEDs Can Be Placed

IEDs may be placed anywhere. A bomber wants to succeed without being caught. The level of security and the awareness of personnel will determine where and how an IED will be placed. Common areas where IEDs might be placed include the following:

Outside areas: trash cans, dumpsters, mailboxes, bushes, storage areas, and parked vehicles.

Inside buildings: Inside mail rooms, restrooms, trash cans, planters, inside desks or storage containers, false ceilings, utility closets, areas hidden by drapes or curtains, behind pictures, boiler rooms, under stairwells, recently repaired or patched segments of walls, floors, or ceilings, or in plain view.

In the event that a suspicious device is found, notify the proper authorities in accordance with existing bomb threat procedures. Security personnel should initiate and coordinate the evacuation in accordance with existing procedures, if necessary. Prior to their arrival, immediate actions should be taken.

Do not panic! Using adequate cover (frontal and overhead) get as far away from the device as possible. Keep away from glass windows that can become lethal fragmentation.

Do not look out the window to see what is going on! If the device is located outside the building, get low to the floor and go to the other side. Increasing your distance from a suspicious device increases the chances of survival after a detonation.

WARNING! Secondary devices are always a possibility. A common tactic is to detonate a device attracting then detonate a second device to inflict heavy casualties.

Appendix A

Auto Search Checklist

How to Search
Start with a 360° sweep, looking around and under vehicle. Do not focus your attention on the vehicle to be searched. Be alert for booby traps and secondary devices. Inspect the area for suspicious items such as wire, tape, or string. You may spot a suspicious object underneath or attached to the vehicle without approaching it.

Be systematic, start and finish your search at a predetermined point.

Look for
Suspicious packages or items in, on, attached, or under the vehicle

Tool marks on vehicle or other indications of forced entry

Where to Search
Exterior:

- Exhaust pipe (ensure nothing inside)
- Inspect the gas tank
- Fuel entry point and neck of fuel tank
- Underneath the vehicle
- Wheel wells, tires and brakes

Interior:

- Under the seats, front and rear
- Under dashboard, driver's side and passenger side
- Under the headrest
- Sun visor
- Any areas where you think a bomb could be concealed

WARNING! Do not sit in or move the vehicle prior to searching the engine and trunk compartments.

Engine compartment:

- Raise hood slowly while searching for hanging wires, tape, or packages attached to the underside
- Check the battery and wiring
- Scan the firewall (rear wall of engine compartment)
- Open the air cleaner
- Be familiar with the general appearance of an engine and components.

Trunk or luggage storage area:

- Slowly raise the trunk while inspecting underside for suspicious items such as wires, string or packages
- Inspect rear wall of trunk (back or rear seat)

- Inspect wiring on rear light assemblies
- Check spare tire (let a little air out)

Appendix B

Building and Room Searches

The search should be systematic, thorough, and quick. Two-person search teams and people most familiar with the building or room have proven to be the most effective and efficient method.

How to Search

Do not alter existing environmental conditions.

Listen for suspicious or unusual sounds after entering the room, background noise may mask sounds such as ticking or buzzing.

Because a radio-controlled device may be present and pick up on stray RF, as well as pose a hazard to electric blasting caps, do not use hand-held radios for communication within thirty-five feet of suspicious items or areas not properly searched and cleared.

Prior to entering a room, and during a search, check for trip wires, and possible indications of pressure-sensitive devices .

Be systematic. Using one's body as a reference, search from floor to waist, from waist to chin, from chin to ceiling. Do not forget to check false ceilings if applicable.

Inspect wall hangings, plants, or other decorations.

If a Suspect Item Is Encountered

Evacuate and secure the area.

Notify the proper authorities in accordance with your existing bomb plan.

—Taken from *http://www.state.gov/documents/organization/19692.pdf*

Device Containment

As a homeland security specialist, you will not be called upon to move, transport, or disarm an IED. Such devices are only to be handled and disarmed by qualified, certified members of an Explosive Ordnance Disposal (EOD) team. EOD members are usually members of special law enforcement or military units, or occasionally a highly trained, private contractor.

These units have special training and material to positively identify, contain, transport, and disarm an explosive device.

Navy EOD Joins Forces with Army, Helps Clear Ordnance Out of Baghdad

BAGHDAD, Iraq (NNS)—While much of the media's attention remains focused on the hunt for weapons of mass destruction in Iraq, U.S. Navy

Explosive Ordnance Disposal (EOD) personnel are diligently working to protect coalition troops and Iraqi citizens from smaller and more deadly tools of individual devastation.

Buried mines, unexploded ordnance, rocket-propelled grenades, and objects called Improvised Explosive Devices, or IEDs, are just a few of the malicious objects threatening the future peace and stability of Iraq.

For the past six months, fourteen Navy EOD technicians from Norfolk, Virginia, and currently assigned to Special Operations Task Force 56 based in Bahrain, have been fully integrated into U.S. Army EOD units spread throughout Baghdad, responding to daily calls from U.S. and coalition military police, Iraqi police, and even Iraqi citizens, to investigate suspicious objects. While conditions are improving daily in Iraq, there are still those opposed to the U.S. presence who continue to attack people and infrastructure with explosives designed to wreak havoc on military convoys, innocent civilians and ultimately, the rebuilding process.

"Probably the biggest threat to coalition personnel in Iraq, and especially in Baghdad, comes from the enemy hiding explosives within mostly commonplace objects, such as cola cans, trash bags, and even MRE [Meals-Ready-to-Eat] packages, making them very dangerous IEDs," said Navy Chief Petty Officer Charles Hashek, who is working with the Army's Third Brigade Combat Team (BCT) operating in Baghdad. Hashek is the current Navy EOD record holder thus far in his one-month-old deployment, with twenty-four disarmed IEDs.

"One of the positive aspects of the work we're doing is that we're all gaining a lot of experience in handling IEDs. We've had to continually adjust our tactics and how we employ ourselves and our equipment in order to keep up with the changing tactics of the enemy. We're keeping a long list of lessons learned to pass down to our training commands."

"Neither the Navy nor the Army has ever dealt with this number of IEDs in such a short period of time," said Army Lt. Col. Tim Eberhard, commander of all EOD forces in country.

"Thirty-seven teams handle between 3,800 to 4,000 incidents per year in the U.S. Here in Iraq, our teams have responded to more than 4,500 IED calls in the past 3 months alone."

Small, inexpensive, easily constructed, and now with relatively sophisticated remote-detonation capability, material for constructing IEDs is easy enough to find.

"Any explosives that can be looted, stolen, or easily obtained are used by the insurgents to make IEDs," explained Army 1st. Sgt. Larry Cushing. "The city has ammunition all over the place—in schools, mosques, and even hospitals. We find it everywhere, from World War I-era bombs to rocket-propelled grenades."

Insurgents simply steal the hardware, remove the explosives, and pack the material into items that would normally not warrant a passing glance. In a densely packed city teeming with loose trash on sidewalks, streets, and in buildings, IEDs are almost impossible to find until it is too late.

The solution for reducing and ultimately eliminating the IED threat is to collect this unexploded ordnance (UXO) and destroy it using demolition procedures in controlled environments. The challenge is moving the UXO from locations throughout the country to captured ammo holding areas (CAHAs) or safe-holding areas (SHAs), then destroying the weapons in safe disposal areas (SDAs).

"We are now moving roughly 60 five-ton truckloads of ammunition per day out of Baghdad alone," said Eberhard. "With the help of the 4 civilian contracting companies we recently hired, we should be able to get up to 100 truckloads per day. That should give you an idea of just how much ammo is still out there."

The joint Navy and Army EOD forces of Third BCT dispose of about 2,000 to 2,500 pounds of ordnance each week. Any arms not destroyed by coalition EOD forces will be stored for possible future use by the Iraqi army currently being developed and trained by coalition forces.

Although a few of the Navy EOD members had previously worked with Army personnel in exercises such as Bright Star in Egypt, most had never before operated with their counterparts. Fortunately, thanks to their common language revolving around "blowing stuff up," these unique teammates quickly bonded into cohesive units capable of effectively working together to save lives and Iraqi property.

"The Navy is strong on water, and the Army is strong on land," said Army Sgt. Keith Adams. "Since we've been working together, we've tried to use each other's strengths to our advantage. I wish we worked more together during our training, but at least the situation here is giving us a chance to learn from each other."

Army Sgt. Micah Long agreed. "At first there were challenges. The Navy teams are organized differently than our Army teams, for example the Navy's team leader is an E-7 [Chief Petty Officer]. Our team leader is an E-6 [Staff Sgt.]. Our teams are also different sizes, and some of the equipment we use is different. But overall, because we have the same goals, the integration is working," Long said.

Navy EOD's ability to deploy quickly with minimal equipment and personnel also worked in the Army's favor.

"Navy EOD teams are highly mobile, and with the Army already stretched a bit thin, it made sense for us to step in and integrate with their highly capable teams already in place," Hashek said. "U.S. forces have never had to deal with IED situations like this before. Our primary challenges revolve around Baghdad's urban environment and not having enough interpreters

Explosive disposal robot. *Courtesy of the Military Picture Library/Corbis Images.*

to assist us in dealing with the crowds that result from our presence during IED calls. We're not doing training missions out here."

The teams expect to be in country until at least after Christmas. But even though they'd like to be home with their families during the holidays, these dedicated sailors and soldiers know their mission is important.

"I miss my family, but I love the work," Long said. Hashek agreed, "It's been an experience so far. It feels good to be contributing to the future of Iraq."

—Taken from *http://www.freerepublic.com/focus/news/1003664/posts*

The following information comes from a private group specializing in EOD operations.

Identify, prioritize, and execute research and development projects that satisfy interagency requirements to more safely and effectively render terrorist devices safe. Particular emphasis is placed on technologies that safely diagnose and defeat improvised explosive devices (IEDs), improvised chemical and radiological devices, and vehicle-borne improvised explosive devices (VBIED).

The Improvised Device Defeat (IDD) subgroup develops prototype hardware and advanced techniques to render-safe improvised terrorist devices as well as information and training systems for conducting operational and tactical threat assessment of terrorist devices. These systems enhance the operational capability of the military explosive ordnance disposal (EOD) and civilian bomb squad community.

Focus Areas

Defeat
Military EOD technicians and civilian bomb squad personnel must be able to defeat and/or render-safe improvised terrorist devices. Develop defeat technologies to enhance the capabilities of bomb technicians to render improvised terrorist devices safe. Develop defeat technologies for explosive, chemical, radiological, and vehicle-borne terrorist devices.

Diagnostics
Develop technologies to nonintrusively determine terrorist device type by function. Provide rapid diagnostic capability for large devices including Vehicle Borne Improvised Explosive Devices (VBIED). Focus is placed on those elements of diagnostic technology necessary to address the current Defense Technology Objectives for diagnostic analysis of improvised explo-

sive devices in the areas of remote and nonintrusive identification of explosive compounds; operational evaluation of neutron interrogation technology; and non-intrusive detection of anti-handling devices associated with improvised explosive devices (IED).

Emerging Explosive Threats

Develop tools, equipment and procedures for bomb technicians to safely and effectively defeat improvised devices built from improvised materials to include nonideal explosives. Analysis of the materials and mixtures that are emerging from threat devices will determine their performance characteristics and provide a better solution for detection and defeat of these devices.

EOD Operational Tools

Responding to an Improvised Explosive Device incident requires detailed coordination and planning by the bomb technician's on scene commander or officer in charge. Develop enhanced command and control tools, data management software, and other critical incident technologies to increase the safety and effectiveness of the EOD and bomb disposal communities. Provide latest intelligence, technical, and operational trends through community outreach programs.

Remote Control Vehicles (RCVs)/Tools

Develop technologies to improve the performance and reliability of robotic systems for EOD and bomb squad technicians. The increasing complexity of the terrorist threat forces bomb technicians to conduct the majority of their missions remotely. Develop and integrate remote technologies and techniques including advanced robotic platforms, manipulation, control systems, navigation technologies, payloads, and communications.

Discussion Questions

1) "IED" stands for _____ _____ _____.

2) To improvise means to create something out of necessity, using whatever _____ are _____.

3) A primary safety rule for addressing an IED threat is: If a suspected device is encountered, it should not be _____, and the area should be _____.

4) Never pick up or disassemble a pipe bomb or any other IED, even if _____ _____ _____.

5) If a pipe bomb is filled with high explosive, then it is basically a _____ _____.

6) Devices fired by an unsuspecting person who disturbs an apparently harmless object or performs a presumably safe act are said to be _____ _____.

7) IEDs may be placed in everyday items such as _____ cans.

8) Specially teams that are trained and equipped to inspect, transport and disarm IEDs are known as _____ _____ _____ teams.

9) An IED placed and transported inside a common conveyance such as a car, van, or truck is known as a _____ _____ Improvised Explosive Device or VBIED.

10) Another important IED safety rule is to always _____ that there is more than one device present.

Answers

1) Improvised Explosive Device

2) Materials, available

3) Handled, secured

4) Someone else has

5) Hand Grenade

6) Booby trapped

7) Soda

8) Explosive Ordnance Disposal

9) Vehicle Borne

10) Assume

6 The Nuclear and Radiological Threat

Atomic bomb explosion. *Courtesy of Bettman/Corbis Images.*

Overview:

"My God, what have we done?" wrote Robert Lewis, the co-pilot of the B-29 bomber nicknamed "Enola Gay," when he looked back over his shoulder at the enormous mushroom cloud rising over the Japanese city of Hiroshima. World War II was ending, but the era of nuclear arms had just begun.

Since then the world has had to deal with the awesome theat of nuclear and radiological warfare, through both the spectre of full-scale global thermonuclear war, as well as through the notion of nuclear terrorism or low-intensity conflict. This chapter will begin your examination of addressing the catastrophic menace represented by nuclear or radiological weaponry.

Chapter Objectives:

- *Explain what is a nuclear and radiological device.*
- *Define the threat of nuclear proliferation.*
- *Explain the threats of a nuclear/radiological weapon including blast, fallout, radiation, shockwave, and psychological anxiety.*

"Nuclear" deals with the energy released or absorbed during reactions taking place at the nuclei of atoms. "Radioactivity" refers to the property of having atoms break up and send out radiation capable of penetrating bodies and producing electrical and chemical effects.

The discovery of the ability to split atoms revolutionized much of modern science, including the ability to make terrible weapons. In the summer of 1945, although the war in Europe had been won by the allies, the war in the Pacific raged on. Imperial Japan had shown the ability and willingness to fight to the death rather than surrender. When it looked as if victory over Japan might take additional years and millions of lives on both sides, President Harry Truman made a decision to use the new atomic bomb against the Japanese. On August 6, 1945, and August 9, 1945, the U.S. Army Air Corps dropped two atom bombs on the cities of Hiroshima and Nagasaki respectively. The carnage, loss of life, and utter destruction caused in just seconds by these single bombs was equal to the devastation of traditional mass bombings involving hundreds of bombers and thousands of conventional bombs. The thought that the United States now possessed a new super-bomb that could eliminate entire cities at a time convinced Japan it was most prudent to issue a surrender.

Since the end of the World War II, huge arsenals of nuclear weapons were developed. The Cold War became a long, tense standoff between ideological rivals each with nuclear arsenals sufficient to destroy the world several times over.

Since the end of the Cold War, new concerns regarding elements of complete nuclear weapons falling into the hands of terrorists or desperate rogue nations have escalated dramatically.

The homeland security specialist in the new world must be prepared to address and function in the face of nuclear and radiological threats.

The Specialized Threat of Nuclear and Radiological Weapons

The attacks of September 11, 2001, have provided a wake-up call for facing the threat of nuclear terrorism. The Nuclear Control Institute, since its inception in 1981, has been analyzing the risks of nuclear terrorism and seeking to alert policymakers and the public to the danger. There was a solid basis for concern long before the attacks of September 11.

Iran threatened attacks against U.S. reactors as early as 1987. Trial testimony has revealed that Osama bin Laden's Al Qaeda training camps offered instruction in "urban warfare" against "enemies' installations" including power plants. It is prudent to assume, especially after the highly coordinated surprise attacks on the World Trade Center and the Pentagon, that bin Laden's soldiers have done their homework and are fully capable of attacking nuclear plants for maximum effect. It is also clear that bin Laden was seeking nuclear explosive materials (plutonium or highly enriched uranium) and know-how for building atomic bombs, and other dangerous nuclear materials for use in "dirty bombs" to spread radioactive contamination with conventional high explosives.

In 1986, the Nuclear Control Institute, in cooperation with the Institute for Studies in International Terrorism of the State University of New York, convened the International Task Force on Prevention of Nuclear Terrorism, comprised of twenty-six nuclear scientists and industrialists, current and former government officials, and experts on terrorism from nine countries. The report issued by the task force, along with more than twenty commissioned studies, remains the most definitive examination of nuclear terrorism in the unclassified literature.

The task force warned that the "probability of nuclear terrorism is increasing" because of a number of factors, including "the growing incidence, sophistication, and lethality of conventional forms of terrorism;" the vulnerability of nuclear power and research reactors to sabotage; and weapons-usable nuclear materials to theft. The task force's warnings and its recommendations for reducing vulnerabilities, many of which went unheeded, are all the more relevant in today's threat environment of sophisticated and suicidal terrorists dedicated to mass killing and destruction.

Recent Developments

There is now intense national and international attention to the risks of nuclear terrorism. The possibilities that Al Qaeda might acquire the materials and the knowledge for building nuclear weapons or "dirty bombs," or might attack commercial nuclear-power facilities to trigger a nuclear meltdown, are of particular concern. The Nuclear Control Institute has been alerting the public and policymakers to these risks, seeking emergency measures to reduce the vulnerabilites, and monitoring and assessing the responses of industry, governments and international agencies.

What follows are some of the key issues pertaining to the risks of nuclear terrorism:

Are reactors adequately protected against attack?
For nearly twenty years, the Nuclear Control Institute (NCI), has pressed the U.S. Nuclear Regulatory Commission, to upgrade security at nuclear power plants. In 1994, we and the California-based Committee to Bridge the Gap finally succeeded in getting NRC to require nuclear-power plant operators to install defenses against truck bombs, although we remain concerned that these protective measures are inadequate to defend against the larger bombs used by terrorists since the 1993 truck-bomb attack against the World Trade Center.

Current NRC security regulations do not address the magnitude of threat demonstrated by the September 11, 2001, attacks. NRC standards require that nuclear plant operators protect against a much smaller number of attackers than involved in these attacks. Yet, even under the current weak standards, the armed guards at nearly half of the nuclear plants tested in NRC-supervised security exercises have failed to repel mock terrorist attacks or prevent simulated destruction of redundant safety systems that in real attacks could cause severe core damage, meltdown, and catastrophic radioactive releases.

This outcome is all the more worrisome because the NRC's mock terrorist exercises severely limit the tactics, weapons, and explosives used by the adversary, do not test plant defenses against attacks from the air or from the water, and do not test whether guards could repel an attack on the spent-fuel pools at plant sites that contain many times more deadly radioactivity than the reactor cores. In addition, in response to industry complaints that the exercises are unfairly severe, the NRC is now preparing to shift responsibility for supervising the exercises to the plant operators themselves. Current events clearly demonstrate that nuclear power plant security is too important to be left to industry self-assessment or to the level of protection that industry is willing to pay for. The heightened security at nuclear plants since 9/11 still falls far short of the military-type protection we have recommended. The NRC is undertaking a "top to bottom" review of plant security with no indication of how long it will take to complete and implement or what additional measures will be required.

Despite nuclear industry claims to the contrary, it is highly unlikely that nuclear-power reactor containment domes are robust enough to withstand a direct hit from a jumbo jetliner. Dr. Edwin Lyman, NCI's scientific director, has calculated that a direct, high-speed hit by a large commercial passenger jet "would in fact have a high likelihood of penetrating a containment building" that houses a power reactor. "Following such an assault," Dr. Lyman said, "the possibility of an unmitigated loss-of-coolant accident and significant release of radiation into the environment is a very real one." Such a release, whether caused by an air strike, or by a ground or water assault, or by insider sabotage could result in tens of thousands of cancer deaths.

Could terrorists build nuclear weapons?
A study prepared for Nuclear Control Institute by five former U.S. nuclear weapons designers concluded that a sophisticated terrorist group would be capable of designing and building a workable nuclear bomb from stolen plutonium or highly enriched uranium, with potential yields in the kiloton range. This risk must be taken seriously, particularly in light of documented attempts by Al Qaeda to acquire nuclear material and nuclear-weapon design information. Despite claims to the contrary from plutonium-fuel advocates in the nuclear power industry, effective and devastating weapons could be made using "reactor-grade" plutonium, hundreds of tons of which are processed, stored, and circulated around the world in civilian nuclear commerce.

Would we know if fissile materials were stolen?
Less than eighteen pounds of plutonium or fifty-five pounds of highly enriched uranium are sufficient to make a nuclear bomb, but these materials circulate in civilian nuclear commerce by the ton. A crucial defense

against nuclear terrorism and nuclear proliferation is to end civilian commerce in plutonium and highly enriched uranium and to convert military stocks of these nuclear explosives into non-weapon-usable forms as soon as possible. Even the International Atomic Energy Agency (IAEA), a staunch promoter of nuclear power, has acknowledged an urgent need to improve protection of civilian and military nuclear materials at plant sites as well as in transit.

Nuclear Control Institute has long been a critic of the inability of IAEA inspections and other "safeguards" measures to detect large process losses of plutonium and highly enriched uranium or to ensure adequate protection against thefts of these materials in transit and in storage. IAEA physical-security standards now only apply to international shipments of nuclear materials, not to the facilities where these materials are processed, stored and used. Because of these shortcomings, we may not even know if materials that could be used in nuclear weapons is missing.

The vulnerabilities of Russian nuclear installations have been well documented, but protection of many Western facilities is also inadequate. Shortcomings in security of materials and warheads have even been documented in the U.S. nuclear-weapons complex. The situation in such emerging nuclear-weapon states as India and Pakistan is even more troubling. Contingency responses to theft and smuggling of materials or warheads must be further developed, and technical capabilities for finding and disarming terrorist bombs must be improved.

Are nuclear weapons vulnerable to theft?

Although generally better secured than nuclear materials, there is still a possibility that nuclear weapons could be stolen by terrorists. In 1986, the NCI\SUNY International Task Force on the Prevention of Nuclear Terrorism raised concerns about the vulnerability of tactical nuclear weapons to theft. Since the 1991 collapse of the Soviet Union, the United States and Russia have removed nearly all their tactical nuclear weapons from overseas deployment. However, there has been continued speculation that some number of Soviet "suitcase bombs" (small portable nuclear weapons) remain unaccounted for, with unconfirmed reports that they have been obtained by Al Qaeda. Also, security weaknesses have been identified at nuclear weapons laboratories and other installations in both Russia and the United States. Further, the security of India and Pakistan's embryonic nuclear arsenals is uncertain, as is the question of whether weapons in these states are secured by Permissive Action Link (PAL) systems (coded, electronic locks). In the United States, the Nuclear Emergency Search Team (NEST) is a highly secretive federal inter-agency group that has had the responsibility for more than twenty years for locating and de-activating terrorist nuclear weapons, but its technical ability to fulfill this daunting mission if the need arose remains uncertain.

How vulnerable are Russian weapons, fissile materials, and reactors?
Since the collapse of the Soviet Union in 1991, the uncertain status of nuclear weapons, fissile materials, and nuclear scientists in Russia and other former Soviet republics are widely regarded as posing perhaps the most immediate threat of nuclear proliferation and nuclear terrorism. Despite significant assistance from the United States over the last ten years, many of Russia's nuclear facilities seem poorly secured, and there is still no comprehensive, verifiable system of nuclear materials accountancy. No one even knows for certain how much nuclear weapons material the Soviet Union produced. With confirmed incidents of Russian-origin fissile materials turning up for sale on the black market, this danger is more than hypothetical.

Controversy also rages over how to dispose of plutonium recovered from dismantled Russian warheads. The Russian government and the Bush Administration plan to fabricate excess Russian and U.S. plutonium into mixed-oxide fuel ("MOX") for irradiation in nuclear-power reactors (including Russia's BN-600 prototype fast breeder reactor). However, a safer, less costly, and more secure alternative would be to combine the plutonium with highly radioactive waste in molten glass. This "immobilized" plutonium, embedded in massive, highly radioactive glass blocks, could be directly disposed of in a geologic repository, and would prevent the circulation of tens of tons of plutonium in civilian commerce throughout Russia (as well as the United States) that the MOX-fuel approach would necessitate. (More information on plutonium disposition is available at www.nci.org/nci-wpu.htm).

NCI has supported U.S. assistance to secure Russia's nuclear weapons, materials and facilities under the Defense Department's Cooperative Threat Reduction Program ("Nunn-Lugar") since its inception in 1991. NCI has played a leading role in advocating the shutdown of Russia's military plutonium production reactors, and has strongly and successfully opposed Russian proposals to convert these reactors to bomb-usable HEU fuel rather than closing them or converting to low-enriched uranium fuel.

Are "dirty bombs" a major terrorism risk?
"Dirty bombs," known also as radiation dispersal devices (RDDs), are weapons that use conventional explosives to disperse radioactive materials, thereby augmenting the injury and property damage caused by the explosion. The capability of an RDD to cause significant harm is strongly dependent on the type of radioactive material used and the means used to disperse it. Other important variables include location of the device and prevailing weather conditions.

Radioactive materials that could be employed in RDDs range from radiation sources used in medicine or industry to spent nuclear fuel from nuclear power plants. In general, the physical protection requirements for radioactive sources widely used in commerce are quite lax; however, the largest radiotherapy sources typically contain no more than a few hundred curies of gamma-emitters like cesium-137 or cobalt-60. Sources of this size, if removed from their shielded containers, could present an acute hazard to individuals within the vicinity (tens of meters) of the source. However, an effective dispersal of the material would tend to dilute the concentration downwind of the site of detonation to relatively low levels quickly. Acute radiation hazard would probably be confined to an area of a few hundred meters' radius around the site for a ground-level release. However, the occurrence of localized areas of contamination further downwind would be a possibility, depending on the meteorology.

Standard modeling of these events in the midst of densely populated urban areas indicates no acute fatalities from radiation exposure and few cancer deaths. However, these models do not take into account the additional consequences that might occur from radioactive contamination of wounds suffered by people injured during the blast, which could cause additional internal contamination, or direct radiation exposure, which could impair the immune systems of burn victims and thwart their recovery.

The most concentrated sources of large quantities of radioactive isotopes are contained in spent nuclear fuel from power plants, but these sources are relatively inaccessible due to their size (several meters in height), weight (half a metric ton) and radiation barrier (thousands to tens of thousands of rem per hour surface dose). A single spent fuel assembly typically can be transported only in a shielded shipping cask weighing many tons. However, if such a package, usually containing radioactive inventories hundreds or thousands of times greater than those of the medical sources, could be acquired by terrorists or sabotaged during transport in an urban area, severe consequences could result, including thousands of latent cancer fatalities.

—Taken from *http://www.nci.org/nci-nt.htm#book*

Nuclear Proliferation

Executive Summary

Draft Special Report, Mr. Robert Banks (United Kingdom), Nov. 1994

Nuclear proliferation is one of the principal threats to international security. Nuclear weapons technology, once only available to the most technologically advanced nations, is now within reach of virtually any nation with a modest or relatively modest scientific and industrial base, provided it has the determination and the resources.

Events in North Korea and recent reports of nuclear smuggling from the former Soviet Union have highlighted this problem at a critical time. Next year, the 164 signatories of the nuclear Non-Proliferation Treaty (NPT) must meet to decide whether to renew the treaty. Indefinite and unconditional renewal is the goal of most industrialized nations but this outcome is far from being assured. The last review conference, in 1990, finished without producing an agreed text due to disputes in several important areas.

One central dispute was whether the nuclear weapons nations had done enough to reduce their own nuclear arsenals. This issue could still raise substantial disagreements, despite the remarkable progress in arms control since 1990. Progress towards a complete ban on nuclear testing will be one key issue, and it remains to be seen whether enough progress will be made to satisfy some NPT parties who see this as the "yardstick" for assessing progress in nuclear disarmament. Other arms control initiatives will clearly influence the outcome of the NPT conference, including the proposal to cap the production of fissile material for weapons purposes and to place surplus military stocks of fissile material under international safeguards.

Other factors might include the nuclear weapons nations agreeing to provide stronger security assurances to the non-nuclear weapons states. Whatever the outcome of the Renewal Conference, efforts to curb nuclear proliferation must continue. Since the war to liberate Kuwait from Iraqi occupation, the International Atomic Energy Agency has shown itself to be far more than a "toothless tiger," but it must be given the resources and the freedom to strengthen its work in preventing nuclear proliferation.

And the international community must show that it has the resolve to deal firmly with nations outside the Non-Proliferation Treaty as well as those nations that violate the Treaty.

Introduction*

1. Nuclear proliferation is one of the gravest threats to international security in the post-Cold War world. A nation acquiring nuclear weapons could menace neighboring nations and—by acquiring suitable missile technology—could pose a far more widespread threat. During 1994, the dangers of nuclear proliferation have been vividly highlighted by three particular developments:

   - North Korean nuclear activities and the crisis arising from North Korea's refusal to permit international inspection of its nuclear facilities.
   - Evidence of "leakage" of nuclear-related materials from Russia and other former Soviet states.
   - The assertion by Pakistan's former Prime Minister, Mr. Nava Sharif that his country had indeed created and deployed nuclear weapons.

2. Events of this kind have underlined the importance of dealing with nuclear proliferation and have focused even more attention on the Non-Proliferation Treaty (NPT) Renewal Conference which will take place in New York in April and May 1995. At the last NPT Review Conference in 1990, many differences emerged among the participants to the extent that the conference closed without producing an agreed text. Although several of the sources of disagreement in 1990

have subsided, renewal of the NPT is certainly not assured. And fail-ure to renew the NPT would be a major blow to efforts to curb nuclear weapons proliferation.

3. The purpose of this report is to survey recent regional developments in nuclear proliferation and to assess the challenges to the non-pro-liferation regime. The Report concludes with recommendations for improving the likelihood of NPT renewal and for strengthening the non-proliferation regime.

Recent Developments in Nuclear Proliferation

The Middle East

The Middle East has long been regarded as a key problem area for the non-proliferation regime. The region's volatile combination of tension, hostil-ity, and activity related to weapons of mass destruction poses many serious challenges.

Israel

Israel is thought to have begun developing nuclear weapons in the early 1970s, allegedly in cooperation with South Africa. According to some esti-mates, Israel could very rapidly make up to one hundred nuclear warheads operational. Israel maintains that it will not be the first state in the region to introduce nuclear weapons. This is usually taken to mean that weapons are held one step short of final assembly. The military nuclear program is centered on the Dimona nuclear research center in the Negev desert.

Israel has not admitted that it has a military nuclear program since this would no doubt lead to an adverse international political reaction. On the other hand, it has not sought to deny its existence too vigorously, thereby making any potential aggressor cautious about military confrontation.

Pressure is mounting on Israel to renounce its military nuclear activities and accede to the Non-Proliferation Treaty. Its military nuclear potential is seen as a key motive for other nations in the region to maintain an interest in nuclear weapons technology and other weapons of mass destruc-tion such as chemical arms. In December 1993, the United Nations Gen-eral Assembly adopted a resolution sponsored by Egypt which called upon Israel to forswear ownership of nuclear weapons and to become a signa-tory to the NPT. The Middle East peace process might lead to movement in this direction and Israel's prime minister, Yitzhak Rabin, has expressed willingness to make bilateral agreements with neighboring states on cre-ating a nuclear-free zone.[1] Israeli opinion seems divided over United States President Bill Clinton's proposal for a global ban on fissile material pro-duction.[2] Some government officials have expressed support for the pro-posal while others have expressed reservations, arguing that Israel's future defense options should not be limited by any agreement.

Iraq

The Iraqi nuclear program, uncovered by United Nations inspectors after the war to liberate Kuwait from Iraqi occupation, showed the inadequacy of existing international measures to control nuclear proliferation. Iraq's progress towards building nuclear weapons surprised the international community and was one of the main reasons for re-appraisals of proliferation controls.

The dismantlement of Iraq's military nuclear potential is still in progress, and it was recently reported that three shipments of nuclear fuel (enough to produce one or two crude nuclear weapons) were transferred from Iraq to Russia for reprocessing. This was believed to be the last nuclear material in Iraq. According to Hans Blix, the Director General of the IAEA, as a result of twenty-one inspection missions in Iraq, the IAEA has concluded that "in all essential aspects, the nuclear weapons program is mapped and is either destroyed or neutralized."[3] Even so, the search continues for some important equipment and documents.

In late 1993, Iraq agreed to the permanent monitoring of facilities related to the development and production of weapons of mass destruction in accordance with United Nations Security Council Resolution 715. This monitoring system is now in place, but the raising of economic sanctions is not likely to be discussed by the Security Council until these have operated satisfactorily for some time. Iraq now poses no imminent threat to the non-proliferation regime but, without external monitoring of relevant facilities, it could make rapid progress in military nuclear technology. At present, it seems that the international community will have to maintain a watchful eye over Iraq.

Iran

Despite acceding to the Non-Proliferation Treaty in 1970, Iran is believed to have pursued a limited military nuclear program since the 1970s, with only a brief lull after the 1979 Islamic revolution. There were reports in 1993 about Iranian efforts to recruit nuclear weapons scientists and purchase nuclear weapons from the former Soviet Union but these allegations remain unsubstantiated.

In 1985, Iran purchased a nuclear reactor from China and plans to buy two additional 300 MW reactors from the same source. Iran is trying to complete construction of a nuclear reactor which was being built by Siemens of Germany but which Siemens will not complete due to the German government's concern about Iranian nuclear activities. In addition, negotiations are taking place between Iran and Russia over the construction of a nuclear power plant. Financial problems, however, have essentially frozen these projects for the time being. Iran's interest in nuclear power, despite its large reserves of fossil fuels, naturally raises questions about Iranian motives.

Iran's military nuclear facilities are reportedly located in Isfahan, Karaj, and Mohalem Kalayah. Iran's technical cooperation with nations such as Pakistan, China, and India is viewed with suspicion and Iran is often cited as one of the possible customers for nuclear materials smuggled out of the former Soviet Union. IAEA inspections at declared nuclear facilities and have found nothing untoward, but visits have not taken place at undeclared sites. Iranian government officials vehemently deny military nuclear activities. In January 1993, for instance, Iranian President Ali Akbar Hashemi Rafsanjani declared that Iran "cannot afford to purchase [and] will never try to purchase" nuclear weapons.[4] That declaration was reinforced by Iran's vice president and head of its nuclear program, Reza Amrollahi, who stated that Iran would promote the idea of the nuclear-free zone in the Middle East.

The CIA has been quoted as believing that Iran could acquire nuclear weapons in about a decade. The International Institute of Strategic Studies has stated that if Iran does have a military nuclear program, it is still in its early stages and Iran cannot hope to produce its own nuclear weapons before the end of the century.

Syria

Syria has long been cited as posing a proliferation risk. It allegedly began a military nuclear program in 1979 and has not provided the IAEA with full information on its nuclear activities. In 1991, China reported to the IAEA the potential sale of a 30 KW research reactor to Syria. The IAEA blocked the sale and Syria subsequently reduced its nuclear activities. Economic difficulties also seem to have played a part in the scaling down of Syria's nuclear program.

Libya

Libya operates a small Soviet-built research reactor at Tadzhura about twenty-five kilometres from Tripoli. Since 1980, Libyan nuclear activities have been under IAEA safeguards. Concern about Libya, however, does not center on its small indigenous program but rather on its alleged desire to obtain a complete nuclear weapon and to fund the development of an "Islamic bomb" by other nations. Over the years, Libya is rumored to have approached China, Pakistan, and India with offers to purchase nuclear weapons. More recently, there have been indications that Libya has been behind efforts to obtain nuclear weapons material from the former Soviet Union.

Algeria

Algeria's nuclear activities were under suspicion for a long time due to its refusal to accede to the Non-Proliferation Treaty, and these suspicions were further reinforced in 1991 by American intelligence reports which provided details of the Ain Oussera nuclear research complex that included a power reactor purchased from China. Some reports suggested that, once complete, this facility would produce enough fissile material to manufacture one bomb per year. In January 1992, Algeria succumbed to international pressure and declared that it would accede to the Non-Proliferation Treaty. Although it has not yet done so, it has signed an inspection and safeguards agreement with the International Atomic Energy Agency.

South Asia

India and Pakistan jointly pose one of the most serious and immediate pro-liferation threats. Their nuclear activities combined with political and ter-ritorial disputes give rise to grave concern. In testimony before the American Congress, the director of the Central Intelligence Agency, James Woolsey, said that the arms race between India and Pakistan represents "the most probable prospect for the future use of weapons of mass destruction, includ-ing nuclear weapons."[5] Both India and Pakistan are believed to have the capacity to build nuclear weapons in a very short space of time. As with Israel, their denials of actual possession of nuclear weapons are probably based on the weapons being held just short of final assembly.

India

India detonated a "peaceful" nuclear explosive device in 1974 but main-tains that it does not have and does not plan to develop nuclear weapons. According to proliferation specialists, however, India probably possesses between fifty and one hundred nuclear weapons.

The politics and tensions in the region—notably past and potential con-frontations with China and Pakistan—are seen as India's motives for pur-suing a clandestine military nuclear program. India is not a party to the Non-Proliferation Treaty on the grounds that it should be "universal and non-discriminating." In other words, India sees the Non-Proliferation Treaty as legitimizing the status of the declared nuclear weapons states while plac-ing other nations in a position of permanent inferiority. Some Indian nuclear facilities are under IAEA safeguards, and negotiations are continuing to extend these. In 1993, India, for the first time, reported information on ura-nium resources to the IAEA. Even so, there seems little prospect of India accepting safeguards on all its nuclear activities. India has refused to accept a United States-sponsored agreement with Pakistan for a joint cap on mil-itary nuclear activities, but some progress has been made in recent years to defuse the covert nuclear arms race in the region. India and Pakistan do exchange lists of nuclear sites—which are not revealed to any other nations—as part of a nonaggression agreement regarding nuclear facili-ties and India has proposed a "no-first-use" agreement with Pakistan along with the establishment of a communications "hot line."

These actions, however, have done little to lessen fears that a large-scale conflict between India and Pakistan could escalate into a nuclear con-frontation. Another factor fueling concerns about nuclear proliferation and regional stability is India's program to develop ballistic missiles with ranges between 250 and 2,500 kilometres which could be used to carry nuclear weapons.

Pakistan

Pakistan's military nuclear program is believed to have begun in 1962 at the Kahuta uranium enrichment facility. It is now thought able to assemble five to ten nuclear devices, which would make it the third largest unofficial nuclear power after Israel and India. Pakistan claims that it has the ability to manufacture nuclear weapons but it has made the political decision not to do so. Shortly after her election in 1993, Prime Minister Benazir Bhutto confirmed that Pakistan would continue with its nuclear program but later issued a directive banning all public statements on nuclear power.

In August 1994, Navaz Sharif, who was the prime minister of Pakistan for thirty months until July 1993, declared that Pakistan had acquired a nuclear weapons capability. He was quoted as saying, "I confirm Pakistan possesses an atomic bomb," at a rally in the disputed area of Kashmir. He declared that any attack against Kashmir could trigger a nuclear holocaust.[6] Pakistan's present prime minister, Benazir Bhutto, denounced this assertion as a "highly irresponsible statement" but declined to elaborate further.[7] Other Pakistani officials then restated the position that Pakistan had acquired the ability to manufacture nuclear weapons but had taken a policy decision not to do so and that the use of nuclear technology was confined to peaceful purposes.

The end of the Cold War had a substantial effect on Pakistan's relations with nations outside South Asia. The withdrawal of Soviet forces from Afghanistan combined with heightened international concern about nuclear proliferation led to increased pressure on Pakistan to abandon its military nuclear program and join the Non-Proliferation Treaty as a non-nuclear state. One important factor in this process was American legislation known as the Pressler amendment. This blocked American military and economic assistance unless the President certified that Pakistan did not possess nuclear weapons. In 1990, President Bush was unable to certify this, so aid was cut off, the most significant effect being the freezing of a delivery of F-16 aircraft which Pakistan has partly paid for. This block is still in place.

Regarding international agreements on non-proliferation such as acceding to the NPT or supporting prohibitions on the production of fissile material, Pakistan's position is that it will only support such moves if India does likewise.

East Asia

North Korea

On March 12, 1993, North Korea announced that it would withdraw from the Non-Proliferation Treaty. Having acceded to the NPT in 1985, North Korea cited Article X of the treaty which allows a party to withdraw at three months notice if extraordinary events jeopardize a party's supreme national interests. That decision followed an IAEA demand to mount a special inspection at the Yongbyon nuclear complex that was suspected of—among other things—housing an undeclared reprocessing plant from which nuclear materials were being diverted for military uses.

For the following three months, negotiations took place to try to resolve the issue. After a great deal of diplomatic effort mainly involving the United States, on June 11, 1993, one day before North Korea's withdrawal would have come into effect, North Korea agreed to suspend its withdrawal and announced that it would permit IAEA inspectors to apply safeguards at declared sites (though not at the facilities at the center of the dispute).

There is no need to provide a detailed chronology of subsequent events. Essentially, the United States led diplomatic efforts to make North Korea comply with IAEA demands to establish the precise status of North Korea's nuclear program. Economic sanctions by the United Nations were frequently mooted but there was resistance to this idea mainly from China, which is North Korea's main trading partner. The stakes in negotiations were high, with North Korea maintaining that sanctions would be sufficient cause for "pitiless" war with South Korea and its allies.

The situation became even tenser when North Korea decided to remove fuel pins from a nuclear reactor and did so in such a way that it became impossible for IAEA inspectors to determine their history. The reactor in question had been shut down for a time in 1989 and North Korea may then have replaced some of the fuel pins and removed plutonium from the original ones. When the fuel pins were removed in May 1994, North Korea allowed IAEA inspectors to watch the process but would not allow them to mark some pins for subsequent study. After removal, the 8,000 pins were also mixed up at random thus preventing their history from being established by later analysis.

In May and June 1994, there was much discussion of the types of sanctions that might be applied to North Korea, and it seemed that the United States, Japan, and South Korea would phase in sanctions in the absence of more comprehensive United Nations sanctions. Then, in mid-June, former President Jimmy Carter visited North Korea on what was described as a "private visit," although he appeared to be acting as an unofficial emissary for the United States. Whatever the precise status of his visit and the agreements he reached with President Kim Il Sun, the net effect was that North Korea and the United States returned to the negotiating table. North Korea apparently agreed to freeze its nuclear program while negotiations took place. On July 8, after only one day of negotiations, Kim Il Sung died and negotiations were suspended until August.

The negotiations in August 1994 made remarkable progress. North Korea agreed to replace its graphite-moderated nuclear reactors with light-water reactors which produce less plutonium. It also agreed to freeze the construction of new reactors, cease nuclear reprocessing, and close the laboratory at the center of the dispute. North Korea further agreed to remain party to the Non-Proliferation Treaty and to allow the implementation of IAEA safeguards. For its part, the United States agreed to provide replacement reactors and to make arrangements for interim energy alternatives.

Fulfilling its side of the agreement will probably cost the United States about $10 billion.

Several issues must still be resolved—whether, for instance, the 8,000 fuel pins now in storage will remain in North Korea or be shipped to a third country for reprocessing—but the crisis appears to have now passed.

Other East Asian Nations

The crisis over North Korea could have led to a far larger nuclear proliferation problem. Other nations in the region such as Taiwan, South Korea, and Japan have advanced civil nuclear industries and the presence of a nuclear-armed North Korea could have led them to re-appraise their commitment to the Non-Proliferation Treaty. In July 1993, for instance, Japan had voiced reservations about the indefinite extension of the NPT and although it subsequently adopted the goal of indefinite extension, this position could understandably have been undermined by the presence of an unpredictable nuclear threat on its doorstep. In the past, South Korea and Taiwan have had to be persuaded to redirect their nuclear program to allay proliferation concerns and they too might have reconsidered their options if faced by a clear failure of the non-proliferation regime in the region.

South America

Until the early 1980s, Brazil and Argentina were often cited as substantial proliferation threats. Both had nuclear programs thought capable of producing nuclear arms by the end of the century, and the rivalry between the two nations suggested that they might pursue military nuclear options. By 1985, however, civilian governments had come to power in both Brazil and Argentina. Although certain disturbing nuclear activities remained outside international safeguards, relations between the two nations improved and they introduced bilateral monitoring schemes.

In recent years, further progress has been made as tensions have continued to diminish. Both nations have signed safeguards agreements with the IAEA and have become party to the Treaty of Tlatelolco which creates a nuclear-weapons free zone in Latin America. They have also ratified the Quadripartite Agreement involving the IAEA and the Brazilian-Argentine Agency for Accounting and Control of Nuclear Materials (ABACC) which essentially introduces proliferation controls equivalent to full-scope safeguards. Argentina has also decided to accede to the Non-Proliferation Treaty irrespective of Brazil's position.

The former Soviet Union[8]

The breakup of the Soviet Union posed several extremely important problems related to the fate of its nuclear arsenals and extensive nuclear infrastructure. Although only Russia among the new republics can sustain a military nuclear weapons program, the transition to non-nuclear weapons status by the other republics is not straightforward.

Following the breakup of the Soviet Union at the end of 1991, former Soviet nuclear weapons remained in Belarus, Kazakhstan, Russia, and Ukraine.

In May 1992, these republics signed the Lisbon Protocol which was added to START I, the nuclear weapons reduction agreement reached by the United States and the Soviet Union in July 1991. Under the Lisbon Protocol, Belarus, Kazakhstan, and Ukraine agreed to transfer all former Soviet nuclear weapons to Russia. These republics also agreed accede to the Non-Proliferation Treaty as non-nuclear weapons states "in the shortest possible time."

The transfer of tactical nuclear weapons was completed by the middle of 1992 despite disagreements between Ukraine and Russia. It rapidly became evident that dealing with the former Soviet Union's nuclear legacy would severely strain the resources of the new republics, so several Western nations began to provide assistance. The most significant assistance is that provided by the United States which, under its "Nunn-Lugar" program, allocates $400 million per year to assist with demilitarization of all kinds. So far, $1.2 billion has been allocated. In addition, the United States agreed to purchase the highly enriched uranium from dismantled nuclear warheads. The proceeds of this sale—possibly $12 billion over 20 years—are to be distributed among the former republics according to a formula agreed among themselves.

Russia

Russia, as the successor state to the former Soviet Union, is a party to the Non-Proliferation Treaty as nuclear weapons state. Russia and the United States are implementing START I and START II, which will reduce their strategic nuclear warheads to 3,500 each by the year 2003. While Russia has an impressive nuclear weapons infrastructure, it was never intended to cope with nuclear disarmament on the present scale. Storage facilities for nuclear warheads and fissile material are stretched and coping with plutonium will be especially difficult. A Russian-American joint venture is investigating a plutonium-burning nuclear reactor and Japan has offered to help in this area, too, but such projects will not come to fruition quickly enough to circumvent the need for large-scale plutonium storage.

In deciding how to deal with Russia's plutonium stockpile, a central problem is that Russia tends to regard plutonium as an asset which has been expensive to develop and which should therefore be used in some way. The United States, on the other hand, tends to view it as a liability which should be rendered unusable and disposed of as soon and as safely as possible. In June 1994, Russia and the United States signed an agreement on plutonium production whereby Russia agreed to close its "dual-use" plutonium manufacturing reactors (located in Tomsk-7 and Krasnoyarsk-26) by the year 2000. Both nations also agreed that their military reactors which have already been closed—this covers all American weapons reactors—will not resume operations at any time. The United States also agreed to help Russia develop alternatives for producing the heat and electricity now generated by its plutonium-producing reactors.

Ukraine

Ukraine inherited 1,800 nuclear warheads from the former Soviet Union. The arsenal included 176 strategic nuclear missiles (130 obsolescent SS-19s and 46 modern SS-24s) along with about 50 strategic bombers equipped with about 500 cruise missiles and gravity bombs. Following Ukraine's emergence as an independent state, a heated debate arose about its nuclear status. This multifaceted debate was fueled by tensions with Russia, the absence of a clear security framework for the nation, severe economic problems, and the feeling that nuclear weapons were being renounced without any compensation or adequate international recognition. Some felt that nuclear weapons could provide a security guarantee against potential Russian aggression while others felt that the key issue was obtaining proper compensation for the fissile materials extracted from the warheads which were perceived as rightfully owned by Ukraine. A number of Ukrainian experts proposed that the warheads should be dismantled at Ukrainian facilities rather than in Russia.

In November 1993, the Ukrainian parliament ratified START I, but attached thirteen reservations limiting its implementation and omitting Article V of the Lisbon Protocol which stipulated that Ukraine should join the NPT as a non-nuclear weapons state. This led to a political deadlock at the trilateral negotiations between Russia, the United States, and Ukraine that was partly overcome on January 14, 1994, when the three countries signed a statement that confirmed Ukraine's obligation to become a non-nuclear state. In the subsequent joint communique, the American and Russian presidents declared that after the implementation of START I and Ukrainian accession to the Non-Proliferation Treaty, the two countries would "reaffirm their commitment to Ukraine . . . to respect the independence and sovereignty of the existing borders" of the country.

The agreement also provided for compensation to Ukraine. In return for the fissile material in the warheads concerned, Russia agreed to provide nuclear fuel for Ukrainian power reactors and wrote off some of Ukraine's debt. The United States agreed to provide $177 million to assist with weapons dismantlement, and Ukraine stands to gain about $1 billion over the next 20 years for its share of the proceeds of the sale of former Soviet fissile material to the United States. All this prompted a new vote in the Ukrainian parliament which dropped the earlier reservations attached to START I ratification and the Lisbon Protocol.

In March 1994, United States Defense Secretary William Perry pledged to contribute an additional $100 million to assist Ukrainian nuclear disarmament. The withdrawal of strategic nuclear warheads from Ukraine began in March 1994, when 60 warheads were transported to Russia in exchange for 120 nuclear fuel assemblies for the Chernobyl power station.

In July, shortly after his election as Ukrainian president, Mr. Leonid Kuchma confirmed that his country will respect its previous obligations to remove all nuclear weapons and to join the NPT as a non-nuclear-state. During a visit to Kiev in August 1994, United States Vice President Al Gore received a firm commitment that Ukraine would join the Non-Proliferation Treaty in the near future. While all this gives grounds for optimism that Ukraine will shortly accede to the Non-Proliferation Treaty and will transfer nuclear weapons based there to Russia, there is still some prospect that further difficulties could arise. Factions within parliament could still try to obstruct NPT accession and the dismantlement of weapons on Ukrainian soil. Even so, for the moment, it appears that Ukraine might well be a party to the NPT before the 1995 Review Conference. In this context, it should be noted that Ukraine is negotiating a full-scope safeguards agreement with the IAEA that would permit inspections of all Ukrainian nuclear activities except those associated with nuclear weapons still based on its soil.

Kazakhstan

Kazakhstan inherited a substantial part of the Soviet strategic nuclear infrastructure including 104 ten-warheaded SS-18 missiles and 40 Tu-95MS "Bear-H" bombers armed with AS-15 cruise missiles. In addition, Semipalatinsk, the former Soviet Union's main nuclear weapons testing site, is in Kazakhstan. Although the transfer of nuclear weapons to Russia has been less troublesome than from Ukraine, problems have emerged. For instance, serious doubts were raised over the safety of nuclear weapons in Kazakhstan following reports that Russian personnel had been prevented from performing maintenance on some nuclear warheads. According to an agreement signed in March 1994, all nuclear weapons will be transferred to Russia within fourteen months.

In 1993, Kazakhstan applied for IAEA membership and, like Ukraine, is negotiating a full-scope safeguards agreement. On February 14, 1994, Kazakhstan acceded to the Non-Proliferation Treaty. This followed agreements with Russia and the United States on security guarantees and the provision of assistance for nuclear weapons dismantlement.

Belarus

Belarus inherited seventy-two mobile SS-25 missiles that quickly pledged to transfer to Russia for dismantlement. With commendable speed and no political wrangling, Belarus ratified START I in April 1993, and transfers of strategic systems began in mid-1993. This process is expected to be complete by 1995. Belarus joined the Non-Proliferation Treaty in July 1993 as a non-nuclear state.

Nuclear Smuggling

In recent months, nuclear smuggling from the former Soviet Union has caused great concern. For several years, there have been warnings that nuclear materials might be smuggled out of the former Soviet Union. Declining living standards combined with instances of lax security provided motives and opportunities for criminal sales of nuclear materials. In 1992, for instance, Mr. Gennadi Novikov, head of the nuclear safety service at the Chelyabinsk-70 nuclear plant, warned of the declining security standards. In addition, the Russian media have provided accounts of breaches in security at military and civil nuclear installations. For example, the Russian press reported in March 1993 that eleven kilograms of uranium 238 were stolen from the Arzamas-16 nuclear research and development center and that local law enforcement authorities were investigating "dozens" of similar cases.[9] Police in St. Petersburg reportedly recovered several kilograms of highly enriched uranium and several journalistic investigations left little doubt about the existence of a nuclear black market.[10]

Russian authorities have long been aware of attempts to penetrate security at nuclear installations but, until recently, seemed confident none had succeeded.

Several contradictory accounts appeared in early 1994. According to one press story, Russia reported that eleven attempts had been made in 1993 to steal uranium from power plants compared with three attempts in 1993. All attempts were reported to have failed.[11] Other reports suggested that there were 900 attempts of illegal penetration into nuclear plants and 700 attempts to steal secret documents while some suggest materials rather than documents were involved.[12]

During 1994, accounts of nuclear smuggling became more frequent and more widespread. In the early months of 1994, Interpol was reported to be investigating 30 serious cases of nuclear smuggling, including the theft of 250 kilograms of uranium from a plant in Glazov and 123 grams of uranium stolen from the Chernobyl nuclear power plant. Then several particularly disturbing cases were uncovered by police in Germany. In May 1994, police discovered 6 grams of extremely pure plutonium in a garage in Tengen-Weichs near Stuttgart[13], and in June they seized 0.8 grams of highly enriched uranium in Landshut, Bavaria. At the beginning of August, German police arrested a Columbian and two Spaniards who arrived in Munich on a flight from Moscow carrying about 350 grams of 87 percent pure plutonium in the form of a powdered oxide. It transpired that this was supposedly part of a four-kilogram deal worth $250 million. Only a few days later, German police arrested a man in Bremen who was trying to sell a much smaller quantity of plutonium.

At first, Russia denied that any of the materials originated there. The spokesman for Russia's Federal Counter-Intelligence Service, Sergei Vasilyev, claimed that "not a single gram of plutonium-239 has gone missing from storage in Russia."[14] Analysis of the materials, however, pinned down its origin to military production centers in Russia. High-level intelligence meetings took place between Germany and Russia with the result that President Yeltsin gave an assurance that nuclear security would be tightened and that cooperation in dealing with nuclear smuggling would be "broader and deeper."

The latest cases in Germany seem to represent only the tip of a growing nuclear smuggling iceberg. In 1991, there were 41 cases of nuclear smuggling; in 1992, 158 cases; and in 1993, 241 cases.[15] Incidents are not confined to Germany. Bulgarian police have in one operation seized nineteen containers of radioactive material including a quantity of plutonium, although the amount and its purity were not revealed. The Bulgarian Committee for the Use of Atomic Energy for Peaceful Purposes said that an investigation in 1993 had found seventy-five unregistered establishments where radioactive material was being used.[16] Hungarian police arrested two Hungarians who were trying to sell radioactive material believed to come from Russian nuclear fuel rods.

Furthermore, at the end of August 1994, Russia reported that it had arrested two men who had been trying to steal eleven kilograms of low-grade nuclear fuel from the Arzamas-16 nuclear complex east of Moscow.[17]

As regards the potential customers for nuclear materials, suspicion has centered on Iran, Pakistan, and North Korea.

It is important to place incidents of nuclear smuggling into context. Many cases reportedly involve bogus material or radioactive material with no nuclear weapons applications. Furthermore, many—although not all—of the seizures of weapons-related material involve extremely small quantities. This does not mean that there is any cause for complacency but nor does it mean that security at weapons-related sites has been seriously compromised. The six grams of plutonium found in a German garage, for instance, was indeed manufactured at the weapons facility Arzamas-16, but material from there was subsequently distributed to non-weapons laboratories which could have been the source of the leak.[18] Similarly, some highly enriched uranium and plutonium probably came from laboratory instruments, naval reactors, or experimental research reactors. Dangerous as these materials are, they are not as dangerous as weapons-grade material.

All that said, there are serious threats to proliferation through nuclear smuggling from the former Soviet Union. International experts from the IAEA, who have visited Ukraine and Kazakhstan in recent months to prepare for safeguards agreements on civil nuclear facilities, have been greatly alarmed by instances of lax security: weapons grade material held in low-security civilian laboratories, highly enriched uranium lying in open-access storage rooms, and so on. There is no reason to assume that conditions are any different in other former Soviet republics, several of which possess nuclear material and facilities which could raise proliferation concerns.

The 1995 NPT Renewal Conference

The Non-Proliferation Treaty is the foundation upon which all other efforts to prevent the spread of nuclear weapons are based. It was opened for signature on July 1, 1968 and entered into force on March 5, 1970. So far, 164 nations have acceded to the treaty and only 28 have not done so.[19] The NPT is re-inforced by a variety of regional arrangements such as Euratom, the Antarctic Treaty, the Treaty of Tlatelolco, and the South Pacific

Nuclear Free Zone. There are also bilateral agreements such as those between Argentina and Brazil, and India and Pakistan. There is also the Nuclear Suppliers Group —also known as the London Club —which has harmonized export controls on nuclear materials and technologies. Finally, there is the International Atomic Energy Agency which operates safeguards on the use of nuclear material and technology to which parties to the NPT are committed.

IAEA safeguards include an accounting system to reveal, within a conversion period (i.e., before the state concerned has had time to assemble a nuclear weapon), any diversion of "significant quantities" of nuclear materials; a containment system for sensitive materials to limit the possibility of access; and a monitoring system, comprising cameras, radiation detectors, and closed-circuit television able to detect illegal traffic in materials, equipment, or technologies. Safeguards can be applied in two ways. Non-nuclear weapons states who are party to the NPT have a "full-scope" or comprehensive safeguards agreement with the IAEA. This means that all nuclear material in the nation concerned is monitored by the IAEA. Nations who are not party to the NPT can purchase materials and technologies from other nations who are party to the NPT, but these items must be placed under IAEA safeguards.

Since the Gulf war, the IAEA has been given the freedom to act on information supplied by outside sources such as national intelligence agencies. It has also determined, after a legal re-appraisal of its rules, that it can mount special inspections in nations which have signed full-scope (also known as comprehensive) safeguards agreements with the IAEA. These inspections can take place at locations chosen by the IAEA, whether or not the inspected state has declared them to the IAEA. Essentially, full-scope safeguards give the IAEA the right to verify all nuclear material in the relevant state and to apply safeguards to all nuclear activities within the state. The inspected state has the right to be consulted but, in the final analysis, it is obliged to permit an inspection to take place. If the objection is maintained or if inspections are frustrated, the IAEA can refer the matter to the United Nations Security Council, as happened with North Korea.

Another development which should enhance non-proliferation efforts is that the Nuclear Suppliers Group agreed in 1992 that all significant new transfers to non-nuclear weapons states would be conditional on the recipient having a full-scope safeguards agreement with the IAEA.[20] The only exceptions would be cases where the transfer is deemed essential for the safe operation of existing facilities and even then safeguards must be applied to the facilities in question.

The NPT specifies that it must be reviewed every five years and that after twenty-five years, a renewal conference should be held to decide whether the NPT will remain in force "indefinitely, or shall be extended for an additional fixed period or periods." Preparatory meetings have already taken place for this renewal conference and, so far, it appears that the indefinite renewal sought by many nations is by no means a foregone conclusion. Before looking further at the prospects for renewing the NPT, it is useful to summarize what are seen as the achievements and failures of the treaty.

NPT Achievements and Failures

The NPT has been neither a complete success nor a complete failure. On the positive side, it has made nuclear weapons proliferation more difficult for would-be proliferators. In the late 1960s, it was feared that dozens of nuclear weapons states might emerge over the next few decades. In fact, there are now probably only three additional de facto nuclear weapons nations: Israel, India, and Pakistan. Another nation, South Africa, actually did produce nuclear weapons but has now abandoned them and has committed itself to full-scope IAEA safeguards. In addition, the NPT has successfully promoted the peaceful use of nuclear energy by allowing nations to develop nuclear energy under IAEA monitoring and with IAEA and other international assistance. It has also provided motivation for the nuclear weapons nations to work toward nuclear disarmament, as they are obliged to do under the NPT. Whether they have done enough has been a subject of acrimonious debate at previous review conferences, but the prospect of regular scrutiny at these conferences has provided some impetus for disarmament. Another NPT strength is that it provides the legal basis for dealing with nations conducting questionable nuclear activities.

On the negative side, experience with Iraq showed that even a party to the NPT can make great progress toward building nuclear weapons with only modest scientific and industrial resources provided it has the will, the ingenuity, and the resources. Another problem is that the treaty is discriminatory in that it enshrines the nuclear weapons status quo and places different obligations on nuclear weapons nations and non-nuclear weapons nations. Its crisis management and enforcement provisions are open to criticism in that sanctions or actions to be taken against violations are not mandatory but instead are at the discretion of the United Nations Security Council. Some of treaty's definitions are unclear. These include the definition of "manufacture" of a nuclear weapon, so that a nation could assemble all the key components of a nuclear weapon but would not be deemed to have manufactured a nuclear weapon unless these components were brought together. The definition of a "significant quantity" of fissile material is also open to question as are the allowable margins of error in accounting for fissile material.[21]

Toward Renewal

There is general agreement that modifying the NPT is likely to be too cumbersome and attempts to do so are likely to result in deadlock and, perhaps, a failure to renew the treaty. Similarly, replacing the NPT with a new treaty has been ruled out since a new treaty is unlikely to attract the nearly universal membership of the NPT. The broad goal of all the NATO nations, Russia, and many other nations is therefore to seek indefinite, unconditional renewal and to enhance non-proliferation efforts. Not all participants are likely to support these goals. Mexico, for instance, has proposed a five-year extension followed by indefinite renewal only if an agreement has been reached on banning all nuclear weapons testing. Only Iran has declared its opposition to indefinite renewal, but other nations are known to feel that extension for fixed periods would be an effective way of applying pressure on the nuclear weapons states to disarm.[22]

A key issue for the non-nuclear weapons states is whether the nuclear weapons states have fulfilled their NPT obligation to "pursue negotiations in good faith on effective measures relating to the cessation of the nuclear arms race at an early date and to nuclear disarmament." At the last review conference in 1990, this was among the principal areas of disagreement. Since then, of course, dramatic reductions in nuclear weapons have occurred and—as noted earlier—nuclear disarmament is proceeding so rapidly that it is stretching the resources available for safe dismantlement and storage of nuclear weapons and material. Even so, many non-nuclear weapons nations have identified a complete ban on nuclear testing as the "yardstick" for deciding whether the nuclear weapons states are living up to their commitments. This linkage is hotly contested by the nuclear weapons nations, and indeed there is no formal link between a test ban and the NPT.

Without going into the details, a complete test ban is being negotiated by the Conference on Disarmament in Geneva, but there is very little prospect that an agreement can be reached before the NPT renewal conference. The latest round of negotiations finished in early September without agreement. France and China apparently opposed an early agreement, arguing that this would "freeze" a Russian and American technical advantage, and China also insisted on the right to conduct "peaceful nuclear tests," a distinction not recognized by other nations.[23] China's continued nuclear testing— the latest was on June 9, 1994—is distinctly unhelpful, particularly when the other nuclear weapons states have imposed moratoria on their nuclear tests. With only two months of negotiating time before the NPT renewal conference, the chairman of the negotiations has said, "It would take a minor miracle for us to complete [a nuclear test ban treaty] in time for next year's non-proliferation conference. There are many non-aligned countries who believe that without a comprehensive test ban there can be no non-proliferation convention."[24]

It remains to be seen whether sufficient progress will be made toward a test ban treaty to mollify the nonaligned nations. It might be that other actions will strengthen the case for indefinite renewal. Foremost among these has been the Clinton Administration's proposal to cease producing fissile material for weapons purposes and to place surplus material under international safeguards. This arrangement would apply equally to the nuclear weapons states as well as the threshold states, so it should not be seen as discriminatory. It would limit weapons production and would move material from dismantled weapons out of the military domain, so that it would be politically more difficult to reclaim the material for weapons purposes in the future. Russia has declared its support for this proposal—most recently in President Yeltsin's speech at the United Nations on September

26, 1994—and, as noted earlier in this report, has agreed to close its plants which produce fissile material for military purposes.

On March 23, 1994, the United States announced the transfer of seven tons of plutonium and fifteen tons of HEU from national to IAEA authority. Further transfers are planned for fissile materials "no longer needed for United States defense program." At present, none of the other declared nuclear weapons states is believed to be producing new fissile material for weapons, so the threshold states are probably the key obstacle to an international agreement. In any event, support for this initiative by the nuclear weapons states might increase the likelihood of NPT renewal, bearing in mind that the key threshold states—Israel, India, and Pakistan—are not party to the NPT.

Other actions to aid renewal could involve positive and negative security assurances by the declared nuclear weapons nations. Positive assurances are pledges to come to the aid of non-nuclear weapons nations if they are threatened by nuclear weapons. Negative assurances are declarations that the nuclear weapons nations will not use or threaten to use nuclear weapons against non-nuclear weapons states. Assurances along these lines were given during the Cold War but they were qualified because both sides wished to reserve the right to use nuclear weapons against each other's allies under certain circumstances.[25] The changed security environment after the end of the Cold War should make it possible to issue less cautious assurances.

Finally, the NPT renewal conference will take place against a background of increasing concern about the divisions between the developed and the developing world. The developing world is increasingly dissatisfied with what it views as lukewarm commitments to development assistance. The NPT provides an undertaking to assist with the development of nuclear energy but this form of assistance is not as attractive as it once was. A more solid commitment to development assistance by the developed world would greatly improve the atmosphere at the NPT conference. Possibilities include the developed nations setting a date for meeting their goal of providing 0.7 percent of GDP in development aid and providing adequate funds for the Rio agreements.[26]

Beyond 1995
The most likely outcome of the NPT Renewal Conference seems to be renewal indefinitely or for a fixed period. The least likely outcome is complete rejection of the NPT. Another possibility, however, is that the conference will fail to agree on renewal. Experts are divided about what this would mean in practice. One view is that since the conference is supposed to address the duration of renewal, a hung conference would not terminate the treaty. On the other hand, the absence of a decision does not mean that it would be automatically extended indefinitely. The prevailing view seems to be that "while the conference is still in session or has been adjourned for a further session to be convened, the NPT continues provisionally."[27]

No matter what the outcome, efforts will continue to strengthen nonproliferation efforts. These will certainly include further enhancement of IAEA safeguards. Since the Gulf War, the IAEA safeguards approach has certainly become more robust, and the new provisions for Special Inspections played an important role in dealing with North Korea. Even so, the Director General of the IAEA, Dr. Hans Blix, has noted that the Chemical Weapons Convention indicates that there is less reluctance to accept a more intrusive inspection regime than was possible when IAEA safeguards were established.[28] There is support for movement in that direction, but other problems of a much more fundamental nature must be addressed to bring it about.

At present, the frequency of inspections is related to the amount of fissile material a nation possesses. On that basis, Japan and Germany absorb about 60 percent of the IAEA's safeguards budget and Canada accounts for a further 10 percent.[29] Although this principle is nondiscriminatory, it is difficult to see this as an appropriate use of scarce resources. Furthermore, IAEA safeguards resources are indeed scarce. Despite the additional burdens of new responsibilities in Iraq, North Korea, Argentina, and Brazil, the safeguards budget has been more or less static at $65 million for 8 years. Activities also had to be cut by about 12 percent when Russia and other CIS nations were unable to pay their contributions, although payments have now resumed.[30]

It certainly seems appropriate that the IAEA be given additional resources to deal more effectively with its new burdens. And it should be noted that reducing the definitions of "significant quantities" and "material unaccounted for" would make safeguards more complex and expensive.

One option for lightening the IAEA's burden would be to create regional safeguards organizations, such as EURATOM, to operate in the Middle East, South Asia, and Africa.

Another action could be to develop mandatory United Nations sanctions on nations which are not party to the NPT or which violate its provisions. This would certainly be controversial but would indicate that the international community takes nuclear proliferation seriously and insists upon the universal application of the NPT.

Conclusion

In sum, there are many actions which would help achieve NPT renewal and which would enhance efforts to prevent nuclear proliferation. The achievement of a complete ban on nuclear tests would clearly increase the chances of indefinite renewal but renewal probably does depend on this factor alone. Progress in that direction along with a good record of success in other aspects of nuclear arms control might suffice. The cessation of fissile material production for weapons purposes and the placing of surplus weapons material under IAEA authority is one such measure which was not even on the horizon at the last NPT Conference.

It seems that there is scope for positive and negative security assurances and these should be examined by the declared nuclear weapons states. Collective declarations by these nations could even be considered.

Regarding efforts to enhance non-proliferation, there is clearly scope for cooperation between East and West as a means of curbing nuclear leakage from the former Soviet Union. A great deal is already being done in this context in the form of assistance for weapons dismantlement, security of nuclear facilities and materials, and research funding for weapons scientists to work in nonmilitary areas. These programs deserve support and should be supplemented by additional assistance in export control implementation.

Regarding nuclear safeguards, there is clearly much scope for redirecting resources so that they reflect proliferation risk rather than simply the scale of national nuclear programs. An extremely strong case can also be made for increasing the IAEA's safeguards budget. At the same time, inspection arrangements should be studied further to see if it is possible to provide the IAEA with the same sort of inspection rights that are associated with the Chemical Weapons Convention.

There should also be detailed consideration of the sanctions which should be imposed on nations which are not party to the NPT and which have nuclear programs. At the very least, these should be excluded from international nuclear trade unless they submit to full-scope IAEA safeguards. For nations which violate the NPT, a clear decision to impose specific sanctions should be agreed. Nations who intend to violate the Treaty should be left in do doubt that their actions will have clear consequences.

Endnotes

* The Rapporteur would like to thank Dmitry Eustafiev for his asistance in preparing this report.

[1] Another factor which may influence Israel is that the Dimona nuclear facility is said to be approaching the point where large investments will be necessary to continue operations.

[2] This proposal is discussed later in this report.

[3] Cited in *The Non-proliferation Review*, Program for Non-proliferation Studies, Monterey Institute of International Studies, Spring–Summer 1994, Vol. 1, No.3, p. 101.

[4] Washington Post, January 2, 1993, cited in *The Non-proliferation Review*, Program for Non-proliferation Studies, Monterey Institute of International Studies, Winter 1994, vol. 1, No. 2, p. 104.

[5]Mitchell Reiss, "South Asia and Nuclear Proliferation: a Future Unlike the Past" *RUSI Journal,* December 1993, pp. 63–67, and Christopher Bellamy, "Islamabad Races Secretly to Build Nuclear Arsenal," *The Independent,* 19 August 1994.

[6]Tim McGirk, "Pakistan Has Bomb, ex-PM Admits," *The Independent,* 24 August 1994.

[7]"Bhutto Denounces A-Arms Warning," *International Herald Tribune,* 25 August 1994.

[8]Previous Reports have addressed nuclear dismantlement issues in some detail, so this section concentrates on the specific issues related to nuclear proliferation.

[9]*Komsomolskaya Pravda* (Moscow), 5 March 1993, p. 1.

[10]Kirill Belyaninov, "Nuclear Nonsense, Black-Market Bombs, and Fissile Flim-Flam," *The Bulletin of the Atomic Scientists,* March/April 1994, pp. 44–50.

[11]"Uranium Trail Hots Up," *Financial Times,* 10 February 1994.

[12]"Russian Nuclear Theft Increases," *The Daily Telegraph,* 10 February 1994, and "Europe Alert Over Threat of Nuclear Terrorism," *The European,* 18 March 1994.

[13]The plutonium in this case was 99.7 percent pure. Weapons-grade plutonium is believed to be 96 percent pure.

[14]"From Russia with Love," *Financial Times,* 22 August 1994

[15]"Split on How to Stop Nuclear Smugglers," *The Independent,* 8 September 1994.

[16]"Sofia Police Raid Nets Nuclear Haul," *The Guardian* 15 September 1994.

[17]"New Russian Nuclear Theft," *The Daily Telegraph,* 25 August 1994.

[18]"The Plutonium Racket," *The Economist,* 20 August 1994.

[19]Of the latter, Algeria, Argentina, Chile and Ukraine have declared their intention to accede; Kyrgyzstan and Moldova have ratified the treaty but not yet deposited their letters of accession; Andorra and Monaco are principalities whose foreign policies are controlled by other nations; Micronesia, Tajikistan, and Turkmenistan are considering accession; Serbia and Montenegro claim membership as the sole successor states to Yugoslavia but this is in dispute; Brazil and Vanuatu have taken no action on the NPT but are participating in regional non-proliferation arrangements; India has rejected accession on the grounds that the Treaty is discriminatory; Pakistan has stated its willingness to accede at the same time as India; Angola, Bosnia and Herzegovina, Comoros, Djibouti, Eritrea, Israel, Macedonia, the Marshall Islands, and Palau have taken no action regarding the NPT; Oman and the United Arab Emirates have cited Israeli nuclear capabilities as the reason for not acceding; and Cuba has taken no action on the NPT, although it has declared that it would participate in the Latin American Nuclear Weapons Free Zone when other Latin American parties brought it into force, which they have now done. ("Non-Signatories of the Nuclear Non-Proliferation Treaty," *Arms Control Today,* July/August 1994, p. 28.

[20]*Inventory of International Non-proliferation Organizations and Regimes.* 1994 Edition. Programme for Non-proliferation Studies, Monterey Institute of International Studies.

[21]The significant quantity of highly enriched uranium 235 is 25 kilograms; uranium 233, 8 kilograms; and plutonium, 8 kilograms. In fact, some experts have argued that these quantities are eight times larger than that needed in a sophisticated weapon. The allowable quantities of "material unaccounted for" in large facilities can exceed the amounts required to make several nuclear weapons, even using current definitions of significant quantities.

[22]Edward Mortimer, "Terms Still to Be Decided," *Financial Times*, 12 September 1994.

[23]"Nuclear Testing Set to Continue," *The Guardian*, 8 September 1994.

[24]Ibid.

[25]Edward Mortimer, "Terms Still to Be Decided," *Financial Times*, 12 September 1994.

[26]This topic is addressed in the Scientific and Technical Committee's Draft General Report [AL 232 STC (94) 7].

[27]John Simpson and Darryl Howlett, "The NPT Renewal Conference: Stumbling Towards 1995," *International Security*, Summer 1994, pp. 41–71.

[28]Dr. Hans Blix, "The Dual Challenge of a Nuclear Age," *IAEA Bulletin*, January 1993, pp. 33–39.

[29]David Fischer, Ben Sanders, Lawrence Scheinman, and George Bunn, "A New Nuclear Triad. The Non-Proliferation of Nuclear Weapons, International Verification and the International Atomic Energy Agency," Programme for Promoting Nuclear Non-Proliferation, Mountbatten Centre for International Studies, University of Southampton, September 1992, p. 28. These nations, incidentally, make great efforts to reduce the burdens that the safeguards impose on the IAEA.

[30]Zachary Davis and Warren H. Donnelly, "The International Atomic Energy Agency: Strengthen Verification Authority?" *CRS Issue Brief*, Congressional Research Service, 3 November 1993.

—Taken from *http://www.fas.org/irp/threat/nato_nuke.htm*

Fact Sheet on Dirty Bombs

Background

In order to better inform the public on what a dirty bomb is and what terrorists might intend to try to accomplish in setting off such a weapon, the following information is provided. Given the scores of exercises—federal, state, and local—being staged to assure that all emergency response organizations are properly equipped, trained, and exercised to respond to terrorist chemical, biological, or radiological attack, we believe members of the public, as well as news organizations, will value some concise, straightforward information.

Basically, the principal type of dirty bomb, or Radiological Dispersal Device (RDD), combines a conventional explosive, such as dynamite, with radioactive material. In most instances, the conventional explosive itself would have more immediate lethality than the radioactive material. At the levels created by most probable sources, not enough radiation would be present in a dirty bomb to kill people or cause severe illness. For example, most radioactive material employed in hospitals for diagnosis or treatment of cancer is sufficiently benign that about 100,000 patients a day are released with this material in their bodies.

However, certain other radioactive materials dispersed in the air could contaminate up to several city blocks, creating fear and possibly panic and requiring potentially costly cleanup. Prompt, accurate, nonemotional public information might prevent the panic sought by terrorists.

A second type of RDD might involve a powerful radioactive source hidden in a public place, such as a trash receptacle in a busy train or subway station, where people passing close to the source might get a significant dose of radiation. A dirty bomb is in no way similar to a nuclear weapon. The presumed purpose of its use would be therefore not as a weapon of mass destruction but rather as a weapon of mass disruption.

Impact of a Dirty Bomb
The extent of local contamination would depend on a number of factors, including the size of the explosive, the amount and type of radioactive material used, and weather conditions. Prompt detectability of the kind of radioactive material employed would greatly assist local authorities in advising the community on protective measures, such as quickly leaving the immediate area, or going inside until being further advised. Subsequent decontamination of the affected area could involve considerable time and expense.

Sources of Radioactive Material
Radioactive materials are widely used at hospitals, research facilities, industrial, and construction sites. These radioactive materials are used for such purposes as in diagnosing and treating illnesses, sterilizing equipment, and inspecting welding seams. For example, the Nuclear Regulatory Commission, together with 32 states which regulate radioactive material, have over 21,000 organizations licensed to use such materials. The vast majority of these sources are not useful for constructing an RDD.

Control of Radioactive Material
NRC and state regulations require licensees to secure radioactive material from theft and unauthorized access. These measures have been stiffened since the attacks of September 11, 2001. Licensees must promptly report lost or stolen material. Local authorities make a determined effort to find and retrieve such sources. Most reports of lost or stolen material involve small or short-lived radioactive sources not useful for an RDD.

Past experience suggests there has not been a pattern of collecting such sources for the purpose of assembling a dirty bomb. Only one high-risk radioactive source has not been recovered in the last five years in the United States. However, this source (Iridium-192) would no longer be considered a high-risk source because much of the radioactivity has decayed away since it was reported stolen in 1999. In fact, the combined total of all unrecovered sources over a five-year time span would barely reach the threshold for one high-risk radioactive source. Unfortunately, the same cannot be said worldwide. The U.S. Government is working to strengthen controls on high-risk radioactive sources both at home and abroad.

What People Should Do Following an Explosion

- Move away from the immediate area—at least several blocks from the explosion—and go inside. This will reduce exposure to any radioactive airborne dust.
- Turn on local radio or TV channels for advisories from emergency response and health authorities.
- If facilities are available, remove clothes and place them in a sealed plastic bag. Saving contaminated clothing will allow testing for radiation exposure.
- Take a shower to wash off dust and dirt. This will reduce total radiation exposure if the explosive device contained radioactive material.
- If radioactive material was released, local news broadcasts will advise people where to report for radiation monitoring and blood and other tests to determine whether they were in fact exposed and what steps to take to protect their health.

Risk of Cancer

Just because a person is near a radioactive source for a short time or gets a small amount of radioactive dust on himself or herself does not mean he or she will get cancer. The additional risk will likely be very small. Doctors will be able to assess the risks and suggest mitigating measures once the radioactive source and exposure level have been determined.

It should be noted that potassium iodide (KI) would not be protective except in the very unlikely event that the dirty bomb contained radioactive iodine isotopes in large quantities. Radioactive iodine isotopes are not particularly attractive for use in an RDD for a variety of technical reasons. KI only protects the thyroid from radioactive iodine, but offers no protection to other parts of the body or against other radioactive isotopes.

A number of federal agencies have responsibilities for dealing with possible detonations of dirty bombs. Reporters or other interested parties may wish to check out their websites. In addition, their offices of public affairs stand ready to promptly answer press questions on the subject or to provide access to experts in and out of government. Their websites and phone numbers follow:

Department of Energy: www.energy.gov/; tel 202-586-4940
Environmental Protection Agency: www.epa.gov; tel 202-564-9828
Nuclear Regulatory Commission: www.nrc.gov; tel 301-415-8200
Federal Emergency Management Agency: www.fema.gov;
   tel 202-646-4600
Department of Justice: www.usdoj.gov; tel 202-514-2007
Federal Bureau of Investigation: www.fbi.gov; tel 202-324-3691

Department of Health and Human Services: www.hhs.gov;
   tel 202-690-6343
Department of Homeland Security: www.dhs.gov; tel 202-282-8010
Transportation Security Administration: www.tsa.gov/public/;
   tel 571-227-2829
National Nuclear Security Administration: www.nnsa.doe.gov/;
   tel 202-586-7371

Taken from *http://www.nrc.gov/reading-rm/doc-collections/fact-sheets/dirty-bombs.html*

Atomic "Suitcase" Weapons

In 1997, the public became aware of a Russian nuclear device they had not known even existed—the so-called suitcase bomb. These devices were made for the Soviet KGB. One of these bombs had an explosive charge of one kiloton, equivalent to one thousand tons of TNT. If a device like this made its way to the United States, it could destroy everything within a half-mile radius of the Capitol in Washington, DC. Within hours, prevailing winds would carry the nuclear fallout throughout Washington.

An Interview with Dr. Alexei Yablokov

Do "backpack" nuclear weapons exist?
Yes, small atomic charges exist. They are very small. Several dozen kilos, thirty kilos, forty kilos. I spoke with people that made them, I saw them. The American specimens can be seen on the Internet, they can be seen on photographs, they can even be seen in the movies. I have never seen Russian analogies, I have only seen American ones, but Russian ones do exist, because I spoke with people who made them, and I believe these people, these people knew what they were talking about. And there was data published about it. . . Some was published in the newspaper of a town in the south of the Urals in a little paper, and it said there that the prominent achievement is that they have manufactured a miniature atomic charge. . . No one knows how many exist. . . Lebed mentioned that there's 48, or 150, but no one knows for certain.

How powerful are they?
Their power is about one kiloton, possibly less, but a powerful charge. You cannot destroy Moscow or London, but the Kremlin, you can destroy. . . . Capitol Hill can be wiped out by such a bomb. . . .

Why were you raising the issue?
I talk about tactical nuclear arms, and including mini-nukes, nuclear cases, because I believe that, after the end of the Cold War, the situation with nuclear arms has become much more dangerous. During the Cold War, everything was under strict control, now it's not the case anymore. Now, it's becoming clear to us that tactical nuclear arms pose a great threat in people's minds. People think that, "Well, the American president and the Russian president have nuclear cases and only after the president presses a button in it, then something happens." But that's not the case regarding tactical nuclear arms. If we've got tactical nuclear arms and small brief-

case bombs, a terrorist version of it, it's not going to be up to the president to decide where and at what time to set the bomb off. So, tactical nuclear arms exist under less control than the strategic nuclear arms. The power is much smaller of tactical ones, but the control is also much weaker. Therefore, it now poses a greater threat to society, that's why I keep talking about it.

We know that Chechnyan leaders announced that they've got two nuclear bombs. But we checked it out, and it seems that it's not the case. Palestinian terrorists also made statements to that effect, they said they've got several atomic bombs which they've purchased in the Soviet Union, but, hopefully, they are also bluffing. But, in reality, the danger comes from within the country, from within Russia. We've got about one hundred organizations of a fascist nature. These fascist organizations have got many military who know where these bombs are located, who know how to use them. And if, inside the country, there's a struggle for power, and these fascists and nationalists get hold of these bombs—there's a small chance, but there is that chance, much smaller than Chechnya or Palestine—but, if that happens, that will be terrible. That's why I'm talking about this, that's why tactical nuclear arms, these small nuclear bombs, ought to be destroyed as soon as possible. . . .

When this scandal with the nuclear mini-bombs erupted, and when it became clear to me that tactical nuclear arms poses a greater threat than strategic ones, I sent a letter to President Yeltsin saying that I would hate to publish all the data but I'd like to draw your attention to this and take measures. I had a call from the Kremlin, from the Defense Council . . . a decision was taken . . . it was deemed necessary to make a ruling which would impose more strict control over tactical nuclear arms. I was told that such a decree would be worked out, and I offered my own draft of such a decree and I sent such a draft to the President [and the Defense Council]. I don't know what the state of affairs is now, it's been three months since I submitted my draft decree. . . .

Did you ever talk to General Lebed about this?
I never spoke with General Lebed about this question. I don't know what General Lebed thinks. I've only heard his statement, and I saw it printed in newspapers. When General Lebed was the secretary of the Security Council, someone mentioned this weapon to him, and he appointed a special commission to look into the matter, and this commission was headed by one of his aides, with whom I'm acquainted. And he gave an interview and he said that the commission's been investigating, . . . and they have found [these weapons], they've established that they exist, there is no doubt about the fact that they exist, they know where they are, the only question is, have they been able to locate all? They said they'd found several dozen, but it's not clear whether they've managed to locate all existing.

Why did you testify before the U.S. Congress?
. . . On the request of [Representative] Weldon, whom I know for a long time, I made a statement in the Committee on National Defense, in the

[House]. And we spoke on the dangers of the tactical nuclear arms. Sometimes you have to go to America and make a statement there, or, like when Lebed spoke about these problems here, no one listened to him. But when he gave an interview to Reuters, the entire world heard about it, and our people back at home began to worry, too. So I agreed, at the request of Congressman Weldon, to appear before the . . . committee. . . Because, the problem, as I said, is a very worrying one and concerns us all.

What was the reaction in Russia to your statements in America?
When I returned, an independent newspaper . . . published a dirty article, accusing me of being an American spy. They insisted that Yablokov is an American spy and that he is using ecological organizations in order to collect classified data. It's all lies. I was so indignant that I filed a court case against [the paper]. And the press secretary of the Atomic Ministry, I sued him as well. And this court case will take place a few days from now.

Can you tell me about your work?
All my life I was a biologist, but, towards the end of Gorbachev's perestroika, I began to be interested in ecology. Towards the end of Gorbachev's perestroika, I believed that it's time to take part in political life. I was elected to the Soviet Parliament, I was Deputy Chairman of the Ecological Commission of Russia. But before the collapse of the Soviet Union, Boris Yeltsin offered me to become his aide in charge of ecological affairs, and for three years, I was his aide in charge of ecology. Recently, I was chairman on a commission on ecological security. Now I've finished my work in administration, and I've returned to the Science Academy. And also to the ecological politics in Russia. It's a small ecological organization, and our goal is to help the government to resolve urgent ecological problems. . . .

Do you think Russian officials are misleading the public opinion?
The fact that they mislead the public is absolutely clear. When Lebed first talked about it . . . he said that he tried to locate all the small atomic charges, but he was unable to do that because he was sacked. The first official reaction was that Lebed is mad, he is talking rubbish. And then I said, no, it's possible, because I spoke to people who manufactured the briefcase bomb. And then this flow was centered on me, all these lies. The federal intelligence . . . , the former KGB, [announced] that this is impossible. The press secretary for the Defense Ministry said, "We know what atomic bombs are, we have never heard of briefcase bombs." The ministry for Atomic Energy said the very same thing, that we've never heard of anything like that. But, if I'm looking at a photograph of these devices, I know they've been made, simply on the Internet. My American friends say, why don't you have a look on the Internet, there are photographs there of small, portable, American-made bombs. And then, bit by bit, people began to say, of course, yes, they exist, but Yablokov is disclosing state secrets. What state secrets are we talking about? . . . We insisted that we have full parity in terms of nuclear arms, that we have everything that the Americans have got; this was our official position. So, if I'm looking at a [picture] of an American weapon, I must be sure that we have an analogy. . . .

An Interview with General Vladimir Dvorkin

President Yeltsin's former science advisor, Alexei Yablokov, testified to the American Congress regarding the so-called suitcase bombs, the small, atomic demolition devices. Can you confirm the existence of these weapons?

I don't really know anything about these devices. I know that some small devices of this type existed both in the United States and in Russia, but why they should be needed in a suitcase format, that's something really for terrorists; I don't think they can really fulfill any kind of deterrence function. . . But even if they did exist, this kind of mobile nuclear bombs or devices, this is something that would have to be reproduced on a regular basis. Made again. Any kind of nuclear device or bomb has a shelf life. And once the service life has run out, then the charges on these devices become more dangerous. They become more dangerous for the people that are actually in possession of them.

You're referring to the tritium, the half-life of some of the materials?

Not only, there are a lot of other factors that lead to the decreased efficiency of devices like that. . . But I don't know anything about the system, and I don't really see why it would make sense. But the most important answer would be that I don't know this field. . . .

General Lebed, when he came and testified before the Congress, evidently said that at one point he had known about them, evidently. And he had tried to account for all of them and couldn't find some of them. Then when a team tried to inquire about it later, he said that he was under investigation for revealing state secrets for even having talked about it. Do you know anything about that end of the story at all?

Well, I've heard about this incident. I can tell you that Lebed is probably the least informed person as far as this topic is concerned. I considered him a big specialist, really, an expert in the military folklore. That's really where it stops.

He says that he was charged with actually making an accounting of these things. Was he not a general, highly placed enough to know?

Well, theoretically, he could have dealt with these issues only when he was the secretary of the Security Council. That was a very short period of time, and he had quite a few other problems to deal with. But he could not be qualified to even deal with this issue, in principle, because that's outside of his expertise.

An Interview with Matthew Bunn

Were we ever able to confirm that suitcase bombs existed?

Not that I'm aware of. Both United States and Russia of course built tactical nuclear weapons that were quite small in size. . . We had, for example, what we called atomic demolition munitions, that were designed to be carried in a backpack. . . I doubt that there was ever anything that was specifically designed to be carried in something that looked like a suitcase, though I couldn't rule it out. My personal judgment is that there probably aren't one hundred or twenty or however many suitcase bombs that are missing in the former Soviet Union, although I would guess that Lebed, when he made his initial statements, probably in good faith believed there were. The way the Russian accounting system works, everything is accounted for on paper. And there's reams of gigantic paper log books. You could easily imagine a situation where Lebed sent somebody to check at a particular facility, and there's a 19-year-old guard there, and he looks in the book and says, "Gee, there's supposed to be one hundred here and it turns out there are only thirty." And the reason is, there's another log book over here that the 19-year-old forgot about, that describes how many had been shipped off to such-and-such a place to be dismantled, or something like that. . . .

Could [Lebed] have been talking about the backpack-size devices rather than suitcase bombs?
Sure. He could have been. I wouldn't want to speculate as to exactly what it was Lebed was trying to communicate. In some of the subsequent interviews he gave, he back-pedaled significantly and just said, "Well, it's a possibility that these things might be missing," rather than, "They are definitely missing, and here's how many are missing." So it's a bit hard for me to parse exactly what he really thinks is the situation.

Congressman Weldon said that we thought that the KGB might have commissioned a suitcase-size specimen of the small atomic demolition device, as a thing to sell to terrorists specifically. Does that wash with anything you know?
I don't think it was as something to sell to terrorists. It was something, I believe, for the KGB's use, was the claim. Alexei Yablokov made that claim in print, in the Russian press. I haven't looked at the intelligence in enough detail to follow that. But it was denied by essentially everyone in a position of authority in the Russian military and nuclear system. . . .

An Interview with General Eugene Habiger

Yeltsin's former Science Advisor, Alexei Yablokov, came to the United States last year and testified about suitcase bombs that KGB or somebody was making for terrorist use. Do we know whether these things existed? If so, do the Russians now know where they all are?
Yes, we knew they existed. Suitcase nuclear bomb is, I think, a little optimistic. It's certainly something that . . . I would be hard-pressed to carry. It's fairly big and it's fairly heavy. The Russians, again from what I saw, go to great lengths in the accountability of their nuclear devices. We are spending a lot of money under Nunn-Lugar to automate that system. Our system is very automated, and we test it on a regular basis. The Russian system is more manpower-intensive. It's pretty much a stubby pencil and a spreadsheet kind of thing. But I was shown how they account for their nuclear weapons. And I was told that these smaller devices are included in that same accountability system. I mean, General Yakoulev took me in his office—General Yakoulev is the commander-in-chief of the Rocket Forces—

and showed me an IBM computer screen, and . . . Yakoulev can track where every nuclear weapon is in his system by serial number. I couldn't do that from my headquarters. . . If the Russians were as deadly serious about the accountability of the nuclear weapons that I saw and have been involved with, I can only surmise that they have the same concerns with the smaller weapons. There have been a number of Russians that have come over here and thrown a grenade on the table of some of our Congressional committees, saying that there lot of loose suitcase bombs out there. I don't think so. . . .

An Interview with Congressman Curt Weldon

Could you tell me how you first found out about the existence of suitcase bombs?

Over the past several years in my work with Russia and its leaders, I have reached out to have conversations with all the senior leaders of the various factions in Russia, one of whom is General Alexander Lebed, a very prominent official credited with ending both the Chechnyan war and the war in Moldova.

On my second meeting with him in Moscow last May [1998], with a delegation of five or six other members, I was discussing with him the security of Russia's nuclear arsenal, and the status of conditions in the Russian military. This was not a meeting that any press attended, there was no press conference before the event or after the event, it was a quiet, off-the-record meeting to discuss in an intelligent way . . . what were his perceptions relative to Russian control of their nuclear arsenal and their conventional forces. And he gave us . . . examples of his concerns, examples of senior Soviet military leaders being forced out, being embarrassed and having to resort to illegal operations to make a living, and how we should be worried in the West because these very successful and capable soldiers and leaders were now having to resort to selling off technology that presents a real danger for the world. He went into the status of Russian nuclear submarines being decommissioned, with no place to store them, no means to take apart these nuclear submarines, and the terrible problem that Russia has today with . . . nuclear submarines being stored in ports potentially subject to an earthquake or another incident that could cause terrible degradation of the environment.

And then he went into . . . what he reported to Boris Yeltsin as Secretary of the National Security Council. He said one of his assignments was to account for 132 suitcase-size nuclear weapons that the Soviet Union had manufactured during the sixties, the seventies and the eighties, much like we manufactured in our country, even though today we no longer have small atomic demolition munitions, we've destroyed them all. . . . He said he could only find forty-eight. We were startled. We said, "General, what do you mean, you can only find forty-eight?" He said, "That's all we could locate. We don't know what the status of the other devices were, we just could not locate them."

The Russian media tried to portray Lebed as trying to gain notoriety for his campaign. There was nothing of that at all occurring. There were no media present. Two months later, after I returned to the United States and I debriefed our intelligence community to give me their assessment of what Lebed had said, I filed my trip report, as is required by members of Congress. In the trip report, I mentioned General Lebed's comments. A producer for "60 Minutes" . . . contacted me, and she said, "Congressman, did General Lebed really say this?" And I said, "Absolutely." She then asked to interview me and went over to Moscow and interviewed General Lebed. That was the first contact by a member of the media, and that was at the end of July, early August. That story then ran nationally in America on "60 Minutes," and following that there was a tremendous outcry. The Russian government denounced Lebed, the Russian media called him a traitor, they denied that he would know anything about these demolition devices. In some cases, senior Russian leaders denied they ever built these devices and said, "This is a fabrication, that Lebed is totally wrong." I then invited my good friend Dr. Alexei Yablokov to come to Washington in October, because he also knew something about these devices. And in a public hearing, Dr. Yablokov . . . said that he knew scientists who had worked on these devices. And in fact he said that he thought part of the problem in accounting for them may have been because some of his colleagues who worked on these devices told him they were building them for the KGB, and therefore if they were being built for the KGB, they may not have been included under the counting of the Ministry of Defense, an entirely separate operation. So therefore, he encouraged us to work jointly with his country to work together to see if in fact we could locate and then destroy these devices. It was not an attempt by him to embarrass his country, it was an attempt by him to get to the facts and the heart of the issue. Again, Yablokov was treated terribly by the Russian media. They called him a traitor, they said he was coming over to America and giving false information.

Finally, I went to Russia on my thirteenth trip out of fourteen or fifteen that I've taken, last December, and I requested, besides my other meetings, a meeting with the Defense Minister, Minister Sergeyev, as you know, General of the Chief Command Staff for some twenty years. And I said to General Sergeyev, after a wide range of topics that we discussed in a session that lasted well over an hour, I asked him specifically, "One, did you build small atomic demolition munitions, as we suspect you did? Two, do you know where they are? And three, have you destroyed them all?" And to me he said, "Yes, we did build them, we are in the process of destroying them, and by the year 2000 we will have destroyed all of our small atomic demolition devices, the so-called nuclear suitcases." Now, I have no reason to doubt General Sergeyev. In fact, I have a lot of respect for him. He impressed me very much in the meeting that I had with him. But again, I don't know whether or not we in fact know that they have the whereabouts known of each of these devices. I have confidence that what he told me is true. They will destroy all the devices that they currently know the whereabouts of. That's not the question. The question is what about devices that Russia may not have an accounting of? Do they exist? Do we have an accurate way of counting them?

How big are these things?

Well, it depends upon what you describe as a suitcase. Our understanding is that Russia manufactured three different types of these devices, most of them able to be carried by two people. Some able to be carried by one strong person. The typical size would be maybe like a large trunk, or in perhaps like a large suitcase, probably weighing someplace in the neighborhood of fifty to one hundred pounds. These devices would be self-activated, which means you would not have to have some central command, as you do the long range missiles, but rather that [the] individual controlling that device could in fact set that device for activation and actually activate it . . . independently from some central command. But these are devices that, yes, could be carried portably. There's no reason why they couldn't be put on a barge or a ship and floated into a harbor. And the devastation that they would present to that area would be beyond anyone's imagination.

What is the scale of damage that a terrorist could do with one of these things?

First of all, it would change the whole face of the earth in terms of our outlook on terrorism. Because you're not talking about a bomb that would blow up perhaps one part of one building, as we saw in Oklahoma, or you see repeatedly in London. You're talking about a bomb, a device with a capability of one kiloton of destruction, which is a massive capability that would cause severe destruction of a major inner city area, perhaps causing a multitude of buildings to collapse with the people inside of them. So you'd have a massive loss of life, you'd have massive radioactive contamination and you'd have massive havoc, unlike any that we've prepared for in the past. Just the threat of that kind of incident alone can change the face of the world in terms of the way we deal with terrorists. That's why a full accounting of these kinds of weapons has got to be the number one priority of both the United States and Russia.

And following on this issue of small nuclear devices is the whole issue of tactical nuclear weapons. I mean, one of the things that is not included in arms control negotiations between the United States and Russia are tactical nukes. Tactical nukes are smaller devices that can wreak havoc. They, too, in the wrong hands, could cause massive destruction and loss of life. And that's why in our discussions with Russia we must include the beginning of a formal counting process and the beginning of a limitation process on tactical nuclear weapons, not just those long range ICBMs. Because I would argue that the potential for a small atomic demolition device or a tactical nuclear device is even greater than the possibility of an accidental launch of a long range ICBM.

Lebed has said that he's been prevented really from talking about the suitcase bombs. What's going on there? Why isn't he allowed to talk freely about what is potentially a problem for the world?

I think it's partly because the Russian government and the media have tried to portray him as creating sensational stories in the West, when that was not his original intent. The sensationalization of the story came about by the Russian government and the Russian media itself, in response to Lebed's interview on "60 Minutes." What Lebed asked for and what Yablokov asked for were deliberate, very detailed efforts by our country to assist Russia, not to create any embarrassment for Russia, but for us to assist . . . them in helping them deal with the problem. . . I think Russia took a very defensive posture that these two individuals were out to embarrass the motherland. When I totally read the opposite. I read their attempts to interact with us [as] a pleading for us to come in and assist Russia in identifying these devices, locating them, using whatever detection means we have, and then destroying them. Something that we should be doing together. Again, as a country, America has not always handled nuclear materials in the most correct manner possible, and so this is not an attempt to try to embarrass Russia, but rather to focus on the potential problem that could come about from one of these devices, be they small atomic demolition nuclear suitcase or a tactical nuke, from getting into the wrong hands.

General Lebed is now in a position where the state prosecutor is investigating him for disclosure of state secrets. Do you think that in retaliation for speaking to you?

I asked General Lebed about this when he appeared before my committee just earlier this year, and he said it's interesting that they could charge him if in fact he didn't know what he was talking about. If, as they said, he didn't know what he was talking about, how could they charge him with a crime? If they're in fact charging him with a crime, then that must indicate he did know what he was talking about, in which case it means the Russian government was lying all this period of time when they said he did not know what he was talking about. But either way, it's not a state secret. General Sergeyev has told me, a member of Congress, that they made these devices, that they are in fact are in the process of destroying them. So that's in the public realm. And to somehow try to create some false accusation against General Lebed or Alexei Yablokov is just demeaning, I think, to a country that I have a great deal of respect for. I respect the Russian people, and I desperately want to assist them in this time of difficulty, but taking the steps to overreact and to pass tighter restrictive laws, as they've done, only hurts the democracy that's just beginning to take hold there.

—Taken from *http://www.pbs.org/wgbh/pages/frontline/shows/russia/suitcase/*

Contingency Planning for a Nuclear/Radiological Attack

Statement of Rose Gottemoeller
Senior Associate of the Carnegie Endowment for
International Peace

Before the Senate Subcommittee on International Security,
Proliferation and Federal Services
Committee on Governmental Affairs

November 7, 2001

This is a critical time to review weapons of mass destruction (WMD) technologies and materials and examine the effectiveness of export controls to curb these threats. Suddenly, the press is full of terrible scenarios: Nuclear weapons in the hands of Osama bin Laden. A suitcase bomb detonating in the middle of the Golden Gate Bridge. A radiological bomb spewing plutonium over the White House, creating a keep-out zone in central Washington that could last for many years. After reading about threats such as these, many people are worried. I commend the Subcommittee on International Security, Proliferation and Federal Services for confronting these complex and difficult issues in the search for new answers.

I would like to begin my remarks by examining the nuclear and radiological threats, how they differ, and what the level of concern should be about them. In describing these threats, I will also summarize the kind of technological challenge that they present to any would-be proliferator, whether state-sponsored, or non-state actors with a terrorist agenda. I will then move on to discuss the nuclear and radiological threats that, in my view, deserve more attention than they currently receive. I will conclude by commenting on how export controls have related to the nuclear nonproliferation regime and peaceful uses of nuclear technologies in the past, and offer my view of how they should relate in the future.

Nuclear and Radiological Weapons: The Threats and the Technologies
A simple nuclear device of the Hiroshima design is actually not the easiest nuclear capability for a proliferator to acquire, be he a terrorist or a rogue state actor. Although the design is now almost fifty years old, the Hiroshima device, also called a "gun-type" weapon, requires a large amount of nuclear material to achieve a nuclear explosion. We assume that 15–30 kg of highly enriched uranium or 3–4 kg of plutonium are needed for a sophisticated nuclear weapon. [1] Cruder devices may require more. One estimate, for example, places the likely size of a Pakistani weapon at around 1,500 pounds. [2] Therefore, although achieving a workable trigger device and other components would not be a trivial matter, the principal barrier to acquiring a nuclear weapon is the large amount of weapons-usable material that is needed.

For this reason, international nonproliferation policy has stressed keeping nuclear material production and enrichment technologies out of proliferators' hands. The crisis begun in 1994, when North Korea threatened to pull out of the Non-proliferation Treaty, was over its production of plutonium at the Yongbyon reactor. The more recent disagreement with Russia over its potential sale of laser isotope enrichment technology to Iran is another example. In all cases, the acquisition of sufficient nuclear material to achieve a nuclear detonation is the goal of would-be proliferators; it is the goal of U.S. non-proliferation policy to prevent that acquisition.

Following the breakup of the Soviet Union in 1991, the possibility that large amounts of weapons-usable material could be stolen from former Soviet nuclear facilities has become a major concern for the non-proliferation policy community worldwide. What would have had to be achieved through years of arduous and expensive production, enrichment and separation work—a sufficient amount nuclear material to build a bomb—could be acquired in an instant through thievery. Therefore, in the past decade, an enormous amount of attention and significant U.S. dollars ($173 million in FY '01 alone) have been spent on cooperating with Russia and the other states in the region to enhance the physical protection of weapons-usable materials in facilities that housed the Soviet weapons complex.

These sites stretch in an archipelago across the former Soviet territory—a vestige of Stalin's mania to spread industrialization to every corner of the Soviet land. In the case of nuclear production, facilities were especially located in remote areas, away from prying eyes and imprudent questions. In addition, operational weapons such as those deployed with the Russian Navy are often located at remote bases in areas such as the Arctic and Far East. The United States is currently working with the Ministry of Atomic Energy and Russian Navy to improve security of nuclear material and weapons at ninety-five sites in Russia and the former Soviet Union. [3] This program complements and strengthens efforts to control exports of nuclear technology. Barriers to the acquisition of weapons-usable nuclear material, in short, take several forms.

In contrast to bombs that would produce a nuclear detonation, radiological weapons are a simpler capability for a proliferator to acquire, if only because the threat in the case of a radiological device exists in a wide spectrum. The spectrum could range from low-level nuclear waste planted as a package in an urban location, through highly toxic nuclear material exploded as a "dirty bomb," using conventional explosives to spread it over a wide area. At the extreme end of the spectrum would be an aircraft attack on a nuclear facility that would turn the facility itself into a radiological weapon. As Mohamed El Baradei, the director-general of the International Atomic Energy Agency (IAEA), has said, "We are not just dealing with the possibility of governments diverting nuclear materials into clandestine weapons programs. Now we have been alerted to the potential of terrorists targeting nuclear facilities or using radioactive sources to incite panic, contaminate property and even cause injury or death among civilian populations." [4]

It is important to stress the differences among the types of radioactive materials that may come into play in a radiological attack. Since 1993, the IAEA has tracked 175 cases of trafficking in nuclear materials and 201 cases of trafficking in radioactive materials used for medical and industrial purposes. Of all of these cases, however, only eighteen involved small amounts of plutonium or highly enriched uranium, the "weapons-usable" material that is required to make a nuclear bomb. [5]

Therefore, a radiological attack would most likely involve lower-level radioactive material or even nuclear waste. Depending on what the material was and the amount of conventional explosive that was used to spread it around, it would potentially sicken people and contaminate large swaths of territory. However, it would not kill thousands of people outright, as would a nuclear explosive blast. Relatively few people, for example, were killed in the immediate aftermath of the 1986 accidental explosion at the Chernobyl nuclear reactor. They were mostly the firefighters who were bravely fighting the blaze, and were dead within a few days from radiation exposure. A thirty-kilometer area around Chernobyl remains a contaminated keep-out zone today, however, and many people have suffered thyroid and other illnesses that are directly related to the Chernobyl disaster.

But even a small amount of low-level nuclear waste, if planted in an urban setting, would have the potential to sow considerable panic unless authorities were quickly able to neutralize the incident in the public's mind. Chechen operatives, for example, planted low-level nuclear material in a park in Moscow in the mid-1990s and brought television cameras to the site to advertise that they had a "nuclear capability." The Russian authorities were quickly able to convey to the public that the material did not amount to a serious threat, thereby neutralizing the incident and preventing widespread panic. Similar quick action to analyze and clarify for the public the nature of radiological threats should be an important goal of public policy in the current environment, both in the United States and in other countries where such incidents might occur.

Nuclear and Radiological Threats Deserving More Attention

In my view, we now must begin to strike a balance between the most dangerous nuclear threats, and the less lethal but profoundly disruptive radiological threats. For many years, we have rightly emphasized in our non-proliferation policy preventing weapons-usable nuclear material and weapons-related technologies from falling into the hands of would-be proliferators—the most urgent and dangerous threat to counteract, given that a taboo against using nuclear material in a terrorist attack seemed to be operating. Nowadays, however, the taboo has disappeared. As David Albright, president of the Institute for Science and International Security, has said, "You'd always reach the point where you'd say, 'yes, a terrorist could theoretically do it' . . . and you'd look at the terrorists and say . . .

'they're not capable or they don't want to.' That's what's changed. Al Qaeda could do it, and they want to." [6]

Given the disappearance of this taboo, the relative ease with which a proliferator might acquire nuclear or radioactive material for use as a radiological device is a cause for strong concern. I believe, therefore, that radiological threats deserve greater attention in our efforts to secure nuclear materials and technologies then they have had in the past. At the same time, we cannot short-change the priorities that we have placed on preventing the proliferation of weapons-usable material and weapons-related technologies. We have to do both.

But resources are limited, and new funding for non-proliferation and nuclear threat reduction activities will have to compete with other urgent priorities in the conduct of the U.S.-led campaign against terrorism. Clearly, ongoing programs in the nuclear threat reduction arena should continue. They are receiving resources, and should not be interrupted in any way.

I would, however, like to suggest that we focus immediately on three new priorities as threats that deserve more attention. Given the demand on resources, we should also consider new methods of funding such projects, which I will specifically suggest in one case. The three priorities that I would suggest are (1) halting the production of weapons-grade plutonium in Russia, (2) securing nuclear facilities that remain vulnerable in the former Soviet Union, and (3) improving security at nuclear reactors and other sites where lower-level (non-weapons-usable) nuclear material is stored or used. The order in which these priorities are presented does not in any way reflect their relative importance. In my view, each of them is critical, and should be given serious and urgent consideration.

The first priority is halting the production of weapons-grade plutonium in Russia, which also deserves consideration as a project that could benefit from new methods of funding. The shutdown of plutonium production reactors in Russia has been a long-standing goal of the U.S. nuclear threat reduction programs. Originally built to pump out plutonium for the Soviet bomb program, the reactors now provide heat and electricity to the cities of Tomsk and Krasnoyarsk. In the process, they continue to produce a ton-and-a-half of weapons-grade plutonium every year, adding to Russian stocks that are well over one hundred tons already. Since it takes about four kilograms to build a nuclear bomb, the Tomsk and Krasnoyarsk reactors are producing every year enough plutonium for over 300 new bombs.

The Bush Administration, however, has not been enthusiastic about the shutdown plan, which involves replacing the three plutonium reactors with fossil fuel alternatives. They have apparently argued that we should not be building fossil fuel plants in Russia when the Russians could be building them themselves. The Bush team does have a point. The Russian Federation is no longer in such desperate straits as it was a decade ago. Indeed, while the U.S. economy has ceased growing, the Russian economy is growing at an annual rate of over 5 percent. Russia should therefore be in a position to shoulder more of the responsibility for nonproliferation priorities.

I believe that we should not take this argument too far, since the size of the Russian economy is still miniscule compared to that of the United States. As one Russian counterpart commented when he heard about the $40 billion supplemental that has been put in place in the United States to fund post-September 11 requirements, "That is more than double the entire Russian defense budget for this year." To square this circle, perhaps Russia could focus on programs, such as shutdown of the plutonium reactors, that the United States finds difficult to fund. At the same time, we could take special action to help the Russians to finance such programs.

One good idea in the funding arena is the so-called "debt-for-security" swap that Senators Biden and Lugar have proposed in new legislation. Under this concept, we would forgive Soviet-era debt in exchange for Russia putting rubles into non-proliferation programs. These swaps would have to be carefully structured. Moscow and Washington would have to agree firmly in advance what the priorities will be, and what schedule will be followed to achieve them. The shutdown of the Tomsk and Krasnoyarsk reactors, for example, would have to be decided in advance as an absolute and urgent priority.

In addition to new rubles, some new dollars should go into priority programs as well. The second priority that I would suggest, securing nuclear facilities that remain vulnerable in the former Soviet Union, falls into this category because it is a straightforward expansion of the existing Material Protection, Control and Accounting (MPC&A) program. This expansion would enable us to counter the potential for nuclear theft. Every time we go into a Russian nuclear site, we immediately survey it to decide what "quick fixes" are needed to urgently upgrade security. Is there a splintered old door that needs to be replaced on a nuclear storage building? Do windows need to be bricked up or equipped with bars? Does underbrush need to be cleared away from the perimeter, so no one can sneak up to the building unseen? These "quick fixes" can generally be completed within three months, if the weather cooperates.

If we began next April, the start of the summer construction period, within nine months we could complete quick fixes on all of the facilities in the Russian weapons complex that so far have not been touched under the MPC&A program. The Russian government would have to agree to give the United States access to the sites, and the U.S. Government would have to move fast to get all the planning and paperwork in place before April. But it could be done, and would give a huge boost to the nuclear security of the United States, Russia, and the rest of the world community.

The third priority, improving security at nuclear reactors and other sites where lower-level (non-weapons-usable) nuclear material is stored or used, addresses the radiological threat that has taken on a new importance in the wake of September 11. Traditionally, U.S. cooperation with the countries of the former Soviet Union to reduce the risk of nuclear proliferation has emphasized so-called higher value material and facilities—sites associated with the weapons complex and especially with nuclear material that can be used in the manufacture of nuclear weapons. Uranium, for example, must be enriched to a level above 20 percent before it is considered a proliferation threat in current U.S. programs. Materials below 20 percent enrichment have been considered a lower priority.

Given that radiological threats have taken on a new importance, programs to address them should also take on a new importance. One simple step that the United States could accomplish, for example, would be to restore the funds for international nuclear safety in the federal budget. For nearly a decade, the United States has been working with the countries of the former Soviet Union to upgrade the safety of Soviet-built nuclear reactors. The focus of the program has been precisely on safety, the rationale to prevent another Chernobyl-style disaster.

It has largely been successful in achieving these goals, and in fact, the permanent shut-down of the last Chernobyl reactor was accomplished in December 2000. For that reason, the program is slowly ramping down, dropping from over $30 million in FY 99 to just $10 million in the FY '02 budget. This program could be quickly ramped up in order to improve security at nuclear reactors and other sites where lower-level (non-weapons-usable) nuclear materials are stored. It could be extended not only to Russia and the former Soviet Union, but also to other countries around the world where such facilities are vulnerable.

How Export Controls Relate to the Nuclear Nonproliferation Regime
With regard to export controls, there is one essential difference between nuclear weapons, and chemical and biological weapons. Chemical and biological weapons are both banned by international protocols, and thus there is a global norm against them. Clearly both chemical and biological weapons are related to a host of dual-use technologies, which complicates efforts to control their proliferation. However, the ban represents a useful prohibition that somewhat simplifies the export control problem.

Nuclear weapons differ in that an essential deal was reached in the Nonproliferation Treaty (NPT), permitting five states to retain nuclear weapons, and other countries who agree to remain non-nuclear weapon states to acquire nuclear technology for peaceful purposes. Trade in support of these peaceful uses of nuclear technology has grown up over the years, principally relating to nuclear energy systems, but also related to medical, agricultural, and other technologies.

This situation is complicated by the fact that many of the peaceful uses of nuclear technology were born along with weapon uses, employing very similar technologies. The Tomsk and Krasnoyarsk reactors, producing weapons-grade plutonium at the same time they are producing heat and electricity for civilian populations, are extreme examples of this phenomenon, but they serve to illustrate the point. During the first fifty years of the nuclear era, it has often been complicated to distinguish between weapon and peaceful uses of the atom.

In this complicated environment, an export control regime has nevertheless grown up in the form of the Nuclear Suppliers Group (NSG), which makes use of mechanisms such as trigger lists of dual-use items to steer trade in nuclear technologies. The NSG has been an effective instrument, and no doubt will go through further development and improvement to address new challenges, such as the presence of nuclear weapons in South Asia. As this topic will receive full attention in the following panel on export control, I will not delve into further detail on it, but instead consider the future of nuclear export controls in a strategic sense.

Increasingly, those who are engaged in nuclear technology development, particularly for electricity generation purposes, are interested in new approaches that have limited cross-over to the weapon sector. They want to avoid the situation inherent in Tomsk and Krasnoyarsk, rather than continuing to proceed along that trajectory. For that reason, the nuclear industry today is beginning to concentrate on developing proliferation-resistant reactors that will minimize the production of weapons-usable material in their cycles. Ideally, proliferation-resistant reactors would burn up plutonium rather than breed it.

Although such reactors may be twenty years or more from commercial application, it is important that a new strategic approach is developing in the nuclear industry. The industry is emphasizing proliferation resistance along with other attributes such as minimization of nuclear waste, and stringent design for safety and security. If this trend develops successfully, it will simplify the export control problem for nuclear technologies. It may also prove to be the best way to fulfill the promise of peaceful nuclear uses in the Non-proliferation Treaty.

—Taken from *http://govt-aff.senate.gov/110701gottemoeller.htm*

Contingency Planning for Response to Radioactive Material Emergencies

Introduction

Part P provides for preparedness and response to events involving actual or potential release of radioactive material by specifying the content and exercise of a licensee contingency plan. Certain licensees are required to evaluate and prepare to respond to any release of radioactive material in an accident.

By addition of this Part P, the requirements for immediate containment, rescue, notifications, and securing the scene of an event are now located separate from Part C (Licensing of Radioactive Material) in the Suggested State

Regulations for Control of Radiation (SSRCR) of the Conference of Radiation Control Program Directors (CRCPD).

The U.S. Nuclear Regulatory Commission regulations upon which Part P is based—in particular 10 CFR 30.4, 30.32(i), 30.72 Schedule C, 40.31(i), 40.31(j), 40.34(f) & 70.22(i)—were published by April 7, 1989 (54 FR 14051), Emergency Preparedness for Fuel Cycle and Other Radioactive Material Licenses (10 CFR parts 30, 40, and 70), effective April 7, 1990. The U. S. Nuclear Regulatory Commission considers their adoption a matter of compatibility for an Agreement State. CRCPD considers these regulations essential to a Naturally Occurring and Accelerator Produced Radioactive Material (NARM) Licensing State. Cognizance was also taken of the June 22, 1995 (60 FR 32430-32442), Emergency Planning Licensing Requirements for Independent Spent Fuel Storage Facilities (ISFSI) and Monitored Retrievable Storage facilities

(MRS), 10 CFR Part 72, Final Rule.

General
The purpose of Part P stated in Section P.1 is for a licensee to be prepared to respond to an event involving actual or potential release of radioactive material.

The term "Contingency" in the title of Part P emphasizes planning and preparedness to respond to multiple eventualities. An effort was made to achieve consistency with response planning and practices between and among multiple types of radiological, and also nonradiological, preparedness and response perspectives, including that of the International Atomic Energy Agency and under the Comprehensive Environmental Response, Compensation and Liability Act as implemented by the U.S. Environmental Protection Agency and the State agencies.

Decisions to include or exclude certain detailed provisions of this part were based primarily on the peer review recommendations of CRCPD Committee E-6, Emergency Response Planning.

Key definitions are provided in Section P.3. For clarity of definition in Part P, reliance was placed upon 2001 Rationale for Part P NUREG-1140, A Regulatory Analysis on Emergency Preparedness for Fuel Cycle and Other Radioactive Material Licensees (January 1988). The U.S. Environmental Protection Agency, Federal Emergency Management Administration, U.S. Department of Energy, and U.S. Department of Transportation also have significant roles in emergency preparedness. Some Part P definitions are based on EPA 400-R-92-001, Manual of Protective Action Guides and Protective Actions for Nuclear Incidents, May 1992. In addition, cognizance was taken of the relevant International Atomic Energy Agency (IAEA) guides, including the International Nuclear Event Scale for prompt communication of safety significance and IAEA Safety Series I, numbers 115 and 109.

As prescribed by P.4, a license application must either (1) provide a contingency plan for responding to any accident in which specified quantities of radioactive material (Appendix A to Part P) could be released from the licensed site or (2) show that 0.01 Sievert (1 rem) total effective dose equivalent or 0.05 Sievert (5 rems) to the thyroid will not be exceeded by any accident. The applicant's dose calculation may take into account the factors in Section P.5.

The applicant's contingency plan must contain the information in Sections P.6a. through P.6l. Section P.7 requires comment on the contingency plan to be solicited from offsite response organizations including, but not limited to, local fire, police, ambulance and hospital services.

Section P.8 relates Part P to the public information requirements of the Emergency Planning and Community Right-to-Know Act of 1986, Title III, Pub. L. 99-499, pertaining to hazardous materials. Sections P.9 and P.10 specify required training, drills and exercises.

Section P.11 specifies what must be done in cases when the plan is put into action. Section P.12 specifies how often the contingency plan is to be revised and how revision is to be done. Section P.13 contains record-keeping requirements.

This part was based upon existing US Nuclear Regulatory Commission and state regulations (AR indicates Arkansas, CO indicates Colorado, and IL indicates Illinois). Wording was used for some provisions from AR RH-403g, adopted August 15, 1990, CO 3.9.11, effective January 1, 1994, and IL 330.500.

Part P is not intended to regulate radioactive material "in transport." See 49 CFR 172.600-604, in particular 49 CFR 172.602. Part P may relate to a licensed shipper or a facility with potential responsibility for an offsite radioactive material transportation accident.

Specific Provisions
Section P.1—Purpose. Part P specifies requirements on a licensee for accidents only. The relationship of "accident" and "incident" is that in the International Basic Safety Standards and International Atomic Energy Agency International Nuclear Event Scale. This is reflected in P.2b. and later in Part P. The key distinction between accident and incident is whether a public dose limit is likely to be exceeded or not. The International Atomic Energy Agency usage fits a wider range of licensees than United States government agency usages and is more self-consistent and less confusing. The International Atomic Energy Agency usage differs semantically from (1) the use of the word "incident" in reporting abnormal occurrences and also (2) the fixed facility definition 2001 Rationale for Part P of "nuclear incident" (EPA 400-R-92-001, p. 1–1), which includes "accidents," both "deliberate or accidental" releases, and the possibility of release "in sufficient quantity to warrant consideration of protective actions" (EPA 400-R-92-001, p. 1–1 & A-2).

Section P.3—Definitions. The definitions in Part P have been judiciously crafted for clarity in their application by state radiation control staff. For example, some planners use a definition of "abnormal exposure condition," defined as when a source, or the radiation from it, is not under control. The Part P definitions do not include abnormal exposure or potential exposure in order to avoid the multiple and often confusing meanings of "exposure" in radiation protection and hazardous material regulation.

As used in this part, "accident" is defined (1) semi-quantitatively in relation to public dose in excess of regulatory limits (consonant with both 10 CFR and the International Atomic Energy Agency), then (2) also in relation to consequences of the unintended event and whether facility protection or safety are degraded. The phrase "in sufficient quantity to warrant consideration of protective actions" is from the definition of a "nuclear incident" in EPA 400-R-92-001.

Some definitions of "accident" refer to the loss of normal control of a source. This is not included in Part P.

Some definitions include "loss" of radioactive material. For Part P, "release" is sufficient.

Other phrases considered but not included in the definition of "accident" were: "unauthorized release of radioactive material due to human error or negligence, system failure, an act of God, or defective components," as well as theft.

Although NRC does not specifically define "accident," it does list classifications of accidents as being alerts or site area emergencies, for example, 10 CFR §30.32h(3)(iii).

The definition of alert is essentially identical to 10 CFR §30.4, which says alert means events may occur, are in progress, or have occurred that could lead to a release of radioactive material but that the release is not expected to require a response by offsite response organizations to protect persons offsite. The preferred singular "event" is used for definiteness and enforceability, rather than plural "events."

CRCPD proposed a similar definition, enhanced slightly. CRCPD proposed that "alert" be defined to mean an accident has occurred, is in progress, or is imminent which involves actual or potential degradation of the level of safety of the facility and requires response, possibly including that off-duty staff of the facility or offsite response organizations report to duty stations. During an alert, the potential release of radioactive material is not expected to require a response by offsite response organizations to protect persons offsite unless the situation becomes more serious. The phrase "may occur" is too general and isn't time-bound, so the word "imminent" is used. The references to "off-duty staff" and "duty stations" help make very clear the distinction between "alert" and "site area emergency."

NRC found the proposed Part P definition to be sufficiently different from 10 CFR §30.4 that it may cause confusion. The differences cited are the additional information provided (type of on-site and off-site response and "unless the situation becomes more serious"). NRC staff believed this information best provided in guidance. The U.S. Nuclear Regulatory Commission stated in a June 12, 2000 letter that the definition should 2001 Rationale for Part P be essentially identical to meet compatibility category A, as defined in Office of State and Tribal Programs (STP) Procedure SA-200.

A definition of "emergency" is added in the sense of EPA 400-R-92-001 (danger to life and property).

The definition of "Emergency Planning Zone" is from federal guides.

The definition of "evacuation" is from EPA 400-R-92-001, p. A-1.

The definition of "event" is meant to be general.

The definition of "exercise" is from federal guides.

A definition of "facility" or "fixed facility" is not included at this time.

A definition of "general emergency" is added in brackets. This would possibly apply in a state evaluating an irradiator facility accident or fire at a radiopharmaceutical laboratory and if a state were to at some future time regulate certain U.S. Department of Energy facilities. The 1989 and 1995 U.S. Nuclear Regulatory Commission NUREG documents and Federal Register notices upon which Part P is based do not anticipate this class of response for non-nuclear-power-plant licenses.

NRC in its June 12, 2000, letter to CRCPD cites the Statements of Consideration for the NRC emergency plan rule (54 FR 14054, April 7, 1989), based on NUREG-1140:

"For nuclear power plants, a general emergency means there is a possibility of very large releases that could cause acute radiation effects miles from the plant. Neither releases nor doses of those magnitudes could result from accidents at fuel cycle or other radioactive materials facilities. Therefore, the general emergency class is not used for these facilities."

States are advised to consider this premise in deciding whether to include or exclude the bracketed definition of "general emergency."

A definition of "immediate" is included ("15 minutes" is from NUREG-0654), with provision for flexibility.

A definition of "incident" as used internationally is included. Incident is not used at this time in any regulatory requirement of Part P. NRC in its June 12, 2000, letter to CRCPD suggested that use of the term "incident" has the potential to cause confusion on the part of licensees. "Incident" is not used in NRC regulations. NRC recognizes that the way Part P distinguishes "incident" from "accident," only an event at level of significance to safety higher than an incident, that is, an alert or site area emergency, requires a contingency plan. Reference to "incident" is deleted from P.6e. to avoid confusion.

The definition of "offsite response organizations" is taken from wording in 60 FR 32430-32442, modified by replacing "for example" with "including, but not limited to," and replacing "medical" with "ambulance and hospital services."

The definition of "projected dose" is from EPA 400-R-92-001, p. A-2.

The definition of "protective action" is from 10 CFR. For comparison, the definition in EPA 400-R-92-001, p. A-2, is: "An activity conducted in response to an incident or potential incident to avoid or reduce radiation dose to members of the public (sometimes called a protective measure)."

The definition of "protective action guide" is condensed from EPA 400-R-92-001, p. A-3, which has: "The projected dose to reference man, or other defined individual, from an accidental release of radioactive material at which a specific protective action to reduce or avoid that dose is warranted."

The definition of "relocation" is from EPA 400-R-92-001, p. A-3.

The definition of "sheltering" is from EPA 400-R-92-001, p. A-3.

The definition of "site" is generically adapted from state radiation regulations (e.g. CO '1.4). It includes the term "restricted area," which is defined in Part A, and also includes a sub-definition of site boundary which is from 10 CFR §20.1003.

The definition of "site area emergency" is essentially identical to 10 CFR §30.4 which says site area emergency means events may occur, are in progress, or have occurred that could lead to a significant release of radioactive material and that could require a response by offsite response organizations to protect persons offsite. The preferred singular "event" is used for definiteness and enforceability, rather than plural "events."

CRCPD proposed a similar definition, enhanced slightly. CRCPD proposed that "site area emergency" be defined to mean that an accident has occurred, is in progress, or is imminent which involves actual or probable major failures of facility functions needed for the protection of the public. A site area emergency will require contact with offsite response organizations to protect persons offsite.

NRC found the proposed Part P definition to be sufficiently different from 10 CFR §30.4 that it needs to meet compatibility category A, as designated in Office of State and Tribal Programs (STP) Procedure SA-200. NRC's definition is said (June 12, 2000, letter) to set the threshold for a site area emergency at events that could lead to a significant release and could require a response by offsite response organizations to protect persons off-site. NRC interprets the Part P definition to use a higher threshold than the NRC's "could require" contact with off-site response organizations to protect persons off-site, with the result that a site area emergency is declared sooner by NRC. A site area emergency is declared sooner by the licensee under NRC regulations.

Section P.4—Dose Evaluation and Contingency Planning. A 10 mSv effective dose equivalent is used, consistent with the U.S. Nuclear Regulatory Commission administrative threshold to determine whether a contingency plan is required. AR uses 5 mSv. "Projected dose" is "in the absence of protective actions," thus, the 10 mSv administrative level (10 times the 10 CFR Part 20 annual limit for an individual member of the public) is in part because in practice (1) actual dose may well be less than 1 mSv and (2) the plan is to prepare (and help prevent) a potential as well as an actual accident. For IAEA, "accident" is at the prescribed public total effective dose equivalent limit, while "incident" is 0.1 of the total effective dose equivalent limit for a member of the public.

Since Appendix A, footnote 1, provides for combinations of materials, "quantities" is used in P.4 and the title to Appendix A.

The word "maximum" was not included, since it adds no meaning to "not exceed."

Section P.5—Evaluation of Potential Dose. Part P uses language from Illinois, "may take into account whether," rather than 10 CFR and Arkansas, which use "One or more of the following factors may be used to support an evaluation submitted under this section."

NRC in its June 12, 2000, letter observed that the rationale for not including §30.32g(2)(vii) is that it is included in P.5e.

Section P.5b.—Evaluation of Potential Dose. The wording "because of the way it is stored or packaged" (AR) is used rather than "due to the method of storage or packaging" (IL).

Section P.5f.—Evaluation of Potential Dose. The phrase "or larger than" (IL) is added to the 10 CFR phrasing.

Section P.5g.—Evaluation of Potential Dose. "Other factors appropriate for the specific facility" as included by NRC, AR & CO but excluded by IL, is not added to P.5g. The CRCPD believes P.5e. includes this flexibility.

Section P.6—Contents of a Contingency Plan. Part P uses IL "shall" rather than AR "must."

To make explicit the accountable and dynamic nature of the contingency planning document, Part P includes "in separate sections having each page labeled with a date and revision number."

Section P.6e.—Contents of a Contingency Plan. P.6e. includes both incidents and accidents, since the ALARA principle applies to both. Radiological exposure controls for both onsite and offsite response personnel are to be included.

Section P.6h.ii.—Contents of a Contingency Plan. This provision is based on 60 FR 32441. Notification is by telephone only, since facsimile or electronic mail can go for hours or days before being read. Arrangements for backup communication and 24-hour capability are required.

Section P.6h.iii.—Contents of a Contingency Plan. This provision is from 60 FR 32441.

Section P.6j.ii.—Contents of a Contingency Plan. The phrase "radiation workers and non-radiation workers including off-site responders" was substituted for "personnel" in order to be explicitly consistent with the recent clarification in 10 CFR of radiation and non-radiation worker and to make it clear that training include responders.

Section P.6k.i.—Contents of a Contingency Plan. Quarterly is a usual frequency of communication drills.

Section P.6k.ii.—Contents of a Contingency Plan. A bi-ennial frequency is required, with at least one drill in between which combines some of the principal functional areas of the licensee's emergency response capabilities.

Section P.6k.iv.—Contents of a Contingency Plan. The most probable scenario may be a minor event. Drills and exercises are to deal with events up to and including the maximum credible accident.

Section P.6k.v.—Contents of a Contingency Plan. Since it can be helpful to have participants think about an exercise in advance, the question of whether scenarios are announced or unannounced is left to be "prescribed in the contingency plan." NUREG-0654 evidently doesn't require that participants not know the scenario, although 10 CFR §30.32(i)(3)(xii) stipulates that the scenario "shall not be known to most exercise participants."

Section P.7—Comment from Offsite Response Organization. 60 FR 32433 discusses whether amendments should also be subject to 60-day comment specification.

The phrase "including, but not limited to, local fire, ambulance, and hospital emergency response officials" was added for explicitness.

Section P.11b.—Plan Implementation. The word "immediately" (IL) is used, consonant with the definition in P.3j. 10 CFR and AR include "not later than one hour after the licensee declares an emergency." Per 60 FR 32435, one commenter on ISFSI emergency response advocated 15 minutes.

Section P.12a.—Plan Revision. 10 CFR "report" is modified to "provide" (meaning "send in").

Section P.12b.—Plan Revision. Plan revisions are to be "in writing," to make explicit that Agency approval is to be documented not just verbal.

Based on comments, the second sentence was added: "For information purposes only, updates of individual names, titles, assignments of responsibility, and telephone numbers are to be reported to the Agency and to affected offsite response organizations within 30 days."

Appendix A—Quantities of Radioactive Materials Requiring Consideration of the Need for a Contingency Plan for Responding to a Release. In the table (10 CFR Part 30.72, Schedule C) of "quantities of radioactive materials requiring consideration of the need for an emergency plan for responding to a release," naturally occurring and accelerator-produced radioactive materials are covered by limits for "any other beta-gamma emitter," "any other alpha emitter" and other special case.

Matters for Future Consideration

These matters for future consideration came from state radiation control agency comments and from federal and state agency documents used by the working group.

1. The working group will consider the following regarding definitions in Sec. P.3:
    a. The relationship of event to "accident" and "incident" in the International Basic Safety Standards and International Atomic Energy Agency International Nuclear Event Scale, deserves closer comparison to usages in the United States.

    Information on the International Nuclear Event Scale is readily available at:

    http://www.iaea.org/ns/nusafe/nusafe3/ineimage.htm
    http://www.iaea.org/worldatom/Periodicals/Factsheets/English/
        ines.html
    http://www.iaea.org/ns/nusafe/nusafe3/ines.htm

    b. The definition of "emergency" could be refined in comparison to the usages of the U.S. Environmental Protection Agency and Federal Emergency Management Agency.
    c. The word "demonstration" may be preferable to "exercise."
    d. A definition of "facility," or reference to one elsewhere, for example, "fixed facility" or "facility alert," could be made.
    e. A definition of "protective measure," used as different from "protective action" by some possession-only license holders to distinguish between onsite and offsite emergency preparedness needs, could be added.
    f. A definition of "release fraction" could be included.
    g. Define "respirable size range" in relation to Sec. P.5c., perhaps by citing an American National Standards Institute or similar reference.
    h. Re-examine the basis for and perceived differences between NRC's and the IAEA-based proposed CRCPD usages related to site area emergency.
    i. Define "solubility" in relation to Sec. P.5c., perhaps by citing an American National Standards Institute or similar reference.

2. The working group will consider deriving specific release fraction values for naturally occurring radionuclides to be added to the table in Appendix A, "Quantities of Radioactive Materials Requiring Consideration of the Need for a Contingency Plan for Responding to a Release." This matter is interrelated with the potential necessity of calculations using revised methods and definitions prior to modifying table entries.
   a. An updated methodology could be used to calculate estimated offsite dose and to relate the release fraction to the calculated total effective dose equivalent. An updated methodology would use and likely replace the present basis, as found in pages 70–101 of U.S. Nuclear Regulatory Commission NUREG-1140, January 1988.
   b. The table values at present do not reflect differences in the chemical state of an element and also the type of material (paper, metal, liquid, etc.) as they might modify the release fraction.
   c. The table values pertain to releases which are airborne. Scenarios exist for waterborne releases that require a response plan.
   d. An updated methodology will likely use a revised definition for release fraction.
   e. Release fraction table values could be calculated for specific naturally occurring and accelerator produced radionuclides (in particular 226Ra, 57Co, 67Gallium, 111In, and 201Thallium). These nuclides could then be added to the table in Appendix A.

3. The working group will consider adding additional specifications of the kind usually required for nuclear power plants, uranium enrichment facilities or an interim spent fuel storage installation. Some of these specifications may be more appropriately included in regulatory guidance. Alternatively, such specifications could be added to Part P in brackets, as optional regulatory language. Requirements which could be considered include the following:
   a. Sec. P.6b.: When radioactive material inventories or industrial applications change, the license should be required to change the offsite release scenarios, making the contingency plan inventory- and process-specific.
   b. Sec. P.6d.: Specifications for the type of monitoring, for example, area monitors.
   c. Sec. P.6e.: Description of radiological exposure controls should specifically state how exposure is estimated (whether based on source term measurements or field airborne radioactivity detectors) and minimized, including how authorization, if any, to exceed limits or guidelines is obtained.
   d. Sec. P.6e.: Description of radiological exposure controls should explicitly state whether respirators will be used, and, if so, whether they're maintained and whether workers receive medical exams.

e. Sec. P.6g.ii.: Description of responsibilities should explicitly state the role of site Radiation Protection Officer. State radiation control programs expect the Radiation Protection Officer to be responsible, since the Radiation Protection Officer will usually have the best information regarding current uses and inventory.

f. Sec. P.6g.iii.: Capabilities and notification procedures of offsite response personnel should be documented, with clearly defined roles and 24-hour telephone and pager numbers.

g. Sec. P.6g.iii.: The description should identify how contractors will be coordinated.

h. Sec. P.6j.ii.: Hazard training should conform to specifications of the Occupation Safety and Health Administration for hazardous waste operations (HAZWOPER).

i. Sec. P.6k.i.: Communications drills should be monthly.

j. Sec. P.6k.ii.: Radiological/health physics drills should be conducted every year with a medical emergency every other year.

k. Sec P.6k.iii.: Fire/ambulance services should be invited to participate every other year.

l. Sec. P.6k.v.: Explicitly state a frequency of unannounced drills or exercises (being unannounced is not necessary every time).

m. Sec. P.10a.: An exercise should be conducted each year and deficiencies corrected before the subsequent drill or exercise is conducted.

n. Sec. P.10b.: Be more explicit about who is to do the critique and evaluation, for example, the licensee Radiation Protection Officer.

o. Sec. P.10c.: Here or in a footnote, be explicit as to whether the Agency is required to participate. The Agency should observe or participate every two years.

p. Sec. P.12: A process for maintaining, updating and distributing controlled copies to onsite and offsite response organizations and to the public should be required.

4. In Sec. P.4, a 1 mSv (100 mrem) may be a more consistent threshold for requiring a contingency plan. As an alternative, a smaller scale of contingency planning (strictly onsite emergency planning) could be required for the 1 mSv to 10 mSv range.

5. Clarify how the thyroid (iodine) special dose limit, included by the U.S. Nuclear Regulatory Commission in 1989, is best understood in relation to total effective dose equivalent.

6. By analogy to the environmental report requirement for some radioactive material licensees, consider providing discretion to the Agency by adding "Notwithstanding P.4a., if the Agency determines a credible accident may affect the quality of the human environment by reason of exposure to radiation, a contingency plan for mitigation shall be included in the application."

7. A question which remains is whether to require delineation of an "emergency planning zone" of set radius, for example 10 miles, or perhaps 1-5 miles as regarded appropriate for an Interim Spent Fuel Storage Installation by the U.S. Nuclear Regulatory Commission in the June 22, 1995, 60 FR 32430-32442, Emergency Planning Licensing Requirements for Independent Spent Fuel Storage Facilities (ISFSI) and Monitored Retrievable Storage Facilities (MRS), 10 CFR Part 72, Final Rule.

8. Part P contains minimal requirements for public information. If a reasonable likelihood existed for offsite consequences of a credible accident, a public education program could let people know ahead of time, possibly through a warning system. If protective action by the public is part of the contingency plan, a description of how the public will be trained in what might happen and how to perform the action (such as removal and disposition of contamination). If no such likelihood exists, the licensee's contingency plan could still describe who is responsible for public information and how news releases will be coordinated.

9. Consider whether Part P might be strengthened by a provision for the Agency to take possession of radioactive material in emergency.

10. Consider whether Part P might be strengthened by a provision for the Agency to assert Agency authority for access to accident site for specific purposes.

11. Consider whether Part P might be strengthened by a provision for the Agency to have certain capabilities in place.

—Taken from *http://www.crcpd.org/SSRCRs/P%20rat%202001.pdf*

U.S. Environmental Protection Agency— Nuclear Terrorism Response

What is EPA's role during a radiological emergency?
(http://www.epa.gov/radiation/rert/respond.htm)

What EPA does during a radiological emergency response depends on the type of emergency that occurs. In some cases EPA leads and coordinates other federal agencies in the response. In other cases, EPA provides technical support and guidance.

When does EPA lead?
EPA leads and coordinates the federal response to accidents involving all radiological materials not regulated or owned by another federal agency. These materials include lost radiation sources, sources of unknown origin, and naturally occurring materials such as radium. In addition, EPA leads the U.S. response to foreign radiological accidents or events that have the potential to affect the United States or its territories (for example, Chernobyl; Ukraine; and Tokaimura, Japan).

As Lead Federal Agency, EPA has a number of responsibilities:
- provide overall coordination of federal response actions
- recommend protective actions to state and local officials to minimize the radiological hazards to people in affected areas and the environment
- coordinate releases of federal information to the public, and provide status reports on all aspects of the emergency to Congress, the White House, and other stakeholders
- coordinate with the Department of State on the international aspects and notifying other countries.

When does EPA support other organizations?

For radiological emergencies involving materials regulated or owned by another federal agency, EPA actively supports the Lead Federal Agency and the affected state and local governments:

- conducting environmental monitoring, sampling, and data analysis
- assessing the national impact of any release on public health and the environment through the Agency's Environmental Radiation Ambient Monitoring System
- providing technical advice on containment and cleanup of the radiological contamination
- assisting in site restoration and recovery

Whether in a leadership or support role, EPA has the option of sending its Radiological Emergency Response Team, RERT, to the accident scene. The RERT is a team of multidisciplinary, specially trained staff from EPA headquarters, its national radiation laboratories, and the Agency's ten regional offices. The team provides critical scientific and technical support to state and local governments and to other federal agencies.

Exercises

Exercises test and validate plans and procedures, test the readiness of response capabilities, and increase the confidence and skill of personnel. In addition, exercises identify weaknesses so that corrective actions can be taken to improve performance during an actual response. Interagency exercises also allow the various agencies' personnel to become familiar with each other and learn to coordinate and operate together.

EPA's Radiological Emergency Response Team (RERT) has participated in many exercises simulating radiological emergencies involving nuclear power plants, Department of Energy weapons and waste storage facilities, and military sites.

Types of Exercises

RERT participates in exercises that range from informal "walk throughs" to highly complex, realistic simulations of actual emergencies. Exercises fall into three main categories: tabletop exercises, command post exercises, and field exercises.

Table Top Exercises (TTX)

During a tabletop exercise or TTX, participants test an emergency response plan and its standard operating procedures by informally "walking through" a hypothetical emergency. The TTX allows policy-making officials and key staff with emergency management responsibilities to identify and resolve problems with the emergency plan.

Command Post Exercise (CPX)

A CPX is more extensive than a tabletop exercise in that it usually involves activities in other than a conference room atmosphere. It usually focuses on a single response or activity, for example, command and control. It can also involve limited deployment of equipment for a specific purpose.

Field Exercises (FTX)

An FTX is more extensive and realistic than either a tabletop or command post exercise. Activities extend beyond a conference room or operations center, taking place in a field environment over several days. An FTX tests many functions in an emergency plan in realistic situations.

Example Exercises

The table and text below provide examples of the exercises in which EPA's Radiological Emergency Response Team has participated. They are field exercises unless otherwise indicated.

Wasatch Rings II

In April 2001, the Utah Olympic Public Safety Command and the FBI co-sponsored a Field Training Exercise in Salt Lake City, Utah. The exercise scenario involved numerous incidents occurring in Utah during the 2002 Olympic Winter Games, including an explosion involving radiological material and mass casualties. The exercise provided an opportunity for various public safety organizations supporting the Games at the local, state, and federal levels to test their Olympic operations and crisis and consequence management procedures.

TOPOFF/National Capitol Region (NCR) Exercise

Held in May 2000, TOPOFF (Top Officials) was a large-scale national exercise mandated by Senate Report 105-235. Per the Senate Report's direction, the exercise, which was co-chaired by the Attorney General and the director of FEMA and coordinated with the National Security Council, was designed to involve top federal, state, and local government officials in responding to terrorist attacks involving weapons of mass destruction (WMDs).

TOPOFF consisted of simultaneous chemical and biological incidents in Denver, Colorado, and Portsmouth, New Hampshire. A concurrent exercise, National Capitol Region 2000, involved a radiological release in the Washington, DC, area. The exercise was the largest federal, state, and local counter-terrorism response exercise ever undertaken.

Exercise	Scenario	Participants
Wasatch Rings II (2001)	various incidents, including an explosion involving radiological material, at the 2002 Olympic Winter Games	FBI, FEMA, EPA, NRC, other federal agencies, State of Utah, numerous local responders
TOPOFF/National Capitol Region (NCR) Exercise (2000)	simultaneous chemical, biological, and radiological attacks in Regions 1, 3, and 8	National Security Council, FEMA, FBI, EPA, other federal, state, and local responders
INEX-2/CANATEX 3 (1999)	accident at a Canadian nuclear power plant	IAEA, Canada, numerous European countries, eleven U.S. agencies
Western Roundup (1998)	fire at former radium dial production facility	federal state and local responders
Digit Pace II (1997)	propane truck collides with truck carrying nuclear weapons, causing explosions/ release of radiation	DOD, EPA, FEMA, state, local government, and other federal agencies
Lost Source (1997)	unshielded 100-curie iridium-192 source found in trash truck at landfill	EPA, NRC, FEMA, state, local government
Digit Pace I (1996)	train collides with Safe Secure Trailer causing fire/ release of radiation	DOE, federal, state, and local responders
MIRRORED IMAGE 96 (1996)	threat of a radiation dispersal incident following the disappearance of a container of spent nuclear fuel	DOD, FEMA, DOE, EPA, other federal, state, and local responders
OLYMPIC SPARKLER (1996)	explosion of a radiation dispersal device (RDD)	EPA
Display Select (1995)	accident with nuclear weapon being loaded on submarine causes plutonium release	DNA, federal, state, and local military and civilian governments
RADEX-94 (1994)	response to radiological emergency in Arctic	State of Alaska, AEPS and Northern Forum emergency response groups, EPA, DOS
Diaz Tabletop (1993)	earthquake cracks underground storage tank causing explosion and hydrogen release	DOE Hanford

Exercise	Scenario	Participants
Fremont (1993)	propane tank explodes causing release of radiation at adjacent facility	Westinghouse Hanford Co., States of Oregon and Washington, EPA, DOE, NRC, USDA
FRMAC-93 (1993)	general emergency at commercial nuclear power plant	State of Nebraska, Ft. Calhoun Nuclear Power Plant, other agencies
INEX-1 Tabletop (1993)	response to a foreign radiological incident	Canada, State of NY, DOE, USDA, HHS, NRC, DOS, EPA, and other federal agencies

INEX-2/CANATEX 3

On April 27–28, 1999, the United States participated as a border country in the Canadian regional INEX-2/CANATEX 3 exercise. Canada, the United States, IAEA, and numerous European nations participated in the exercise. A total of eleven U.S. agencies were involved, including EPA, the Department of State, the Department of Energy, the NRC, and FEMA. The overall purpose of the Canadian regional INEX-2 exercise was to allow participating countries to assess their emergency preparedness by responding to a simulated nuclear power plant accident. Each country acted on the scenario information it received, thereby testing pre-existing emergency plans, communication equipment and procedures, and personnel.

Western Roundup Exercise

In September 1998, federal, state, and local emergency responders held a radiological exercise near Austin, Texas. In the scenario, a fire occurs in an abandoned industrial warehouse that produced instrument gauges using luminous paint containing radium during World War II. The exercise was designed to improve coordination, and exchange knowledge between federal, state, and local agencies.

Digit Pace II

In 1997, the Department of Energy and the Defense Special Weapons Agency co-sponsored a full-field weapons exercise at Kirtland Air Force Base in Albuquerque, New Mexico. Participants included the Department of Defense, EPA, the Federal Emergency Management Agency, other federal agencies, and state and local governments.

The exercise simulated a propane truck colliding with a truck carrying nuclear weapons. The resulting explosions released radioactive material into the environment and surrounding community.

The exercise was the first test of DOE's role as a Lead Federal Agency under the *Federal Radiological Emergency Response Plan.*

Lost Source

In 1997, several federal agencies sponsored a two-part, lost source exercise. It included a tabletop exercise in September and a field exercise in October 1997.

In the exercise scenario, a trash truck arrived at a landfill facility carrying a load containing radioactive material—an unshielded, 100 Curie iridium-192 source.

The exercise tested the capability to mount a multi-agency response to a radioactive material release on a regional scale.

Digit Pace I

In 1996, The Department of Energy sponsored the exercise Digit Pace I at Kirtland AFB in Albuquerque, New Mexico. It involved federal, state, and local responders.

In the exercise scenario, a train collided with a Safe Secure Trailer carrying nuclear weapons, causing a fire and the release of radioactive materials. (A Safe Secure Trailer is specially designed for transporting nuclear materials. As its name implies, it is built for security and to withstand severe impacts.)

The exercise tested the effectiveness and coordination of the participants. It focused on the ability of the Department of Energy to lead other federal agencies, provide strategic policy guidance and federal oversight, and coordinate with state and local governments during an emergency.

Mirrored Image 96

Exercise Mirrored Image 96 was held in March 1996 in Atlanta, Georgia, in preparation for the 1996 Summer Olympic Games. The exercise scenario involved the theft of a container from a shipment of spent nuclear fuel and an attempt to extort money from the Atlanta Committee for the Olympic Games, threatening to disrupt the Games if demands were not met. FEMA, the U.S. Department of Energy, and the Georgia Emergency Management Agency activated response teams for the exercise. Additional support was provided by DOE, the Department of Defense, EPA, and FEMA to assess the situation, protect the public, and bring about the recovery of the nuclear material. The Command Post Exercise included over 300 personnel representing 47 organizations.

Olympic Sparkler

Held in April 1996, Exercise Olympic Sparkler was an EPA Headquarters exercise focusing on the role of EPA's National Incident Coordination Team in response to a simulated explosion of a radiation dispersal device in the Atlanta, Georgia, area. The exercise was designed to test EPA plans and procedures used to respond to a terrorist threat or incidents involving radiation disposal among a civilian population.

Display Select
In 1995, the Defense Nuclear Agency sponsored a nuclear weapons accident exercise at the Naval Weapons Station in Yorktown, Virginia, for federal, state, and local military and civilian responders.

The exercise simulated the accidental explosion of a weapon being loaded onto a submarine. The explosion led to a major release of weapons-grade plutonium that spread throughout the surrounding area.

The exercise tested response procedures among participants and explored the relationship between the Federal Radiological Emergency Response Plan and the Federal Response Plan.

International Emergency Exercise (INEX-I) Tabletop Exercise
The May 1993 exercise, INEX-1, included representatives from Canada; the State of New York; the Departments of State, Energy, Agriculture, and Health and Human Services; the Nuclear Regulatory Commission; and other federal agencies.

In the exercise scenario, involving two fictitious countries, a reactor accident in Acciland threatened the neighboring country of Neighborland.

INEX-1 tested the ability of Canada and the United States to respond jointly to an emergency involving both countries. The exercise resulted in recommendations that work groups cross-train in both Canadian and U.S. procedures and in provincial and state procedures. Recommendations also included refining Lead Federal Agency communication procedures between Canada and EPA.

Diaz Tabletop Exercise
In June 1993, the Department of Energy, Hanford Office held the Diaz Tabletop exercise in Richland, Washington.

In the exercise scenario, an underground tank cracked during an earthquake, releasing hydrogen. As the earthquake caused instruments to short out, sparks ignited the hydrogen. The resulting explosion and fire propelled radioactive material beyond the site boundary and burned 5,000 kg of the waste.

The exercise tested the technical component of the Federal Radiological Emergency Response Plan for response to a general emergency at a Department of Energy facility.

Federal Radiological Monitoring and Assessment Center FRMAC-93
In 1993, the states of Nebraska and Iowa and participating federal agencies conducted an exercise in Omaha, Nebraska. With the cooperation of the Ft. Calhoun Nuclear Power Station the exercise scenario simulated a general emergency at a nuclear power plant.

During emergencies at a Department of Energy facility or commercial nuclear power plant, DOE sets up and operates the Federal Radiological Monitoring and Assessment Center. It is an ad hoc center for collecting and analyzing monitoring data during an emergency. Following the emergency, DOE turns the center over to EPA for long-term management.

The exercise tested this technical component of the *Federal Radiological Emergency Response Plan.*

Fremont

In September 1993, about 150 emergency personnel took part in the Fremont exercise in Richland, Washington. The exercise involved people from the states of Washington and Oregon and from Westinghouse Hanford Company, the company that operates the Hanford Reservation facilities for the Department of Energy. Participating agencies included EPA, the Department of Energy, the Nuclear Regulatory Commission, and the Department of Agriculture.

In the initial scenario, a propane tank, located adjacent to the fictitious 299 EX Facility, exploded, releasing radioactive material. The release prompted a declaration of general emergency. Responders had to shelter the general population living in the downwind path of the simulated *plume.*

This exercise tested the full breadth of response functions under the *Federal Radiological Emergency Response Plan.*

International Radiological Exercise-94 (RADEX-94)

In 1994, EPA's International Radiological Exercise in Anchorage, Alaska, involved a number of regional, state, and federal organizations:

- Emergency Response Working Group of The Arctic Environmental Protection Strategy
- Environmental Health and Emergency Response Project of The Northern Forum
- EPA's Office of Radiation and Indoor Air
- Department of State
- Alaskan Department of Environmental Conservation.

EPA was the Lead Federal Agency, responsible for coordinating federal participation and developing the exercise scenario. In the exercise scenario, a fictitious country, Articland, experienced a release of radioactive material from a nuclear power plant.

The exercise addressed international concern about the capability of member nations to respond to a radiological emergency affecting the Arctic.

Radiological Emergency Response Team

The Radiological Emergency Response Team (RERT), based in EPA's Office of Radiation and Indoor Air and regional offices, responds to emergencies involving releases of radioactive materials. Working closely with EPA's Superfund Program as well as federal, state, and local agencies, the RERT responds to emergencies that can range from accidents at nuclear power plants to transportation accidents involving shipments of radioactive materials to deliberate acts of nuclear terrorism.

What does RERT do during a radiological emergency?

Staff from ORIA's National Air and Radiation Environmental Laboratory (NAREL) in Montgomery, Alabama, and its Radiation and Indoor Environments National Laboratory (R&IENL) in Las Vegas, Nevada, provide monitoring and assessment services both at the labs and at the response site, if needed.

How quickly can the RERT respond?

Field teams (teams that go to the scene of the emergency) can begin deployment six hours after notification. Shortly after arriving at the scene, the RERT begins environmental measurement and guidance activities: monitoring, sampling, and laboratory activities and providing state and local authorities with advice on protecting local residents from exposure to harmful radiation levels.

The team is on standby alert at all times and, if needed, can drive its mobile emergency response vehicles to any site in the United States within two to four days.

How does the RERT prepare for emergencies?

To maintain readiness, the RERT works with other federal agencies and state and local governments to develop and fine-tune plans for responding to nuclear emergencies. To test these plans, Team personnel continually update their multidisciplinary skills, hold practice exercises, and provide training to other organizations charged with responding to radiological emergencies.

How big is the RERT?

There are approximately 75 team members stationed at EPA's two national radiation laboratories and EPA headquarters in Washington, DC. EPA can send a few specialists or all of the team members to the site emergency. Headquarters RERT members support field operations activities from the Agency's Emergency Operations Center.

What type of vehicles and equipment does RERT use?

The RERT has both laboratory and emergency management vehicles:

- a mobile command post
- a mobile radiation laboratory
- two commercial delivery-van-based mobile laboratories
- two sample preparation laboratories
- a van equipped to scan for gamma radiation.

These mobile facilities can can be driven to the scene of an emergency. Local VHF and long-distance communication capabilities help them keep in touch with response personnel from other agencies.

The RERT also has handheld equipment used to survey the emergency area:

- alpha, beta, and gamma scanning equipment
- air sampling equipment

- protective equipment for personnel
- personal dosimeters, used to measure an individual's radiation dose

What role do EPA's national radiation laboratories play?

The National Air and Radiation Environmental Laboratory in Montgomery, Alabama, and the Radiation and Indoor Environments National Laboratory in Las Vegas, Nevada, provide monitoring and assessment services at the lab and at the scene of an accident. Both the Las Vegas and Montgomery laboratories have mobile labs, equipped for radioanalytical services, including gamma spectroscopy, alpha/beta analyses, and liquid scintillation analyses. RERT field staff send samples requiring more extensive analyses back to NAREL and R&IENL.

Discussion Questions

1) A terrorist organization building a nuclear device, a stolen nuclear weapon, or a sabotaged nuclear reactor are all concerns for security planners when considering nuclear terrorism.

       True   False

2) Dirty bombs are also known also as radiation dispersal devices (RDDs).

       True   False

3) A dirty bomb would be most likely constructed from a fully functional, stolen nuclear missile.

       True   False

4) The unauthorized proliferation of former Soviet nuclear weapons technology is not regarded as a major global threat.

       True   False

5) Most experts agree there is no such thing as an atomic "suitcase bomb."

       True   False

6) For nuclear power plants, a general emergency means there is a possibility of very large releases that could cause acute radiation effects miles from the plant.

       True   False

7) The use of a nuclear device by a terrorist could cause massive loss of life, destruction, and contamination, as well as create massive psychological trauma.

       True   False

8) Dirty bombs would be difficult to construct because radioactive material is hard to come by and is almost never found in common-place settings such as hospitals and research facilities.

       True   False

9) A nuclear incident" may include "accidents," both "deliberate or accidental" releases, and the possibility of release "in sufficient quantity to warrant consideration of protective actions."

       True   False

10) Since the most common nuclear events would be classified as a "minor incident," these small scale events make for good drill scenarios.

       True   False

Answers

1) True

2) True

3) False

4) False

5) False

6) True

7) True

8) False

9) True

10) True

Homeland Security Program Development Team

Project Director
Daniel Byram, MA

Daniel Byram brings over twenty years of law enforcement experience to his role as an educator. He has been involved for more than thirty years in program management, tactical security operations, intelligence operations, and law enforcement.

He has been widely involved in training and program development for law enforcement agencies and businesses, including the creation of a covert operations training program for law enforcement special operations personnel; the development of hostage rescue and crisis survival responses for covert operations personnel; and the designing of a "blueprint" for corporate terrorism response for the Insurance Education Association.

Daniel, with Dr. Julie Brown, designed the model for the homeland security degree programs offered in the Corinthian College network, and he brought together experts from across the United States and Canada to develop the program materials.

Daniel holds a master's degree in Human Behavior and has provided over fifteen years of leadership in the post secondary educational experience. Mr. Byram is currently the National Director of Security, Justice and Legal Programs for Corinthian Colleges, Inc.

Team Leader
Jeff Hynes

Jeff Hynes has twenty-three years of experience with the Phoenix Police Department and currently serves as Commander. He has managed the advanced training for the department in defensive tactics, firearms, driving, and physical fitness and wellness. He also coordinated and facilitated the yearly forty-hour in-service advanced training tactical module for 2,700 police officers, handles curriculum review, records keeping, and facilitates the yearly Citizen's Forum. Mr. Hynes has served as a liaison between the Phoenix Police Department and other federal, state, and local agencies' proficiency-related training at the Arizona Law Enforcement Training Academy.

Commander Hynes received his bachelor's degree in Police Science and holds a master's degree in Educational Leadership. He is currently finishing his doctorate in Education from Northern Arizona University and is an adjunct faculty member of several state and community colleges.

Jeff has also received numerous national, state, and Phoenix Police Department Excellence Awards and nominations for Outstanding Community Based Policing Initiatives.

Team Leader
Jean Goodall

Dr. Jean Goodall's diverse career has been distinguished by the broad range of experiences she has had in her community that give her firsthand knowledge of the link between the criminal justice system and government operations. Throughout her efforts in this field, she has interlaced her strong background in public administration and teaching.

Following her study of criminology and public administration, she completed a master's degree in Criminal Justice. Dr. Goodall has worked for over thirty years with legal issues in the criminal justice environment. She has also combined a master's degree in Management and a doctorate in Public Administration with knowledge gleaned from numerous FBI, CBI, OEM, and weapons seminars, camps and schools. She has received specialized FEMA training regarding emergency management and homeland security. This in-depth combination provides Dr. Goodall with a unique perspective on the role of the civil and criminal justice system in homeland security issues.

Dr. Goodall holds a teaching certificate from Colorado and has twelve years experience in adult education at the university level. She recently served as the chairman of the Criminal Justice Department at Blair College, in Colorado Springs, Colorado.

Team Leader
Julie Brown, MD

If ready response to disasters is the mark of an exemplary security specialist, Dr. Julie Brown's career sets an excellent example. Whether she's been the physician assisting with refugees or a member of the crime-prevention posse for the sheriff's department of Maricopa County, Arizona, Dr. Brown has actively engaged in disaster management throughout her career.

An experienced professional in forensic pathology, law enforcement, and disaster medicine, Dr. Brown is a registered nurse and became a physician in 1988. She serves on several federal-disaster teams that respond to a variety of disasters.

Her areas of study include nursing, biology, psychology, human behavior, medicine, and general business. She has a teaching certificate in biology, psychology, and the medical sciences and has extensive experience as an educator at the college level. She received an MBA in General Business from the University of Phoenix. She formerly served as the program manager for business and accounting for Corinthian College.

Subject Matter Expert
Richard Wilmot, General (retired) United States Army

General Richard Wilmot comes from a varied and unusual career in both the government and private sectors. Before retiring from the Army, General Wilmot, a Vietnam War veteran, held several key positions in the defense sector, including Commanding General of the U.S. Army Intelligence Center and School and Director of Intelligence Systems in the Pentagon. General Wilmot commanded troops at every grade from second lieutenant to brigadier general.

Having been in 106 countries, his life story is replete with unusual true adventures. In Afghanistan he was an advisor to the Afghan rebels when they were fighting the Soviet Union in the mid-1980s. This foray alone has resulted in many interesting anecdotes, realizations, and a broad understanding of events that are tied to the international terrorist situation we now face.

Today, General Wilmot is a successful entrepreneur and an international businessman. He practices leadership in tense areas of the world, where leading in crisis situations leaves no room for error. He is a motivator, a strategic planner, a consultant, and an international speaker. The stories of his adventures provide unusual insight into terrorist situations we face today. He is a graduate of Michigan State University, the U.S. Army War College, the Industrial College of the Armed Forces, and the Command and General Staff College.

Subject Matter Expert
Jane Chung—Examiner, CSC LA Joint Drug Intelligence Group

The analysis of intelligence data is Jane Chung's expertise. As an examiner for the Los Angeles Joint Drug Intelligence Group (LA JDIG), she provides analytical support for narcotics cases for the LA JDIG's Southwest Border Team. She researches commercial and law enforcement databases, evaluates and analyzes the data extracted, and presents the findings to the case agent and other analysts.

Jane's experience with data analysis includes work in international intelligence. In Kosovo, she conducted over 800 personnel interviews to determine the threat level against U.S. forces. She has also developed intelligence threat and damage products focusing on foreign intelligence services, terrorist, paramilitary, law enforcement, political, and criminal organizations. Jane managed the classified segment of the Migrated Defense Intelligence Threat Data System (MDITDS) database for the U.S. Army Europe Analytical Control Element.

Jane graduated in 1998 from the University of California, Irvine, with her bachelor's degree in Criminology, Law and Society.

Subject Matter Expert
Stewart Kellock, Ost J CD Detective 897, Toronto Police Service

With twenty-six years of policing for the Toronto Police Service and serving with the military, Stewart Kellock offers a hands-on perspective to anti-terrorist intelligence. He has a strong and varied investigative background that includes working with a major crime unit, leading multi-unit investigations, and investigating several major political incidents. Stewart has plains clothes experience, and has worked with Provincial Weapons Enforcement and Intelligence. He is currently attached to the anti-terrorist unit of Intelligence Support.

Stewart has extensive military experience. He was commissioned in 1981 and currently holds the rank of Captain. Most recently he was the Leadership Company Commander at 32 CBG Battle School. Previously he was an intelligence officer at LandForce Central Area Headquarters, where he was involved in numerous intelligence operations, both domestic and international. His most recent international mission was commanding the Regional Crime Squad as part of the contingent of the United Nation's Mission in Kosovo.

Stewart majored in International Terrorism at Humbar College and has completed numerous courses in military training and policing. He currently serves as the Unit Training Officer for the 53 Division Canadian Regional Unit.

Subject Matter Expert
James McShane, MPA—Deputy Chief (retired) —Executive Officer, Narcotics Division New York City Police Department

James McShane was second in command of the 2,300 person Narcotics Division of the New York City Police Department where he was responsible for all narcotics enforcement activities in New York City, including all "Buy and Bust" operations, as well as the investigation of all narcotics complaints. He directed all major narcotic investigations in New York City.

James has a law degree and is a member of the Bar of the State of New York and has been admitted to practice in the U.S. Supreme Court and the Federal Courts of New York. He also holds permanent certification as a New York Secondary School Teacher and a New York City teacher's license. James taught math and served as the Dean of a South Bronx High School where he taught, counseled students, and adjudicated conflicts.

James received his bachelor's degree in Communications from Fordham and was a Fulbright scholar and lecturer at the Police College of Finland in Helsinki. He attended the Police Management Institute at Columbia University School of Business, and received a master's degree in Public Administration from Harvard University's Kennedy School of Government.

Subject Matter Expert
Bruce Tefft — Senior Associate, Orion Scientific Systems

Bruce Tefft is a well-seasoned intelligence investigator with twenty-two years of service in foreign affairs and intelligence operations as Headquarters Branch Chief and Field Chief of Station in the Central Intelligence Agency's Directorate of Operations. He served in several African countries, Europe, South Asia, and the Middle East. His multiple responsibilities and activities with the CIA varied from developing and teaching intelligence collection and analysis courses, and running intelligence collection and counter-terrorist operations against Islamic fundamentalists, to developing and implementing logistics and training programs for over

1,000 U.S. and foreign personnel. He planned and organized the first joint CIA-FBI-US Military operation and successfully captured a foreign terrorist.

Bruce has managed liaison relationships and operations with major Allied Nation intelligence organizations and U.S. Government departments such as State and Defense; the Federal Bureau of Investigation; the Drug Enforcement Agency; Defense Intelligence Agency; Defense HUMINT Service; and the U.S. Marine Corps.

He is currently a successful executive as the Senior Associate of Orion Scientific Systems and is the counter-terrorism advisor to the New York City Police Department. He has a bachelor's and a master's degree in History and received his law degree from the University of Denver in 1974.

Subject Matter Expert
Lieutenant Colonel Xavier Stewart

Throughout the last twenty years, LTC Xavier Stewart has been widely recognized for distinguished service in his military career and in the healthcare field. He joined the Army National Guard following the Marine Corps and is the Commander of a Weapons of Mass Destruction Civilian Support Team with the Pennsylvania National Guard. His military duties have included assignments within the Military Police, Military Intelligence, Physical Security, Military Academy, and Medical Arena bringing him several prestigious honors including three Meritorious Service Metals and the Guarde Nationale Trophy for Outstanding Service. He is currently a member of the Executive Advisory Board for Homeland Security and has been recognized by Congress with a Congress Special Award.

With a doctorate in Public Health, LTC Stewart has held numerous faculty positions in respiratory therapy programs, rehabilitation services, biology, physician assistant, and nurse practitioner programs. He has been recognized as one of the Top Ten Respiratory Care Practitioners by the AARC Journal and is listed in Who's Who Among College Professors, Who's Who in America, and Who's Who in the World. LTC Stewart is a board certified Forensic Examiner and is board certified in Forensic Medicine. He is currently a first responder as a nationally registered EMT, HAZMAT firefighter and former deputy sheriff.

He is a graduate of Command and General Staff College and earned a master's in Education with a concentration in Health Services.

Subject Matter Expert
Christopher J. Wren

Christopher Wren is a Security Specialist whose talents have repeatedly been tested in the field. During the Olympic games in Atlanta, where he was responsible for athlete and venue security, he assisted in the design and evaluation of security plans for three high profile locations. While the Director of Security for a large downtown Phoenix Hotel, he was responsible for completely overhauling the hotel security monitoring system to include state-of-the-art cameras, motion censors, and sound monitors. Christopher's training in dignitary/VIP protection brought him a commendation from the White House Security Detail for his assistance in protection of the President and Vice-President of the United States.

As a commissioned law enforcement officer, Christopher coordinated security efforts with federal, state, and local law enforcement agencies, and he has over four years experience in the planning, set-up, and supervision of threat assessment teams. He currently serves on the Homeland Defense Planning and Advisory Team for Phoenix, Arizona.

Christopher served in the U.S. Marine Corps, receiving the rank of Meritorious Sergeant, and was awarded the Navy/Marine Corps Achievement Medal for Excellence. He has studied criminal justice and vocational education and has special training in advanced detective work, media relations, negotiation techniques for first responders, and technical aspects of covert operations.

Subject Matter Expert
D. James Stanger

Dr. James Stanger, a prolific author and PhD, is the Director of Certification and Product Development at ProsoftTraining. His credentials include Symantec Technology Architect, Convergence Technology Professional, CIW Master Administrator, Linux+, and A+. He has led certification development efforts in these proficiencies for various organizations including ProsoftTraining, Symantec, and Linux Professional Institute. Dr. Stanger's specialties include network auditing, risk management, business continuity planning, intrusion detection, and firewall configuration. He has coordinated audits for various clients, which have recently included Brigham Young University, Fuelzone.com, and the William Blake Archive.

An author, Dr. Stanger has created titles for Symantec Education Services, designed executive training seminars concerning firewall and Virtual Private Network (VPN) management, and written other titles concerning security, Cisco routing, and system administration for many companies.

In addition to his development work, Dr. Stanger finds time to serve on several certification boards and advisory councils where, among his many responsibilities, he works to ensure that exams remain relevant and protect certification exam intellectual property.

Subject Matter Expert
Matt Pope, CPP

Matt Pope is the founder of The Security, Integrity and Perception Standard, a private consultancy, which advises on the impact of global security and business integrity on government and economic stability. He also specializes in identifying and creating cutting-edge marketing trends, services, and technologies to improve homeland security and public trust.

Matt has sixteen years experience in business, public safety, and military force protection. He is certified in professional security management, and holds a degree in political science. Most recently, Matt developed a specific expertise with contemporary issues of public security and integrity, privacy legislation, and security ethics. He has worked with some of the world's leading corporations on a broad range of security and emergency planning projects. Matt also serves as an adjunct instructor of homeland security and has written extensively on topics relating to security, law, contingency planning, ethics, privacy, and legislation.

Subject Matter Expert
Lieutenant Kevin Kazmaier

With over twenty years of experience in law enforcement, Lieutenant Kevin Kazmaier has an extensive background in explosive devices, SWAT, and special operations. A member of the International Association of Bomb Technicians and Investigators since his certification as a bomb technician in 1987, he has taught many courses in firearms and advanced explosive technique.

Lieutenant Kazmaier is a graduate of Protective Operations courses from the Association of Chiefs of Police, Secret Service Debriefings, the United States Army Military Police School, and the Phoenix Police Department. He has worked as a consultant for America West Airlines and has provided security at such events as the Super Bowl, the Senior PGA Tour, and the World Series.

Lieutenant Kazmaier holds an A.A.S. in Law Enforcement and a bachelor's degree in Social Justice Professions.

Subject Matter Expert
Harold M. Spangler, MD

Dr. Harold M. Spangler is Chief Resident of Emergency Medicine at North Carolina Baptist Hospital and Bowman-Gray School of Medicine. He is board certified in Emergency Medicine and holds licenses as an Advanced Cardiac Life Support Instructor, an Advanced Trauma Life Support Provider, and a Basic Trauma Life Support Instructor.

After receiving a bachelor's degree in Biology, Dr. Spangler went on to receive honors throughout medical school graduating from Jefferson Medical College, Thomas Jefferson University in Philadelphia, Pennsylvania. He is a member of the American Medical Association, the American College of Emergency Physicians, the North Caroline Chapter of ACEP, and the National Association of EMS Physicians.

Subject Matter Expert
Alan Pruitt, CPP

Alan Pruitt's extensive expertise has made him an integral part of the development of the Homeland Security Specialist Program at Bryman

College in San Jose, California, where he currently serves as the Homeland Security Program Chair. His experiences in the field of intelligence investigation and gathering are diverse. They include his duties as a Marine Corps intelligence officer, his work in corporate security, and his service as a licensed private investigator.

In the military, Alan served as a Counterintelligence Agent with the U.S. Army National Guard and as a Counterintelligence Specialist with the U.S. Marine Corps. His military education introduced him to the skill of tactical intelligence photography and he completed courses in counterintelligence and qualified as an anti-terrorist instructor. He was awarded the Navy Commendation Medal from the Secretary of the Navy for superior achievements in security management.

A member of the California Association of Licensed Investigators and the Association of Certified Fraud Examiners, Alan has over 18,000 hours of investigative experience. His many corporate clients have included Paramount Pictures, the Department of Justice, and the U.S. Customs Service.

He holds a bachelor's degree in Business Management and is a member of the American Society of Law Enforcement Trainers and the American Society of Industrial Security.

Subject Matter Expert
Steve Martin—Security Operations CEO

Steve Martin has over twenty-one years of international experience in the government and private sectors. His career highlights are wide-ranging in the fields of international security, communications, management, business, and paralegal.

As a Special Agent with the Defense Department's National Security Agency, Steve faced the complexities of providing physical security for NSA/CSS personnel and facilities. His overall mission was to create and maintain security activities that detected and protected against acts of espionage, sabotage, and terrorism. His accomplishments include authoring complex government policies and procedures, team leading for the NSA Strategic Planning Sessions, and coordinating actions and policies on counter-terrorism and counter-intelligence measures. He has trained security officers, managing many of the duties of a 500-man NSA police force. He lectures at home and abroad on security and advanced technology.

When Steve was with the NSA he maintained a liaison with his counterparts in other government agencies and private industry. In 1993, he founded a private, multi-division company of which he is part owner. From this vantage, he is able to provide a very informed analysis of the critical need in homeland security for entrepreneurial enterprise.

Subject Matter Expert
Master Sergeant Rocky Dunlap

Master Sergeant Rocky Dunlap retired as Program Manager and Inspector General Team Member for the Air Force Space Command

Explosive Ordnance Disposal at Peterson Air Force Base. In this capacity, he oversaw command objectives relating to anti-terrorism issues; homeland defense initiatives; conventional, nuclear and biological improvised devices; weapons of mass destruction; and reducing the vulnerability of Air Force Space Command installations within the United States and abroad. He was responsible for six major installations and nine remote sites worldwide. Master Sergeant Dunlop established the first regional post 9/11 bomb squad in the Department of Defense to combat weapons of mass destruction. He led NASA's pyrotechnic recovery operations of the Columbia Space shuttle disaster.

He is a graduate of many military courses that deal with weaponry, terrorism, and disaster control. He completed courses in anti-terrorism, weapons and ordinance disposal, chemical and biological school, counter insurgency, nuclear, and HAZMAT first responders and has studied to be a post-blast investigator.

Master Sergeant Dunlop a bachelor's degree in Workforce Education and Development, an AS in Explosive Technology and currently holds the highest certification possible for a Department of Defense Bomb Technician.

Subject Matter Expert
Mr. William Oberholtzer

William Oberholtzer, a military consultant with Vector Incorporated, provides expertise on weapons of mass destruction to a variety of security and defense teams. As Chief of Weapons of Mass Destruction Counter Technology Integration, William provides the National Guard, civilian emergency response agencies and those of the first responder community with recommendations on organization, training, and equipment alterations best suited to meet unit requirements.

Credited with making major contributions toward the establishment of the nation's premier Weapons of Mass Destruction Civil Support Team, he also developed the organization and curriculum requirements for the National Weapons of Mass Destruction and Counter Terrorism Training and Simulation Center in response to initiatives pertaining to homeland defense.

William has a bachelor's in Education Administration and master's degree in Management and Human Relations. He graduated from Defense Systems Management College and has many FEMA courses and certifications to his credit, including: Emergency Program Manager and Emergency Preparedness, Radiological Emergency Management and Response, Hazardous Material, and the Role of the Emergency Operations Center.

Subject Matter Expert
Dr. Victor Herbert

Dr. Victor Herbert has dedicated a lifetime to teaching and administration. He is currently Dean of Instruction for the New York City Fire Department (FDNY) where he coordinates all training for FDNY personnel and directs FDNYC, AmeriCorp, and Fire Safety Education. He came to this position following his work in public and higher education.

With a master's degree in English Education and a doctorate in Educational Leadership, he taught English and Spanish and went on to win the Fund for the City of New York's award as Educator of the Year in 1983. After obtaining a number of professional certificates in educational administration and Spanish, he received a Fulbright Award to study relationships between Mexico and the United States. He has traveled extensively throughout Latin America.

Besides his teaching positions, Dr. Herbert has assumed many roles in public school administration working as department chair, principal, and school superintendent in school districts in New York, Arizona, and Connecticut. Dr. Herbert has been an associate faculty member at Chapman University, Arizona State University, Norwalk Community College, and St. Joseph's College in New York. His expertise has enabled him to teach both technical and academic subjects. He also has directed several programs for emergency responders in the acquisition of Spanish.